www.wadsworth.com

wadsworth.com is the World Wide Web site for Wadsworth and is your direct source to dozens of online resources.

At *wadsworth.com* you can find out about supplements, demonstration software, and student resources. You can also send email to many of our authors and preview new publications and exciting new technologies.

wadsworth.com
Changing the way the world learns®

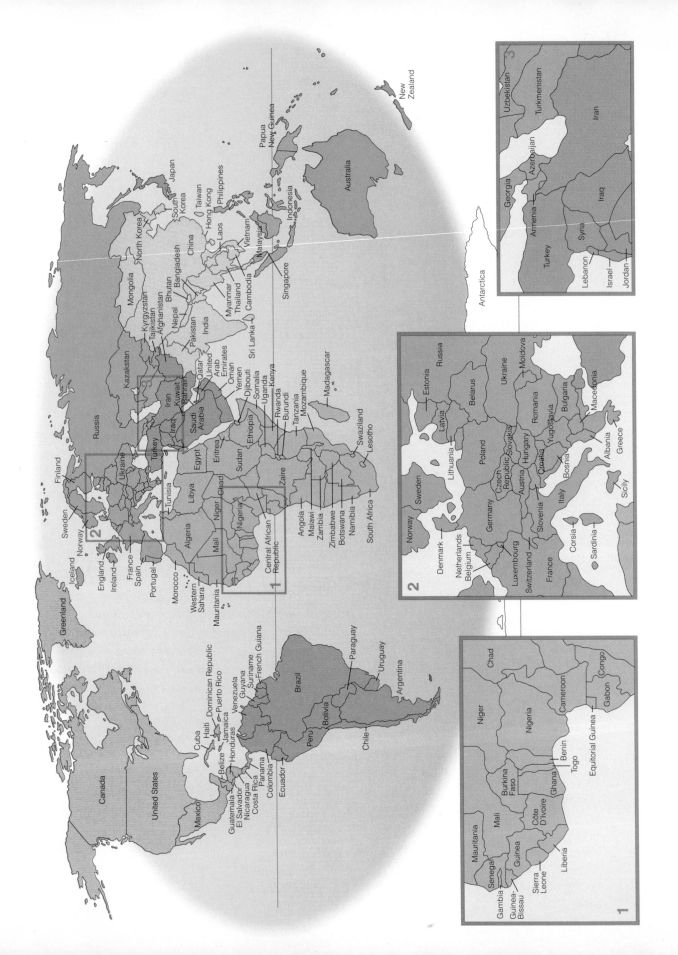

CULTURAL ANTHROPOLOGY

SEVENTH EDITION

Serena Nanda
John Jay College of Criminal Justice
City University of New York

Richard L. Warms
Southwest Texas State University

WADSWORTH

THOMSON LEARNING

*Australia • Canada • Mexico • Singapore • Spain
United Kingdom • United States*

WADSWORTH

THOMSON LEARNING

Anthropology Editor: Lin Marshall
Development Editor: Robert Jucha
Assistant Editor: Analie Barnett
Editorial Assistant: Reilly O'Neal
Marketing Manager: Matthew Wright
Project Manager: Jerilyn Emori
Print Buyer: Mary Noel
Permissions Editor: Joohee Lee
Production Service: Cecile Joyner/ The Cooper Company

Text and Cover Designer: Liz Harasymczuk
Photo Researcher: Terri Wright
Copy Editor: Peggy Tropp
Illustrator: Scientific Illustrators
Cover Image: Angela Fisher/Robert Estall Photo Agency
Cover Printer: Phoenix Color Corp.
Compositor: Thompson Type
Printer: Quebecor World Book Services, Taunton

For permission to use material from this text,
contact us by
Web: http://www.thomsonrights.com
Fax: 1-800-730-2215   **Phone:** 1-800-730-2214

Library of Congress Cataloging-in-Publication Data
Nanda, Serena.
   Cultural anthropology / Serena Nanda, Richard L. Warms.—7th ed.
        p.   cm.
Includes bibliographical references and index.
   ISBN 0-534-55739-2
   1. Ethnology.   I. Warms, Richard L.   II. Title.
GN316 .N36 2002
306—dc21   00-050969

Wadsworth/Thomson Learning
10 Davis Drive
Belmont, CA 94002-3098
USA

For more information about our products, contact us:
Thomson Learning Academic Resource Center
1-800-423-0563
http://www.wadsworth.com

International Headquarters
Thomson Learning
International Division
290 Harbor Drive, 2nd Floor
Stamford, CT 06902-7477
USA

UK/Europe/Middle East/South Africa
Thomson Learning
Berkshire House
168-173 High Holborn
London WC1V 7AA
United Kingdom

Asia
Thomson Learning
60 Albert Street, #15-01
Albert Complex
Singapore 189969

Canada
Nelson Thomson Learning
1120 Birchmount Road
Toronto, Ontario M1K 5G4
Canada

To
Ruth Freed
and
Benjamin and Nathan

PHOTO CREDITS

1 and vii (top) Jean Pierre Dutilleux
3 Courtesy of Ronald Coley
7 A. Pierce Bounds/Pictor
10 Jessie Tarbox/Photo courtesy of the Missouri Historical Society
18 and vii (bottom) Peter Weit/CORBIS/Sygma
20 American Museum of Natural History, Special Collections
24 Lynn Kilgore
26 Courtesy Meredith Small
28 Don Johanson/Institute of Human Origins
31 Institute of Human Origins
35 National Museums of Kenya
36 Kenya Museums of Natural History
37 William Turnbaugh/The Museum of Primitive Art and Culture
38 Border Cave—Courtesy, Fred Smith
40 © Jim Cartier, Photo Researchers, Inc.
42 Courtesy of David Glassman
48 and viii Irven DeVore/Anthro-Photo File
51 United States Postal Service
54 © 1998 Jose Azel/Aurora
57 (left) Michael Justice/The Image Works (right) Courtesy of Charles Brooks
63 Courtesy of Serena Nanda
64 Courtesy of Serena Nanda
70 and ix (top) Sonia Katchain/Photo Shuttle: Japan
77 Courtesy of James Hamilton
78 Tomas D. W. Friedman/Photo Researchers, Inc.
79 (left) © Pictor (right) Andre Durland/Bettmann/CORBIS
84 Adam G. Sylvester/Photo Researchers, Inc.
86 © Mathias Oppersdorff/Photo Researchers, Inc.
87 Barry Kass/Anthro-Photo File
88 Paul Souders/Stone
92 and ix (bottom) Courtesy of Serena Nanda
94 Courtesy of Colorado University
104 Joe Viesti/Viesti Associates, Inc.
105 Paul Conklin/Pictor
111 AP/Wide World Photos

114 The Harold Lloyd Estate and Film Trust
122 and x John Eastcott/Yva Momatiuk/Woodfin Camp & Associates
126 Courtesy of Serena Nanda
127 Marcello Bertinetti/Photo Researchers, Inc.
129 © Mark S. Wexler/Woodfin Camp and Associates
133 Welsh/The Gamma Liaison Network
135 (left) Bob Daemmrich/Stock, Boston (right) Joe Viesti/Viesti Associates, Inc.
136 © Bob Daemmrich/Stock, Boston
140 © Catherine Karnow/Woodfin Camp & Associates
144 and xi (top) © Charles Gupton/Stock, Boston
146 Stan Wayman/Photo Researchers, Inc.
149 Irven DeVore/Anthro-Photo File
152 © David Austen/Stock, Boston
155 Courtesy of Serena Nanda
157 F. Jack Jackson/Bruce Coleman Inc.
161 Robert Caputo/Stock, Boston
168 and xi (bottom) © Georg Gerster/Photo Researchers, Inc.
170 Jonathan Kirn/Stone
174 Leon Patenburg/Index Stock Photography, Inc.
176 (left) Jim Olive/Pictor (right) Robert Frerck/Odyssey Productions
178 Bettmann/CORBIS
186 © Joel Gordon
189 © Randa Bishop/Pictor
190 Alan Oddie/PhotoEdit
194 and xii Courtesy of Chander Dembla
201 © Evan Hurd/CORBIS/Sygma
205 Abu Lughod/Anthro-Photo File
206 Courtesy of Jean Zorn
209 Courtesy of Serena Nanda
211 Spencer Grant/Photo Researchers, Inc.
215 © Earl & Nazima Kowall/CORBIS
218 and xiii (top) Courtesy of Soo Choi
225 Terry Eiler/Stock, Boston
229 Courtesy of Tom Curtin
240 and xiii (bottom) Abu Lughod/Anthro-Photo File
243 © David Austen/Stock, Boston
245 Courtesy of Serena Nanda
248 H. Armstrong Roberts, Inc./Camerique Stock Photography
249 © Pablo Corral V/CORBIS
252 Betty Press/Woodfin Camp & Associates
253 Jean Pierre Dutilleux
256 © Mike Yamashita/Woodfin Camp & Associates
262 and xiv Mark & Evelyn Bernheim/Woodfin Camp & Associates
266 Michael Dwyer/Stock, Boston
269 © Austin MacRae

271 Irven DeVore/Anthro-Photo File
273 Courtesy of Serena Nanda
275 Napoleon Chagnon/Anthro-Photo File
282 North Wind Picture Archives
286 and xv Sharon Chester/Comstock Inc.
288 © Kevin Horan/Stock, Boston
289 Kolvoord/The Image Works
291 © Nubar Alexanian/Stock, Boston
292 Barry Iverson/Woodfin Camp & Associates
296 AP/Wide World Photos
298 Courtesy of The Hispanic Society of America
308 and xvi (top) © Katsuyoshi Tanaka/Woodfin Camp & Associates
312 Courtesy of Serena Nanda
315 © AFP/CORBIS
317 Serena Nanda
319 Nik Wheeler/CORBIS
323 Courtesy of Cultural Survival
325 © L. P. Winfrey/Woodfin Camp & Associates
334 and xvi (bottom) Courtesy of Serena Nanda
338 Courtesy of Yuko Miyazaki
342 Bob Burch/Bruce Coleman Inc.
345 Bettmann/CORBIS
347 © AFP/CORBIS
350 © Chris Lisle/CORBIS
352 George Holton/Photo Researchers, Inc.
353 Bettmann/CORBIS
357 Jacques Charlas/Stock, Boston
358 Courtesy of Serena Nanda
359 The Granger Collection
364 and xvii © Gianni Dagli Orti/CORBIS
366 Courtesy of Serena Nanda
367 George Haling/Photo Researchers, Inc.
369 © Phil Borden/PhotoEdit
371 Alexander Marshack
372 Unknown Artist Mano Poderosa/The Brooklyn Museum
374 Jerry L. Thompson/Courtesy of the Museum for African Art, New York
375 Wendy Bass/Viesti Associates, Inc.
377 Otto E. Nelson/The Metropolitan Museum of Art, Gift of Lincoln Kristein, 1959
379 Juan Gimenez/Martin/Dahesh Museum
381 Wendy Bass/Viesti Associates, Inc.
384 and xviii Barbara Backer
386 Antman Archives/The Image Works
389 H. Armstrong Roberts, Inc.
395 Courtesy of Richard Warms
397 Paul S. Howell/The Gamma Liaison Network
404 (left) © Bill Bachmann/Stock, Boston (right) David Frazier/Photo Researchers, Inc.
408 © Peter Turnley/CORBIS

CONTENTS

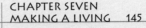

PREFACE

Cultural Anthropology, Seventh Edition, is designed to increase students' understanding of the globally interconnected world in which they live, the human past and present, and the unity and diversity that characterize the human species. Cultural Anthropology enables students to "make sense" of the behavior and cultures of peoples unlike themselves as well as gain insight into their own behavior and society.

Cultural Anthropology introduces fundamental concepts, theories, methods, data, and references in ways that are exciting and informative for students who intend to major in anthropology as well those who may take only one or two courses in the subject. The topics included in the text cover the full range of cultural anthropology, and are presented in the order most frequently taught in anthropology classrooms. Each chapter can stand separately, however, and the chapters can be fairly easily rearranged to reflect particular course emphases.

The main perspective of this book is ethnographic. Ethnography is the fundamental source of the data of anthropology, and knowledge of a broad range of ethnographic examples is essential to students. Ethnography draws people to anthropology. It engages them and encourages them to analyze and question their own culture. Ethnographic examples are used extensively in every chapter of Cultural Anthropology. In addition, each chapter contains one or more multipage ethnographies, labeled "In the Field," that provide additional detail on specific cultures. These ethnographic features have been chosen to illuminate cultures, situations, and histories that students will find particularly fascinating.

Cultural Anthropology takes a broad, optimistic, and enthusiastic approach to the discipline of anthropology. We believe that the significant rethinking of basic concepts now going on in anthropology is a sign of the growth and vitality of the field rather than its demise. Cultural Anthropology describes the major issues, debates, and theoretical approaches in anthropology in a balanced manner, drawing analysis, information, and insight from many different perspectives.

This Seventh Edition of Cultural Anthropology continues the collaboration between Serena Nanda and Richard Warms. Warms' specialties in West Africa, anthropological theory, and social anthropology complement Nanda's in India, gender, law, and cultural anthropology. The results have been synergistic. Our experiences, readings, discussions, and debates, as well as feedback from reviewers and professors who have adopted previous editions, have led to the production of a textbook that reflects the energy and passion of anthropology. We have revised extensively, rewritten, added hundreds of new references, and emphasized what we believe to be the best of current thinking in our field. Writing this book continues to be an exciting intellectual adventure for us, and we believe that working with it will promote students' growth as well.

In addition to our ethnographic focus, the Seventh Edition continues many of the successful innovations of earlier editions. We continue to use full-color photographs and illustrations to catch the eye and engage the mind. We find that our students are intensely visual. Well-chosen photographs make them think about the text's critical points. The photographs help students visualize other cultural patterns and suggest ways for them to think about their own. All photographs have explanatory captions identifying their source and linking them with the text.

Also continued is our treatment of theory as a critical component of anthropological thought, both in Chapter 4, "The Idea of Culture," and in a special Appendix, "A Brief Guide to Anthropological Theory," which offers concise descriptions of major schools of thought in anthropology from the nineteenth century to the present.

NEW IN THIS EDITION

We have made a number of significant changes and additions to the Seventh Edition, based partly on recent developments in the field of anthropology and partly on the valuable feedback we have received from our adopters and reviewers. Following is a synopsis of the changes you will encounter in the Seventh Edition.

• With this edition, we introduce a new chapter, Chapter 2, "Human Evolution." The chapter covers Darwin's theory of natural selection, distinctive characteristics of primates and their social lives, basic descriptive information about the major species of human ancestors, and material on human variation. It is written in a clear, jargon-free, accessible style. It is not necessary to read the chapter to understand the rest of the book, so instructors who do not normally cover evolution need not assign it. However, we feel confident that both students and professors will appreciate this useful and engaging material.

• Chapter 6, "Learning Culture Throughout Life," expands the idea of learning culture beyond the early years of life. This chapter (formerly Chapter 5) also has new information on male and female initiation rituals, learning culture in adulthood, old age, and death.

• Chapter 12, "Political Organization," and Chapter 13, "Social Stratification in Contemporary Societies: Class, Caste, and Race," have been reorganized. Information about different types of political organization has been concentrated in the first of these chapters, while the second explores issues of stratification in contemporary societies with special attention to race in the United States and caste in India.

• In this edition we inaugurate a new Chapter 14, "Ethnicity." Ideas about ethnicity have come to play an increasingly important role in anthropological theorizing and teaching. This new chapter explores theoretical perspectives on ethnicity, the ways in which nation-states shape ethnicity, and relations between nation-states and indigenous peoples. The chapter incorporates an extensive section on immigration, along with ethnic and cultural diversity in the United States, that students will find extremely relevant to their own experiences.

• Previous editions of *Cultural Anthropology* have concluded with a chapter on applied anthropology. For the Seventh Edition we wished to integrate applied anthropology more tightly into all sections of the text. With this aim in mind, we have created a new feature called "Anthropology Makes a Difference." All chapters now include a boxed feature that gives a concise description of an application of anthropology to a real-world problem. These boxes cover issues such as drug use, Ebonics, development projects, business anthropology, family violence, and conflict resolution. Students frequently ask about the uses of anthropology. This feature helps to answer that question in terms relevant to students' experiences.

• We have modified the name of our boxed ethnography features to "In the Field." We hope that this new designation conveys the excitement of conducting anthropological studies in real-world situations. More substantively, we have added several new ethnographies, including the Pintupi of Australia (Chapter 7), the Asante of Ghana (Chapter 12), and new Chinese immigrants in San Francisco (Chapter 14). In addition, you will find new, nonboxed ethnographic information about police officers in Los Angeles, childhood among the Inuit, ethnic violence in Yugoslavia, and the Saami of Norway.

• Also new to this edition is a running glossary. In addition to the glossary at the end of the book, you will find critical terms defined at the bottom of the page on which they are introduced. Anthropological terminology may be new for first-time students, and this learning aid will facilitate both comprehension and study.

• The last major addition to *Cultural Anthropology,* Seventh Edition, is in many ways the most significant. The Seventh Edition is more completely integrated with Internet resources than any other beginning cultural anthropology textbook. Within the last several years, the Internet has become an indispensable resource for both the scholarly community and the general public. We believe strongly that the Internet provides new opportunities for learning, research, and collaboration. As a result, we have constructed a web site for this book that provides valuable tools for the instructor and student. The enriched web content includes photo essays and film clips for most chapters, which visually demonstrate key concepts in the chapter. Each chapter has hot links to key web sites, which we believe will increase the students' enthusiasm for anthropology. A further explanation of how the text, Internet resources, and web site work together is provided at the end of this preface.

CHAPTER OVERVIEW

Each chapter is organized so that the main ideas, secondary ideas, important terms and definitions, and ethnographic material stand out clearly. The entire text has been thoroughly updated reflecting the important anthropological work of the 1990s.

Chapter 1, "Anthropology and Human Diversity," focuses on anthropology as a discipline whose subject is human diversity. This chapter introduces the major perspectives of anthropology and the subfields of the discipline. It highlights race as a social construction and the many ways anthropology contributes to a sensitive understanding of human difference. Issues of race, gender, and the nature of cultural interpretation are introduced.

Chapter 2, "Human Evolution," is a new chapter designed to give introductory students a background in the theory of evolution by natural selection, the physical and social characteristics of primates, and the major groups of fossil human ancestors. The chapter concludes with a section on human variation that highlights the biology of human traits commonly used in "racial" classification.

Chapter 3, "Doing Cultural Anthropology," considers postmodern as well as more traditional perspectives on ethnography. The chapter begins with historical background, describing the contributions of Boas and Malinowski. It includes detailed descriptions of a field study in India and new ethnographic research on the use of illegal drugs in the United States. It explores doing ethnography in one's own culture, the dilemmas of the "native anthropologist," and concludes with a section on the cross-cultural survey method.

Chapter 4, "The Idea of Culture," is designed to expose students to a range of theoretical positions in anthropology by examining the way different anthropologists have understood the idea of culture. In addition to introducing students to the history of theory in anthropology, it demonstrates that different theoretical positions lead anthropologists to ask different sorts of questions and do different sorts of research. We present anthropology as an exciting arena in which different understandings and interpretations jostle for position.

Chapter 5, "Language," provides a solid background for anthropological linguistics. Phonology, morphology, and other elements of linguistics are discussed. There are special highlights on language acquisition and language experiments with apes. A section on sociolinguistics addresses the speech patterns of men and women in American society, linguistic minorities, and cross-cultural communication. A newly updated and expanded section explores nonverbal communication.

Chapter 6, "Learning Culture Throughout Life," has been substantially redesigned. It examines human development in cross-cultural perspective, beginning with a section on the cultural construction of stages of human development. An ethnography comparing the values and practices of preschools in China, Japan, and the United States highlights the ways in which child-rearing practices are related to cultural values, as does a new section on childhood learning among the Inuit. The material on "coming of age," in the United States and other cultures, has been expanded to include new information on women's coming of age ceremonies. There are new sections on learning in adulthood, featuring a description of the education of police officers in Los Angeles, and on death and dying in cross-cultural perspective.

Chapter 7, "Making a Living," brings cultural adaptation into focus. It examines the major human food-getting strategies through four extended ethnographies describing foraging, pastoralism, horticulture, and agriculture. Included is a new ethnographic example of foraging from the Great Australian Desert, along with descriptions of the pastoral Yarahmadzai of Baluchistan, the horticultural Lua' of Thailand, and Egyptian peasant villagers. The chapter concludes with a section on earning a living in the contemporary global economy.

Chapter 8, "Economics," explores the nature of economic behavior and economic systems in cross-cultural perspective. Special attention is paid to issues of access to resources, the organization of labor, systems of distribution and exchange (including classic examples such as the potlatch and the Kula ring), and reactions to the spread of capitalism. The ethnography focuses on female pieceworkers in Turkey and explores the relationship between traditional modes of production and the international marketplace.

Chapter 9, "Marriage, Family, and Domestic Groups," has been largely retained from the previous edition. It focuses on types of family systems and their relationship to other parts of culture. It includes an ethnography about the Tiwi of North Australia and a new section on culture, domestic violence, and the cultural defense.

Chapter 10, "Kinship," introduces the major kinship ideologies and the kinds of social groups formed by kinship. A case study on the process of inheritance in a Korean village emphasizes some of the realities of human behavior as they interact with kin, as contrasted to the cultural ideals of kinship systems. The ethnography, a personalized account of an anthropologist participating in the kinship systems of the United States and India, makes the normally difficult topic of kinship accessible to students and enjoyable to read.

Chapter 11, "Gender," brings together an historical perspective on the examination of gender in cultural anthropology with current research on the role of women in hunting societies, the relationship between women and power, changes in women's roles as a result of European contact, and an examination of the effects of "development" and multinational corporations on women. The emphasis of this chapter is on the construction of gender, using ethnographic data on the construction of masculinity in Spain and the construction of the Hijra role, an alternative gender role in India. The Anthropology Makes a Difference box features Chinese women workers in the global economy.

Chapter 12, "Political Organization," has been substantially rearranged. The chapter begins with a description of social differentiation in egalitarian, rank, and stratified societies. It goes on to explore the issue of power and social control before turning to a systematic discussion of leadership, social control, and conflict resolution in bands, tribes, chiefdoms, and states. The new ethnography on the precolonial Asante highlights the interactions among power, wealth, and the development of the state.

Chapter 13, "Social Stratification in Contemporary Societies: Class, Caste, and Race," expands our coverage of these vital aspects of anthropological theorizing and research. It explores explanations for social stratification before turning to detailed discussions of caste in India and race in the United States and Brazil, and an updated section on the changing nature of caste in modern India. The ethnography focuses on downward mobility among the middle class in the United States.

Chapter 14, "Ethnicity," is a new chapter that enlarges upon our coverage of this topic in earlier editions. The chapter begins by exploring theoretical perspectives on ethnicity, then turns to the relationship between ethnicity and the nation-state, showing the ways in which ethnicity is historically situated. The discussion of ethnic conflict is illustrated by examples from the former Yugoslavia. A section explores the relationship between nation-states and indigenous peoples, using an extended ethnographic example of the Saami reindeer herders of Norway. The second half of the chapter explores ethnicity and cultural diversity in the United States, particularly as these relate to immigration. The ethnography focuses on new Chinese immigrants in San Francisco.

Chapter 15, "Religion," takes an eclectic approach that focuses on the ecological and social functions of religions as well as on the ways that religions operate symbolically and emotionally to give meaning and order to life. It includes detailed information about the world of spirits and sacred powers, the nature and structure of religious ritual, and religious practitioners. An ethnography on the Rastafarians and extensive information on the Ghost Dance Religion and Native American Church show the roles of religion in social change and resistance.

Chapter 16, "The Arts: Expressing Cultural Identities," is integrated around the theme of how cultural identities are expressed through art, performance, and sports. Material on how cultures represent others, as well as themselves, uses ethnographic data on European Orientalism and Mexican folk dances of the Conquest. The chapter's ethnography, on the emergence of a new identity for the Toraja of Indonesia linked to tourism and art, carries through the chapter's theme.

Chapter 17, "Culture Change," takes an historical perspective on the subject, exploring the ways in which the expansion of the power of today's wealthy nations fundamentally changed cultures throughout the world. Sections on the era of Western exploration, colonialism, economic development, and problems of urbanization, population growth, and instability highlight the speed of change and the inequities of wealth and power. An ethnography on African soldiers drafted into the French colonial army focuses attention on a little-known aspect of the African colonial experience.

TEACHING FEATURES AND STUDY AIDS

Each chapter includes outstanding pedagogical features to help students identify, learn, and remember key concepts and data. As befits a text in which ethnographic material holds so central a role, the major features within each chapter are the 21 boxed **In the Field** ethnographies. The ethnographies provide interesting and enjoyable information designed to engage students' interest and provide a context for thinking about more abstract concepts. **Locator maps** accompany all ethnographies. **Critical thinking questions** at the end of each

ethnography tie the ethnography firmly to the material presented in the chapter and open opportunities for discussion of the role of anthropology in the modern world.

The In the Field ethnography boxes are supplemented by three additional boxed features:

- **Globalization** boxes are found in most chapters of the text. They are designed to provide interesting examples that draw students' attention to the ways in which all peoples and cultures are interconnected. The Globalization boxes raise issues that students will find interesting and professors can use to spark classroom discussion.
- **Cultural Focus** boxes are found intermittently throughout the book. They provide more in-depth coverage of specific topics that parallel the general concepts discussed in the chapter. Examples include nonhuman primate communications in Chapter 5, an historical perspective on culture and personality studies in Chapter 6, Religion and Ecology in Chapter 15.
- **Anthropology Makes a Difference** boxes, described previously, provide examples of situations in which anthropology is applied to help address today's real-world issues.

Each chapter also has several learning aids to help students understand and retain the chapter's information:

- **Study questions** at the beginning of each chapter, keyed to major topics covered, help students focus their attention on the critical issues in each chapter.
- A **running glossary** of key terms is found at the bottom of the pages.
- **Summaries,** arranged as numbered points at the end of each chapter, recap critical ideas and aid study and review.
- **Key Terms** are listed alphabetically at the end of each chapter, for quick review.
- **Suggested Readings** that are interesting and accessible to the introductory student are listed at the end of each chapter.
- **Internet Resources** conclude each chapter and give a summary of all the integrated Internet resources for that chapter. These resources include photo essays, video clips, hot

a day, seven days a week, are *American Anthropologist, Current Anthropology,* and *Canadian Review of Sociology and Anthropology.* Contact your Wadsworth/Thomson Learning representative for more information.

WebTutor WebTutor is a content-rich, web-based teaching and learning tool that helps students succeed by taking the course beyond classroom boundaries to an anywhere, anytime environment. WebTutor is rich with study and mastery tools, communication tools, and course content. Professors can use WebTutor to provide virtual office hours, post syllabi, set up threaded discussions, track student progress with the quizzing material, and more.

ACKNOWLEDGMENTS

It gives us great pleasure to thank the many people who have been associated with this book. We are most appreciative of the helpful comments made by reviewers of the Seventh Edition: Dorothy K. Billings, Wichita State University; Rebecca Cramer, Johnson County Community College; Karen Daar, Glendale College; Sharon McCormick Derrick; Roya Falahi, Joliet Junior College; B. Garrity-Blake, East Carolina University; Huma Ahmed Ghosh, San Diego State University; Carol Hayman, Austin Community College; Gary Heidinger, Roane State Community College; Susan Lees, Hunter College–CUNY; Christopher D. Mayer, Cowley County Community College; Lars Rodseth, University of Utah; Esther Skirboll, Slippery Rock University.

We also want to thank the reviewers of the Sixth Edition for their comments, which we found helpful: Thomas F. Aleto, Bloomsburg University; Caroline B. Brettell, Southern Methodist University; Gregory R. Campbell, University of Montana; T. Virginia Cox, Boise State University; Robert Dirks, Illinois State University; E. Paul Durrenberger, University of Iowa; Nicholas Freiden, Marshall University; AnnCorinne Freter, Ohio University; Mary Kay Gilliland, Pima Community College; Barbara Hoffman, Cleveland State University; Susan A. Johnson, University of Rhode Island; Ronald Kephart, University of North Florida; Jay Longshore, Community College of Phila-delphia; Jerome S. O'Neal, Spokane Falls Community College; Harold Prins, Kansas State University; Cathy A. Small, Northern Arizona University; Mara Kent Skruch, Anne Arundel Community College; Dianne Smith, Santa Rosa Junior College; and Daryl White, Spelman College.

Our colleagues within our respective institutions and outside as well have been most generous in sharing their wide and deep knowledge. For their support we would like to thank Brit Bousman, Kojo Dei, Bert Erhart, Stanley Freed, Jim Garber, David Glassman, Joan Gregg, Ana Juarez, Owen Lynch, R. Jon McGee, Michael Newman, F. Kent Reilly, and Stephen Wooten.

For the use of photographs we would like to thank Kathleen Adams, Charles Brooks, Soo Choi, Ronald Coley, Kojo Dei, Chander Dembla, Joan Gregg, James Hamilton, Ray Kennedy, Yuko Miyazaki, Marilyn Omifunke Torres, and Jean Zorn. We would also like to thank Sunil Chopra and Mrs. Raksha Chopra, invaluable informants on the intricacies of North Indian kinship terminology, and Paisley Joy Gregg for her research assistance.

We gratefully acknowledge the support of our universities and the help of the staffs at our departments at John Jay College of Criminal Justice and Southwest Texas State University. We are particularly grateful to Sharan Smith and Glenda S. Bailey of Southwest Texas State University and Linda John of John Jay College. In addition, many of our students have contributed ideas, reflections, and labor to this project, and we thank them collectively.

Our families continue to form an important cheering section for our work, and we thank them for their patience, endurance, and just plain putting up with us.

We are deeply grateful to the people at Wadsworth, particularly our editors, Lin Marshall and Bob Jucha, for their support, their encouragement, and their insight. In addition, we wish to thank the following persons at Wadsworth for their assistance: Jerilyn Emori, Mathew Wright, and Analie Barnett. Finally, we would like to thank Cecile Joyner and The Cooper Company, who shepherded us through the production process. The knowledge, editing skills, and superb suggestions made by the many people involved in the production of this book have greatly contributed to it.

USING THE WEB SITE IN CONJUNCTION WITH THE TEXT

Cultural Anthropology, Seventh Edition, was written in conjunction with the accompanying web site to provide the reader with an enhanced, integrated learning experience of both text and online material. Throughout the chapters of the text you will find in the margins this icon **WWW**, indicating that additional information on this topic can be found on the accompanying web site. Because anthropology is, among the social sciences, the richest in employing visual information, the web site draws heavily upon photographs and video. Depending on your Internet connection and the speed of the modem you are using, this may affect the way you use the web site.

At the end of each chapter, under "Internet Resources," you will find a quick summary of all the links identified by the icons for that chapter. To find the Internet Resources, log onto the accompanying web site, Anthropology Online: The Wadsworth Anthropology Resource Center (http://anthropology.wadsworth.com). Then click on the following: Student Resources_Cultural Anthropology_Nanda/Warms 7th Edition. Enter the following (use all lowercase):

USER NAME: nandawarms
PASSWORD: website

At the Student Resources page, select the chapter you are studying. You will find material on all the links listed for that chapter, and much more. The enrichment material on the web site takes three forms:

1. Links to highly relevant, stable web sites that provide additional material on the topic.
2. Links to photo essays drawn largely from photographs taken by the text's authors. Each essay includes a short written description placing the photographs within the anthropological context.
3. The third link, found in most chapters, is a video link. Anthropologists were among the first social scientists to make use of film in their studies, and the field has a rich tradition of ethnographic filmmaking. Wadsworth has arranged with one of world's leading producers and distributors of anthropological films, Documentary Education Resources, to bring you these video clips. Additional information about the films, along with discussion questions, places the film in context.

Finally, for each chapter there is a reminder to access InfoTrac College Edition for keyword searches and articles relevant to the chapter.

ABOUT THE AUTHORS

Serena Nanda is professor emeritus of anthropology at John Jay College of Criminal Justice, City University of New York. Her published works include *Neither Man nor Woman: The Hijras of India,* winner of the 1990 Ruth Benedict Prize; *American Cultural Pluralism and Law;* and *Gender Diversity: Cross-Cultural Variations.*

Richard Warms is associate professor of anthropology at Southwest Texas State University. His published works include *Anthropological Theory: An Introductory History,* as well as journal articles on commerce, religion and ethnic identity in West Africa, African exploration and romanticism, and African veterans of French colonial armed forces.

CULTURAL ANTHROPOLOGY

Jean Pierre Dutilleux

ANTHROPOLOGY STUDIES CULTURES ALL OVER THE WORLD IN ITS ATTEMPT TO UNDERSTAND THE SIMILARITIES AND DIFFERENCES AMONG HUMAN BEINGS. IN ALL CULTURES, WIDOWS HAVE A SPECIAL STATUS, BUT THE FORMS OF MOURNING RITUALS DIFFER. DURING THEIR MOURNING PERIOD, THESE WIDOWS IN PAPUA NEW GUINEA MUST WEAR THESE FORTY-POUND NECKLACES. AS A RESULT, THEY ARE UNABLE TO BEND AND CAN ONLY DRINK FROM A SPRING WITH THE HELP OF A BAMBOO ROD.

CHAPTER ONE

ANTHROPOLOGY AND HUMAN DIVERSITY

What are the aims of cultural anthropology?

In what ways does anthropology differ from other social sciences?

What are the different subfields within anthropology?

How do anthropologists understand human biological diversity?

How does anthropology help us understand our own and other cultures?

How have changes in the world affected the practice of anthropology?

As long as human beings have existed they have faced fundamental problems. Among these are how to feed, clothe, and house themselves, how to determine rights and responsibilities, how to lend meaning and poignancy to their lives, how to live with each other, and how to deal with those who live differently. Human cultures are the answers people have devised to these basic questions. The goal of **anthropology**—the comparative study of human societies and cultures—is to describe, analyze, and explain different cultures, to show how groups have adapted to their environments and given meaning to their lives.

Anthropology is comparative in that it attempts to understand similarities and differences among human cultures. Only through the study of humanity in its total variety can we understand who we are as human beings, our potentials and our perils. In an era when people from different cultures are increasingly in contact with each other, and when most people in the world live in multicultural and multiethnic nations, these are important goals.

Anthropologists study our species from its beginnings several million years ago up to the present. We study human beings as they live in every corner of the earth, in all kinds of environments. Some anthropologists are even trying to project how human beings will live in the future, exploring the possibilities of space stations and communities on other planets. This interest in humankind throughout time and in all parts of the world distinguishes anthropology as a scientific and humanistic discipline.

In other academic disciplines, human behavior is usually studied primarily from the point of view of Western society. Human nature is thought to be the same as the behavior of people in the modern industrial nations of Europe and North America. Anthropologists insist that human nature is not so easily accessible.

Human beings everywhere consider their own behavior not only right, but natural. Our ideas about economics, religion, morality, and other areas of social life seem logical and inevitable to us, but others have found different answers. For example, should you give your infant bottled formula or should you breast-feed

anthropology The comparative study of human societies and cultures.

not only your own child but, like the Efe of Zaire, those of your friends and neighbors as well (Peacock 1991:352)? Is it right that emotional love should precede sexual relations? Or should sexual relations precede love, as is normal for the Mangaian of the Pacific (D. Marshall 1971)? What should we have for lunch: hamburgers and fries, or termites, grasshoppers, and hot maguey worms, all of which are commonly eaten in certain regions of Mexico (Bates 1967:58–59)? In anthropology, concepts of human nature and theories of human behavior are based on studies of human groups whose goals, values, views of reality, and environmental adaptations are very different from those of industrial Western societies.

Anthropologists bring a holistic approach to understanding and explaining. To say anthropology is **holistic** means that it combines the study of human biology, history, and the learned and shared patterns of human behavior and thought we call culture in order to analyze human groups. Holism separates anthropology from other academic disciplines, which generally focus on one factor—biology, psychology, physiology, or society—as the explanation for human behavior. Anthropology seeks to understand human beings as whole organisms who adapt to their environments through a complex interaction of biology and culture.

Because anthropologists use this holistic approach, they are interested in the total range of human activity. Most anthropologists specialize in a single field and a single problem, but together they study the small dramas of daily living as well as spectacular social events. They study the ways in which mothers hold their babies or sons address their fathers. They want to know not only how a group gets its food but also the rules for eating it. Anthropologists are interested in how human societies think about time and space and how they see colors and name them. They are interested in health and illness and the significance of physical variation. Anthropologists are interested in sex and marriage and in giving birth and dying. They are interested in folklore and fairy tales, political speeches, and everyday conversation. For the anthropologist, great ceremonies and the ordinary rituals of greeting a friend are all worth investigating. When presented out of context, some of the behaviors anthropologists study seem strange or silly, but every aspect of human behavior can help us to understand human life and society.

SPECIALIZATION IN ANTHROPOLOGY

The broad range of anthropological interest has led to specialization of research and teaching. The major divisions of anthropology are cultural anthropology, linguistic anthropology, archaeology, physical or biological anthropology, and applied anthropology.

CULTURAL ANTHROPOLOGY

Cultural anthropology is the study of human culture and society. A **society** is a group of people who depend on one another for survival or well-being. Traditionally, societies are thought of as occupying a specific geographic location, but modern transportation and electronic communication have made specific locales less important. Societies are increasingly global rather than local phenomena.

The **WWW** icon refers you to additional information about a topic, which can be found on the book's website at **http://anthropology.wadsworth.com.** See the list of all web links at the end of each chapter under "Internet Resources." Additional information about these links can be found in the preface.

holistic/holism The physical proposition that the whole is greater than the sum of its parts. In anthropology, an approach that focuses on the elements of culture, the relationships among these elements, and the relationship of culture to biology and environment.

cultural anthropology The study of human behavior that is learned rather than genetically transmitted, and that is typical of groups of people.

society The set of social relationships among people in their statuses and roles within a given geographical area.

culture The learned behaviors and symbols that allow people to live in groups. The primary means by which humans adapt to their environments. The way of life characteristic of a particular human society.

As Chapter 4 will show, culture is an extremely complex phenomenon. **Culture** is the major way in which human beings adapt to their environments and give meaning to their lives. It includes human behavior and ideas that are learned rather than genetically transmitted, as well as the physical objects produced by a group of people.

Cultural anthropologists attempt to understand culture through the study of its origins, development, and diversity as it changes through time and among people. They bring many research strategies to this task. They may focus on the search for general principles that underlie all cultures or examine the dynamics of a particular culture. They may explore the ways in which different societies adapt to their environments or how members of other cultures understand the world and their place in it.

Cultural anthropologists are often particularly interested in documenting and understanding the ways in which cultures change. They focus on the roles played by power and coercion in change, as well as humans' ability to invent new technologies and social forms and modify old ones. An understanding of the dynamics of culture change can play an important role in determining public policy, and one goal of cultural anthropology is to be able to contribute productively to public debate about social, cultural, and technological change.

LINGUISTIC ANTHROPOLOGY

Language is the primary means by which people communicate with one another; as such, it is a fundamental part of what it means to be human and an essential part of all human cultures. The field of anthropology that is concerned with language is called **linguistics.** Anthropological linguists study linguistic variation, the ways in which human languages have developed, the ways in which they are related to one another, how language is learned, and the relationship between language and other aspects of culture. One aim of anthropological linguistics is to understand the processes of thought and the organization of the human mind as they are expressed in language.

ARCHAEOLOGISTS ATTEMPT TO RECONSTRUCT PAST CULTURES BY STUDYING THEIR MATERIAL REMAINS, AS IN THIS DIG AT AN EARLY SETTLER CABIN IN TEXAS.

Courtesy of Ronald Coley

ARCHAEOLOGY

Archaeology is the study of past cultures through their material remains. Archaeologists thus add a vital time dimension to our understanding of cultures and how they change. Many archaeologists study **prehistoric** societies—those for which no written records have been found or no writing systems have been deciphered. However, even when an extensive written record is available, as in the case of Ancient Greece or Colonial America, archaeology can help us increase our understanding of the cultures and lifeways of those who came before us.

The archaeologist does not observe human behavior and culture directly but reconstructs them from material remains or artifacts. An

---

linguistics A field of cultural anthropology that specializes in the study of human languages.

archaeology The subdiscipline of anthropology that focuses on the reconstruction of past cultures based on their material remains.

prehistoric Societies for which we have no usable written records.

artifact is any object that has been made, used, or altered by human beings. Artifacts thus include pottery, tools, garbage, ruins of buildings, burials, and whatever else a society has left behind.

In the popular media, archaeology is mainly identified with spectacular discoveries of prehistoric and ancient cultures, such as uncovering the tomb of the Egyptian king Tutankhamen, and people often think of archaeologists as collectors of ancient artifacts. But the principal task of archaeology is to infer the nature of past cultures based on the patterns of the artifacts they have left behind. Archaeologists work like detectives who slowly sift and interpret evidence. The context in which things are found, the location of an archaeological site, and the precise position of an artifact within that site are critical to interpretation. In fact, these may be more important than the artifact itself. Contemporary archaeologists are much more interested in understanding and explaining their finds in terms of what they say about the behavior that produced them than in creating collections.

PHYSICAL OR BIOLOGICAL ANTHROPOLOGY

The human ability to survive under a broad range of conditions is based primarily on the enormous flexibility of cultural behavior. The capacity for culture, however, is grounded in our biological history and physical makeup. Human adaptation is thus biocultural; that is, it involves both biological and cultural di-

mensions. Therefore, to understand fully what it is to be human, we need a sense of how the biological aspects of this adaptation came about and how they influence human cultural behavior.

Biological (or **physical**) **anthropology** is the study of humankind from a biological perspective. Biological anthropology includes numerous subfields, such as skeletal analysis, or osteology; the study of human nutrition; demography, or the statistical study of human populations; epidemiology, or the study of patterns of disease; and primatology.

Biological anthropology is probably best known for the study of human evolution and the biological processes involved in human adaptation. **Paleoanthropologists** search for the origins of humanity, using the fossil record to trace the history of human evolution. They study the remains of the earliest human forms, as well as those of nonhuman forms that can suggest something about human origin and development. We explore some of the findings of paleoanthropology in Chapter 2.

Another subspeciality of biological anthropology, called **human variation,** is concerned with physiological differences among modern humans. Anthropologists who study human variation map physiological differences between modern human groups and attempt to explain the sources of this diversity.

Since the human species evolved through a complex feedback system involving both biological and cultural factors, biological anthropologists are also interested in the evolution of culture. Our unique evolutionary history resulted in the development of a biological structure, the human brain, capable of inventing, learning, and using cultural adaptations. Cultural adaptation, in turn, has freed humans from the slow process of biological adaptation: Populations can invent new ways of dealing with problems almost immediately, or adopt them from other societies. The study of the complex relationship between biological and cultural evolution is the link among biological anthropology, cultural anthropology, and archaeology.

Because early human populations were hunters and gatherers, biological anthropologists

---

artifact A material remain of a past culture; any object made or modified by human beings.

biological/physical anthropology The subdiscipline of anthropology that specializes in the study of humankind from a biological perspective. It includes osteology, nutrition, demography, epidemiology, and primatology.

paleoanthropology The subdiscipline of anthropology concerned with tracing the evolution of humankind in the fossil record.

human variation The subdiscipline of anthropology concerned with mapping and explaining physical differences among modern human groups.

study contemporary foraging societies in order to fill in the fragmentary physical evidence left by early humans. In addition to studying living human groups, biological anthropologists study living nonhuman **primates,** members of the order that includes monkeys, apes, and humans. Primates are studied for the clues that their chemistry, physiology, morphology (physical structure), and behavior provide about our own species. At one time primates were studied mainly in the artificial settings of laboratories and zoos, but now much of the work of biological anthropologists involves studying these animals in the wild. Jane Goodall and Dian Fossey are two well-known anthropologists who studied primates in the wild. Fossey, who died in 1985, worked with gorillas in Rwanda. Goodall works with chimpanzees in Tanzania.

Applied Anthropology

Although anthropology is mainly concerned with basic research—that is, asking the big questions about the origins of our species, the development of culture and civilization, and the functions of human social institutions—anthropologists also put their knowledge to work to solve human problems. **Applied anthropologists** use their insights and research techniques to analyze social, political, and economic problems and develop solutions. In this book, we have chosen to highlight some of the work of applied anthropologists. Each chapter includes a box titled "Anthropology Makes a Difference." There, you will read about some of the exciting ways anthropologists are involved in the practical worlds of business, medicine, public policy, law enforcement, and communication.

Specialists in each of the subfields of anthropology make contributions to applied work. For example, in cultural anthropology, experts in the anthropology of agriculture use their knowledge to help people with reforestation, water management, and agricultural productivity. Anthropologists who study legal and criminal justice systems address such problems as drug abuse or racial and ethnic conflict. Al-

ternative forms of conflict resolution, such as mediation, which grew out of anthropological studies of non-Western societies, are now being used in American courts, as adversarial litigation proves itself unequal to the task of resolving civil disputes. Psychological and educational anthropologists contribute to the more effective construction and implementation of educational and mental-health policies, and medical anthropologists apply their cross-cultural knowledge to improve health care, sanitation, diet, and disease control in a variety of cultural contexts.

Archaeologists' research about what Americans throw into the garbage is being used to help solve the nation's garbage crisis—a problem partly caused by consumerism—and to address more theoretical problems, such as how eating habits differ in different social classes (Rathje and Murphy 1993).

Biological anthropologists shed light on some of the major diseases of the modern industrial world by comparing our diet and lifestyle with those of prehistoric and contemporary hunter-gatherer peoples who do not suffer from heart disease, high blood pressure, and diabetes (Eaton and Konner 1989). **Forensic anthropologists** use their knowledge of human skeletal biology to discover information about the victims of crimes, aiding in law enforcement and judicial proceedings.

These examples only hint at the many different subjects and methods of the anthropological specialties. The comparative and holistic perspective of anthropology emphasizes connections between human culture and the environment as well as the links among different elements of culture. The anthropological perspective often demonstrates the complexity of human problems and the difficulty of their

---

primate A member of a biological order of mammals that includes human beings, apes, and monkeys as well as prosimians (lemurs, tarsiers, and others).

applied anthropology The application of anthropology to the solution of human problems.

forensic anthropology The application of biological anthropology to the identification of skeletized or badly decomposed human remains.

A LITTLE HISTORY

Anthropology has a long tradition of being vitally involved in real-world problems. The founders of American anthropology, people such as Franz Boas and Margaret Mead, thought of anthropology as a "reformer's science" and spoke frequently and eloquently on the social, economic, and political problems of their day. Their tradition continues today. Throughout the twentieth century, anthropologists have done important applied work and spoken forcefully on critical issues.

In the early years of the century, Franz Boas fought against the racism of white American society and the proposition that blacks were intellectually inferior to whites. Starting in 1894, and continuing until the end of his life, Boas repeatedly attacked the racist assumptions of most white scientists. Boas, a man of his era, never entirely freed himself from racism, but his correspondence shows deep empathy with African Americans and support for their political struggle (V. Williams 1996). Boas's anti-racist work, as well as that of his students, provided critical elements of the arguments presented by the NAACP before the Supreme Court in *Brown* v. *Board of Education,* the 1954 case that ended legal segregation in American schools (L. Baker 1998).

During the Second World War, anthropologists were drawn into politics and the effort to defeat the Axis powers. Margaret Mead was first active as a member of the Committee on National Morale, which attempted to mobilize social scientists in anthropology, psychology, and sociology for the war effort. As the war progressed, she moved to Washington and became the executive secretary of the Committee on Food Habits, which advised the government on rationing policies as well as nutritional programs designed to feed both Americans and refugees. After the war, this committee evolved into the Committee on Living Habits and eventually laid the groundwork for UNESCO, the United Nations Educational, Scientific, and Cultural Organization (Howard 1984).

After the end of World War II, the attentions of anthropologists turned increasingly to issues of economic development. One famous example was the Vicos Project. In the 1950s and 1960s, a team of anthropologists led by Allan Holmberg and Mario Vasquez attempted to devise a series of programs to help improve the living conditions for Indians on the Vicos hacienda in Peru. The Vicos Project was an early example of integrated development. Instead of focusing on a single aspect of culture change, anthropologists attempted to guide the Indians toward self-sufficiency, the promotion of human dignity, and political independence (Holmberg et al. 1965). Education was combined with changes in agricultural practices, in land ownership, and in the ways people were paid for their labor. The Vicos Project proved to be an important model for other development projects around the world. (You can see a nice photo essay about the Vicos Project at http://etext.lib. virginia.edu/VAR/collier/collier.html).

In the past 25 years, practical application of anthropological ideas has become increasingly important in the world of business and politics. Until the late 1970s, most applied anthropologists were members of university anthropology departments who did some applied work, and interest in applied anthropology remains strong with many of these departments today. However, applied anthropologists are increasingly found outside of university settings. The American Anthropological Association (n.d.) reports that more than half of all new PhD's in anthropology since 1985 have taken jobs in research institutes, nonprofit associations, government agencies, world organizations, or private corporations. There are many local and national organizations of applied anthropologists. Two of the most prominent are the National Association of Practicing Anthropologists and the Society for Applied Anthropology. You can find a wealth of information about careers in anthropology by visiting the "frequently asked questions" section of the Society's website at http://anthap.oakland.edu.

solution. Because politicians and the public generally want quick fixes to social problems, anthropological knowledge is not applied as widely as it could be. Indeed, perhaps the major contribution of anthropology has not been in applying its knowledge but in significantly affecting how people think about themselves in relation to others.

WHAT WE LEARN FROM ANTHROPOLOGY: UNDERSTANDING HUMAN DIFFERENCES

A major contribution of anthropology is to demonstrate the importance of culture, or learned behavior, in human societies. Anthropology enables us to look more critically at popular ideas about human nature; indeed, the anthropological perspective challenges the notion that there is such a thing as a single, stable, scientifically observable human nature. Anthropology demonstrates that what is considered natural in one culture is not necessarily considered natural in all cultures. The notions of natural, unnatural, and supernatural may be absent in other cultures or have different meanings than in American culture.

ETHNOCENTRISM IS THE NOTION THAT ONE'S OWN CULTURE IS SUPERIOR TO ANY OTHER.

ETHNOCENTRISM

When we look at people who are different from ourselves, we are often in the position of a deaf man who sees a bunch of people with fiddles and drums, jumping around every which way, and thinks they are crazy. He cannot hear the music, so he doesn't see that they are dancing (Myerhoff 1978). Similarly, a person who does not hear the music of another culture cannot make sense of its dance. In other words, if we assume that the understandings, patternings, and rules of other cultures are the same as our own, then the actions of other people may seem incomprehensible. One of the most important contributions of anthropology is its ability to open our ears to the music and meaning in other cultures. It challenges and corrects our ethnocentrism.

Ethnocentrism is the notion that one's own culture is superior to any other. It is the idea that other cultures should be measured by the degree to which they live up to our cultural standards. We are ethnocentric when we view other cultures through the narrow lens of our own culture or social position.

The American tourist who, presented with a handful of Italian lire, asks "How much is this in real money?" is being ethnocentric—but there is nothing uniquely American about ethnocentrism. People all over the world tend to see things from their own culturally patterned point of view, through their own cultural filters. They tend to value what they have been taught to value and to see the meaning of life in terms of their own culturally defined purposes. For example, when the people living in Highland New Guinea first saw European outsiders in the 1930s, they believed that the Europeans were the ghosts of their ancestors. It was the only way that these people could initially make sense of what they were seeing (Connolloy and Anderson 1987). Most peoples in the world regard their own culture as superior, and many consider peoples from other cultures to be less than human.

Although most peoples are ethnocentric, the ethnocentrism of Western societies has had greater consequences than that of smaller, less technologically advanced, and more geographically isolated peoples. The historical circumstances that led to the spread of Western culture have given its members a strong belief in its rightness and superiority. Westerners have been in a position to impose their beliefs and practices on other peoples because of their superior military technology and because their

ethnocentrism Judging other cultures from the perspective of one's own culture. The notion that one's own culture is more beautiful, rational, and nearer to perfection than any other.

industrial technology provides an abundance of consumer goods that other people quickly learn to want. The rapid acceptance of the trappings of technological society often leads people in industrialized cultures to believe that their social institutions are superior to those of others.

Although ethnocentrism gets in the way of understanding, some ethnocentrism seems necessary as a kind of glue to hold a society together. A group's belief in the superiority of its own way of life binds its members together and helps them to perpetuate their values. When a culture loses value for its people, they may experience great emotional stress and even lose interest in living. They may be rapidly absorbed by other groups and their culture lost.

To the extent that ethnocentrism prevents building bridges between cultures, however, it is maladaptive. When one culture is motivated by ethnocentrism to trespass on another, the harm done can be enormous. It is but a short step from this kind of ethnocentrism to **racism**—the belief that some human populations are superior to others because of inherited, genetically transmitted characteristics. The transformation from ethnocentrism to racism underlies much of the structural inequality that characterizes modern history.

HUMAN BIOLOGICAL DIVERSITY

Anthropology contributes to our understanding of genetically transmitted differences among human groups, as well as those that result from learning. In comparison to closely related species, the human species shows extremely low levels of morphological (skeletal) and serological (blood type) diversity. However, one of the important outcomes of human evolution is the wide diversity in human form. Some people are short, others are tall; skin color covers a spectrum from very dark to very light; some people have slight builds, others are husky. The degree to which humans vary is even more startling when less obvious differences, such as blood type and other biochemical traits, are taken into account. Moreover, this biological diversity follows geographic patterns, with people from the same region tending to share more traits with each other than they do with people from distant lands. Some of these variations are discussed in greater detail in Chapter 2.

THE CULTURAL CONSTRUCTION OF RACE

A particularly salient aspect of culture in the United States is the assumption that this range of human diversity is best understood as a small number of biologically separate races. Over the past two centuries, scientists have struggled to create a consistent system to identify and classify these races. It may come as a surprise to learn that despite hundreds of years of labor by enormously creative and intelligent researchers, no agreed upon, consistent system of racial classification has ever been developed. Furthermore, other cultures construct racial categories differently than Americans do (see Chapter 13 for an example).

Anthropology in the United States has always been concerned with questions of race. At the turn of the century, Franz Boas, one of the founders of modern American anthropology, argued passionately for **biopsychological equality**—the notion that although individuals differ, all human beings have equal capacity for culture. Before World War II, however, many physical anthropologists attempted to create systems to divide humanity into races and rank them. Today most anthropologists agree that there is no way of doing this and that race, as a biological characteristic of humans, does not exist (Shanklin 1994).

In biological terms, no group of humans has ever been isolated for long enough to make it very different from others. Thus, anthropologists understand systems of racial classification as reflecting social patterning rather than biological reality. Prejudice and racism are certainly realities, but they are not rooted in biological differences between people (Kilker 1993;

---

racism The belief that some human populations are superior to others because of inherited, genetically transmitted characteristics.

biopsychological equality The fact that all human groups have the same biological and mental capabilities.

L. Reynolds 1992). Human beings are truly all members of a single race.

The notion that races are not biological categories might seem unusual, and it is worth a brief detour to point out the problems with the notion of biological race. These problems are many, but three are extremely important: the arbitrary selection of traits used to define races; the inability to adequately describe within-species variation through the use of racial categories; and the repeated independent evolution of so-called racial characteristics in populations with no genetic relationship.

Each human being is a collection of thousands of characteristics such as skin color, blood type, tolerance to lactose (milk sugar), tooth shape, and so on. Variations in these traits result from both genetic and environmental factors as well as interactions between the two. There is no way to weight the importance of any trait in determining racial classification—no reason, for example, why blood type should be intrinsically more or less important than lactose tolerance or hair shape. However, schemes of racial classification select a very small number of traits and ignore others. Such systems typically assume that the traits they have selected have a very strong genetic basis and that these traits are more significant than others, which they ignore. The problem with such schemes is that they identify races that are simply the result of the particular traits the researchers have chosen. In other words, if different traits were chosen, different races would result. Jared Diamond (1994) notes that identifying a race on the basis of lactose tolerance is as valid as basing a racial group on any other trait. However, if we did so, we would group Norwegians, Arabs, north Indians, and some Africans into one race, while excluding other peoples.

It is no accident that the characteristics the members of many cultural groups, including Americans, choose are visible traits such as skin color, eye shape, nose shape, and hair texture. These factors are chosen not because they are particularly important biologically but because they are easily visible and make assigning an individual to a race rather simple. Using blood types, lactose intolerance, or dry versus wet earwax to determine race would be as good (or bad) as other means of defining racial groups, but because such traits are not easily seen, they would be socially useless.

Variation within socially constructed races also presents enormous problems. Obvious and obscure physical differences between members of the same so-called race are enormous, typically exceeding differences between average members of racial groups. In fact, studies using biological measures make it clear that individual differences between people are much greater than racial differences. In other words, measured genetically, you are about as different from another person of your race as you are from another person of a different race.

To illustrate the importance of variation with races, imagine lining up all the students on your campus according to the color of their skin. Assuming the student population is large enough, all skin tones, from the very light people at one end of the line to the very dark people at the other, would be represented. The vast majority of people would fall in between. At what point would white become black? Are people who stand close to each other in the line necessarily more closely related than those who stand further apart? In fact, there is no way to tell who is related to whom by looking at the line.

Finally, the traits that are typically used to define races have arisen repeatedly and independently throughout the world and are the result of common forms of evolution. Most theories of race assume that people who share similar racial characteristics share similar origins. The fact that traits arise recurrently, however, means that this assumption is faulty: people who share similar traits are not necessarily more closely related to each other than to people of other races.

It is often imagined, for example, that all black people are descendants of a group of central Africans and all white people are descendants of a group who lived in the Caucasus Mountains. In fact, this is biological nonsense. To illustrate this point, consider people from the Central African Republic, New Guinea, and France. People from Central African Republic and New Guinea are both likely to have

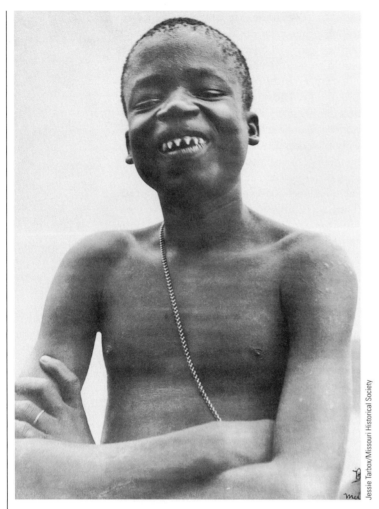

Jessie Tarbox/Missouri Historical Society

OTA BENGA, A PYGMY, WAS BROUGHT TO THE UNITED STATES FOR THE AFRICA EXHIBIT AT THE ST. LOUIS WORLD'S FAIR IN 1904. IN 1906, HE WAS BRIEFLY EXHIBITED AT THE MONKEY HOUSE IN THE BRONX ZOO IN NEW YORK. THE IMPLICATION OF THE EXHIBIT WAS THAT PEOPLE SUCH AS OTA BENGA WERE MORE SIMILAR TO CHIMPANZEES THAN TO WHITE AMERICANS. SUCH EXHIBITIONS REINFORCED THE MISTAKEN NOTION THAT AFRICANS WERE BIOLOGICALLY INFERIOR TO EUROPEANS.

dark skins and share other features. People from France are likely to have white skins and look different. From this, one might conclude that Central Africans and New Guineans are

racialism An ideology that claims there are biologically fixed races with different moral, intellectual, and physical characteristics that determine individual aptitudes and that such races can be ranked on a single hierarchy. Racialists propose that political action should be taken to order society so that it reflects this hierarchy.

more closely related to each other than either is to the French. This is incorrect; the French and the Central African are more likely to share a common inheritance than either is with the New Guinean. This is only logical. A person could walk from France to Central Africa (although this would take a long time), whereas New Guinea, off the coast of Australia, is halfway around the world, separated by water.

RACISM AND RACIALISM

Racism is contempt for people who have physical characteristics different from your own. In Western culture, racism is often combined with racialism. **Racialism** is an ideology based on the following suppositions: There are biologically fixed races; different races have different moral, intellectual, and physical characteristics; an individual's aptitudes are determined primarily by his or her race; races can be ranked on a single hierarchy; and political action should be taken to order society so that it reflects this hierarchy (Todorov 1993:90–96).

The combination of racism and racialism is a particularly pernicious mixture, merging very weak scientific reasoning with agendas for political or social action. Nonetheless, such notions, couched in scientific language, are repeatedly used to buttress the oppression of ethnic minorities, particularly blacks, in the United States as well as many other nations. *The Bell Curve* (Herrnstein and Murray 1994), a popular pseudoscientific account of the effect of racial differences in American society, is only one recent example.

Because race is not a meaningful biological classification, the notion that perceived differences between social groups in characteristics such as intelligence, athletic abilities, perseverance, and creativity are caused by racial inheritance has no biological validity and must be dismissed. People who wish to argue that racial groups have differing biologically based abilities must first show that such groups are biologically distinct. This has not been done and is probably impossible to do.

One of the most important things we can learn by studying anthropology is that although racism is an important social fact, the big differences among human groups are the result of culture, not biological inheritance or race. All human beings belong to the same species, and the biological features essential to human life are common to us all. A human being from any part of the world can learn the cultural and behavioral patterns of any group she or he is born into. Adaptation through culture and the potential for cultural richness and creativity are part of a universal human heritage and override any physical variation among human groups.

ANTHROPOLOGICAL APPROACHES TO CULTURE

Anthropologists have devised critical research and analysis tools in their quest to understand culture. In this section we examine some of the most important ones: cultural relativism, and emic and etic approaches to analysis. We also examine recent trends in anthropological analysis.

ANTHROPOLOGY AND CULTURAL RELATIVISM

Anthropology helps us understand peoples whose ways of life are different from our own but with whom we share a common human destiny. However, we can never understand a people's behavior if we insist on judging it first. **Cultural relativism** is the notion that a people's values and customs must be understood in terms of the culture of which they are a part. Cultural relativists maintain that, for the sake of scientific accuracy, anthropologists must suspend judgment in order to understand the logic and dynamics of other cultures. Observers who view the actions of other people simply in terms of the degree to which they correspond to the observers' notions of right and wrong systematically distort the cultures they observe.

Cultural relativism is a fundamental research tool of anthropology. It is distinct from moral relativism—the notion that because no universal standard of behavior exists, people should not judge between good and evil. Anthropo-

logical methods may require researchers to suspend judgment but not to dispense with it entirely. Anthropologists are not usually moral relativists and are not required to approve of all cultural practices. However, it is possible to understand other cultures without approving of them. Anthropologists insist that every culture has a logic that makes sense to its own members. It is our job to understand that logic, even if we do not approve of it or wish that culture for ourselves.

Using the anthropological technique of cultural relativism helps us to see that our own culture is only one design for living among the many in the history of humankind—a much needed corrective for ethnocentrism. Our culture is an adaptation to one kind of environment with a particular level of technology, and it came into being under a particular set of historical circumstances. An outsider's view of our culture and its historical context is an important contribution anthropology can make to understanding and constructively addressing our society's problems.

From its beginnings, anthropology held out a dual promise: contributing to the understanding of human diversity, and providing a cultural critique of our own society (Marcus and Fischer 1986). By becoming aware of cultural alternatives, we are better able to see ourselves as others see us and to use that knowledge to make constructive changes in our own society. Through looking at the "other," we come to understand ourselves.

EMIC AND ETIC APPROACHES TO CULTURE

Virtually all anthropologists subscribe to the notion of cultural relativism, but they take a variety of perspectives in their attempt to understand culture. Anthropological descriptions of culture are often characterized as either emic or etic, terms drawn from the study of language.

cultural relativism The notion that there are no universal standards by which all cultures may be evaluated. Cultures must be analyzed with reference to their own histories and culture traits understood in terms of the cultural whole.

ETHNOGRAPHY

BODY RITUAL AMONG THE NACIREMA

Anthropologists have become so familiar with the diversity of ways different peoples behave in similar situations that they are not apt to be surprised by even the most exotic customs. In fact, if all of the logically possible combinations of behavior have not been found somewhere in the world, anthropologists are apt to suspect that they must be present in some yet undescribed tribe. . . . In this light, the magical beliefs and practices of the Nacirema present such unusual aspects that it seems desirable to describe them as an example of the extremes to which human behavior can go. The Nacirema are a North American group living in the territory between the Canadian Cree, the Yaqui and Tarahumare of Mexico, and the Carib and Arawak of the Antilles. Little is known of their origin, although tradition states that they came from the east. . . .

Nacirema culture is characterized by a highly developed market economy which has evolved in a rich natural habitat. While much of the people's time is devoted to economic pursuits, a large part of the fruits of these labors and a considerable portion of the day are spent in ritual activity. The focus of this activity is the human body, the appearance and health of which loom as a dominant concern in the ethos of the people. While such a concern is certainly not unusual, its ceremonial aspects and associated philosophy are unique.

The fundamental belief underlying the whole system appears to be that the human body is ugly and that its natural tendency is to debility and disease. Incarcer-ated in such a body, man's only hope is to avert these characteristics through the use of the powerful influences of ritual and ceremony and every household has one or more shrines devoted to this purpose. The rituals associated with the shrine are not family ceremonies but are private and secret. The rites are normally only discussed with children, and then only during the period when they are being initiated into these mysteries. I was able, however, to establish sufficient rapport with the natives to examine these shrines and to have the rituals described to me.

The focal point of the shrine is a box or chest which is built into the wall. In this chest are kept the many charms and magical potions without which no native believes he could live. These preparations are secured from a variety of specialized practitioners. The most powerful of these are the medicine men, whose assistance must be rewarded with substantial gifts. However, the medicine men do not provide the curative potions for their clients, but decide what the ingredients should be and then write them down in an ancient and secret language. This writing is understood only by the medicine men and by the herbalists who, for another gift, provide the required charm. The charm is not disposed of after it has served its purpose, but is placed in the charm-box of the household shrine.

Beneath the charm-box is a small font. Each day every member of the family, in succession, enters the shrine room, bows his head before the charm-box, mingles different sorts of holy water in the font, and proceeds with a brief rite of ablution. The holy waters are secured from the Water Temple of the community, where the priests conduct elaborate ceremonies to make the liquid ritually pure.

In the hierarchy of magical practitioners, and below the medicine men in prestige, are specialists whose designation is best translated "holy-mouth-men." The Nacirema have an almost pathological horror of and fascination with the mouth, the condition of which is believed to have a supernatural influence on all social relationships. Were it not for the rituals of the mouth, they believe that their teeth would fall out, their gums bleed, their jaws shrink, their friends desert them, and their lovers reject them.

The daily body ritual performed by everyone includes a mouth-rite, but in addition, the people seek out a holy-mouth-man once or twice a year. These practitioners have an impressive set of paraphernalia, consisting of a variety of augers, awls, probes, and prods. The use of these objects in the exorcism of the evils of the mouth involves almost unbelievable ritual torture of the client. The holy-mouth-man opens the client's mouth and, using the above mentioned tools, enlarges any holes which decay may have created in the teeth. Magical materials are put into those holes. In the client's view, the purpose of these ministrations is to arrest decay and to draw friends. The extremely sacred and traditional character of the rite is evident in the fact that the natives return to the holy-mouth-men year after year, despite the fact that their teeth continue to decay.

It is to be hoped that, when a thorough study of the Nacirema is made, there will be careful inquiry into the personality structure of these people. One has but to watch the gleam in the eye of a holy-mouth-man, as he jabs an awl into an exposed nerve, to suspect that a certain amount of sadism is involved. If this can be established, a very interesting pattern emerges, for most of the population shows definite masochistic tendencies. For example, a portion of the daily body ritual performed only by men involves scraping and lacerating the surface of the face with a sharp instrument. Special women's rites are performed only four times during each lunar month, but what they lack in frequency is made up in barbarity. As part of this ceremony, women bake their heads in small ovens for about an hour. The theoretically interesting point is that what seems to be a preponderantly masochistic people have developed sadistic specialists.

The medicine men have an imposing temple, or latipsoh, in every community of any size. The more elaborate ceremonies required to treat very sick patients can only be performed at this temple. These ceremonies involve not only the priests who perform miracles, but a permanent group of vestal maidens who move sedately about the temple chambers in distinctive costume and headdress.

The latipsoh ceremonies are so harsh that it is phenomenal that a fair proportion of the really sick natives who enter the temple ever recover. Despite this fact, sick adults are not only willing but eager to undergo the protracted ritual purification, if they can afford to do so. No matter how ill the supplicant or how grave the emergency, the guardians of many temples will not admit a client if he cannot give a rich gift to the custodian. Even after one has gained admission and survived the ceremonies, the guardians will not permit the neophyte to leave until he makes still another gift.

The supplicant entering the temple is first stripped of all his or her clothes. Psychological shock results from the fact that body secrecy is suddenly lost upon entry into the latipsoh. A man whose own wife has never seen him in an excretory act suddenly finds himself naked and assisted by a vestal maiden while he performs his natural functions into a sacred vessel. This sort of ceremonial treatment is necessitated by the fact that the excreta are used by a diviner to ascertain the course and nature of the client's sickness. Female clients, on the other hand, find their naked bodies are subjected to the scrutiny, manipulation, and prodding of the medicine men. The fact that these temple ceremonies may not cure, and may even kill the neophyte, in no way decreases the people's faith in the medicine men.

In conclusion, mention must be made of certain practices which have their base in native esthetics but which depend upon the pervasive aversion to the natural body and its functions. There are ritual fasts to make fat people thin and ceremonial feasts to make thin people fat. Still other rites are used to make women's breasts larger if they are small, and smaller if they are large. General dissatisfaction with breast shape is symbolized in the fact that the ideal form is virtually outside the range of human variation. A few women afflicted with almost inhuman hypermammary development are so idolized that they make a handsome living by simply going from village to village and permitting the natives to stare at them for a fee.

Our review of the ritual life of the Nacirema has certainly shown them to be a magic-ridden people. It is hard to understand how they have managed to exist so long under the burdens which they have imposed upon themselves. But even such exotic customs as these take on real meaning when they are viewed with the insight provided by Malinowski when he wrote: "Looking from far and above, from our high places of safety in the developed civilization, it is easy to see all the crudity and irrelevance of magic. But without its power and guidance early man could not have mastered his practical difficulties as he has done, nor could man have advanced to the higher stages of civilization."

Critical Thinking Questions

1. The Nacirema raise many critical issues for anthropologists. You may have realized that they are modern Americans, but many readers do not. How can anthropologists ensure that their analyses of culture are not as strange and foreign to members of those cultures as the Nacirema are to us?

2. An interpretation that makes no sense to members of the culture being described is not necessarily wrong. Outsiders may be able to perceive essential truths invisible to members of a culture. Has Miner uncovered any basic truths about American culture? Does his analysis of "body ritual" make us look at our own practices in new and productive ways?

3. It's fun to try your own hand at describing the Nacirema. Can you write a description of a Nacirema cultural practice that is similar to this one? What sorts of things might you learn from trying to do so?

Source: Horace Miner, "Body Ritual Among the Nacirema." From *The American Anthropologist,* 1956, 58:503–507.

Anthropologists using the **emic** perspective seek to understand how cultures look from the inside and what one must know in order to think and act as a native. To this end, they analyze cultures using concepts and distinctions that are meaningful to the members of the culture they are studying. The aim of emic research is to generate understanding that a native would find meaningful or to help cultural outsiders gain a sense of what it might be like to be a member of the culture being described.

Anthropologists using an **etic** perspective seek to derive principles or rules that explain the behavior of members of a culture and can be used to compare one culture with another. The methods of analysis, concepts, and distinctions used by etic anthropologists may not be part of the native's cultural awareness, or may even be in conflict with it. However, the aim of etic research is to generate useful scientific theories. It is by this criterion, which may lie outside the native's ability to judge, that etic research is tested.

The debate over whether the emic or etic perspective is more appropriate for the goals of anthropological research is ongoing. However, these arguments often overlook the complementary relationship between the two perspectives. Emic and etic analyses answer different questions about the nature of culture. Furthermore, the attempt to see another culture from the inside (the emic perspective) helps develop our ability to look at our own culture from the outside (an etic perspective). Anthropology, like good poetry, makes the strange familiar and the familiar strange (Spiro 1995).

ANTHROPOLOGY IN A CHANGING WORLD

From the late nineteenth through the mid-twentieth century, when anthropology was developing as a field of study, much of the world was held as colonies by the world's most powerful nations. Additionally, these nations often held ethnic minorities and traditional societies as subjugated populations within their own borders. It was frequently among these colonized and oppressed peoples that anthropologists worked. For example, British and French anthropologists worked among colonized people in Africa. American anthropologists often worked with Native American populations or Pacific Islanders in areas under U.S. control.

Doing anthropological research under such conditions had several implications. First, communities had little control over whether or not to accept an anthropologist. If the government assigned anthropologists to a village, the residents had to accept them. They had no choice in the matter. Second, anthropologists did not have to be responsive to the political or economic needs of the people among whom they worked. Finally, very few of the people among whom anthropologists worked either knew how to read European languages or had access to the libraries and bookstores where anthropological works were available. This meant that anthropologists had little fear their work could be contradicted by those about whom they wrote. Although anthropologists during these times frequently did outstanding work, the conditions under which they worked inevitably affected their descriptions of society.

After World War II, international conditions began to change. Most colonies held by Western powers received their independence in the 1960s. Political liberties were longer in coming in areas held by the Soviet Union, but by the close of the twentieth century the vast majority of people lived in independent nations. Furthermore, education in Western languages has become increasingly available, and communication by radio, television, telephone, and the Internet has become ubiquitous.

The effects on anthropology have been profound. In order to work, anthropologists must now negotiate with independent governments. Community members have much more say than before in deciding to accept anthropologists. Anthropologists can be certain that at least some of the people they work with will hear about or read about the results of their

---

emic (perspective) Examining society using concepts, categories, and distinctions that are meaningful to members of that culture.

etic (perspective) Examining society using concepts, categories, and rules derived from science; an outsider's perspective, which produces analyses that members of the society being studied may not find meaningful.

STONE AGE TRIBES

Introductory anthropology students often imagine that anthropologists go off to study groups that are wholly unaffected by the modern world and uncontaminated by its practices. For better or worse, this is not the case: There have been no such groups for a long time. Members of industrialized cultures had reached virtually every group of people in the world by the time of World War I.

Two exceptions are interesting to note. In the 1930s, the Leahy brothers, Australian gold prospectors, made contact with the peoples of Highland New Guinea. They provided a fascinating pictorial account of this encounter (Connolloy and Anderson 1987). In the early 1970s, anthropologists and journalists hailed the discovery of the gentle Tasaday, a "Stone Age" tribe living in the Philippines. However, it is now widely suspected that the Tasaday were a hoax (Berreman 1990; Headland 1992).

Today, anthropologists are apt to find that the people they work with wear T-shirts with the names of American cities or professional sports teams, drink Coca-Cola, and watch CNN and MTV. They often know more about what is going on in the world than the anthropologists themselves. Anthropologist Robert Hitchcock reports that in October 1995, during the O. J. Simpson murder trial, he spoke to an elderly Ju/'hoansi man about hunting. "This man, who was sitting in the sand working sharpening a poison arrow, looked up at me and said, "Well, do you think OJ's guilty?" (Hitchcock 1997:1).

research. Additionally, anthropologists now come from many of the communities that anthropologists have traditionally studied. These anthropologists, as well as many others, raise hard questions about the nature of the discipline (Yanagisako and Delaney 1994; Rosaldo 1993; Said 1993; Marcus 1992; di Leonardo 1991; Hooks 1989; Clifford and Marcus 1986). They challenge the accuracy of past anthropological reporting and raise doubts about the ability of anthropologists to accurately describe cultures. They urge anthropologists to consider exactly whose story gets told and why.

Issues such as these present interesting theoretical challenges to anthropology. But they are also very important because anthropological research often has political implications. As contemporary social groups, whether nations or smaller units within nations, search for identity and autonomy, cultural representations become important resources, and traditions once taken for granted become the subject of heightened political consciousness. **Indigenous peoples,** as well as minority groups within nations, want their cultures to be represented to the outside world in ways acceptable to them and are holding anthropologists responsible for the political impact of their work.

Anthropologists have responded to these challenges in a variety of ways. For example, anthropologists have become much more explicit about the exact conditions under which their data were collected. They increasingly present their work using multiple viewpoints, trying to tell the story of a culture from the perspective not only of the detached social scientist but also of men, women, and children with the society under study. Additionally, many have become politically active, fighting for the rights of oppressed minorities and traditional peoples throughout the world.

The challenges to anthropology and the discipline's response to them have caused enormous controversy. Some theorists insist that anthropology must be committed and engaged. They argue that it is the duty of anthropologists to defend the rights of the oppressed and present the views of those who have not previously been heard. Others argue that such political engagement distorts anthropological

indigenous peoples Groups of people who have occupied a region for a long time but who have a minority position and usually little or no influence in the government of the nation–state that ultimately controls their land.

research and that anthropologists should be concerned with gathering data as objectively as possible and using it to increase our theoretical knowledge of the underlying dynamics of human society (see D'Andrade, Scheper-Hughes, et al. 1995 for a good example of this debate).

We firmly believe that anthropology benefits from lively discussion of its role and meaning. The participation of anthropologists from many backgrounds as well as members of the communities anthropologists study makes the discipline richer and the debate more useful. As Chapter 4 shows, no single understanding of culture commands the devotion of all anthropologists or ever has. Many anthropologists believe that our studies should become more reflective on issues of politics, history, and context (R. Lee 1992a). Others insist on a commitment to the generation of theories that transcend these same factors. Regardless of these differences, anthropologists are dedicated to understanding the nature of human diversity and similarity; to exploring the context, depth, origins, and, occasionally, the poetry of human experience. Most anthropologists hope that, with the help of such understanding, we will leave the world a better place than we found it.

SUMMARY

1. Anthropology is a comparative study of humankind. It studies human beings in the past and the present and in every corner of the world.

2. Anthropology is holistic. It studies the whole range of human social, political, economic, and religious behavior as well as the relationships among the different aspects of human behavior.

3. Anthropology focuses on what is typical within a human group, rather than on differences among individuals.

4. The aim of anthropology is to discover and explain the similarities and differences among human groups.

5. Biological anthropology focuses on human characteristics that are transmitted genetically.

6. Cultural anthropology focuses on culture, the learned and shared ways of behaving typical of a particular human group. Anthropologists also study culture in general and attempt to discover laws of cultural development that apply to the whole of humankind.

7. Archaeology is a specialty in cultural anthropology. Archaeologists study societies that existed in the past and did not leave written records.

8. Linguistics is a specialty in cultural anthropology. Linguists study the history, structure, and variation of human language.

9. Applied anthropologists not only do basic research but also apply their knowledge to solving human problems.

10. Anthropology stresses the importance of culture in human adaptation. It asserts that critical differences among individuals are cultural rather than biological.

11. Anthropology reduces ethnocentrism, or looking at and judging other people through the narrow perspective of one's own culture.

12. Anthropology demonstrates that race is not a valid scientific category but rather a social and cultural construct.

13. Anthropology introduces the concept of cultural relativism, which means that anthropologists refrain from judging the values and practices of other cultures until they understand them.

14. By taking the outsider's view of our own society and culture, we can understand it more objectively and perhaps use this understanding to make more rational changes in our own lives.

15. Anthropology can present both emic and etic views of culture. Emic anthropology attempts to describe the organization and meaning that a culture's practices have for its members. Etic anthropology tries to determine the causes and consequences of particular cultural patterns that may be beyond the awareness of members of the culture being studied.

16. With the end of colonialism, the theories and practices of anthropology are being challenged by peoples whose cultures have traditionally been studied by anthropology.

KEY TERMS

anthropology

applied
  anthropology

archaeology

artifacts

biological/physical
  anthropology

biopsychological
  equality

cultural
  anthropology

cultural relativism

culture

emic

ethnocentrism

etic

forensic
  anthropology

holistic/holism

human variation

indigenous peoples

linguistics

paleoanthropology

prehistoric

primate

racialism

racism

society

SUGGESTED READINGS

Anderson, Barbara G. 1999. *Around the World in 30 Years: Life as a Cultural Anthropologist.* Prospect Heights, IL: Waveland Press. Anderson describes her experiences as an anthropologist in ten cultures, including the United States, France, Thailand, Japan, Russia, and Corsica. In each chapter she highlights principles of anthropology, as well as describing both the successes and failures of life as an anthropologist in the field.

DeVita, Philip R., and James D. Armstrong. 1993. *Distant Mirrors: America as a Foreign Culture.* Belmont, CA: Wadsworth. An entertaining series of articles with a serious message: how U.S. culture looks to foreign anthropologists. This book gives the United States a chance to "see ourselves as others see us."

Gould, Stephen Jay. 1982. *The Mismeasure of Man.* New York: Norton. A brilliant and important book that attacks the theories of biological determinism in a well-argued and carefully documented manner.

Grindal, Bruce, and Frank Salamone (Eds.). 1995. *Bridges to Humanity: Narratives on Anthropology and Friendship.* Prospect Heights, IL: Waveland. A collection of fourteen essays by anthropologists, who explore the process of anthropological research

and the often very personal meanings it has for them. This book explores the ways that anthropology changes our understanding of others and of ourselves.

Malik, Kenan. 1996. *The Meaning of Race.* New York: New York University Press. A provocative and stimulating discussion of the development of the idea of race in the history and culture of Western society. Malik focuses specific attention on recent events, particularly the end of the Cold War.

Shanklin, Eugenia. 1994. *Anthropology and Race.* Belmont, CA: Wadsworth. A brief and highly readable review of the history of the idea of race. The book emphasizes the inability of scientists to find a consistent biological basis for race.

Spradley, James, and David W. McCurdy (Eds.). 2000. *Conformity and Conflict: Readings in Cultural Anthropology.* Boston: Allyn and Bacon. A classic but frequently updated collection of readings that covers a broad range of topics, demonstrating both anthropological principles and theoretical approaches.

INTERNET RESOURCES

The following Internet resources appear in this chapter. Please log on to the Wadsworth anthropology website: **http://anthropology. wadsworth.com**. Click on the Nanda/Warms *Cultural Anthropology* page. Then select the Student Resources section, where you will find a complete presentation of these links and more.

- The website of the American Anthropological Association, page 2
- Link to Wadsworth's Applied Anthropology Resource Center, page 5
- A photo essay on the biological unity and variation among humans, page 8
- Access to the Study Guide to InfoTrac College Edition for Anthropology Students

RESEARCHER DIAN FOSSEY (1932–1985) WAS A PIONEER OF OBSERVING PRIMATE BEHAVIOR IN THE WILD. UNDERSTANDING PRIMATE
BEHAVIOR HELPS TEACH US ABOUT THE PLACE OF HUMANS IN THE NATURAL WORLD.

CHAPTER TWO

HUMAN EVOLUTION

What is Darwin's theory of evolution by natural selection, and how well accepted is it?

What characteristics do humans have in common with our nearest nonhuman relations, and where do these characteristics come from?

Do complex social lives and the use of tools distinguish humans from the members of all other species?

Who were our ancestors, the Australopithecines, Homo habilis, *and* Homo erectus, *and how did they live?*

How are modern-day humans different from our earlier ancestors?

If all human beings are members of a single species, how come we look so different from one another?

Speculation about the history of humanity and the natural world plays an important role in most societies. The notion that human beings came from earlier life forms was well developed among ancient European philosophers. In the sixth century BCE, the Greek thinker Anaximander of Miletus speculated that humans arose from fish. A century later, his disciple Xenophanes of Colophon used evidence of fossil fish from numerous places around the Mediterranean to support Anaximander's theory. Echoes of this theory are found in the work of other Greek philosophers.

Several centuries later, the Roman philosopher Titus Lucretius Carus (99–55 BCE) proposed a theory of evolution that, in some senses, sounds almost modern. In the fifth book of his great work, *De Rerum Natura,* Lucretius anticipated Darwin by suggesting that some creatures became extinct when they failed to leave sufficient offspring, while others prospered "by cunning or by valor, or at least by speed of foot or wing."

Although modern human behavior is almost totally learned and cultural, it rests on a biological base. It is expressed in the brains and bodies of actual human beings. These brains and bodies were shaped by the process of evolution. Thus, evolution has shaped our behavior. For example, we have highly accurate depth perception and hands with opposable thumbs and the ability to manipulate objects with great precision. These features, which developed over the course of evolution, are absolutely fundamental to the cultural behavior of modern humans. Members of all cultures are adept tool users. Humans make tools ranging from fishhooks and spears to microprocessors and satellites. The use of such tools is basic to human life and helps to shape the patterns of subsistence, learning, and communication within society. Our ability to make and use sophisticated tools is based on our capacity to accurately gauge the positions of objects in space and manipulate them with great precision. If we were not able to do these things, human culture would be vastly different, if it existed at all.

While human cultures are vastly different, human bodies and brains are all very similar. All human beings share a common evolutionary heritage. We became who we are biologically under specific historical and environmental conditions. Understanding our evolutionary history is vital to cultural anthropologists because it tells us about the physical, material base upon which all culture is built, and thus informs us about the things that all humans have in common. As we learn about evolution, we gain insight into what it means to be human, the ties that bind us to one another, and our relationship to the nonhuman world.

DARWIN AND NATURAL SELECTION

In the eighteenth and nineteenth centuries, scientists in Europe and North America proposed many different theories of evolution. It was Charles Darwin's theory of evolution by **natural selection,** however, that proved the most convincing scientific explanation of the variety and history of life on earth.

Darwin, the son of a prominent medical doctor, was born in England in 1809. He was educated at Cambridge University, where he studied to become a minister. Perhaps the central event of Darwin's life was his five-year voyage of discovery, from 1831 to 1836, aboard HMS *Beagle.* Darwin made numerous contributions to scientific discovery during the voyage, but most important, he collected the data that would enable him to formulate his theory of evolution by natural selection.

It took Darwin a long time to publish his ideas on evolution. He returned from his travels in 1836, and though he produced several books about his experiences and discoveries, he did not publish his theory on evolution for more than twenty years. Understanding the implications of his thesis and deeply concerned about its reception, Darwin spent much of this time gathering additional evidence. The work

CHARLES DARWIN AS A YOUNG MAN. DARWIN'S THEORY OF NATURAL SELECTION REVOLUTIONIZED EVOLUTIONARY THOUGHT BECAUSE IT ACCURATELY SHOWED HOW EVOLUTION OCCURRED.

might never have been published during his lifetime, but in 1858 Darwin received word that another scientist, Alfred Russell Wallace, had independently arrived at similar conclusions and intended to publish them. Darwin and Wallace presented their work together at the Linnean Society of London in July 1859, and it was published in the society's journal the following year. Despite this joint publication, Darwin's name is more closely associated with evolution than Wallace's—probably because Darwin, rather than Wallace, spent much of the rest of his very productive life (he died in 1882) expanding and defending the theory.

THE THEORY OF NATURAL SELECTION

Darwin's notion of natural selection is both powerful and elegant. It is a relatively simple set of ideas with profound consequences. Because it is based on things that are easily ob-

natural selection The mechanism of evolutionary change; changes in traits of living organisms that occur over time as a result of differences in reproductive success among individuals.

servable, such as variation among members of a species, most of its elements are easy to verify and extremely difficult to refute. As a result, Darwin's theory has been highly durable.

Darwin began by pointing out the great variety of nature. He observed that no two living things, even those of the same species, are quite alike. Living things not only vary in their external appearance but exhibit subtle differences of internal structure as well.

Variation among members of a species comes from many sources. All living things are subject to **mutations,** or random changes in genetic material. Mutations result from external environmental sources, such as background radiation or contact with chemical agents. They may also result during the process of sexual reproduction. Mutations are the ultimate source of all variation. Sexual reproduction and the movement of individuals and groups from place to place result in the mixing of genetic material and also create new variations. Isolation can play an important role as well. Imagine that a small number of individuals is separated from a larger population. By chance, some members of the small group have a characteristic relatively rare in the larger population—say, a sixth finger on their right hand. The descendants of this small, isolated group will have an unusually large percentage of individuals with six fingers, compared with the larger population from which they were separated. This process is known as **genetic drift.**

Darwin went on to observe that most creatures, human and nonhuman, did not survive long enough to have offspring. They fell victim to predators, contracted diseases, or perished through some defect in their biological makeup. Though it is apparent to us that very few animals survive to reproductive age, with the advent of modern medicine we are used to the idea that most human children will survive. However, before the development of sanitation in the nineteenth century and antibiotics in the twentieth, vast numbers of children died very young. For example, more than 40 percent of all deaths in London between 1813 and 1820 were children under ten years old (Roberton 1827). Even today, in the world's poor nations, large numbers of children die before they reach the age of five. In 1998, for example, more than 20 percent of children died before the age of five in Angola, Burkina Faso, Malawi, Mali, Sierra Leone, and several other African nations. More than 10 percent died in Iraq, Myanmar, and Nepal (World Bank 2000).

Darwin argued that, in most cases, those creatures that survived did so for some reason. That is to say, their survival was not a random occurrence. There was something about them that favored their survival. Perhaps they blended well with a background and so were more difficult for predators to see, or they had a bit more resistance to a disease. Perhaps their shape made them a bit more efficient at getting food, or their digestive system a bit better at processing the food they did find. (See Figure 2.1.)

Darwin was profoundly affected by the economic and social philosophy of his era, particularly the works of Adam Smith and Thomas Malthus. Both of these philosophers had emphasized the role of competition in human social life. In the 1770s, Smith had argued that competition among firms increased their productivity and led to social betterment. A quarter century later, Malthus wrote that because human population levels rose much faster than agricultural production, struggles over resources were inevitable. Darwin, synthesizing these two positions, gave competition and struggle a prominent role in his theory. He argued that life involved constant struggle. Creatures competed with many others for food and with members of their own species for mates. Those who had traits that suited them well to their environment tended to win this struggle for nutrition and reproduction. Thus, Darwin combined the struggle-for-food element of Malthus's work with the notion drawn from Adam Smith that competition leads to betterment.

Darwin further argued that those who won this struggle for survival were able, in some way, to pass some of the traits that led to their success to their offspring. Thus, each subsequent generation would include more and more individuals with these traits and fewer without.

mutation A random change in genetic material; the ultimate source of all biological variation.

genetic drift Changes in the frequencies of specific traits caused by random factors.

(a) **Ground finch**
Main food: seeds
Beak: heavy

(b) **Tree finch**
Main food: leaves, buds, blossoms, fruits
Beak: thick, short

(c) **Tree finch** (called woodpecker finch)
Main food: insects
Beak: stout, straight

(d) **Ground finch** (known as warbler finch)
Main food: insects
Beak: slender

FIGURE 2.1

BEAK VARIATIONS IN DARWIN'S GALÁPAGOS FINCHES.
DARWIN FOUND MANY DIFFERENT SPECIES OF FINCH ON
THE GALÁPAGOS, EACH WITH A BEAK SPECIALIZED FOR A
PARTICULAR TYPE OF FOOD.

Darwin reasoned that, over the course of millions of years, this process could give rise to new species and all of the tremendous variation of the natural world.

Darwin's theory of evolution by natural selection is sometimes referred to as "survival of the fittest," but this phrase was coined by the social theorist Herbert Spencer, not by Darwin himself. Although Darwin reportedly approved of Spencer's phrase, it is misleading for modern readers. When Spencer spoke of fit-

ness, he thought of wealth, power, and physical strength. But when Darwin spoke of fitness, he meant reproductive success: Creatures better adapted to their environment tend to succeed in the struggle for food and mates, passing on their traits, while those less well adapted tend to disappear. Modern readers tend to understand fitness the way Spencer did, equating it with strength or intellect. So, it sounds as if Darwin's theory actually says the strong and smart survive. But this is incorrect. Strength and intelligence do not necessarily guarantee reproductive success. They are not important for all creatures or environments. Consider the tree sloth, the famous South American tree-dwelling mammal. Sloths are neither particularly strong nor intelligent, yet their continually growing teeth, multichambered stomachs, protective coloring, and habit of sleeping most of the day and night adapt them well to their tropical forest environment.

EVOLUTION, POLITICS, AND RELIGION

Darwin's theory of evolution is highly controversial, particularly in the United States. It is extremely important to point out, however, that virtually all of the debate about evolution is religious and political rather than scientific. The majority of the world's religions have stories about the ways in which animals and humans came to live on the earth. Evolution challenges a literal reading of these stories, and for this reason it has been strongly resisted by leaders and congregations in some religions. It is important to note that not all religious people argue against evolution. The Catholic Church, for example, declared that evolution was compatible with Christian teachings in 1950, half a century ago. Pope John Paul II repeated and expanded this position in 1996. Many theologians in a great variety of religions agree that evolution is consistent with the teachings of their tradition. In official publications and conference proceedings, the United Presbyterian Church, the Episcopalian Church, the Unitarian Church, the United Methodist Church, and the Central Council of American Rabbis have all supported evolution and opposed the teaching of "scientific" creationism in public schools (Lieberman and Kirk 1996).

Whether the religious agree or not, Darwin's theory of evolution by natural selection has withstood more than 140 years of intensive scientific scrutiny. Today there is no meaningful scientific challenge to evolutionary theory. In fact, evolution has become part of the basic framework of all biological sciences. Just as it is impossible to imagine a science of physics without the theory of gravity, so too modern biology, biochemistry, and many other fields of scientific endeavor are grounded in evolution and all but unthinkable without it.

The fact that scientists who study biology overwhelmingly agree on the basic principles of evolution and natural selection does not mean there are no disputes among them. Scholars argue about the speed of evolution and the precise conditions under which it occurs. There is much discussion about the historic relationships of plants and animals and how they should be classified. Scientists debate the appropriate evolutionary place of specific fossil human ancestors. It is important to understand, however, that all of this debate takes place within the context of evolution. All sides in these arguments agree with the basic principles of natural selection, though they may differ about the specific applications.

HUMANS AND OUR NEAREST RELATIVES

When people think about human evolution, they generally associate the idea with the notion that human beings evolved from apes or monkeys. It is important to understand that this is incorrect. Rather, modern-day humans and modern-day gorillas and chimpanzees evolved from common ancestors. The distinction is critical. First of all, it is biologically inaccurate to say that humans evolved from modern-day great apes. But perhaps as important, saying so leads to a misunderstanding of evolution.

Saying that humans evolved from gorillas or chimpanzees suggests that humans are more evolved than these animals. However, no creature can be any more evolved than another. We can only imagine that we are more evolved if we believe that intellect or ability to alter the environment is the most important criterion of evolution. However, that is an extremely human-centered way of looking at biology. We could as easily say that producing the greatest number of related species or the greatest number of individuals is the best measure of evolution. If we were to take these criteria seriously, it would be clear that insects are far more "evolved" than humans. For example, there are believed to be more than 8,000 species of ants, comprising countless individuals. By contrast, there is only a single species of humans, comprising a mere 5 billion individuals. Realizing that humans and our nearest nonhuman relations evolved from a common ancestor promotes the understanding that humans, gorillas, chimpanzees, and other animals are all equally evolved. They just evolved in different ways and under different environmental circumstances.

OUR SHARED ANCESTOR AND COMMON CHARACTERISTICS

Once we understand that humans and our nearest relatives evolved from a common ancestor, the next question we should ask is who that ancestor was. The question is not easily answered: so far, no fossil that is clearly ancestral to both humans and chimpanzees or humans and gorillas has been found. However, other fossil finds, as well as information gained from a series of biochemical dating techniques, enable us to know a good deal about the creature even though we have not yet found it.

Biological anthropologists use the fossil record and a variety of techniques based on the study of DNA, blood protein, blood-clotting agents, and immunology to try and determine when the animals that were the common ancestors of humans and other primate species lived. Evidence from a variety of sources yields similar dates. It shows that the creatures that became humans and apes split from those that gave rise to the monkeys of Europe, Africa, and Asia about 20 million years ago. We last had a common ancestor with orangutans between 10 and 13 million years ago. Human ancestors diverged from the ancestors of chimpanzees

Lynn Kilgore

TO LIVE IN TREES, PRIMATES SUCH AS THIS WHITE-HANDED GIBBON DEVELOPED VERY ACUTE HAND-EYE COORDINATION.

and gorillas between 5 and 8 million years ago (Sibley and Ahlquist 1987; Sibley, Comstock, and Ahlquist 1990; Spuhler 1989; Templeton 1985, 1986; Marks, Schmidt, and Sarich 1988; Holmquist, Miyamoto, and Goodman 1988; Pilbeam 1996).

Our common ancestry means that humans, chimpanzees, gorillas, and other primates have many similarities. All primates originated as tree-dwelling mammals, and many of our commonalities come from this **arboreal** ancestry. To survive in the three-dimensional world of trees, primates needed grasping hands and feet that could be used in climbing and could hold branches firmly. Often their hands and feet have fully opposable thumbs. To live in trees, primates developed very acute eyesight; most see in great detail and in color. Additionally, tree dwellers need very accurate depth perception. Misjudging the precise location of an object, such as a branch or a piece of fruit, can easily lead to a fall and death. In primates, accurate depth perception comes from overlapping fields of vision. Primates have eyes that face forward, near the front of their heads. The field of vision of each eye overlaps the other. The result is that we, and other primates, see objects close to us from two slightly different angles at once.

arboreal Tree-dwelling.

Our brains use the slight differences in the images produced by each eye to accurately compute the distance to the object. This completely unconscious process is known as stereoscopic vision. Reliance on hand-eye coordination developed along with the expansion of the areas of the brain involved in vision, motor skills, and the integration of the two.

Life in the trees also involved reductions in some sensory capacities. For example, terrestrial mammals generally have a highly developed sense of smell. Both predators and prey rely heavily on smell to detect each other. In the trees, smell plays a much weaker role. Most scent molecules are heavy and tend to accumulate at ground level. Further, breezes make scent a less dependable indicator of direction than it is on the ground. As a result, primates have a reduced sense of smell compared to most other mammals.

PRIMATE SOCIAL LIFE

WWW Primates, particularly apes and humans, have a larger brain compared to their body weight than do other animals, and many have extremely complicated social lives. While human social life clearly differs greatly from that of our closest ape relations, there are some similarities as well. By examining the characteristics of primate social lives, we may be able to find basic patterns shared by all primates, including humans. We may also learn the ways in which humans are fundamentally different from our primate relations.

Almost all primates live in social groups, and these have several different sorts of structure. Gorillas live in groups consisting of a single adult male and numerous adult females and their offspring. Chimpanzees, on the other hand, live in groups that include several adult males and several adult females and their offspring. Gibbons as well as several species of monkey live in monogamous pairs, while several species of monkey from Central and South America live in groupings with one female and two males (Jolly 1985).

The core of primate societies is the bond between mothers and their infant offspring. With the possible exception of elephants, the mother-infant bond is stronger among pri-

DISAPPEARING PRIMATES

Learning about primate behavior is basic to understanding human evolution. Knowing how creatures are both like ourselves and different from ourselves helps us comprehend what it means to be a human being. However, throughout the world, primates are increasingly endangered. Although no species of primate has become extinct in the past century, many are on the verge of disappearing today. The World Conservation Union identifies about 15 percent of the approximately 620 primate species as either endangered or critically endangered. This means that many of these species will disappear in the coming decades unless people take active steps to preserve them.

One key factor threatening primate populations is destruction of habitat. The tropical forests where most primates live are threatened by expanding human populations and commercial exploitation. As human populations expand, people bring new lands into cultivation, destroying primate habitat as they do so. In addition, international demand for hardwoods and tropical produce also encourage the felling of forests and the establishment of agricultural plantations. In some areas, the combination of population increase and commercial demand has resulted in the destruction of more than 90 percent of the original habitat for some primates.

Primates face other problems, too. Political turmoil can have horrific effects on animal populations and is of fundamental concern. A good example is the fate of the wildlife in the central African nations of Rwanda and Congo. These nations are home to many primates species, including some of the only remaining groups of mountain gorillas. They are also plagued by civil war, economic turmoil, and genocide. As farming and market systems collapse, populations desperate to survive turn to hunting primates and other animals for food. People desperate for a little cash are willing to sell any animal body parts that might be used as medicine or to provide souvenirs to wealthy outsiders. Thus, the fate of wildlife is linked to that of humans. As long as people are desperately poor and live in nations in turmoil, wildlife will be threatened. Protecting endangered species in these areas must involve more than simply constructing preserves. Viable, politically and economically secure lifestyles must be found for the human as well as the animal populations.

Many groups are involved in attempting to protect the lives and habitats of endangered primates. Some of these are Conservation International (www.conservation.org), The Dian Fossey Gorilla Fund International (www.gorillafund.org), Primate Conservation Inc. (www.primate.org), and the World Wildlife Fund (www.worldwildlife.org).

---

mates than any other animals. Infants spend most of their time in very close contact with their mother and travel by clinging to their mother's belly. In many primate species, if a mother dies, the offspring will be adopted by other adult females. Often an adopter is a family member of the deceased mother, and grandmothers may play an important role in parenting (Fairbanks 1988).

The intense bonding between mother and offspring is an ideal ground for teaching and learning. Primates have an enormous ability and need to learn. Young primates learn initially by imitating their mother's actions. In this way, they discover where to find food and water as well as which other animals are dangerous and which can be approached safely.

As primates grow older, play becomes central to their interaction with their age-mates, and they may spend most of their waking hours playing. Most play is intense, repetitive, and physical. By playing, primates refine their physical skills, explore their world, and practice solving problems. It is important to understand that primates are motivated to learn because much of learning, like play, is highly pleasurable for them (Fagan 1993).

In most primate societies, both males and females develop dominance hierarchies; that is, they are ranked as superior or inferior to one another. These hierarchies exist both within and between genders. Although such hierarchies, particularly among males, are created and maintained by shows of aggression, anthropol-

Courtesy Meredith Small

GROOMING IS AN ESSENTIAL ELEMENT OF SOCIAL BEHAVIOR IN MANY PRIMATE SPECIES, AS AMONG THESE LONGTAIL MACAQUES.

cific. That is, a low-ranking female might give way to higher rank in competition for food but will defend her baby against all others, regardless of rank.

In addition to displays of aggression, primates have many means of reconciliation. One of the best known, grooming, is common among members of the same sex as well as members of different sexes. Inferior-rank animals groom their superiors, and friends groom friends. Among chimpanzees, baboons, and others, friends may hug, pat each other, or hold hands. A variety of other behaviors, including lip smacking and male–male mounting behaviors, are used to establish, reestablish, or maintain friendly relations between individuals and cohesion within the group.

ogists believe that overall they serve to limit the amount of aggression with societies; once the hierarchy is established, lower-ranking individuals are less likely to challenge those with more status than might otherwise be the case.

The critical benefit of high rank is greater access to food, sex, and other resources. There is also evidence that high-ranking individuals reproduce more frequently than those of low rank. However, this is controversial. Although it is true that high-ranking males are frequently seen having sex, both by anthropologists and by members of their own species, there is evidence that low-ranking males also have frequent sex—they just do it covertly. Thus, even though high-ranking males have better reproductive chances, those of lower rank are not always effectively prevented from fathering offspring.

Among most primates, dominance hierarchies result from a great many individual encounters. Thus, while the presence of a hierarchy prevents constant conflict, rankings are not absolutely fixed. Aggression among animals does occur, and patterns of dominance within the group may change. Furthermore, it is important to note that rank may be context spe-

termite fishing The learned use of twigs or blades of grass to extract termites from their mounds characteristic of some groups of chimpanzees.

TOOL USE AMONG PRIMATES

The use of tools is fairly common among nonhuman animals. Many different animals build nests; some, like sea otters, use rocks, twigs, or leaves to get at their prey. However, these capacities seem qualitatively different from the extremely complex and varied tool manufacture and use among humans. Nonhuman primates also use tools, but in ways that seem different both from the behavior of animals such as sea otters and from humans.

Monkeys use sticks and branches to threaten others or defend themselves when they are threatened. Some Japanese macaques wash their food, use water to separate grains of wheat from sand, and play with rocks (Strier 2000; Huffman and Quiatt 1986; Jurmain et al. 1997). However, the most sophisticated tool use is found among chimpanzees and bonobos. Two well-documented examples of chimpanzee and bonobo tool use are termite fishing and the use of leaf sponges.

Termite fishing involves the use of a stick or blade of grass. After carefully selecting a stick, chimpanzees modify it, by stripping off leaves and any other material that might interfere with the task at hand. They place these tools in termite mounds, wait until the termites begin to feed on them, then withdraw them to eat the termites. Chimps make leaf sponges by taking leaves, chewing them, and then using the resulting wad of material to soak up water from tree hollows and other places difficult for them to access. They also use leaves to clean their fur and pick their teeth. Both termite fishing and the use of leaf sponges are complex actions requiring foresight and planning.

It is particularly interesting that behaviors such as termite fishing and leaf chewing are not species-wide. Rather, some groups of chimpanzees do them and others do not. This implies that such practices are learned behavior passed along as part of the knowledge of the social group, very much like human culture. It is also interesting that among all primates who use tools, it is females who first develop tool-using skills. Further, females generally become more adept at tool use than males (Strier 2000).

THE EVOLUTION OF HUMANS

Human beings and our nearest ape relations have been following separate courses of evolution for the past 5 to 8 million years. In this time, our species has developed in systematic ways. Our early ancestors were relatively few in number and geographically confined to Africa. In 1999, the world's population topped 6 billion, and humans live on every continent. Our early ancestors did not depend heavily on tools, and their cultures left few material remains. They were certainly able to learn, and depended on learning for their survival. However, the range of their learning was probably small. Today, people make millions of different sorts of tools and other material items. We transform our landscape in radical and novel ways. Our ability to learn is vastly greater than that of our early ancestors, and our environment demands that we innovate, applying our learning in new and original ways.

The history of human evolution is thus a narrative of movement. Human beings have spread from our African origins to inhabit most of the globe. This means we have adapted to living in many different climates and ecosystems: surviving in temperate areas involves different skills than living in the tropics, and living in the rain forest is different from living in the desert. The primary methods by which humans and our ancestors adapted to the different demands of their environments included finding new foods, making new tools, developing clothing, and controlling fire. In other words, we have adapted through changing our behavior. The gradual spread of humans and our ancestors reflects our history of gradually increasing dependence on learned, cultural behavior.

NAMING NAMES

Human ancestors, like those of other species, are generally referred to by their scientific names. All human ancestors, as well as current-day humans, are members of the biological family *Hominidae.* Within this family, individual ancestors are known by the names of their genus and species. A **genus** is a group of similar species.

Among living creatures, there is a relatively simple guideline for determining if similar animals are members of the same or different **species.** If a male and female are capable of producing fertile offspring, they are members of the same species. If they can produce no offspring at all, or if the offspring are infertile, they are members of different species. For example, horses and donkeys are similar, but their offspring, mules, are infertile. Therefore, we must say they are members of different species. With extinct creatures, such as our fossil ancestors, no such test can be performed. Therefore, determining species membership is much more speculative.

Human ancestors and modern-day people fall into two genera (the plural of genus): *Australopithecus* and *Homo.* Some anthropologists argue that the earliest of our ancestors fall into a third genus, *Ardipithecus,* but whether these fossils are different enough from *Australopithecus* to constitute a separate genus is still debated. Modern people, *Homo sapiens,* are members of

genus In biological classification, a group of similar species.

species In biological classification, a group of organisms whose members are similar to one another and are able to reproduce with one another but not with members of other species.

THERE'S EVIDENCE!

Reconstructions of the evolutionary history of human beings are based on data. But how do anthropologists find the data, and how do they figure out when human ancestors lived?

Many of the data used to build our theories of human evolution are found in the form of fossils. Fossils may be of a great many different kinds. Sometimes they are bones; sometimes they are impressions left by bones (or, in the case of fossil footprints, by behavior). On occasion, even fossil imprints of hair, skin, and soft tissues may be found.

Fossilization of any kind is a rare event, and not all things fossilize equally well. In general, the larger and harder something is, the longer it takes to decay, and hence the greater chance it will become fossilized. Teeth are the hardest part of the body, and hence the most easily fossilized. Skulls and leg bones are large and thus found more frequently than smaller bones such as ribs. Soft tissue parts of the body, such as skin and internal organs, decay very rapidly and are rarely found.

Finding fossils involves luck, skill, and the use of careful, scientific methodology. Finding a fossil-bearing site is often extremely difficult. Anthropologists know that certain geological formations are much more likely to bear fossils than others, and they use techniques such as aerial and ground-based surveys, satellite imagery, and radar to try to locate fossils within these regions. However, luck and chance also play a large role. Experienced fossil hunters can sometimes go for many years without a major find.

Once a fossil-bearing site is found, excavation proceeds in a highly controlled manner. The area is extensively photographed and precisely mapped. Researchers usually divide it into a grid and systematically examine each section. The positions of fossils or artifacts are carefully recorded. Each item to be removed is given a number, and extensive notes are made about it. Soil is carefully analyzed for the remains of any fossilized plant or animal material that could provide clues about the ancient environment. To be sure that nothing is missed, dirt removed from the site is passed through wire screens.

One critical aspect of analyzing finds is determining their dates. Dating is a complex and highly technical procedure. Many different dating techniques are available. Some of these are potassium/argon (K/Ar) dating, carbon 14 (C14) dating, thermoluminescence, and paleomagnetic dating. Each technique has advantages and disadvantages. C14, for example, is probably the best-known dating technique, but is only useful for dating organic material less than 40,000 years old.

Many of the critical finds in human evolution have been dated using the K/Ar method. Potassium 40 (K40), a radioactive form of potassium, decays into argon at a steady, predictable rate. The heat of volcanic eruptions drives all argon (Ar) from rock or ash. Afterwards, the only new source of argon is K40. Thus, measuring the amount of Ar in volcanic rock or ash tells investigators when these materials erupted from volcanos and provides a reliable date for the fossils found in such material.

It is important to note that dating techniques such as K/Ar provide date ranges rather than precise calendar dates. Dates are generally specified as plus or minus a certain number of years. For very ancient finds, these date ranges can be quite large. Thus, we are not able to determine the exact year when an ancient ancestor lived. But, using K/Ar, we can reliably know the date range for many fossils.

AS FRAGMENTS OF A HOMINID FIND ARE COLLECTED, EACH LOCATION WHERE A PIECE IS DISCOVERED IS MARKED WITH A FLAG. HERE, YOEL RAK OF TEL AVIV UNIVERSITY AND THE INSTITUTE OF HUMAN ORIGINS FLAGS THE PRECISE LOCATION FOR EACH FRAGMENT OF THE AUSTRALOPITHECUS AFARENSIS CRANIUM DISCOVERED AT HADAR IN 1992.

Don Johanson/Institute of Human Origins

the genus *Homo*. *Australopithecus* and *Homo* each include numerous species. See Figure 2.2.

THE EARLIEST HUMAN ANCESTORS

From an anatomical perspective, the critical thing that differentiates humans and our ancestors from modern-day apes and their ancestors is **bipedal** locomotion. Unlike any other primate, humans and our ancestors walk habitually on two legs. Although chimpanzees, gorillas, and some other primates are capable of walking or running on two legs for short distances, their habitual stance is on all fours. Bipedalism involved substantial anatomical changes. See Figure 2.3. Skulls and pelvises of bipeds are shaped differently than those of animals that walk on all fours. In addition, the feet of human ancestors are specialized for walking, whereas their hands are generalized for a wide variety of tasks. When anthropologists are able to find fossils of these bones, bipedalism is easily inferred.

Among human ancestors, bipedalism appeared far earlier in the fossil record than increased brain size or the use of stone tools. In fact, bipedalism played a critical role in the development of these features of humanity. Bipedal locomotion freed the hands, allowing our ancestors to carry things for long distances and make tools. Further, creatures standing on two legs have a wider view of their surroundings and can walk efficiently for long distances.

In addition to bipedalism, particular aspects of tooth number, size, shape, and enamel are critical in tracing human ancestry. The specific qualities of teeth are important because different species have different dental characteristics and can be identified on that basis. Further, teeth are the hardest parts of the body and, for that reason, are the most frequently preserved. Hence, they are the most commonly found fossils.

The earliest evidence currently available for a creature generally considered ancestral to humans is a single jawbone, found near Lothagam, a town in northeastern Kenya, and called the Lothagam mandible. It has been dated to approximately 5.5 million years ago. Several additional bone fragments found at Mabaget and Tabarin, also in Kenya, date from between 5 and 5.1 million years ago.

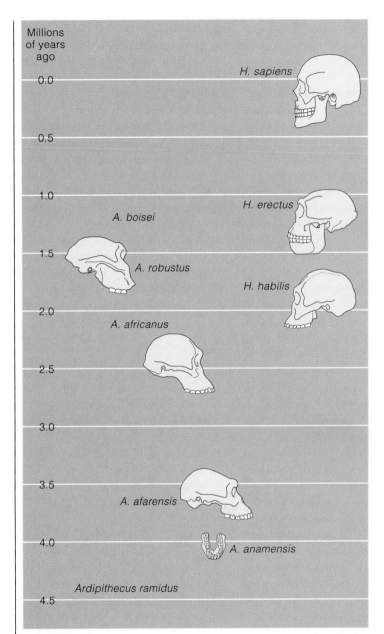

FIGURE 2.2

A PLAUSIBLE VIEW OF EARLY HUMAN EVOLUTION. A. IS AUSTRALOPITHECUS; H. IS HOMO.

The earliest, most substantial evidence for human ancestors comes from the Awash River in northeastern Ethiopia. In the early and mid-1990s, teams of anthropologists led by Tim

bipedalism Walking on two feet, a distinctive characteristic of humans and our ancestors.

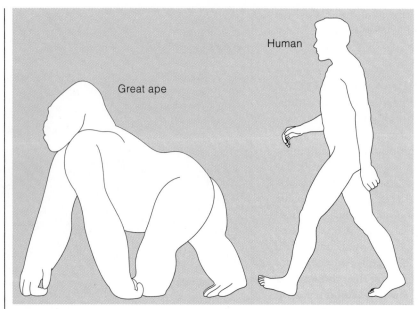

FIGURE 2.3

THIS DRAWING ILLUSTRATES BIPEDALISM. LOWER LIMBS ARE ELONGATED, AS SHOWN BY THE PROPORTIONAL LENGTHS OF VARIOUS BODY SEGMENTS (E.G., IN HUMANS THE THIGH COMPRISES 20 PERCENT OF BODY HEIGHT WHILE IN GORILLAS IT COMPRISES ONLY 11 PERCENT).

White of the University of California discovered the remains of more than 40 individuals who lived approximately 4.4 million years ago. They named these creatures *Ardipithecus ramidus* (Whilte, Suwa, and Asfaw 1995). These ancestors had large jaws and small brains compared to modern humans. Many of their teeth and other aspects of their jaw shape were similar to those of modern-day chimpanzees. Despite this, evidence from their pelvic bones, skulls, and forelimbs indicate that they were bipedal. Reconstructions of the environment they lived in shows a flat plain covered with open woodland and dense forests. This reinforces the notion that bipedalism first evolved in wooded areas rather than on grassy plains as many anthropologists had earlier believed (Wolde-Gabriel, White, and Suwa 1994) and suggests that these ancestors may have spent much of their time living in the trees.

australopithecines Members of an early hominid genus found in Africa and characterized by bipedal locomotion and small brain size.

THE AUSTRALOPITHECINES

Perhaps the best known and best described of the early hominid fossils are the **australopithecines.** Beginning with Raymond Dart's discovery of "Taung Child" in 1924, more than 10,000 individual australopithecine fossil bones have been found, comprising several hundred individuals. Many of the most exciting finds have been made in the past ten years. The earliest australopithecine fossils are from northern Kenya and are between 4.2 and 3.9 million years old. The most recent, from South Africa, are only about 1 million years old. Though australopithecines are found only in Africa, they were a diverse and complex group of creatures who persisted for a very long stretch of time.

The oldest australopithecine fossils come from the northern border of Kenya and were discovered in 1995 by Meave Leakey (see In The Field, page 32, for details about the Leakey family). They are between 4.2 and 3.9 million years old. Additional early australopithecine finds include the remains of 23 individuals found at Laetoli in northern Tanzania, and a collection of more than 6,000 specimens representing at least 40 individuals found at Hadar in the Afar region of Ethiopia.

Two of these finds are among the most famous in the history of anthropology. In 1974, at Hadar, a team led by Donald Johanson found an australopithecine skeleton they dubbed "Lucy." "Lucy" is unusually complete; more than 40 percent of the bones are present. With such a full skeleton, anthropologists were able to answer definitively many questions about the way australopithecines looked, stood, and moved. The second remarkable discovery was made by Mary Leakey, working at Laetoli in Tanzania. She and her team found a well-preserved bed of volcanic ash that was deposited about 3.5 million years ago. Many animals had walked across the ash when it was fresh, leaving their footprints behind. The ash bed had been covered by other materials and, as a result, the footprints had been very

"LUCY," AN UNUSUALLY COMPLETE AUSTRALOPITHECUS SKELETON, WAS DISCOVERED AT HADAR, ETHIOPIA, IN 1974.

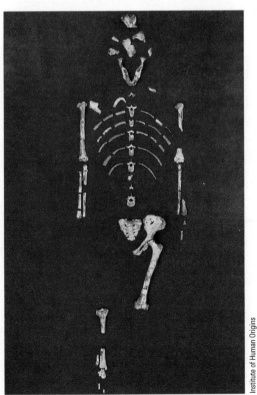

Institute of Human Origins

well preserved. Leakey's research recovered thousands of prints from at least 20 different species, but the most interesting part of her find is two footprint trails clearly made by australopithecines. One of the trails was made by two individuals who were probably walking together. The second trail was made by three individuals. Two of these were walking together and the third, a smaller individual, was walking in the footprints left by the larger of the first two.

This plethora of fossil finds reveals a great deal about the australopithecines and their lifestyles. Though they varied substantially, these "gracile" australopithecines were generally small, standing between 3.5 and 5 feet tall and weighing between 65 and 100 pounds (McHenry 1992). Compared to modern humans, they had relatively small brains. The average modern human brain is 1300 cubic centimeters; australopithecine brains varied from about 400 to 500 cubic centimeters. Their faces protruded, and they had relatively large and slightly overlapping canine teeth. Although their hips and lower limbs were a bit different from those of modern people, they were fully bipedal.

The "gracile" australopithecines lived in a variety of arid and semiarid environments in eastern and southern Africa. The ecology of these locales during the era of australopithecines varied from dry grasslands to bushland and forest. The size and shape of their teeth strongly suggests that they were **omnivores.** Although the "gracile" australopithecines probably used tools made of wood or bone, such tools have not survived, and no stone tools are associated with the earliest australopithecine remains. Many people think of ancient human ancestors as hunters who preyed on large animals. However, the lack of stone tools, combined with australopithecines' relatively small size and lack of claws or very large canine teeth, has led many researchers to conclude that they ate fruit and vegetable foods, insects, and small animals. They probably scavenged for remains left by larger predators, but it is unlikely that

omnivore An animal that eats both plant and animal foods.

I N T H E F I E L D

FOSSIL HUNTERS

Mary Leakey (1913–1996) was perhaps the greatest single fossil hunter of the twentieth century. Among her numerous finds were the 1959 discovery of the australopithecine fossil "Zinjanthropus" and the "Laetoli footprints," the fossilized footprints of two or three ancient hominids, probably *Australopithecus africanus.*

Mary Leakey was the daughter of the popular British landscape artist Erskine Nicol. She spent much of her childhood in the Dordogne in France, a region particularly rich in human prehistory. From an early age, Leakey was fascinated by these archaeological treasures. Leakey was precocious, but she was a rebellious student and was expelled from two Catholic schools. She audited courses in archaeology and geology at the University of London, but, although later in life she was to receive many honorary degrees, she never earned a university diploma.

In 1933, friends introduced her to Louis Leakey. He was the son of missionaries and had grown up in Kenya. He studied at Cambridge University and by 1930 had a PhD. Despite the fact that he was married, with a child and a pregnant wife, Louis and Mary began an affair. In 1935 he returned to Africa, taking Mary with him (and leaving his wife in England). In 1936, his first wife sued him for divorce, and later that year he married Mary. Mary and Louis eventually had three children. Of these, Richard and his wife Meave have become extremely important fossil hunters.

Louis had hoped for a job in England, but the scandal surrounding his divorce and remarriage as well as some contro-

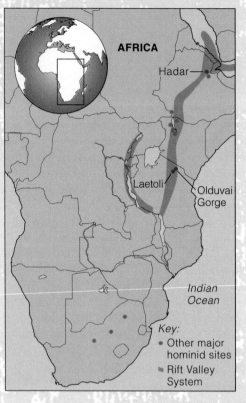

AFRICA

Hadar

Laetoli

Olduvai Gorge

Indian Ocean

Key:
● Other major hominid sites
▪ Rift Valley System

versy over his fossil finds made this impossible. From the mid-1930s until the late 1950s, Louis and Mary searched East Africa for human ancestor fossils with little success. Although Mary found the first fossil skull of an extinct primate called *Proconsul,* as well as many tools and sites, a truly big find eluded them.

On July 17, 1959, the Leakeys were waiting for their friends Armand and Michaela Denis to arrive. The Denises were naturalists who, along with their cameraman Des Bartlett, made popular nature films for British television. The Leakeys had agreed to let them film their Olduvai excavations and had paused in their research to allow them time to come to the site. Louis was sick in bed, and Mary decided to take her two dogs for a walk over to a site they were not actively working, which Louis had named for his first wife. Mary Leakey later wrote:

There was indeed plenty of material lying on the eroded surface.... But one scrap of bone that caught and held my eye was not lying loose on the surface but projecting from beneath. It seemed to be part of a skull.... It had a hominid look, but the bones seemed enormously thick—too thick, surely. I carefully brushed away a little of the deposit, and then I could see parts of two large teeth in place in the upper jaw. They *were* hominid. It was a hominid skull, apparently *in situ,* and there was a lot of it there. I rushed back to camp to tell Louis, who leaped out of bed, and then we were soon back at the site looking at my find together. (Leakey and Leakey 1984/1996:47–48)

What Mary had found was Zinjanthropus.

Needless to say, when the Leakeys' naturalist friends and their cameraman arrived, it was the excavation of Zinjanthropus that they filmed. Zinjanthropus was important for two reasons: it was the first australopithecine found outside of South Africa, and it provided strong indication that not all australopithecines were directly ancestral to modern humans. Finding Zinjanthropus also made the Leakeys' careers. Whereas before they had struggled along in obscurity with very limited funds, they soon found themselves international celebrities and the recipients of many grants. From the early 1960s to the early 1980s, Mary and Louis (who died in 1972) ran large and very successful projects at Olduvai and other African locations. Mary later wrote:

The reason why "Zinj" was so important to us was that he captured the public imagination.... If we had not had Des Bartlett and his film camera on the spot to record the discovery and excavation of the skull, this might have been much harder to achieve. Zinj made good television, and so a very wide public had the vicarious excitement of "being there when he was dug up." (Leakey and Leakey 1984/1996:48)

Louis Leakey had the academic credentials, and he was a charismatic speaker with an eagle eye for outstanding publicity opportunities. Thus, until his death, he was the public face of their projects. However, it was Mary and their children who actually made most of the fossil finds. Mary's relationship with Louis was problematic; he had frequent affairs with other women and the couple grew apart. Looking back on their lives, it is clear that Mary was not only the better fossil finder but, despite her lack of an earned degree, her meticulous work and caution probably made her the better scientist as well.

I n 1974, a team led by Donald Johanson (1943–) discovered "Lucy," one of the best-known human ancestors. Johanson's parents had immigrated from Sweden to Chicago, where his father worked as a barber, eventually saving enough to buy his own shop. However, Johanson's father died when he was two, and he and his mother moved to Hartford, Connecticut. There, he lived next to the Hartford Theological Foundation and came to know the German-educated anthropologist Paul Leser, who became his mentor and inspired him to become an anthropologist. In 1959, Leser brought Johanson a *New York Times* article about the Leakeys' discovery of Zinjanthropus. He decided then, at the age of 16, to become an anthropologist and hunt fossils in Africa's Great Rift Valley.

As a graduate student at the University of Chicago, Johanson worked on chim-

panzee dentition with Albert Dahlberg. When he learned that F. Clark Howell was planning a trip to Omo in Ethiopia to look for australopithecines, especially teeth, he convinced Howell to offer him a job on the expedition. This first experience in 1970 led to yearly trips to Ethiopia between 1972 and 1974. It was on the 1974 trip that Johanson found Lucy.

Johanson later wrote that he had been planning to spend the morning of November 30, 1974, catching up on paperwork, but Tom Gray, an American graduate student who was with the team studying fossil plants and animals of the region, asked Johanson to show him Locality 162 of the large Hadar site. Johanson, who believes that luck plays a large role in finding fossils, was feeling lucky that morning, so they jumped in a Land Rover and headed for the field.

Johanson and Gray went to the site and surveyed it for a couple of hours, looking for any fossils that might catch their eyes. They were almost finished when they decided to survey a little gully. Johanson later wrote:

The little gully in question was just over the crest of the rise where we had been working all morning. It had been thoroughly checked out at least twice before by other workers, who had found nothing interesting. Nevertheless, conscious of the "lucky" feeling that had been with me since I woke, I decided to make that small final detour. There was virtually no bone in the gully. But as we turned to leave, I noticed something lying on the ground partway up the slope.
"That's a bit of hominid arm," I said.
"Can't be. It's too small. Has to be a monkey of some kind."
We knelt to examine it.
"Much too small," said Gray again. I shook my head. "Hominid."

"What makes you so sure?" he said.
"That piece right next to your hand. That's hominid too."
"Jesus Christ," said Gray. He picked it up. It was the back of a small skull. A few feet away was part of a femur: a thighbone. "Jesus Christ," he said again. We stood up, and began to see other bits of bone on the slope: a couple of vertebrae, part of a pelvis—all of them hominid. An unbelievable, impermissible thought flickered through my mind. Suppose all these fitted together? Could they be parts of a single, extremely primitive skeleton? No such skeleton had ever been found—anywhere. (1981/1996:56)

Johanson and Gray went back to camp elated. That afternoon they brought the entire team back to work on the site. Complete excavation took three weeks, but by the evening of the first night it was clear that Johanson and Gray had made a truly exceptional find. The fossil bones they uncovered did belong to a single individual, and much of the skeleton was present.

That first night we never went to bed at all. We talked and talked. We drank beer after beer. There was a tape recorder in the camp, and a tape of the Beatles song "Lucy in the Sky with Diamonds" went belting out into the night sky and was played at full volume over and over again out of sheer exuberance. At some point during that unforgettable evening—I no longer remember exactly when—the new fossil picked up the name of Lucy and has been so known ever since, although its proper name—its acquisition number in the Hadar collection—is AL 288-1. (1981/1996:58)

"Lucy" was a critical find. There are fossil hominids that are older, and fossil ho-

---

Fossil Hunters (continued)

minid skeletons that are more complete, but "Lucy" is the oldest most complete we have. As with the Leakeys' discovery of Zinjanthropus, Lucy brought fame and funding to Johanson and his team. Since the 1970s they have continued to work in the Ethiopian desert, as well as many other locations, and have unearthed many additional fossils, including the fossils of 13 ancient individuals in 1975 and a 1.8-million-year-old *Homo habilis*

skeleton in 1986. In 1981, Johanson founded the The Institute of Human Origins, a multidisciplinary research organization dedicated to the recovery and analysis of the fossil evidence for human evolution.

Johanson has played a critical role in popularizing the study of human evolution. He has coauthored several books about evolution aimed at general audiences, including *Lucy: The Beginnings of*

Humankind (1981) and *Blueprints: Solving the Mystery of Evolution* (1989). He has also hosted programs on public television.

Source: Excerpts reprinted by permission of Waveland Press, Inc., from *Quest for the Past: Great Discoveries in Archaeology,* Second Edition (Prospect Heights, IL: Waveland Press, Inc. 1994). All rights reserved.

---

they hunted large animals. The fact that remains of numerous individuals are commonly found together suggests they were social animals living in small groups.

About 2.5 million years ago, global weather turned cooler, and this seems to have resulted in the evolution of several new hominid species. One group of these new animals is called the "robust" australopithecines, though they are sometimes known by the older name *Paranthropus.* The "robust" australopithecines tended to be slightly larger than the "graciles," but the ranges for both height and weight clearly overlap. More important, "robust" australopithecines had much heavier skulls, reinforced with bony ridges. They also had substantially larger teeth and jaws. Such factors strongly suggest that these creatures were adapted for chewing heavy, coarse material. They were probably vegetarian. "Robust" australopithecines lived in Africa until about 1 million years ago and do not seem to be ancestral to modern humans.

HOMO HABILIS AND RUDOLFENSIS

www At roughly the same time as some "gracile" australopithecines were evolving into "robust," others gave rise to a new genus, *Homo.* Between 2.3 and 2.5 million years

ago, the earliest members of this group, **Homo habilis** and *Homo rudolfensis* emerged. Although there are important technical differences between *habilis* and *rudolfensis,* they are generally quite similar. Most fossil finds of this era belong to *habilis,* and in this section we will focus on them.

Several physical features distinguish *Homo habilis* from the australopithecines. Perhaps most important, *habilis,* like all members of *Homo,* had brains that were quite large compared to the size of their bodies. Beyond that, their teeth were smaller than australopithecine teeth, their skulls higher, and their faces protruded less. *Homo*'s legs and arms were also somewhat different from those of the australopithecines. Legs tended to be longer (probably resulting in an increase in walking speed), whereas arms tended to be shorter.

One thing that clearly distinguishes *habilis* is the presence of stone tools. Although some australopithecines may well have used wood or bone as tools, *habilis* clearly learned to work stone into a variety of useful shapes. New discoveries suggest that toolmaking appeared quite early; *habilis* were making fairly sophisticated sets of tools as early as 2.3 million years ago (Steele 1999). Toolmaking was clearly a critical factor in human evolution. Human ancestors had relatively small teeth. But by using tools, they could match the biting and chewing abilities of much larger, more powerful animals. Thus, using tools led to improvements in nutrition, which in turn favored those individuals and

---

Homo habilis A species of early human found in Africa. *Homo habilis* were present between 2.5 and 1.8 million years ago.

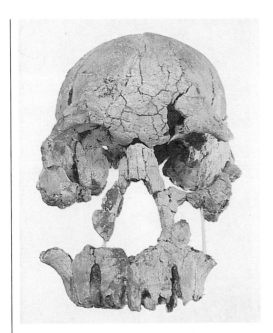
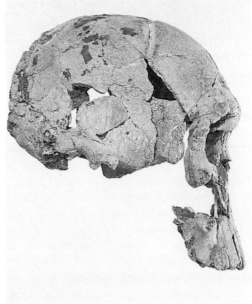

National Museums of Kenya

A NEARLY COMPLETE HOMO RUDOLFENSIS CRANIUM FROM LAKE TURKANA IN EAST AFRICA.

groups best able to make and use tools. In the course of evolution, our ancestors develop both the fine motor and the mental skills to make and use tools of ever greater sophistication.

The habitat of *habilis* was a grassland with far fewer trees than were available to the earlier "gracile" australopithecines. Their dentition suggests that they were omnivores, competing with members of other species for both plant and animal foods. The fact that Oldowan tools are designed for cutting and bashing rather than hunting strongly suggests that *habilis* rarely killed large animals. Like their australopithecine predecessors, they probably hunted small animals and scavenged the remains of larger ones. Stone rings found at Olduvai indicate that *habilis* probably built shelters for protection from predators and cold weather.

The earliest remains of *habilis* are from east and southern Africa, and it had been believed that the species was limited entirely to Africa. However, new finds cast doubt on this position (Hwang et al. 1995; Swisher et al. 1994). A variety of fossils from Indonesia and China are more than 1.8 million years old, and Oldowan-style tools found in Pakistan and France have dates of between 1.6 and 2 million years ago. If it is true that *habilis* spread out of Africa,

some of our understanding of them will need revision. Such geographic dispersion would suggest that *habilis* was more adaptable, and more dependent on culture, than was previously thought. Much more research and analysis needs to be done before we understand the relationship of the European and Asian finds to those from Africa.

HOMO ERECTUS

The earliest **Homo erectus** fossils come from northern Kenya and are about 1.8 million years old. *Homo erectus* fossils show some substantial changes over the earlier *Homo habilis*. One of the most important of these changes is in body size. *Erectus* were substantially larger than *habilis*. Many may have been roughly the same size as modern-day people. For example, the 1.6-million-year-old skeleton of a 12-year-old *erectus* boy was found in the mid-1980s, at Lake Turkana in Kenya. It is estimated that, had the

Homo erectus A species of early human found in Africa, Asia, and Europe. *Homo erectus* were present between 1.8 million and about 200,000 years ago.

boy grown to maturity, he would have been at least 6 feet tall.

Homo erectus brain size increased along with body size. The average brain volume for *erectus* is about 1,000 cubic centimeters. Some *erectus* had brain sizes of up to 1,250 cubic centimeters, placing them within the range of modern humans.

Erectus was also substantially more "robust" than *habilis.* Not only is the *erectus* skull larger, its bones are heavier. There is a heavy ridge of bone above the eyes, and the cranial bone is thick. The thick bones and heavy reinforcing features suggest very strong jaw muscles. Compared to modern humans, *erectus* skulls appear squat. In modern humans, the maximum width of the skull is above the ears, but in *erectus* the skull's widest point is below them.

The name *erectus* might seem to suggest that this species was the first human ancestor to walk upright, but as we have seen, this is not the case. Bipedalism is very ancient in human ancestry; all of our ancestors, back to the australopithecines, walked on two legs. However, there is a reason this particular fossil is called *erectus.* Because the finder of a new fossil species has the right to name it, the names of the different species reflect the history of discovery. The first *erectus* fossils were found by the Dutch Army surgeon Eugene Dubois in the 1890s, years before any of the australopithecines were discovered. Dubois, believing he had found the oldest human ancestor who walked upright, named his discovery *erectus.*

One reason *erectus* was found earlier than the fossils of earlier bipedal species was that its geographic spread was much greater than that of any earlier hominid. Although there is some evidence of *habilis* remains outside of Africa, clearly *erectus* inhabited much of Africa, Europe, and Asia. Major *erectus* finds have been made in East, North, and South Africa, Spain, the Middle East, China, and Indonesia.

From this wide geographic dispersal, we know that *erectus* was able to adapt to life in a great variety of different ecological and climatic settings. Since much of the era of *erectus* occurred during the Ice Ages, climatic variation was probably even greater than today. In order to thrive in these varying habitats, *erectus* became increasingly dependent on culture.

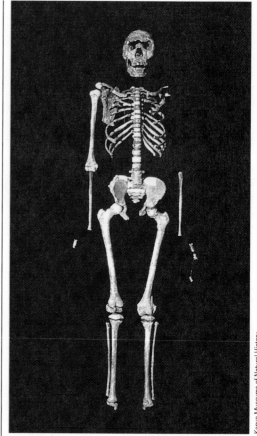

Kenya Museums of Natural History

WT 15000 FROM NARIOKOTOME, KENYA, IS THE MOST COMPLETE HOMO ERECTUS SPECIMEN YET FOUND.

One important window on *erectus* culture is provided by human and animal remains and artifacts found at Zhoukoudian, near Beijing, in China. Anthropologists, working in this area since the 1920s, have recovered remains from more than 40 individuals and more than 100,000 artifacts. Zhoukoudian was inhabited between about 450,000 and 230,000 years ago. Its inhabitants made choppers, scrapers, points, and awls from stone. They also used deer antlers for tools, and possibly skulls for "drinking bowls" (Jia and Weiwen 1990). There are also the remains of fires. In some places, the ash layers are more than 18 feet deep. But, though most anthropologists agree that *erectus* was capable of controlling and using fire, it is not known if they were able to make it.

Homo erectus almost certainly lived by hunting, scavenging, and gathering. Remains in

Spain show that human ancestors were capable of hunting and butchering elephants half a million years ago. Remains of deer and wild horses have been found at Zhoukoudian. However, many of the bones at *erectus* sites show the marks of carnivore teeth as well as cut marks from tools. This strongly suggests that much of the meat consumed by *erectus* was scavenged. Debris at many other sites show that *erectus* also ate a wide variety of wild fruits, vegetables, tubers, and eggs.

Winters at many *erectus* sites are very cold, so it is likely that *erectus* made clothing of animal skins. Although no such clothing has survived, there is some evidence of needles among the bone tools found at Zhoukoudian.

Little is known about *erectus* social or religious life. The fact that they killed large animals meant that large amounts of meat had to be consumed rapidly. This suggests that social groups were relatively large and probably included complex mechanisms for distributing food, and perhaps other goods. One tantalizing if grim bit of evidence about possible religious beliefs comes from Zhoukoudian. It is clear that the brains of some Zhoukoudian individuals were removed after their death, but why this was done is unknown. It could have been cannibalism; perhaps it was part of a religious ritual; or maybe individuals just wanted to use the empty skull case as a drinking vessel.

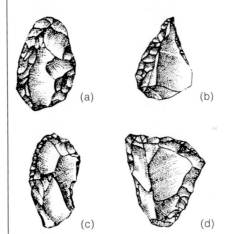

FIGURE 2.4

(TOP) A HOMO ERECTUS HAND AX (BIFACE). (BOTTOM) SMALL HOMO ERECTUS TOOLS: (A) SIDE SCRAPER, (B) POINT, (C) END SCRAPER, AND (D) BURIN (A TOOL USED TO MAKE GROOVES IN WOOD, STONE, LEATHER, BONE, OR ANTLER).

HOMO SAPIENS

The critical anatomical distinctions between *Homo erectus* and **Homo sapiens** lie in the volume and shape of the skull. On the average, *Homo sapiens* clearly have substantially larger brains than *erectus. Sapiens* skulls lack the heavy bony ridging above the eyes and the thick skull bone of the *erectus.* In addition, while *erectus* had a squat skull with little forehead, the *sapiens* skull is high and vaulted with a large forehead.

The skeletal changes between *erectus* and *sapiens* reflect the tight interrelationship of learned behavior and biological evolution. *Erectus* tools were relatively crude. Using them in hunting required hunters to attack their quarry at close range, exposing them to substantial physical danger from the prey. In this situation, thick, heavy skull bones helped protect their brains from injury. As human ability to learn increased and weaponry improved, animals could be hunted from greater distance, and this favored the lighter-boned, bigger-brained *sapiens.*

Homo sapiens A species of human found throughout the world. The earliest *Homo sapiens* appeared about 500,000 years ago.

The details of the transition between *Homo erectus* and *Homo sapiens* are complex. By about half a million years ago, some *erectus* groups were becoming more like *sapiens*. Bones from locations throughout the Old World attest to ancestors who had lighter-boned, more rounded skulls than *erectus*. However, these fossils still show the bony ridging above the eyes typical of *erectus*. Between 300,000 and 100,000 years ago, this brow ridging disappears in many of the fossils found in Africa. However, the brain size of all of these fossils is somewhat below that of modern people. About 130,000 years ago, **Neandertals,** with brain sizes overlapping and sometimes larger than those of modern people, appeared in Europe and in some parts of the Middle East. They were present until about 35,000 years ago. At about the same time as Neandertals appeared in Europe, anatomically modern people, *Homo sapiens sapiens* appeared in Africa. By about 35,000 years ago, *Homo sapiens sapiens* had spread throughout the range of all other *Homo* and was the only form present.

Since the 1980s, there has been much debate over the interpretation of these fossils and dates. Anthropologists have used the fossil as well as molecular and genetic data to try to discover the relationship between the different forms of *erectus* and *sapiens*. Some anthropologists propose a **multiregional model.** They argue that different populations of *Homo sapiens* evolved from different populations of *Homo erectus*. In other words, in many places, more or less simultaneously, *Homo erectus* populations became increasingly like modern *Homo sapiens*. Proponents claim that this explanation is supported by the fossil record and accounts for some anatomical differences between modern human populations.

A second prominent theory is the **replacement model,** sometimes called the Out of Africa model. This theory proposes that *Homo sapiens sapiens* evolved from an earlier *Homo* form in Africa about 125,000 years ago. Between that time and 35,000 years ago, this new species spread out from Africa to inhabit virtually all the world. When *Homo sapiens sapiens* ran into Neandertals or other archaic forms of *Homo sapiens,* they outcompeted them but did not mate with them. The result was that anatomically modern people replaced all others.

A third theory, the **hybridization model,** provides a middle ground between the other two. It claims that *Homo sapiens sapiens* spreading out of Africa did mate with earlier archaic *Homo*.

Although each of the three theories has its proponents, there is increasing agreement that the replacement model best explains the fossil, biochemical, and cultural data. Biochemical and genetic evidence analyzed in the 1980s and 1990s strongly suggests that all modern humans had common ancestors in Africa about 125,000 years ago. Recent analyses of DNA extracted from a 29,000-year-old Neandertal specimen found in southern Russia (Ovchinnikov et al. 2000) have confirmed earlier findings (Krings et al. 1997) suggesting that Neandertals and modern human beings last shared a common ancestor more than 500,000 years ago.

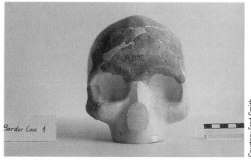

THIS SKULL OF AN ANATOMICALLY MODERN HUMAN WAS FOUND AT BORDER CAVE IN SOUTH AFRICA. IT HAS BEEN DATED TO BETWEEN 100,000 AND 90,000 YEARS AGO, MAKING IT ONE OF THE EARLIEST EXAMPLES OF HOMO SAPIENS SAPIENS.

Courtesy Fred Smith

Neandertals Members of a population of archaic *Homo sapiens* that lived between 130,000 and 35,000 years ago.

multiregional model A theory that seeks to explain the transition from *Homo erectus* to *Homo sapiens* by arguing that different populations of *Homo sapiens* are descendant from different populations of *Homo erectus*.

replacement model The theory that modern people evolved first in Africa and then spread out to inhabit virtually all the world, outcompeting or destroying other human populations in the process.

hybridization model A theory that seeks to explain the transition from archaic to modern *Homo sapiens* by proposing that modern and archaic forms interbred.

Thus, Neandertals and modern humans are not very closely related. In addition, although Neandertals and other archaic *Homo* made numerous sophisticated tools, the number and complexity of these tools pales in comparison to tools made by *Homo sapiens sapiens.*

HOMO SAPIENS CULTURE

Material remains show us that complex culture is not limited to modern *Homo sapiens.* Archaic forms such as Neandertal were clearly cultural. Good evidence of this comes from burial practices. Several examples of burial of the dead by Neandertals have been found.

One of the best-known examples is at Shanidar Cave in Iraq. There, anthropologists found the remains of nine individuals, four of whom were intentionally buried. These remains are between 45,000 and 60,000 years old. Two factors make the burials particularly interesting. First, high concentrations of pollen in the graves shows that the bodies were buried with flowers. This strongly suggests that Neandertals had complex, symbolic rituals for the burial of the dead, and possibly a belief in an afterlife. Second, one of the Shanidar individuals, a male known as Shanidar 1, was clearly severely injured during his life. He was blind in one eye, his right arm had atrophied from injury, and he would have walked with difficulty. Yet Shanidar 1 clearly survived in this condition for many years. This finding strongly suggests that Neandertals cared for and supported this disabled individual.

We should be careful, however, to avoid romanticizing Neandertal life. New evidence from Moula-Guercy cave in France shows that some Neandertals practiced cannibalism (Defleur, White, and Valensi 1999). Evidence gathered there shows that 100,000 years ago, Neandertals used the same butchery techniques on game animals and other Neandertals (Culotta 1999). That some Neandertals practiced cannibalism should not come as a great surprise. After all, within the past hundred years, people have used cannibalism under conditions of extreme deprivation, and as part of religious rituals.

Homo sapiens sapiens made tools of much greater sophistication and efficiency than any prior species. For example, with a pound of flint, Neandertals could make about 40 inches of blade; with the same amount of stone, *Homo sapiens sapiens* could make anywhere between 10 and 40 feet of blade (Bordes 1968). The tools of these early people are characterized not only by their efficiency but also by their variety: stone blades, scrapers, chisel-like tools called burins, as well as tools of bone, awls, needles, and tools for scraping and smoothing leather. In addition to utility, many of these tools show clear aesthetic qualities, something not true of tools made by earlier species. One critical innovation was the compound tool, made of several wood, bone, and stone pieces bound together. Ax heads were hafted to wood or bone handles; blades of stone were set in wooden handles. One of the best-known innovations of the era was the spear thrower, or **atlatl,** a hooked piece of wood or bone used to increase the power with which a spear can be thrown (see Figure 2.5). The variety of *Homo sapiens sapiens* tools and the learning involved in their manufacture suggest that this species had much more complex culture than any earlier creature.

Although many of the best-known early tools come from Europe, some of the earliest examples come from Africa. For example, extremely complex bone tools, probably designed to spear fish, have been found in eastern Congo. Though their dating is controversial, they are believed to be between 180,000 and 75,000 years old. If these dates are correct, the tools are considerably older than any *Homo sapiens sapiens* material found in Europe (Yellen et al. 1995).

The ability of humans to hunt using complex, efficient tools might have had a devastating effect on their environment. For example, *Homo sapiens sapiens* entered Europe during the Ice Age. At that time, much of the land was a vast tundra supporting an abundance of animal life, particularly large herd animals. Shortly after modern people appeared, more than 50

---

atlatl A spear thrower; a device used to increase and extend the power of the human arm when throwing a spear.

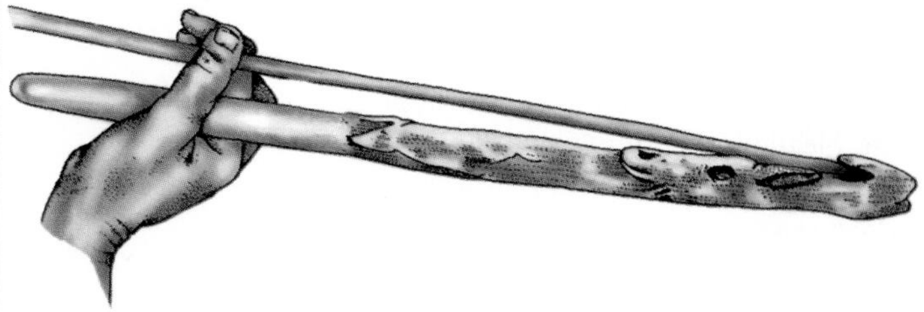

FIGURE 2.5

HOMO SAPIENS SAPIENS USED SPEAR THROWERS (ATLATLS) TO INCREASE A SPEAR'S POWER AND RANGE. NOTE THE CARVING.

VENUS OF WILLENDORF, AUSTRIA. "VENUS" FIGURINES ARE STYLIZED REPRESENTATIONS OF WOMEN MADE BETWEEN 30,000 AND 40,000 YEARS AGO.

genera of large mammals became extinct. Since small mammals survived and there is no evidence of drought, it is possible that hunting by humans was responsible for these extinctions.

In addition to tools, early people left many symbolic and artistic remains. Among the best known of these are the so-called "**Venus" figurines** and cave paintings. "Venus" figurines are small carvings of women sculpted in a variety of materials, including stone, bone, and wood, and made between 30,000 and 20,000 years ago. About 40 intact figures have been discovered, along with fragments of at least 80 more (McDermott 1996). Many depict women with exaggerated breasts and buttocks. The first of these statues was found in 1864, and controversy about their meaning and importance has raged since. They have been variously interpreted as art for art's sake (Ucko and Rosenfeld 1967), fertility magic (Burenhult 1993), representations of female deities (Gimbutas 1989), erotic images made for male pleasure (Guthrie 1984), and ordinary women's views of their own bodies (McDermott 1996).

The cave paintings are perhaps the most spectacular of the cultural remains left by early *Homo sapiens sapiens*. The earliest of them were made about 32,000 years ago, and the most recent are about 10,000 years old. There are some cave painting sites in southern Africa, but most of the best-known sites are in Europe, particularly in France and Spain. Some of the most spectacular of these are Altamira Cave in

Spain, discovered in 1879, Lascaux Cave in France, discovered in 1940, and the recently discovered (1994) Grotte Chauvet in France. It is very possible that, around the globe, people of this era painted on areas that were exposed to the weather. However, it is only in well-protected caves that this art survives.

Most cave paintings depict animals such as wild bulls, horses, deer, bison, mammoth, lion, and bear. There are also frequent realistic representations of human hands and stylized human figures. The techniques used in making cave art were sophisticated. Many different colors of pigment were used. In some places, the artists used naturally occurring bulges and dips in the rock to make their portrayals more realistic. In others, they partially sculpted the rock, using a technique called bas-relief, to make their work more dramatic.

Cave art is found in many different settings. Some of the most spectacular images are found deep in caves. In these locations, there is little sign of human habitation. Although people certainly

"Venus" figurines Small stylized statues of females made in a variety of materials by early modern humans.

visited these sites, it is clear that they did not live there. In other places, there are clear indications that people lived among their paintings.

As with the "Venus" figurines, there is no agreement among scholars on the correct interpretation of cave art. Since many of the images are of animals that were commonly eaten, one interpretation is that these images were drawn as part of ceremonies intended to magically increase the chances of a successful hunt. Strauss (1991), on the other hand, argues that the paintings contain encoded information about hunting techniques and other information useful for survival in the harsh conditions of the Ice Age. A third interpretation holds that the paintings depict things seen by shamans in altered states of consciousness and that the caves were painted for religious rituals (Lewis-Williams and Dowson 1988). Since the paintings were made by many different artists over a 20,000-year period, show many different subjects, and are painted in different kinds of space, it is very unlikely that any single theory can explain them all.

About 10,000 years ago, the last of the Ice Ages ended. As temperatures rose, the ecosystems that had supported these ancient cultures changed, and for many people new ways of living became essential. As the wild animals associated with the Ice Age tundra disappeared, in some areas people turned increasingly to the domestication of both plants and animals. Dogs were domesticated between 14,000 and 10,000 years ago (Mestel 1994). People in the Middle East were beginning to use rye by about 13,000 year ago but did not become dependent on farming until about 10,000 years ago (Pringle 1998).

The move from hunting herd animals to domesticating plants and animals involved substantial increases in the amount of work humans had to do. It almost certainly led to an upturn in rates of disease, increased physiological stress, a reduction in well-being, and a decline in nutrition (Larsen 1995). However, it also made it possible to support a larger population than ever before. Cities, kingdoms, and empires could emerge, using domesticated plants and animals as food sources. Thus, the origin of current industrialized society lies in this move to dependence on domesticated plants and animals 10,000 years ago.

HUMAN VARIATION

As we saw in Chapter 1, the notion of race in human beings has enormous historical and sociological importance, but no biological validity. No agreed upon, scientific way to divide humanity into a set number of races, no matter how large, has ever been found. Biological analysis makes it clear that human populations are neither sharply genetically distinguished from each other, nor do they constitute distinct evolutionary sublineages of humanity (Templeton 1998). Further, there is no evidence that traits such as skin color commonly used to determine race are of any more significance than any of the thousands of other traits that make up a human being. Nonetheless, it is true that there is enormous variety among human beings. The historical, cultural, and sociological effects of human variation are discussed further in Chapter 13. The systematic variation of biological traits among human beings is also an important subject for anthropological investigation. In this section we discuss a few prominent examples of variation.

Many human traits show **clinal distributions.** A cline is a geographical gradient, and a map of clines shows the systematic variation in the frequency of a trait from place to place. Blood type provides a good example. All human beings have type A, type B, or type O blood. The letters refer to the presence of specific antigens on the surface of the blood cells. Antigens are involved in the body's immune system, and when foreign antigens are detected, the body attempts to eliminate them. The frequency of blood type varies geographically. In far northeastern Europe and northern Russia, between 25 and 30 percent of the population has type B blood. This number declines steadily as you move south and west. In Spain, in the far southwest, only between 10 and 15 percent of the population has type B blood (Mourant, Kopec, and Domaniewska-Sobczak 1976). The pattern of blood type distribution around the world leads many anthro-

clinal distribution The frequency of change of a particular trait as you move geographically from one point to another.

FORENSIC ANTHROPOLOGY

Forensic anthropologists apply their knowledge of physical anthropology to the identification of skeletal or badly decomposed human remains. Their goal is to discover information that can assist in the detection of crime and the prosecution of those responsible. When human remains are found, forensic anthropologists are often called in to determine the age, sex, ancestry, and stature, as well as the manner of death of the individual. This information is used to identify the deceased and to determine if a crime has been committed.

The work of forensic anthropologists is often vital in settling humanitarian issues. In the past two decades, forensic anthropologists have frequently been called upon to discover the identities of victims of political violence. A good example comes from Guatemala, where members of the Guatemala Forensic Anthropology Foundation are exhuming mass graves and examining bones to chronicle the nation's bloody 36-year civil war. More than 40,000 individuals disappeared during the war. Most were the victims of government death squads who, in the

FORENSIC ANTHROPOLOGIST DAVID GLASSMAN EXAMINES A SKULL.

Courtesy of David Glassman

late 1970s and early 1980s, kidnapped and murdered many whom they believed to be their opponents. With the evidence provided by anthropologists, Guatemalans are beginning to confront their brutal past. Karen Fisher, one of Guatemala's leading human rights activists, has said

"When you've hidden secrets for years and years, the truth is going to heal your wounds, but it will take time; it won't be easy" (Moore 1998). More recently, forensic anthropologists have been involved in identification efforts in Bosnia and Kosovo.

---

pologists to believe that there must be some selective agent involved. In other words, it is widely believed that having one blood type or another gives specific advantages and disadvantages under different environmental conditions. However, no one has yet convincingly demonstrated what those advantages or disadvantages are.

The gene associated with the disease sickle cell anemia is another good example of a trait that follows a clinal distribution. The sickle cell gene is common in areas that have a high in-

cidence of malaria, particularly certain regions of West Africa, India, and the Middle East (see Figure 2.6). Inheriting the gene from a single parent confers a degree of immunity to malaria; inheriting it from both produces sickle cell anemia. In some areas where malaria is particularly prevalent, as much as 20 percent of the population may have the trait. As one moves away from these areas, the frequency of the gene for sickle cell declines steadily.

Skin color is one of the most obvious aspects of human variation, and historically it has been

While the identification of victims of atrocities often makes the news, most forensic anthropologists work closer to home, identifying the victims of violent crime. In 1998, for example, certified members of the American Board of Forensic Anthropology were called in to work on almost 1,700 cases in the United States. David Glassman, a board-certified forensic anthropologist working in Texas and a professor of anthropology at Southwest Texas State University, says he works on approximately 30 forensic cases each year. A case begins when a law enforcement agency or medical examiner's office calls for help in discovering the identity and cause of death of an individual whose remains have recently been found. Sometimes, it turns out that the remains are nonhuman; at other times, it is determined that they are archaeological; but in the vast majority of cases, the remains are from a recent violent crime.

The next step is the recovery of the body. Sometimes this has already been done by the law enforcement agency, but frequently anthropologists are called upon to assist and supervise the procedure. Sometimes bodies are found complete and in good preservation, but often they are found skeletalized, burnt, fragmentary, or in other various stages of decomposition. Glassman reports that he has recovered bodies in rock shelters, forests, under water, and in many other environments. In one case, he was called in to remove a body lodged in a metal pipe three feet underground, adjacent to a remote mountain road. To extract the skeletal remains, Glassman had to crawl into the pipe, slowly pushing dirt and debris out along his body until he was able to reach them.

After the body has been recovered, the anthropologist's job is to establish both the individual's identity and the cause of death. To do this, the bones and any other remains are analyzed to determine the sex, age, estimated time since death, ancestry, and stature of the individual, as well as any unique identifying marks such as healed fractures or skeletal abnormalities that might be useful in making a positive identification. In some cases, facial reconstructions are made to provide a likeness of the deceased. Analysis of the fracture patterns visible in the bones provides specific information about the cause of death. Glassman has analyzed fractures indicative of blunt trauma, sharp trauma, stabbing, gunshot, and hanging, as well as combinations of these. One particularly brutal case involved machete and gunshot wounds to the face, as well as ax and knife wounds to other parts of the body.

In every case, forensic anthropologists are required to produce a report of their findings. These reports are used by law enforcement agencies to match the bodies with missing persons reports and, if foul play is suspected, to prosecute the individuals believed to be responsible. In most cases the anthropologist's work ends with the delivery of the report, but Glassman says that at least once a year he is required to testify as an expert witness at a criminal trial.

You can find additional information about forensic anthropology at the web site of the American Board of Forensic Anthropology (www.csuchico.edu/anth/ABFA). You can find illustrated but fairly technical information on sex, age, stature, and other aspects of identification at the Osteo Interactive (medstat.med.utah.edu/kw/osteo/index.html).

the primary basis for constructing systems of racial classification. Although skin color is a complex trait and we do not entirely understand it, we do know quite a bit about the geographic distribution of skin colors and their adaptive significance.

Skin color in humans, and in many other mammals, follows a clinal distribution. The darkest colors are found in bright, tropical regions, and the lightest colors in far northern or southern areas where there is much less sunlight. As one travels, for example, from equatorial Africa to northern Europe, skin color becomes progressively lighter.

The primary factor in all colors of skin is a pigment called **melanin.** Melanin is produced by special cells in the skin called melanocytes. All human beings have about the same number of melanocytes. However, the amount of

melanin A pigment found in the skin, hair, and eyes of human beings, as well as many other species, and responsible for variations in color.

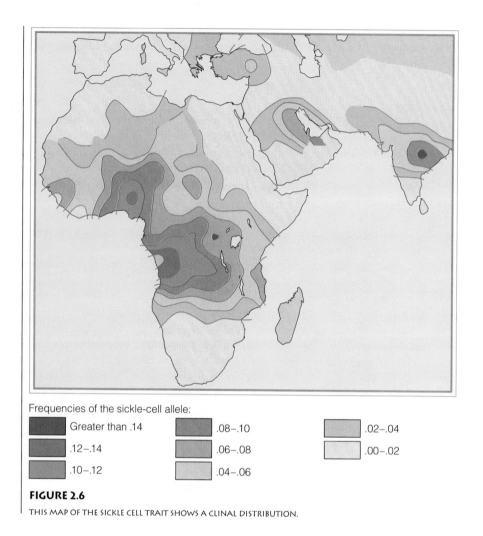

Frequencies of the sickle-cell allele:

Greater than .14

.12–.14

.10–.12

.08–.10

.06–.08

.04–.06

.02–.04

.00–.02

FIGURE 2.6

THIS MAP OF THE SICKLE CELL TRAIT SHOWS A CLINAL DISTRIBUTION.

melanin (and the size of melanin particles) produced by the melanocytes differs among human populations. These discrepancies in melanin production create differences in skin color.

There is a clear relationship between melanin, ultraviolet light, and skin cancer. High levels of ultraviolet light are found in tropical areas and can cause genetic mutations in skin that lead to skin cancer. Some types of skin cancer can easily spread to other parts of the body and cause death. The damage caused by ultraviolet radiation is particularly important in the first 20 years of life. Melanin in the skin absorbs ultraviolet rays and hence protects people from this form of cancer. Australia, a largely tropical nation, which, because of colonization and immigration by northern Europeans, has a majority light-skinned population, provides a good

example of the relationship between skin color and ultraviolet radiation. The skin cancer rates in Australia are the highest in the world, 10 times greater than in the United States; up to 60 percent of the population will be treated for skin cancer at some point (Skin Cancer Research Foundation 1998).

Since human ancestors evolved in bright, tropical East Africa, they probably had very dark skin (although they did not necessarily look like dark-skinned peoples today, and they are certainly no more closely related to modern dark-skinned people than to light-skinned people). As people moved away from areas with very high amounts of sunlight (and hence ultraviolet) they tended to lose skin color. Following the logic of evolution, this could not have occurred simply because high levels of ultraviolet protection were no longer necessary. In order for any trait to disappear, those possessing it must be at some reproductive disadvantage. That is to say, those without the trait must leave more offspring than those with it. We have already seen that in tropical areas, dark skin colors confer the advantage of protection from ultraviolet. In northern latitudes, light skin color must confer some reproductive advantage.

There are two leading theories to account for the precise advantage conferred by light skin color in northern latitudes. The first concerns vitamin D. Vitamin D plays a critical role in bone growth, particularly in infants and children. Although people get some vitamin D from food sources such as fish oils and egg yolks, most vitamin D is produced by the body. Ultraviolet light interacts with special cells in human skin to produce the chemical precursors to vitamin D. Children with insufficient exposure to sunlight do not produce enough vitamin D. This insufficiency results in the bone disease **rickets,** which leads to deformation of the pelvis. Women with deformed pelvises have great difficulty giving birth. Before modern medicine and caesarian sections were available, they often died in childbirth.

The link between ultraviolet light, vitamin D, and rickets probably plays a critical role in determining skin color. Melanin in skin protects from skin cancer by absorbing ultraviolet light. However, in doing that it also reduces the amount of ultraviolet light available to interact with the cells that are critical in the manufacture of vitamin D. Thus, people with dark skin are less efficient at producing vitamin D than people with light skin. In bright, tropical areas where there is a great deal of ultraviolet present, this inefficiency makes no difference. People are exposed to so much ultraviolet radiation that everyone produces adequate amounts of vitamin D. However, in far northern and southern areas, where there are few hours of daylight for much of the year and the cloud cover is often very dense, there is much less ultraviolet light present. In such places, efficiency at vitamin D production is at a premium, and people with light-colored skin are at an advantage. People with dark skin are more likely to get rickets.

While there is very good evidence supporting this hypothesis (Molnar 1983), it has also come in for criticism. Robins (1991) for example, argues that rickets was only a problem in urban industrial societies where people lived indoors, frequently in crowded slum conditions. It would not have much of an effect on people who foraged or farmed outdoors, and thus it is unlikely that it had any effect on changes in skin coloration that happened thousands of years ago. He further states that although darker skin does indeed produce vitamin D less efficiently than lighter skin, the difference is not large enough to injure health, except under modern conditions.

An alternative explanation for skin color difference is based on the reaction of different people to cold weather. Studies on soldiers from World War I through the 1950s showed that those with dark skin color were about four times more likely to suffer frostbite than soldiers with light skin (Boas and Almquist 1999: 296; Post, Daniels, and Binford 1975). Thus, it might also be true that light skin color somehow confers a degree of protection against cold weather. However, if such a relationship exists, the biological mechanisms behind it are unknown.

Racial classification based primarily on skin color has been a compelling fact of human history for at least the past 500 years. On the basis of the color of their skin, some people have been enslaved, oppressed, and subjected to public scorn and humiliation. Others have been given special rights and privileges. This fact demonstrates the ability of people to create worlds of symbolic, cultural meaning around simple, biological aspects of the world. It shows the enormous power of culture. However, as we have seen, skin color is a complex trait that has to do with adaptation to environment. In and of itself, it has neither particular meaning nor importance. It does not serve as a good marker for other biological characteristics and has no biological connection with any particular cultural traits. Skin color is simply an evolution-

rickets A childhood disease characterized by softening and bending of leg and pelvis bones. Rickets is related to dietary insufficiency of vitamin D and/or calcium.

ary reaction to physical factors such as ultra-violet light, vitamin D, and cold weather. The notion that the historical exposure of a population to ultraviolet radiation or extremes of temperature has anything at all to do with cultural, intellectual, or physical superiority or inferiority is obviously ridiculous.

SUMMARY

1. Though human behavior is almost entirely learned, it rests on a biological base that is the product of our evolutionary history.

2. Darwin's theory of evolution by natural selection shows how humans and other species came to exist. The theory notes that there is much variation among members of all species, but most that are born do not survive to reproduce. Those that do reproduce pass some of the traits that favored their survival on to their offspring.

3. While there is a great deal of religious and political controversy over Darwin's ideas about evolution, virtually all biologists and anthropologists agree that the basic elements of Darwin's theory are correct.

4. Human beings and other primates share common ancestry. Our closest relations are with chimpanzees and gorillas. Common ancestry gives all primates many similarities, including grasping hands and excellent three-dimensional vision.

5. Humans and other primates are highly social animals. Mothers and infants form very strong bonds, and these favor teaching and learning. As primates grow, they interact more with their own age group and play becomes essential to learning. Dominance hierarchies are extremely common in primate societies. Position within these hierarchies is decided by both birth and individual action.

6. The earliest fossil remains for human ancestors are about 4.4 million years old. These creatures had large jaws and small brains but were bipedal (walked on two legs). They have been named *Ardipithecus ramidus.*

7. Between 4.2 million and 1 million years ago, a diverse group of creatures called australopithecines lived in eastern and southern Africa. Australopithecines were bipedal and small-brained. They probably lived in part by scavenging.

8. When the weather turned cool about 2.5 million years ago, some australopithecines evolved into specialized vegetarian "robust" australopithecines. They are not ancestral to modern humans. Others evolved into *Homo habilis.*

9. *Homo habilis* are distinguished by somewhat larger brains and the use of simple stone tools. They were probably omnivores, but it is unlikely that they were able to hunt large animals.

10. By about 1.8 million years ago, *Homo erectus* had appeared. These creatures had large bodies and brains. Their remains are found in many places in Europe, Africa, and Asia. They made more sophisticated tools than *Homo habilis* and probably were able to control fire. They were clearly much more dependent on culture than earlier species.

11. By half a million years ago, some *Homo erectus* had become "sapienized." *Homo sapiens* are distinguished by substantially larger brain capacity and more complex culture than earlier forms. Between 300,000 and 35,000 years ago, there were several different forms of archaic *Homo sapiens,* including Neandertals.

12. Modern *Homo sapiens sapiens* appeared first in Africa about 125,000 years ago. By 35,000 years ago, modern people had replaced all archaic forms worldwide. *Homo sapiens sapiens* clearly had much more sophisticated tools than all other forms.

13. *Homo sapiens* culture is extremely complex. Neandertals buried their dead and clearly had religious beliefs. "Venus" figurines and cave paintings attest to the highly developed artistic talents of human ancestors more than 30,000 years ago.

14. The human species shows enormous variety. Many human traits such as blood type or the presence of sickle cell show systematic change over space. Such a pattern is called a clinal distribution.

15. Although skin color has been of critical cultural and historical importance, it has no special biological importance. It is simply an evolutionary adaptation to ultraviolet radiation. One prominent theory holds that melanin protects skin from cancer in sunny areas but interferes with vitamin D production in areas with little sunlight. Hence, dark skin colors are found in sunny areas and light skin colors in areas with less sun.

16. The fact that skin color is implicated in so much of history is an indication of our remarkable ability to invest aspects of the world with symbolic, cultural meaning and of the absurdity of racism.

KEY TERMS

arboreal	multiregional model
atlatl	mutation
australopithecine	natural selection
bipedalism	Neandertal
clinal distribution	Oldowan tools
genetic drift	omnivore
genus	replacement model
Homo sapiens	rickets
Homo habilis	species
Homo erectus	termite fishing
hybridization model	"Venus" figurines
melanin	

SUGGESTED READINGS

Dawkins, Richard. 1996. *Climbing Mount Improbable.* New York: Norton. Dawkins is one of the great popular writers in evolution and is noted for his insistence that natural selection occurs on the genetic rather than individual or population level. In this work, he argues that the universe is a product of the laws of physics rather than any divine being. Dawkins's other popular books include *River Out of Eden: A Darwinian View of Life* (1995), *The Blind Watchmaker* (1986), and *The Selfish Gene* (1976).

Dennett, Daniel C. 1995. *Darwin's Dangerous Idea: Evolution and the Meanings of Life.* New York: Simon and Schuster. An outstanding, well-written introduction to evolution and some of its implications. The book covers the historical development of the theory of evolution, challenges to the Darwinian theory, and what evolution might be able to tell us about understanding human consciousness.

Gould, Stephen J. 1998. *Leonardo's Mountain of Clams and the Diet of Worms: Essays on Natural History.* New York: Harmony Books. Gould, one of the best authors on evolution, writes monthly essays for *Natural History* magazine about evolution and the history of science. Many of his books, including this one, are collections of the best of these essays. Other titles include *Full House: The Spread of Excellence from Plato to Darwin* (1996), *Eight Little Piggies: Reflections in Natural History* (1993), and *The Mismeasure of Man* (originally issued 1981, updated 1996).

Stringer, Christopher, and Robin McKie. 1997. *African Exodus: The Origins of Modern Humanity.* New York: Holt. Stringer and McKie present a power-ful overview of the origins of modern humanity. They describe the evolutionary history of humanity but focus on the distinctions between modern *Homo sapiens* and other human relations such as Neandertal. They also examine visible racial and ethnic distinctions.

Tattersall, Ian. 1998. *Becoming Human: Evolution and Human Uniqueness.* New York: Harcourt Brace. Tattersall, the curator of anthropology at the American Museum of Natural History, uses genetics, evolutionary theory, primate anatomy, and archaeology to explain the story of human evolution. This book shows the ways our ancestors adapted to their environments and the effects those adaptations had on our evolutionary history. Another Tattersall title, *The Fossil Trail: How We Know What We Think We Know About Human Evolution* (1995), examines the history of fossil discoveries and their interpretation.

Weiner, Jonathan. 1994. *The Beak of the Finch: A Story of Evolution in Our Time.* 1994. New York: Knopf. This popular account documents the work of Peter and Rosemary Grant on the Galapagos Islands. The Grants have spent more than 20 years documenting changes in populations of Darwin's finches. The Grants' work, including the documentation of DNA changes among the birds, shows the ongoing power of Darwinian evolution. Weiner's recent work, *Time, Love, Memory* (1999), is about the science and the biologists involved in the analyses of the relationship between behavior and genetics in fruit flies.

INTERNET RESOURCES

The following Internet resources appear in this chapter. Please log on to the Wadsworth anthropology website: **http://anthropology.wadsworth.com**. Click on the Nanda/Warms *Cultural Anthropology* page. Then select the Student Resources section, where you will find a complete presentation of these links and more.

- A photo essay on the Olduvai Gorge, page 34
- A video link: an interview with Jane Goodall, page 24
- Link to website on the evolution of humans, page 27
- Access the Study Guide to InfoTrac College Edition for Anthropology Students

AN IMPORTANT PART OF DOING CULTURAL ANTHROPOLOGY IS ASKING QUESTIONS AND LISTENING CAREFULLY TO THE ANSWERS, AS WELL AS OBSERVING AND PARTICIPATING IN THE LIFE OF THE SOCIETY THEY ARE STUDYING. HERE, ANTHROPOLOGIST ALAN RUMSEY HAS A CONVERSATION WITH A MEMBER OF A HIGHLAND NEW GUINEA SOCIETY.

Irven DeVore/Anthro-Photo File

CHAPTER THREE

DOING CULTURAL ANTHROPOLOGY

What are the aims of ethnography and fieldwork?

How does an anthropologist do an ethnographic field study?

How has ethnography changed in the past century?

How do the personalities, social status, and culture of anthropologists affect their ethnographies?

What are the special opportunities and problems in doing anthropology in one's own society?

What are some of the ethical problems raised by ethnography?

How do anthropologists use ethnographic data?

In attempting to understand human diversity, cultural anthropologists have developed particular methodologies for gathering data and developing and testing theories. The controlled laboratory situation of the physical sciences is, for both technical and ethical reasons, of little use in cultural anthropology. Anthropologists can hardly go out and start a war somewhere to see the effect of warfare on family life. Nor can they control in a laboratory all the factors involved in examining the impact of multinational corporations on villages in the Amazon rain forest. Instead, they look to the existing diversity of human cultures. In place of the artificially controlled laboratory, anthropologists rely on the ethnographic method and cross-cultural comparison.

The **ethnographic method** is the gathering and interpretation of information based on intensive, firsthand study of a particular culture. The written report of this study is called an **ethnography.** In **ethnology,** or cross-cultural comparison, the ethnographic data from different societies are analyzed to build and test hypotheses about social and cultural processes.

Cultural anthropology encompasses a wide range of activities and specialties: solitary fieldwork in a remote location, delving into historical archives, testing hypotheses using statistical correlations from many different societies, administering a community health care clinic, and working with indigenous peoples to exhibit their art in a museum. But all of these diverse activities are based on ethnography, which is not only the major source of anthropological data and theory but also an important part of most anthropologists' experience. We thus begin this chapter with a discussion of ethnography and then turn to some of the ways in which ethnographic data are used in cross-cultural comparison.

ethnographic method The intensive study of a particular society and culture as the basis for generating anthropological theory.

ethnography The major research tool of cultural anthropology; includes both fieldwork among people in society and the written results of fieldwork.

ethnology Comparative statements about cultural and social processes that are based on cross-cultural ethnographic data.

ETHNOGRAPHY AND FIELDWORK

Ethnography is the written description and analysis of the culture of a group of people based on fieldwork. **Fieldwork** is the firsthand, intensive, systematic exploration of a culture. Although fieldwork includes many techniques, such as structured and unstructured interviewing, mapping space, taking census data, photographing and filming, using historical archives, and recording life histories, the heart of anthropological fieldwork is participant-observation. **Participant-observation** is the technique of gathering data on human cultures by living among the people, observing their social interaction on an ongoing daily basis, and participating as much as possible in their lives. This intensive field experience is the methodological hallmark of cultural anthropology. Typically, the field experience results in an ethnography—that is, an in-depth description and analysis of a particular culture.

The goal of fieldwork is to gather as much information as one can on a particular cultural system, or on a particular aspect of a culture that is the focus of the fieldworker's special interest. The data are written up to present as authentic and coherent a picture of the cultural system as possible. The holistic perspective of anthropology developed through fieldwork. Only by living with people and engaging in their activities over a long period of time can we see culture as a system of interrelated patterns. Good fieldwork and ethnography are based both on the fieldworker's ability to see things from the other person's point of view (the emic perspective) and on the ability to see patterns, relationships, and meanings that may not be consciously understood by a person in that culture (the etic perspective).

Observation, participation, and interviewing are all necessary in good fieldwork. The anthropologist observes, listens, asks questions, and attempts to find a way in which to participate in the life of the society over an extended period of time.

Anthropology, like every other scientific discipline, must be concerned with the accuracy of its data. Anthropology is unique among the sciences in that a human being is the major research instrument, and other human beings supply most of the data. At least in the initial stages of research—and usually throughout the fieldwork—anthropologists have to rely to a great extent on informants as well as observation for their data. **Informants** are people through whom the anthropologist learns about the culture, partly by observation and partly by asking questions. Many people in a society may act as informants, but most anthropologists also have a few key informants with whom they work. **Key informants** are people who have a deep knowledge of their culture and are willing to pass this knowledge on to the anthropologist. Anthropologists often develop deep rapport with their key informants, and even lifetime friendships (Grindal and Salamone 1995). These key informants are essential not only for explaining cultural patterns but also for introducing anthropologists to the community and helping them establish a network of social relationships. The establishment of trust and cooperation in these relationships is the basis for sound fieldwork.

In the early stages of fieldwork, the anthropologist may just observe or perform some seemingly neutral task such as collecting **genealogies** (family trees) or taking a census. Within a short time, however, he or she will begin to participate in cultural activities. Participation is the best way to understand the difference between what people say they do, feel, or think and what they actually do. It is not that informants deliberately lie (although they may), but rather, when they are asked about some aspect of their culture, they may

fieldwork The firsthand, systematic exploration of a society. It involves living with a group of people and participating in and observing their behavior.

participant-observation The fieldwork technique that involves gathering cultural data by observing people's behavior and participating in their lives.

informant A person from whom anthropologists gather cultural data.

key informant A person particularly knowledgeable about his or her own culture who is a major source of the anthropologist's information.

genealogy A family history; a chart of family relationships.

WWW

RUTH BENEDICT'S MAJOR WORK, PATTERNS OF CULTURE, WAS A BEST-SELLER IN THE UNITED STATES WHEN IT WAS PUBLISHED IN THE 1930S. IT IS STILL WIDELY USED IN COLLEGE ANTHROPOLOGY COURSES. BENEDICT WORKED TIRELESSLY WITH FRANZ BOAS TO DEMONSTRATE TO AMERICANS THAT IDEOLOGIES OF RACIAL SUPERIORITY HAD NO BASIS IN SCIENCE. THE WORK OF RUTH BENEDICT, HER MENTOR FRANZ BOAS, AND HER STUDENT MARGARET MEAD HAD A DEEP AND WIDESPREAD INFLUENCE ON HOW AMERICANS THINK ABOUT CULTURAL DIVERSITY. HER CONTRIBUTIONS ARE RECOGNIZED BY HER PICTURE ON A UNITED STATES STAMP.

give the cultural ideal, not what actually happens. This is especially true when the outsider has higher social status than the informant. For psychological or pragmatic reasons, the informant wants to look good in the anthropologist's eyes. Participation also forces the researcher to think more deeply about culturally correct behavior and thus sharpens insight into culture beyond that learned by observation alone.

ETHNOGRAPHY IN HISTORICAL PERSPECTIVE

Anthropology began in the last quarter of the nineteenth century as a comparative science; although its first practitioners were not field-workers, fieldwork and ethnography soon became its defining characteristics (Stocking 1992). For a number of reasons, the earliest ethnographers concentrated their studies on the small-scale, technologically simpler societies that had developed for thousands of years outside the orbit of European culture. One reason was the fear that much of the traditional culture of these societies was disappearing under the assault of Western culture, and so their cultures needed to be recorded as soon as possible. Another reason was that these cultures were sufficiently homogenous that patterns and processes of culture could be more easily perceived than was possible in the large, technologically complex, heterogeneous societies of the West. In addition, it was necessary to look at societies outside the orbit of Western society in order to learn about the very diverse ways of being human.

European interest in cultural differences was enormously intensified by the fifteenth-century expansion of European power, which brought Europeans into contact with cultures that were very different from their own. This interest continued to develop and, by the eighteenth and nineteenth centuries, laid the foundation for the emergence of anthropology.

Anthropologists attempted to grapple with the significance of the cultural differences between Europeans and other cultures, initially by placing the cultures they encountered on evolutionary scales of cultural development. In these scales, characterized by different stages of technology and social institutions (such as the form of family or type of religion), European culture was placed at the pinnacle and these other, "primitive" societies were viewed as earlier forms of its own development.

The earliest observers of the societies later studied by these nineteenth-century anthropologists were typically amateurs—travelers, explorers, missionaries, and colonial officers who had recorded their experiences in remote corners of the world. In the nineteenth and early twentieth centuries, much of anthropological theory, including much of cultural evolutionary theory, was developed by "armchair anthropologists" who had not done fieldwork themselves and who based their theories on the often ethnocentric and unsystematic writings of the amateurs.

By the early twentieth century, fieldwork and ethnography had become the hallmarks of cultural anthropology. Twentieth-century anthropologists hoped that detailed ethnographies would illuminate the richness and human satisfactions in a wide range of cultures and increase respect among Europeans and North Americans for peoples whose lives were very different from their own. Particularly after the devastation, demoralization, and disenchantment with European civilization following World War I, academically trained ethnographers began doing intensive fieldwork in distant places and among peoples whose cultures were not only different from but often in striking contrast to Western culture (Tedlock 1991). This emphasis on fieldwork is linked particularly with the names of Franz Boas in the United States and Bronislaw Malinowski in Europe.

Franz Boas, the primary influence in anthropology in the United States in the first half of the twentieth century, turned away from armchair anthropology and urged anthropologists to do more fieldwork before small non-Western cultures disappeared. Boas himself produced an enormous amount of ethnographic data on Native American cultures, particularly those of the Pacific Northwest. For Boas, the status of anthropology as a science would depend on the most complete and objective gathering of ethnographic data on specific cultural systems. He insisted that grasping the whole of a culture could be achieved only through fieldwork.

Malinowski, whose fieldwork was carried out in the Trobriand Islands, saw as an essential goal that the ethnographer "grasp the native's point of view, his relation to life, to realize his vision of his world" (1922/1961:25). Only an anthropologist who could learn to think, feel, and behave as a member of another culture could enter into another cultural experience. And this could be done only through fieldwork—living among the people, observing their behavior firsthand, and participating in their lives. With the publication of Malinowski's unmatched ethnographies of the Trobriand Islands, doing fieldwork and writing ethnography became the dominant activities identified with cultural anthropology.

Boas and Malinowski together set the high standards for fieldwork, the unique methodology of cultural anthropology. The major criterion of good ethnography that grew out of their work was that it grasp the native point of view objectively and without bias. This goal was based on the assumptions of **positivism,** an **empirical scientific** approach that dominated the nineteenth and most of the twentieth centuries. Positivism and empiricism emphasized the possibility and desirability of observing and recording an objective reality. Anthropology reflected this scientific view: The basis of the ethnographic method was the confidence that trained, neutral investigators could, through observation of behavior, comprehend the objective reality of a culture.

After World War I, and even more so after World War II, cultural anthropology took yet another turn, expanding fieldwork and ethnography to peasant and urban societies, which were enmeshed in more complex regional and national systems. Gathering data on such societies required some changes in the way fieldwork was practiced, as the study of these "part cultures" is not amenable to the same holistic perspective derived from the study of a small-scale, seemingly isolated culture. This shift to the study of smaller units in complex societies led to new methodologies as well as new theories about culture, in particular about the relationships of small-scale cultures to larger systems. Indeed, in today's global community, the connections between cultures are so central that no society, no matter how seemingly remote, can be studied as if it existed in cultural isolation.

positivism A philosophical system concerned with positive facts and phenomena and excluding speculation on origins or ultimate causes.

empirical science An approach to understanding phenomena based on the attempts to observe and record a presumed objective reality.

ETHNOGRAPHIC DATA IN THE GLOBAL ECONOMY

In today's global economy, ethnographic data have a new commercial value. Huge multinational pharmaceutical companies, for example, continually search for new natural habitats in hopes of finding new miracle drugs. These searches sometimes include interviews with native healers, who are most knowledgeable about medicinally effective plants in their environments, but much of the multinationals' research relies on digging out information from ethnographic publications.

Once ethnographic and ethnobotanical data are published, they are in the public domain, and multinational corporations or governments may use the data with no legal obligation to get permission from the societies who are the source of the information or to remunerate the members of those societies financially or in any other way (Greaves 1995).

Concern over this issue is part of a larger issue of the cultural rights of indigenous people to protect their own cultural knowledge and cultural products. In many cases, these areas of knowledge and products are associated with secret societies and practices, and their dissemination beyond their original cultural borders violates important religious values.

The increasing concerns of indigenous people over the appropriation of their cultural knowledge will undoubtedly affect fieldwork and ethnography, as these peoples exercise greater control over what ethnographers can publish. Recognition of the cultural and intellectual property rights of indigenous peoples and efforts to protect those rights are some of the adaptations ethnography must make in a changing world characterized by a global economy and global communication.

CHANGING DIRECTIONS IN ETHNOGRAPHY

Since the 1970s, many of the assumptions of twentieth-century fieldwork and ethnography, including confidence in the possibility of discovering an objective reality, have become the subject of intense debate in anthropology (Lee 1992). These debates result from the postmodern perspective that is gaining importance in anthropology and the humanities. **Postmodernism** holds that all knowledge is influenced by the observer's culture and social position and that there is no single objective reality but rather many partial truths, depending on one's frame of reference. Postmodernism has resulted in intense reflection on why, how, and with what goals cultural anthropologists have done, are doing, and should be doing ethnography.

Under the influence of postmodernism, cultural anthropology today is significantly more sensitive to issues of history and power than has been true in the past. Because in most twentieth-century ethnographic encounters, the ethnographer came from a much more powerful (and frequently colonial) culture than the "ethnographic subject," this history is particularly important in understanding early anthropologists' interpretations and representations of cultures other than their own (Said 1978).

Postmodernism has also challenged the ethnographer as the sole, or even most authoritative, voice in representing a culture. From a postmodern perspective, ethnographies are "stories," just like other stories about experienced reality, and the ethnographer's voice is only one of many possible representations. Thus, some postmodern cultural anthropologists are experimenting with different styles of

postmodernism A theoretical perspective focusing on issues of power and voice. Postmodernists suggest that anthropological accounts are partial truths reflecting the background, training, and social position of their authors.

ANTHROPOLOGISTS USUALLY HAVE SEVERAL KEY INFOR-MANTS UPON WHOM THEY DEPEND FOR MUCH OF THEIR CULTURAL UNDERSTANDING AND INTRODUCTION INTO THE SOCIAL NETWORKS OF A SOCIETY. HERE, ANTHRO-POLOGIST ROBERT BAILEY WORKS WITH THE NGALI NGALI OF THE ITURI FOREST IN ZAIRE.

By the 1990s, the trickle of interest in field-work methods and ethnography itself had "turned into a flood," and the "observation of participation" became a central focus of cul-tural anthropology (Tedlock 1991:69). The contemporary concerns of cultural anthropol-ogists—issues of subjectivity and objectivity in fieldwork, bias in the interpretation of field data, the accuracy of traditional ethnographic representations of culture, the relationship of ethnography to anthropological theory, and the usefulness of the culture concept itself—are viewed differently by different anthropolo-gists. Depending on their theoretical persua-sions, anthropologists may see postmodernism as a threat to anthropology's status as a science, a crisis that threatens the demise of ethnogra-phy, or merely a fad that will soon moderate or disappear. In fact, while almost all contem-porary ethnographies now include some re-flection about the conditions under which the fieldwork was carried out, ethnography con-tinues to be dominated by fairly straightfor-ward cultural descriptions and analyses.

Although the status of cultural anthropol-ogy as a science is indeed an important issue, ethnographic writing that focused almost ex-clusively on general patterns of culture, de-scribing cultural norms and structures, often seemed to omit the lifeblood of a culture, leaving out variation and individuality, in-cluding the individuality of the ethnographer. With a few notable exceptions—for example, E. E. Evans-Pritchard's classic, *The Nuer* (1940/ 1968)—only occasionally, in an introduction or a preface, were explicit accounts of the field-work process included in ethnographies. Until the 1970s, few ethnographies considered, in any central way, how interactions between eth-nographer and informants affected the gather-ing, interpretation, and writing up of data.

Two early first-person, experiential accounts of fieldwork were those of Laura Bohannan, writing under the name Elenore Smith Bowen, of her work in Africa, presented as a thinly disguised fictional account (1964), and that of Hortense Powdermaker, *Stranger and Friend* (1960), which included accounts of her field-work outside the United States as well as in

ethnography in which fiction, poetry, and multiple voices (of which the ethnographer's is only one) provide varying representations of cultural realities (see, for example, K. Brown 1991; R. Abu-Lughod 1993; Harding and Myers 1994). It must be remembered, how-ever, that these multiple voices are still selected and presented by the ethnographer.

The view that ethnography is just another story about reality increased anthropological interest in how ethnographers give authority to their narratives—that is, how they make their representations about other cultures believable (Geertz 1988). The postmodern emphasis on ethnography as narrative also raises questions about how the projected audience for an eth-nography, as well as the cultural and political position of the ethnographer, shapes the inter-pretation and representation of other cultures.

the American South and in Hollywood. By the 1960s and 1970s, more ethnographies appeared in which the observation of participation had a central place, along with more traditional cultural descriptions. These concerns have now moved from the margins of anthropology to the center (though a center that continues to be shared by other interests and issues).

Observing their participation leads anthropologists to reflect more consciously on how their own status, personality, and culture shape their view of others, and how they personally interact with "the other" to produce cultural data. Thus, there is a new focus on the interaction between the self and the other—the ethnographer and her or his informants—and the kinds of communication they engage in, as part of or even central to both the fieldwork experience and the written ethnography. Fieldwork and ethnography, from this perspective, become a dialogue, a coproduction between the self and the other, the ethnographer and the native informant (Crapanzano 1980).

The effects of these changes have been more productive in some areas than in others. A postmodern perspective, for example, has clearly contributed to the ethnography of what Westerners call the Middle East. Western views of the Middle East, the Muslim religion, and Arab culture have been very significantly biased by historical encounters between Islam and Christianity, the historical colonization of the Middle East by Western powers, the contemporary politics of the Middle East, and the 1991 Gulf War (Said 1978, 1993; S. Hale 1989). As one anthropologist (Waines 1982:652) noted, too much of the anthropological literature "assumes *a priori* the existence of a universal Islam which mysteriously moulds behavior 'from above.'" These assumptions have, until quite recently, resulted in neglect of other factors in studying the Middle East, such as history, economics, political dynamics and ideologies, the formation of social classes, and the diversity and variety of cultural contexts. Middle Eastern realities are more complex than anthropologists have generally portrayed them.

An unreflective and ethnocentric view of the Middle East particularly affected the study of gender, which overemphasized Islam as *the* cultural determinant of gender roles and women's status; the dominance of a shame/ honor dichotomy focused on women's sexuality; the complete domination of men paralleled by the total submission of women, symbolized by veiling; and the sharp segregation between the two sexes. The overemphasis on separation and subordination in gender relations, for example, led to a neglect of study of the places, such as the family or the workplace, where men and women meet and interact.

THE INFLUENCE OF FEMINIST ANTHROPOLOGY ON ETHNOGRAPHY

Middle East ethnography raises important questions about both ethnocentrism and gender bias in cultural anthropology, but both of these biases extend beyond the Middle East. Questioning the power of gender bias in both ethnography and cultural theory has been a significant contribution of feminist anthropology (further discussed in Chapter 11). Historically, much fieldwork was—and continues to be— done by men who have limited, or even no, personal access to women's lives. This is particularly true in cultures where men and women lead very separate lives and are often hostile to each other, as in New Guinea (Hammar 1989) or the Middle East, where cultural notions of honor and shame severely restrict the interactions of men and women who are not related (L. Abu-Lughod 1987).

The description of whole cultures based on male activities grew out of an assumption that the most important cultural activities are dominated by men. A good example is the work of Malinowski himself. His descriptions of exchange among the Trobriand Islanders almost completely excluded women's gift exchanges, an omission rectified more than 50 years later by a woman anthropologist whose restudy of the Trobriand Islands focused on exchanges among women (Weiner 1976).

Gender bias had its effect not only on the accuracy of ethnographies, but also on the development of theories about culture. When the

ETHNOGRAPHY

AN ETHNOGRAPHIC FIELD STUDY IN INDIA

Charles Brooks is an American anthropologist who carried out field research on the impact of foreign Hare Krishnas in India. The followers of Hare Krishna, with their orange robes and shaved heads, their public processions and festivals featuring drums and cymbals, and their vegetarian food, are well known in the United States. Brooks worked not in an isolated, small-scale society, but rather in a large town in the very complex society of India. The following description of his fieldwork shows what anthropologists actually do as they go about understanding cultures. Although each fieldwork project is different, there are certain common steps: choosing the problem, choosing the site, locating informants, gathering and recording the data, and analyzing and writing up the results.

CHOOSING THE PROBLEM

Like much contemporary fieldwork, Brooks's approach to the culture he was studying was holistic, yet focused on a number of specific questions. Through his graduate study, Brooks had become interested in religion and change in India. This interest formed the background of his research. Brooks was also aware of the most visible representation of Indian religion in the United States, the International Society for Krishna Consciousness (ISKCON), also called the Hare Krishna. The Hare Krishna movement began in India as a way of spreading the worship of the Hindu god Krishna. In this religion, devoted worship to Krishna is the main path to religious or spiritual enlightenment. Krishna worship was brought to the United States in the 1960s by an In-

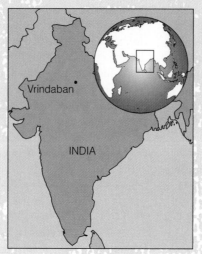

dian monk, Swami Bhaktivedanta, who aimed to save Westerners from what he saw as their materialism and atheism. His movement was very successful in the United States and Europe, attracting many converts from the counterculture of the 1960s. As part of their commitment to their new religion, many of these people went to India to help spread Krishna consciousness in the land where it originated.

Brooks was fascinated by this process, and his research was guided by an overarching question: "How did a Western cultural version of Hare Krishna fit itself into the religious culture of India?" In order to answer this larger question, Brooks broke it down into smaller questions, which would actually guide his research. These questions included "In what specific types of situations did foreign and Indian Krishna followers interact?" "What were the similarities and differences in how foreigners and Indian devotees understood the symbols, rituals, meanings, and goals of Krishna worship?" "How did Indians react to foreigners who claimed they were Hindus—and Hindu priests at that?" "What opinions did Indians have about Westerners who were in India to spread the word about a religion that was

originally Indian?" "Because Hindus believe that foreigners cannot become Hindus, as ISKCON members claim they have become, how was this paradox resolved?" "How did ISKCON's presence in India affect both Hindu religious culture and the Indian and Western Krishna followers who encountered each other?" In sum, Brooks was interested in the subjective experience of individuals from two different cultures who had come together through participation in the same religion.

PICKING THE RESEARCH SITE

Sometimes anthropologists have a particular site in mind when they begin their fieldwork, but in many cases they have only a general idea about a location that might suit their research interests. The ultimate choice involves some practical matters, such as the availability of housing, health care, and transportation, but the major consideration is whether the site will allow the researchers to answer the questions they are interested in. Because Brooks wanted to study social interaction between foreign and Indian devotees to Krishna, his main criterion was to find a location where such interaction took place.

Anthropologists generally use the first month or so of their fieldwork to look over possible sites (this has changed somewhat today, when thanks to cheaper airfares, many graduate students take an initial trip of several months to pick a research site, and then return for the longer fieldwork trip). Brooks's initial choice for his research was the sacred pilgrimage town of Vrindaban, where Krishna is said to have been born and lived for part of his life. This town has many temples and religious sites dedicated to Krishna worship, and Brooks knew that ISKCON had also set up a temple there. He made

Michael Justice/The Image Works

Courtesy of Charles Brooks

(LEFT) THE HARE KRISHNA MOVEMENT HAS SPREAD THROUGHOUT EUROPE AND THE UNITED STATES. THIS PROCESSION IS IN RUSSIA. CHARLES BROOKS'S ETHNOGRAPHY IS AIMED AT UNDERSTANDING HOW WESTERN HARE KRISHNA DEVOTEES WERE INTEGRATED INTO THE INDIAN CITY OF VRINDABAN, A CENTER FOR KRISHNA WORSHIP. (RIGHT) ONE OF BROOKS'S KEY INFORMANTS WAS GOVIND KISHORE GOSWAMI, A BRAHMIN PRIEST AND THE OWNER OF THE PILGRIM'S HOSTEL WHERE BROOKS LIVED DURING HIS RESEARCH. HERE GOSWAMI IS PICTURED WITH HIS WIFE AND SON DURING HOLI, A FESTIVAL IN WHICH PEOPLE SPRINKLE EACH OTHER WITH COLORED WATER.

an initial visit to discover whether significant social interaction took place among the Indian and foreign pilgrims and residents in Vrindaban and whether any Indians worshipped at ISKCON's temple. When he saw that such interactions did occur, and that the ISKCON temple attracted many Indian pilgrims, Brooks decided that this would be an appropriate site for his fieldwork.

Brooks chose as his residence a place where many foreign and Indian people stay while they are on pilgrimage at Vrin-

daban. As a neutral site, it would not associate Brooks with any particular religious faction. This would allow him greater access to a variety of social situations than if he had stayed at a place identified with a particular religious sect or temple. In addition, this residence was centrally located in the town and situated near a principal pilgrimage destination where Brooks could observe from his rooftop rooms the constant movement of pilgrims and the many cultural performances that were held in the adjacent public courtyard.

Having found a suitable place to stay, Brooks turned his attention to beginning the research project.

COLLECTING AND RECORDING DATA

In anthropology, as in every science, method is connected to theory. The way we collect our data is related to the questions we hope our research will answer. Because Charles Brooks's main interest was in the way people create meanings for their behavior through social interaction, participant-observation was his major method of collecting data. Only in this way did Brooks feel he could develop the "intimate familiarity and sensitivity to the social world" he wished to understand (Brooks 1989:235). In order to do this, he also had to take account of his own role as an anthropologist in these interactions.

Because the initial step of participation is to find a role through which to interact with others, Brooks defined his role as someone looking for personal development, and also as a research scholar who had been certified by the Indian government to study Vrindaban's culture and history. Both these roles were familiar and valid to pilgrims and town residents. In order to more effectively participate in the religious culture of the town, without identifying himself with any particular faction, Brooks wore Indian clothing and accessories that were typical of Indians in Vrindaban but were not specifically identified with any particular religious sect.

Because of the public nature of many of the religious interactions Brooks wished to understand, gaining entry to these situations and observing behavior was not difficult. And because he had learned Hindi, the main language used for social interaction in this part of India, he rarely

needed an interpreter. But recording his observations presented more of a problem. Many anthropologists use tape recorders or take notes at the time of observation, but in other cases this hinders interaction. On one occasion early in his research, when Brooks was recording an interview in a small notebook, one of his key informants, a guru told him, "When you are ready to learn, come back without your notebook." From that point he stopped taking notes on the spot and waited until an encounter was over before writing it up. To help him remember and keep track of the many details of an interaction and record them in a consistent way, he developed a schematic flowchart into which he could fit his daily observations. A different flowchart was kept for each separate interaction, and each chart incorporated information on the actors, the content of their interaction, the symbols used, the goal of the interaction, and its conclusion. In addition, he also recorded his experiences in a more impressionistic way in a journal.

Second to participant-observation in its importance for collecting data, Brooks also used unstructured, open-ended interviews. The goal of these interviews was to explore a particular topic in depth, such as the meaning of a particular symbolic object used in religious practice.

Many of his interviews were with groups of informants. These were helpful in comparing the ways different individuals interpret a symbolic object or act, whereas in the individual interviews people could speak about more private matters. This was the format he used for collecting life histories. The individual interviews were taped and more structured, organized around preset questions, but Brooks also allowed the conversations to develop on their own if an informant showed a particular interest in or knowledge of a subject. Twenty-two of these life histories were collected, and they were particularly valuable in giving information about the background from which informants developed their interpretations of religious phenomena.

Brooks also used random verbal surveys to discover the castes and backgrounds of the pilgrims and town residents, and to learn their opinions and attitudes toward the foreign devotees in Vrindaban. He initially tried to use a written questionnaire to gather this kind of information but dropped that method as counterproductive. First, written questionnaires were foreign to Vrindaban culture and thus not very effective. Second, although Brooks assured informants of their confidentiality, many people were nervous at the idea of writing down private in-

culture of a small society is based on information from just one segment of the community—that is, men—the culture appears to be much more homogeneous than it really is. This erroneous picture may also perpetuate oppres-

sion of women by ignoring their perspectives on their own culture, which differ from men's. As we will see in Chapter 11, the recognition of the **androcentric bias** of anthropology has led to a new concern with the lives, thoughts, and activities of women, and also to a new interest in men's lives and activities and the whole subject of gender and sexuality.

These new emphases in ethnography are further evidence of the diversity and dynamism

androcentric bias The distortion in anthropological theory and ethnography focusing primarily on male activities or male perceptions of female activities.

formation. Finally, the use of such formal documents might be interpreted to confirm the belief of many Indians that all Americans in India are working for the CIA.

Hardly any anthropologist could be found today who does not take a camera to the field. Brooks used photographs in several specific ways related to his research project: documenting the physical aspects of Vrindaban's religious complex, such as the temples and pilgrimage sites; documenting the different people who visited and lived in Vrindaban and their clothing and appearance as a way of preserving a record of cultural diversity; and photographing the sites and participants of social interactions as an aid to remembering and interpreting them.

ANALYZING AND INTERPRETING THE DATA

Brooks's data indicate significant interaction between Indians and foreigners in Vrindaban. The ISKCON temple is accepted as a legitimate place of worship for Indian devotees of Krishna, and ISKCON members are accorded legitimacy as Krishna devotees by Indians. The interaction of people from different cultures in the religious complex of Krishna worship has led to changes in the meanings of the symbols involved in this worship.

On a more theoretical level, Brooks's research challenges some popularly held conceptions about Indian culture and society, especially concerning the importance of caste in social interaction.

As the study uncovered some ways that outsiders—the foreigners—could be accepted in a Hindu religious and social universe, it opened up new perceptions of social organization in India. Brooks found that in religious settings, caste identity, which is normally essential in social interaction, could be subordinated to evaluations of the sincerity of a person's devotion. The acceptance of foreigners as Hindus and even Brahmins highlights the complexity of Indian culture and demonstrates its flexibility—its ability to deal with novel and contradictory situations. Thus caste, which has popularly been viewed as a rigid hierarchy, can be deemphasized, superseded by other social statuses, or held irrelevant for determining individual social position.

In the case of Vrindaban, as is true in many other parts of India, religion is of prime importance in determining individual social position and social interaction. Religious competence and extreme devotion can actually override caste as indicators of rank and status. The fact that foreigners can be considered Brahmins in India shows that our understanding of caste may be incomplete and even incorrect—that Brahmin status, for example, may be achieved as well as acquired by birth.

Like all good ethnography, Brooks's study of one town in India has a wider application, as it reveals the processes by which social reality is transformed into a meaningful universe. As people from different parts of the world increasingly come into contact with one another and participate in common social systems, they are forced to rethink traditional cultural concepts and their own and others' cultural identities.

Critical Thinking Questions

1. How might the social processes revealed in Brooks's study apply to the multicultural society of the United States?
2. If you were to study a situation in the United States like the one Brooks studied in India, what groups would you study and why?

Source: Based on Charles Brooks, *The Hare Krishnas in India*. Princeton, NJ: Princeton University Press, 1989.

that have always characterized the history of anthropology. Discussions and debates over theory and method in contemporary anthropology highlight the wide range of approaches cultural anthropologists bring to the question of what it means to be human. Anthropology focuses on the "other" as well as ourselves; its goals embrace those of a comparative science as well as a unique, humanistic inquiry. Thus, many ethnographies continue to emphasize "objective" descriptions of a culture, while other, more experimental ethnographies try in different ways to incorporate the many voices that make up a culture. In their field studies, some anthropologists still try to be the proverbial "fly on the wall," observing and reporting from the position of outsider, but political activism and advocacy for the people one is studying have also come to be important goals. In meeting the challenges of a changing world, anthropologists are increasingly reflecting on the work they do and its place in the contemporary global society. These reflections have raised new issues and new interests in doing ethnography.

SPECIAL PROBLEMS IN CONTEMPORARY ETHNOGRAPHY
STUDYING ONE'S OWN SOCIETY

The demand for more self-conscious fieldwork means that anthropologists need to be more aware of their own reactions in the field and to see themselves not only as the instrument of observation but also as the subject of observation. These observations of the self emerge as part of the interaction with others that is central to fieldwork and can be the source of the special insights that make fieldwork such an exciting but risky enterprise for cultural outsiders. The emphasis on more reflective fieldwork and ethnography affects all anthropologists but particularly anthropologists studying their own societies, or **native anthropologists.**

When anthropologists study a culture different from their own, their main methodological task is to perceive cultures emically (that is, from the point of view of its members). Although training in anthropology is designed to increase awareness and perhaps ultimately overcome cultural bias, even well-trained anthropologists slip into projecting their own culturally determined feelings and perceptions on other peoples. In studying their own cultures, anthropologists must try to maintain the social distance of the outsider because it is all too easy to take for granted what one knows. In addition, as distinguished anthropologist Margaret Mead once noted, remaining objective, or relativist, may be easier when confronting problematic patterns, such as cannibalism or infanticide, in other cultures than when con-

fronting problematic situations such as child neglect, corporate greed, or armed conflict in one's own society.

Some of the problems and the rewards of studying one's own culture are found in the work of Barbara Myerhoff, an American anthropologist. Myerhoff contrasted her earlier work with the Huichol of northern Mexico with her work among elderly Jewish people in an urban ghetto in California (1978). She notes that in the first case, doing anthropology was "an act of imagination, a means for discovering what one is not and will never be." In the second case, fieldwork was a glimpse into her possible future, as she knew that someday she would be a "little old Jewish lady." Her work was a personal way to understand that condition. Because in North American culture the lives of the elderly poor are often "invisible," Myerhoff's ethnography of elderly Jewish people who had struggled to overcome and had triumphed in many small ways over the disabilities of being old and poor in North America was, for her, a valuable and rare experience: that of being able to rehearse and contemplate her own future.

In other cultures, both similar and different problems arise for cultural insiders. Although Middle Eastern ethnography has substantially improved through the work of native women anthropologists, their fieldwork accounts suggest that the ethnographer's insider/outsider position still poses special difficulties in cultures where women's public activities are limited and where respectability, honor, and shame are central cultural values (Altorki and Fawzi El-Solh 1988). Anthropologist Lila Abu-Lughod started her fieldwork among the Bedouin accompanied by her father, a circumstance that first irritated and embarrassed her. But she later concluded that her father's insistence that a "young, unmarried woman traveling alone on uncertain business" would be suspect and "have a hard time persuading people of her respectability" was culturally appropriate. This was all the more true because Abu-Lughod had lived in the West and was subject to the negative stereotypes the Arabs have of the morals of Western women. Abu-Lughod had confi-

native anthropologist An anthropologist who does fieldwork in his or her own culture.

dence that she could overcome this suspicion by her own culturally sensitive behavior, but she did not realize until she reflected on her fieldwork that a young woman alone would be seen to have been abandoned or alienated from her family. This would cast doubts on her respectability (1987:9) and hinder her fieldwork, or even make it impossible, among the conservative Egyptian Bedouin whom she was studying.

Another dilemma experienced by many anthropologists, but particularly poignant for native anthropologists, is whether one should be a disinterested researcher or an advocate for the people one studies and whether it is possible to be both. Delmos Jones, an African American anthropologist in the United States, experienced some of these conflicts in studying the role of voluntary organizations in effecting political and social change in African American urban communities (1995). An important finding of his research emphasized the contradictory demands on organizational leaders, who often had to compromise their members' expectations in order to remain effective with local power establishments. Leaders sometimes emphasized the importance of these connections with powerful outsiders to stifle dissent within their organizations' staff and membership.

Jones's finding on dissension between the leadership and the membership of these organizations presented him with a dilemma, one that rested partly on his being a native anthropologist. On the one hand, Jones acknowledged that he was given access to the leadership of the community organizations *because* he was African American and because he shared their concern about improving the position of African Americans in the United States. On the other hand, many of the members and staff of the organization were more suspicious of Jones because they identified him with the leaders (who had given permission for the study) toward whom they were antagonistic. Nor was his finding of dissension between the group's leadership and their membership palatable to the leadership. Jones asked himself whether he should omit reporting on the socially destructive aspect of the organization's tension between

its leadership and its members in the interest of racial unity or whether he should describe how racial unity could be used as a slogan by the leadership to silence dissent among the organization members.

Reflecting on his research experience, Delmos Jones concluded that although being a cultural insider offers certain advantages for an anthropologist, such as access to the community, it also poses special dilemmas, particularly when the group being studied has been oppressed by the larger society. Indeed, he noted that the very concept of a native anthropologist is itself problematic. As he and other native anthropologists have pointed out, an individual has many identities, which include those of race and culture but also of gender and social class. Being a native in one identity does not make one a native in all one's identities (Narayan 1993; Cerroni-Long 1995). Furthermore, for all anthropologists who share Delmos Jones's view that the most important goal of research and ethnography is to demonstrate the ways in which social systems may exploit, alienate, and repress human possibilities, both cultural insiders and cultural outsiders face similar dilemmas.

As "exotic" cultures disappear, it becomes much more difficult for Western anthropologists to limit themselves to studying "others," and many more anthropological studies are being carried out in North America and Europe by natives of those cultures. But whether it is Western or non-Western anthropologists studying their own societies, the dimensions of native anthropology will become increasingly important as subjects for reflection.

On this subject, M. N. Srinivas, a distinguished anthropologist from India who has studied his own society, coined the term *thrice born* for what he called the ideal anthropological journey. First, we are born into our original, particular culture. Then, our second birth is to move away from this familiar place to a far place to do our fieldwork. In this experience we are eventually able to understand the rules and meanings of other cultures, and the "exotic" becomes familiar. In our third birth, we again turn toward our native land and find that the

ANTHROPOLOGISTS STUDY THE USE OF ILLEGAL DRUGS

Anthropologists have an important contribution to make to our understanding of the use and abuse of controlled substances. In the 1960s and 1970s, the identification of a drug addict "subculture" drew anthropologists into the world of substance abuse and addiction (Schensul 1997). Ethnography was a particularly suitable methodology for studying street drug scenes and their participants.

Most social science models of drug use and distribution treat drug users and sellers as "deviants," separate from the larger population, and indeed focus on "drug addicts" as criminal deviants, operating outside of larger social networks and cultural norms. Psychopharmacological models of drug use, which emphasize intrapsychic and chemical "causes" of substance abuse, also fail to consider the social and cultural contexts of drug-related behavior.

Anthropologists, in keeping with their broader holistic perspective, have introduced structural and cultural models as alternatives to the deviant and psychomedical models. Structural models aim at connecting the individual drug user and seller with the larger, structural features of the society, and particularly its political economy (Hamid 1990, 1998; Waterston 1993). Anthropologist Ansley Hamid, for example, demonstrates that patterns of drug-related violence cannot be understood only in terms of an individual's impulsive or economically motivated behavior, but rather vary as a result of the ways in which political decisions and economic processes impact on neighborhoods, families, and kinship networks. Hamid's work goes beyond the view of mainstream America—particularly the media and law enforcement—to show that drug use and distribution are not the work only of the "alienated, the deviant, or the diseased," but are integrated with larger economic and political issues, particularly those affecting the transformation of minority neighborhoods.

This focus on the structures within which drug use and distribution are embedded makes ethnography a particularly valuable methodology, both for examining the links between drug users and sellers and their communities, and for examining the cultural meanings that users and sellers attach to their drug-related behavior (see, for example, Williams 1989; Sharff 1997; Bourgois 1989; Maher 1997).

Anthropologist Kojo Dei, in his ethnography of Southside, a lower-class African American neighborhood in a suburban county bordering a major urban center in the Northeast, found that the residents of this community view drugs in a quite different way than that encoded in the laws and mainstream cultural norms of middle-class America. In this community, smoking marijuana is common. Although in public most adult residents of Southside give lip service to the view that "drugs are a major social problem," in private they express different views. Many Southside residents note that alcohol and nicotine—two legal addictive drugs—do more harm than marijuana. The community's view of a "drug addict" is a person who cannot function because of his or her drug use—a definition different from that of the social service and medical professions, who define addiction in terms of physical withdrawal symptoms. And, unlike law enforcement perspectives, the community's main concerns are the violence and other criminal activities associated with the use and distribution of both illegal drugs and alcohol rather than the use and distribution of illegal drugs as such (Dei 1996).

As Jagna Sharff's (1997) study of a Puerto Rican neighborhood in New York also shows, the sale of illegal drugs may even be viewed positively in poor communities, such as Southside, as a way for young men (few women are involved

familiar has become exotic. We see it with new eyes. Despite our deep emotional attachment to its ways, we are able to see it also with scientific objectivity (quoted in Myerhoff 1978).

Srinivas's ideal anthropological experience is becoming more real for many anthropologists today. It is also an experience completely consistent with one of anthropology's original goals: that of eventually examining our own cultures in the same objective way that we have examined other cultures, and of bringing what we learn back home.

in drug distribution; Maher 1997) to help out their families financially. Indeed, many of the young men who distribute drugs in Southside view selling drugs as "work" and a legitimate, if not legal, path to achieving the American Dream through the capitalist model of entrepreneurship. In addition to the money, many of these young men prefer selling drugs to "working for the white man." Unlike the inner-city youth in Katherine Newman's (1999b) study, who are willing to work in dead-end jobs in the fast-food sector of the economy in order to get ahead, Dei's informants in Southside consider these jobs "kid stuff."

Much "drug scene" ethnography by anthropologists has been used in formulating more effective services and risk reduction programs for those using drugs, such as AIDS education and needle exchange programs (Singer 2000). Ethnography also reveals where anti-drug-use programs are ineffective. In Southside, for example, the Drug Abuse Resistance Education (DARE) program, run by the school district, is largely ineffective because it is taught by police officers in uniform, whom the black community generally distrust.

Anthropology, then, through its holistic perspective on the individual, its eth-

Courtesy of Serena Nanda

KOJO A. DEI (RIGHT), AN ANTHROPOLOGIST FROM GHANA, DOES ETHNOGRAPHIC FIELDWORK AMONG AFRICAN AMERICAN YOUTH IN A MAJOR CITY IN THE UNITED STATES. THE FOCUS OF DEI'S ETHNOGRAPHY IS ON HOW THE CULTURAL MEANINGS OF SUBSTANCE USE AND ABUSE WITHIN INNER-CITY COMMUNITIES BOTH SUPPORT AND DIVERGE FROM THOSE IN THE LARGER SOCIETY. AN ESSENTIAL RELATIONSHIP IN DEI'S ETHNOGRAPHIC FIELDWORK IS WITH HIS KEY INFORMANTS, AMONG THEM PRINCE AFRIKA.

nographic methodology, and its multi-level analysis of culture and society, has much to contribute to the formulation of policy regarding what is considered by many to be a major social problem in the United States.

ETHICAL CONSIDERATIONS IN FIELDWORK

Ethical considerations come up in every fieldwork experience, and anthropologists are always required to reflect on the possible effects of their research on those they study. Three main ethical principles that must guide the fieldworker are obtaining the informed consent of the people to be studied, protecting them from risk, and respecting their privacy and dignity. The current concern with ethics in participant-observation is an important, often agonizing

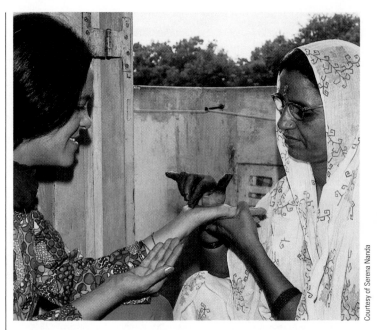

Courtesy of Serena Nanda

ANTHROPOLOGISTS PARTICIPATE IN THE ACTIVITIES OF THE SOCIETIES THEY ARE STUDY-
ING, AS WELL AS OBSERVING BEHAVIOR AND ASKING QUESTIONS. HERE THE ANTHRO-
POLOGIST IS HAVING HER HANDS PAINTED WITH MEHNDI AS PART OF A HINDU RITUAL
THAT A WIFE PERFORMS FOR THE WELFARE OF HER HUSBAND.

matter, much more so than in the past, and is surrounded by both professional codes and federal regulations (Murphy and Johannsen 1990). Some serious transgressions of ethical conduct, such as the past participation of anthropologists in counterinsurgency work, have caused concern within the profession. Fieldwork is based on trust, and as anthropologists involve themselves in a continually expanding range of research situations, ethical dilemmas will increase.

In trying to address these issues, the American Anthropological Association (1983) has adopted a statement of ethics, which holds that the anthropologist's paramount responsibility is to those being studied. Anthropologists must do everything within their power to protect the physical, social, and psychological welfare of the people they study and to honor their dignity and privacy. This includes the obligation to allow informants to remain anonymous when they wish to do so and not to exploit them for personal gain. It also includes the responsibility to communicate the results of the research to the individuals and groups likely to be affected, as well as to the general public.

Anthropologists' obligations to the public include a positive responsibility to speak out, both individually and collectively, in order to contribute to an "adequate definition of reality" that may become the basis of public opinion, public policy, or a resource in the politics of culture. Thus, anthropologists must not only carry on fieldwork in a manner that appropriately involves working in collaboration with their informants but also do ethnography in a way that most accurately represents both the culture and the collaborative dialogues through which cultural description emerges. All of these issues are particularly pertinent in ethnography that is focused on social problems, such as the use and abuse of illegal substances.

NEW ROLES FOR THE ETHNOGRAPHER

Another important issue affecting fieldwork and ethnography is that, contrary to the situation in the late nineteenth and early twentieth centuries, anthropology today is well understood in many of the societies that anthropologists study. People from those societies are attending universities in greater numbers, and some have become anthropologists themselves. In some cases, members of the societies studied resent anthropological representations of themselves; in other cases, ethnographic data are viewed as useful to a society, serving as a basis for the revitalization of traditional cultural elements and the creation of cultural identities that have been nearly effaced by Western impact (Feinberg 1994).

In societies where different versions of a culture are competing for validation as "authentic" in the construction of national identities, both anthropological data and anthropologists may be incorporated as important sources of cultural authority. When Kathleen Adams carried out her fieldwork among the Toraja of Sulawesi, Indonesia, she found her informants already quite sophisticated about ethnography. On her third day there, one of the Toraja told her, "As an anthropologist, you should write a book about the *real* Toraja identity and history, both the good and the bad . . . [the] authentic and the true . . . the Toraja without make-up" (Adams 1995).

Toraja society was traditionally based on a ranking of aristocrats, commoners, and slaves. In the last several decades, however, for a variety of reasons, including wage labor outside the region and income from tourism, lower-status people had begun to achieve some wealth. As the aristocrats became more insecure about the relevance of their own royal genealogies, anthropological accounts became an important resource, shoring up their claims to noble status, and elite Toraja competed for anthropological attention. Indeed, Adams became a featured event on tourist itineraries in the region as tour guides led their groups to the home of her host, not only validating his importance in the village but also bolstering the tourists' experience of the Toraja as a group sufficiently remote to be studied by anthropologists.

The manipulation of anthropologists by the local politics of culture is another of the changed conditions reinforcing our recognition that the concept of a bounded, isolated tribal or village culture is no longer a viable basis for ethnography. Whether working in cities, villages, or with tribal groups, almost all ethnographers must take into account the interaction of these local units with larger, even global social structures, economies, and cultures. It may mean following informants from villages to their workplaces in cities or collecting genealogies that spread over countries or even continents. This new conceptual framework raises questions about how typical one's unit of study is within a larger cultural pattern, or even whether it is a culturally legitimate unit at all. In addition to expanding the research site, contemporary ethnographers more often use techniques other than participant-observation, such as questionnaires, social surveys, archival material, government documents, and court records.

CROSS-CULTURAL COMPARISON

The gathering of good ethnographic data through participant-observation is the hallmark of cultural anthropology and the foun-

dation on which anthropological theories are built. Under the influence of anthropologists such as Bronislaw Malinowski and Franz Boas, the aim of anthropological fieldwork was the description of a total cultural pattern. Today, however, many anthropologists go into the field with the aim of focusing on specific theoretical problems, much as Charles Brooks did in his study of the Hare Krishna in India. Some of these field studies may be comparative, studying the same cultural pattern or social institution in several cultures, as in the comparative study of preschools in China, Japan, and the United States described in Chapter 6. However, these comparative approaches still depend on intensive field studies of particular societies and are well within the definition of the ethnographic method.

An entirely different kind of cross-cultural comparative method is the **cross-cultural survey,** or **controlled cross-cultural comparison.** The goal of the cross-cultural survey is to test generalizations about culture, using statistical correlations of culture traits based on a wide survey of many different cultures. The database for the cross-cultural survey method is the **Human Relations Area File (HRAF).** The HRAF is an extensive filing system containing ethnographic data about hundreds of societies, past and present, from the main ethnographically distinguished areas of the world: Africa, Asia, native North and South America, and Oceania. Combining ethnographic information about these societies from books and articles, the HRAF cross-indexes hundreds of cultural features. Thus, it makes accessible information about specific cultural patterns in a particular society, and it also facilitates inquiry about cultural patterns that are found in association with each other.

Thousands of different kinds of questions can be answered by the cross-cultural survey

---

cross-cultural survey (also called **controlled cross-cultural comparison**) A research method that uses statistical correlations of traits from many different cultures to test generalizations about culture and human behavior.

Human Relations Area File (HRAF) An ethnographic database including cultural descriptions of more than 300 cultures.

method (Ember and Ember 1996). For example, in the 1950s, when divorce was becoming more common in the United States and the increasing divorce rate was causing some alarm, anthropologist George Murdock, one of the important pioneers in this methodology, used the HRAF to determine how marriage instability in the United States compared with that of other cultures (1950/1996).

Using a **random sample** of eight societies from each of the five major ethnographic divisions of the world, Murdock ascertained that 39 of the 40 societies in his sample made provision for the termination of marriage through divorce. When Murdock surveyed his sample for the frequency of divorce, he found that while 15 societies had more stable marriages than the United States, 24 societies (60 percent of the sample) had less stable marriages. He also investigated the grounds for divorce and found that the great majority of societies recognized only certain grounds as adequate and few societies condoned divorce for a "mere whim." The most common bases for divorce were incompatibility, adultery, barrenness or sterility, impotence or frigidity, economic incapacity or nonsupport, cruelty, and quarrelsomeness.

Murdock concluded from his cross-cultural survey that the American divorce rate was well within the limits that "human experience has shown that societies can tolerate with safety." He also concluded that most societies, even those with high divorce rates, are not indifferent to family stability and that societies with lower divorce rates usually have social devices such as marriage payments, arranged marriages by parents, and prohibitions against adultery to support marital stability.

Most often, the cross-cultural survey is used to test hypotheses about cultural correlations and causes. For example, anthropologist Donald Horton used this method to test his theory that the primary function of drinking alcohol is to reduce anxiety (Horton 1943). One of the many hypotheses he tested as part of his larger theory was that drinking alcohol would be related to the level of anxiety in a society and that a major source of anxiety would be economic insecurity.

To test this hypothesis, Horton first classified societies in the HRAF for which there was information on drinking behavior into those having high, moderate, or low subsistence insecurity. He then classified the same societies into those having high, moderate, or low rates of insobriety. Horton found a significant statistical correlation between high subsistence insecurity and high rates of insobriety. After finding significant statistical correlations for many of the other hypotheses generated from his theory, Horton considered his theory confirmed.

The cross-cultural survey has both advantages and disadvantages. A major advantage of the method is that it encourages formulating hypotheses, which can then be tested by finding statistically significant correlations between two or more cultural traits. A problem, however, is whether the correlations found have explanatory power—that is, whether they indicate causality. For example, although Horton's study found a statistically significant correlation between economic insecurity and high rates of insobriety, his findings cannot confirm that subsistence insecurity *causes* high rates of insobriety. To confirm causality one needs to test the association of many different features and to disprove alternative hypotheses.

Another problem with the cross-cultural survey is ambiguity about what constitutes a particular cultural trait and how to measure it. Because the cross-cultural survey method uses cultural traits taken out of context, it is not always clear that a trait has the same meaning in the different societies in which it is found. Insobriety, for example, would be constructed differently in different cultures, and its measurement may be somewhat arbitrary. Still another problem is that for many societies, information on the particular cultural trait the investigator wants to measure may be missing from the ethnographic source. Because most of the ethnographic data in the HRAF were collected without HRAF categories in mind, not all societies have data on all of the same

random sample A selection of items from a total set, chosen on a random, or unbiased, basis.

cultural patterns. Anthropologists using the cross-cultural method have tried to overcome these problems in different ways, and many continue to find the method of substantial advantage.

Carol and Melvin Ember, anthropologists prominently associated with the cross-cultural survey method, note that cross-cultural surveys help to prevent generalizing about human nature or making assumptions about cultural correlations based on only a few cultures (Ember and Ember 1996). They note that the thousands of cross-cultural surveys carried out have produced conclusions that support common-sense expectations and also hold some surprises. On the question of violence, for example, cross-cultural comparative studies confirm that societies that have a lot of violence in one aspect of culture tend to have a lot of violence throughout the culture. Societies that more often engage in warfare, for example, also tend to have a high degree of other forms of violence, such as homicide, assault, wife beating, capital punishment, and male socialization practices that permit or encourage aggression. Such studies, like George Murdock's study on divorce noted earlier, are also important in putting contemporary social problems in cross-cultural perspective, providing new insights into possible solutions.

Undoubtedly, as more anthropologists learn to use the HRAF through the annual Summer Institutes in Comparative Anthropological Research sponsored by the Human Relations Area Files and the National Science Foundation, cross-cultural comparisons will become an increasingly important part of anthropologists' work. The use of cross-cultural surveys and the HRAF database underscores the need for good ethnography. The use of both methods confirms anthropology's status as the most humanistic of the sciences and the most scientific of the humanities.

An ethnography is the written account of a culture based on fieldwork.

2. An essential ability in fieldwork is to see another culture from the point of view of members of that culture. Bronislaw Malinowski and Franz Boas were two twentieth-century anthropologists whose meticulous fieldwork set a standard for the profession.

3. In the global economy and with the global reach of information, ethnographic data, particularly from indigenous cultures, is increasingly being used for commercial purposes. This has led to greater activism by anthropologists, working with indigenous peoples, to find ways to protect cultural knowledge and products.

4. With the postmodern emphasis on multiple voices in ethnography, anthropological accounts of other cultures increasingly describe the fieldwork experience and raise questions about how anthropologists' status and culture influence their perceptions and representations of other cultures.

5. Charles Brooks's field experience in India illustrates the steps in doing fieldwork: choosing a research problem, picking a research site, finding key informants, collecting and recording data, and analyzing and interpreting the data.

6. Doing fieldwork in the anthropologist's own culture presents similar and different problems from doing fieldwork in another culture. Although native anthropologists may have advantages of access and rapport in some cases, they also experience special burdens more intensely, such as whether to expose aspects of the culture that may be received unfavorably by outsiders.

7. Anthropological ethics require protecting the dignity, privacy, and anonymity of the people one studies and not putting them at risk in any way. This may require extra caution when the research setting is a site of illegal activity, such as drug use.

8. In addition to ethnography, anthropologists may also use the rich ethnographic data of the HRAF in cross-cultural surveys in order to test hypotheses about human behavior and cultural processes.

SUMMARY

1. The main method of cultural anthropology is ethnography, or the intensive, firsthand study of a particular society through fieldwork. The major technique in fieldwork is participant-observation.

KEY TERMS

androcentric bias

controlled cross-cultural comparison

cross-cultural survey

empirical science

ethnographic method

ethnography

ethnology

fieldwork

genealogy

Human Relations
Area File
(HRAF)

informant

key informant

native
anthropologist

participant-
observation

positivism

postmodernism

random sample

SUGGESTED READINGS

Agar, Michael. 1996. *The Professional Stranger: An Informal Introduction to Ethnography* (2nd ed.). New York: Academic Press. Agar's informal and often humorous style makes this a good source on the whys and hows of ethnography for the introductory student.

Behar, Ruth, and Deborah A. Gordon (Eds.). 1995. *Women Writing Culture.* Berkeley: University of California Press. This edited volume, which includes articles from many different cultural perspectives and ethnographic sites, illuminates the relationships between women and anthropology through reflective, innovative, and experimental writing.

Bernard, Russell H., and Jesus Salinas Pedraza. 1995. *Native Ethnography: A Mexican Indian Describes His Culture.* Walnut Creek, CA: Altamira Press. An innovative ethnography based on native-researcher collaboration, in which Salinas's ethnography of his own people, written in his own language, was guided, translated, and annotated by the American anthropologist.

Descola, Phillipe. 1996. *The Spears of Twilight: Life and Death in the Amazon Jungle.* New York: New Press. An account of classical anthropological fieldwork among the Achuar of the Ecuadorian Amazon that interweaves the personal and the ethnographic. Starting out as a search for the isolated "exotic," the author finds he must also consider historic contacts in understanding Achuar culture.

DeVita, Philip R. (Ed.). 2000. *Stumbling Toward Truth: Anthropologists at Work.* Prospect Heights, IL: Waveland. An anthology of original and often amusing articles by anthropologists who have been taught some important lessons by their informants in the process of doing fieldwork.

di Leonardo, Micaela. 1998. *Exotics at Home: Anthropologies, Others, American Modernity.* A wonderfully insightful, provocative book about ethnography, anthropology, and its impact on American cultural images of the "other," both abroad and at home. The author argues for the necessity of an interdisciplinary approach and a political economy perspective if anthropology is to achieve its historic potential for making the world a better place.

Malcolm Young. 1993. *In the Sticks: Cultural Identity in a Rural Police Force.* Oxford: Clarendon Press. A fascinating ethnography by an anthropologist who spent more than 30 years on the English police force, it describes his "culture shock" as well as some of the pitfalls of planned change among the police in England.

INTERNET RESOURCES

The following Internet resources appear in this chapter. Please log on to the Wadsworth anthropology website: **http://anthropology.wadsworth. com**. Click on the Nanda/Warms *Cultural Anthropology* page. Then select the Student Resources section, where you will find a complete presentation of these links and more.

- A video link: Margaret Mead Taking Note, page 51
- A website on the changing directions in ethnography, page 53
- A photo essay on male and female roles in the Middle East, page 55
- Access the Study Guide to InfoTrac College Edition for Anthropology Students

ANTHROPOLOGISTS AGREE THAT ALL HUMANS HAVE CULTURE, BUT DISAGREE ON ITS MEANING AND FUNCTION. IN THIS PICTURE, NOVICE MONKS FROM THE ZOJOJOI TEMPLE IN TOKYO SETTLE DOWN TO ENJOY A PIZZA AT A PIZZA HUT RESTAURANT. DO WE UNDERSTAND THEIR MEAL IN TERMS OF ADAPTATION, ECONOMICS, SYMBOLISM, DIFFUSION, OR ACCULTURATION?

CHAPTER FOUR

THE IDEA OF CULTURE

How do anthropologists understand culture?

In what ways can culture be considered an adaptation?

How do people use culture to organize and give meaning to their lives?

In what ways is culture a system?

To what extent do members of a group share a single culture?

How does culture change?

People in industrialized cultures that emphasize individualism sometimes think of culture as something that restrains them and deprives them of freedom, but without it, human beings would not be human beings. Although culture is not easy to define precisely, practically everything humans perceive, know, think, value, feel, and do—in short, almost everything that makes us human—is learned through participation in a sociocultural system. Even things that strike us as natural often are cultural.

The few well-documented cases of children isolated from society in the early years of life bear out this statement. One of these cases, known as the "wild boy of Aveyron" (Itard 1806/1962), is of exceptional interest. In 1799, a boy of about 12 was captured in a forest in Aveyron, France. He was brought to Paris, where he attracted huge crowds who expected to see the "noble savage" of the romantic eighteenth-century philosophical vision. Instead, they found a boy whose

eyes were unsteady, expressionless, wandering vaguely from one object to another . . . so little trained by the sense of touch, they could never distinguish an object in relief from one in a picture. His . . . hearing was insensible to the loudest noises and to . . . music. His voice was reduced to a state of complete muteness and only a uniform guttural sound escaped him . . . he was equally indifferent to the odor of perfume and to the fetid exhalation of the dirt with which his bed was filled . . . [his] touch was restricted to the mechanical grasping of an object. [He had a] tendency to trot and gallop [and] an obstinate habit of smelling at anything given to him . . . he chewed like a rodent with a sudden action of the incisors . . . [and] showed no sensitivity to cold or heat and could seize hot coals from the fire without flinching or lay half naked upon the wet ground for hours in the wintertime. . . . He was incapable of attention and spent his time apathetically rocking himself backwards and forwards like the animals in the zoo.

According to Jean-Marc-Gaspard Itard, the young psychologist who undertook to educate the boy, whom he called Victor, Victor's apparent subnormality was not caused by incurable mental disease or want of intelligence but by the lack of participation in normal human society. Itard's account of Victor's education makes fascinating reading. It underscores the fact that human potential can be realized only within the structure of human culture and through growing up in close contact with other human beings. Without the constraints imposed by a specific culture, we are not more free, but rather totally unfree in that none of our human qualities and abilities can develop. But what is culture?

DEFINING CULTURE

In 1873, Sir Edward Burnett Tylor, sometimes called the father of anthropology, introduced the concept of culture as an explanation of the differences among human societies. Tylor defined culture as the "complex whole which includes knowledge, belief, art, law, morals, custom, and any other capabilities acquired [learned] by man as a member of society" (1920:1), and he defined anthropology as the scientific study of human culture. Tylor's definition sounds straightforward enough, but it is actually very different from that used by anthropologists today. Tylor went on to suggest that culture was found to a greater or lesser extent among all the world's peoples. For him, there was a single, universal human culture, which members of different societies possessed to different degrees. As far as we know, no modern anthropologist holds this position. Anthropologists certainly agree that anthropology is the study of culture, but they now think of culture as something fully possessed by all human societies. Tylor's notion of one universal culture has been replaced by the modern idea of a great many different cultures.

Today, anthropologists generally agree that all cultures share, in some degree, the following six characteristics:

1. Cultures are made up of learned behaviors. People are not born knowing their culture. They learn it through a process called enculturation (discussed more fully in Chapter 6). Learning culture is a continuous process. We start learning our culture the day we are born, and we are still learning things at the time of our death.
2. Cultures all involve the use of language and symbols. A **symbol** is simply something that stands for something else. In cultures, people manipulate language and symbols to create systems of ideology or statements about the way the world should be. However, many different such statements are likely to be found within any culture.
3. Cultures are to some degree patterned and integrated. That is, the elements of culture stand in some logical relationship to one another. However, as we shall see below, the degree of coordination among elements of culture is hotly disputed.
4. Cultures are in some way shared by members of a group. Every human being has an individual personality. Studying that is the domain of psychology. Each person must also interact with others and thus must share a framework of interaction with them. However, people who share this framework do not necessarily approach it in the same way.
5. Cultures are in some way adaptive. That is, cultures contain information about how to survive in the world. Of course, cultures also contain much that is maladaptive.
6. All cultures are subject to change. Whether propelled by its internal dynamic or acted upon by outside forces, no culture remains static. However, the speed with which cultures change may vary enormously from place to place and time to time.

Based on this list, we might define culture as the learned, symbolic, at least partially adaptive, and ever-changing patterns of behavior shared by members of a group. Although anthropologists might agree to this broad definition, such accord would cover up enormous disagreements over what the definition really means. While anthropologists agree on culture's basic characteristics, they disagree on how to interpret them, their relative importance, the ways in which they should be studied, and what sorts of things anthropologists should try to learn about cultures. No consensus has ever emerged on the precise definition of culture, nor on the proper means to study it.

Anthropologists disagree about the definition of culture because different ideas about which aspects of culture are fundamental rep-

symbol Something that stands for something else; central to culture.

resent different theoretical positions. Theory lies at the heart of anthropology, and each theoretical position directs those who adopt it to study a different aspect of society.

The notion of culture is like a window through which one may view human groups. Just as the view changes as one moves from window to window of a building, so the anthropologist's understanding of society changes as he or she moves from one definition of culture to another. Just as two windows may have views that overlap or may show totally different scenes, definitions of culture may overlap or reveal totally different aspects of society.

In this chapter, we explore the nature of culture and some aspects of anthropological theory by presenting several different ideas about the nature of culture, each of which tells us something about what it means to be human. We examine culture as a system of human adaptation to the world, a way that humans understand the world around them, and a way that people give meaning to their lives. We discuss the debate over the degree to which cultures are integrated systems and examine the question of whether members of a culture really share values and norms. Finally, we explore some of the ways cultures change. This discussion is not meant to be an exhaustive description of the ways anthropologists see the world. Rather, it is intended to give you some of the flavor of the lively debate about the nature of human society within anthropology and allow you to reexamine some of the things that we perhaps take for granted in our own and other societies.

Table 4.1 provides a very brief list of key theoretical schools in anthropology and their understanding of culture. These schools are summarized in more detail, and key works within them are listed, in the Appendix.

CULTURE IS THE WAY HUMAN BEINGS ADAPT TO THE WORLD

Human beings, like other living creatures, have biological needs. They need a secure supply of food and adequate conditions under which they can live and raise their young. Like many other creatures, humans have psychological needs as well. These needs include safety, growth, and movement. Other animals fill their needs primarily through biological **adaptation.** For example, a lion uses speed and sharp teeth and claws to capture and eat its prey. Humans are singularly lacking in offensive biological weaponry. Left to get our food like the lion, we would surely starve.

Culture is the principal tool we use to feed ourselves. That is, human beings, in groups, develop forms of knowledge and technologies that enable them to get the necessary energy from the environment and make life more secure. This knowledge and technology forms a core of culture that can be passed from generation to generation and group to group. Thus, for people, culture plays a role similar to that played by tooth, claw, and muscle for the lion. Lions are biologically adapted to their world, whereas humans adapt culturally.

Cultural adaptation has some distinct advantages over biological adaptation. Because humans adapt through learned behavior, they can change their approach to solving problems more quickly and easily. Creatures whose adaptations are primarily biological change slowly. Furthermore, biological or evolutionary change is based on the presence of more highly adapted variations within the gene pool of a species. These variations occur as chance mutations. If the variations happen not to be present, no change is possible. For example, imagine a species of fish living in a pond of fresh water. If the pond is polluted by industrial waste, all will die except those that, by chance, have a genetic makeup that allows them to survive in polluted water. These will go on to give birth to the next generation of fish. If such a variation does not exist, none will survive and the fish will become extinct. There is no way a fish can learn how to live in the polluted water. Either the genetic variation that allows some of them to survive is present or it is not. Human beings, on the other hand, can learn to live in polluted environments. They can develop ways to clean the environment or mechanisms to enable their

adaptation The ways in which living populations relate to the environment so that they can survive and reproduce.

TABLE 4.1

SOME MAJOR ANTHROPOLOGICAL SCHOOLS OF THOUGHT AND THEIR UNDERSTANDINGS OF CULTURE

THEORY NAME	UNDERSTANDING OF CULTURE	CRITICAL THINKERS
Nineteenth-century evolutionism	A universal human culture is shared, in different degrees, by all societies	E. B. Tylor (1832–1917) L. H. Morgan (1818–1881)
Turn-of-the-century sociology	Groups of people share sets of symbols and practices that bind them into societies.	Emile Durkheim (1858–1917) Marcel Mauss (1872–1950)
American historical particularism	Cultures are the result of the specific histories of the people who share them.	Franz Boas (1858–1942) A. L. Kroeber (1876–1960)
Functionalism	Social practices support society's structure or fill the needs of individuals.	A. R. Radcliffe Brown (1881–1955) Bronislaw Malinowski (1884–1942)
Culture and personality	Culture is personality writ large. It both shapes and is shaped by the personalities of its members.	Ruth Benedict (1887–1948) Margaret Mead (1901–1978)
Cultural ecology and neo-evolutionism	Culture is the way in which humans adapt to the environment and make their lives secure.	Julian Steward (1902–1972) Leslie White (1900–1975)
Ecological materialism	Physical and economic causes give rise to cultures and explain changes within them.	Morton Fried (1923–1986) Marvin Harris (1927–)
Structuralism	All cultures reflect the universal biological structure of the human mind.	Claude Levi-Strauss (1908–)
Ethnoscience and cognitive anthropology	Culture is a mental template that determines how members of a society understand their world.	Harold Conklin (1926–) Stephen Tyler (1932–)
Sociobiology	Culture is the visible expression of underlying genetic coding.	E. O. Wilson (1929–) Jerome Barkow (1944–)
Anthropology and gender	The roles of women and the ways societies understand sexuality are central to understanding culture.	Sherry Ortner (1941–) Michelle Rosaldo (1944?–1981)
Symbolic and interpretive anthropology	Culture is the way in which members of a society understand who they are and give their lives meaning.	Mary Douglas (1921–) Clifford Geertz (1926–)
Postmodernism	Because understanding of cultures most reflect the observer's biases, culture can never be completely or accurately described.	Renato Rosaldo (1941–) Vincent Crapanzano (1939–)

Note: Theoretical positions in anthropology represent sophisticated thinking and cannot be summed up in a single line. This table is not intended to reflect the complexity of the theories it describes.

survival within it. People can teach these to others. No biological change is necessary.

Lions hunt and eat today in much the same way as they have for tens of thousands of years. The vast majority of human beings today do not live like humans of three or four generations ago, let alone our distant ancestors. Our means of feeding ourselves, our culture, has changed. **Plasticity**—the ability to change behavior in response to a wide range of environmental demands—has allowed human beings to thrive under a wide variety of ecological conditions.

Cultural adaptation has some disadvantages too. Misinformation, leading to cultural practices that hinder rather than aid survival, may creep into human behavior. For example, before 1820 most Americans considered the tomato to be poisonous and therefore did not use this valuable food source. Cultural practices that encourage overpopulation, destructive depletion, or contamination of natural resources may lead to short-term success but long-term disaster. Further, it is clear that many human practices are not adaptive, even in the short run. Political movements such as policies of ethnic cleansing and genocide that urge people to murder their neighbors may benefit their leaders, but it is hard to see any meaningful way in which they are adaptive. A normal lion will always inherit the muscle, tooth, and claw that lets it survive. Normal humans, on the other hand, may inherit a great deal of cultural misinformation that hinders their survival.

Anthropologists who view culture as an adaptation tend to be concerned with people's behavior, particularly as it concerns their physical well-being. They ask questions about subsistence technology and its relationship to family structure, religion, and other elements of culture. They are concerned with the ways in which cultures adapt to specific environments and the ways in which cultures have evolved. Anthropologists concerned primarily with these types of issues may identify themselves as belonging to theoretical schools including **cultural ecology, cultural materialism, neo-evolutionism, neo-Marxism,** and **sociobiology** (McGee and Warms 2000).

CULTURE IS THE WAY HUMANS ORGANIZE THE WORLD

Human beings are unable to see everything in their environment. Instead, we pay attention to some of our surroundings and disregard others. When you walk into a classroom, for example, you probably notice friends and other students, the professor, video equipment, and additional features of the room that are germane to learning and teaching. You might spend an entire semester without ever noticing cracks in the wall, the pattern of the carpeting, the type of ceiling tile, or perhaps even the color of the walls. Yet these things are as physically present in the room as the chairs and your friends.

You see certain things in the classroom and overlook others because you come to the room as a student and organize its contents in that context. Some of the things in the room, such as professors and friends, you classify as important and worthy of notice. Others, such as the color of the walls, you discount and may not notice at all. It is virtually impossible to see things without organizing and evaluating them in some manner.

If you actually paid as much attention to the cracks in the wall, the patterns on the floor, and the humming of the ventilation system as you did to the professor's lecture, not only would you be likely to fail the class, but you would live in a world that was overwhelming and impossibly confusing. Only through fitting our perceptions and experiences into systems of classification can we comprehend our lives and act in the world. A human without the ability to organize and classify would be paralyzed, frozen by an overwhelming bombardment of random sensations.

plasticity The ability of humans to change their behavior in response to a wide range of environmental demands.

cultural ecology A theoretical approach that regards cultural patterns as adaptive responses to the basic problems of human survival and reproduction.

cultural materialism A theoretical perspective that holds that the primary task of anthropology is to account for the similarities and differences among cultures and that this can best be done by studying the material constraints to which human existence is subject.

neo-evolutionism A theoretical perspective concerned with the historical change of culture from small-scale societies to extremely large-scale societies.

neo-Marxism A theoretical perspective concerned with applying the insights of Marxist thought to anthropology; neo-Marxists modify Marxist analysis to make it appropriate to the investigation of small-scale, non-Western societies.

sociobiology A theoretical perspective that explores the relationship between human cultural behavior and genetics.

IN THE FIELD

BUILDING A HOUSE IN NORTHWESTERN THAILAND

The importance of adaptation to the environment is more easily seen in some areas of culture than in others. For example, the ways in which humans satisfy their basic needs for food, shelter, and safety, although part of a culturally constructed reality, are more directly adaptive to the physical environment than, say, art. The material culture of societies with simple technologies is based on adaptive strategies that have developed slowly over long periods of trial and error and are well suited to their physical environments, even when the people in the society cannot say why they do things in a certain way.

Anthropologist James Hamilton found this out the hard way when he tried to build a house for himself while doing fieldwork among the Pwo Karen of northwestern Thailand (Hamilton 1987). To learn about house construction, Hamilton carefully observed the details of building a house. Karen houses are essentially wooden-post structures, raised about six feet off the ground, with bamboo walls, peaked roofs, and a veranda. There are no windows; the space between the thatch of the roof and the height of the walls serves for light and ventilation. The kitchen is in the house, with a water-storage area on one side of the veranda. This is an important feature

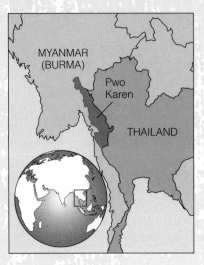

MYANMAR (BURMA)

Pwo Karen

THAILAND

of a house because Karen customs of sociability require that visitors and guests be offered water.

While Hamilton knew a great deal about Karen house construction, when he went to build his own home, he decided to incorporate his own, American notions of what a proper, comfortable house should be. First of all, because the climate was very hot, he insisted that his house be in a shaded area under some tall trees. The Karen villagers suggested that this was a bad location, but failed to dissuade him. Like most Americans, Hamilton also liked his lawn—a wide grassy area in front of his house—and protested when the villagers started pulling up the grass. He said he was not concerned about the snakes and scorpions that might be in the grass; besides, he had a flashlight and boots in case he had to go out at night. In a traditional Karen house, a

person cannot stand up straight because the side walls are less than five feet high. In order to accommodate his belief that people ought to be able to stand up in their houses, Hamilton lowered the floor to about two feet off the ground. Furthermore, because the Karen house is dark and, to Americans, rather small, Hamilton decided to have his kitchen outside the house. Despite Karen grumbling that this was not the proper way to build a house, he built an extension on one side of the house with a lean-to roof covering made of leaves, and this became his kitchen. Finally, when the Karen started to cut off the long overhanging thatch from the roof, Hamilton asked that they let it remain, as it gave him some privacy from eyes peering over the wall, which did not meet the top of the house.

After the house was finished and Hamilton had lived in it for a while, he found out why the Karen did not like the alterations he had made to their traditional design. This part of Thailand has a heavy rainy season. Because the house was under the trees, the roof could not dry out properly and it rotted. In addition, so many twigs and branches fell through the roof that it became like a sieve, barely providing any protection from the rain at all. The slope of the lean-to over the kitchen was not steep enough; instead of running off, the water came through the roof. That whole side of the house roof had to be torn off and replaced with a steeper roof, made of sturdier and more expensive thatch.

Methods of organizing and classifying are not individual but products of a group. You are not the only one who thinks that the students and professors in a classroom are more important than ceiling tiles; that perception is probably shared by all students and professors. Anthropologists have long proposed that all members

of a culture share similar ways of organizing and classifying. In this view, culture is the mental model people use to organize and classify and ultimately to understand their world.

Different cultures clearly have different models for understanding and speaking about the world, and the ways people classify elements

The nice lawn combined with the reachable thatch of the roof offered too great a temptation for the local cows, who tried to eat it. One morning Hamilton woke to find his lawn covered with piles of cow dung, with hundreds of dung beetles rolling little balls of dung all around the yard. He cut off the thatch overhang that was left under the trees and pulled up all the grass.

Because the house had been built low to the ground (by Karen standards) in a shady, cool, wet area, there was insufficient ventilation and drying in and around the house to prevent mildew. This meant that Hamilton had to sweep the walls and wipe all leather objects once a week and tightly seal all his anthropological tools, including field notes, camera, film, tape recorder, and typewriter.

The Karen house, like houses everywhere, has symbolic meanings and reflects the social organization and worldview of a people. But there is no getting around the fact that it must also be built within the constraints imposed by the physical environment. Although some alterations have been made in the Karen house over the past 80 years, reflecting some changes in social organization, Hamilton learned the hard way that Karen house design was extremely well adapted to the environment, and not easily tinkered with.

JAMES HAMILTON'S HOUSE. HAMILTON'S AMERICAN NOTIONS OF HOUSE BUILDING DID NOT WORK WELL IN THE JUNGLES OF THAILAND.

Courtesy of James Hamilton

Critical Thinking Questions

1. James Hamilton's experience shows that even though traditional Karen housing ideals did not match American notions of housing, they were well adapted to their environment. What particular design features of housing are adaptations to the environment where you live?
2. Is housing in the United States generally well adapted to the environment? Consider both modern and older construction. Is modern construction better adapted to the environment than older construction?
3. Because it is a physical object, it is easy to see a house as an adaptation. But intangible things such as social structure and family type can also be adaptations. For example, the Shoshone Indians lived in the deserts of the American West and supported themselves by hunting animals and gathering plants. They lived in family groups of fewer than 20 people. In what way was living in such small groups an adaptation to their environment?

Adapted from James W. Hamilton, "This Old House: A Karen Ideal." In Daniel W. Ingersoll, Jr., and Gordon Bronitsky (Eds.), *Mirror and Metaphor: Material and Social Construction of Reality.* Lanham, MD: University Press of America, 1987.

of their environment provide many examples. For instance, Bamana children in Mali classify some kinds of termites as food. Americans think of all termites as pests. In English, the verb *smoke* describes the action of ingesting a cigarette and *drink* describes the action of consuming a liquid. However, in the Bamana language, you use the same verb, *min,* for smoking and drinking. Americans think rainbows are beautiful and take pleasure in pointing them out to each other. Lacondon Maya consider rainbows dangerous and frightening, and it is highly inappropriate to point one out to another person (McGee, personal communication).

Tomas D. W. Friedman/Photo Researchers, Inc.

THE CHINESE UNDERSTANDING OF HEALTH AND SICKNESS IS VERY DIFFERENT FROM THAT OF MOST NORTH AMERICANS. ANTHROPOLOGISTS WHO STUDY ETHNOMEDICINE FOCUS ON UNDERSTANDING THE WAYS MEMBERS OF DIFFERENT CULTURES CLASSIFY DISEASES AND THEIR TREATMENTS.

One way of thinking about culture is as a codification of reality—a system of meaning that transforms physical reality, what is there, into experienced reality. Dorothy Lee (1959:1), an anthropologist interested in the different ways people see themselves and their environments, described her perception of reality as she looked out the window of her house: "I see trees, some of which I like to be there, and some of which I intend to cut down to keep them from encroaching further upon the small clearing I made for my house." But she noted that Black Elk, a holy man of the Oglala (Sioux) "saw trees as having rights to the land, equal to his own. He saw them as the standing peoples, in whom the winged ones built their lodges and reared their families."

Many anthropologists believe that each culture has a particular way of classifying, and hence understanding, the world. Their interest is in describing the systems of organization and classification used by individual cultures, and their goal is to enable strangers to sort experience in the same way as the native would. Such anthropologists belong to the theoretical schools of **ethnoscience** and **cognitive anthropology.** Recently, there has been great interest in **ethnobotany,** or understanding the way members of different cultures classify plants (Schultes and von Reis 1995; Warren, Slikkerveer, and Brokensha 1995), and **ethnomedicine,** understanding the way they perceive health, sickness, and healing (Balick, Elisabetsky, and Laird 1996).

Other anthropologists believe that although the details of a system of classification may be unique to individual cultures, there are grand overall patterns to these systems that are common to all humanity. Such anthropologists compare the myths and beliefs of different cultures to isolate common patterns. Many believe that these reflect a universal underlying patterning of human thought: the tendency to divide everything into two opposing classes (male/female, good/bad, right/left), as well as a third class that crosses the boundary between these two. The study of this aspect of culture is generally called **structural anthropology.**

ethnoscience A theoretical approach that focuses on the ways in which members of a culture classify their world and holds that anthropology should be the study of cultural systems of classification.

cognitive anthropology A theoretical approach that defines culture in terms of the rules and meanings underlying human behavior, rather than behavior itself.

ethnobotany An anthropological discipline devoted to describing the ways in which different cultures classify plants.

ethnomedicine An anthropological discipline devoted to describing the medical systems of different cultures.

structural anthropology A theoretical perspective that holds that all cultures reflect similar deep, underlying patterns and that anthropologists should attempt to decipher these patterns.

CULTURE IS THE WAY HUMANS GIVE MEANING TO THEIR LIVES

Human beings not only classify the world, but they also fill it with meaning. Members of every culture imbue their world with stories and symbols. Ideas, words, and actions have not only practical value but symbolic meaning and emotional force. Human behavior signifies something. The central histories, legends, and lore of religions and cultures are not simply

FOOTBALL IN THE UNITED STATES AND BULL FIGHTING IN SPAIN ARE BOTH POPULAR BECAUSE THEY ILLUSTRATE IMPORTANT THEMES OF THEIR RESPECTIVE CULTURES. THEY ARE EXCITING IN PART BECAUSE THEY TELL STORIES LOADED WITH CULTURAL MEANING.

stories; they have powerful emotional resonance for us. People are literally willing to fight and die for their religious and moral beliefs. Actions, such as flag burning or the desecration of religious symbols, that challenge the central meanings of our culture often bring immediate and passionate response. As anthropologist Clifford Geertz puts it, a human being is "an animal suspended in webs of significance which he himself has spun." To put this another way, a culture is a story people tell themselves about themselves. Culture is the way people understand who they are and how they should act in the world. It is the context within which human actions can be understood.

Anthropologists try to understand this cultural context in several different ways. Some are concerned with analyzing the central symbols of culture. In many societies, these are found in religious rituals. Such symbols reflect the deepest concerns of the culture's members in ways that are often difficult to articulate.

Among the Ndembu of East Africa, for example, the mudyi tree is a central symbol. Its chief characteristic is that it has a white, milky sap. For the Ndembu, the tree has many meanings, and it plays important roles in girls' puberty rites. It symbolizes breastfeeding, the

relationship between mother and child, inheritance through the mother's family line, and at the most abstract level, the unity and continuity of Ndembu society itself (Turner 1967). To understand the role the mudyi tree plays in Ndembu society is to have penetrated deeply into the Ndembu view of the world.

As anthropologists attempt to understand culture, they sometimes turn to the tools of literature. A novel is fiction, a story, but it gains its poignancy from its relationship to the real-life experience of its readers. Culture itself is often like a novel. That is, it consists of actions, ideas, and stories through which we not only participate in our community but come to reflect on ourselves and our society. Through actions, ideas, and stories we not only make our lives, but make our lives meaningful. Just as a literary critic might analyze a novel, so an anthropologist might analyze a culture as a text.

For example, consider the American fascination with football. American football has little appeal outside the United States, but here it draws more fans than any other sport. In order to explain its popularity, analysts have studied the key themes of the game. They point out that the game is heavily laden with sexuality. Dundes (1980) notes that the vocabulary

CULTURE AND HIV

The theoretical perspective anthropologists take makes a critical difference in the ways they understand problems and the solutions they are likely to propose. A good example comes from work on AIDS prevention around the world. Some of this work focuses on physical and material aspects of AIDS prevention. Other work focuses on understanding the ways in which people think about sex. Work in the first of these perspectives treats culture primarily as a set of material practices—things people do. Work in the second perspective suggests that culture is more about the ways in which people understand themselves and the world—a mental template. In this case, the two perspectives are not mutually exclusive, and both provide insights about how to reduce the spread of HIV.

Anthropologists have applied a materialist focus to the transmission of HIV among intravenous drug users. People who inject heroin or other drugs are at high risk for HIV and AIDS because they share needles. Anthropological research shows that they do so because their dominant concern is the need to inject drugs, and clean needles are frequently unavailable. Many drug users cannot afford to buy their own "works" (syringes and related paraphernalia). Additionally, where it is illegal to own a needle without a prescription, as it is in many states, they fear carrying their own works. They may borrow needles from friends or rent them in "shooting galleries." These practices increase the transmission of HIV (Singer, Irizarry, and Schensul 1991). Anthropological research also shows that

overwhelmingly, addicts would use clean needles if they were available and would not share them with other people (Carlson et al. 1996).

Research on needle use has led applied anthropologists to conclude that the primary problem is access to clean needles. Thus, they advocate a material solution: government or other agencies should fund free needle distribution or exchange programs. By the mid-1990s, many major American cities had implemented such programs. Three of the best known were in Hartford and New Haven, Connecticut, and Oakland, California. However, such programs have faced staunch political resistance (Heimer et al. 1996). For example, a successful needle-exchange program in Windham, Connecticut, was closed after a political campaign during which it was blamed for virtually all of the city's drug-related problems. However, the end of the program did not cause any improvement in the city's drug problems and led to increases in syringe sharing and a black market in syringes, crippling the city's ability to protect its citizens against HIV and other drug-related problems (Broadhead, Van Hulst, and Heckathorn 1999).

Anthropologist Eric Ratliff (1999), in contrast, took an approach that focused on people's understanding of sex and AIDS. Ratliff examined the ways in which exotic dancers in the Philippines understood sex, love, and their future marital prospects. He found that because people generally looked down on "sex workers," even dancers in Go-Go bars who frequently exchanged sex for money and gifts did not think of themselves

purely in those terms. They tended to define first-time sex encounters for money as "sex work." Since they saw what they were doing as a job, it was acceptable for them to demand that their clients use condoms. However, the women tended to see additional sexual encounters with the same individual as part of building a relationship with a "boyfriend" that could turn into marriage and take them away from their lives as prostitutes. Because of this redefinition, they were unlikely to demand that their partners continue to use condoms. Ratliff notes that those in charge of AIDS prevention programs make a grave error when they define "sex workers" and prostitutes simply as women and men who sell sex for money. These individuals often see themselves as seeking long-term relationships based on love. AIDS prevention programs may be effective in promoting the use of condoms among such people when they have sex with a client for the first time. However, because repeat visitors are likely to be defined as boyfriends rather than customers, condom use declines and AIDS prevention programs may fail.

There are many resources for additional information on programs to treat, prevent, and cure HIV and AIDS. Statistics and information on HIV/AIDS from many nations can be found at the Joint UN Program on HIV/AIDS website at www.unaids.org. Additional information can be found at the websites for AIDS Action Committee (www.aac.org), The Names Project (www.aidsquilt.org), and The Gay Men's Health Crisis (www.gmhc.org), among others.

of football is full of sexual overtones (ends, making a touchdown in the end zone, scoring, going all the way). Football uniforms accentuate male physique: enlarged head and shoulders, narrow waist, and a lower torso "poured into skintight pants accentuated only by a metal codpiece" (Arens 1975). Dressed this way, men tackle each other, hold hands, hug each other, and pat each other's bottoms. But sexuality is not the only important aspect of the sport. Football is, in Geertz's terms, "playing with fire" (1973b). It is attractive to us because, more than other sports, it manipulates some of the most dangerous and controversial themes in American culture. These include masculine identity, the violence and sexuality underlying competition between men, the social role of women, the relationship of the individual to the coordinated group, rules and their infringement, gaining and surrendering territory, and racial character (Oriard 1993:18). As we watch football, we see these issues displayed and manipulated or implied. Football is a game, but it is also a commentary on American culture. It is a text that we read, and those who would understand Americans must learn to read it as well.

Anthropologists who analyze culture in these ways generally refer to themselves as **interpretive** or **symbolic anthropologists.** They try to uncover and interpret the deep emotional and psychological structure of societies. Their methods are those of the humanities rather than the sciences; that is, they deal with meaning and interpretation rather than measurement and experiment. Their goal is to understand the experience of being a member of a culture and to make that experience available to their readers (Marcus and Fischer 1986).

CULTURE IS AN INTEGRATED SYSTEM—OR IS IT?

One of the key ideas of anthropology is the notion of holism (see Chapter 1). Franz Boas, who is often considered the founder of modern American anthropology, taught that cultures are systems composed of parts that stand in certain relations to one another. European

anthropologists often compared culture to a biological organism. Just as an animal is composed of different organs that stand in certain relations to one another (the heart pumps the blood, the lungs supply it with oxygen, the liver purifies it, and so on), so a culture is composed of subsystems that stand in certain relations to one another. For example, the subsistence system provides food, kinship and political systems determine how it is produced and distributed, religion provides motivation and justification for the distribution system, and so on.

This organic analogy has two implications, one widely accepted by modern anthropologists and one heavily criticized. The first implication is that a change in one part of such a system affects other parts of the system. For example, a change in the way people get their food may well result in a change in family structure. If people get their food by hunting and gathering, they may have a loose family structure. If they change to agriculture, with its heavier demands for coordination and direction, their family structure will probably become more rigid.

The second—and controversial—implication of seeing cultures as analogous to organic systems is that cultures are stable. We think of biological systems as composed of parts that work together to keep the entire organism alive and well. The lungs do not suddenly declare war on the liver. If they do, a doctor is called to try to restore balance and proper functioning. Thinking of cultures as systems suggests that, similarly, all their parts work in harmony to keep the system functioning properly. But do cultures really work like this?

Consider the relationship between the American family and the workplace. Does the family system really fit well with the demands made by jobs? Most Americans probably want to maintain long-term marriage commitments,

interpretive or **symbolic anthropology** A theoretical approach that emphasizes that culture is a system of meaning and proposes that the aim of cultural anthropology is to interpret the meanings that cultural acts have for their participants.

raise families, and live middle-class lifestyles. Most jobs in the United States provide inadequate income for this purpose. Furthermore, jobs often require mobility, long hours, and flexibility, conflicting with the demands of the family. Americans must negotiate these conflicts among the lifestyle they desire, the demands of their families, and the requirements of their jobs. For most people, there is no way to satisfy all of these demands simultaneously. Some interests are always sacrificed to others.

In the United States and elsewhere, conflict may also exist between different groups in society. Institutional arrangements within and between societies may favor one group over another. Societies may be divided into castes, or individuals of a particular ethnic origin may be relegated to undesirable positions. Social stratification in India and the United States is explored more fully in Chapter 13.

In socially stratified societies, different groups have different and often opposing interests, which creates conflict. For example, consider a modern factory. Both the workers and the owners want the company to do well, but within this context, the owners hope to maximize their profit and the workers want to maximize their pay. Because increases in the cost of labor come at some expense to profits, there is a structural conflict between the owners and the workers. This conflict has the potential for erupting in violence. In the late nineteenth and early twentieth centuries, labor strikes in the United States repeatedly resulted in death and injury as security forces, police, the national guard, and the army battled strikers. Even during World War II, a time we usually think of as characterized by great internal solidarity, the United States experienced 14,471 strikes involving 6,774,000 workers (Brecher 1972).

There is nothing uniquely American or modern about the conflict engendered by the different and sometimes opposing demands that cultures impose. People in nonindustrialized societies must also handle conflicting commitments to their families and other social groups, such as secret societies or religious associations, to which they belong. Nonstratified societies may have less conflict than those with separate castes, ethnic groups, or classes, but relations within them are not entirely peaceful. The interests of men and women may differ, as may those of the old and young. In the modern world, nonindustrialized and nonstratified societies must often deal with the demands of governments and markets as well.

Thus, in all societies, social life may be characterized by conflict as well as concord. Culture may well be a system, but if so, it is a system composed of parts that rub and chafe against each other. Such parts do affect each other, but they do not necessarily work smoothly together.

Anthropologists who believe that culture is highly integrated have tried to work out the precise relations of one aspect of culture to another. In the first half of the twentieth century, **functionalists** such as A. R. Radcliffe-Brown and Bronislaw Malinowski tried to demonstrate the ways in which separate parts of society affected each other and operated together. They examined kinship in relation to politics as well as many other aspects of culture. For example, Radcliffe-Brown argued that religion reinforced the social structure of a society by giving individuals a sense of dependence, reinforcing the notion that people receive comfort and succor from society but must submit to its control (1952/1965:176).

More recently, **ecological functionalists** have focused on the relationship between the environment and society. For example, Marvin Harris, whose theoretical position, called cultural materialism, is very close to ecological functionalism, examined the Indian Hindu taboo on eating beef (1966). Despite widespread poverty and periodic famine in India, Hindus refuse to eat their cattle. Although this may seem ridiculous to outsiders, it makes good ecological sense. Cows are important in India, not as a food source but because they provide dung for fertilizer and give birth to bullocks,

functionalism The anthropological theory that specific cultural institutions function to support the structure of society or serve the needs of individuals in society.

ecological functionalism A theoretical perspective that holds that the ways in which cultural institutions work can best be understood by examining their effects on the environment.

the draft animals that pull plows and carts, which are essential in agriculture. If a family ate its cows during a famine, it would deprive itself of the source of bullocks and could not continue farming. Thus, Harris argued that the Hindu religious taboo on eating beef is integrated with the Indian subsistence system.

Although the notion that different aspects of culture have specific functions is widely accepted in modern anthropology, many anthropologists have turned away from the idea that in "normal" times, societies should run smoothly. Some insist that elements of discord may be more important than those of agreement. Anthropologists who study social change, such as neo-evolutionists, may see the clash of interests within cultures as a key source of cultural transformation. Other anthropologists, particularly postmodernists (see Chapter 3), look at culture and society as battlegrounds where individuals and groups fight for power and the right to control the interpretation of culture.

CULTURE IS A SHARED SYSTEM OF NORMS AND VALUES— OR IS IT?

Imagine that a person had his or her own private integrated system of classification and meaning, which was shared with no one else. What would that person be like? He or she would live in a world where objects and actions made sense to him or her but had completely different meanings for others. This would certainly create problems in interactions with others. Such a person would undoubtedly be isolated and would probably be considered insane. It is clear that at some level, members of a culture must share ways of thinking and behaving.

Norms and values are two sorts of ideas that members of a culture might share. **Norms** are the ideas members of a culture share about the way things ought to be done. For example, in the United States it is expected that when two adults are introduced, they will shake hands. Norms seem to cluster around certain identities, roles, or posi-

tions in society. The members of each culture have ideas about how people such as parents, politicians, or priests ought to behave. **Values** are shared ideas about what is true, right, and beautiful that underlie cultural patterns and guide society in response to the physical and social environment. For example, in contrast to many other societies, the United States is significantly oriented toward the value of technology—the idea that humans can and should transform nature to meet human ends.

Human behavior is not always consistent with cultural norms or values. What people do and what they say they do are not exactly the same. For example, among upper-middle-class Hindus living in large cities in India, the norm of social equality among all classes of society is widely accepted. However, this norm is considerably different from actual behavior, which rarely involves social interaction between people of the highest and lowest castes on a basis of equality.

Norms may also be contradictory and can be manipulated for personal and group ends. For example, in India people believe that women should be in their home and not "moving about" with their friends. They also believe that women should spend a lot of time in religious activities. Modern Indian women use the second of these ideals to get around the first. By forming clubs whose activities are religious, they have an excuse to get out of the house to which their elders cannot object too strongly.

These examples raise important questions about norms and values. How do we determine the norms and values of any society? Do all people in society agree on these things? How many people must agree on something before it is considered a norm or a value? Who gets to decide these sorts of things? Historically, anthropologists tended not to worry too much about these issues, assuming that the small non-Western societies they studied were homoge-

norm An ideal cultural pattern that influences behavior in a particular society.

values Culturally defined ideas of what is true, right, and beautiful.

Adam G. Sylvester/Photo Researchers, Inc.

NOT EVERYONE IN A CULTURE MUST CONFORM. WHILE CULTURES DEMAND A CERTAIN AMOUNT OF CONSENSUS, PEOPLE WHO ARE MEMBERS OF A SINGLE CULTURE OFTEN SHOW GREAT VARIABILITY IN KNOWLEDGE, STYLE, AND BELIEFS.

nous. It followed from this assumption that people in such societies always acted in the same way in the same situation and attached the same meanings and values to cultural patterns. As early as 1936, however, Ralph Linton, an important American anthropologist, noted that not everyone participates equally in a culture.

Research in the past 25 years in particular has shown that even in small societies, norms are elusive. Individuals differ in their knowledge, understanding, and beliefs. For example, one might expect that in a small fishing society all members would be able to agree on the proper names for different kinds of fish, but on Pukapuka, the small Pacific atoll studied by Robert Borofsky (1994), this is not the case. Even experienced fishermen disagreed much of the time.

subculture A system of perceptions, values, beliefs, and customs that are significantly different from those of a larger, dominant culture within the same society.

Differences among individuals or groups within a society may be pronounced when values and beliefs are at issue. A close look at societies with significant sex segregation, such as those in New Guinea (Hammar 1989) and the Amazon (Murphy and Murphy 1974), makes it clear that men and women do not attach the same meanings to many of the myths and rituals that maintain the system of male dominance.

Issues concerning the degree to which people share a single culture are even more obvious in larger societies. Sometimes the term **subculture** is used to designate groups within a single society that share norms and values significantly different from those of the dominant culture. The terms *dominant culture* and *subculture* do not refer to better and worse, superior and inferior, but rather to the idea that the dominant culture is the more powerful in a society.

Dominant cultures retain their power partly through control of institutions such as the legal system, which criminalizes some subcultural practices that conflict with the dominant cul-

COLUMBUS

The controversy surrounding the role and importance of Christopher Columbus in American culture shows the interconnections among cultures and the way these may result in conflicts about beliefs and values. In 1892, most people in the United States saw Columbus as the forerunner of a confident and progressive nation (Royal 1992). The 400th anniversary of his arrival in the Americas was greeted with celebration throughout the country. There were parades and speeches. Statues, including the one at Columbus Circle in New York City, were erected. Chicago held the Columbian Exposition, a fair with "authentic" ethnic displays from around the world. These were intended to demonstrate the march of human progress to the pinnacle of social and technological achievement represented by white European and American societies (Yewell 1992:171). The "Pledge of Allegiance" was written for this event.

The 500th anniversary, in 1992, was a completely different story. Americans could not agree on the proper way to commemorate the event or whether it should be celebrated at all. There were no large fairs, no new versions of the "Pledge of Allegiance."

Historical circumstances explain the difference between the two occasions. In 1892, almost all of those with wealth and power in the United States were of European descent. Furthermore, hundreds of thousands of Italians had recently come to the country (Gallo 1981:14). Celebrating Columbus legitimized the presence in the United States of people of European descent and the place of Italian Americans within the nation. Citizens of non-European descent had little voice in the nation at that time. In 1992, the situation had changed. Native Americans, Latinos, and others who saw themselves as the descendants of pre-Columbian Americans had gained a degree of power and spoke loudly against the celebration. Other, more recent migrants from Asia and the Middle East had little connection to Columbus. The result was intense debate over the symbolic position of Columbus in American history. The debate made it clear that for some Americans Columbus was a hero whose discoveries made our civilization possible, but for others he was a villain who brought death and cultural destruction to the Americas. Still others saw him as a figure of no particular importance. This example illustrates the idea that American culture is not a set of beliefs and values that all Americans share, but an arena within which issues of conflict and consensus over such norms and values are played out.

ture and threaten to undermine its power (Norgren and Nanda 1996). Additionally, dominant cultures often control the flow of information through which people get their images of subcultures. Hence, they have a powerful means of encouraging people to perceive subcultures in stereotypical ways.

Although in some situations domination of one group by another may be extreme, it is rarely complete. People contest their subjugation through political, economic, and military means. Sometimes, when domination is extreme, they are only able to do so through religious faith and tales that cast themselves in positions of power and their oppressors in weak roles (Scott 1992).

The result of struggles between groups in society is that norms and values, ideas we sometimes think of as timeless and consensual, are constantly changing and being renegotiated. This dynamic process involves conflict and subjugation as well as consensus. Understanding the process is critical because such cultural ideas influence and are influenced by real issues of wealth, power, and status.

In the United States, for example, do we see individuals as responsible for their own destinies or as the product of social circumstances? This question goes to the root of a social norm, is extremely complicated, and has very important political ramifications. In the standard version of the American Dream, people compete with one another to achieve material success. The result is that the hardest-working, best-qualified individuals succeed. A corollary to this view is that the rich and powerful deserve their wealth and power while the poor and weak have only themselves to blame. This is

THE AMISH ARE MEMBERS OF AN AMERICAN SUBCULTURE. THEY HAVE CUSTOMS, LANGUAGE, AND VALUES DIFFERENT FROM THOSE OF MOST AMERICANS.

neatly captured in the American expression "If you're so smart, why ain't you rich?"

While belief in the virtue of hard work seems central to American society, there is considerable dissent on its relation to outcomes. In order for people's hard work to be justly rewarded, everyone must start out with a more-or-less equal chance for success. Some Americans insist that people do start out with approximately equal chances, that failure is thus the responsibility of the individual, and that society bears little responsibility for helping people to succeed. Others reject this notion, proposing instead that some people are born with particular advantages. Thus, success or failure depends to a considerable extent on accidents of birth and the many forms of prejudice institutionalized in American society. It follows that society has an obligation to provide services and programs that benefit historically oppressed groups. This point of view is

culture and personality A theoretical perspective that focuses on culture as the principal force in shaping the typical personality of a society as well as on the role of personality in the maintenance of cultural institutions.

common among the poor and among members of minority groups (Hochschild 1995). For example, a 1996 poll showed that most African Americans believed that racism was a big problem in the United States and that the police and the legal system were severely prejudiced against them (J. Anderson 1996:64).

Believing either that blame for failure is individual or that family and ethnic background plays the most important role in social advancement does not make one individual more or less "American" than another. However, which of these notions is held by those in power is critical. It determines public support for social welfare programs that, for good or ill, have direct economic impact on the lives of many Americans. Anthropological analysis helps to show that even though the vast majority of people who live in the United States consider themselves Americans, they do not necessarily share a common set of beliefs. Different groups may participate in the same culture in different ways.

To avoid the predicament of the insane person described at the beginning of this section, members of a culture must have a great deal in common. As we have seen, however, determining exactly what they share is not easy. Anthropologists have generally assumed that people need to share information in order to form a society (Borofsky 1994). It may well be, however, that people share certain information because they have learned how to interact with one another. In other words, shared ideas and the sense of community may be the result of human interaction rather than its cause.

Historically, the notion of culture as a shared set of norms and values was associated with American anthropology in the first half of the twentieth century. Anthropologists such as A. L. Kroeber, Robert Lowie, Ruth Benedict, and Cora DuBois saw shared norms and values as central to culture. Many of these thinkers, particularly Lowie, Benedict, and DuBois, shared a theoretical perspective usually known as **culture and personality.** Benedict (1934) in particular viewed culture as personality writ large and tried to identify and describe the beliefs, values, and psychological characteristics that were central to individual cultures. In

© Mathias Oppersdorff/Photo Researchers, Inc.

contrast, some contemporary **feminist,** neo-Marxist, and postmodern anthropologists hold that culture is a context in which norms and values are contested. Rather than assuming a cultural core of shared beliefs and values, these anthropologists try to describe the processes through which norms and values are both subverted and maintained. They often focus on the role of governments and other institutions in that process. This issue is more fully examined in Chapters 12, 13, and 14.

CULTURE IS CONSTANTLY CHANGING

In the popular press or movies, one often hears of "Stone Age peoples." The implication is that a group of people has been living in precisely the same way for thousands of years. This romantic notion is, as far as we know, incorrect. All cultures have histories of change, and no one belongs to a culture that is stuck in time. In fact, one of the implications of the notion that culture is based on contention as well as on consensus is that cultures are likely to experience constant change. This is not to say that all cultures change at the same speed. The pace of change in traditional cultures may have been much slower than in modern cultures. Cultural change may happen in small increments, or it may happen in revolutionary bursts. However, no culture is timeless. The source of cultural change may be the internal dynamic of a society, or it may originate outside the society. Like other aspects of culture, change often involves issues of conflict and oppression as well as consensus and solidarity. As we will see in Chapter 17, invasions by members of foreign cultures, revolutions, and epidemic diseases have all been sources of cultural change.

Anthropologists have traditionally discussed cultural change in terms of innovation, invention, and diffusion. An **innovation** is a variation of an existing cultural pattern that is accepted or learned by members of a society. Most innovations are slight modifications of already existing habits of thought and action. An innovation can be the result of delib-

INNOVATION OFTEN INVOLVES CRAFTING FAMILIAR THINGS FROM NEW MATERIALS. IN NIGER, A CRAFTSMAN FASHIONS SANDALS FROM OLD TIRES.

erate experimentation, or it can come about unintentionally.

An **invention** is the combination of existing cultural elements into something altogether new. Although we are likely to think of inventions as technological, invention is not limited to the material aspects of culture. New art forms and new ideas can also be considered inventions.

All inventions involve human ingenuity and creativity, and these exist in the same quantities in all societies. However, even geniuses are limited by the nature of their cultures. Had Einstein been born among a group that did not have Western notions of science, he could never have "invented" the theory of relativity.

feminist anthropology A theoretical perspective that focuses on describing and explaining the social roles of women.

innovation A new variation on an existing cultural pattern that is subsequently accepted by other members of the society.

invention New combinations of existing cultural elements.

Paul Souders/Stone

IN THE MODERN ECONOMY, TRAITS SPREAD RAPIDLY FROM ONE CULTURE TO ANOTHER. CAPITALISM AND MASS COMMUNICATION AFFECT EVERY CULTURE AND TOUCH ALMOST ALL THE WORLD'S CITIZENS.

If Beethoven had been a Bororo (a member of a Brazilian hunting, gathering, and gardening group), he would never have composed a symphony. An old cliché has it that we all stand on the shoulders of giants. This means that everyone in a culture builds on what has gone before.

Diffusion is the spread of cultural elements from one culture to another. Although both small and large changes can come from within a society or through contact with other societies, it is usually direct cultural contact that results in the most far-reaching changes. That is why cultures located on major trade routes tend to change more rapidly than those in more isolated places. However, because no human society has ever been isolated for a long time from all others, diffusion has always been an important factor in culture. This implies that "pure" cultures, free from outside influences, have never existed.

As with innovation and invention, people may reject diffused cultural traits or may alter them to fit a new cultural setting. Thus, cultural elements that move from one society to another often undergo changes in both form

and meaning as they become part of an existing cultural pattern. For example, American football had its origins in British rugby. Football was born when American colleges modified rugby rules in the late nineteenth century (Oriard 1993:26–27). It took on new meanings and has become a central symbol of American culture. Rugby is not nearly as important in British society. Changes in the meanings of cultural elements are particularly important in archaeology. Archaeologists who find the same material item in two different cultures cannot assume that it has the same meaning in both.

Sometimes, new cultural practices are adopted because they have advantages that are immediately apparent to virtually all members of the culture. For example, steel knives are more versatile and flexible than stone knives. They resist breakage and require less care. It would be extremely difficult to find a society anywhere in the world that has retained stone knives for other than ceremonial purposes once they have access to steel knives. Similarly, in the United States, CD recordings replaced vinyl LPs within a few years because they were more portable and virtually free of the problems of scratching, static, and degradation typical of vinyl records.

Often, however, cultural change involves conflict and clashing of interests within and between societies. Innovations and inventions often do not benefit all segments of a society or do not benefit all segments equally. New agricultural techniques, for example, may benefit the wealthy landowner but impoverish small land holders. New technologies may face powerful resistance from those who have invested heavily in older ones. For example, FM radio broadcasting is clearly superior to AM broadcasting; it has greater fidelity and is much less susceptible to static and interference. FM broadcasting was invented in 1933, but because of the resistance of CBS, NBC, and its parent company RCA, extremely powerful corporations heavily invested in AM technology, FM did not gain popularity until the late 1960s (T. Lewis 1991).

Like innovation, diffusion is often accompanied by conflict. Cultures often confront one another in war, and people who are captured or colonized by others are forced to assume new cultural practices. New rulers may require

diffusion The spread of cultural elements from one culture to another through cultural contact.

but how far does it travel

that traditions be abandoned. Economic demands by governments or creditors often compel the adoption of new technologies and practices. Although these processes happen in most places where cultures confront one another, they have been particularly important in the past 500 years. During this time, cultures have been increasingly tied together in an economic system centered in Northern Europe, North America, and Japan. We examine this process more fully in Chapter 17. The expansion of powers located in these regions has involved the diffusion of cultural traits to all areas of the world. Such diffusion has sometimes been peaceful, but often it has involved conflict and unspeakable violence (Wolf 1982).

The rapid pace of cultural change and diffusion, particularly in the past 100 years, raises the question of cultural homogenization. Are cultural differences being erased? Are we all being submerged in a single global culture? There is no simple answer to these questions. On one hand, modern technological culture now penetrates virtually every place on earth. People in almost every country have access to radio, tape recorders, telephones, television, and other aspects of modern technology. On the other hand, this access is extremely uneven. The world may be a global village, but not all parts of it are equally close to the center. The vast majority of electronic communication, for example, is located in the industrialized nations. People in rural African villages may have radios, but they are unlikely to be connected to the Internet any time soon.

The world dominance of industrialized nations has affected cultures everywhere, but rather than annihilating local culture, the result may be what Ortiz (1947) has described as **transculturation.** Cultural traits are transformed as they are adopted, and new cultural forms result. Radio is again a good example. Developed by industrialized societies, it has spread throughout the world, promoting the culture of consumption through advertising. But radio can be used to broadcast messages of resistance and cultural preservation as well as the messages of the society where it originated.

Ayatollah Khomeini, the leader of the 1979 Iranian revolution, provides a good example of the revolutionary use of technology. Kho-meini was virulently anti-Western, but tape recordings were essential to the success of his revolution. In 1978, more than 100,000 tapes of Khomeini's sermons were circulating in Iran (Taheri 1986:213). Late that same year, the Ayatollah went into exile in a suburb of Paris. During the four months he was there, he used the telephone to keep in touch with key supporters in Iran and gave 132 radio, television, and press interviews (Taheri 1986:228). Khomeini's use of the tools of technological society was fundamental to the success of his anti-Western revolution. Issues of cultural globalization and resistance to it are explored further in Chapters 16 and 17.

Anthropologists have traditionally worked in tribal and peasant societies. Because such cultures have been profoundly affected by their contact with industrial societies, anthropologists of most theoretical orientations have been interested in change. The study of cultural change has special interest for applied anthropologists, particularly those who work on issues in the economic development of poor nations.

RETHINKING CULTURE

In the opening paragraphs of this book, we defined culture as the answer people have devised to the basic questions of human social life. These questions concern things such as how to feed oneself, how to live with other groups, and how to lend meaning to life. In considering ways to explore and understand these cultural answers, anthropologists have looked at different aspects of culture. The studies they have done reflect the facets of culture they chose to explore. In this chapter, we have described some of these different ways of looking at culture. Taken together, they do not make up a unified whole but rather involve contending views of what it means to be human.

Anthropologists are always involved in fractious debate over the nature of culture. For example, recent issues of the *Anthropology Newsletter* have carried a heated debate on whether

transculturation The transformation of adopted cultural traits, resulting in new cultural forms.

anthropology should draw its models and methods from natural sciences such as biology and physics, or humanities such as philosophy and literary criticism (Benfer 1996; D'Andrade 1995; Dow 1996). However, as Geertz has written, "Anthropology in general, and cultural anthropology in particular, draws the greater part of its vitality from the controversies that animate it. It is not much destined for secured positions and settled issues" (1995:4). Debates within anthropology are not a sign of the collapse of the discipline but rather of its continuing vitality. In debate, we arrive at new understandings of ourselves and our subject matter. We come to a keener appreciation of the nature of culture and, ultimately, what it means to be human.

SUMMARY

1. Culture is an essential aspect of being human. The few recorded cases of children raised in isolation show that growing up as a member of society is absolutely fundamental to human development.

2. Culture is the learned, symbolic, at least partially adaptive, and ever-changing patterns of behavior shared by members of a group. However, this broad definition conceals great controversy. Anthropologists differ on which aspects of culture are most important. Different definitions of culture lead to different theoretical positions, different research questions, and different areas of study.

3. Many anthropologists understand culture as the major adaptive mechanism of the human species. Whereas other animals adapt through biological mechanisms, humans satisfy their needs for food, shelter, and safety largely through the use of culture. Cultural adaptation has both advantages and disadvantages.

4. Alternatively, cultures may be thought of as mental templates for organizing the world. In this view, cultures are ways of understanding the world. Every culture has a system of classification through which its people identify and organize the aspects of the world that are most important to them. In order to understand a culture, the anthropologist must first comprehend its systems of classification.

5. Culture may also be a way of understanding ourselves. A culture is a collection of symbols and meanings that permit us to understand others and ourselves. Through culture we experience our humanity. It is the web of significance that gives meaning to our lives and actions. The job of the anthropologist is to comprehend the central symbols and meanings of a culture.

6. Cultures, in some ways, are systems. That is, they are composed of parts that are related to one another. Changes in one aspect of culture result in other changes as well. At the same time, conflict is common in all cultures. If culture is a system, its parts do not fit together easily or well.

7. Cultures are collections of norms, or guidelines for behavior, and values or ideals. Norms and values are not necessarily consistent. Individuals manipulate them, and groups battle over them. Norms and values are subject to constant renegotiation as different groups within society vie for power. They involve conflict and subjugation as well as accommodation and consensus.

8. Cultures are constantly changing. There have been no "Stone Age people" since the Stone Age. Anthropologists have traditionally discussed cultural change in terms of innovation, invention, and diffusion. Many cultural traits that we think of as being solidly American are the result of diffusion from other cultures.

9. Cultural change often occurs as part of the domination of one culture by another. This process has occurred throughout human history, but it has been particularly important in the past few centuries. The process of expansion of Western capitalist culture to all areas of the world has entailed massive and often violent cultural change.

10. Different anthropological views of culture do not present a complete and coherent picture. Anthropologists argue bitterly over the proper definition of culture and the right way to understand it. It is through such argumentation that our understanding of culture progresses.

KEY TERMS

adaptation	**ecological functionalism**
cognitive anthropology	**ethnobotany**
cultural ecology	**ethnomedicine**
cultural materialism	**ethnoscience**
culture and personality	**feminist anthropology**
diffusion	**functionalism**

innovation

interpretive or symbolic anthropology

invention

neo-evolutionism

neo-Marxism

norm

plasticity

sociobiology

structural anthropology

subculture

symbol

transculturation

values

SUGGESTED READINGS

Borofsky, Robert (Ed.). 1994. *Assessing Cultural Anthropology.* New York: McGraw-Hill. This book of essays by modern anthropologists analyzes critical issues in current anthropology. The authors reflect on the history of anthropology and speculate on its future. Each essay includes a brief analysis by the editor.

Harris, Marvin. 1968. *The Rise of Anthropological Theory.* New York: Harper & Row. Harris's book is challenging reading, but it is one of the best-known analyses of the history of anthropological theory. The book is an essential source, but because Harris evaluates all thinkers according to the degree to which they conform to his own theoretical position—cultural materialism—it must be read critically. Harris has recently published an updated statement of his theoretical position, *Theories of Culture in Postmodern Times* (1999). In addition to this and other scholarly works, Harris has also written a series of popular books on anthropology, including *Cows, Pigs, Wars, and Witches* (1974), *Cannibals and Kings* (1977), *Why Nothing Works* (1981), and *Our Kind: Who We Are, Where We Came From, Where We Are Going* (1989). All of these well-written books explain cultural practices from Harris's theoretical perspective.

Kuper, Adam. 1999. *Culture: The Anthropologist's Account.* Cambridge, MA: Harvard University Press. Analyzing the history and importance of the idea of culture in the twentieth century, Kuper argues that an emphasis on culture as a set of ideas has failed to produce a useful anthropology, leading instead to academic obscurantism. He argues that anthropologists should focus on political and economic forces, social institutions, and biological processes.

Marcus, George E. 1998. *Ethnography Through Thick and Thin.* Princeton, NJ: Princeton University Press. In this collection of essays, spanning the years 1980–1997, Marcus charts the changes in the ways anthropologists have pursued anthropology from a postmodern perspective. This volume is the latest in a series of influential books written or edited by Marcus, including *Anthropology as Culture Critique* (1986), *Writing Culture* (1990), and *Rereading Cultural Anthropology* (1992).

McGee, R. Jon, and Richard L. Warms (Eds.). 2000. *Anthropological Theory: An Introductory History* (2nd ed.). Mountain View, CA: Mayfield. A comprehensive introduction to theory in anthropology, this edited volume contains essays by critical theoretical thinkers as well as detailed annotations and commentary by McGee and Warms.

Rosaldo, Renato. 1989. *Culture and Truth: The Remaking of Social Analysis.* Boston: Beacon Press. This collection of essays deals with the nature of culture and the process of writing about it. Rosaldo's clear writing style and gift for storytelling makes this one of the most readable introductions to the postmodern position in anthropology.

Stocking, George. 1995. *After Tylor: British Social Anthropology 1888–1951.* Madison: University of Wisconsin Press. Stocking, one of the most important historians of anthropology, has edited a series of books on the history of anthropology. The books are collections of his essays as well as essays by leading current anthropologists. Other titles include *The Ethnographer's Magic and Other Essays in the History of Anthropology* (1992), *Colonial Situations: Essays on the Contextualization of Ethnographic History* (1991), and *Romantic Motives: Essays on Anthropological Sensibility* (1989).

INTERNET RESOURCES

The following Internet resources appear in this chapter. Please log on to the Wadsworth anthropology website: **http://anthropology.wadsworth.com**. Click on the Nanda/Warms *Cultural Anthropology* page. Then select the Student Resources section, where you will find a complete presentation of these links and more.

- A website on theory in anthropology, page 72
- A photo essay on shared system of norms and values, page 83
- A video link: changing images of Native Americans, page 87
- Access the Study Guide to InfoTrac College Edition for Anthropology Students

HUMAN LANGUAGE, WHICH CONSISTS OF WORDS AND GESTURES, IS AN ESSENTIAL PART OF HUMAN ADAPTATION. EVEN WHEN CONVEYING PRACTICAL INFORMATION, AS IN THIS INTERACTION BETWEEN ISRAELI BEDOUIN IN A MARKETPLACE, HUMAN LANGUAGE IS UNIQUE IN HAVING THE CAPABILITY OF RECREATING COMPLEX THOUGHT PATTERNS AND EXPERIENCES IN WORDS.

Courtesy of Serena Nanda

Chapter Five

LANGUAGE

How does human language differ from the communication systems of other animals?

How do humans acquire their language?

What are some characteristics of human languages, and how are languages structured?

What is the relationship among language, thought, and culture?

What are some nonlinguistic ways in which humans communicate?

How do languages change?

Communication is the act of transmitting a message that influences the behavior of another organism. Communication, and hence interaction, in all animal species depends on a consistent set of signals by which individuals convey information. These signals are channeled through visual, olfactory, auditory, and tactile senses.

Many animals use sounds and movements to communicate, or share, information. Such communication can be quite complex. For example, a scout honeybee uses stereotyped and patterned movements to communicate information about the direction and distance of a field of pollen-bearing flowers to others in its hive. But although bees can say a lot about where flowers are, they cannot say much about anything else. Crows caw as a signal of danger, and crickets chirp when they are ready to mate. Among primates, far greater amounts of information can be transmitted about many more subjects.

While communication among animals is critical to their survival, it is quite limited compared to human language. Animal systems of verbal communication are referred to as **call systems.** They are restricted to a set number of signals generally uttered in response to specific events. Human language, on the other hand, whether spoken, signed, or written, is capable of recreating complex thought patterns and experiences in words. Our linguistic abilities allow enormous variety in how we act, think, and adapt to our surroundings. Without human language, human culture could not exist.

Language makes possible the exchange of abstract and highly complex thoughts, and these play a crucial role in the maintenance of the social relationships within human societies. Without language, it would be impossible to socialize children into the intricate workings of their cultures, to teach others how to make anything but very simple tools, or to pass on the traditions, rituals, myths, and religious beliefs that instill a sense of group identity and maintain social order.

ORIGINS AND DEVELOPMENT OF HUMAN LANGUAGE

Like the communication systems of all animals, human language reflects the particular character of our adaptation. Because it is a creative and open system, it is extremely flexible and can

communication The act of transmitting information that influences the behavior of another organism.

call system Form of communication among nonhuman primates composed of a limited number of sounds that are tied to specific stimuli in the environment.

CULTURAL FOCUS

NONHUMAN PRIMATE COMMUNICATION

Studies of nonhuman primate communication, especially gestures and vocalizations, have been done in the field (see Goodall 1968), among captive groups, and in laboratory settings (Miles 1978; Terrace 1979). Baboons in the wild constantly transmit information to one another. Lip-smacking, grunts, stares, poses, and screams are all part of their communication system. One long-term study of rhesus monkeys revealed more than 120 behavioral patterns that are used in communication.

Because chimpanzees are thought to be among humans' closest relations, their communication system is of great interest to social scientists. Wild chimpanzees, like other primates, exhibit a wide variety of communicative behaviors, such as the apparent use of gestures and physical contact to express feelings. For example, when they meet in the forest, "old friends" kiss and hug, pat each other on the head, or rest a hand on the thigh of the other. In addition to gestures, chimpanzees use calls to communicate. These calls are distinctive—a *waa* bark for danger, a series of soft moans for worry, a hooting to communicate excitement caused by the presence of an abundance of food, and screams and squeals of fear (V. Reynolds 1965). However, a primate

SOME PHYSICAL ANTHROPOLOGISTS STUDY THE BEHAVIOR OF OUR NEAREST PRIMATE RELATIONS. IN THIS PICTURE, NIM SIGNS "DOUBLE APPLE" TO HIS TRAINER, JOYCE BUTLER, AT COLORADO UNIVERSITY.

Courtesy of Colorado University

call system is not the same as human language. Although intonation can intensify the meaning of a call—for example, from "danger" to "extreme danger"—a chimp can signal only immediate danger. A second important limitation is that parts of calls cannot be recombined to generate new information; each call appears to have just one meaning.

While primates use calls in the wild, anthropologists have been very interested in whether or not they have the capacity to learn human-like language. One research strategy involves teaching languages (usually either a version of American Sign Language or a language specially designed for experimental purposes) to higher primates, especially

communicate new ideas and abstract concepts. Language and human culture probably evolved together. The more elaborate the culture of human ancestors grew, the more complex the system of communication among people had to become. Conversely, increases in the sophis-

tication of communication led to increases in the complexity of culture (Salzmann 1993:88).

No one really knows how human language originated, but one of the most widely accepted theories of language origin was proposed by Charles Hockett in the 1970s. Hockett suggested that language evolved in two steps. The first step, which he called **blending,** occurred when human ancestors began to produce new calls by combining two old ones. Hockett called

blending The combination of two calls to produce a new call; a hypothesized early phase in language evolution.

chimpanzees and gorillas. The results of studies based on this strategy show that chimpanzees are capable of much more complex communication than they demonstrate in the wild. One famous ape language study concerned Washoe, a chimpanzee who was raised in a human environment and taught American Sign Language (Gardner and Gardner 1967). After learning about ten signs, Washoe spontaneously began to produce new combinations of signs. Ultimately, researchers claimed she was able to master more than 85 signs. Even more impressive, without human intervention, Washoe has been able to teach more than 50 of these signs to her adoptive son Loulis (Fouts and Fouts 1989). Much attention has been focused recently on pigmy or Bonobo chimpanzees. Researcher Sue Savage-Rumbaugh has taught Kanzi, a Bonobo chimpanzee, a vocabulary of about 150 signs. She claims that he is able to arrange these signs into sentence-like strings that use a very basic syntax different from that of English. Further, researchers argue that Kanzi has responded appropriately to more than 500 sentences of spoken English (Savage-Rumbaugh, Shanker, and Taylor 1998).

While the data from experiments with Washoe, Loulis, Kanzi, and many other primates is certainly impressive, it is also controversial. It is not clear whether the remarkable achievements of these animals reflect true language abilities or simply training and unconscious cuing and projecting on the part of researchers. In his attempt to train a chimpanzee, for example, Terrace (1983) reported a lack of any true humanlike language abilities. His study has been criticized by other researchers, however, who claim that it was not conducted within a proper social environment and that he used inappropriate research methods.

The theoretical question underlying the ape language studies is whether human language is a completely separate and unique form of communication. The experiments suggest that the answer to this question is extremely complicated. On the one hand, the results show that some primates, particularly Bonobo chimpanzees, have much greater linguistic abilities than previously recognized. On the other hand, the experiments demonstrate that, despite enormous effort in training, no chimp, or any other animal, has ever developed greater linguistic skill than a very young child. There are two possible explanations. Perhaps chimps are learning language in ways that are similar to those used by humans, and they have simply reached the limit of their linguistic ability. If so, then language is a continuum: chimps and humans are similar in the nature of their linguistic abilities; humans just have much more of that ability. Alternatively, perhaps chimps learn language poorly because they must learn it in ways fundamentally different from those used by people. Maybe human infants learn language spontaneously because their biology compels them to learn it, whereas chimps must learn by rote memorization. If that is the case, then their linguistic abilities are not only different in quantity but different in kind from our own.

One thing is clear: human language is the result of our own particular evolutionary history. Human language is unique in terms of its great complexity and the importance of its role in human adaptation. We may be able to teach other animals simple humanlike languages, but these languages are not essential to them. In contrast, the use of highly complex language is fundamental to human culture.

this kind of communication **prelanguage.** He pointed out that blending would greatly increase the number of possible messages in a call system but that a system based on blending would still be limited compared to modern language.

The second step in the evolution of language was what Hockett called **duality of patterning.** At this stage, human ancestors acquired the ability to produce arrangements of blended sounds. By this means, a limited number of blended sounds could be combined into a virtually limitless number of utterances (Hockett

prelanguage A language of human ancestors consisting of blended sounds; a hypothesized phase in the evolution of language.

duality of patterning The ability to produce arrangements of blended sounds; the hypothesized second step in the evolution of language.

1973:106). Although prelanguage and early language sounded nothing like modern language, we can use current-day English to get a sense of blending and duality of patterning. Blending would be like combining two words to make a third word (for example, combining *breakfast* and *lunch* to make *brunch*). Duality of patterning would be like combining the sound units that compose the words *breakfast* and *lunch* to make a great many different new words, such as *bench, bunch, chest, fun, less, lust,* and so on (Salzmann 1993:84).

Estimates of when language emerged vary tremendously. Some anthropologists argue that language emerged with the appearance of modern human beings some 50,000 to 150,000 years ago (Salzmann 1993; J. Clark 1989). Others insist that it occurred much earlier. The development of language required physical changes in the brain, the ear, and probably the vocal apparatus. Therefore, at least in theory, the fossil record may provide us with some information on when modern language emerged (P. Lieberman 1984; Laitman 1984; Falk 1984). Recent analyses of fossil anatomy support an early date for the evolution of language (Wilkins and Wakefield 1995; Schepartz 1993). Schepartz (1993:119), for example, suggests that analyses of the brains and vocal tracts of human ancestors provide evidence for the existence of language at the time of the origin of the genus *Homo,* about 2 million years ago.

CHARACTERISTICS OF LANGUAGE

Human language is a unique system of communication, distinct from any other animal communication system in three ways: conventionality, productivity, and displacement.

conventionality The notion that, in human language, words are only arbitrarily or conventionally connected to the things for which they stand.

productivity The idea that humans can combine words and sounds into new meaningful utterances they have never before heard.

displacement The capacity of all human languages to describe things not happening in the present.

Conventionality describes the association between a meaningful sequence of sounds and an object, action, or idea. In human language, a limited number of sounds (hardly any language uses more than 50) are combined to refer to thousands of different things and experiences. Words stand for things simply because speakers of a language agree that they do. The animal is no more a *dog* than it is a *chien* (French), a *perro* (Spanish), or a *kutta* (Hindi).

It is conventionality—the capacity to separate the vocal symbol from its referent—that is absent in the call systems of most nonhuman animals. If, like them, we had to use a different sound for every item of meaning, we would wind up with either a very small vocabulary or an impossibly large number of sounds. It is the ability to recombine sounds to create new meanings that makes human language such an efficient and effective communication system.

Not only is human language efficient, it is also infinitely **productive.** Humans constantly forge new combinations of words. The following sentence uses words in a series that you have probably never heard before; yet it can be easily created and understood by any English-speaking person: "I don't know the man who took the spoon that Horace left on the table that was lying upside down in the upstairs hallway of the building that burned down last night" (Southworth and Daswani 1974). Speakers of any human language can generate an almost infinite number of such sentences. The productive capacity of human language, sometimes called *openness,* makes it an extremely flexible instrument for communication, capable of conveying all kinds of new information.

The third distinguishing characteristic of human language is **displacement**—the ability of language to convey information about something not in the immediate environment. We can describe things that happened in the past, will or may happen in the future, exist only in the mind, and are hypothetical (may not happen at all). This feature of human language allows us to think abstractly.

Among other animals, communication is generally about the present and the particular: A particular threatening object is in a particular place at this particular time. Human language generalizes; it categorizes some objects and events as similar and other objects and events as dissimilar. Humans can talk about a particular tree ("The tree in front of my house needs trimming") and also about trees in general ("Trees provide shade and are pleasant on hot days"). Language allows trees to be differentiated from bushes, bushes from flowers, and flowers from grass.

Hundreds of thousands of natural and manufactured objects have significance for human beings. Taking command of this incredibly complex world means classifying objects and events in an orderly way. Human language is the most effective means for doing exactly that. These qualities of human language—conventionality, productivity, and displacement—allow humans to make plans, understand and correct mistakes, and coordinate their activities. They also give our species a distinct advantage over other animals.

By translating experience into language, humans build up a storehouse of knowledge that can be transmitted to new members of the group. Although some of the things humans teach one another could be learned without language, teaching through language is more efficient and adaptive than relying on the slower and often clumsy process of imitation used by other animals. Furthermore, some human behavior patterns, such as religion, law, and science, would not be possible without the symbolizing capacity of human language. It is through this capacity for accumulating experience and passing it on by teaching others in the social group that human culture has developed.

Although at one time many anthropologists and linguists believed that contemporary human languages could be classified into primitive and civilized, less complex and more complex, inferior and superior, we know today that this is not so. All human languages are similar in that they possess a well-defined system of sounds, finite in number and combined to form words, phrases, and sentences according to definite rules, and all languages can be used for abstract thought. Although the vocabulary of each language reflects what is important in a particular physical and sociocultural environment, every language has a vocabulary adequate to deal with that environment. Vocabulary can be expanded in any language, with new words added as cultural change requires.

ACQUIRING LANGUAGE

The fact that linguistic symbols are nearly all arbitrary—that is, they are conventions by which certain sounds are attached to certain objects and events—emphasizes the social aspect of language. In this sense, language is a part of culture. An individual learns a language only by interaction with other human beings who speak that language. An individual from any human population, if taken at birth and brought up in a different society, will grow up speaking the language of the group in which he or she is raised. The normal physical and mental apparatus of human beings everywhere allows them to learn any language with equal ease.

If you are wondering what language a human being would speak if he or she were not taught any particular language, the answer is none. Herodotus, the ancient Greek historian, reported that the Egyptian pharaoh Psammetichus ordered two infants reared where they could hear no human voices in order to learn the original language of humankind. Psammetichus assumed that the children would "naturally" talk in the language of their ancestors. To his ears, their babbling sounded like Phrygian, which he concluded was the original human language. King James IV of Scotland supposedly tried a similar experiment, and he claimed that the two infants spoke Hebrew. Biblical scholars of his time asserted that Adam and Eve had spoken Hebrew, and people believed that it was the original, natural language of all humans.

The development of human language in children is illustrated by cases of children brought up in isolation such as Victor, the "wild child" of Aveyron (see Chapter 4). Victor could understand much of what he heard, but although he lived in human society until he was 40, he never learned to speak like others. The same was true of Genie, a child discovered in the 1970s by social workers in California. Genie had been locked in an attic for the first 12 years of her life. With training and good living conditions, she rapidly acquired a large vocabulary but never mastered English syntax. For example, she spoke in sentences like "Genie have Momma have baby grow up" (Pinker 1994:292).

Cases such as Genie's suggest that people raised in isolation are able to learn vocabulary but are incapable of mastering the full grammar of their language. This implies that there is a critical period of language development for humans. All children are capable of learning language before the age of six, but thereafter it becomes increasingly difficult, and after puberty it is very rare (Pinker 1994:293). You have probably experienced the time-limited nature of human ability to learn language. All college students (and indeed all people) speak the language they learned as children with ease and fluency. Most, however, struggle to learn a second language in college, and very few will ever learn to speak it with the proficiency of a native speaker.

Studies of how children learn language indicate that human beings may have an innate predisposition or mechanism for learning language patterns or rules. A child exposed to a language automatically begins to learn it. Furthermore, all human children go through the same stages of language learning, which appear in the same sequence regardless of the language being learned. Children actually take the initiative in learning language. They recognize the sounds of their language within days after birth. By the time children are six months old, their babbling includes consonant and vowel sequences and repetitive patterns.

Most adults do not consciously know the rules of the languages they speak, certainly not well enough to teach them to children. What happens is that children are surrounded by a flow of sounds, words, and intonations. They not only imitate these but also take the initiative in forming combinations of words they may never have heard before but that are consistent with the rules of the language. Even when children do not understand what they are saying, they can speak grammatically, using the different parts of speech in correct relation to one another.

The realization that children surrounded by language learn it spontaneously has led to an increased interest in the biological basis of human language. On one level, the human brain and body are clearly biologically adapted for language. Not only are the visual and auditory areas of the brain directly connected to each other, but both areas are directly connected to the area concerned with touch. Thus, human children are able to make the association between the visible image, the feel of an object, and the sound pattern or word used to designate it, even though the word itself is an arbitrary symbol. Furthermore, the structure of human air and food tracts is different from that of our closest ape relations. Among apes, food and air pass through separate passageways. As anyone who has ever tried to speak while eating knows, in humans the food and air tracts are connected. This increases the possibility of choking but also greatly expands our ability to make different sounds.

At a second level, many linguists, led by Noam Chomsky, have speculated that there is a **universal grammar**—a basic set of principles, conditions, and rules that forms the foundation of all languages (Chomsky 1975). This universal grammar forms the foundation of all human language. Language is thus an innate property of the mind. Children learn language by applying this unconscious universal grammar to the sounds they hear. They mentally process the sequences of words in their parents' speech to figure out the grammar of their parents' language, matching their utterances to those they hear until their version matches, or almost matches, the one being used around them (Pinker 1994).

One good way to understand universal grammar is by using the analogy of computer languages. A computer language is a set of symbols and rules in which instructions that a computer

universal grammar A basic set of principles, conditions, and rules that underlie all languages.

can follow are written (see Figure 5.1). Some examples are Fortran, Pascal, C, and Basic. A programmer uses a language to write a program. Many different kinds of programs can be written using a single computer language. However, because they all ultimately derive from the same set of principles and rules, they have certain fundamental similarities. In the same way, Chomsky and his followers argue, each individual is born with an instinctive universal grammar, analogous to a programming language. A child "programs" his or her language by interacting verbally with other people. The result is that although humans speak many different languages, they all share fundamental underlying similarities.

The computer analogy is not perfect. Programming a computer is a conscious, voluntary task. Children learn language automatically, apparently without conscious effort. Furthermore, no computer application has yet been able to equal the subtlety and complexity of human language.

There is substantial evidence for this view of language. Pinker (1994:52–53), for example, points out that people who have a rare genetic disease called Williams syndrome have extremely low IQs and cannot learn tasks such as tying their shoes or telling left from right. However, such people often speak very well. They understand complex sentences and are fond of unusual words. This strongly suggests that language competence is not part of general intelligence. Another bit of evidence comes from the study of hearing-impaired children. When such children are raised by hearing parents who use sign language, their proficiency at signing is often much greater than that of their parents. The parents have generally learned sign language late in life and do not use it with particular fluency. But deaf children are able to learn sophisticated and grammatical sign language from their parents' often unsophisticated and ungrammatical version of it. This indicates that children must have an innate ability to process language (Pinker 1994:38).

Most anthropologists agree with Chomsky's notion of a biological basis for language but point out that mastery of vocabulary and syn-

```
TYPE STRING = PACKED ARRAY[1..40] OF CHAR;
     PART = RECORD
                DESCR : STRING;
                ID : INTEGER;
                COST : REAL
                END; (*RECORD*)
     NAME = ARRAY[1..20] OF CHAR;

VAR INFILE, OUTFILE : TEXT;
    MAIL : FILE OF NAME;
    WORDS : FILE OF STRING;
    INVTRY : FILE OF PART;
    LETTER : NAME;
    WORD : STRING;
    APART : PART;
```

FIGURE 5.1

MANY SORTS OF COMPUTER PROGRAMS MAY BE WRITTEN IN A SINGLE LANGUAGE SUCH AS PASCAL. THOUGH SUCH PROGRAMS MAY BE VERY DIFFERENT, THEY WILL SHARE UNDERLYING RESEMBLANCES. SIMILARLY, ALL HUMAN LANGUAGES MAY SHARE CHARACTERISTICS OF AN UNDERLYING UNIVERSAL GRAMMAR.

tax is only part of language learning. Children must also learn to be members of a speech community. That is, they must learn the social rules about how to use language to participate in their society. These rules include when to speak and when not to speak, whom to speak to and in what manner, what to talk about, and many other aspects of participation (Duranti 1997:20–21). Thus, although the acquisition of language is based in biology, the acceptable use of speech to participate in a community must be learned culturally.

Additionally, there are many different cultural scenarios through which language is actually learned. For example, Locke (1994) notes that in societies where children are the focus of much attention, their desire to share a social and emotional relationship with the people around them may propel them to learn some aspects of language through imitation. As an example, he points to an infant talking on a toy telephone. The child "babbles, pauses, babbles again. . . . Although no words may be spoken, the infant obviously takes pleasure in acting and sounding like the rest of us" (1994:

438). Ochs and Schieffelin (1984) note that American parents spend a great deal of time talking with their infants and encouraging them to speak. The Kaluli of Papua New Guinea, on the other hand, rarely talk to their infants at all, except for an occasional rebuke. Although American and Kaluli children learn to speak at the same speed and with equal competence, Kaluli and American speech patterns may be different as a result of these early experiences. Thus, language acquisition, though not controlled by culture, may very well be influenced by it.

THE STRUCTURE OF LANGUAGE

Every language has a structure: an internal logic and a particular relationship among its parts. **Descriptive** or **structural linguistics** is the study of the structure and content of specific languages. Descriptive or structural linguists assume that language can be separated from other aspects of culture and studied without any direct reference to the social context in which speaking takes place (Hickerson 1980:3). Their work suggests that the structure of any language consists of four subsystems: **phonology** (a system of sounds), **morphology** (a system for creating words from sounds), **syntax** (a series of rules for combining words into meaningful sentences), and **semantics** (a system that relates words to meaning).

PHONOLOGY

People use a vast number of different sounds in language. The **International Phonetic Alphabet (IPA)** was developed to record all these sounds. A glance at the IPA (Figure 5.2) shows the complexity of the sound systems used in human speech. All people are biologically capable of making all the several hundred possible sounds listed on the chart. These sounds are referred to as **phones.** A phone is simply any sound that is used as part of a human language.

Although humans use a huge number of sounds, any particular language uses only a relatively small number of phones. Sounds used in one language may be absent in other languages. English, for example, does not use the click sound of the language of the Ju/'hoansi (!Kung) of southern Africa or many of the tonal sounds of Chinese. Furthermore, combinations of sounds are used in different ways in different languages. For example, an English speaker can easily pronounce the *ng* sound in thing at the end of an utterance but not at the beginning; however, this sound is used in the initial position in Bambara, a language of Africa (compare the ease of saying *thing* with the difficulty of saying *ngoni,* the name of a musical instrument in Bambara).

The set of phones used in a particular language are referred to as the phonemes of the language. A **phoneme** is the smallest sound unit that distinguishes meaning within a given language. An example will help to make this clear. In **Standard Spoken American English (SSAE),** the English accent you generally hear on network news broadcasts, the sound /d/ in the English word *den* and /th/ in *then* are phonemes. The words *den* and *then* have different meanings, and this difference in meaning is indicated by the initial consonant sound (/d/ or /th/). Spanish also uses these sounds, but in Spanish these two sounds are **allophones;** that is, both phones indicate only one phoneme. In Spanish, the sounds /d/ and /th/ may be slightly different, but they do not

descriptive or **structural linguistics** The study and analysis of the structure and content of particular languages.

phonology The sound system of a language.

morphology A system for creating words from sounds.

syntax The part of grammar that has to do with the arrangement of words to form phrases and sentences.

semantics The subsystem of a language that relates form to meaning.

International Phonetic Alphabet (IPA) A system of writing designed to represent all the sounds used in the different languages of the world.

phone A sound made by humans and used in any language.

phoneme The smallest significant unit of sound in a language. A phonemic system is the sound system of a language.

Standard Spoken American English (SSAE) The form of English spoken by most of the American middle class.

allophones Two or more different phones that can be used to make the same phoneme in a specific language.

The INTERNATIONAL PHONETIC ASSOCIATION
ði ɪntəˈnæʃənəl fəˈnɛtɪk əsousiˈeɪʃn

Reproduction of The International Phonetic Alphabet
(Revised to 1993, Updated 1996)

THE INTERNATIONAL PHONETIC ALPHABET (revised to 1993)

CONSONANTS (PULMONIC)

	Bilabial	Labiodental	Dental	Alveolar	Postalveolar	Retroflex	Palatal	Velar	Uvular	Pharyngeal	Glottal
Plosive	p b			t d		ʈ ɖ	c ɟ	k g	q ɢ		ʔ
Nasal	m	ɱ		n		ɳ	ɲ	ŋ	ɴ		
Trill	ʙ			r					ʀ		
Tap or Flap				ɾ		ɽ					
Fricative	ɸ β	f v	θ ð	s z	ʃ ʒ	ʂ ʐ	ç ʝ	x ɣ	χ ʁ	ħ ʕ	h ɦ
Lateral fricative				ɬ ɮ							
Approximant		ʋ		ɹ		ɻ	j	ɰ			
Lateral approximant				l		ɭ	ʎ	ʟ			

Where symbols appear in pairs, the one to the right represents a voiced consonant. Shaded areas denote articulations judged impossible.

CONSONANTS (NON-PULMONIC)

Clicks		Voiced implosives		Ejectives	
ʘ	Bilabial	ɓ	Bilabial	ʼ	as in:
ǀ	Dental	ɗ	Dental/alveolar	pʼ	Bilabial
ǃ	(Post)alveolar	ʄ	Palatal	tʼ	Dental/alveolar
ǂ	Palatoalveolar	ɠ	Velar	kʼ	Velar
ǁ	Alveolar lateral	ʛ	Uvular	sʼ	Alveolar frictive

VOWELS

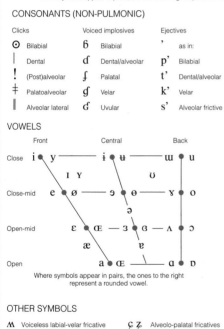

Where symbols appear in pairs, the ones to the right
represent a rounded vowel.

OTHER SYMBOLS

ʍ	Voiceless labial-velar fricative	ɕ ʑ	Alveolo-palatal fricatives
w	Voiced labial-velar approximant	ɺ	Alveolar lateral flap
ɥ	Voiced labial-palatal approximant	ɧ	Simultaneous ʃ and x
ʜ	Voiceless epiglottal fricative		
ʢ	Voiced epiglottal fricative	Affricates and double articulations can be represented by two symbols joined by a tie bar if necessary.	
ʡ	Epiglottal plosive	k͡p t͡s	

SUPRASEGMENTALS

ˈ	Primary stress	foʊnəˈtɪʃən
ˌ	Secondary stress	
ː	Long	eː
ˑ	Half-long	eˑ
̆	Extra-short	ĕ
.	Syllable break	ɹi.ækt
ǀ	Minor (foot) group	
ǁ	Major (intonation) group	
‿	Linking (absence of a break)	

TONES & WORD ACCENTS

	LEVEL			CONTOUR	
e̋	or ˥	Extra high	ě	or ˩˥	Rising
é	˦	High	ê	˥˩	Falling
ē	˧	Mid	ɛ̋	˩˩˥	High rising
è	˨	Low	ɛ̀	˩˩˩	Low rising
ȅ	˩	Extra low	ɛ̃	˥˩˥	Rising-falling etc.
ꜜ	Downstep		↗	Global rise	
ꜛ	Upstep		↘	Global fall	

DIACRITICS

Diacritics may be placed above a symbol with a descender, e.g. ŋ̊

̥	Voiceless	n̥ d̥	̤	Breathy voiced	b̤ a̤	̪	Dental t̪ d̪
̬	Voiced	s̬ t̬	̰	Creaky voiced	b̰ a̰	̺	Apical t̺ d̺
ʰ	Aspirated	tʰ dʰ	̼	Linguolabial	t̼ d̼	̻	Laminal t̻ d̻
̹	More rounded	ɔ̹	ʷ	Labialized	tʷ dʷ	̃	Nasalized ẽ
̜	Less rounded	ɔ̜	ʲ	Palatalized	tʲ dʲ	ⁿ	Nasal release dⁿ
̟	Advanced	u̟	ˠ	Velarized	tˠ dˠ	ˡ	Lateral release dˡ
̠	Retracted	i̠	ˤ	Pharyngealized	tˤ dˤ	̚	No audible release d̚
̈	Centralized	ë	̴	Velarized or pharyngealized	ɫ		
̽	Mid-centralized	e̽	̝	Raised	e̝ (ɹ̝ = voiced alveolar fricative)		
̩	Syllabic	ɹ̩	̞	Lowered	e̞ (β̞ = voiced bilabial approximant)		
̯	Non-syllabic	e̯	̘	Advanced Tongue Root	e̘		
˞	Rhoticity	ɚ	̙	Retracted Tongue Root	e̙		

FIGURE 5.2

THE INTERNATIONAL PHONETIC ALPHABET CAN BE USED TO WRITE ANY LANGUAGE. ITS LETTERS ARE
BASED ON PHYSICAL ASPECTS OF SOUND PRODUCTION SUCH AS TONGUE POSITION.

distinguish words from one another. Rather, these sounds are used in different contexts (/d/ at the beginning of a word and /th/ in the middle of a word). A person who says *nada* using the consonant sound in *dia* will still be understood to be saying "nothing," although people may think the accent is "wrong" or "foreign."

English has many cases in which a single phoneme may be indicated by many phones; as in Spanish, different sounds do not necessarily serve to distinguish words. For example, the English phoneme /t/ includes at least six different phones (Ladefoged 1982). Consider the /t/ sounds in *stick, tick,* and *little.* The /t/ sound in each of these words is different. As you say the /t/ sound in one word after another, you can feel your tongue change position. Now, hold your hand in front of your mouth and say *stick* and then *tick.* Although the /t/ in each of these words might sound the same to you, you will feel a puff of air as you say the /t/ in *tick* but not when you say *stick.* This demonstrates that the sounds are different, even though you may have a difficult time hearing the difference.

Most languages use only about 30 phonemes in their structure. By an unconscious process, the native speaker not only learns to make the sounds used in the language but also to differentiate between sounds that are significant (phonemes) and those that are not. The ordinary person does not consciously think about the phonemic pattern of his or her language. Only when trying to learn another language, or hearing someone with a thick foreign ac-

cent speak our own, do we become aware of the variation in sounds and phonemes.

MORPHOLOGY

A **morpheme** is the smallest unit of a language that has a meaning. In English, *-s,* as in *dogs,* means "plural"; *un-* as in *undo,* means "negative"; *-er,* as in *teacher,* means "one who does." Because *-s, un-,* and *-er* are not used by themselves but only in association with another unit of meaning, they are called **bound morphemes.** A morpheme that can stand alone, such as *giraffe,* is called a **free morpheme.**

A **word** is the smallest part of a sentence that can be said alone and still retain its meaning. Some words consist of a single morpheme. *Giraffe* is an example of a single-morpheme word. *Teacher* has two morphemes, *teach* and *-er. Unlocks* has three morphemes: *un-, lock,* and *-s.*

Languages differ in the extent to which their words tend to contain only one, several, or many morphemes and in their rules for combining morphemes. Some languages, such as English and Chinese, are **isolating.** They have relatively few morphemes per word, and the rules for combining morphemes are fairly simple. **Agglutinating** languages, such as Turkish, allow a great number of morphemes per word and have highly regular rules for combining them. **Synthetic** languages such as Mohawk or Inuktitut (an Arctic Canadian language) have words with a great many morphemes and complex, highly irregular rules for their combination. In agglutinating or synthetic languages, translating a single word may require an entire English sentence. For example, the Inuktituk word *qasuirrsarvigssarsingitluinarnarpuq* contains ten morphemes and is best translated as "someone did not find a completely suitable resting place" (Bonvillain 1997:19).

Even in isolating and agglutinating languages, the rules used to combine morphemes into words can be quite complex. For example, one of the rules of English morphology is that the morpheme for plural, *-s,* follows the element it is pluralizing. Things are not quite that easy, however. In English, the plural of *dog* is made by adding *-s,* but the plural of *child* is made by adding *-ren.* A grammar therefore specifies not

---

morpheme The smallest unit of a language that has a meaning.

bound morpheme A unit of meaning that must be associated with another.

free morpheme A unit of meaning that may stand alone as a word.

word The smallest part of a sentence that can be said alone and still retain its meaning.

isolating Languages that have relatively few morphemes per word and relatively simple rules for combining morphemes.

agglutinating Languages that allow a great number of morphemes per word and have highly regular rules for combining them.

synthetic Languages that allow a great many morphemes per word and have complex, highly irregular rules for their combination.

only the general rules of morpheme combination but also exceptions to the rules and the rules for different classes of exceptions.

SYNTAX

Syntax is the arrangement of words to form phrases and sentences. Languages differ in their syntactic structures. In English, word order is important because it conveys meaning. The syntax of the English language gives a different meaning to these two sentences: "The dog bit the man" and "The man bit the dog." However, word order is not equally important in all languages. In Latin, for example, the subject and object of a sentence are indicated by word endings rather than word order.

When they analyze the syntactic structure of a language, descriptive linguists establish the different form classes, or parts of speech, for that language. All languages have a word class of nouns, but different languages have different subclasses of nouns, frequently referred to as genders. Gender classification can apply to verbs, indefinite and definite articles, and adjectives, all of which must agree with the gender classification of the noun.

The use of the term *gender* seems appropriate in the Romance languages (Spanish, French, and Italian), as well as in many others, because nouns are divided into masculine and feminine subclasses. In addition to these, German and Latin have a neuter subclass. However, some languages have a great many different subclasses. For example, Kivunjo, a language spoken in East Africa, has 16 subclasses (Pinker 1994:27). Although the word *gender* may be used to describe these classes, they have nothing to do with sex roles. Papago, a Native American language, provides another example of a linguistic gender division that has nothing to do with sex roles. The Papago divide all the features of the world into two genders, or classes: "living things" and "growing things." Living things include all animated objects, such as people and animals; growing things refer to inanimate objects, such as plants and rocks.

Applying the rules of grammar turns meaningless sequences of words into meaningful utterances, but sometimes grammar seems to have a meaning of its own. We can recognize a sentence as grammatical even if it makes no sense. To use a now classic example (Chomsky 1965), consider the following sentences:

"Colorless green ideas sleep furiously."
"Furiously sleep ideas green colorless."

Both sentences are meaningless in English. But the first is easily recognized as grammatical by an English speaker, whereas the second is both meaningless and ungrammatical. The first sentence has the parts of speech in English in their proper relation to each other, so it seems as if it should make sense. The second sentence does not.

SEMANTICS: THE LEXICON

A **lexicon** is the total stock of words in a language. The relationship between culture and language is clearly seen in a lexicon. In industrial societies, the lexicon contains many words reflecting technological complexity and specialization. In technologically simpler societies, the lexicon has few such words. The lexicon of any culture reflects what is most important in that culture. For example, whereas the average American can name only about 50 to 100 species of plants, members of societies based on hunting and gathering or on gardening can typically name 500 to 1000 species of plants (Harris 1989:72). Such lexical specialization is not limited to nonindustrial societies. Germans in Munich have a vocabulary of more than 70 words to describe the strength, color, fizziness, clarity, and age of beer (Hage 1972, cited in Salzmann 1993:256).

Because vocabulary reflects the way people with a certain culture perceive their environment, anthropologists use it as a clue to understanding experience and reality in different cultures. Through vocabulary, anthropologists attempt to get an insider's view of the world less influenced by the anthropologist's own classification system. This perspective has long been used in studying the vocabulary for kin-

---

lexicon The total stock of words in a language.

LANGUAGES BUILD FOCAL VOCABULARIES AROUND IDEAS AND THINGS IMPORTANT TO THEIR SPEAKERS. GERMANS IN MUNICH HAVE MORE THAN 70 WORDS TO DESCRIBE BEER.

one critical way in which individuals in a culture are introduced to their physical and social environments. Anthropologists have long hypothesized that, as a result, the language a person speaks has a critical impact on the way he or she perceives and conceptualizes the world.

THE SAPIR-WHORF HYPOTHESIS

In the first half of the twentieth century, Edward Sapir and his student Benjamin Lee Whorf investigated the ways in which the use of a particular language affected the way its speakers understood the world. Sapir and Whorf believed that languages had a compelling influence on thought. Sapir wrote:

> Human beings do not live in the objective world alone . . . but are very much at the mercy of the particular language which has become the medium of expression for their society. . . . The fact . . . is that the "real world" is to a large extent unconsciously built up on the language habits of the group. No two languages are ever sufficiently similar to be considered as representing the same social reality. The worlds in which different societies live are distinct worlds, not merely the same world with different labels attached. (1949b:162)

In other words, different languages represent different ways of understanding the world. For example, if my language has only one term—*brother-in-law*—for my sister's husband, my husband's brothers, and my husband's sisters' husbands, I am led by my language to perceive all these relatives in a similar way. Thus, vocabulary, through what it groups together under one label and what it differentiates with different labels, shapes our perception of the world.

Sapir and Whorf proposed a set of ideas that have come to be called the **Sapir-Whorf hypothesis.** The hypothesis proposes that concepts such as time, space, and matter are not the same for all people but are conditioned by the structure of our language. Thus, we perceive the world in certain ways because we talk about the world in certain ways. Further, cultural ideas and behavioral norms are

ship, which gives good clues to the nature of family relations in a culture. In English, for example, the term *brother-in-law* can include my sister's husband, my husband's brother, and the husbands of all my husband's sisters. The use of a single term for all of these relations reflects the similarity of a woman's behavior toward all the men in those different kinship statuses. Hindi, a language of North India, has separate terms for my sister's husband (*behnoi*), my husband's elder brother (*jait*), my husband's younger brother (*deva*), and my husband's sisters' husbands (*nandoya*). The variety of words in Hindi reflects the fact that a woman treats the members of each of these categories differently.

LANGUAGE AND CULTURE

We have seen how language reflects the ways in which cultures divide up their physical and social environment as well as the ideas, objects, or relationships cultures emphasize. But language does more than just reflect culture: It is

Sapir-Whorf hypothesis The hypothesis that perceptions and understandings of time, space, and matter are conditioned by the structure of a language

ENDANGERED LANGUAGES

Members of many cultures see their culture as rooted in their language. It is clear that for many people there is a tight bond between retaining their language and keeping their cultural identity. It is therefore of great concern to anthropologists that languages are increasingly disappearing. Linguist Michael Krauss (1992) has estimated that about 10,000 years ago there may have been as many as 15,000 different languages spoken in the world. Today that number has been reduced to 6,000, and Krauss estimates that in the next 100 years, 90 percent of these will either vanish entirely or be spoken only by a few very old people.

Various factors may cause the disappearance of a language. It may die when all of its speakers are killed by disease or genocide. Government policies may deliberately seek to eliminate a language. For example, for much of the nineteenth and twentieth centuries, the U.S. government had an active policy of eliminating the languages of Native Americans. Students in Bureau of Indian Affairs schools were punished and humiliated for speaking their native languages (Crawford 1992). Today, people who are members of linguistic minorities often abandon their languages because they find it more prestigious or more profitable to speak another.

Although there is probably no way to make sure all of today's languages will still be spoken in the future, some successes are possible. The Navajo, Arapaho, and Northern Ute, as well as several other Native American tribes, have adopted policies to promote the use of their native languages (Crawford 1992). Anthropologists and linguists can help by providing dictionaries, guides to grammar, and a basic library of texts showing the language in use. The most fundamental element of any program to preserve or restore language, however, is the will and desire of the people who speak it to preserve their own language.

THE SPREAD OF WESTERN-STYLE EDUCATION, AS IN THIS CLASSROOM IN NAIROBI, KENYA, HAS LED TO THE DISAPPEARANCE OF MANY LANGUAGES. SOME ANTHROPOLOGISTS ESTIMATE THAT IN THE NEXT 100 YEARS, 90 PERCENT OF LANGUAGES CURRENTLY SPOKEN WILL VANISH.

Paul Conklin/Pictor

C U L T U R A L   F O C U S

GENDERLECTS: CONVERSATION BETWEEN MEN AND WOMEN

Sociolinguist Deborah Tannen is the author of the best-seller *You Just Don't Understand: Men and Women in Conversation,* as well as several additional titles about the difficulties that men and women in the United States have in speaking to each other. According to Tannen, women speak and hear a language of connections and intimacy, while men speak and hear a language of status and independence. Thus, she says, communication between men and women can be like cross-cultural communication, prey to a clash of conversational styles. Instead of different dialects, Tannen says, men and women speak different genderlects.

Where do women and men learn these different ways of speaking and hearing? According to Tannen, boys and girls grow up in different worlds of words. Boys tend to play outside, in large groups that are hierarchically structured. Their groups have leaders who tell others what to do and how to do it, and resist doing what other boys propose. It is by giving orders and making them stick that high status is negotiated. Another way boys achieve status is by taking center stage to tell stories and jokes, and by sidetracking or challenging the stories and jokes of others. Boys' games have winners and losers and elaborate systems of rules that frequently are the subject of arguments.

Boys also boast of their skill and argue about who is best at what.

Girls, on the other hand, tend to play in small groups or in pairs; the centers of girls' social life are best friends. Within the group, intimacy is key: differentiation is measured by relative closeness. In their most frequent games, everyone gets a turn. Many of their activities do not have winners and losers. Though some girls are certainly more skilled than others, girls are expected not to boast about it, or show that they think they are better than the others. Girls don't give orders; they express their preferences or suggestions. They don't grab center stage, so they don't challenge each other directly. And much of the time, they simply sit together and talk. Girls are not accustomed to jockeying for status in an obvious way; they are more concerned that they be liked.

Tannen characterizes these differences between male and female use of words as report-talk versus rapport-talk.

For most women, the language of conversation is primarily a language of rapport—a way of establishing connections and negotiating relationships. The emphasis is on displaying similarities and matching experiences. From childhood, girls criticize peers who try to stand out or appear better than others.

For most men, talk is primarily a means to preserve independence and negoti-

ate and maintain status in a hierarchical social order. This is done by exhibiting knowledge and skill, and by holding center stage through verbal performance such as storytelling, joking, or imparting information. From childhood, men learn to use talking as a way to get and keep attention.

Misunderstandings are caused by genderlect differences in conversation between men and women because women often want the "gift of understanding," while men tend to give the "gift of advice." Tannen illustrates this in the story of a woman who was hospitalized after being seriously injured in an accident. Because she hated being in the hospital, she asked to come home early. But once home, she suffered increasing pain. In response to her expressions of pain, her husband said, "Why didn't you stay in the hospital where you would have been more comfortable?" The wife felt hurt because to her, her husband's comment implied that he did not want her at home. She did not view his suggestion as a response to her complaints about her pain, but rather viewed it as an independent expression of his preference not to have her at home.

Research on differences in public and private speaking in the United States supports Tannen's view that men and women have different ways of speaking.

---

encoded in language. Thus, we act the way we do because we speak a certain language.

Most anthropologists today would agree that language is closely related to culture and does help to mold our understanding of the world. Few, however, would argue that it has the iron

grip on our thinking that Sapir and Whorf proposed. Anthropologists have attempted to test the hypothesis with mixed success. Harry Hoijer (1964) applied it to the Navajo. Many aspects of Navajo grammar (such as the conjugation of active verbs and the reporting of

For example, it is a common stereotype that women don't tell jokes. Although the stereotype is wrong, it is true that women are less likely than men to tell jokes in large groups, especially groups that include men. Whereas men are more likely to tell jokes when they have an audience, many women are reluctant to tell jokes in front of people they don't know well. This is consistent with Tannen's view that women are more likely to talk in a situation that is more private, where the audience is small, familiar, and perceived to be members of a community, than in a more public situation that requires speakers to claim center stage and prove their abilities.

The dominant male style of competition and the contrasting female style of cooperation and affiliation lead to different approaches to conflict, and these are reflected in language. To most women, says Tannen, conflict is a threat to connection, to be avoided at all costs. Disputes are preferably settled without direct confrontation. But to many men, conflict is that necessary means by which status is negotiated, so it is to be accepted and may even be sought, embraced, and enjoyed. Thus, male report-talk is part of a larger framework in which many men approach life as a contest.

Differences in attitudes toward conflict show up in daily conversations, says Tannen. Women's tendency to hate arguing often places them in the role of peacemaker. This reflects a general tendency among women to seek agreement as a way of establishing affiliation, whereas men often use competition to accomplish affiliative ends.

As evidence of other differences between men and women that are reflected in genderlects, Tannen describes the results of a class assignment requiring her students to record an ordinary conversation in which someone described personal experiences. She reports that all 14 men told stories about themselves, whereas of the 12 women, only 6 told stories about themselves. In addition, for the most part, the stories that men told made them look good, whereas many of the women told stories that made them look foolish.

Much research confirms the notion that men and women approach life in different ways, that these differences are the result of patterns of socialization, and that they find expression in patterns of language. However, some sociolinguists criticize Tannen for her lack of emphasis on the relationship of genderlects to the power differences between men and women in American society (Kramarae 1992). Unlike other sociolinguists writing about gender differences in language (see Penelope 1990), Tannen's work does not directly challenge or question the importance of patriarchy, reflected in many linguistic features of the English language (Burke 1994), nor does she take into account the factors of race and class hierarchies as these affect speech behavior. Feminist critics particularly note that Tannen's emphasis on genderlects as a difference in style distracts attention from the important conflicts of interest and status between men and women in American society, which may equally be the cause of different speech behavior. In that case, it would be less important to understand the style of the other, as Tannen advises, than to analyze and challenge it. Beyond these criticisms, it is well to remember that genderlects are tendencies rather than absolutes. They may describe the linguistic behavior of the majority of men and women in American society, but there are numerous exceptions. Many women enjoy public speech and confrontation, and many men prefer private speech and strive for agreement.

Source: Adapted from Deborah Tannen, *You Just Don't Understand: Men and Women in Conversation.* New York: William Morrow, 1991. Copyright 1990 Deborah Tannen, PhD. By permission of HarperCollins Publishers, Inc.

actions and events) emphasize movement. Hoijer found parallels to this linguistic emphasis on motion in many aspects of Navajo culture. In Navajo mythology, for example, gods and culture heroes restlessly move from one place to another, seeking by their motion to perfect the universe. However, this sort of evidence is quite weak. Consider that like their Navajo counterparts, Greek cultural heroes such as Odysseus move restlessly from place to place, but the Greek language is utterly different from Navajo.

THE INDIAN AND THE WHITEMAN

Understanding the relationship between language and ethnocentrism is an essential part of the ethnography of communication. The following is a joke told by the Western Apache. It shows how cultural values are unintentionally encoded in verbal and nonverbal communication. The teller of the joke is poking fun at what he sees as European American ethnocentrism. It is for the reader to determine whether the joke teller is being ethnocentric as well.

Scene: It is a clear, hot evening in July. J and K have finished their meal. The children are sitting nearby. There is a knock at the door. J rises, answers the knock, and finds L standing outside.

J (playing the part of the Whiteman): Hello, my friend! How're you doing? How you feeling, L? You feeling good? (J now turns in the direction of K and addresses her.)

J: Look who here, everybody! Look who just come in. Sure, it's my Indian friend, L. Pretty good, all right. (J slaps L on the shoulder and, looking him directly in the eyes, seizes his hand and pumps it wildly up and down.)

J: Come right in, my friend! Don't stay outside in the rain. Better you come in right now. (J now drapes his arm around L's shoulder and moves him in the direction of a chair.)

J: Sit down! Sit right down! Take your loads off you ass. You hungry? You want crackers? Maybe you want some beer? You want some wine? Bread? You want some sandwich? How about it? You hungry? I don't know. Maybe you sick. Maybe you don't eat again long time. (K has now stopped what she is doing and is looking on with amusement. L has seated himself and has a look of bemused resignation on his face.)

J: You sure looking good to me, L. You looking pretty fat! Pretty good all right! You got new boots? Where you buy them? Sure pretty good boots! I glad . . .

(At this point, J breaks into laughter. K joins in. L shakes his head and smiles. The joke is over.)

This joke is one of an inventive repertoire among the Western Apache known as Whiteman jokes—elaborate satirical routines that the Apache do for one another as a way of expressing their sense of difference from European Americans. These jokes are part of a process of social criticism and self-definition. In them, the Apache try to make sense of the whites with whom they have had to deal for a long time and to confer order on Apache experiences with European Americans. In these jokes, Apaches play at being Whitemen, imitating them in speech and nonverbal gestures and behavior.

When Western Apaches stage joking imitations of whites, they portray them as gross incompetents in the conduct of social relations. Judged according to Apache standards of what is right and normal, the joke teller's actions are intended to seem extremely peculiar and wrong. This joke shows the different ways in which whites appear to the Apache as ignorant of the proper way to comport themselves in public situations.

In the first line of the joke, the use of "my friend" indicates the Apache view that European Americans use this word much too loosely, even for people whom

---

The use of grammatical gender presents yet other difficulties for the Sapir-Whorf hypothesis. In the Romance languages, it is necessary to distinguish masculine from feminine nouns; in Chinese, Turkish, and Farsi, it is not. This difference is interesting, but it tells us nothing about relations between men and women in these cultures. And the lack of gender classes for nouns and adjectives in English does not correspond to any culturally perceived equality between male and female.

THE ETHNOGRAPHY OF COMMUNICATION

Many anthropologists in the first half of the twentieth century focused on describing languages and on understanding them as systems of

it is clear they hold in low esteem. Among the Apache, a friend is a person one has known for many years and with whom one has strong feelings of mutual confidence and respect. "How you feeling?" as a question to a mere acquaintance is a breach of personal privacy for the Apache and indicates an unnatural curiosity about the inner feelings of other people.

The second line of the joke criticizes what the Apache view as the unnecessary and embarrassing attention given to the individual in social situations by whites. Among the Apache, entering and leaving a group should be done unobtrusively to avoid causing anyone to feel socially isolated and uncomfortable. In the use of the personal name L, the joke teller contrasts the Apache view of a name as an item of individually owned and valued property with the European American behavior, which uses such names loosely and without propriety. Also, the repetition of the name indicates the Apache view that Whitemen must have bad memories, because they continually remind themselves whom they are talking to. The humor is heightened when J slaps L on the shoulder and looks him in the eye. The Apache view such behavior as aggressive and insolent. Among them, adult men are careful to avoid touching each other in public, as this is viewed as an unwarranted encroachment on the private territory of the self.

In the third and fourth lines, J demands that the visitor immediately sit down and eat. These actions suggest that the European American is bossy and imply that the guest is a person of little account whose wishes may be safely ignored. The rapid-fire questions and repetitions about food are viewed by the Apache as a form of coercion, and the line "Maybe you sick" contrasts with the Apache belief that talking about trouble can increase its chances of happening.

In the final line, the attention J pays to L's physical appearance and new boots is another example to the Apache of how Whitemen force others into self-consciousness and embarrassment. Because this kind of remark appears to be well received among European Americans, however, the Apache conclude that Whitemen are deeply absorbed with the surfaces of themselves, an absorption that is related to their need to be regarded as separate and distinct from other people.

To the Apache, Whitemen often seem insensitive in the ways they conduct themselves in the presence of Indian people. The Whitemen stories are a rare opportunity for European Americans to be on the receiving end of a "native" perspective.

Critical Thinking Questions

1. The Whiteman joke includes numerous examples of inappropriate speech in Apache culture. As the analysis shows, knowing what is inappropriate speech and why it is improper involves considerable understanding of the way the Apache see the world. What sorts of things are inappropriate speech in American culture, and what do they tell you about the way Americans see the world?

2. For better or worse, ethnic jokes are common in American culture. The success of such a joke often depends on the ability of the teller to imitate effectively the accent and linguistic style of the people about whom the joke is told. Why is imitating accents central to these jokes? What sorts of information are conveyed by such imitation?

3. In telling this Whiteman joke, J is doing a parody of European Americans, commenting on their ethnocentrism in their dealings with Western Apaches. Is J, by doing this, also being ethnocentric? If so, is there any difference between J's ethnocentrism and that of the people he parodies?

Source: Joke from Keith Basso, *Portraits of "the Whiteman."* New York: Cambridge University Press, 1979. Reprinted by permission of the publisher.

---

thought independent of the ways in which people actually speak. In the past 25 years, anthropologists have increasingly turned to understanding speech performance: the actual encounters that involve verbal (and also accompanying nonverbal) communication between human beings. This specialty is called **sociolinguistics.** Sociolinguists observe verbal behavior among different individuals and groups in society.

The sociolinguist attempts to identify, describe, and understand the cultural patterning of different speech events within a speech community (society or subsociety). For example, a political speech has different purposes and is

sociolinguistics A subdiscipline of anthropology that focuses on speech performance.

limited by different norms from those for a political discussion among friends. And different cultures have different norms regarding political speeches: who can participate as speaker and audience, the appropriate topics for such a speech, what kinds of cultural themes can be used, where such speeches can take place, the relationship between the speaker and hearer, the language used in a multilingual community, and so forth.

Sociolinguists are interested in the ways in which speech varies depending on a person's position in a social structure or social relationship. In some cultures, different speech forms are used depending on whether the speaker and hearer are intimate friends, acquaintances on equal footing, or people of distinctly different social statuses. French, German, and Spanish, among other languages, have formal and informal pronouns and conjugations that are not found in English. The rules for their use vary from culture to culture. In France, parents use the informal term to address their children, but children use the formal term to their parents. In the Spanish spoken in Costa Rica, many people use three forms: The informal *tu* may be used by an adult speaking to a child (or lover), the formal *usted* is used among strangers, and an intermediate term, *vos,* may be used among friends. In India, the status of a husband is higher than that of a wife, and among most Hindi speakers a wife never addresses her husband by his name (certainly not in public) but uses a roundabout expression that would translate into English as something like "I am speaking to you, sir."

In many speech communities, the ordinary person knows and uses more than one language. Sociolinguists are interested in the different contexts in which one or the other language is used. The language a person chooses to use can be a way of solidifying ethnic or familial identity or of distancing oneself from another person or group.

An interesting example of this is Apache Whiteman stories. This speech performance, which developed out of the interaction be-

tween Native Americans and the larger society, was described in the Ethnography box on pages 108 and 109. The fact that Whiteman stories are never told to Whitemen underscores William Labov's point that the anthropologist must hear people speak in their natural settings in order to grasp their full linguistic creativity.

LANGUAGES AND DIALECTS

All human groups have language, and all languages are equally sophisticated and serve the needs of their speakers equally well. A language cannot make its speakers more or less intelligent, sexist, sophisticated, or anything else. Individual knowledge of vocabulary may vary, as may the artfulness with which an individual communicates, but every human being speaks with equal grammatical sophistication. Despite this, in American society (and many others with social hierarchies), some usages are considered "correct" and others are taken to be examples of poor grammar. Two examples with which most people are familiar are the use of *ain't* and the use of the double negative, as in "I don't got no money." In fact, there is no scientific reason why "is not" is superior to "ain't" or why "I don't have any money" is superior to "I don't got no money." In either case, the constructions are logical and consistent, and there is no linguistic reason to prefer one over the other. The fact that in each case one is labeled "proper" and the other is considered poor construction is a social rather than a linguistic issue. (By the way, double-negative constructions such as "I don't got no . . ." are not examples of two negatives' making a positive. Linguistically, they are simply two-part negatives, which are used in many of the world's languages. For example, French uses the words *ne* and *pas* to make a negative, as in "Je ne parle pas," meaning "I don't talk.")

In a hierarchical society, the most powerful group generally determines what is "proper" in language. The grammatical constructions used by the socially dominant group are considered to be a language, and deviations from them are often called **dialects.** Linguist Max Weinreich has defined a language as a dialect with an army and a navy (quoted in Pinker 1994:28). By this he meant that whether some-

dialects Forms of a language that deviate from the form used by the socially dominant group.

thing is considered a language or a dialect is determined by the power of those who speak it rather than by any objective linguistic criteria.

William Labov's classic study of language patterns in New York City is an outstanding example of the relationship among hierarchy, power, and the ways people speak. Labov (1972) noted that elites and working-class people have different vocabularies and pronounce words differently. Some forms are associated with higher socioeconomic status and are considered "proper." Such speech is privileged or automatically granted higher status. Other forms, particularly those associated with lower socioeconomic status, are stigmatized and considered incorrect.

Labov found that many speakers use several different forms of speech. Not only do people vary their vocabulary and pronunciation in different contexts, but the degree of such variation is related to the social class of the speaker. People at the bottom of the social hierarchy do not vary their speech much from casual talk to careful speech. Upper-middle-class people, whose pronunciation normally falls midway between the privileged and the stigmatized forms, also show little variation. The most extreme variations are exhibited by members of the lower middle class, who use the stigmatized forms in casual speech but the privileged forms in careful speech.

Labov's study might be interpreted as demonstrating that those on the bottom do not vary their pronunciation because they have little hope of moving up socially, those at the top do not vary their pronunciation because they are secure in their social position, and those in the middle (lower middle class) vary their pronunciation most because they are "social climbers" and therefore are the most sensitive to behaving in "correct" ways.

In any case, Labov's study makes clear what many of us know but do not like to admit: We do judge a person's social status by the way he or she speaks. The function of speech is not limited to communicating information. What we say and how we say it are also ways of telling people what we are socially, or, perhaps, where we want to be.

The relationship between speech and social hierarchy has been a particularly important issue

PEOPLE SUCH AS THE GULLAH, WHO SPEAK IN A DIALECT, ARE OFTEN SOCIALLY STIGMATIZED AND TOLD THEY SPEAK INCORRECTLY. HOWEVER, THEIR LANGUAGE IS NOT IN ANY TECHNICAL SENSE INFERIOR.

in American society. In the 1950s and 1960s, educational psychologists argued that the poor, and particularly members of ethnic minorities, were handicapped by their language. They suggested that the general cultural deprivation of such people led them to use language that was coarse, simple, and irrational. Furthermore, the use of impoverished language perpetuated the economic poverty and social marginalization of these groups. Such scholars argued that if people could be taught to speak standard English they would be able to think logically, and this ability would lift them from poverty (Bereiter and Engelmann 1966; Engelmann and Engelmann 1966).

EBONICS

Social critics of the 1960s considered many varieties of English to be inferior, including Appalachian English, Dutchified Pennsylvania English, Hawaiian Creole, Gullah, and emergent Hispanic Englishes. However, **Ebonics**—also known as **Black English Vernacular**

Ebonics A form of English commonly spoken among rural and urban African Americans of working-class background.

Black English Vernacular (BEV) See **Ebonics**.

(BEV) or **African American Vernacular English (AAVE)**—spoken by many African Americans, is perhaps the most widely known stigmatized variety. Ebonics has deep roots in the African American community, and although not all Americans of African origin speak it, it has become emblematic of blacks in the minds of many Americans. For various reasons, it is particularly deep-rooted among African Americans of working-class backgrounds, whether rural or urban. This form of speech has been heavily criticized. Arthur Jensen even argued that the deficiencies of Ebonics provided evidence for genetic intellectual inferiority of Africans.

Research beginning in the 1960s demonstrated that notions about the linguistic inferiority of Ebonics were baseless. It is indeed a different variety from Standard Spoken American English (SSAE), the language spoken by most of the American middle class, but it is in no way linguistically inferior. Like every other language, it is fully systematic, grammatical, symbolic, and certainly no barrier to abstract thought. A good example, taken from the work of William Labov (1972:217), is the following interview with Larry, a 15-year-old core member of the Jets, an inner-city street gang.

Interviewer: But, just say that there is a God, what color is he? White or black?
Larry: Well, if it is a God . . . I wouldn't know what color, I couldn' say—couldn' nobody say what color he is or really would be.
Interviewer: But now, jus' suppose there was a God.
Larry: Unless'n they say. . . .
Interviewer: No, I was jus' saying jus' suppose there is a God, would he be white or black?
Larry: He'd be white, man.
Interviewer: Why?
Larry: Why? I'll tell you why. 'Cause the average whitey out here got everything, you dig? And the [black man] ain't got shit, y'know? Y'understan'? So-um-for-in order for that to happen, you know it ain't no black God that's doin' that bullshit.

African American Vernacular English (AAVE) See **Ebonics.**

It is clear from this dialogue that there is nothing wrong with Larry's thinking. The argument he presents is sophisticated and logical.

Although Larry's English does not sound like SSAE, it is neither less complicated nor less abstract. It simply follows different rules. Some of the changes in the rules of syntax are quite rudimentary. For example, where SSAE uses the word *there* as a meaningless subject ("If there is a God"), Ebonics uses the word *it* ("If it is a God"). Like SSAE, Ebonics allows certain kinds of contractions. In both SSAE and Ebonics, in certain circumstances you may contract the verb *to be.* In SSAE, for instance, "you are" may be replaced with "you're," or "I am" may become "I'm." In Ebonics, "If you are bad" may be replaced with "If you bad" (Pinker 1994:30). Other differences between Ebonics and SSAE can be explained with similarly simple rules. The analysis of Ebonics demonstrates that this variation of English is rich and potent, with a distinct, consistent pronunciation, vocabulary, and grammar. Further, through the works of authors such as Langston Hughes, Maya Angelou, and many others, it has enormously enriched American literature (Rickford and Rickford 2000).

Despite the fact that objectively Ebonics is simply a language like any other, it is stigmatized in American society. The degree to which the use of Ebonics is a political issue in the United States was shown by the furor that erupted over the 1996 proposal by the Oakland (California) School Board to use it to aid in the teaching of SSAE. This decision by a single school board soon became a national controversy (Monaghan 1997). You can read more about the Ebonics controversy in the Anthropology Makes a Difference box in this chapter.

The fact that many Americans of all races, even many of its speakers, consider Ebonics not just different from but inferior to Standard Spoken American English burdens many African Americans with a difficult problem. To speak naturally within the family and community, black children must learn one variety of English, Ebonics. But when these children enter school or have to deal with people who are not members of their community, they gener-

EBONICS

Anthropologists have played a vital role in the controversy surrounding the place of Ebonics, or African American Vernacular English, in educating American children. The story goes back to the 1970s in Ann Arbor, Michigan. In that year, a federal court ruled that the city's public schools were denying African American elementary-school students their civil rights by failing to teach them to speak, read, and write standard English as an alternative to the Black English (now called Ebonics) that was their native dialect. The court said that failure on the part of the schools to recognize and use Ebonics as a basis for teaching standard English denied African American children an equal opportunity to succeed in school and thus in later life.

An important part of the expert testimony was provided by William Labov, a sociolinguist who had conducted extensive ethnographic research in the language patterns of speakers of nonstandard English in the United States. Labov's research showed that Ebonics is a distinct linguistic system, as capable as standard English of expressing complex and abstract ideas, rather than an impoverished and deficient language. Labov argued that Ebonics has many features in common with Southern dialects, and that it also has distinct marks of an Afro-Caribbean ancestry, reflecting earlier origins of the African American community (Labov 1983:31).

Labov's testimony focused on the elements of Ebonics that interfered with its speakers' learning how to read and speak in standard English. Based primarily on Labov's testimony, the judge charged the Ann Arbor school district with finding ways to provide its teachers with training in Ebonics so that they could more adequately teach children who speak it to read and function in standard English.

The issue reemerged in December 1996, when the school board of Oakland, California, drawing on Labov's research, passed a resolution that encouraged teachers to understand and use Ebonics in the teaching of standard English. The school board's resolution ignited a nationwide furor. Legislators in several states introduced bills banning the teaching of Ebonics. Hearings were held in the U.S. Senate, where Senator Faircloth of North Carolina denounced Ebonics as "absurd" and described it as "political correctness gone wild" (Sanchez 1997). An editorialist for *The Atlanta Constitution* announced, "This movement is an 'Ebonic plague' that will kill this country faster and deader than our old enemies in Moscow ever dreamed of doing" (Matthews 1997). As in the earlier case, sociolinguists played an important role in the controversy. Labov as well as several others provided critical testimony at the Senate hearings. The Linguistic Society of America, at its January 1997 annual meeting, unanimously approved a resolution stating that the Oakland decision was both linguistically and pedagogically sound (Rickford 1997). The controversy became so intense that the Oakland School Board dropped the word Ebonics (though not the general substance of its resolution) from its proposals in April 1997.

In the heat of debate over Ebonics, many critical points seemed to be lost. First, linguists had shown in the 1960s and 1970s that Ebonics was a distinctive and complex language. Second, no one suggested that students should simply be taught Ebonics. Rather, the school board proposed the use of Ebonics to help students read and write in Standard American English. Finally, numerous studies have shown that using Ebonics to teach reading and writing in Standard American English is more effective than conventional techniques (Rickford 1997). While the precise role Ebonics should play in the classroom remains an important subject for debate, the Ebonics controversy shows both the importance of anthropological research and the need for anthropologists to keep their findings in the public eye.

John Rickford of Stanford University is a leading scholar on Ebonics. He maintains a large website where you can read about Ebonics and the Oakland schools controversy (www.stanford.edu/~rickford). Other good resources are pages for dialects and Ebonics at the Center for Applied Linguistics (www.cal.org) and the National Institutes of Health working group on African American English (www.umass.edu/aae).

The Harold Lloyd Estate and Film Trust

IN THIS PICTURE FROM THE 1923 FILM "SAFETY LAST," HAROLD LLOYD SATIRIZES THE OBSESSIVE CONCERN WITH TIME COMMON IN AMERICAN AND BRITISH CULTURE.

ally have to learn to communicate in SSAE, which may almost be experienced as a foreign language. Most speakers of Ebonics, through school, exposure to mass media, and the need to work in the world outside the local community, become effective speakers of several varieties of English. Like others who are bilingual, speakers of Ebonics often engage in code switching. **Code switching** is the ability of speakers of two languages to move seamlessly between them. Those who code switch use each language in the setting that is appropriate to it. However, some Ebonics speakers do not become fluent in SSAE, leaving them at a disadvantage in their attempts to operate beyond the local community.

The study of Ebonics shows the advantages of an anthropological approach. Much of the misunderstanding of Ebonics came from the conditions under which it was studied. Sometimes it was studied in schools, a place often viewed by Ebonics speakers as a hostile environment. Other studies were performed in artificial situations designed by psychologists to carry out linguistic studies. To be understood,

code switching The ability of speakers of two (or more) languages to move seamlessly between them.

however, the verbal capacities of Ebonics speakers had to be studied within the cultural context in which they were developed. This very anthropological perspective is similar to that presented in other studies in this chapter. As we saw with the Apache Whiteman story, language use differs depending on its audience, and it may be only within the ethnic community that the linguistic capacities of speakers are fully realized.

NONVERBAL COMMUNICATION

In addition to speaking, all humans use a variety of other methods to communicate. Birdwhistell, one of the pioneers of research in nonverbal communication, argued that in any social situation, almost two-thirds of communicated meaning comes from nonverbal cues (1955). To quote Edward Hall (1959), another influential analyst of nonverbal behavior, "time talks" and "space speaks." The study of nonverbal communication is divided into numerous fields—among them, artifacts, haptics, chronemics, proxemics, and kenesics. Although a full analysis of these is beyond the range of this book, we will present and discuss each of them briefly.

In the context of nonverbal communication, the analysis of artifacts refers to understanding the messages sent by clothing, jewelry, tattoos, piercings, and other visible body modifications. For example, among the Tuareg, a people of the Sahara whose men are veiled, the position of the veil is an important part of nonverbal communication (R. Murphy 1964). A Tuareg man lowers his veil only among intimates and people of lower social status. When he is engaged in an encounter in which he does not wish to commit himself to a particular course of action, he wears the veil very high on the bridge of his nose so that the other party can read as little as possible from his facial expression. In the United States, we are very aware of the use of artifacts to send messages about ourselves. A pierced ear means something different than a pierced lip or tongue. Some students come to class in torn jeans and T-shirts; others wear designer labels or a white shirt and tie. All are trying to send messages about who they are.

Haptics refers to the study and analysis of touch. Touch carries important meaning in all societies. Handshaking, pats on the back or head, kisses, and hugs are all ways we communicate by touch. Many American males, for example, believe that much is communicated by the particular quality of a handshake. Strong, firm handshakes are taken to indicate power, self-confidence, and strength of character, whereas weak or limp handshakes may be interpreted as suggesting lack of interest, indecisiveness, or effeminacy. Americans generally feel free to use their left hands for virtually anything, but in many cultures, particularly in the Middle East, people scrupulously avoid the use of their left hands for eating, handling money, and many other social interactions. The left hand is considered unclean, and using it is generally unacceptable.

Analysts have frequently divided the world's societies into "contact" cultures and "noncontact" cultures (Hall 1966; Montagu 1978). Contact cultures are found in the Middle East, India, the Mediterranean, and Latin America. In these regions, people interact at very close distances and touch one another frequently. In "noncontact" cultures, including those of northern Europe, North America, and Japan, people generally avoid physical contact. The contact/noncontact dichotomy is simplistic and does not accurately reflect the variability and complexity of actual interaction. For example, people in Western "noncontact" cultures in certain instances may expect relatively high degrees of contact when conversing, even with strangers (Burgoon, Buller, and Woodall 1996).

In many cultures, there is a strong relationship between touch and power. In public social relationships, the person who touches another is likely to have more power than the person who is touched. Thus, bosses touch their subordinates, but workers are not likely to touch their bosses. Research shows that in the United States touchers are likely to be perceived as more assertive, strong, and dominant than nontouchers (Leathers 1997:126).

Researchers interested in **chronemics** study the different ways that cultures understand time and use it to communicate. People in different cultures are likely to have different notions of the importance of time. For example, in North American culture, what are we saying to a person when we show up for an appointment 40 minutes late? Are we saying something different if we show up 10 minutes early? Is a Latin American who shows up late for an appointment saying the same thing?

The American concern with the precise measurement of time is suggested by the prominence of clocks in public places such as town squares and on banks and other commercial buildings. Most Americans wear watches and make sure that they are set accurately. Ferraro (1994) notes that the American obsession with accurate timing and schedules is often viewed negatively by members of other cultures. Keeping to a schedule often means rushing through appointments and thus sacrificing meaningful interpersonal relations to the rigors of timing.

Edward Hall (1983) divided cultures into those with monochronic time (M-time) and those with polychronic time (P-time). The United States and northern European countries exemplify M-time cultures. Hall argued that people in M-time cultures think of time as inflexible and organize their lives according to time schedules; in P-time cultures, time is understood as fluid, much more emphasis is placed on social interaction than on schedules, and human activities are not expected to proceed like clockwork. According to Victor (1992), time in P-time cultures simply exists. Being late for an appointment conveys virtually none of the unspoken messages that the same action would in an M-time culture.

Like the contact/noncontact dichotomy, the division of cultures into M-time and P-time seems to capture a basic truth about cultural variation but is overly simplistic. There is enormous variability within cultures. For example, how long an individual is kept waiting for an appointment may have more to do with power

---

haptics The study and analysis of the cultural use of touch.

chronemics The study of the ways in which members of different cultures understand and use time.

than with either polychronic or monochronic perceptions of time. People may be on time for their superiors but keep their subordinates waiting.

Proxemics is the study of social space, which is understood differently in different cultures. Americans, for example, tend to focus on objects and think of the space between them as empty, whereas Japanese tend to focus more on space and assign specific meanings to it. For example, Americans name streets in their cities, whereas Japanese name the intersections (Leathers 1997).

Researchers in proxemics identify three different sorts of space (Hall 1968, Rapoport 1982). First is the built environment: homes, buildings, parks, and how they are arranged. Such arrangements are referred to as fixed-feature space. For example, the number of rooms it is appropriate to have in a house and the relation of these rooms to one another are aspects of fixed space that vary from culture to culture. The second type, semi-fixed-feature space, refers to the placement of furniture, equipment, and decoration within an environment. Furniture, for example, has very clear communicative functions. Consider the placement of a desk within a professor's office. The office may be arranged so that the professor sits behind the desk and the student in front, or the desk may be off to the side so that the student and professor sit much closer to each other. The third type, non-fixed-feature space, refers to the space that individuals maintain around their bodies.

Hall (1968) identified three different ranges of personal communicative space: intimate distance, from 1 to 18 inches; personal distance, from 18 inches to 4 feet; and social distance, from 4 to 12 feet. He suggested that communication among friends ideally happened at personal distance, whereas lovers and very close friends communicated at intimate distance and relative strangers at social distance. However, interpersonal communication difference is

clearly affected by circumstances, culture, gender, and aspects of individual personality. We speak to strangers at a much closer distance in a movie or a classroom than we would in an unconfined space. In the United States, women talk to each other at closer distances than men, as do mixed-gender pairs. In Turkey, on the other hand, both men and women talk at close distances with members of their own sex but at very large distances with each other (Leathers 1997).

Finally, **kenesics** is the study of body position, movement, facial expressions, and gaze. Birdwhistell (1952) identified eight parts of the body that could be used to send messages: total head, face, neck, trunk, shoulder-arm-wrist, hand, hipjoint-leg-ankle, and foot. In other words, virtually all body movements can have significance. But, of course, not all do. We use our posture, our visual expression, eye contact, and other body movements to communicate interest, boredom, and many other things. However, it is clear that not all the movements of our body carry social meaning. Clifford Geertz (1973b) famously suggested that the job of an ethnographer was learning to tell the winks from the twitches—that is, to tell the meaningful communication from the meaningless. Geertz meant this metaphorically, but those who study kenesics do it literally.

The case of smiling is a particularly interesting example of kinesic research. There is very good evidence that smiling, and some other facial expressions, are biologically based human universals. There are no societies in which people do not smile. In fact, smiling is not only characteristic of human beings; our nearest nonhuman relations, chimpanzees and gorillas, smile as well. Moreover, smiling is a reasonably good indicator of happiness or nonviolent intent among all peoples. In any society, social interactions are more likely to have a positive outcome if people are smiling than if they are frowning or scowling. However, it is also true that a smile does not mean the same thing in all cultures. Americans generally equate smiling with happiness, but anthropologists report that people in many cultures smile when they experience surprise, wonder, or embarrassment (Ferraro 1994). A recent book on in-

proxemics The study of the ways in which different cultures use space.
kenesics The study of body movement, facial expressions, and gaze.

TABLE 5.1

THE GREAT VOWEL SHIFT

THE MIDDLE ENGLISH VOWEL	SHIFTS TO THE MODERN ENGLISH VOWEL	THE MIDDLE ENGLISH WORD	PRONOUNCED TO RHYME WITH MODERN WORD	BECOMES THE MODERN WORD
i	aj	mis	piece	mice
u	aw	mus	moose	mouse
e	i	ges	place	geese
o	u	gos	close	goose
ɛ	e	brɛk	trek	break
ɔ	o	brɔk	squawk	broke
a	e	namə	comma	name

ternational business advises American managers that in Japan, happiness hides behind a straight face and that the Japanese often smile to make their guests feel comfortable rather than because they are happy (R. Lewis 1996:267). However, researchers Matsumoto and Kudoh (1993) found that despite substantial differences between American and Japanese interpretations of smiles, members of both cultures agreed that smiling faces were more sociable than neutral faces. Nagashima and Schellenberg (1997) found that similarities far outweighed differences in interpretation of smiles by American and Japanese college students.

LANGUAGE CHANGE

Language, like other aspects of culture, shows both stability and change. **Historical linguists** study the ways in which languages change over time. Historical linguistics can be applied to phonology, morphology, or vocabulary.

CHANGING SOUNDS

When we imagine people speaking English hundreds of years ago, we often think of them as using different words than we do, but otherwise sounding pretty much like us. This is quite incorrect. Not only does the vocabulary of a language change, but the phonemes used

to make words change as well. Linguists attempt to discover laws or rules that describe the ways in which the phonemes of a language have shifted.

A good example of this process is the change in the sounds of English that linguists call the Great Vowel Shift. Between 1400 and 1600, the sounds of many English vowels changed in systematic ways. Table 5.1 gives some examples of the ways in which the sounds changed. The Great Vowel Shift is one of the main reasons why many English words do not seem to be spelled the way they sound. Their current spelling reflects the way the words were pronounced before the shift took place (Fromkin and Rodman 1998).

CHANGING SYNTAX

In any language, the rules by which words are formed into meaningful utterances may also change over time. English again provides some excellent examples of this principle. Modern English is tightly tied to word order. In a modern sentence, the subject comes before the verb and the object comes after the verb. However, in Old English, as in Latin, the endings of

historical linguistics A branch of linguistics concerned with discovering the histories of languages.

nouns indicated whether they were subjects or objects. Thus, the order of words within the sentence was less important. Sentences could occur either as subject-verb-object or subject-object-verb. For example, in Old English, the two sentences "The dog bit the child" and "The dog the child bit" would have the same meaning and be equally grammatical.

CHANGING LEXICON

The vocabulary of a language also undergoes both internal and external changes. Words change their meanings. For example, in Old English, the word *silly* meant "happy." By the time of Middle English, it meant "naive," and now it has come to mean "foolish" (Fromkin and Rodman 1998). New words are constantly added to language. In the past ten to twenty years, an entire vocabulary has grown up around computers and the Internet. Words such as *software, dot-com, disk drive, gigabyte, e-mail,* and *snail mail* would have been unintelligible to most people in 1980.

Many words come into language as borrowings from other languages. As cultures come into contact, cultural items are borrowed, and frequently the original name for the item is kept. Pajamas are an item of clothing borrowed from India, and we have kept the original Indian word, incorporating it into the English vocabulary. In other cases, words or combinations of words already present in the language are applied to new cultural items. Some Native American groups, upon seeing their first horses (introduced by the Spanish), called them "ten dogs," and North Americans refer to their automobiles in terms of "horsepower."

Historical linguists use data on internal linguistic change to discover the relationships between different languages. Languages may be similar because of historical contact between cultures and resultant borrowing. However, if the similarities among languages are numerous, regular, and basic, it is likely that these languages are derived from the same ancestral language.

Historical linguists use a technique called glottochronology to learn about the historical connections among genetically related languages. Linguists have identified a **core vocabulary** of 100 or 200 words that designate things, actions, and activities likely to be named in all the world's languages (see Table 5.2). **Glottochronology** is a statistical technique that uses this core vocabulary to estimate the date of separation of related languages. Researchers have found that a 100-word core vocabulary is likely to change at the rate of 14 percent per thousand years (Salzmann 1993:108). Based on this figure, by computing the percentage of shared basic vocabulary words among related languages, historical linguistics can estimate how long ago they separated from a single ancestral language. Glottochronology is widely applied but has always been controversial. Critics charge that it is based on the assumption that core vocabularies change at a constant rate, whereas in fact the rate of change may vary (Renfrew 1989).

Comparative linguistics has been successful in documenting the relationships among many languages and grouping them into language families. Although this work has been done in greatest detail for Indo-European languages, the technique has also been applied to non-European languages.

Comparative linguistics is an important way of tracing cultural and historical processes. Through reconstruction of a protolanguage, comparative linguistics can also tell us something about the culture of the people who spoke that language. For example, the reconstructed vocabulary of proto-Indo-European contains words for trees and animals that existed in northern Europe, suggesting that this may have been the home of the original Indo-Europeans.

Traditional linguists have been concerned mainly with internal language change. Sociolinguists are interested in language history or the study of historical events that affect language change. Some of the contemporary problems they study have to do with the impact of

core vocabulary A list of 100 or 200 terms that designate things, actions, and activities likely to be named in all the world's languages.

glottochronology A statistical technique that linguists have developed to estimate the date of separation of related languages.

TABLE 5.2
THE 100-WORD CORE VOCABULARY

I	fish	hair	eat	moon
you	bird	head	bite	star
we	dog	ear	see	water
this	louse	eye	hear	rain
that	tree	nose	know	stone
who	seed	mouth	sleep	sand
what	leaf	tooth	die	earth
not	root	tongue	kill	cloud
all	bark	claw	swim	smoke
many	skin	foot	fly	fire
one	flesh	knee	walk	ash
two	blood	hand	come	burn
big	bone	belly	lie	path
long	grease	neck	sit	mountain
small	egg	breasts	stand	red
woman	horn	heart	give	green
man	tail	liver	say	yellow
person	feather	drink	sun	white
black	hot	full	good	dry
night	cold	new	round	name

SOURCE: Salzmann 1993:108

industrialization, acculturation, social stratification, and national politics as these relate to changes in language structure and language use. Sociolinguists are also interested in the social factors within a society that affect changes in both structure and language use.

SUMMARY

1. All animals communicate. However, human communication differs from that of other animals in its flexibility and its ability to convey new ideas and abstract concepts.

2. Researchers have trained some animals to use language in very sophisticated, humanlike ways. However, the use of language is a fundamental part of human adaptation. As far as we know, it does not play this role for any other species.

3. Conventionality, productivity, and displacement are key characteristics of human language. Conventionality is the idea that the meaning of any word is based on the agreement of speakers of a language rather than on characteristics intrinsic to the word. Productivity means that humans can produce and understand an infinite number of utterances they have never said or heard before. Displacement is the ability of human languages to describe things and actions not immediately present in the environment.

4. A child takes the initiative in learning language and learns to speak grammatically without being taught grammatical rules. This suggests that human beings have a precultural, or innate, language-learning capacity. However, this potential for speech is realized only through interaction with other human beings speaking a human language.

5. All languages have structure. The subsystems of a language are a sound system (its phonology), a morphology, syntax, and a lexicon. Phonemes are minimal sound units used within a language. Morphemes are the units that carry meaning, syntax is the combination of morphemes used to produce meaningful utterances, and the lexicon links words to their meanings.

6. The Sapir–Whorf hypothesis is the notion that because grammar and vocabulary influence perception of the environment, speakers of different languages perceive their worlds in fundamentally different ways. There is some evidence to support this notion, but most linguists argue that the similarities among languages far outweigh their differences and that language does not have a systematic effect on thought or perception.

7. Sociolinguists focus on the cultural patterning of speech. They study the different forms of speech within communities and the ways in which speech varies depending on a person's position in a society and relationships to others. In North American culture, one critical area of study is the speech differences between men and women.

8. Stratified societies often have many different forms of language. When this is the case, some forms are often considered to be correct and others improper or inferior. Although society may stigmatize some forms of speech, there is no scientific sense in which one grammatical pattern or accent is better or worse than another.

9. Humans everywhere communicate nonverbally as well as verbally. In every society, people use gestures, facial expressions, posture, and time to communicate with one another. However, the meaning of a gesture or expression may vary greatly from culture to culture.

10. Language changes. Historical linguists are interested in internal linguistic change. Comparative linguists attempt to discover which languages are related. Sociolinguists are interested in the historical and social factors in language change.

11. Linguists seek regularities in the ways in which languages change over time. Glottochronology is a technique that uses the regularity of change in a core vocabulary to discover the historic relationships among languages.

KEY TERMS

African American Vernacular English (AAVE)
agglutinating
allophones
Black English Vernacular (BEV)
blending
bound morpheme
call system
chronemics
code switching
communication
comparative linguistics
conventionality
core vocabulary
descriptive or structural linguistics
dialect
displacement
duality of patterning
Ebonics
free morpheme
glottochronology
haptics

historical linguistics
International Phonetic Alphabet (IPA)
isolating
kenesics
lexicon
morpheme
morphology
phone
phoneme
phonology
prelanguage
productivity
proxemics
Sapir–Whorf hypothesis
semantics
sociolinguistics
Standard Spoken American English (SSAE)
syntax
synthetic
universal grammar
word

SUGGESTED READINGS

Bauman, Richard, and Joel Sherzer (Eds.). 1989. *Explorations in the Ethnography of Speaking.* Cambridge: Cambridge University Press. This collection of classic case studies in linguistic anthropology spans traditional societies in the Americas, Africa, and Oceania, as well as English-, French-, and Yiddish-speaking communities in Europe and North America and African American communities in North America and the Caribbean.

Brenneis, Donald, and Ronald K. S. Macauley (Eds.). 1996. *The Matrix of Language.* Boulder, CO: Westview. A collection of essays that covers recent debates in the study of language and culture. Brenneis and Macauley's volume introduces students to current work in language and socialization, gender, the ethnography of speaking, and language in social and political life.

Goodluck, Helen. 1991. *Language Acquisition: A Linguistic Introduction.* Oxford: Blackwell. A technical introduction to language acquisition that relies heavily on Chomsky's work. Goodluck's book is a must for anyone who would like a detailed understanding of the ways children learn language.

Pinker, Steven. 1994. *The Language Instinct.* New York: William Morrow. A readable introduction to the highly technical field of linguistics. Pinker explains Noam Chomsky's theory of language and provides evidence for the innateness of language. Pinker has recently published a follow-up volume, *Words and Rules: The Ingredients of Language* (1999).

Rickford, John Russell, and Russell John Rickford. 2000. *Spoken Soul: The Story of Black English.* New York: Wiley. This lively and well-written account by a Stanford linguistics professor and a journalist is aimed at both a novice and professional audience. The authors trace the history of Black English and explore the issues and controversies surrounding Ebonics and the Oakland School Board case.

Salzmann, Zdenek. 1993. *Language, Culture, and Society: An Introduction to Linguistic Anthropology.* Boulder, CO: Westview. In this recent and thorough introduction to linguistic anthropology, Salzmann covers topics such as phonology, grammar, historical linguistics, and performance.

Scollon, Ronald, and Susan Wong Scollon. 1994. *Intercultural Communication.* Oxford: Blackwell. This book provides an introduction and practical guide to concepts and problems of intercultural communication. It focuses particularly on language differences between Asians and Westerners and pays particular attention to issues of gender and language within businesses and professional organizations.

Tannen, Deborah. 1990. *You Just Don't Understand: Women and Men in Conversation.* New York: William Morrow. A substantial contribution to the sociolinguistics of gender, this book is a witty, easy-to-read best-seller that uses research findings and everyday experiences to drive home the point that men and women follow different norms of speaking. Tannen has published several "follow-up" volumes, including *Talking from 9 to 5* (1994) and *Gender and Discourse* (1996).

INTERNET RESOURCES

The following Internet resources appear in this chapter. Please log on to the Wadsworth anthropology website: **http://anthropology.wadsworth. com**. Click on the Nanda/Warms *Cultural Anthropology* page. Then select the Student Resources section, where you will find a complete presentation of these links and more.

- A link to a major linguistics website, page 100
- A photo essay on nonverbal communications, page 114
- Access the Study Guide to InfoTrac College Edition for Anthropology Students

John Eastcott/Yva Momatiuk/Woodfin Camp & Associates

ALL CULTURES, NO MATTER HOW SEEMINGLY REMOTE, ARE PART OF THE CONTEMPORARY WORLD SYSTEM. THESE MAORI CHILDREN FROM NEW ZEALAND LIVE IN A BICULTURAL SOCIETY WHERE THEY NEED TO LEARN THE SKILLS OF THEIR TRADITIONAL CULTURE AND THOSE OF THE POSTINDUSTRIAL WORLD.

CHAPTER SIX

LEARNING CULTURE THROUGHOUT LIFE

What are some cultural differences in the construction of human development?

How does the informal transmission of culture occur?

How is formal and informal enculturation linked to cultural values?

What are some of the meanings and functions of male and female initiation?

How does the cross-cultural perspective of anthropology contribute to our understanding of illness, old age, and death?

Human beings, more than any other animal, depend on the social, rather than biological, transmission of the knowledge necessary for survival. Human infants cannot survive without the care of other people. They cannot get food, cannot move around, cannot cling, and cannot force adults to respond to their needs. Although the complex human brain gives us the capacity for learning, it also means that humans develop slowly and need the support of other humans to survive. Human social organization and culture provide the basic context in which humans learn from others while being protected by them. Although other animals, particularly nonhuman primates, also have this capacity and live in groups, no other animal species depends as much as humans on taught and learned behavior.

The long period of dependency is the price *Homo sapiens* pay for their big brain and its enormous potential for learning. This long period of total dependency on the group provides the opportunity for the transmission of culture and reinforces the power of culture in human life. Human infants become adults only by growing up in a particular human society. Thus, the infant grows into a child and later into an adult not simply as a human, but as a particular kind of human: a Kwakiutl, Trobriand Islander, Briton, or Tahitian. Indeed, for many societies, the definition of human being is identical to their own cultural identity. Every society has developed both informal and formal means of **enculturation,** or transmitting its culture, so that children grow up to be responsible and participating adults and so that the society is socially as well as biologically reproduced.

BECOMING A SOCIAL PERSON

Although all cultures nurture human infants and children so that they grow up into acceptable adults, the way in which human development is conceptualized is culturally variable. Cultures vary in their understanding of when

enculturation The ways in which humans learn to become members of their society.

life begins and the point at which one becomes accepted by one's society as a human being (Morgan 1996). Culturally variable timing in the recognition of fetuses, newborns, and young children as social persons is linked to many factors: the productive basis of society, the relations between the sexes, the social stratification system, the culturally defined divisions of the life cycle, attitudes toward death, and particularly, to infant mortality rates.

In cultures where infant mortality is high, a period of time passes before a child undergoes **social birth.** At this point, the infant's survival appears more likely, and it is the social birth rather than the biological birth that is often marked by ritual. Among the Toda of India, for example, the newborn is not considered a person until the age of three months, after which a "face opening" ceremony takes place. The infant is brought outdoors, its face is unveiled at dawn, and it is introduced to the temple, to nature, to buffaloes, and to its clan relatives (Morgan 1996:28). Naming an infant, an important widespread marker of social personhood, also varies cross-culturally. In the United States the newborn is named almost immediately after birth, but in other cultures naming is delayed for months or even years. Delayed social recognition of an infant occurs among the Arunta of Central Australia, where a very premature child is not considered a human being but an animal that by mistake went into the pregnant woman's body. In Ghana, mother and newborn are confined to the house for the first seven days after birth to ascertain that the newborn is a human, not a spirit child. If the child dies within this period, the parents are not permitted to mourn but must show joy at being rid of an unwelcome guest. Similarly, in Truk, in the South Pacific, abnormal or deformed infants were not considered humans but rather ghosts, and among the Tallensi of Africa, twins were not considered definitely human until a month after birth (Morgan 1996:25–26).

In the poverty-stricken region of northeastern Brazil, a child is not considered a social

person until it shows physical and emotional signs of being able to survive (Scheper-Hughes 1992). Children here are mainly raised in single-parent families, and their very low-paid working mothers cannot care for their children during the day nor can they afford to hire caretakers. Since older children are expected to be in school or working, babies are frequently left at home alone, a condition under which many weaker babies die. Children who are born small, wasted, and weak, who are passive, do not suck vigorously, and have little resistance to disease are considered to have an "aversion to living." If they develop acute symptoms, such as convulsions, they are left to die, because it is believed there is no hope for them. Their deaths are viewed as "nature taking its course" or as indicating that the child "wants to die." In the absence of a firm expectation that a child will survive, mothers learn to distance themselves emotionally from vulnerable infants. As very devout Catholics, the mothers believe that allowing "nature to take its course" in child death is cooperating with God's plan and not a sin. The child is believed to become an angel, flying up to a heavenly home. The infant is buried with little ceremony and no tears. Mothers are told that if they cry, their tears will dampen the little angel's wings so that she or he cannot fly to heaven. The graves of these infants are not marked and are never visited; they are soon used for other dead infants and quickly become anonymous. This cultural pattern, which delays the social recognition of a weak infant, functions as a pragmatic survival strategy, notes anthropologist Nancy Scheper-Hughes—a rational response to desperate economic conditions.

Cultural patterns of delayed recognition of social personhood contrast with cultural patterns in the largely affluent United States and shed new light on the intense debate over abortion policy. The American abortion debate is really about when one becomes a social person. Almost all Americans agree that biological birth marks the entrance of a new human being into society, but abortion opponents insist that becoming a social person occurs before birth. They hold that a fetus or embryo is a social person with established rights. In other

social birth   Time at which an infant is considered a person.

societies, where biological birth and social birth are not identical, an infant who dies before social birth has died before it was born, and killing such an infant is not considered murder.

CROSS-CULTURAL VARIATION IN CHILD REARING

The recognition of human status is the beginning phase in human development. Beginning with birth, all humans then pass through developmental phases, each characterized by an increase in the capacity to deal with the physical and social environment. At each phase, the biologically based physical, mental, and psychological potentials of the individual unfold, within a specific cultural context. Physically, the infant gains muscular coordination. From an immobile creature barely able to control the movement of its eyes and limbs, the infant begins to be able to lift its head, focus its eyes, sit up, creep on all fours, stand, and then walk by itself. Mentally, it increases its capacity to differentiate and classify objects and people in the environment. Its curiosity increases. Human infants take an active role in trying new ways of behaving and exploring the world around them. Psychologically, the infant increasingly develops a sense of itself and others. As the infant grows, it learns to modify its demands so that it will meet with success in its social environment. The infant becomes increasingly able to distinguish what actions will bring gratification and what actions will be met with no response or negative responses from others. In thousands of different ways, through the attempts to satisfy its needs, the human infant slowly develops into a social person.

The human needs for physical gratification, emotional contact with others, the expansion of mental and physical capacities, and the development of self, although universal, are not acknowledged or marked in the same ways in all cultures. Some stages of life taken for granted in the United States as natural and universal—infancy, childhood, adolescence, middle age, old age—have been culturally constructed in response to specific social and economic factors. Among these factors are the necessity for record keeping in state bureaucracies, such as schools, and institutional reliance on chronological age in obtaining financial benefits such as social security. Childhood is not universally given the attention as a distinct stage of life that it receives in Western cultures. Indeed, it was only recognized as a developmental stage in Western societies after the introduction of formal schooling in the sixteenth and seventeenth centuries (Aries 1962:412). As the concept of childhood evolved, so did new expectations about the nature of children and the behavior appropriate to childhood.

Child-rearing practices in all cultures are designed to produce adults who know the skills, norms, and behavior patterns of their society—the cultural content. But the transmission of culture involves more than just knowing cultural content. It also involves patterning children's attitudes, motivations, values, perceptions, and beliefs so that they are in harmony with their society (which itself adapts to external requirements of the physical and social environment).

As an example, we will take a closer look at child rearing among the Inuit, a hunting people of the Arctic. Inuit child-rearing practices teach a child to deal with a world that is regarded as a dangerously problematic place, in which making wrong decisions might well mean death (Briggs 1991l). The physical hazards of the extreme Arctic environment in which the Inuit live include treacherous weather and deceptive landscapes, continuously altering under changing conditions of wind, ice, snow, and light.

Inuit adapt to the conditions of uncertainty in their environment by maintaining a "constant state of alertness" and an "experimental way of living." Children and adults constantly test the limits of danger and their own individual abilities to cope with it. Thus, developing skills for solving problems quickly and spontaneously is a central principle of Inuit child rearing. Children are brought up to constantly test their physical skills, in order to extend them and to learn their own capacity for pain and endurance (Stern 1999).

The initiative for learning skills rests largely with the child; no pressure is put on children

CULTURE AND PERSONALITY STUDIES: AN HISTORICAL PERSPECTIVE

The relationships among culture, child rearing, and personality have been a long-term interest of anthropologists. **Psychological anthropologists** try to understand how culture may affect psychological processes such as cognition, emotions, attitudes, personality, concepts of the self, and self-esteem.

One early approach in culture and personality studies was to test Freudian psychoanalytical theories, which had become very influential in the United States, in non-Western cultures. One of Freud's major concepts, for example, was the **Oedipus complex**—the sexual attachment of the male child to his mother, accompanied by hatred and jealousy toward his father. Freud claimed that the Oedipus complex was universal. Anthropologist Bronislaw Malinowski (1927/1953) attempted to show that the Oedipus complex, as Freud defined it, did not exist in the Trobriand Islands. Trobriand society is **matrilineal;** that is, the kinship group is organized around a woman and her descendants. Therefore, the mother's brother, rather than the father, is the primary authority in the family. **Incest taboos** in this society are strongest for brothers and sisters, not mothers and sons, and a boy's major unconscious rivalry is directed toward his maternal uncle, not his father (for a critique, see Spiro 1982).

Between 1920 and 1950, anthropologists such as Margaret Mead (1928/1971), Ruth Benedict (1934/1961), and Edward Sapir (1949a) analyzed broader relationships between culture and personality. They painted these relationships in impressionistic strokes, characterizing whole societies, including complex nations, in terms of a basic personality type. Some early culture and personality studies, influenced by Freudian theory, put particular emphasis on child-rearing practices such as feeding, weaning, and toilet training (for example, DuBois 1944; Kardiner 1945).

After the 1950s, anthropologists used data from the Human Relations Area Files to conduct controlled cross-cultural comparisons, seeking connections among child-rearing practices, personality, and other cultural and social patterns. John Whiting and Irvin Child (1984), for example, used a large cross-cultural sample to test the proposition that systems of curing illness would use techniques that reflected sources of gratification in early child rearing. Thus, a culture in which children were indulged in sources of oral gratification, such as feeding, would tend to use oral medicines for curing illness. Whiting and Child also hypothesized the reverse of this relationship: An aspect of child rearing that was frustrating and promoted anxiety would be used to account for illness. If a culture frustrated a child's oral gratification—by withholding food, for example—that culture would be likely to see disease as something that enters the body through the mouth. Both hypotheses were validated statistically, and the work proved to be a major step

BODILY GRACE AND EMOTIONAL RESTRAINT IN BALI IS TAUGHT EARLY IN CHILDHOOD THROUGH THE DISCIPLINE OF RITUAL DANCE.

toward more refined methods of demonstrating the relationships among child-rearing practices, personality development, and other aspects of culture.

As part of the effort to more precisely demonstrate the relationship of personality development to other aspects of culture, Beatrice Whiting and others compared childhood in six cultures, including the United States (1963). The study's basic thesis was that personality emerges in response both to a society's economic and social arrangements, including division of labor and residence patterns, and to the cultural values reflected in its child-rearing patterns.

psychological anthropology A specialization in cultural anthropology that seeks to understand the relation between psychological processes and cultural practices.

to learn. If they imitate an adult activity, however, they will be encouraged to continue it and help their elders. Children are not encouraged to ask questions, which is considered in-

AS A WAY OF ADAPTING TO A HARSH ENVIRONMENT, INUIT CHILDREN ARE TAUGHT TO BE AUTONOMOUS AT AN EARLY AGE.

terfering and aggressive. Rather, when confronted with a problem situation, they are expected to observe closely, to reason, and to find solutions independently. They watch, practice, and are then tested, frequently by adults' asking them questions. In this way, they learn to think for themselves.

For example, when traveling on the featureless, snow-covered tundra, an adult may ask a child, "Where are we?" "Have you ever been here before?" "In what direction is the town?" (Briggs 1991:270). Children will not be given the correct answer but will have to figure it out for themselves. This technique is also applied to social relationships. When company arrives, a child will be asked, "Who is this person to you?" "Where [in this room] is your mother's sister?" This mode of training accustoms children to thinking in terms of problems to be solved. It also habituates them to

setting problems for themselves, as practice in learning the correct answers.

A key Inuit child-training technique is setting problems for the child to solve within the context of "play." The play often tests the limits of things—objects, people, situations—and provides an opportunity to learn the consequences of various actions. In early childhood, both boys and girls play with material objects by taking them apart and trying to put them back together, sometimes unsuccessfully. This develops careful attention to detail, to noting relationships among details, to patient trial and error, and to a mental recording of results for future reference. Children experience a great deal of autonomy to experiment without fear of sanction, other than the real sanctions imposed by the materials themselves.

The emphasis on experiential learning means that Inuit children are less physically restrained or verbally reprimanded than children in many other cultures. Compared to American middle-class mothers, for example, Inuit mothers are more willing to permit a child to experiment with potentially harmful behavior so that the child learns not to repeat it. Inuit do not consider it helpful to learning for one person to try to persuade others, influence their actions, criticize them, suggest alternatives, or question motives. Social control among the Inuit is indirect. Children are taught to anticipate the needs of others and fulfill them without being asked to do so, and to passively but firmly resist others' encroaching on them.

In addition to being physically adept and independent, Inuit children must learn to be cooperative and emotionally restrained. Under the conditions of their closely knit and often isolated camp life, expressions of anger or aggression are strongly avoided. The Inuit consider maturity as the exercise of reason, judgment, and emotional control, and it is thought to grow naturally as children grow. The Inuit

Oedipus complex Defined by Freud as the sexual attachment of a male child to his mother, accompanied by hatred and jealousy of the father.

matrilineal A rule that affiliates a person to kin of both sexes related through females only.

incest taboos Prohibitions on sexual relations between relatives.

I N   T H E   F I E L D

ETHNOGRAPHY

PRESCHOOLS IN JAPAN, CHINA, AND THE UNITED STATES

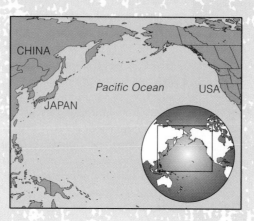

With the world growing more technologically and informationally complex, schooling in industrialized societies now begins earlier than in the past. Preschool is becoming a widespread educational institution. Preschools, like other transmitters of culture, both reflect and stimulate change in the societies in which they operate. In the following cross-cultural comparison, we see some of the similarities and differences in preschool philosophies and practices found in Japan, the United States, and China in the mid-1980s. It will be interesting to see how preschools respond to the economic and social changes that have taken place in China since the late 1980s, as individual initiative becomes a more important part of the economy and pressure continues for democratization, both inside and outside the country.

The enculturation practices of China and Japan, which put more emphasis on the group than does the culture of the United States, are nevertheless very different from each other. This should give us pause before we make generalizations about the "East" versus the "West." These comparative enculturation studies are also an important corrective to Western psychological theories that emphasize separation from the family and individuation of the self as central to psychological well-being and mature adult personality. With some notable exceptions (see Roland 1988), the Western psychological yardstick of individuation is the one against which other cultures are often judged and found wanting.

Increasing numbers of children are being enrolled in preschools in Japan, China, and the United States. In China, preschools provide an alternative child-rearing process for the single-child family, which the Chinese believe results in "spoiling" children. In Japan, where families are becoming smaller, urban middle-class Japanese families believe that preschools help their children learn to function as part of a group, which is central to being human in Japanese culture. Preschools now enroll almost 95 percent of four-year-olds in Tokyo. In the United States, the increase in preschool attendance is a response to the growing number of working mothers, the high divorce rate, and the concerns of single-parent families. In New York City, 60 percent of four-year-olds attend preschool.

In a methodologically unique study, researchers Joseph Tobin, David Wu, and Dana Davidson sought to uncover the connections among preschool, enculturation, and cultural values. They used ethnography, interviews, videotaping, and parent, teacher, and administrator responses to the videotapes of their own and other schools. Often the responses of members of one culture to the videotapes of the preschool in another culture were most useful in clarifying both the overlaps in cultural values and the most significant contrasts.

Japanese teachers, parents, and preschool administrators have a clear idea of the cultural values they are trying to impart. Among the most important are empathy, gentleness, social consciousness, kindness, cooperativeness, obedience, enthusiasm, energy, liveliness, and perseverance. But values more often associated with the West, such as independence, individuality, and creativity, are also considered important. These values also find a place, albeit a less important one, in the Japanese preschool.

One way in which Japanese preschools teach empathy and compassion is by encouraging the older children to help smaller children, and even infants (where an infant day care center is attached to the preschool). As one administrator said, "[This] is . . . important for the older children because it gives them a chance to experience what it feels like to take care of another person . . . to develop empathy and to learn to know and anticipate the needs of another" (p. 34).

Responsiveness to a group is also taught by emphasizing student-student, rather than student-teacher, interactions. This is facilitated by larger classes and a higher student-teacher ratio than in the United States. For Japanese preschool teachers and administrators, a large (to Americans) class size (of around 30 children for one teacher) better reflects the complexity of the outer world and gives each child a chance to deal with a wider diversity of children and situations. As one Japanese educator commented about the American preschool, "I understand how this . . . small class size can help young children become very self-reliant and independent. But [there seems] something kind of sad or lonely about a class that size. Don't American teachers worry that children may become too independent? I wonder how you teach a child to become a member of a group in a class that small?" For preschool teachers in Japan, this emphasis on "groupism" makes possible the fullest expression of what it means to be human: the experience of camaraderie, and of unity with something larger than the self.

Another way in which Japanese preschools encode Japanese values is through their handling of children who misbehave. Both Americans and Chinese watching the videotape of the Japanese preschool were concerned about the misbehavior of a boy named Hiroki. He "disrupted" the class by shouting out answers to all the teacher's questions; he poked, pushed, and punched the other children; he prevented the children from cleaning up after an activity by throwing their materials off the porch. The class teacher did not "punish" Hiroki in any way. She did not tell him to stop doing any of the things he was doing. When a child came inside the school to tell her about Hiroki's behavior, she suggested that the child find ways of dealing with Hiroki herself. Both the teacher and school administrator believed that their method—ignoring Hiroki's behavior—was the most effective way to deal with him. It also encouraged the other children to feel that it was their responsibility, as members of the group, to help Hiroki correct his behavior. Japanese preschool teachers take great care not to isolate a disruptive child from the group by singling him out for punishment or censure or excluding him from a group activity. Whenever possible, they avoid direct confrontations with children. Indeed, as noted earlier, teachers try to limit any kind of intense interaction with the children on a one-to-one basis.

The treatment of Hiroki contrasts significantly with the way "disruptive" children are treated in American and Chinese preschools and elicited condemnation by both Americans and Chinese viewing the Japanese videotape. Despite the American emphasis on "freedom" in preschool enculturation, there are strict rules and clear limits on acceptable behavior. One of the rules is "no fighting." American teachers intervene in disputes and fights, encouraging children to resolve conflict by verbalizing their feelings instead of hitting.

In the American preschool, when two boys, Mike and Stu, were fighting over blocks, the teacher separated the boys with her arms. After getting each boy to tell his side of the argument, the teacher said, "Let's not have any fighting; Mike, can you tell Stu what you want with words instead of grabbing? . . . Stu, when Mike took the block from you, how did you feel? Did you tell him that made you angry? Did you feel angry?" (p. 152). The teacher gave both children a chance to "explain" what had happened and how they felt about the conflict. This approach is consistent with the American emphasis on teaching children to express their needs and feelings, and the importance of words for social as well as cognitive development.

In another case, a child, Kerry, would not put away the toys he had played with. After repeated exhortations, the teacher kneeled down, put her face directly in front of his, and repeated her command to clean up his blocks. She reminded Kerry that each child is responsible for cleaning up toys they use. When Kerry still refused, the teacher made him sit on the "time-out" chair to "think about it until you are ready to clean up."

The "legalistic" and verbal emphasis in the American preschool was perceived

ENCULTURATION IN JAPAN, IN BOTH FORMAL AND INFORMAL SETTINGS, EMPHASIZES THE IMPORTANCE OF THE PEER GROUP AS A WAY FOR CHILDREN TO LEARN EMPATHY, COOPERATION, SELF-DISCIPLINE, AND CONCERN FOR THE GROUP. PRESCHOOL AND ELEMENTARY SCHOOL TEACHERS IN JAPAN TRY NOT TO INTERFERE IN CHILDREN'S PLAY AND CONFLICTS, LETTING THEM WORK OUT SOLUTIONS ON THEIR OWN.

negatively by both the Chinese and the Japanese videotape viewers, but for somewhat different reasons. Chinese viewers felt that the American teacher should have intervened in a more authoritarian fashion, telling a misbehaving child "forcefully that that kind of behavior is unacceptable and just will not be tolerated." Japanese teachers tended to feel that the American teachers intervened too much and that the long conversations about feelings "were too heavy handed."

What emerged from this study of Chinese preschool practices in the mid-1980s was an emphasis on both socialist ideology and modernizing the Chinese economy. Teachers and administrators articulated principles of control, collectivity, selflessness, and comradeship as the main values children need to learn. In short, they reflected an ideology that holds social responsibility as more important than individual pleasure. Unlike the Japanese and the Americans, the Chinese teachers and administrators also explicitly emphasized the government's responsibility for protecting children's health, hygiene, and physical well-being. Thus, the Chinese provide "whole care boarding schools" for young children whose mothers work at night, as well as daytime preschools.

Much of the Chinese criticism of the American and Japanese preschools was based on the Chinese view that children must develop a commitment to the nation's good and not merely their own individual happiness. Chinese preschool officials look with great disapproval on the tendency of Chinese parents to "spoil" their children—making them weak, willful, and bad-tempered by "coddling them too much." Chinese preschool administrators and teachers applied the terms "spoiled" and "selfish" to what they considered the intolerable behavior of Hiroki in Japan and Kerry in the United States. The Chinese are particularly concerned about "spoiling" because of the

large number of single-child families, a result of China's stringent population control policies. Thus, preschools in China, more than in Japan and particularly the United States, see their job as "correcting" bad influences that the family may have on a child.

The Chinese view "order" and "governing" as very important preschool tasks. Even more than the Japanese, the Chinese expressed disapproval of the American teacher's "punishing" Kerry by making him take a "time out." The Chinese teachers gave voice to a philosophy that emphasizes controlling children before they misbehave, or as one teacher put it, "before they even know they are about to misbehave."

The idea of preventing serious deviance by monitoring others' behavior and stepping in before deviance becomes serious is central in Chinese culture (Bracey 1985). Teachers place great importance on molding children's behavior through verbal comparison and praise. For example, in getting children ready for supper,

a teacher said, "Now let's see. Who is sitting properly? How about Chen Ling—is he sitting properly? Who knows what is wrong with the way he is sitting? Should he be fiddling with his hands? Look at Lin Ping. Is she sitting nicely? See how straight her back is. See how she has her hands behind her back?"

Chinese teachers, more like the Americans and less like the Japanese, also believe that a teacher should intervene immediately when children misbehave. Chinese preschool teachers see their main task as controlling children's behavior, calmly, consistently, and without anger. The emphasis is less on punishing bad behavior than on explaining, modeling, and praising desirable behavior. For the Chinese, the best way to ensure desirable behavior in children is for a teacher to "take charge" in a classroom, providing order and structure, so that the child will internalize control and not experience it as imposed from the outside (p. 95). Both the traditional Chinese values of Confucianism and contemporary Chinese po-

believe that children have both the ability and the wish to learn. Educating a child thus consists of providing the necessary information, which sooner or later the child will remember. Scolding is seen as futile. Children will learn when they are ready; there is no point in forcing children to learn something before they are ready to remember it. Inuit elders consider it demeaning to do "serious battle" with a child; for an adult to express anger shows a lack of judgment. They also believe that frequent scolding makes a child hostile, rebellious, and impervious to the opinions of others. Constraints and sanctions are subtle and nonpunitive.

Inuit child rearing is directed at adjusting to a close-knit, traditionally isolated world in which survival depends on cooperation, calmness, innovative problem solving, visual and spatial acuity, and physical dexterity in a phys-

ically demanding environment. Child rearing in China, Japan, and the United States, described in the Ethnography box above, is quite different. In these societies, child-rearing practices are geared to the social, economic, and political conditions of life in socially, technologically, and informationally complex societies. These societies are integrated into a global economy, characterized by economic specialization, social stratification, and a high premium on conformity.

COMING OF AGE IN CROSS-CULTURAL PERSPECTIVE

All cultures have changing expectations of an individual at different points in the life course, as new capacities unfold or diminish. At each

litical ideology emphasize that character is shaped by experience and that teachers bear an important responsibility in inculcating self-restraint and correct behavior in children.

American and Japanese comments were very critical of the Chinese preschools, which parents and teachers found "overly regimented." One example was the practice of having all the children go to the bathroom together, boys lined up on one side, girls on the other. They were particularly appalled at the Chinese "whole boarding school" for young children. The Chinese, however, view these practices not as harsh treatment, but as expressions of care and concern. They responded to American criticism by asking how, in the absence of boarding schools, Americans take care of children whose mothers work at night?

The many differences in preschool policies and practices in Japan, China, and the United States are based on fundamentally different cultural values. These values concern the nature of children, the importance of the mother-child bond, and the social value of the group in relation to the individual. The belief of many Americans that children belong exclusively to their parents, in nuclear family homes, is not shared by the Japanese and Chinese. However, they attach different cultural values to "groupism" and teach group orientation in different ways and with different outcomes. The Chinese believe that selflessness and collectivism are best taught outside the family, by the school. For the Japanese, too, preschool should teach children sensitivity to the needs of the group, but it also provides opportunities for children to develop playfulness and imagination. American parents, too, cite "getting along in a group" as an important aim of preschool. However, they are much more concerned with the intellectual and creative development and happiness of the individual child. They expect these to be the focus of preschool policies and practices.

As formal educational institutions expand in these three cultures, and in other societies around the world, anthropologists are increasingly studying the ways children are enculturated outside the home, as well as within it.

Critical Thinking Questions

1. What values are emphasized in the American preschool, and how are these values taught?
2. What are the most important value contrasts between China, Japan, and the United States, as viewed through their preschools?
3. How does child rearing in each of these cultures differ from that of the Inuit?

Source: Adapted from Joseph J. Tobin, David Y. H. Wu, and Dana H. Davidson, *Preschool in Three Cultures: Japan, China, and the United States.* New Haven: Yale University Press, 1989.

of these points, individuals learn what is necessary for the new roles associated with these changing expectations. The cultural learning that takes place in childhood is particularly important, but the teaching and learning of culture continues throughout life.

Adolescence, like childhood, is culturally variable in its recognition as a distinct stage of life. In the United States, adolescence is associated with the physiological changes of puberty; in other societies, adolescence, as a socially constructed stage of life, is not recognized. One important contribution of Margaret Mead's classic study, *Coming of Age in Samoa* (1928/1971), was her finding that the idealism, psychic conflict, and rebellion against authority that Americans view as an inevitable part of adolescence did not occur in Samoa. Rather, in Samoa, as in many societies, an individual's transition from childhood to adulthood involved a gradually increasing participation in society, with little psychological trauma.

WWW In many societies, although the stage of adolescence is not recognized, the passage of children into adulthood is marked by rituals. In spite of their cross-cultural variability, these are often categorized together as **initiation rituals,** or coming of age.

MALE INITIATION RITUALS

Beginning with the work of Arnold van Gennep on rites of passage (1960), initiation rituals have attracted much anthropological attention.

initiation ritual A ritual that marks the passage from childhood to adult status.

Van Gennep viewed **rites of passage** as a way of publicly and ceremonially acknowledging a change of social roles, or a passage from one social group to another. These rites were performed at important life crises, such as puberty, marriage, and death. Their function was to reduce the traumatic effects of such transitions both on the society and on the individual by formalizing and ceremonializing them.

Most subsequent anthropological studies focused on the sociological and psychological causes or functions of male initiation. Sociological theories held that male initiation rites primarily expressed and affirmed the enduring order of male relationships and male solidarity. In some societies, they also served to culturally validate male dominance. The most obvious purpose of the rites appeared to be the legitimation of a change of status from child to adult. They often involved an extended period of separation, during which the initiates learned the beliefs, skills, and knowledge necessary to participating as a functioning adult in society. Thus, another function of the rites was the transmission of culture. The social order was reinforced by dramatizing its values in a public context. By taking the child out of the home, initiation rites emphasized the importance of citizenship. An individual was responsible to the whole society, and society as well as the family had an interest in him (Hart 1967).

There are several different psychological theories of male initiation. The Freudian view is based on the Oedipus complex. Initiation rituals are seen as a symbolic means of mastering the universal conflicts generated by boys' identification with their mothers, from whom they must be separated in order to carry out their male adult responsibilities. Evidence for this theory can be found in the work of John Whiting, who showed that male initiation rites are more likely to occur in cultures where there is a strong identification of the boy with his mother and hostility toward the father (Whiting, Kluckhohn, and Anthony, 1967). This may

grow out of sleeping arrangements in which children sleep with the mother apart from the father. In these cases, says Whiting, male initiation rites are necessary to ensure the development of an adequate male role.

Other psychological theories of male initiation rites, particularly those involving bloodletting, explain the rites as symbolic reactions by males to their envy of female procreative ability and the mother-son bond (see, for example, Bettelheim 1962/1996). Margaret Mead noted that male initiation rites frequently involved men ritualizing birth and taking over, as a collective group, the functions women perform naturally. Gilbert Herdt (1981) described the male initiation rites of the Sambia of New Guinea in terms of men's symbolic control over the rebirth of boys, making them into men. Viewed from this perspective, male initiation is a type of fertility cult in which men celebrate and ritually reproduce their control over the fertility of crops, animals, and humans. Particularly in New Guinea, fertility is frequently a male as well as female principle.

Whatever the underlying psychodynamics, male initiation rituals clearly have an important sociological role in moving young people from childhood to adulthood. Radcliffe-Brown (1956), for example, viewed the ordeals, taboos, and solemnity of these rites as essential to communicating the seriousness of life and its duties to the initiates. The sociological and psychological features of initiation rites complement each other. Many are exemplified in the autobiography of a Maasai, Tepilit Ole Saitoti's account of his father's words to him at his own initiation (1986:66)

> "Tepilit, circumcision means a sharp knife cutting into the skin of the most sensitive part of your body. You must not budge; don't move a muscle or even blink. You can face only one direction until the operation is completed. The slightest movement on your part will mean you are a coward, incompetent and unworthy to be a Maasai man. Ours has always been a proud family, and we would like to keep it that way. We will not tolerate unnecessary embarrassment, so you had better be ready.

---

rite of passage A ritual that marks a person's transition from one status to another.

"If you are not, tell us now so that we will not proceed. Imagine yourself alone remaining uncircumcised like the water youth [white people]. I hear they are not circumcised. Such a thing is not known in Maasailand; therefore, circumcision will have to take place even if it means holding you down until it is completed."

My father continued to speak and every one of us kept quiet. "The pain you will feel is symbolic. There is a deeper meaning in all this. Circumcision means a break between childhood and adulthood. For the first time in your life, you are regarded as a grownup, a complete man or woman. You will be expected to give and not just to receive. To protect the family always, not just to be protected yourself. And your wise judgment will for the first time be taken into consideration. No family affairs will be discussed without your being consulted. If you are ready for all these responsibilities, tell us now. Coming into manhood is not simply a matter of growth and maturity. It is a heavy load on your shoulders and especially a burden on the mind. Too much of this—I am done. I have said all I wanted to say. Fellows, if you have anything to add, go ahead and tell your brother, because I am through. I have spoken."

FEMALE INITIATION

The general ethnographic neglect of female initiation rites results partly from androcentric bias (a focus by males on male activities) and partly from the definition of initiation rites as group activities (Lutkehaus and Roscoe 1995). Puberty rituals for girls, generally performed for individuals at their **menarche** (first menstruation), have largely been excluded from anthropological description and theory. In fact, however, such rites occur in more societies than male initiation rites. Recent research on girls' coming of age rituals indicates much cross-cultural variability (Lutkehaus and Roscoe 1995). Sometimes the initiate is isolated from society; sometimes she is the center of attention. Some rituals are elaborate and take years to perform; others are performed with little ceremony.

Welsh/The Gamma Liaison Network

DURING INITIATION, ELDERS IMPART TO YOUNG PEOPLE IMPORTANT INFORMATION THAT WILL ALLOW THEM TO PARTICIPATE AS RESPONSIBLE ADULTS IN THEIR SOCIETY. FEMALE INITIATIONS GENERALLY INVOLVE LESS EMOTIONAL TRAUMA THAN MALE INITIATIONS. FEMALE INITIATIONS THAT INCLUDE CIRCUMCISION, HOWEVER, CAN BE VERY PAINFUL AND HAVE ADVERSE LIFELONG EFFECTS ON HEALTH AND SEXUAL FUNCTIONING.

Several interpretations have been offered for girls' initiation rites. Judith Brown (1965) found that such rites are more likely to occur in societies in which the young girl continues to live in her mother's home after marriage. This suggests that the rites are a way of publicly announcing a girl's status change, because she will spend her adult life in the same place as she spent her childhood. Although the girl may continue to do the same kind of tasks she did as a child, she now has to do them as a responsible adult. The rites are thus the means by which the girl publicly accepts her new legal role. As with boys, girls' initiation rites also teach them what they will need to know as adults. Bemba women explain their elaborate girls' initiation rite called Chisungu (Richards 1956:125) by saying that they "make the girls clever." The word they use means "to be intelligent and socially competent and to have a knowledge of etiquette."

menarche A girl's first menstruation.

Many of the older analytical frameworks of male initiation—transmission of cultural skills and traditions, the social importance of publicly moving individuals from one social status to another, and the channeling of sexuality into adult reproduction—are also relevant to female initiation. Female rites, however, are most productively analyzed on their own terms. Feminist anthropology, along with the current anthropological interest in women's bodies and reproductive experiences as sources of power as well as subordination, has given girls' initiation rites a new ethnographic and theoretical prominence.

Recent ethnography in New Guinea suggests that although girls' initiation rites are individual, they are connected to the larger social whole. These connections are seen in the ritual's sponsors, public observation of the rituals, and the meanings the rituals have as metaphors for other cultural patterns. In addition to making cultural statements about what it means to move from girlhood to womanhood, female initiation rites may also make more general cultural statements about gender and gender relations. Many female initiation rites in New Guinea suggest the complementarity of male and female, rather than male dominance and antagonism between the sexes. In acknowledging gender difference, initiation rites for males and females may convey the message that both male and female powers and potentialities are necessary for social reproduction—that each sex is dependent on the other to complete its personhood and make its contribution, as a father or a mother, to society. Thus, the sexual symbolism of girls' initiation rites may refer not only to male/female sexual relations and biological reproduction, but also to the reproduction of society.

The New Guinea studies also emphasize that initiation rites—for females as well as males—are processual; that is, they move individuals through successive stages of life. Among the Murik, a girl's transition to adulthood does not end with a puberty rite. Rather, the puberty rite is just one ritual step in a series of rites celebrating reproduction, culminating in marriage and the birth of the first child.

Analysis of female initiation provides new insights into the ritual manipulation of the body that is often central to these ceremonies. As expressed in Saitoti's (1986) description of Maasai male initiation rites, the usual explanation of the emotional and symbolic significance of these often painful and traumatic transformations—ordeals, scarification, circumcision, infibulation—is that they are a test of the initiate's preparation for adulthood, and the permanent signs of the initiate's change of status. This emphasis, derived mainly from male initiation, overlooks the importance in body manipulation of the association among sexuality, beauty, and power. In some cultures, like those in New Guinea, this is a prominent theme in both female and male initiation. The attention to the body is not just for health, but also to enhance the beauty and sexual attractiveness of the initiate to members of the opposite sex.

This bodily attractiveness is one form of female power, manifest in procreation. Other forms of power are displayed in female initiation rites as well. Among the Manam of New Guinea, the exchange of valuables plays an important role in female initiation. In the Manam girl's initiation rite, the initiate displays the wealth her parents and clan have contributed for the event, which significantly influences later bridewealth negotiations. The wealth displayed in the initiation rite also affects the social reputation of the kin group who sponsors it.

This recent attention to girls' initiation not only deepens our understanding of cultural worldviews and symbolic meanings within cultures, but also suggests new directions for theorizing about an old topic of cross-cultural interest.

COLLEGE AND COMING OF AGE IN THE UNITED STATES

In contrast to many of the world's societies, American culture does not include a formal initiation ceremony through which young people pass from childhood to adulthood. Nevertheless, some cultural practices signify maturity, and some cultural contexts have particular significance for the transition from youth to

AMONG THE MIDDLE CLASS IN THE UNITED STATES, COLLEGE IS AN IMPORTANT ARENA FOR "COMING OF AGE." DURING A STUDENT'S COLLEGE YEARS, INFORMAL INTERACTION AMONG PEERS IS AS IMPORTANT FOR THE TRANSITION TO ADULTHOOD AS THE FORMAL ACADEMIC PROGRAM AND THE CLASSROOM. THE INFORMALITY OF COMING OF AGE FOR COLLEGE STUDENTS IN THE UNITED STATES CONTRASTS WITH THE FORMAL RITUAL OF COMING OF AGE FOR MALES IN MANY CULTURES. IN THE JEWISH RELIGION, A BOY BECOMES A MAN AT 13 YEARS OF AGE, SIGNIFIED BY THE BAR MITZVAH. AFTER THIS COMING OF AGE CEREMONY, A YOUNG MAN MAY PARTICIPATE IN PRAYERS AT THE SYNAGOGUE AND IN RITUALS FOR THE DEAD.

adulthood. Michael Moffatt's study *Coming of Age in New Jersey* (1989), whose title is modeled on Margaret Mead's famous work in Samoa, suggests that for the American middle class, coming of age may take place in college. Students experience the maturing process as a set of stages, corresponding with the freshman, sophomore, junior, and senior years. College freshmen are seen as foolish and inexperienced, sophomores as "wild men—and women," juniors as having outgrown the juvenile behavior of the college dorm, and seniors as "burnt out," "tired of college," and anxious about the future.

Moffatt found that students attributed their growing maturity in college to the formal and informal learning experiences of undergraduate life. Most important were the social skills they acquired in informal social interaction with other students. An essential skill transmitted through college culture was the ability to take responsibility for oneself. With teachers, guidance counselors, and parents no longer monitoring behavior, and with much more free time, a more flexible schedule, and many more distractions and activities available, students had to make their own decisions about how to allocate their time between work and play.

Another important learning experience for these students was negotiating the complexities of an impersonal university bureaucracy. This experience built skills of persistence and determination that they believed would be very useful in the "real world." And although the students Moffatt studied did not have culturally diverse friendship groups, for many, college was their first experience with any cultural diversity at all. Students believed that their ability to get along in such a diverse environment was an important social skill and contributed to their becoming mature adults.

The college experience is not the same for all students; indeed, it has different outcomes for men and women. And, of course, not all youths in the United States go to college. But Moffatt's study indicates that for students who do attend college away from home right after high school, these four years give some structure to the coming of age process.

LEARNING CULTURE IN ADULTHOOD

All cultures have expectations of adulthood. Although the personality traits and abilities of a mature, socially acceptable person may differ among cultures, becoming an adult in every society involves competence in making a living. In nonindustrialized societies, many of these competencies are learned in childhood and carry over to adult life. In industrialized societies, with their extreme occupational specialization, much cultural learning takes place "on the job." This cultural learning may involve not only new behaviors and skills, but also a new set of attitudes and values. Some occupations are more transforming in this respect than others. One occupational subculture that has persistently attracted attention because of its transformative effect on adult identity and behavior is police work.

In a book aptly titled *Danger, Duty, and Disillusion,* anthropologist Joan Barker (1999) describes the occupational socialization of police officers in the Los Angeles Police Department. As police officers learn their job, their behaviors, their identities, their values, their perceptions of the job, and their concerns change in consistent and predictable ways. As with the transmission of culture in general, not all of what officers are formally taught is learned (that is, incorporated and internalized), and much of what they learn is not formally taught. Though the physical and social environment of the Los Angeles Police Department is quite remote from that of the Inuit, there are some similarities in the perception of the social environment as a dangerous place requiring specific attitudinal and behavioral skills. Like the Inuit, the Los Angeles police perceive their environment as one in which, to survive, they must be calm, bold, and innovative problem solvers, able to defuse conflict.

AN IMPORTANT ASPECT OF POLICE ENCULTURATION IS LEARNING HOW TO PROJECT AUTHORITY WHILE DEFUSING POTENTIALLY DANGEROUS SITUATIONS.

Los Angeles police officers, like those of most large inner-city forces, are formally trained in a Police Academy that explicitly teaches, tests, and evaluates their ability in police functions. Requirements for success include rigorous physical training, respect for authority, and the ability to interact collegially with peers, who will rely on them in dangerous situations.

During and after their Police Academy training, police officers learn to regard their inner-city beats as very dangerous places. In their formal academy training, they are exposed to classes, lectures by experienced street officers, and video presentations of cops being injured or killed on the job. This training teaches cadets strategies for minimizing the risk of injury and death. They learn the police style of driving, the appropriate use of weapons, combat methods, and means of restraint—such as maintaining distance and using the baton or gas—that lower the potential for danger to themselves and their partners. Equally important is academy training in "command presence"—a quality of authority, confidence, and competence whose purpose is to defuse potentially dangerous situations and minimize physical risks.

Once on the street, the rookie's informal education in police work becomes very important. Police learn informally through observing, listening to, and socializing with fellow officers and veteran cops. Developing the attitudes and behaviors of a cop, as opposed to the worldview and conduct of "civilians" (nonpolice), is viewed by the police as perhaps the most vital factor in reaching appropriate police decisions that have life and death consequences. Imitating the actions of veteran street police and listening to their "war stories," jokes, and gossip, both "on the watch" and in after-hours socializing, become essential instruments of education. Police officers cannot be trained for every potential conflict. Successful decision making depends on their acquiring a "police mentality" that will instinctively lead officers to handle situations in a predictable police manner upon which their fellow officers can rely.

As they stay longer and mature on the job, police officers internalize police definitions and perceptions of the world that contrast with those of the general public, including their spouses and nonpolice friends. These contrasting worldviews may become a source of conflict with others not on the force. This transformation of attitudes distances them from nonpolice contacts and frequently imperils their marriages, but it is viewed as an essential job requirement without which their safety on the streets, and that of their partners, cannot be ensured.

During their careers, many police officers move from the inner cities to suburbs populated largely by other law enforcement personnel. Their homes often become fortresses guarded by fences, dogs, and expensive security devices. Their social lives increasingly revolve around their fellow officers, who understand that police scheduling may account for a wife's appearance at a party without her officer husband or his absence from a child's school play. Socializing with other police officers means that there are no hostile questions to field about allegations of police brutality. It allows officers to discuss in supportive intimacy such police-related problems as lawsuits by the public, lack of support from police administration, their disillusion and frustration with a criminal justice system that they perceive as "putting the bad guys back out on the street," the difficulty of marriage to nonpolice spouses, the problem of making ends meet without moonlighting, and concerns over pension losses and retirement.

Retirement among the police, as among other workers in industrial societies, is significantly associated with financial concerns. Like other workers, too, retiring police must deal with emotional issues involving definitions of self. They need to learn not only new behaviors but new attitudes, as they move from the social status of police officer, which has been such an essential part of their lives, to the status of "retired person." Police officers often retire at a relatively young age, as high pension benefits are earned after 25 years on the job. For those in other jobs, who remain in the workforce longer, retirement is also problematical because of its association with aging.

OLD AGE

Aging is a universal human experience. Like other stages in the human life course, aging involves both biological and cultural factors. Old age as a stage in human life is culturally variable, as is the very construction of life stages itself (Keith et al. 1994:323). Individuals learn to understand, enter, and adjust to old age within a matrix of cultural meanings. These meanings are shaped by the material and social conditions of a society and by the specific circumstances of individual lives.

The cultural values of a society are represented by symbols through which aging is experienced. In the United States, for example, the cultural themes of the glorification of youth, competitive self-reliance, and action orientation are expressed in many media images. Nearly 30 years ago, J. Scott Francher (1973) called attention to the role of advertising, particularly the "Pepsi Generation" ads, in purveying images that implicitly denigrate the old. These values continue to be perpetuated through a focus on youth and consumerism, as in the Nike Corporation's "Just Do It" campaign of the 1990s (Sokolovsky 1997:Introduction). With the demographic increase in older age groups, however, more advertising is now aimed at older Americans, ranging from body products that inhibit aging to travel and leisure opportunities. Even as earlier negative images of aging are changing, however, the

MEDICAL ANTHROPOLOGY

Over the past century many branches of medicine have made important advances in preventing disease and improving health care. Yet the modern medical model has serious limitations in dealing with health issues in different cultures and among different ethnic, racial, and class populations in the United States (Helman 1991/1998). Medical anthropology is the study of how people in different cultures and social groups explain the causes of ill health, the meanings they attach to it, the types of treatments they believe in, and whom they turn to when they become ill.

Medical anthropologists adapt the holistic and ethnographic approaches of anthropology to the study of both emotional and physical illnesses in complex societies. Modern biomedicine tends to regard "diseases" as universal entities, regardless of their contexts. Anthropologists have shown, however, that individuals' personality, life experiences, social class, family networks, religion, and culturally patterned fears and health beliefs are a necessary addition to the diagnostic technologies and physiological measurements used by the medical profession. In the early 1960s, medical schools began hiring anthropologists—mainly in departments of psychiatry, behavioral sciences, community and family medicine, community health, and mental health programs—as did international agencies implementing health and development programs in Third World countries. In the later 1970s and 1980s, anthropologists became a part of the Centers for Disease Control, the World Health Organization, U.S. state and municipal health departments, hospitals, private for-profit and not-for-profit health-oriented foundations, research institutes, and similar organizations. More recently, the many challenges to mainstream medicine have provided new openings for medical anthropologists, particularly in AIDS-related organizations (Schensul 1997).

According to medical anthropologist and activist Stephen Schensul (1997), medical anthropologists do much more than provide broad social, cultural and political perspectives on health and health-care institutions. They contribute a unique understanding of the real and potential sociocultural and sociopolitical divisions between medical service providers and their clientele. They provide a data collection methodology emphasizing participant interaction and interviewing, both within communities served by medical institutions and in those medical institutions themselves. Finally, they use their results to improve medical programs from within, increasing a community's ability to make positive changes in the health programs that serve them.

As Schensul suggests, anthropologists are increasingly analyzing the sites and subcultures of the medical profession itself, illuminating how these both influence and are influenced by larger cultural

---

connection of aging with loss, abandonment, and death remains as a negative association with this stage of life.

This association is not universal. In many nonindustrial and economically underdeveloped societies, death is not uniquely associated with old age. In these societies, the human life span is shorter, and death is associated with infant mortality, childhood diseases, and accidents and sickness in adulthood, rather than with old age. Ironically, the association of old age and death in the United States is partly a result of scientific advances that have lengthened the life span. Under these conditions, old age becomes associated with the long dying process or mental deterioration of such "modern" diseases as hypertension, cancer, coronary heart disease, and senility, diseases that are almost absent in some simpler societies.

It is important, however, not to romanticize aging in more traditional societies. In many societies, age itself is not so much a basis for authority or respect; rather, it is whether age brings with it or expands control over resources and knowledge, great accomplishments, or the accumulation of descendants (Counts and Counts 1985:261). In almost all societies, the experience of growing old and the treatment of the elderly are to a large extent dependent on their ability to function productively in society and the availability of resources to care for them. Nor can we stereotype aging in the

patterns. Recently, for example, Sharon R. Kaufman (2000) examined the special facilities for the (seemingly) terminally comatose. Her study explored how the available technology and the specialist medical personnel associated with keeping alive persons in a vegetative state are transforming the concept of the person in American culture.

Even more than physical illness, anthropology has long had an interest in the cultural aspects of emotional disturbance. Jules Henry's brilliant analysis of families with autistic children in *Pathways to Madness* (1973); the collection *Cultural Illness and Health,* edited by Laura Nader and Thomas Maretzki (1973); the pathbreaking holistic study of ghost possession, "The Psychomedical Case History of a Low-Caste Woman of North India," by anthropologists Ruth and Stanley Freed (1985); and the cross-cultural study *Culture and Depression* by Arthur Kleinman and Byron Good (1985) are among the many anthropological contributions to our understanding of mental health and transcultural psychiatry.

In keeping with this interest, as well as newer, more critical anthropological approaches (see Scheper-Hughes 1994), the socialization and training of psychiatric practitioners has recently been the subject of anthropological scrutiny. In a new book, *Of Two Minds: The Growing Disorder in American Psychiatry,* anthropologist Tanya Luhrmann (2000) illuminates the socialization of doctors who specialize in psychiatry in the United States. The major question that shapes psychiatric training is whether mental illnesses such as schizophrenia, depression, and personality disorders are a matter of biological dysfunction best treated pharmacologically, or whether they are the product of psychosocial factors such as family dynamics and early childhood experiences, and thus best treated by psychotherapy.

For anthropology, with its holistic emphasis on the interaction of biology, social relationships, and culture, this question is misdirected. But Lurhmann found that psychiatric training continues to take this either/or approach and that a psychiatric resident has to decide which camp he or she is in by the second year of residency. Once that decision is made, it has enormous implications for the image and treatment of emotional disturbance, not only within the psychiatric profession, but in the larger culture of the United States as well. As Luhrmann points out, the socialization and training of doctors does not occur in a political or economic vacuum. The aggressive marketing by Smith Kline and French of the antipsychotic drug Thorazine in 1954 helped to foster the biomedical approach to mental illness. Since then, managed health care companies, in their efforts to control costs, have severely cut back on psychotherapeutic treatment for the mentally ill, further reinforcing the biomedical approach.

United States as uniformly negative. In fact, about 39 percent of Americans over 65 say they are very happy, but only about 30 percent of people between 18 and 29 say the same thing. Furthermore, those over 65 are about twice as likely to be satisfied with their current financial status as younger people (Stark 1996:419–424).

Where aging is linked to physical decline, a decrease in productive participation in society, and a scarcity of material resources, it is experienced almost everywhere in negative terms—both by the elderly themselves and by the kin or communities who care for them. Thus, a culturally widespread concept is that of the elderly as a "burden." This occurs even in those societies where, unlike the United States, self-reliance or competitive individualism is not a central cultural value. In Japan, where integration and harmony within a group are valued over competitive independence, "becoming a burden" is a source of anxiety among the elderly. This concern arises not because of a generalized cultural fear of incurring obligations, but because of the anxiety of incurring obligations that cannot be reciprocated (Traphagan 1998).

One notable cultural exception to the perception of the very old as a "burden" is found among the Ju/'hoansi of Botswana (Sokolovsky 1997:5; Keith et al. 1994:330). Formerly foragers, the Ju/'hoansi are now mainly seden-

IN MANY SOCIETIES THE CULTURALLY VALUED INTEGRATION OF THE GENERATIONS PROVIDES A POSITIVE ENVIRONMENT FOR THE ELDERLY.

able-bodied, they forage, fetch water, visit, trade gifts, make crafts, dance, sleep, and eat whenever they choose. They live where they want. They do not have fears of pauperization or other anxieties about personal security, interpersonal violence, or abuse. They do not talk about loneliness, and express no desire to live alone. Even the extremely weak are not socially segregated. And all of this in an environment poor in material resources!

Indeed, cross-cultural ethnography reveals a painful paradox: On the one hand, postindustrial technologies have made productive participation in society less dependent on physical vigor and created health technologies that compensate for physical decline. On the other hand, the social and cultural processes attending these technological changes (sometimes called "modernization") have undermined the sources of social support and personal identity through which aging might be viewed in more positive terms (Keith et al. 1994:320).

tary pastoralists and agriculturalists. But their traditional values, particularly their ideology of sharing, remain largely intact. This provides a very positive context for the elderly, even those who are unable to care for themselves. Unlike many societies, among the Ju/'hoansi even the very frail elderly are not targets of ridicule, fear, or anxiety. Indeed, the physical changes of aging, such as declining sexuality, are a frequent subject of conversation and humor (Sokolovsky 1997:35). Although the Ju/'hoansi do link old age with physical decline, elders are also associated with special powers, life-giving activities, and important decision-making roles. This is particularly impressive because, as foragers without property, Ju/'hoansi elders lack the leverage of inheritance to exact compliance from their children.

Ju/'hoansi elders are independent and autonomous. They do what they like. If they are

DEATH AND DYING

To the extent that old age is associated with death, culturally variable attitudes toward dying and death shape attitudes toward the elderly. Many cultures believe that death is not the end of the person, but rather a passage from the world of the living to another world, or spirit realm. This belief offers an active role to the dead, as potential enemies or potential guardians. In the United States, the biomedical perspective is influential in shaping the belief that death is the result of human genetic structure. Nevertheless, American cultural patterns—most prominently, the avoidance of talking and thinking about death—indicate that mainstream American culture is uncomfortable with the idea that death means the end of all individual awareness. For example, honoring the wishes that a dead individual made in life suggests some ambivalence about "the ability of the dead to remain aware of what we, the living, are doing for them" (Kalish 1980:2).

Most cultures are much more explicit about their belief that death is but a transition from one social status to another. Like initiation and marriage, it is a "rite of passage" (van Gennep 1960). In many African societies, the communion between the dead and the living is essential in the social order. Among the indigenous peoples of Australia, the Dreamtime—that long ago time when the ancestors created all the things of the cosmos—is continually brought into the present through intense and elaborate rituals.

The attitude toward dying, the meanings it has for the dying person, and the behaviors imposed on the dying person and the survivors are significantly related to cultural beliefs about death. Among Hindus, beliefs in karma (fate) influence attitudes toward death and dying. Just as the quality of one's life is shaped by one's deeds in previous lives, so the quality of one's death is also believed to be affected by how well one has behaved in life. In contrast to the dominant American cultural pattern, where every effort is made to prolong life, even if that involves permanent, debilitating, and agonizing pain with little hope of cure, in India older persons are taught to prepare positively for death, and to prefer an early death to a long life of pain and suffering. Death is openly talked about among family members, and the acceptance of death's inevitability permits older people to prepare for it emotionally and spiritually (Vatuk 1990:82).

Islam imposes a number of very specific behavioral requirements on persons who know that death is imminent. They must ask forgiveness and forgive others. They must pay off their debts, arrange to have them paid by others, or ask creditors for forgiveness. They must make a will. They must take care of their bodies in certain ways, cleaning their teeth and bodies and putting on clean clothes. The dying person must recite the Quran, and remember God and ask his forgiveness. It is the responsibility of those nearby to remind the dying person of these duties, as well as to perform other duties at the moment of death (Muwahidi 1989:47).

The meaning of death, the proper behavior at death, and even the emotions at death are shaped by culture and transmitted as part of cultural learning. These patterns may be passed on by society's elders or, as in the United States,

become the charge of a specialized profession of funeral directors. In China, from late imperial times until the early twentieth century, the state took the initiative in setting proper norms for the death ritual and printing pamphlets that were disseminated throughout the empire. These instructions covered the correct ritual for commoners and for the elite. They included the correct procedure for public notification of death; the donning of mourning clothes by kin; ritualized bathing of the corpse; the provision of food, goods, and money to the deceased; the preparation of a soul tablet for the domestic altar; music to accompany the corpse and settle the spirit; the sealing of the corpse into an airtight coffin; and the expulsion of the corpse from the community.

A comparative perspective reveals a common cultural pattern surrounding death in nonindustrial and many non-Western cultures: However the dying person is treated, dying takes place within the social community. At the moment of death, if not during the dying process that preceded it, the community responds to death as a matter of public, not merely private, concern. Unlike the passive role assigned to kin in the United States, in other societies surviving kin take an active part in death rituals. The culturally patterned grief reactions and rituals that surround death are aimed at effectively consoling the bereaved persons closest to the deceased and toward reintegrating the society around the loss of the dead person.

Because in every society individuals build long-term, interdependent relationships that produce feelings of attachment and caring, the end of these relationships produces emotional distress and disorganization in every culture. Thus, in spite of cultural differences, there are some universal, or at least very widespread, individual and social reactions to death. In all cultures, people react to death by expressing emotions. Sadness, emptiness, fear, and anger are the most common, although the expression of these emotions differ.

The widespread cultural rituals of death and mourning have multiple functions. Death always raises issues concerning the obligations imposed on survivors: The corpse must be looked after. The deceased must be placed in a new status. The roles vacated by the deceased must be filled and their property disposed of. The solidarity of the group must be reaffirmed. The bereaved must be comforted and reestablished in their relationships to others. The meaning of death, the proper behavior at death, and the parallel shaping of emotional response are, like the cultural patterns involved in other life transitions and crises, transmitted and learned as part of becoming human in a particular culture.

SUMMARY

1. Developing into a fully functioning adult is the result of a complex interaction between universal human capacities and culturally variable child-rearing practices. Enculturation is the culturally specific ways in which human infants are reared to become functioning members of a particular sociocultural system.

2. Cultures differ in their understanding of the different phases of life development, beginning with when an infant or child becomes a social person.

3. Enculturation transmits the skills and knowledge of a culture and shapes the values, attitudes, and personality of the growing child.

4. Psychological anthropology uses ethnography and cross-cultural research to analyze how culture affects psychological processes such as cognition, emotions, personality, and concepts of the self.

5. In many societies, formal educational settings such as preschools are becoming more important in enculturation. A comparison of preschools in China, Japan, and the United States demonstrates the different value systems that underlie enculturation. Chinese preschools emphasize the indi-

vidual's commitment to society over personal pleasures; American preschools emphasize individual cognitive and emotional development; Japanese preschools emphasize sensitivity to the needs of others.

6. In many cultures, male initiation rituals, often marked by painful rites such as circumcision, mark the transition from childhood to adulthood. These rituals, which have a deep emotional impact, also impart information needed to function as a male adult in that society and affirm male solidarity.

7. Anthropologists have suggested that males may experience more discontinuities in enculturation than females because the dependent male child must make the transition to an independent and assertive male role. Male initiation rites help the individual make this emotional transition.

8. Female initiation, often associated with menarche, is marked by group rituals in fewer societies than male initiation and is usually less emotionally traumatic.

9. In the United States, where formal initiation rites are generally lacking, the four-year college experience serves many of the functions of initiation rites in other societies for middle-class youth.

10. Enculturation continues into adulthood. Occupational status, such as among the police, is a particularly important site for the transmission of specialized, culturally patterned skills and attitudes.

11. Medical anthropology studies illness and health, both physical and emotional. These experiences vary among cultures and, in complex societies, among different subcultures. Medical anthropologists apply their ethnographic and holistic perspective to those who receive health care and to the subcultures of health care professionals.

12. Enculturation also continues in the later stages of life, as among the elderly and the dying. These experiences differ widely in different cultures. Where old age is associated with death, loss, abandonment, and isolation, it is almost always perceived negatively. In most non-Western and nonindustrial cultures, the aged and the dying are surrounded by kin and community.

Key Terms

enculturation	Oedipus complex
incest taboos	psychological
initiation ritual	anthropology
matrilineal	rite of passage
menarche	social birth

Suggested Readings

Amit-Talai, Vered, and Helena Wulff (Eds.). 1995. *Youth Cultures: A Cross-Cultural Perspective.* London: Routledge. This collection of ethnographically based studies of young people from a wide range of cultures, including Third World immigrants in Western cities, focuses on these youth in the process of cultural creation and identity formation.

Cohen, Lawrence. 1998. *No Aging in India: Alzheimer's, the Bad Family, and Other Modern Things.* Berkeley: University of California Press. This award-winning book reflects the humanist and post-modernist style of this author's work on India.

Fernea, Elizabeth Warnock. 1995. *Children in the Muslim Middle East.* Austin: University of Texas Press. This book presents a wide range of information about children and teenagers in 15 countries, grouped under the categories of growing up, health, work, education, politics and war, and play and the arts. It touches on such thorny issues as female genital mutilation, child labor, and the involvement of children in national and revolutionary struggles.

Goldman, L. R. 1998. *Child's Play: Myth, Mimesis and Make Believe.* New York: New York University Press. This ethnographic account of children's play among the Huli of Papua New Guinea makes a significant contribution to the anthropological study of play. The focus is on the cultural role of fantasy involving Huli mythic figures.

Sokolovsky, Jay (Ed.). 1997. *The Cultural Context of Aging: Worldwide Perspectives.* Westport, CT: Bergin and Garvey. This volume contains an interesting set of articles edited by one of the first anthropologists to study aging from a cultural perspective.

Internet Resources

The following Internet resources appear in this chapter. Please log on to the Wadsworth anthropology website: **http://anthropology.wadsworth. com**. Click on the Nanda/Warms *Cultural Anthropology* page. Then select the Student Resources section, where you will find a complete presentation of these links and more.

- A link to the websites on the rites of passage, page 131
- A photo essay on Balinese cremation ceremony, page 140
- A link to the website for the Society for Medical Anthropology, page 139
- Access the Study Guide to InfoTrac College Edition for Anthropology Students

INDUSTRIAL AND POSTINDUSTRIAL SOCIETIES INCREASINGLY REQUIRE A LABOR FORCE THAT IS SKILLED, EDUCATED, AND MOBILE.

CHAPTER SEVEN

MAKING A LIVING

How do human cultures impact on their environments?

What are the major ways in which different societies make a living?

What are some of the relationships between subsistence strategies and other aspects of culture and social life?

How can anthropology make a difference in improving food production?

All societies survive by using their environments to provide people with the basic material requirements of life: food, clothing, and shelter. In this chapter, we focus on the different **subsistence strategies,** or ways in which societies transform the material resources of the environment into food.

Anthropology, particularly ecological anthropology, has always been interested in the interactions between human cultures and their environments. Ecological anthropologists seek to understand the effects of the physical environment on human activities and cultures, the effects of human cultures on the physical environment, the interrelationships among human cultures within a physical environment, and how human cultures change their subsistence strategies in response to challenges and threats to their livelihood (Bates and Lees 1996:Introduction). Although we are used to thinking about the physical environment as "natural," it is important to keep in mind that the so-called natural environment is also a cultural construction (Biersak 1999:9).

ronments). Some environments, such as the Arctic or the Great Australian Desert, present extreme challenges to human existence. Such regions are relatively limited in the numbers of people and types of subsistence strategies they can support. The productivity of any particular environment, however, is related to the type of technology used to exploit it. In aboriginal America, for example, the Great Plains supported a relatively small population, living mainly by hunting bison; with intensive mechanized agriculture, the same region can support millions of people. In the same way, a desert area that can support very small numbers of people without irrigation can support much larger populations with irrigation agriculture.

Because of their technological capabilities, humans generally have a strong impact on their environments, greatly affecting the life chances and reproductive rates of other species in their habitats (Bates and Lees 1996:4). Technological development has enabled humans to transform a wide range of materials into sources of usable energy. As a result, humans have been able to create many kinds of artificial environments, such as farms and cities, and many different economic systems and forms of social organization.

HUMAN ADAPTATION AND THE ENVIRONMENT

Human beings, unlike most other animals, live in an extremely broad range of habitats (envi-

---

subsistence strategies The ways in which societies transform the material resources of the environment into food, clothing, and shelter.

Stan Wayman/Photo Researchers, Inc.

IN FORAGING AND HORTICULTURAL SOCIETIES, CULTURAL ADAPTATIONS INCLUDE A VARIETY OF WAYS OF GETTING FOOD, USING SIMPLE BUT INGENIOUS TECHNOLOGIES, AND DEEP KNOWLEDGE OF THE ENVIRONMENT. HERE, A KALAPOLO INDIAN ON THE XINGU RIVER IN CENTRAL BRAZIL FISHES WITH A BOW AND ARROW.

These human technologies and cultural adaptations have led to great increases in **population density,** which in turn have greatly intensified the effects on the environment.

Up until about 10,000 years ago, humans lived by **foraging**—that is, hunting and collecting vegetable food. As tools improved, foragers spread out into many environments and developed diverse cultures, arriving in the Americas and Australia about 25,000 years ago. Foraging sets limits on population growth and density and, consequently, on the complexity of social organization in these societies. About 10,000 years ago, human groups in the Old World began to domesticate plants and animals, a food-producing "revolution" that occurred 4,000 years later in the New World. The transition to food production was actually very gradual, more like evolution than revolution, but it was revolutionary in the possibilities it opened up for the development of complex social organization.

With the increased populations that could be supported by the domestication of plants and animals, **sedentary** village life became widespread. More intensive means of cultivation and animal management developed, and human labor was more closely coordinated and controlled, leading eventually to complex social forms such as the state. Within this general outline of growing control over the environment and human population increase, specific environmental and historical conditions explain the exact sequence of events in any particular place.

Why cultivation did not arise everywhere—and why some populations, such as the abo-

population density The number of people inhabiting a given area of land.

foraging (hunting and gathering) A food-getting strategy that does not involve food production or domestication of animals.

sedentary Settled, living in one place.

riginal peoples of Australia, never made the transition from foraging to food production—has several answers. In some cases, such as in the Arctic, climate and soil composition precluded agriculture. In other cases, such as the fertile valleys of California, aboriginal foraging was so productive there was little pressure to make the transition to food production. Sometimes foraging strategies were actually more dependable than cultivation or animal husbandry, which are more adversely affected by extreme drought. For example, with the introduction of the horse by the Spaniards in the sixteenth century, some Native American Plains cultures, such as the Cheyenne, did so well with bison hunting that they gave up their traditional cultivation strategy. Even today, many foraging and pastoral populations resist abandoning these occupations for cultivation because they prefer the economic, social, and psychological satisfactions of a foraging or pastoral way of life. In these societies, hunting and pastoralism are highly valued occupations, intimately connected to a people's cultural identity, and in some circumstances more productive than agriculture.

In general, **industrialism,** or the replacement of human and animal energy by machines, has greatly increased productivity. In a typical nonindustrial society, more than 80 percent of the population is directly involved in food production; in a highly industrialized society, 10 percent of the people directly produce food for the other 90 percent. At the same time, increasingly complex technology and industrialism have brought new problems, particularly in their impact on the environment.

Many nonindustrial societies have made quite satisfactory adaptations to their environments without modern science and with simple but ingenious technology. This success is partly due to the vast knowledge and understanding these societies have of their environment. In the enormous Amazon **rain forest,** for example, it is not uncommon for people to know the names of hundreds of diverse species of plants and trees. The Kuikuru of central Brazil can identify more than 191 different trees by name, and know the uses of 138 of them. Some of these uses are very specialized, such as the root of a particular tree that is used to

poison dogs (Carneiro 1988:78). A Kuikuru hunter knows the place of each species in the web of forest life and the importance of sustaining the vegetal diversity that provides different animal species with their specialized, preferred foods.

Indigenous peoples of the Amazon forest not only know their environments well but manage their food resources in diverse, complex, and sophisticated ways. Compared to Western "experts" in specialized fields of agriculture or wildlife management, members of many indigenous societies have a more holistic approach to their environment. The Kayapo of the Xingu River basin, for example, view their cultivated garden plots as just the first step in the long-term process of environmental management that ultimately culminates in a mature forest filled with plants that are useful for food, medicine, and building materials, and for attracting useful animals (Posey 1988: 89). The Kayapo carefully manage the soil, protect the ground cover, control humidity, and manage pests, all based on their deep understanding of soil, the properties of fire, and the relation of the seasons to plant growth. Like many other nonindustrial societies, the Kayapo clearly understand the impact of human food-getting activities on the environment. They use this knowledge in efficient but conserving ways as they exploit various food resources.

The environmental problems resulting from industrial and postindustrial society have led to a reawakened interest and respect for the ways in which nonindustrial people have adapted to their environment. In the modern technological age, we too frequently forget that technology must be used to human ends and that economic efficiency is only one of many important values.

A central source of environmental degradation has been the consumer desires and energy needs of industrialized nations. Almost from the moment of European con-

---

industrialism An economic strategy involving the mechanization of production and associated characteristics such as bureaucratization, extreme occupational specialization, and social stratification.

rain forest Tropical woodland characterized by high rainfall and a dense canopy of broad-leaved evergreen trees.

WHERE'S THE BEEF?

Local eating habits have worldwide ecological consequences. In contemporary society, Western appetites for beef are having profound effects on the global environment. In the eighteenth century, the British upper classes acquired a taste for marbleized beef, and eating beef became associated with social status. In the United States, many immigrants viewed the regular eating of steaks and chops as a symbol of their having moved into the middle class. This culturally patterned taste for beef has continued to spread throughout the industrialized nations of the world, especially in the United States and Japan. The proliferation of fast-food restaurants, begun in the United States but now expanding globally, has led to an increased demand for cheap beef. This has resulted in the destruction of enormous swaths of rain forests in Central and South America.

From an investor's point of view, clearing tropical forests for pasturage is the best way to acquire the huge amount of land needed to raise cattle. But ecologically, cattle production is one of the worst land uses for tropical forests (Brookfield 1988). The production of enough ground beef for one hamburger requires the destruction of 200 pounds of living matter, including more than 20 plant species, 100 insect species, and dozens of bird, mammal, and reptile species. Cattle raising is also the most costly kind of food production. Producing one pound of beef takes 2,500 gallons of water, compared with 119 gallons for corn, and 9 pounds of feed, compared with 2 pounds of feed for chicken. In the global economy, "having it your way" at your neighborhood fast-food restaurant translates into environmental consequences thousands of miles away (Rifkin 1993).

---

tact with other parts of the world, European culture affected the environment. The introduction of domestic animals—cattle and sheep—ultimately devastated the carefully managed ecosystem of the Inca empire, which depended on agriculture (Scammel 1989:125). The European fashion for furs almost denuded North America of furbearing animals such as the beaver, and today European consumer demands for tropical hardwoods are leading to devastating logging in tropical forests (Brosius 1999). The European demand for sugar and tobacco resulted in huge areas of monocrop agriculture, which not only transformed the physical environment of the Americas but, with the introduction of African slavery, its social environment as well (Mintz 1985). In the Pacific Northwest of the United States, dam building has affected the ability of salmon to spawn, a concern not only of conservationists but also of Native Americans in this area, for whom salmon are not only an important food but an object of religious awe (Duncan 2000).

MAJOR TYPES OF SUBSISTENCE STRATEGIES

Anthropological understanding of the interactions among culture, making a living, and the environment can be approached by a typology of subsistence strategies. Each strategy uses the environment in different ways, and each has a different impact on the environment. The five basic subsistence strategies identified by anthropologists are foraging, pastoralism, horticulture, agriculture, and industrialism (Y. Cohen 1971).

Foraging depends on the use of plant and animal resources naturally available in the environment. **Pastoralism** primarily involves the care of domesticated herd animals, whose dairy and meat products are a major part of the pastoralist diet. **Horticulture,** or **extensive cultivation,** refers to the production of plants using a simple, nonmechanized technology.

pastoralism A food-getting strategy that depends on the care of domesticated herds.

horticulture (extensive cultivation) Production of plants using a simple, nonmechanized technology; fields are not used continuously.

Iven Devore/Anthro-Photo File

THE JU/'HOANSI OF THE KALAHARI DESERT IN SOUTHERN AFRICA USE A WIDE VARIETY OF RESOURCES TO SECURE THEIR EXISTENCE. IN ADDITION TO HUNTING BIG ANIMALS, THE JU/'HOANSI DEPEND ON GATHERING NUTS AND VEGETABLES AND ON HUNTING SMALLER ANIMALS SUCH AS FOWL.

Agriculture, or **intensive cultivation,** involves the production of food using the plow, draft animals, and more complex techniques of water and soil control so that land is permanently cultivated and needs no fallow period. Finally, industrialism involves the use of machine technology and chemical processes for the production of food and other goods. Within these basic types of subsistence strategies, however, there is much diversity. Furthermore, while any society normally uses one dominant strategy, many societies combine strategies in meeting their energy needs. Today no society, however seemingly remote, lies outside the impact of the industrialized world system.

Each subsistence strategy generally supports a characteristic level of population density (number of persons per square unit of land), and has a different level of **productivity** (yield per person per unit of land) and **efficiency**

(yield per person per hour of labor invested). These criteria, in turn, tend to be associated with characteristic forms of social organization and certain cultural patterns. For example, where local technology allows only limited exploitation of the environment and where safe and reliable methods of artificial contraception are unknown, cultural practices such as sexual abstinence, abortion, and infanticide may be used to limit population growth. Other cultural practices and beliefs also result in limiting population. Late weaning and prohibitions on sexual intercourse after the birth of a child, for example, regulate population by spacing births.

In addition to limiting population, a society can also extend its resource base by trading. Trade occurs in all types of societies, including foragers. In the Ituri rain forest in Central Africa, Mbuti foragers have complex, hereditary exchange relationships with the Lese, their horticultural neighbors (Wilkie 1988). In exchange for meat, mushrooms, honey, building materials, medicine, and agricultural labor, the Mbuti receive manioc, plantains, peanuts, and rice, which together form more than 50 percent of their diet. The Lese also provide the Mbuti with metal for knives and arrowheads; cotton cloth, which is stronger and more colorful than traditional Mbuti bark cloth; and aluminum cooking pots, which are more durable than traditional Mbuti clay pots (Wilkie 1988:123). Trade, of course, also forms the basis of the historical and contemporary global economy, incorporating peoples all over the world engaging in many kinds of food production and manufacturing.

FORAGING

Foraging is a diverse strategy that relies on naturally available food resources. It includes the hunting of large and small game, fishing, and

agriculture (intensive cultivation) A form of food production in which fields are in permanent cultivation using plows, animals, and techniques of soil and water control.

productivity Yield per person per unit of land.

efficiency Yield per person per hour of labor invested.

the collecting of various plant foods. Foragers do not produce food, either directly by planting or indirectly by controlling the reproduction of animals or keeping domestic animals for consumption of their meat or milk. Foraging strategies vary in productivity, but in general, support lower population densities than other subsistence systems. Today, only a very small proportion of the world's people live by foraging, mainly in marginal areas into which they have been pushed by expanding, militarily superior agricultural peoples and states (see map). In the past, however, foragers occupied many diverse environments, including the Arctic tundra and the most arid deserts.

All foragers exploit the diversity of their environments. In spite of the popular stereotype of prehistoric hunters, most foragers actually rely more on vegetal collecting than hunting. One exception is the Inuit of the Arctic circle, whose traditional hunting strategy included almost no collecting of plant food, which is virtually absent in their environment. Typical of most foragers, however, the Inuit food quest followed the seasonal variations of climate, which consists of a long, cold winter during which the water areas become sheets of ice, and a short, cool summer. Inuit culture adapted to the availability of different animals in the different seasons. The coastal Inuit of Alaska depended on whaling and sea resources, particularly seals, while the inland Inuit primarily depended on hunting caribou (Moran 1979). Animals provided not only food, but also resources for Inuit material culture, such as the layered clothing that keeps out the cold yet prevents overheating. In this harsh climate, Inuit survival depended upon their detailed knowledge of their environment and animal behavior, as well as cultural values of patience, innovative problem solving, cooperation, and the avoidance of conflict (Briggs 1991). Because of Inuit reliance on big animals, which are hunted only by men, Inuit women play a less important role in foraging than in most foraging societies. They make a vital contribution to Inuit survival, however, in processing meat for storage, making and repairing clothing, cooking, and caring for children.

As with many other foragers, the twentieth century brought drastic changes in Inuit subsistence strategies (Condon et al. 1996). The introduction of rifles led to a decline in caribou. At the same time, the Western demand for

THIS MAP INDICATES THE DIFFERENT WAYS OF MAKING A LIVING THROUGH CULTIVATION AND ANIMAL HUSBANDRY AS THEY ARE FOUND IN DIFFERENT ENVIRONMENTS.

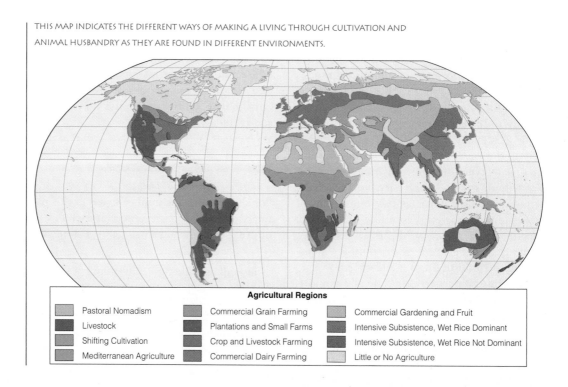

Agricultural Regions

Pastoral Nomadism

Livestock

Shifting Cultivation

Mediterranean Agriculture

Commercial Grain Farming

Plantations and Small Farms

Crop and Livestock Farming

Commercial Dairy Farming

Commercial Gardening and Fruit

Intensive Subsistence, Wet Rice Dominant

Intensive Subsistence, Wet Rice Not Dominant

Little or No Agriculture

fox furs brought the Inuit into the global economy, partly (or largely, depending on the area) replacing subsistence with commercial trapping. Fox trapping provided the Inuit with guns and also with cash, which they used to buy food, tobacco, tea, canvas tents, and clothing. In addition, many Inuit sought employment with the United States government, which established a Distant Early Warning radar installation. Trading posts attracted permanent settlement. Other important sources of income for Inuit today are handicrafts, tourism, and when necessary, welfare payments.

More typical of foraging subsistence is the strategy of the Aborigines of the Australian Desert (see the Ethnography box on pages 152–153), in which a wide range of vegetal foods provides most of their diet. Contrary to popular stereotypes (or prejudice), foraging is not necessarily a "harsh" existence, although in extreme environments, such as the Arctic and the Australian Desert, there may be periods of desperation. In less extreme environments, where predictable vegetal foods can be supplemented by hunting, foragers may experience abundant leisure time and generally good health. Richard Lee estimated that an adult Dobe Ju/'hoansi of the Kalahari Desert in southern Africa, for example, spends only an average of two-and-a-half six-hour days per week in subsistence activities, and a woman can gather enough in one day to feed her family for three days (1984:50–53).

Some general social correlates of foraging are seasonal **nomadism** geared to the availability of game and wild plants; organization of the society into small camps with flexible membership, composed mainly of kinsmen; and seasonal association of larger groups when food is more available.

PASTORALISM

Pastoralism is a subsistence strategy that depends primarily on the products of domesticated herd animals. It is a specialized adaptation to an environment that, because of hilly terrain, dry climate, or unsuitable soil, cannot support a large human population through agriculture, but can support enough native vege-

tation for animals if they are allowed to range over a large area. Because human beings cannot digest grass, raising animals that can live on grasses makes pastoralism an efficient way to exploit semiarid natural grasslands that are otherwise unproductive. Unlike ranching (commercial animal husbandry), in which livestock are fed grain (which could be used to feed humans) to produce meat or milk, pastoralism does not compete directly with humans for the same resources (Barfield 1993:13).

Pastoralists mainly herd cattle, sheep, goats, yaks, or camels, all of which produce both meat and milk. Because the herd animals found in the New World were not of a variety that could be domesticated (with the exception of the llama and alpaca in Peru), pastoralism did not develop as a New World subsistence strategy. The major areas of pastoralism are found in East Africa (cattle), North Africa (camels), southwestern Asia (sheep and goats), central Asia (yak), and the subarctic (caribou and reindeer). Subarctic Old World pastoral societies are divided into five distinct nomadic pastoral zones, each with its own style of animal husbandry and social organization (see map).

Pastoralism can be either transhumant or nomadic. In **transhumant** pastoralism, found mostly in East Africa, men and boys move the animals regularly throughout the year to different areas as pastures become available at different altitudes or in different climatic zones, while women and children and some men remain at a permanent village site. In nomadic pastoralism, the whole population—men, women, and children—moves with the herds throughout the year, and there are no permanent villages.

Pastoralism involves a complex interaction among animals, land, and people. With domestication, animals became dependent on their human keepers for pasture, water, breeding, shelter, salt, and protection from predators. Pas-

nomadism The constant mobility of human groups in pursuit of food (as in foraging) or a form of pastoralism in which the whole social group (men, women, children) and their animals move in search of new pasture.

transhumance A pastoralist pattern in which herd animals are moved regularly throughout the year to different areas as pasture becomes available.

I N   T H E   F I E L D

THE COMPLEX STRATEGY OF AUSTRALIAN FORAGERS

The Pintupi and Gugdja peoples of the Great Sandy Desert of Western Australia survived with a traditional foraging strategy until the mid-twentieth century. Beginning in the 1920s, because of prolonged drought, the Pintupi began moving to mission stations, cattle stations, government settlements, and towns around the desert fringe; the last Pintupi left the Western Desert in 1966 (Myers 1986). From the Pintupi point of view, they left the desert because food was easier to get elsewhere. As with other foraging peoples, the unreliability of water supplies posed a fundamental challenge to survival. For the Pintupi, the key to their long residence in this very arid area was their use of a wide variety of seasonally available plant and animal foods and their detailed knowledge of their environment. Even with a simple technology, this made foraging a generally predictable and reliable strategy, though at certain seasons a very difficult way of life.

These Australian peoples recognize and can name 126 plants serving 138 different social, economic, and medicinal functions. They use more than 75 different plants for edible seeds, and also include in their diet various tubers, fruits, nectars, sap, and edible insects or larvae. Particularly important is the witchetty grub, an insect available all year round. Birds and bird eggs are important dietary resources, with bustards the most common and easily caught. Small mammals are also an occasional source of animal protein. The main constraint on population growth and density is the scarcity of water in the driest and hottest months. Thus, the Western Desert societies consist of small, isolated, family groups, with a population density as low as one person per 150–200 square miles (compared, for example, with 1250 people per square mile in agricultural Java).

Climatic changes are extreme. Average summer temperatures reach 120 degrees, with winter temperatures around 72 degrees. Most critically, rainfall is very low, unpredictable, and evaporates quickly. The availability of food, and particularly water, is the most important influence on the distance people travel, the places they camp, and the length of time they stay in one place.

In the wet season, December through February, families spread across the desert. The intense rainstorms deposit fresh, drinkable water in streambeds, rock pools,

A WIDE VARIETY OF PLANT FOODS AND SMALL ANIMALS PERMIT PEOPLE TO SURVIVE IN THE HARSH ENVIRONMENT OF THE GREAT SANDY DESERT.

© David Austen/Stock, Boston

and cachements. The availability of water permits high mobility; families move great distances to search for food and travel great distances to attend ceremonies. Though water is available, food is scarce at this time of year, limited mainly to fruits, seeds, and tubers left over from the previous year, lizards, and some edible toads. Men and women gather reptiles, which are a main source of protein

toralists, therefore, must be highly knowledgeable about the carrying capacity of the land in proportion to the number of animals raised, as well as about the human relationship to the number of animals needed to provide subsistence (Barfield 1993:6).

The pastoralists described in the Ethnography box on pages 154–155 belong to the sheep and goat pastoralism that lies north of the arid deserts of camel pastoralism and south of the Central Eurasian steppe. It runs along the Mediterranean littoral through the Anatolian and Iranian Plateaus into mountainous central Asia (see map). Nomads here take advantage of changes in elevation, moving their livestock in a regular cycle of migration from lowland winter pasture to highland summer pasture. Herd composition of the total area is diverse, consisting of sheep, goats, horses, camels, and donkeys. Pastoral nomads in this area occupy a specialized ecological niche. Their survival depends upon relationships with their sedentary neighbors, with whom they trade meat animals, wool, milk products, and hides for grain, which constitutes the bulk of their diet, and for manufactured goods.

and fat and are relatively easy to collect. The most common mammals, kangaroos, are not very common at any time of year, but during this season are so widely spread across the desert that they are only infrequently encountered.

At the end of the wet season, plants begin to grow, and the period March through May is called the "green grass time." The temperature is moderate, and families move near the large surface water holes. Tubers are more readily available, and migrating birds become a more important dietary item.

The following season, June and July, called the "cold time," brings the greatest material prosperity. Tubers, large, tasty, and easily collected grass seeds, and fruits are all abundantly available. Edible fruits are collected from 12 different plants, and several species are stored for the "hungry season." People live semipermanently around large water holes, and the women gather tubers while the men engage in ceremonial activities. Night temperatures may drop into the 40s; people often stay up at night around a fire and sleep in the warmer hours of the midmorning.

The spring, August to October, or the "goanna get up time," follows the cold season. Food availability decreases, and temperatures rise steadily, reaching over 100 degrees. The landscape begins to dry

out, and people fall back to large rockholes where there is water. They set fires on the plains to attract game and to stimulate the growth of new grass seeds and tubers for the following year. They hunt goanna (lizards) and kangaroos and gather fruits, bulbs, tubers, and grass seeds, which are both eaten and stored. Men and women spend most of the day gathering.

With the onset of the "hot time," the summer months of November and December, temperatures continue to rise, sometimes reaching as high as 120 degrees. This is the harshest time of year, called the "hungry time." Families travel to the largest rockholes for water, but even these occasionally run dry. Food becomes less available, and many seeds and tubers run out completely. If the rain has not come by December, foraging ceases almost entirely. People try to take it easy to conserve food and water. Women remain in camp looking after the children and the elderly while the men search for food, sometimes traveling as far as 12 miles a day from camp. Average daily intake may be reduced to 800 calories per person. The shortage of water and heat stress prevent the whole camp from moving to areas where food might be more available, and people are thus "trapped" in the areas around the larger water holes. Under conditions of

starvation, people may be fed blood from healthier individuals to get them through the worst weeks. Now the availability of lizards becomes critical, as they may be the only food source if the rains are late.

The extraordinary ability of human beings to adapt to the most extreme environments is well illustrated by the Australians of the Great Sandy Desert. Though constrained materially by their simple technology, their detailed knowledge of their environment has permitted them not only to survive as foragers for thousands of years, but to develop highly complex ceremonial, religious, kinship, and artistic cultural patterns.

Critical Thinking Questions

1. What are the main strategies through which these indigenous Australians survive in their extreme environment?

2. In what ways do seasonal changes in the environment affect Australian subsistence and social life?

Source: Adapted from Scott Cane, "Australian Aboriginal Subsistence in the Western Desert." In Daniel G. Bates and Susan H. Lees (Eds.), *Case Studies in Human Ecology.* New York: Plenum Press, 1996, pp. 17–51.

The key to the pastoralist economy is herd growth, which depends primarily on reproduction by herd female animals. The number of animals needed to support a family is a constant source of pastoralism decision making. Eating or selling too many animals in a single year may lead to insolvency, so that pastoralists must always balance their present needs against future herd production. Pastoralism is a risky business; weather disasters such as drought or storms, disease, or theft can easily decimate a herd. These factors, along with social pressure by the nation-states within which pastoralists

now subsist, are leading to increased sedentization among pastoralist peoples (see Chapter 14, pages 319–321).

Nomadic pastoralist societies tend to be based on **patrilineal** kinship. In Southwest Asia, their characteristic political organization is supratribal confederations, with powerful leaders allied in regional political networks. In the past, they were subordinated to various empires on

patrilineal A rule that affiliates children with kinsmen of both sexes related through males only.

THE YARAHMADZAI OF BALUCHISTAN: A PASTORAL ADAPTATION

The chief problems of adapting to grassland environments revolve around the use of water and pasture. Because of the patchy characteristics of the environment, nomadism is the most common means of securing an adequate supply of these resources. As part of their adaptive strategies, pastoralists have to make important decisions about the size and composition of their herds. These decisions reflect both their evaluation of the diet needed to sustain the group and their need to maintain social exchanges with their neighboring cultivators, because some agricultural contribution to the pastoral diet is always required.

The Yarahmadzai are a patrilineal tribe of several thousand people living in the area of southeastern Iran known as Baluchistan. The total tribal territory is about 3,600 square miles. The plateau on which the Yarahmadzai live is at 5,000 feet and is cut by high mountains. The winters are cold and the summers hot. Some years there is no rain at all, and the maximum tends to be about 6 inches a year, most of which falls in the winter. The main natural vegetation is grass, although some

areas are completely barren. The area is bounded to the east by a vast desert that contains almost no vegetation.

In winter (December, January, and February), each local community of the tribe has a traditional camping area on the plateau consisting of 5 to 20 tents. The herds of goats and sheep are taken out together by shepherds; camels are herded separately by camel boys. At this time, there is practically no vegetation for the animals to eat, and they live primarily on the accumulated fat of the previous spring. During the winter, the entire Yarahmadzai area is barren, so there is no point in moving. Their strategy is to sit tight and protect the animals as best

they can. They compensate for the lack of pasturage by feeding the camels with roots, the goats and sheep with grain, and the lambs and kids with dates, processed date pits, and grain. The people depend on food stores from the previous year during this season. Because this is the rainy season, water is normally available.

In spring (March, April, and May), grass begins to appear and plants to bud. Because of the variability of the rain and winter runoff water from the mountains, the availability of pasture varies from year to year within the territory. Thus, the community does not know beforehand where it will go. After spending some time gathering information about where the pasture is good, the camp packs up and migrates. During the period observed by anthropologist Philip Salzman, his camp moved seven times, covering distances of 5–25 miles. Because even pasturage in a good area is quickly exhausted, all the camps constantly move from place to place.

In the first part of summer (June and July), the pasturage begins to dry up. The Iranian government has introduced some irrigation technology into the area, and many people migrate to these areas to harvest grain. The livestock grazes on stubble and fertilizes the ground with droppings. From March to July, the animals give ample milk both for their young and

the Iranian and Anatolian Plateaus, which had little success in controlling them. For the past 200 years, however, pastoralists have had to adapt to the policies set by distant governments of centralized nation-states, losing much of their political and military autonomy (Barfield 1993:206).

Nomadic pastoralists demonstrate great adaptation, however, particularly in raising animals for exchange rather than subsistence. Pastoralists in most parts of the world now depend

less on consuming the direct products of their herds—meat, wool, milk—and more on the sale of animals and animal products for cash. In this sense, many nomadic pastoralists, like the Saami of Norway, discussed in Chapter 14, are becoming ranchers: pastoral specialists in a cash economy.

Pastoralists today are often successful in adapting their products to local and even global markets. Nomads in Afghanistan and Iran, for example, are highly integrated into national

for human consumption. Milk is consumed in many different forms and is preserved as dried milk solids and butter. The butter is sold or exchanged for other products, mostly grain.

In late summer and early autumn (August, September, and October), the Yarahmadzai migrate to the lowland desert, leaving their winter tents, goats, and sheep on the plateau in the care of young boys. The group makes an 8-day migration to the groves of date palms. During this time, they live in mud huts, harvesting and eating dates and preparing a number of food products for the return journey. Dates, date preserves, and date pits are all needed for consumption in the winter; salt, which is gathered from salt wastes, is consumed year-round; palm leaves are woven into ropes for tying and packing tents and baggage. The date palms are easily cultivated: A river drains into the desert basin, creating a sandy soil with a 5-foot water table into which the date palms sink their roots. Because of the heat, wind, and lack of rain, however, it is not possible for sheep and goats to live there, even for a short time.

In November the group migrates back to the plateau. Those who are also cultivators plant grain at this time, and the women go off to work for cash in nearby towns. As a source of subsistence, this labor is a substitute for the extensive live-

IN CULTURES LIKE THE YARAHMADZAI, WHICH ARE BASED ON NOMADIC PASTORALISM, ALL MEMBERS OF THE GROUP—MEN, WOMEN, AND CHILDREN—MOVE WITH THEIR HERDS THROUGHOUT THE YEAR, AND THERE IS NO PERMANENT SETTLEMENT. WOMEN ARE RESPONSIBLE FOR THE WATER SUPPLY AND TAKE CARE OF THE PROCESSING OF DAILY FOOD, WHILE MEN HERD THE ANIMALS.

Courtesy of Serena Nanda

stock raiding of an earlier era, which has been suppressed by the Iranian government. Pastoralism, date cultivation, and additional sources of subsistence are all necessary to economic survival in such an environment.

Critical Thinking Questions

1. What are the special problems in the pastoralist way of life?

2. How does your diet reflect seasonal change?

Source: Adapted from Philip C. Salzman, "Multi-Resource Nomadism in Iranian Baluchistan." In William Irons and Neville Dyson-Hudson (Eds.), *Perspectives on Nomadism*. Leiden, The Netherlands: E. J. Brill, 1972, pp. 61–69. Reprinted by permission.

and international trade networks. They specialize in selling meat animals to local markets, lambskins to international buyers, and sheep intestines to meet the huge German demand for natural sausage casings (Barfield 1993:211).

Critics of nomadic pastoralism focus on the "tragedy of the commons," claiming that the individual pastoralist's desire to increase the size of his herds inevitably leads to collective overgrazing and the destruction of grasslands. In fact, however, pastoralists are aware of this po-

tential problem and in a variety of ways have restricted access to "common" pasture (Barfield 1993: 214). Indeed, it is more often government policies that restrict nomadic use of pastoralist territories in an attempt to make them productive for agriculture that have directly and indirectly exacerbated environmental degradation.

Pastoralism cannot support an indefinitely increasing population, and many pastoralists have already become sedentary. But with their

ETHNOGRAPHY

THE LUA': SWIDDEN CULTIVATORS IN THAILAND

The traditional livelihood of the Lua' living in the mountains of northern Thailand is swidden cultivation. After clearing a block of land, villagers allow it to lie fallow for about nine years because they understand that in the second year the soil would lose its fertility and there would be too many weeds. Swidden blocks around the village are cultivated in a regular rotational sequence. Each household normally returns to the same field it cultivated ten years before, marking their swidden field boundaries with a row of charred logs.

Every January, village elders inspect the swidden block they expect to use the following year to see whether forest regrowth has been adequate for cultivation. They check to see that fires have not occurred, as that would deplete the soil's fertility. Using long steel-bladed knives, the men clear their fields by felling small trees, leaving stumps about three feet high. They begin with the trees at the bottom of a slope and work uphill so that the falling trees knock down smaller vegetation. They are careful to leave a strip of trees along watercourses and at the top of ridges to prevent erosion and provide seed sources for forest regrowth during the fallow period. They also leave taller trees standing, but trim their branches so they will not shade the crops.

The fields are cleared in January and February and allowed to dry until the end of March, the driest time of the year. In consultation with ritual leaders and village elders, a day is chosen to burn the fields, which requires people to be available to prevent the accidental spread of the fire into forest reserved for future

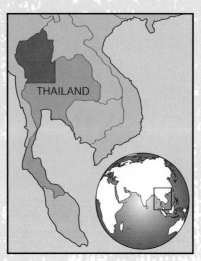

THAILAND

cultivation, or into the village. Toward this end, all the low vegetation is cleared to form a firebreak about 5 meters wide around the swidden block. The slash is consumed by a roaring fire within an hour or so. The men burning the swiddens usually carry guns, hoping game animals such as boar or barking deer will run toward them out of the burning fields, although this happens less today than in the past.

The cultivators first plant cotton and corn, which they sow on the slopes of the fields, and plant yams on the lower, wetter portions. For the next 2 weeks they prop up unburned logs along the contour of the fields to reduce hillside erosion. They mark the boundaries, gather larger logs for firewood, and build fences to keep livestock out of the field. By mid-April they begin to plant the main subsistence crop, upland rice, jabbing the earth loose with a 10-foot iron-tipped planting pole. The hope is that the rice will take root and sprout before the heavy monsoon rains. Different types of rice are sown in different areas of the field. Quick-ripening rice is planted near the field shelter, where it can be easily

watched. Drought-resistant varieties are planted on the drier, sandier tops of the slopes, along with millet.

Each household plants tall-growing sorghum (a cereal grass) to mark out their fields from their neighbors'. Mustard greens, peppers, several varieties of beans, and other vegetables are grown in gardens near the field shelters. Vine plants are grown along the creases in the hillside fields, which are more vulnerable to erosion. By May, weeding begins. The weeders, mainly women and older children, use a short-handled tool to scrape and hack at the weeds on the surface; weeds are not dug or pulled out by the roots.

Both men and women harvest the rice. They use small, handheld sickles, cutting the stems of each bunch of rice close to the ground. The stalks, about three feet long, are laid out to dry for a few days before threshing. At threshing time, women gather large bundles of rice stalks on a threshing floor leveled on the hillside. Young men beat the rice stalks against a threshing mat laid on the floor to knock the rice grains loose; other men beat the broken straw with bamboo threshing sticks to separate the rice grains as completely as possible. As the grain and chaff piles grow, the men shuffle through with their feet, fanning with a woven bamboo winnowing fan to blow away as much dirt as possible. After a second winnowing, the cleaned rice is loaded into baskets and kept in a temporary barn near the field shelter.

Like most horticulturalists, the Lua' maintain a pattern of varied vegetation zones around the village. Mature forests are preserved where villagers are forbidden to cut lumber or make swiddens or gardens. Uncut forest strips are also maintained between swidden blocks, around the village, along streamcourses and headwaters, and at the tops of ridges, all of

SWIDDEN, OR SLASH AND BURN HORTICULTURE, AS PRACTICED TRADITIONALLY IN NORTHERN THAILAND, IS BASED ON A DEEP UNDERSTANDING OF THE FOREST ENVIRONMENT. ALL THE FEATURES OF THE LANDSCAPE ARE TAKEN INTO ACCOUNT AS LUA' BUILD THEIR HOUSES AND PLANT THEIR FIELDS WITH A VARIETY OF CROPS, USED FOR SUBSISTENCE, FOR CASH, AND FOR ANIMAL FODDER.

which reduce erosion. Villagers use the plant growth of fallow fields for grazing and as traditional medicines, dyes for homespun clothing, and material for weaving baskets and building houses. The wild fruits and yams that grow on fallow land are particularly important during food shortages.

The Lua' also keep pigs, water buffalo, cattle, and chickens, which may be sold at local markets for cash. Before the 1960s, when the big fish in the streams were killed by pollution from chemical dumping of agricultural and malaria eradication pesticides, fish were another important addition to the Lua' diet. Hunting also has declined. Since World War II, there has been little game in the forests, though occasionally a forest animal will

fall into a trap set in the fields to catch birds and rats, which can destroy a crop.

Lua' adaptation worked well with its relatively stable population, which until the 1960s was held in check by a high mortality rate (caused largely by smallpox and malaria) and a delayed age of marriage, as men often had to wait until their 20s to accumulate the necessary brideprice. With a limited amount of cultivable land, large families are not seen as an advantage, and the number of women who migrate to the village as brides is generally balanced by the number who move out.

The stability of Lua' land use patterns and population has been changing since the beginning of the twentieth century, as other ethnic groups entered the area

and began to pay rent to the Lua' to farm on their land. By the mid-twentieth century, still other ethnic groups, including the Hmong, also began to settle in the area. These newer settlers were less careful about their swidden practices than the Lua', and the quality of the land began to deteriorate. Like many governments today, the Thai government claims ownership of all forested land and, without distinguishing between good and bad swidden practices, has outlawed all swidden as destructive. This has circumscribed traditional Lua' livelihood.

The Lua' were familiar with more intensive methods of agriculture, including permanently irrigated fields, and some Lua' had already switched to agriculture before the end of the nineteenth cen-

The Lua': Swidden Cultivators in Thailand (continued)

tury. The pressure to substitute intensive cultivation for horticulture has increased, and today, instead of maintaining the diversity of their environment with their swidden-rotation system, the Lua' are homogenizing their land use with irrigated, terraced agriculture. With the increase of cattle and population in the area, sorghum and millet are no longer grown. Fields planted with cotton have also declined and now the Lua' usually buy thread for weaving and cotton clothes. Cattle grazing on the fallow land also means that less grass is available for house construction, and more Lua' now roof their houses with leaves or with corrugated metal if they can afford it. The increase of cash cropping in soybeans has transformed the previously clear and free-flowing streams to muddy, polluted pools, which the Lua' now consider too dirty to wash their clothes in, and year-round irrigation has brought in year-round mosquitoes. Although the Lua' have not been subject to the severe dislocations of some neighboring ethnic groups, such as the Hmong, these changes in Lua' food producing have brought about substantial changes in their economic, social, and ritual lifestyle.

Critical Thinking Questions

1. What do the Lua' need to know about their environment in order to be successful farmers? What do you need to know about your environment in order to be successful?

2. Compare the effects of environmental pollution on the Lua' with its effects on your own life.

Source: Adapted from Peter Kunstadter, "Hill People of Northern Thailand." In J. S. Denslow and C. Padoch (Eds.), *Tropical Forest People.* Berkeley: University of California Press, 1988, pp. 93–110.

knowledge of their environment, creative use of multiple resources, and global demand for their products, pastoralism as a subsistence strategy has a strong future in exploiting the planet's large arid and semiarid zones.

HORTICULTURE

Horticultural societies depend primarily on the production of plants using a simple, non-mechanized technology. An important defining characteristic of horticulture is that cultivated fields are not used permanently, year after year, but remain fallow for some time after being cultivated. This is one of the important contrasts between an extensive and an intensive cultivation strategy. Horticulturalists plant and harvest with simple tools, such as hoes or digging sticks, and do not use draft animals, irrigation techniques, or plows. Extensive cultivation has a lower yield per acre than intensive cultivation and does not use as much human labor as other forms of farming. Traditionally, horticulturalists grow enough food in their fields or gardens to support the local group, but they do not produce surpluses that involve the group in a wider market system with nonagricultural populations. Population densities among horticultural peoples are generally low, usually not exceeding 150 people per square mile (Netting 1977). Despite this, horticultural villages may be quite large, ranging from 100 to 1,000 people.

Extensive cultivation may be practiced in dry lands, such as among the Hopi Indians of northeastern Arizona, who cultivate maize, beans, and squash. However, horticulture is typically a tropical forest adaptation, found mainly in Southeast Asia, sub-Saharan Africa, some Pacific islands, and the Amazon Basin in South America. In these environments, people practice a form of cultivation called **swidden,** or **slash and burn.** In slash and burn cultivation, a field is cleared by felling the trees and burning the brush. The burned vegetation is allowed to remain on the soil, which prevents its drying out from the sun. The resulting bed of ash acts as a fertilizer, returning nutrients to the soil. Fields are used for a few years (one to five) and then allowed to lie fallow for a longer period (up to 20 years) so that the forest cover can be rebuilt and fertility restored. Swidden cultivators require five to six times as much fallow land as they are actually cultivating. Swidden cultivation *can* have a deteriorating

swidden (slash and burn) A form of cultivation in which a field is cleared by felling the trees and burning the brush.

effect on the environment if fields are cultivated before they have lain fallow long enough to recover their forest growth. Eventually, the forest will not grow back, and the tree cover will be replaced by grasslands. Because of the possibility of irreversible ecological deterioration, swidden cultivation is considered both inefficient and destructive by governments in developing nations. However, modern industrial strategies such as logging and giant agribusiness are mainly responsible for the deterioration and disappearance of tropical forests (Sponsel 1995).

Most swidden cultivators grow several crops. Because their gardens do not provide all the necessary proteins for human health, they may also hunt and fish or raise some domestic animals. In New Guinea, for example, domestic pigs are an important source of protein. The horticulturalist Kofyar of Nigeria keep goats, chickens, sheep, and cows. The Yanomamo of the Amazon rain forest hunt monkeys and other forest animals.

Because of the very diverse environments of swidden cultivation, horticulturalists also have diverse cultures. Most horticulturalists shift residences as they move their fields, but some occupy villages permanently or at least on a long-term basis.

AGRICULTURE

In agriculture (sometimes called intensive cultivation), the same piece of land is permanently cultivated with the use of the plow, draft animals, and more complex techniques of water and soil control than are used by horticulturalists. Plows are more efficient at loosening the soil than are digging sticks or hoes. The turning of the soil brings nutrients to the surface. Plowing requires a much more thorough clearing of the land, but it allows land to be used year after year.

Irrigation is also important in intensive cultivation. Although some horticulturalists practice simple methods of water conservation and control, intensive cultivation in dry areas can be carried out only with sophisticated irrigation techniques. In hilly areas, intensive cultivation requires some form of terracing in order to prevent crops and good soil from being washed down the hillside. Preindustrial intensive cultivation also used techniques of natural fertilization, selective breeding of livestock and crops, and crop rotation, all of which increase productivity. Whereas horticulturalists have to increase the land under cultivation in order to support a larger population, agriculture can support population increases by more intensive use of the same piece of land.

Intensive cultivation generally supports higher population densities than horticulture. A dramatic example of the difference in productivity between slash and burn and intensive cultivation is offered by the island nation of Indonesia. Java, which makes up only 9 percent of the Indonesian land area, supports more than two-thirds of the Indonesian population. The "outer islands," which make up almost 90 percent of the land area and support about a third of the population, mainly use swidden cultivation. In Java, intensive wet rice cultivation using elaborate irrigation terraces supports an average of approximately 1,250 people per square mile. This contrasts sharply with the maximum population density of swidden areas, which has been estimated at about 145 persons per square mile (Geertz 1963:13).

The greater productivity of agriculture results not only from more sophisticated technology but also from more intensive use of labor. Farmers must work long and hard to make the land productive. In terraced agriculture, for example, ditches must be dug and kept clean, sluices constructed and repaired, and all terraces leveled and diked. It has been estimated that growing rice under a swidden system requires 241 worker-days per yearly crop, whereas wet rice cultivation requires 292 worker-days a year. Agriculture also requires more capital investment than does horticulture, for which the only necessary tool may be a simple digging stick. In intensive cultivation, apart from the cost of human labor, plows have to be bought and draft animals raised and cared for. Although intensive agriculturalists may have more control over food production, they are also more vulnerable to the environment. By depending on the intensive cultivation of one or two crops, they can face disaster in case of a crop failure. Draft animals may be struck by

I N   T H E   F I E L D

MUSHA: A PEASANT VILLAGE IN UPPER EGYPT

Musha is about 400 miles south of Cairo in the Nile Valley, a fertile agricultural strip between the riverbanks and the desert. Larger than the average Egyptian village, Musha has a population of about 18,000. Most village families own their houses, which, in addition to living quarters, are used for storage, stabling animals, raising poultry, and some agricultural work.

Musha's farmers practice a two-year crop rotation system based on summer crops of cotton, maize, and sorghum and winter crops of wheat, beans, chickpeas, and bersim (a variety of millet). The cycle begins with cotton in the first summer, followed by wheat in the following winter. Maize or sorghum follows in the second summer, or the land may be left fallow. The cycle is completed in the second winter with bersim, lentils, and chickpeas. In addition, there are grape and pomegranate orchards, and farmers raise onions, peppers, watermelons, and other vegetables on small patches for home consumption. Small farmers also depend heavily on the milk, cheese, and butter from water buffalo and the cheese from cows, sheep, and goats. Only water buffalo are regularly eaten and sold.

The traditional technology in Musha relied on either animal power or human effort and a few basic wooden tools. Tools included the short-handled hoe for weeding and irrigation, a small sickle for harvesting, and a digging stick for planting cotton. Shallow plows and threshing sleds were pulled by cows. Winnowing relied on the wind and a winnowing fork and sieves for the final cleaning. Donkeys carried small loads for short distances; camels were used for larger loads and longer distances and for bringing the crops in from the field.

Many changes have occurred in Musha in the past 30 years. Almost all farmers now use machines at least some of the time. The number of tractors has increased enormously, and these also have a mechanism for threshing and for pulling four-wheeled wagons, which transport fertilizer and bring crops in from the field. Farmers now depend on chemical fertilizers and pesticides as well as animal manure.

Pumping machines owned by private farmers began lifting the groundwater to supplement the Nile floodwater for part of the year. With pumps, double-cropping and the cultivation of cotton became possible. Land values increased, leading to the creation of large land holdings and increased demand for labor. In the 1960s, when the completion of the Aswan High Dam brought an end to the flooding of the Nile, the government constructed feed canals, which were linked up to the privately owned pumps and became the main source of water for the fields. The government now supplies water to the canals every other week. The water raised from the canals to the level of the fields flows through a network of ditches until it reaches the fields. The pumps are generally owned by several people, who share the work of guarding and maintaining the pumps, maintaining the ditches, arranging for the distribution of water to the farmers' fields, and keeping accounts. Each farmer provides the necessary labor to open a break in the ditch band so that the water will flow into his field. The farmer pays the owner of the pump a set fee per watering and also pays the pump guard an annual fee. The government is responsible for maintaining the feeder canals and cleans them once a year.

In Musha, wheat and cotton are the most important crops. Wheat, normally planted in November and harvested in May and June, is used for both grain and straw; selling the latter is more profitable because of government-mandated price controls on grain. In order to grow wheat, the farmer must register his acreage with the government and follow government rules on crop rotation. The government-owned village bank authorizes a loan in the form of fertilizer, insecticide, or seed.

After arranging for the distribution of water to his fields, the farmer must hire a driver and tractor (if he does not own one, which many small farmers do not) to plow the fields. Fertilizer and seed are hauled from the village bank to his home and from his home to the field. The fertilizer is then spread by hand.

Wheat is usually harvested by hired laborers using a small sickle. The reaped wheat is bundled into sheaves, which are transported by camel or wagon to the threshing ground at the edge of the village. The grain is threshed using a tractor and drum thresher. Threshing is a long and tedious job. It requires a five-member team to feed the machine, shovel away the threshed grain that has passed through the machine, and hand sheaves to the feed. The threshed grain, winnowed and sifted by specialists who are paid piece rates, is measured and sacked by the winnower, an activity the farmer personally supervises. In the final step, the grain and straw are hauled from the threshing ground back to the storeroom in the farmer's house.

The household is central in agriculture, although extra laborers are hired as needed and household members may work outside the agricultural sector. Women do the housekeeping, care for animals, and make cheese. In Musha they do not work in the fields, as they do in some other parts of Egypt. Children, recruited by labor contractors, cut clover for animals and help harvest cotton. Hired laborers, paid piece rates, generally do the harvesting and bundle the wheat into sheaves. The household head plays a key managerial role in Musha, supervising others, making agricultural purchases, hiring labor, scheduling the use of machinery, and arranging for the water flow into his fields.

Wheat is grown for household use, but also for the market, sold to merchants who sell it in the cities. (Until recently, the government was a major purchaser of grain.) Cotton is sold, in the form of "forced deliveries," to the government. At one time the farmers were obliged to sell their entire cotton crop to the government; other crops could be sold at higher, market prices. For cotton, the farmer is paid a base price at delivery, from which the village bank subtracts the debt of services and products (such as fertilizer). Although the government sets a price relative to the world market price, intended to motivate the farmer to cultivate the cotton properly, the farmers, who know the world market price, often feel cheated by the lower government price. The farmer makes up for these lower prices by paying his workers lower wages.

IN PEASANT VILLAGES IN EGYPT, A FARMER MAKES IMPORTANT DECISIONS REGARDING THE ALLOCATION OF HOUSEHOLD AND EXTRADOMESTIC LABOR, PURCHASES NECESSITIES FOR AGRICULTURE, SCHEDULES THE USE OF MACHINERY, AND NEGOTIATES WITH THE GOVERNMENT FOR THE SALE OF HIS CROPS.

Robert Caputo/Stock, Boston

The profit from farming is uncertain, and most families have several sources of income. Animals are sold in weekly markets through professional brokers who have established trusted relationships built on personal contact. Fruits and vegetables are sold either in the fields or to merchant brokers. In fact, 70 percent of village households derive their major income from activities other than farming: day labor, government jobs, craft trades, specialist agricultural work, remittances from family members who have migrated, or from rents and pensions.

In deciding on their strategies for making a living, the farmers of Musha must adapt to the physical and social environment. Critical in the social environment is government intervention in the agricultural process, which has remodeled the very landscape on which the farmer works. The state makes major investments in agriculture through the irrigation system and other infrastructure projects. It provides agricultural credit for such inputs as seed and fertilizer, relieving the farmers of the need to finance each year's crop from the preceding harvest. The state is also involved in marketing, and state policies, such as importing wheat from the United States, affect the prices it is willing to offer the farmer. The state

---

Musha: A Peasant Village in Upper Egypt (continued)

has a role in setting land ownership policy and makes rules governing land tenancy. These policies have made available large pools of labor, who thus have less bargaining power. The state also affects the labor market by controlling (and permitting or encouraging) migration outside the country, which acts as a safety valve for surplus rural labor. The state also benefits from the remittances in hard currency sent back by migrants.

In addition to interacting with government officials, farmers must also negotiate with the owners of tractors, day laborers, recruiters for child labor, neighbors, contractors for transport animals, and merchants, as well as supervising a complicated agricultural cycle. The farmer must know enough of the traditional skills of farming to supervise the agricultural work and also how to manage a wide range of activities, making important decisions at every step. With the increasing monetization of agriculture, farmers now consciously orient themselves to the market and have become sophisticated in dealing with it. Peasant farmers today are part of a world economy.

Critical Thinking Questions

1. Compare how technological changes have affected the working

environment in Musha with how technological changes have affected the working environment in the United States.

2. Compare the impact of the state on your life with its impact on farmers in Musha.

Source: Adapted from Nicholas Hopkins, "Mechanized Irrigation in Upper Egypt: The Role of Technology and the State in Agriculture." In B. Turner II and Stephen B. Brush (Eds.), *Comparative Farming Systems*. New York: Guilford Press, 1987, pp. 223–247. Reprinted by permission.

---

disease, again affecting the cultivator's ability to produce.

Agriculture is generally associated with sedentary villages, the rise of cities and the state, occupational diversity, social stratification, and other complex forms of social organization, although some states, in Africa for example, have been built on horticultural bases. Horticulturalists grow food mainly for the subsistence of their households, while farmers are enmeshed within larger complex societies. Part of their food production goes to support non-food-producing occupational specialists, such as those in religious or ruling elites. Rural cultivators who produce for the subsistence of their households but are also integrated into larger, complex state societies are called **peasants.**

Musha, the Egyptian village described in the Ethnography box above, exhibits many of the general characteristics of peasant villages. These characteristics include the importance of the household in production, the use of a supplementary labor supply outside the household,

the need of many farmers to depend on part-time work to supplement their income, and the surplus extracted from the cultivator by the state in the form of rent, taxes, and free labor. Although Egypt has a particularly long and well-documented history of state intervention in agriculture, the intervention of the state in Musha is typical of peasant societies generally. The multiple strategies for making a living in Musha highlight the ways in which both physical and social environments provide opportunities but also constrain human choices and shape culture and society.

MAKING A LIVING IN THE INDUSTRIAL AND POSTINDUSTRIAL GLOBAL ECONOMY

The transition to machines and chemical processes for the production of goods was explosive in its effect on many aspects of economy and society. Industrialization led to vastly increased population growth, expanded consumption of resources (especially energy), international expansion, occupational specialization, and a shift from subsistence strategies to wage

peasants Food-producing populations that are incorporated politically, economically, and culturally into nation-states.

labor. Industrial economies are based on the principle that consumption must be constantly expanded and that material standards of living must always go up. This pattern contrasts with tribal economies, which put various limits on consumption and thus are able to make lighter demands on their environments. Industrialism, which promotes rapid resource consumption, has outgrown national boundaries. The result has been great movement of resources and capital and migrations of population, as the whole world has been gradually drawn into the global economy.

Industrial societies always have at least two social classes: a large labor force that produces goods and services, and a much smaller class that controls what is produced and how it is distributed. In addition, there is a managerial class that oversees the day-to-day operation of the workplace.

TAIWAN: TRANSITION TO INDUSTRIALISM IN THE GLOBAL ECONOMY

Taiwan is an example of a nation that is making the transition from agriculture to industrialization within the context of an increasingly global economy (Gates 1987). Until 1958, agriculture was the main occupation for most Taiwanese. Peasant farming in Taiwan was difficult. Farmers grew rice and sugar, both of which require much labor in very uncomfortable conditions. Wet rice growing involves many hours spent knee-deep in muddy water, and sugar cultivation involves extremely heavy labor with dangers of heat prostration, hernia, back trouble, and snake bite. Many Taiwanese, therefore, sought other work when it became available through industrialization.

Much of the work available in industrial society however, is also experienced as difficult and unpleasant. Hard manual work, such as digging building foundations with shovels, is called "bitter labor" by the Taiwanese because of the long hours and low pay. Service work, which includes domestic service, restaurant and hotel work, retail sales, and entertainment (including prostitution, which is encouraged by the militarized economy), also involves long hours and low pay, plus the "emotional labor" of flattering and cajoling potential customers. Factory work is preferred to bitter labor and service, but even this is not easy, especially for the one-third of the factory workforce made up of young women from the countryside. Some young people enjoy the opportunity to leave home, but others become homesick or disillusioned with the dull work routines, the limited opportunities for advancement, and the exploitation. Factory work also entails physical dangers, such as rapid deterioration of eyesight in assembling electronics, and exposure to unguarded machinery and toxic substances. Some factories do not have air conditioning, a particular hardship in the hot, sticky Taiwan summers.

Thus, many Taiwanese have the goal of owning a small business. These businesses typically require little capital. "Shoulder pole" noodle sellers, for example, carry an entire restaurant— stove, cookpot, ingredients, dishes, and stool for the customer—on their shoulders. Other such miniaturized businesses include mending nylon stockings, recycling light bulbs, and manufacturing bean curd, which is sold to larger factories.

Many Taiwanese working-class people, compared to those in many other countries, are in fact relatively well off. But as anthropologist Hill Gates (1987) notes, for every prospering small-business family whose children can attend college and whose shops and factories have become successful in the Asian miracle, dozens of other families' economic and educational struggles are not so well rewarded. Taiwan's working class comprises about 75 percent of its population, in an economy that demands both relatively skilled and relatively inexpensive labor to maintain its position in the global marketplace. Farms and small businesses supply a steady stream of young, cheap workers, who typically move on (or try to) to businesses of their own. They may purchase a truck to start a transport business, take over their parents' small restaurant, or with the right contacts, enter the import-export market. In Taiwan, in spite of the difficulties, striving for upward mobility encourages hard work and does produce modest comfort for workers, as well as very consid-

A SUCCESSFUL AGRICULTURAL INTERVENTION IN BOLIVIA

The holistic approach of anthropologists can make a big difference in the quality and quantity of food production all over the world. This is demonstrated by the work of Alan Kolata, an archaeological anthropologist who, with agronomists and local farmers in a high plateau region of the Andes Mountains in Bolivia, is reviving a system of ancient agriculture.

This region, on the shores of Lake Titicaca, was the site of an ancient culture called the Tiwanaku. By around 1500 BCE, local farmers had developed a system of agriculture that was ingenious in taking advantage of the particular resources of this area while compensating for its deficiencies.

Lake Titicaca, which has the highest elevation of any lake in the world, is slightly salty. It is fed by rivers and springs and receives intense sunlight during the day, but during the growing season the area is subject to severe temperature drops in the evening. Successful farming

Lake Titicaca
BOLIVIA

in this area had to cushion the growing area from these temperature extremes and prevent the seepage of brackish water into the cultivated area.

To adapt to the opportunities and drawbacks of the region, the Tiwanaku farmers constructed a system of raised-bed agriculture. They made a series of plat-

forms, beginning with a foundation layer of cobblestones. Next they added a layer of clay that prevented the salty lake water from seeping into the topsoil. Above the clay was a layer of sand and gravel that promoted drainage, and above that was the fertile soil in which the crops were grown. Surrounding the platforms were canals, filled with water from a river that the farmers rerouted from its natural bed. This water trapped the radiant energy from the intense Andean sunlight, so that an insulating blanket of warm water seeping into the growing soil from the canals protected the crops from evening frosts. These canals of standing water also became an environment for plants, insects, and other organisms that enriched the soil.

After the Spanish conquest in the sixteenth century, these raised fields fell into disuse as the farmers adopted European farming methods. The platforms deteriorated into marshy pasture, although the mounds were still visible around the lake.

erable wealth for those who control the products of that wealth.

CHARACTERISTICS OF INDUSTRIAL AND POSTINDUSTRIAL SOCIETY

Poverty in industrialized societies punishes weakness, failure, or ill fortune in a way that is less true for the subsistence strategies of foraging, pastoralism, and horticulture described earlier in this chapter. Contemporary indus-

bureaucracy Administrative hierarchy characterized by specialization of function and fixed rules.

trial and postindustrial societies, characterized by well-coordinated specialized labor forces, increasingly require mobility, skill, and education for success. The creation of complex global systems of exchange between those who supply raw materials and those who use them in manufacturing, as well as between manufacturers and consumers, has resulted in significant worldwide inequities within and among nations. The rise of a special kind of formal organization called a **bureaucracy,** cultivation oriented primarily toward the market, the predominance of wage labor, and the subsequent loss of control over culture and social institutions are some of the constraints within which

In 1979, anthropological archaeologist Alan Kolata noted the mounds while investigating the remains of the ancient culture in the area. His research indicated that this area had once supported a much larger population. This led Kolata to think about whether reviving this earlier system of agriculture might prove more productive for local farmers than their present methods. Kolata's idea was positively received by local development experts, who were beginning to question industrialized, capital-intensive, irrigation-based agriculture as the only solution to problems of food production in developing nations and were looking for new alternatives more suited to local conditions. By 1987, Kolata was supervising five experimental raised-bed fields to compare current agricultural yields with those produced by traditional post-conquest) farming methods.

The potato yield in the experimental fields was much higher than in the traditional plots, and the experimental fields

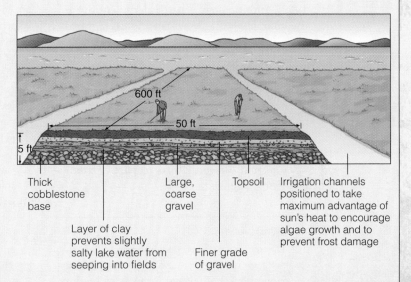

600 ft
50 ft
5 ft

Thick cobblestone base

Layer of clay prevents slightly salty lake water from seeping into fields

Large, coarse gravel

Finer grade of gravel

Topsoil

Irrigation channels positioned to take maximum advantage of sun's heat to encourage algae growth and to prevent frost damage

survived a crucial test: When potatoes and other crops were nearly destroyed by a frost late in the growing season, the crops in the raised-bed fields escaped almost undamaged. Kolata is now spearheading a project to reclaim more land on which to revive this ancient system of agriculture that has proven to be so effective (Kolata 1996). In such ways, basic research in anthropology demonstrates its use when applied to human problems.

people in the modern global economy must struggle to make a living.

The contemporary world is characterized by connectedness and change of a magnitude greater than anything seen earlier. Events in seemingly far-off places have a direct impact on the ways people make a living: A shutdown of oil wells in the Persian Gulf halts generating plants in Ohio. Indians and Koreans are recruited to build cities in the deserts of the Middle East. A woman from the Philippines finds a job as a nurse in New York or a waitress in an Israeli restaurant. For some people, the expansion of the global economy has meant new and more satisfying means of making a living.

However, these opportunities are not equally available to all peoples or to all individuals within a culture. The promise of the global economy is yet to be fulfilled. Meanwhile, it has created many new problems, including degradation of the environment.

Different kinds of livelihood and economic systems all affect the quality of the environment—water, forests, air, animal and plant life. Tropical and other old-growth forests all over the world, critical for the maintenance of biodiversity, have been particularly hard hit. Significant factors here are the corporate and state exploitation of tropical forests to meet consumer demands for tropical forest products and increasing population in nations within which these forests are located. Tropical forest and other environmental conservation efforts have thus become a critical global issue, one in which ecological anthropologists play an important role (see Murray 1986; Kottack 1999; Brosius 1999). Anthropology is particularly sensitive to the complex linkages between local, regional, national, and global contexts that structure the modern world. Anthropologists today can play an important role in shaping government and global economic policies that take into account the environmental impact of different ways of making a living, the values and practices of local cultures, international plant and animal conservation efforts, and corporate- and state-driven efforts to participate in global markets.

SUMMARY

1. Different physical environments present different problems, opportunities, and limitations to human populations. In the quest for survival, humans have had increasingly intensive impacts on their environments as their populations have increased and they have developed more complex forms of social and economic organization. Ecological anthropology examines the interrelationships between humans and their environments.

2. The subsistence (food-getting) pattern of a society develops in response to seasonal variation in the environment and environmental variations over the long run, such as drought, flood, or animal diseases.

3. Modern science and technology are important strategies for successfully exploiting diverse environments. But traditional ways of using the land, based on simple but ingenious technology and vast knowledge of the environment, can also be successful strategies of environmental management.

4. The five major patterns of using the environment to support human populations are foraging (hunting and gathering), pastoralism, horticulture (extensive cultivation), agriculture (intensive cultivation), and industrialism. As a whole, humankind has moved in the direction of using more complex technology, increasing its numbers, and developing more complex sociocultural systems.

5. Foraging, which relies on food naturally available in the environment, was the major food-getting pattern for 99 percent of the time humans have been on earth. Although this way of life is rapidly disappearing, foraging is still a useful adjunct to other subsistence strategies for many societies.

6. Traditionally, the aboriginal peoples of Australia were adept at surviving in harsh desert areas, using their deep knowledge of the wide variety of plants, animals, and other edible resources of their environment. Despite extremes of climate, particularly heat and the absence of water, their seasonal round permitted them to exploit a wide range of resources in their quest for food, and provided them with a reasonably reliable subsistence strategy.

7. Pastoralism involves the care of domesticated herd animals, which alone cannot provide the necessary ingredients for an adequate human diet. Because supplementary food grains are required, pastoralism either is found along with cultivation or involves trading relations with food cultivators.

8. The Yarahmadzai of Baluchistan are a pastoralist society. In addition to their herds, they also use other means of obtaining food: date cultivation, wage labor, and trade.

9. Horticulturalists use a simple, nonmechanized technology. Fields are not used permanently but are allowed to lie fallow after several years of productivity. Horticulture is typically a tropical forest adaptation and requires the cutting and burning of jungle to clear fields for cultivation.

10. The Lua' are swidden cultivators of the mountainous region of northern Thailand. Their major crops are cotton, corn, yams, rice, and sorghum; they also grow vegetables and keep pigs, water buffalo, cattle, and chickens, which they may sell at local markets for cash. The Lua' mixed economy is becoming more typical for horticulturalists in the modern world.

11. Agriculture uses land and labor intensively, with a complex technology that involves plows, irrigation, or mechanization. This food-getting pattern generally supports greater population densities than all but industrial patterns. It is associated with sedentary village life and the rise of the state.

12. Peasants, like those in Musha, Egypt, are cultivators who produce mainly for the subsistence of their households and who are part of larger po-

litical entities, such as the state. For peasants, agriculture is the main source of subsistence, but they also participate in the larger cash economy of the state, engage in wage labor, and have some occupational specialties. Peasant farmers are controlled in many ways by state pricing and other regulatory policies, although at the local level they must also make important decisions about their work.

13. Industrialism is a system in which machines and chemical processes are used for the production of goods. Industrial societies require a large, mobile labor force. They are characterized by complex systems of exchange among all elements of the economy and by social stratification. Taiwan is an example of a society making the transition from peasant agriculture to industrialization.

KEY TERMS

agriculture (intensive cultivation)

bureaucracy

efficiency

foraging (hunting and gathering)

horticulture (extensive cultivation

industrialism

nomadism

pastoralism

patrilineal

peasants

population density

productivity

rain forest

sedentary

subsistence strategies

swidden (slash and burn)

transhumance

SUGGESTED READINGS

Condon, Richard G., with Julia Ogina and the Holman Elders. 1996. *The Northern Copper Inuit: A History.* Toronto: University of Toronto Press. A record of the many social, economic, and material changes experienced by a group of Copper Inuit on the west coast of Victoria Island, former nomadic hunter-gatherers who have become dependent on the modern consumer products of Western society.

Denslow, Julie Sloan, and Christine Padoch. 1988. *People of the Tropical Rain Forest.* Berkeley: University of California Press. A beautifully illustrated, sensitive portrayal of the many peoples who inhabit the tropical rain forests in different parts of the world. The book includes essays on what we can learn from tropical forest peoples and the impact of the modern global economy on their subsistence economies and environments.

Evans-Pritchard, E. E. 1968. *The Nuer.* Oxford: Clarendon Press. *The* classic ethnography of East African pastoralists, with a focus on ecology.

Griffith, David, Ed Kissam, Jeronimo Campseco, Anna Garcia, Max Pfeffer, David Runsten, and Manuel Valdes Pizzini. 1995. *Working Poor: Farmworkers in the United States.* Philadelphia: Temple University Press. A model of field research by a team, this meticulous study of farmwork in California, Texas, Florida, Puerto Rico, New Jersey, and Michigan places this way of making a living in the context of American culture and the global economy.

Lieber, Michael. 1994. *More than a Living: Fishing and the Social Order on a Polynesian Atoll.* Boulder, CO: Westview Press. This ethnography of a tiny Micronesian atoll helps fill the gap in anthropological analyses of fishing as a subsistence strategy. Its focus on the changing context of fishing activities provides useful insights applicable to the issue of overfishing now faced by many Pacific Island peoples.

Roberts, Glenda S. 1994. *Staying on the Line: Blue-Collar Women in Contemporary Japan.* Honolulu: University of Hawaii Press. Based on ethnography in a garment factory in Japan, in which the workers largely speak for themselves, this study adds to our knowledge of the Japanese workplace, which up till now has mainly focused on white-collar employment.

INTERNET RESOURCES

WWW

The following Internet resources appear in this chapter. Please log on to the Wadsworth anthropology website: **http://anthropology.wadsworth. com.** Click on the Nanda/Warms *Cultural Anthropology* page. Then select the Student Resources section, where you will find a complete presentation of these links and more.

- A photo essay on the changing sources of energy in transportation, page 147
- A video link: Foraging: The Alaskan Inuit, page 150
- A link to the websites of major nature conservation organizations, 166
- Access the Study Guide to InfoTrac College Edition for Anthropology Students

AT THE MARKET OUTSIDE THE GREAT MOSQUE IN DJENNE, MALI, AFRICA, TRADITIONAL AND MODERN ECONOMIES MIX AS PEOPLE COME TO BUY AND SELL FOOD AND HANDICRAFTS, AS WELL AS MANUFACTURED GOODS FROM ALL OVER THE WORLD.

CHAPTER EIGHT

ECONOMICS

What is economizing behavior, and how does this concept apply to anthropology?

How are critical resources such as land allocated in various societies?

How do gender and age relate to the organization of labor in different societies?

What is the relationship between the sociopolitical organization of a society and its system of exchange?

What is capitalism, and how does it differ from other ways in which economies can be organized?

Do all groups in a capitalist society participate in the capitalist economy?

All human societies have **economic systems** within which goods and services are produced, distributed, and consumed. In one sense, the economic aspect of culture is simply the sum of the choices people make regarding these areas of their lives. These choices critically determine much of people's lives. For example, choosing to become a farmer rather than an insurance broker may determine where you live, who you are likely to meet, the sorts of behaviors you will expect in your spouse and offspring, and so on. However, such choices are not unlimited; rather, they are constrained by our cultures, traditions, and technologies. Furthermore, our environments set the boundaries within which choices about the production, distribution, and consumption of goods and services are made. To the extent that economic systems are part of culture, people in different cultures have differing sorts of economic behavior.

nomics deals partly with things—with the tools used to produce goods, and the goods themselves. More important, it deals with the relationship of things to people and people to one another in the process of producing, distributing, and consuming goods. Anthropologists are interested in understanding the relationship between the economy and the rest of a culture. One aspect of this relationship is that culture defines or shapes the ends sought by individuals and the means of achieving those ends.

Society and economy are interdependent in other ways. The way in which production is organized has consequences for the institution of the family and for the political system. For example, in southern Mali, where most people live by agriculture and where land is abundant, children can help farm when they are very young. Thus, families tend to have as many children as they possibly can. Large families can cultivate more land and therefore are generally wealthier than small families. Their leaders acquire the political power and social prestige that derives from having wealth and numerous relations.

ECONOMIC SYSTEMS

An economic system is the part of a society that deals with the production, distribution, and consumption of goods and services. Eco-

economic system The norms governing production, distribution, and consumption of goods and services within a society.

DECISIONS THESE STOCK TRADERS MAKE ON THE FLOOR ARE BASED ALMOST ENTIRELY ON PROFIT AND LOSS. HOWEVER, MOST OF THE TIME, OUR DECISIONS ARE MOTIVATED BY OTHER CONSIDERATIONS AS WELL. WE MAY PREFER RELAXATION AND FREE TIME TO FINANCIAL RETURN.

Jonathan Kirn/Stone

Although economists often attempt to do so, it is difficult to separate the economic system from the rest of culture. Economics is embedded in the total social process and cultural pattern. In nonindustrial and kin-based societies, for example, few groups are organized solely for the purpose of production; their economic activities are only one aspect of what they do. Production is carried out by groups such as families, larger kinship groups, or local communities. The distribution, exchange, and consumption of goods is thus embedded in relationships that have social and political purposes as well as economic ones.

ECONOMIC BEHAVIOR

Economics is the study of the ways in which the choices people make as individuals and as members of societies combine to determine

economics The study of the ways in which the choices people make combine to determine how their society uses its scarce resources to produce and distribute goods and services.

economizing behavior Choosing a course of action that pursues the course of perceived maximum benefit.

how their society uses its scarce resources to produce and distribute goods and services. The academic discipline of economics developed in a Western market economy, and there has been much debate within anthropology over its applicability to other cultures (Isaac 1993).

The idea of scarcity is a fundamental assumption of Western microeconomic theory. Economists assume that human wants are unlimited but the means for achieving them are not. If this is correct, organizations and individuals must make decisions about the best way to apply their limited means to meet their unlimited desires. Economists assume that individuals and organizations will make such choices in the way they believe provides the greatest benefit to them. Economists call such choices **economizing behavior.**

Some scholars have equated benefit with material well-being and profit (see Dalton 1961). Will a business firm cut down or expand its production? Will it purchase a new machine or hire more laborers? Where will it locate its plant? Will it manufacture shoes or gloves? How much will be spent on advertising its product? Such decisions are assumed to be motivated by an analysis designed to produce the greatest cash profit and are assumed to be rational—that is, based on the desire to maximize profit.

The notion of financial profit is very limited, however. Consider a choice you may make this evening. After you finish reading this chapter, you may well be confronted with a series of decisions: Should you reread it for better comprehension? Should you study for another course? Should you make a call and get a pizza delivered? Should you go out and socialize with your friends? Of course, there are many other possibilities.

You will make your choice based on some calculation of benefit. However, that benefit is not necessarily reducible to financial profit. It is quite possible for you to believe that you would ultimately make more money by studying and getting higher grades; yet because your choice is set in a context in which making money is not the only element of value, you may choose to socialize instead. We value our friends and our leisure time as well as many other things. Your choice is rational because it is based on some calculation of your needs and goals, but it need not lead to greater profit. If we were to predict your behavior on the assumption that you will always act to increase your material well-being, our predictions would be inaccurate. We would do better by asking what motivates you.

Just as you might value an evening spent with friends over an "A" in this class, members of other cultures might value family connections, community stability, cultural tradition, leisure time, or other things over monetary profit. People everywhere make rational choices based on their needs and their guesses about the future. But culture, values, and institutions provide the framework within which these choices are made. For example, Western culture is dominated by capitalism. We place an extremely high value on wealth and material prosperity and see the marketplace as the primary institution through which those goals can be achieved. In our popular mythology, those who can achieve high levels of wealth and consumption, such as athletes, actors, and entrepreneurs, are held up as role models. We are easily motivated by monetary profit (but not exclusively so). On the other hand, some other societies appear to be in business for their health (Sahlins 1972).

The Hadza, a hunting-gathering people of Tanzania, live in an area with an abundance of animal and vegetable food. Hadza men spend much of their time gambling, and they make no attempt to use leisure time to increase wealth. Surrounded by cultivators, for a long time the Hadza refused to give up their hunting way of life because it would require too much work (Woodburn 1968). Such behavior seems irrational or lazy only if we assume that people should value material wealth over free time. This is clearly not the case among the Hadza, or even among many North Americans.

Enjoyable use of leisure time is only one of the ends toward which human effort may be expended. Increasing social status or respect is another value toward which people may direct their energies. In Western society, **prestige** is primarily tied up with increased consumption and display of goods and services. In some other societies, prestige is associated not with individual display but with generosity and the giving away of goods to others. Those who have much more than others may be considered stingy, and they may lose rather than gain prestige. Conspicuous consumers and stingy people become objects of scorn and may even be accused of witchcraft. Thus, we cannot assume that people's choices are motivated only by material well-being as we understand it.

In order to understand the economies of different cultures, anthropologists face two related problems. They must attempt to analyze the broad institutional and social contexts within which people make decisions, and they must attempt to determine and evaluate the factors that motivate individual decision making. These are important intellectual projects in their own right, but they become crucial in applied anthropology. Applied anthropologists are often concerned with issues of economic development in poor nations. It is very difficult to design programs that promote development in a foreign culture without a thorough understanding of that culture's institutions and the forces that motivate its people.

PRODUCTION

In order to produce, people must have access to basic resources: land, water, and the materials from which tools are made. Every society has norms or rules that regulate access to and control over these resources. In addition, labor must be controlled and organized to make these resources work. Examining these provides insight into the cultural variations in economy.

ALLOCATING RESOURCES

Productive resources are the things that members of a society need to participate in the economy. Thus, access to and control of productive resources are basic to every economy.

prestige Social honor or respect.

productive resources Material goods, natural resources, or information that is used to create other goods or information.

People everywhere require access to land and water. Until relatively recently, in most societies these were the most important resources. But access to tools and the materials to make them, as well as knowledge, also played important roles. Among fishing societies, for example, productive resources include watercraft and elaborate trapping and netting devices that require a great investment of time and labor.

An important point of contrast between economic systems is the extent to which the members of a society have access to productive resources. In general, differential access to resources develops as population and social complexity increase. Small-scale economies have a limited number of productive resources, and most everyone has access to them. Large-scale societies have a great many more resources, but access to them is limited. This can be seen by comparing access to resources among foragers, pastoralists, and extensive and intensive cultivators.

FORAGERS

Among foragers, weapons used in hunting animals and tools used in gathering plants are productive resources. The technology is simple, and tools are made by hand. People take great care to assure that they have access to the tools necessary for their individual survival. For example, among the Hadza of Tanzania, men spend much time gambling. Personally owned objects such as knives, pipes, necklaces, and clothing are routinely gambled. However, a man's bow, bird arrows, and leather bag are never shared or gambled, because these items are essential to survival (Woodburn 1998). As a result, every male always has access to these resources.

Besides tools, land and water are the most critical resources for foragers, and many forms of land tenure are found among them. The requirements of a foraging lifestyle generally mean that a group of people must spread out over a large area of land. The adaptive value of flexible boundaries is directly related to foraging strategies because ranges can be adjusted to a change in the availability of resources in a particular area. This is also related to the abundance and predictability of resources. Where resources are scarce and large areas are needed to support the population, territorial boundaries are not defended. Where resources are more abundant and people move less, groups may be more inclined to defend their territory (Cashdan 1989:42).

The Ju/'hoansi of the Kalahari were typical foragers. Although today most Ju/'hoansi are settled, in earlier times their camps were located near water holes, and the area used by a local group was measured by one day's round-trip walk (about 12 miles from the camp) in all directions. Each camp had a core area of about 6 miles surrounding each water hole. By fanning out from the water hole, camp members gained access to food resources within about 100 square miles. Points beyond this were rarely used. Although camps were moved five or six times a year, they were not moved far. Sometimes the move was only a few hundred yards; the farthest move was about 10 or 12 miles (R. Lee 1968). Ju/'hoansi territories were associated with long-standing residents who were spoken of as owners, although they did not have exclusive rights to the land. Their permission had to be asked when others wished to use the land's resources, but it was rarely refused, although visitors might be made to feel unwelcome (Cashdan 1989:41).

Hunters and gatherers require freedom of movement not only as a condition of success in their search for food but also as a way of dealing with social conflict. Hunting bands are kept small in order to exploit the environment successfully. In such small groups, conflict must be kept to a minimum. When arguments break out, individuals can move to other groups without fear that they are cutting themselves off from access to vital resources. If land were individually or even communally defended against outsiders, the freedom of movement in hunting societies would be severely limited.

PASTORALISTS

Among pastoralists, the most critical resources are livestock and land. Access to grassland and water is gained through membership in corporate kin groups. Within pastoralist camps, all members share equal access to pastures. It is this right of access, rather than ownership, that is important. Livestock, on the other hand, is owned and managed by individual heads of households. Animals produce goods that are directly consumed, such as milk; they are also kept to produce other animals and used in exchange. Because animals must be cared for and fed, maintenance of these productive resources requires substantial time and energy.

Pastoral tribes have traditionally determined access to pasture and migration routes by arrangements with local authorities who have control over these areas. Contemporary pastoralists often establish access to land for grazing livestock by contracts with the landowners of villages through which the pastoralists move in their migrations. These contracts, which must be renewed every year, specify the rent for the pasture, the borders of the area, and the date by which the area must be vacated.

The yak-herding Drokba of northwestern Tibet present an interesting historical example. The Drokba were under the control of large Buddhist monasteries that owned all the grassland. Families were granted rights to use pastures in return for tax payments. Allocation of pastureland was reviewed every third year and altered to fit family herd size and composition. The system worked well because the land could be managed to even out grazing (Barfield 1993:188).

EXTENSIVE CULTIVATORS

Besides land and tools, horticultural societies often require storage facilities. These facilities must be built and maintained. In such societies, land tends to be communally owned by an extended kin group, although rights to use a piece of land may be given to households or even individuals. The users of the land may not sell it or otherwise transfer it, however, because ultimately the land belongs to the larger community. Designated elders or officials of the group often allocate plots to members of the group or heads of households. For example, among the Ibo, swidden farmers in Nigeria, no individual owns land or has permanent rights to it. Instead, land is vested in kinship groups and allocated to individuals by leaders of these groups (Acheson 1989). But even the group that has rights to use the land may not dispose of it at will; land is "inalienable" and may not be sold. With this type of land ownership, few people are deprived of access to basic resources because almost every person belongs to a group within the society. Control over land, therefore, is not a means by which one group can exploit another or exert permanent control over other groups.

In societies based on extensive agriculture, the work involved in clearing, cultivating, and maintaining the land is a large investment and is more important than exclusive title to the land. The rights to cleared and productive land and to the products of that land are vested in those who work it, most often the domestic group or household. Because the user of the land may die while the land is still productive, some system of inheritance of use rights is usually provided for.

Among the Lacandon Maya, for example, individuals may farm any unused piece of land. However, clearing virgin land is very difficult, so individuals retain rights to land they have cleared and are likely to reuse after 10–20 years. People who migrate from the area may lose rights to land they have cleared, but their family retains ownership of any fruit trees that have been planted on it. Should a man die after investing time and labor in clearing and planting land, his wife and children retain rights to use the land (McGee 1990).

Where population densities are low or large areas of land are available for cultivation, rights to land use are very loosely held. For example, among the Machiguenga of Peru, a group with extensive lands, there is little sense of exclusive territory, although it is considered polite to ask permission before foraging near another settlement (Johnson 1989:58). But when specific geographical conditions limit the amount of land available, or when population pressures increase, land shortages do occur, as among the Enga in the New Guinea highlands. There the problem is dealt with primarily by warfare. Most Enga warfare is aimed at driving smaller, weaker groups off their land and annexing it (Johnson 1989:62). Warfare is not the only

IN SOCIETIES WITH INTENSIVE CULTIVATION, THOSE WHO WORK THE LAND ARE NOT NECESSARILY THOSE WHO OWN IT. LAND MAY BE OWNED BY ABSENTEE LANDLORDS OR LARGE COMMERCIAL ORGANIZATIONS. IN THIS PICTURE, MIGRANT WORKERS HARVEST ONIONS ON A FARM IN IDAHO.

Leon Patenburg/Index Stock Photography, Inc.

way land shortages can be dealt with. Sometimes they are alleviated by the development of more efficient technology. In this case, horticulturalists may become intensive cultivators.

INTENSIVE CULTIVATORS

In politically and technologically more complex societies, access to the means of production is likely to be in the hands of a ruling elite. In these societies, intensive cultivation of the land comes to dominate production. Technology becomes more complex, and the material base of a society expands. Productive resources take many forms, including complex tools and the technological knowledge required to make them. Ownership of these critical resources may be limited to a small group whose members thereby gain power over others and control their labor.

In some societies, productive resources become **capital.** Capital resources are continually reinvested in order to generate profit for

capital Productive resources that are used with the primary goal of increasing their owner's financial wealth.

their owners beyond their subsistence needs. Although the use of capital occurs in many different sorts of societies (Berdan 1989), it becomes the principal form of economic organization in capitalist societies (discussed later in this chapter).

Under conditions of intensive cultivation, the material and labor investment in land becomes substantial. As land remains in production, it produces surpluses and can feed more people than those who work it. When this happens, private ownership of land becomes common. Land belongs to individuals by right of sale, and within the limits of the law, the individual who owns it has the right to keep others off and dispose of it as he or she wishes.

Individual land ownership may grow out of population pressures that produce land scarcity and lead to intensified methods of agriculture. Under these conditions, communal control of land creates conflict as people begin to grumble about not receiving their fair share. Those who have improved the land are unwilling to see the investment of their labor revert to a family pool. This may be particularly true in the case of cash crops such as coffee, which require long-term care and yield harvests over many years. Individuals thus become tied to particular plots of land. In a study of land use and rights in the New Guinea highlands, Brown and Podelefsky (1976) found that individual ownership of land was correlated with high population density and intensive agriculture. Individual rights to land (though within the framework of group territory) occurred where plots of land were in permanent use or had a short fallow period (less than six years) and where trees and shrubs had been planted by the owner.

Private or family ownership of rigidly defined fields does not necessarily mean that landowners work their fields. Instead, fields are usually rented to laborers whose efforts support both themselves and the landowners. For example, a study of a rural village in Bangladesh showed that 48 percent of families were functionally landless. Their members had to rent land from large landowners or work for others (Michael Harris 1991:151–155). Under conditions such as these, a peasantry emerges. Peasants are agriculturalists who are integrated into large state-level societies (see Chapter 7). Part of what they produce is taken by a ruling class in the form of rents and taxes.

In societies with peasantries, landowners rather than cultivators are able to claim most of the surplus, and land becomes an economic asset of great value. Landowners enjoy higher levels of consumption and standards of living based on rents and services they receive from the peasants. Landowners use these surpluses to command the services of craft workers, servants, and sometimes armed forces. Intensive cultivation therefore tends to be associated with a political organization characterized by a ruling landowning class and with occupational specialization.

ORGANIZING LABOR

In small-scale preindustrial and peasant economies, the household or some extended kin group is the basic unit of production and consumption (B. White 1980). These groups produce goods mainly for their own use. Their goals are often social or religious rather than strictly monetary. Labor is not a commodity bought and sold in the market; rather, it is one aspect of a role that derives its primary meaning and reward from membership in a social group such as the family.

In Western society, work has very important social implications. It is a source not only of money but also of self-respect, challenge, growth, and personal fulfillment. Political scientist Alan Ryan (1996) has noted, "We do not go to work only to earn an income, but to find meaning in our lives. What we do is a large part of what we are." People work to consider themselves participants in society as well as for financial gain. In the United States, for example, many people say they play the lottery with the dream of striking it rich and never working again. However, in the 1980s, 88 percent of winners of very large lottery jackpots wanted to continue working despite the fact that they had no financial need. In Japan, the number was 93.4 percent (Trice and Beyer 1993).

FIRMS AND HOUSEHOLDS

In most nonindustrial societies, production is based around the household. Anthropologists generally differentiate between the household and the family (Rapp 1991). The **household** is an economic unit—a group of people united by kinship or other links who share a residence and organize production, consumption, and distribution among themselves. The family is an ideological construct—a set of ideas about how people are related to one another and what their mutual obligations are (Narotzky 1997). It is clear that family and household can refer to different groups of people. Households, for example, frequently include servants and lodgers, but these people are not considered family members.

Production and consumption based around kin groups and households are different from those in industrial societies, where the basic unit of production is the business firm. A business **firm** is an institution composed of kin and/or nonkin that is organized primarily for financial gain. Individuals are usually tied to firms through the sale of their labor for wages. Labor is thus a commodity, bought and sold on the market. A firm does not produce goods for the use of its members; the items it produces are sold for profit.

Firms are geared toward economic growth. They can make their decisions primarily on an economic basis and tap large reserves of labor. Even when they are not geared solely to the profit of individual owners, firms are always looking for technological innovation and expansion of productivity.

On the other hand, the structure of households and kin groups as producing units limits their economic growth. In addition to seeking financial gain, households must also fill social and ritual functions. They are limited because

household A group of people united by kinship or other links who share a residence and organize production, consumption, and distribution among themselves.

firm An institution composed of kin and/or nonkin that is organized primarily for financial gain.

Jim Olive/Pictor

Robert Frerck/Odyssey Productions

SEX-ROLE SPECIALIZATION IN CRAFT ACTIVITIES VARIES CROSS-CULTURALLY. IN GHANA MEN DO THE WEAVING, BUT IN THE NAVAJO NATION WEAVING IS A WOMAN'S TASK.

they can draw labor from only a small group. A household cannot easily liquidate if it makes poor choices in the allocation of its resources (M. Nash 1967).

In economies where households are the producing units, there can be little expansion. Thus, large-scale production and mass distribution systems tend not to develop where economic systems are made up entirely of households. However, as we will see in the ethnography of Turkey later in this chapter, household social relations can play an important role in an industrialized economy.

DIVISION OF LABOR BY SEX

The sexual division of labor is a universal characteristic of human society. In every society, some tasks are considered appropriate only for women and others only for men. At some level, the basis for the division of labor between men and women is biological: Only women can bear and nurse children. Thus, caring for infants is almost universally a female role (see Nielsen 1990:147–168). Pregnancy and nursing tend to make women less mobile than men, and this may account for the fact that tasks that require mobility such as hunting large animals and warfare (in nonindustrial societies) are almost exclusively male occupations. As we will see in Chapter 11, however, the extent to which biological sex differences can explain sex-role differentiation is a matter of dispute among anthropologists.

Most anthropologists emphasize the tremendous variation in the sex-related division of labor, and they look for explanations in the environment, food-getting strategy, ideology, and level of sociopolitical complexity of the particular society. Furthermore, as Elizabeth Brumfiel (1991) notes, assigning specific tasks to one gender or another is actually quite complicated. Whether men or women perform a particular chore may depend on how the job is defined, the conditions under which it is done, and the personality of the individual doing it. The Sabarl, island dwellers who live near New Guinea, provide a good example of this. Among them, forms of wealth and labor are unambiguously classified as either male or female. However, women often do men's work and men often do women's work. The Sabarl explain this by quoting the proverb, "Some birds can swim, some fish can fly" (Battaglia 1992:5). Despite this variation, there are important general trends.

In foraging societies hunting is generally men's work and gathering is usually done by women (although, as noted in Chapter 10, there are exceptions). Among the Aché of Paraguay, for example, men hunt almost continually. Women are responsible for gathering food and carrying the family's belongings on their very frequent moves. Although women's work may sound dull, they spend only about 13 hours a week getting food and have much more leisure time than men (Hill, Hawkes, and Hurtado 1985; Hurtado et al. 1985). Where hunting is a communal activity, as among the Mbuti, women and men from several families collectively drive the animals into some central area, although men do the actual killing. In some societies, men and women also work together gathering nuts or fishing in streams (Turnbull 1983).

In societies that practice extensive cultivation, both men and women play important roles in food production. However, there is an inverse relationship between the dietary importance of cultivated food (cultigens) and women's responsibility for food production. As societies depend increasingly on cultigens, men's role in food production increases and women's role decreases (Bossen 1989). In some cases women are responsible for cultivating the basic staples and men raise only the prestige crops used in exchange. In highland New Guinea, for example, women raise sweet potatoes, which are the main food for humans as well as pigs, and men raise sugar, taro, and bananas, which are used only in exchange.

In societies that practice intensive cultivation (agriculture), the general shift toward male dominance in farming activities continues. Wielding the plow is almost always a male task. In irrigation agriculture, women still do weeding and, if rice is grown, transplant the paddy, but men do most of the work in digging irrigation ditches, lifting water from wells and canals, and repairing terraces.

Many new demands are placed on women in farming societies. The time they spend in domestic tasks such as food preservation and processing and caring for domestic animals increases. Furthermore, because women in agricultural societies generally have more children than those in foraging or horticultural societies, time spent in child care increases (Bossen 1989).

Agricultural societies are a good example of the principle that women lose status as the unpaid work they do in the home increases. Flood (1994), for example, reports that as agriculture in Zinacantan, Mexico, has modernized, women's work has been devalued. Many of the goods and services they contributed to the household are now easily available for purchase. At the same time, technological changes in farming have increased men's dependence on the market. The result has been that whereas Zinacantec women are increasingly dependent on men, Zinacantec men are less and less dependent on women. Women's position in society has suffered as a result.

Women's dependence on men in agricultural societies is conditioned by the fact that land is the primary productive resource, and access to land is frequently through men. When societies become more urbanized and families migrate to the cities, women's position is affected. Vincent (1998) compares two generations of women in Mata Chico, Peru. In the 1930s, access to land was critical to peasant livelihoods. Since the only way women and their children could access land was through marriage, they were under great pressure to take husbands. By the 1980s, however, Peru was increasingly urbanized and many occupations were available to both men and women. Since women could support themselves and their children through employment in urban areas they began to remain single longer, and, in some cases chose not to marry at all. Problems faced by women as a result of cultural change in the

INDUSTRIALIZATION OF SOCIETIES LEADS TO ENORMOUS SPECIALIZATION OF LABOR, OFTEN AT THE PRICE OF INDEPENDENCE AND MEANING. IN "MODERN TIMES" (1936), CHARLIE CHAPLIN DRAMATIZED THIS BY PLAYING THE ROLE OF AN ASSEMBLY LINE WORKER.

contemporary world are discussed more fully in Chapter 11.

SPECIALIZATION IN COMPLEX SOCIETIES

Some societies have very simple technologies. For example, although the tools and techniques of foragers are ingenious and fit the requirements of their environment, toolmaking does not require skills beyond those that can be learned through informal socialization. The work involved in making the tools of production can be done by every adult and requires no machines or scarce materials. There is little need for specialization.

Among hunter-gatherers and most horticulturalists, all adult men and women are actively engaged in the quest for food. The few specialists (for example, religious practitioners) are usually part-time specialists who also engage in food production. The characteristic division of labor is not by job but, as we have noted, by age and sex. This contrasts with industrial society, in which production is highly specialized.

The division of labor in society becomes more specialized and complex as the population increases and agricultural production intensifies. Agricultural surpluses are required to support specialists who consume food but do not produce it. These surpluses may be of two kinds: surpluses of perishable goods and surpluses of storable goods. Perishable goods may be used for exchanges, such as the Kula and potlatch described later in this chapter. However, since these goods must be either consumed immediately or left to rot, they rarely lead to high levels of full-time specialization. Storable goods such as grains, on the other hand, can be stockpiled and used to feed large numbers of people over extended periods. The result is that societies based on grain agriculture are able to support large numbers of full-time occupational specialists.

The caste system in India provides an excellent example of occupational specialization. In casted India, only people belonging to particular hereditary kinship groups are allowed to perform certain services or produce certain kinds of goods. Literally thousands of specialized activities—washing clothes, drumming at festivals, presiding over religious ceremonies, making pots, painting pictures—are traditionally performed by various castes within a village or even by villages as a whole.

Industrialization as an adaptive strategy requires the greatest specialization of labor. Only a small proportion of the population is directly involved in producing food. The remainder, supported by these food producers, are involved in countless specializations. A quick glance at the Yellow Pages of a phone book of a major American city gives a good indication of the degree of specialization in American society. Although specialization of production undoubtedly has advantages, in terms of efficiency and the ability to produce large quantities of goods, we must also consider the price to be paid in terms of nonmaterial human values.

DISTRIBUTION: SYSTEMS OF EXCHANGE

In all societies, goods and services are exchanged. In fact, some anthropologists have long theorized that the exchange of goods is one of the fundamental bases of culture. The great French anthropologist Marcel Mauss (1924/1990) theorized that societies were held together by patterns of giving and receiving. He pointed out that gifts invariably must be repaid. Through exchange we are obligated to each other, and in many situations it is better to give than to receive.

There are three main ways in which exchange occurs: reciprocity, redistribution, and market exchange. Although more than one kind of exchange system exists in most societies, each system is predominantly associated with a certain kind of political and social organization (Polyani 1944). Where there is more than one system, each is normally used for the exchange of different kinds of goods and services. Let us look first at reciprocity.

RECIPROCITY

Reciprocity is the mutual give-and-take among people of equal status and is actually a continuum of forms of exchange. Three types of reciprocity are distinguished from one another by the degree of social distance between the exchanging partners. Generalized reciprocity, which is usually carried out among close kin, has the highest degree of moral obligation. Balanced reciprocity is characteristic of the relationship between friends or members of different tribes in a peaceable relationship with one another. Negative reciprocity refers to exchanges between strangers or peoples hostile to one another (Sahlins 1972).

GENERALIZED RECIPROCITY

Generalized reciprocity involves a distribution of goods in which no overt account is kept of what is given and no immediate or specific return is expected. Such transactions are ideally altruistic—that is, without any thought of economic or other self-interest. Assistance is given and, if possible and necessary, returned. In Western society, we are familiar with generalized reciprocity as it exists between parents and children. Parents are constantly giving things and providing services to their children out of love or a sense of responsibility. What would we think of a parent who kept an account of what a child "cost" and then expected the child to repay this amount? What parents

usually expect is some gratitude, love, respect, and the child's happiness.

Generalized reciprocity involving food is an important social mechanism among foraging peoples. In these societies, a hunter or group of hunters distributes meat among the kin group or camp. Each person or family gets either an equal share or a share dependent on its kinship relationship to the hunter.

Robert Dentan (1979:48) describes this system among the Semai of Malaysia:

> After several days of fruitless hunting, a Semai man kills a large pig. He lugs it back to the settlement. Everyone gathers around. Two other men meticulously divide the pig into portions sufficient to feed two adults each (children are not supposed to eat pork). As nearly as possible each portion contains exactly the same amount of meat, fat, liver, and innards as every other portion. The adult men take the leaf-wrapped portions home to redistribute them among the members of the house group.

Similar systems are used by the Ju/'hoansi of the Kalahari and the Inuit (Figure 8.1).

A North American might wonder, What does the hunter get out of it? Aren't some people always in the position of providing and others always receiving? Part of the answer is that hunters gain satisfaction from accomplishing a highly skilled and difficult task (Woodburn 1998). However, in many cases they also receive other rewards. Because all people in the society are bound by the same rules, the system provides everyone with the opportunity to give and receive, though this cannot assure that people actually do give and receive equally. In addition, the hunter may derive a degree of status from his kill. For example, among the Pacaa Nova, a horticultural group in Brazil, distributing meat gives a man prestige and an opportunity to display the culture's most valued trait, generosity. At the same time,

reciprocity A mutual give-and-take among people of equal status.

generalized reciprocity A distribution of goods with no immediate or specific return expected.

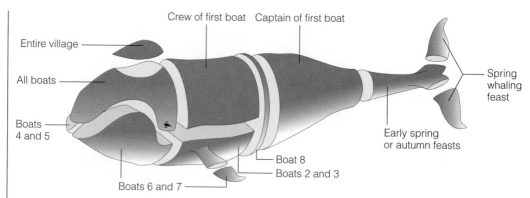

FIGURE 8.1

HUNTING OF WHALES BY THE INUIT INVOLVES TEN TO FIFTEEN BOATS STANDING BY. THE FIRST EIGHT BOATS TO REACH AND HARPOON THE WHALE RECEIVE STIPULATED PORTIONS OF THE MEAT. THE CAPTAIN OF EACH BOAT GETS HIS TRADITIONAL PART OF THE BODY, AND HE SHARES HIS MEAT WITH HIS CREW. THE CAPTAIN OF THE FIRST BOAT GIVES THE SHAMAN A NARROW STRIP CUT FROM THE BELLY BETWEEN THE EIGHTH BOAT'S STRIP AND THE GENITALS. THE TOP OF THE HEAD IS CUT UP AND EATEN AT ONCE BY EVERYONE IN THE VILLAGE. PORTIONS OF THE TAIL ARE SAVED FOR FEASTING IN THE SPRING AND AUTUMN.

Source: Carleton S. Coon, *The Hunting Peoples*. Boston: Little, Brown, 1971, pp. 124–125. By permission of the estate of Carleton S. Coon.

it builds his credit for future reciprocity (van Graeve 1989:66). In small societies, where the good opinion of others is really necessary for survival, the desire not to be thought stingy is a strong motivation to share and to do one's share.

Generalized reciprocity also has important adaptive functions. One hunter and his family probably could not consume the meat from a large animal at one sitting. Without techniques for storing and preserving food, the meat would go to waste if it were not distributed beyond the family.

BALANCED RECIPROCITY

Balanced reciprocity involves a clear obligation to return, within a specified time limit, goods of nearly equal value. The fact that balanced reciprocity is most often called gift giving obscures its economic importance in societies where it is the dominant form of exchange. We are familiar with balanced reciprocity when we give gifts at weddings or birthdays, ex-

balanced reciprocity An exchange of goods of nearly equal value, with a clear obligation to return them within a specified time limit.

change invitations, or buy a round of drinks for friends. In these exchanges, it is always the spirit of the gift and the social relationship between the givers that people say is important. The economic aspect of the exchange is repressed. However, we also know that an unreciprocated gift or a return gift of very different value will evoke negative feelings. Similarly, accepting an invitation involves the obligation to offer an invitation in the future.

The social obligation to give, accept, and return is at the heart of balanced reciprocity. A refusal to receive or a failure to reciprocate a gift is taken as a withdrawal from a social relationship. A gift that is accepted puts the receiver under an obligation to the giver, and if the social relationship is to continue, a return gift must be given. Sometimes, a return gift may be given immediately. In some marriages, friendship compacts, and peace agreements, people may give each other exactly the same types and quantities of goods (Sahlins 1972:194). For example, 100 yams may be exchanged for 100 yams. More often, the payoff is not immediate. In fact, sometimes an attempt to reciprocate the gift immediately is an indication of unwillingness to be obligated and shows that a trust-

THE KULA RING

Bronislaw Malinowski's analysis of the Kula ring is one of the most famous anthropological studies of reciprocal trading (1922/1961). The Kula is an extensive system of intertribal trade among a ring of islands off New Guinea (today part of the nation of Papua New Guinea; see Figure 8.2).

Although many kinds of goods are actually traded, Malinowski reports that from the Trobriand point of view, the most important aspect of the Kula is the trading of two kinds of articles, each of which moves in a different direction. Soulava, long necklaces of red shell, move clockwise, and mwali, bracelets of white shell, move counterclockwise. These items are exchanged between trading partners on the different islands that make up the Kula ring.

On most islands, all men participate in the Kula and some women are allowed to Kula as well (Macintyre 1983; Scoditti and Leach 1983; Weiner 1976). On the Trobriands, however, only high-ranking men can take part. They receive the necklaces or bracelets from their trading partners. Although Kula items can be permanently owned and may be taken out of circulation (Weiner 1976), people generally hold them for a while and then pass them on. Kula trading partnerships are lifelong affairs, and their details are fixed by tradition.

Although on the surface the Kula might appear to be primarily an exchange of goods, Malinowski's intensive fieldwork demonstrated the many complex cultural, social, and psychological meanings the Kula has for the Trobriand Islanders. The trade is infused with a great many cultural norms and values related to Tro-

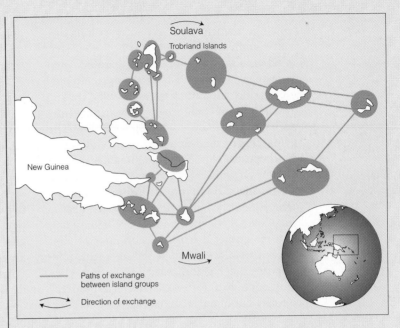

FIGURE 8.2

THE KULA TRADE IS AN EXAMPLE OF RECIPROCITY. NECKLACES (SOULAVA) AND ARMBANDS (MWALI) ARE TRADED AMONG THESE ISLANDS OFF THE COAST OF NEW GUINEA. SOULAVA MOVE CLOCKWISE WHILE MWALI MOVE COUNTERCLOCKWISE.

briand life. Kinship and political structure, magic, prestige, economy, technology, myth, ritual, feasting, and especially friendship and alliance all come together in the Kula. Participants derive prestige from generous behavior during the exchanges, and the Kula gives them an opportunity to display their wealth.

In the absence of a formal government incorporating the different groups that participate in the Kula, this system of reciprocal trade assures that relations among trading partners are relatively friendly. Both the Kula trade itself and the preparations for it reinforce ties among its participants. This contributes to the integration of Trobriand society as well as the

maintenance of economic and social relations among all.

Although Malinowski focused his study on mwali and soulava, other authors (Fortune 1932; Damon 1983; Munn 1983) emphasize that trade in many utilitarian items is carried out as well. Canoes, axe blades, pottery, pigs, and other items are exchanged along with armbands and necklaces as part of the Kula. These objects are often unprocurable in the district to which they are given. This suggests that the Kula trade has important economic functions that may be recognized by the anthropologist but not necessarily by the people involved.

ing social relationship is neither present nor desired (Mauss 1924/1990).

Balanced reciprocity is often characteristic of trading relations among non-Western peoples without market economies. Such trade, which is frequently carried out over long distances and between different tribes or villages, is often in the hands of trading partners, men or women who have a long-standing and personalized relationship with each other. Trading partners know each other's personalities, histories, and other aspects of their social lives. The **Kula ring,** a long-distance system of trade in both valuable objects and commodities that occurs in Oceania, is an outstanding example of personalized trading relationships. The Kula trade is described more fully in the accompanying Cultural Focus box. Plattner (1989a) notes that the greater the risk of economic loss, betrayal of confidence, or unfair dealing, the more important such personalized relations are. They exist not only in societies characterized by reciprocity but in uncertain markets as well.

NEGATIVE RECIPROCITY

Negative reciprocity is the unsociable extreme in exchange. It happens when trade is conducted for the purpose of material advantage and is based on the desire to get something for nothing (gambling, theft, cheating) or to get the better of a bargain (haggling). Negative reciprocity is characteristic of either an impersonal or an unfriendly transaction. As such, it is generally carried out by those who stand as outsiders to one another. Both in industrial society and in tribal and peasant societies, outsiders—however they may be defined—are considered fair game. In a large, complex society where economic dealings are carried out mainly among strangers, abstract principles of

morality develop that should apply to everyone. However, there are areas of commerce where these ideals often are not met. Merchants of used goods, particularly cars and machinery, often have reputations for shady practice. The phrase *caveat emptor,* or "let the buyer beware," neatly captures the notion that the rules of even trade are not always in force.

Tribal and peasant societies often distinguish between the insider, whom it is morally wrong to cheat, and the outsider, from whom every advantage may be gained. Anthropologist Clyde Kluckhohn did important studies of the Navajo in the 1940s and 1950s. He reported that among the Navajo, the rules for interaction vary with the situation; to deceive when trading with outsiders is a morally accepted practice. Even witchcraft techniques are considered permissible in trading with members of foreign tribes (1959).

Another good example of negative reciprocity is the historic relationship between traditional dynastic China and the nomadic empires of Mongolia. For more than a thousand years, the nomadic tribes of Mongolia organized into empires to manage their relationship with China and gain access to its vast resources. The ability of Mongol empires to benefit their constituent tribes was based on their capacity to extract wealth and resources from China. They did this by following a policy of violent raiding and forcing the Chinese government to make tribute payments. Because the nomads were highly mobile, war against them was prohibitively expensive, and the Chinese were repeatedly forced to buy peace from the nomads. The threat of violence lay under the surface of all interactions between the two groups (Barfield 1993:150–155).

REDISTRIBUTION

In **redistribution,** goods are collected from or contributed by members of a group and then given out to the group in a new pattern. Redistribution thus involves a social center to which goods are brought and from which they are distributed. There are many contexts in which redistribution is the mode of exchange. In household food sharing, pooled resources

---

Kula ring A pattern of exchange among trading partners in the Trobriands and other South Pacific islands.

negative reciprocity Exchange conducted for the purpose of material advantage and the desire to get something for nothing.

redistribution A form of exchange in which goods are collected from or contributed by members of the group and then redistributed to the group, often in the form of ceremonial feasts.

GLOBALIZATION

REDISTRIBUTION AMONG NATIONS

When anthropologists discuss redistribution, they are generally speaking of the mechanisms that redistribute wealth within a society. However, there are also economic forces that redistribute wealth among societies, and these are particularly important in the modern world. Changes in the policies by which goods are bought and sold internationally, international trade agreements, the actions of multinational corporations, foreign aid, and loans between national governments are all mechanisms that redistribute wealth among nations. Most Americans know that the United States gives foreign aid to poor nations but may be unaware that international policies tend to favor redistribution of wealth from the poor nations to the wealthy ones.

In 1993, development assistance from the wealthy nations to the 45 poorest nations in the world totaled more than $31 billion. This may sound like a great deal of money, but it is an extremely small part of the world's wealth. For example, foreign assistance from the United States was less than 0.2% of its gross national product (GNP). Total international aid to the world's 45 poorest nations amounted to an average of only $9.20 for each individual. These same nations are deeply indebted to the wealthy nations, together owing more than $440 billion. In most cases, interest payments on the debt alone are greater than the foreign aid received. Thus, even though the wealthy nations give foreign aid, they receive more money from the poor nations than they give.

One result of the movement of wealth from poor countries to rich countries has been a rapidly widening gap between the world's wealthy and poor. According to the United Nations (2000) *Human Development Report,* the gap between the richest and the poorest fifth of the world's population widened from 30 to 1 in 1960 to 74 to 1 in 1995.

---

are reallocated among family members. In state societies, redistribution is achieved through taxation—an obligatory payment on the part of the people in return for which various services are provided by a government. As the Globalization box shows, redistribution can occur between societies as well as within a single society.

Redistribution is especially important as a mechanism of exchange in societies where political organization includes chiefs or bigmen. Such men act as social centers to whom goods and food are contributed by the population. Often these items are redistributed back to the people in communal feasts, which the chief or bigman sponsors to sustain his political power and raise his prestige.

THE POTLATCH

The potlatch of Native American groups of the Pacific Northwest is one example of redistribution in action. In these groups, including the Tshmshan, Tlingit, Haida, Nootka, Bella Coola, and Kwakiutl, social rank-ing was a primary interest. Rank was inherited, but a claim to a rank had to be validated by a potlatch.

A **potlatch** was a feast in which many kinds of wealth were distributed by the chief to the people and to chiefs from other villages, invited as guests. If the distribution of goods at a potlatch was inadequate, the person who gave it might suffer a loss of prestige or others may not accept his claim of rank. In potlatching, an individual represented himself and his group. Potlatches might be held at times when issues of social rank and inheritance were important, such as births, deaths, marriages, or a youth's coming of age (Rosman and Rubel 1971). The number of guests present and the amount of goods given away, or even destroyed, revealed the wealth and prestige of the host chief. The host publicly traced his line of descent and claimed the right to certain symbolic privileges, such as the ownership of a particular song

> **potlatch** A form of competitive giveaway practiced by the Kwakiutl and other groups of the northwest coast of North America.

or dance. Each of these claims was accompanied by feasting and the display and giving away of large quantities of food and manufactured goods, such as blankets, carved wooden boxes, boats, fish oil, and flour.

Potlatches often expressed an ethos of social competition and individual rivalry. When there was a competitive potlatch—that is, when two men competed for the same symbolic privilege—one of the rivals might ostentatiously destroy quantities of property (canoes, blankets, and even slaves) in order to show how great he was and how little his possessions meant to him (Rohner and Rohner 1970).

Potlatch-type feasting is not limited to the Pacific Northwest. Similar practices are found among the Trobrianders, among the Chin in Myanmar (Burma), in Samoa, and in ancient Chinese society (Rosman and Rubel 1971:xii). In Northwest Coast societies, competitive feasts were characterized by boasting, but this is not always the case. In Pohnpei, a Micronesian island, the production and display of food at community feasts is not done with bravado but with modesty. The man who brings the largest and best foods will always protest that someone else's products are better than his own (Bascom 1970).

Anthropologists believe that the boasting typical of the Northwest Coast potlatch intensified when Native Americans began to participate in the cash economy of the Canadians. The outside source of income resulted in the "inflation" of potlatching and greater destruction of goods in the late nineteenth and early twentieth centuries.

The potlatch was ecologically adaptive and provided an important means of redistribution. The desire to gain prestige drove people to produce more than they could immediately consume. It was a way of providing reserves to be used in times of shortage and was particularly necessary where food preservation techniques were not well developed. A system of feasting also provided a way for food surpluses to be distributed among villages that were not

in equally good environments. In lean years, such communities could accept the invitations of chiefs from other villages and receive food in return for the diminished status involved in receiving rather than giving. When things got better, the recipients could become hosts, distributing food and goods to others who needed it and thus regaining some of their lost prestige.

Recent analyses of potlatch have focused on its function as a marker of cultural identity. Although the notion of competition is fundamental to the potlatch, among modern Native American groups such as the Haida (Stearns 1975) and the Northern Athapaskan Tanacross people (Simeone 1995), the potlatch is a symbol of unity. For example, the Tanacross people construct their identity in terms of the contrast between the cooperation they believe exists among native peoples and the competition that exists among nonnatives. The potlatch, with its demands for reciprocity, love, respect, and competence is a central symbol of cooperation (Simeone 1995:162–165) and thus of native identity. The Canadian government outlawed the potlatch between 1884 and 1951. To government authorities, potlatch was a symbol of the otherness and irrationality of Native Americans and their refusal to fully join the Canadian economic system (Bracken 1997).

Today, almost all groups are, to some degree, part of a market economy. In these circumstances, redistributive feasts such as the potlatch have lost most of their economic importance. However, they still retain their power as ceremonial demonstrations of ethnic identity.

LEVELING MECHANISMS

Redistribution of wealth may either increase or decrease the inequality of wealth within a society. **Leveling mechanisms** are practices, values, or forms of social organization that result in evening out the distribution of wealth. Leveling mechanisms force accumulated resources or capital to be used in ways that reduce economic differences. They ensure that social goals are considered along with economic ones.

Leveling mechanisms take many different forms. For example, if an economy is based

leveling mechanism A practice, value, or form of social organization that evens out wealth within a society.

around redistribution, and generosity is the basis of prestige, those who desire power and prestige will distribute as much wealth as they receive. Thus, the powerful may have less wealth than those with less prestige. Another leveling device is redistribution through feasting.

Manning Nash (1967) describes a number of leveling mechanisms that operate in the village of Amatenango, in the Chiapas district of Mexico. One is the organization of production by households. As mentioned earlier, economic expansion and accumulation of wealth are limited where households, rather than business firms, are the productive units. A second factor in Amatenango is inheritance: All of a man's children share equally in his estate. This makes it difficult for large estates to persist over generations. Accusations of witchcraft are a third leveling mechanism. Should anyone in Amatenango manage to accumulate more than their neighbors, members of other families are likely to accuse them of witchcraft. A man who is thought to be a witch is likely to be killed. Witchcraft accusations are most often leveled at those who are rich but not generous.

Finally, Amatenango and many other villages have cargo systems. In a **cargo system,** every year a number of different cargos, or religious offices, must be assumed by men in the village. Assuming such a cargo is an expensive proposition. The officeholder cannot work full time, and the obligations of the cargo involve substantial purchases and donations, which take up some of a family's extra resources. A man must serve in 12 such cargos before he can retire from public life, so the cost continues throughout adulthood. In addition to these 12 offices, there is the alferez, a ritual position filled by a younger man. One of the requirements of this office is sponsoring a community feast, which involves paying for the food and liquor and renting costumes. Men are selected for this prestigious office by their ability to pay, and it is an enormous drain on the economic resources of their households.

Community obligations such as a system of expensive religious offices may help to limit the economic gap between the relatively rich and the poor, but they do not eliminate it. For example, Zinacantan has a system of cargos or religious offices similar to that of Amatenango. Research there showed that men who were rich enough to take on these religious offices remained rich throughout their lives, whereas poor families incapable of filling such offices remained poor (Cancian 1989). Thus, although it does redistribute some of the wealth in the community, the cargo system in Mexican villages seems to have little financial impact on social stratification. Additionally, since holding cargos is prestigious, these offices serve to increase the status of the families that can afford them, further differentiating them from poorer families. Thus, the cargo system may serve to reinforce economic differences among families rather than limit them (Cancian 1989:147).

MARKET EXCHANGE

Market exchange is the principal distribution mechanism in most of the world's societies today. Goods and services are bought and sold at a money price determined, at least in theory, primarily by the impersonal forces of supply and demand. Unlike reciprocity and redistribution, in which the social and political roles of those who exchange are important, a market exchange is impersonal and occurs without regard to the social position of the participants. Market exchange is thus the most purely "economic" mode of exchange, the one in which participants' main concern is in maximizing material gain. In a society where the market system is the key economic institution, social or political goals are usually less important than financial goals. Organization around predominantly economic purposes and activities is a dominant feature of social life.

The penetration of the market varies among societies. Theoretically, in a market society, if one has enough money, everything is available for purchase. In practice, all societies limit what

cargo system A ritual system common in Central and South America in which wealthy people are required to hold a series of costly ceremonial offices.

market exchange An economic system in which goods and services are bought and sold at a money price determined primarily by the forces of supply and demand.

CAPITALISM IS THE PREDOMINANT FORM OF ECONOMIC ORGANIZATION IN INDUSTRIAL-IZED NATIONS, BUT PEOPLE IN EVERY SOCIETY ARE AFFECTED BY CAPITALIST MARKETS.

may be purchased legally. In many traditional societies, people gain access to key factors of production such as land and labor through kinship or obligations of reciprocity and redistribution. In such places, markets may not exist or may be limited to trading a very small number of goods. Western society is overwhelmingly dominated by market exchange. However, for moral, social, and political reasons, governments limit trade in certain goods. For example, there are restrictions on the sale of drugs, guns, children, and college degrees.

CAPITALISM

In the modern world, most societies that rely primarily on market exchange are capitalist. Productive resources become capital when they are used with the primary goal of increasing their owner's financial wealth. In capitalism, this becomes the most common (though not the only) use of such resources. **Capitalism** is further characterized by three fundamental attributes. The first is that most productive resources, the capital goods, are owned by a small portion of the population. Factories, farms, service corporations, and equipment of all sorts

capitalism An economic system in which people work for wages, land and capital goods are privately owned, and capital is invested for individual profit.

are owned primarily by banks, corporations, and wealthy individuals. The second attribute is that most individuals' primary resource is their labor. In order to survive, people sell their labor for wages. For example, most Americans work for large or small corporations that they do not own, or they are employed by government. For their work, they receive a salary or an hourly wage. The third attribute of capitalism is that whatever wages workers receive, the value of their contribution to production is always greater. This difference is the profit that accrues to the capitalist, who owns the productive resources (Plattner 1989b: 382–384).

The fact that most modern economies are dominated by capitalist market exchange does not mean that people always experience their economy in terms of buying and selling at whatever price the market will bear. Work always has a social component, which may mask capitalist relations. That is, capitalism may occur within the context of other sorts of relationships. Buying and selling, even when done to maximize profit, may be understood by participants in terms of reciprocity and redistribution. The Ethnography box on pages 188–189 of women in urban Turkey shows that even in a capitalist context, labor may occur within the framework of kinship. Workers may understand their labor as a contribution to family solidarity rather than an economic transaction between them and their employers. This understanding (or misunderstanding) cushions a system whose primary beneficiaries are not the worker's family members but the owners of productive resources. It makes high levels of exploitation possible.

In the past 300 years, capitalism has become the predominant economic system around the world. The expansion of this system, centered in northern Europe, North America, and Japan, has transformed traditional economies worldwide. As capitalism has spread, through conquest, colonization, and trade, nations and cultures have become increasingly united in a complex integrated economy (Wallerstein 1995).

It would be difficult to find any people in the world today not affected by capitalist markets. For the most part, members of traditional societies enter the market as low-wage labor-

ANTHROPOLOGY MAKES A DIFFERENCE

DOING BUSINESS

Anthropologist Francisco Aguilera has been consulting with businesses for more than 25 years. In that time, he has seen the idea of using anthropologists in business consulting go from obscurity to prominence. Today, major corporations such as Intel, Motorola, Hewlett-Packard, and Xerox make use of anthropologists in analyzing their own organizations and in market research designed to tailor their products, services, and publicity to the public. Anthropologists have become popular consultants because while focus groups and opinion surveys explore what people say, anthropologists using participant-observation focus on what people actually do.

Aguilera notes that anthropological research is particularly useful in the modern corporate context. While old-style corporations thought of themselves as fixed organizations with rigid boundaries, the new emphasis is on open production groups and an extension of networks across the organization's boundaries to embrace customers, suppliers, and competitors in partnerships, alliances, and service delivery. In this situation, decision making based on ethnographic description and comparison is essential.

Aguilera says that while other social science disciplines can and do offer consulting to business, anthropologists have some unique gifts to bring to the table. First, culture is the mainstay of anthropology, and anthropologists have better ways of talking about it than members of other disciplines. Second, anthropologists understand that boundaries are artificial, so they seek to understand the entire environment of the business and its employees. Finally, because of the participant-observer methodology of ethnography and the multilevel analysis that makes sense of ethnographic data, anthropologists are more likely to comprehend the fuller meaning of informants' reports than are practitioners of those disciplines that rely heavily on other forms of data collection and analysis.

Paco Underhill's work presents an excellent example of the use of anthropological techniques in business research. For more than 20 years, Underhill has used observation, photography, and interviews to study the ways people shop. He is the founder of the consulting firm Envirosell (www.envirosell.com), which advises clients such as McDonalds, The Gap, and Microsoft on how best to appeal to consumers. Some of Underhill's discoveries include the "transition zone" and the "butt brush." The transition zone is the area near the entrance to a store. Underhill observed that people need time to slow down and get used to a new environment, so they rarely purchase items from displays of merchandise that are within 12 or 15 steps of the front of the store. He also pointed out that women in particular will avoid purchasing items on low shelves in narrow aisles, because bending to reach such goods exposes them to being "butt brushed," or bumped from behind. Men are much less prone to avoid being jostled in this way. Underhill has summarized many of his findings in a popular book, *Why We Buy: The Science of Shopping* (1999).

In addition to consulting for businesses, many anthropologists have gone on to found businesses or work directly for them. Anthropologist Steve Barnett, for example, is a vice president at Citicorp who uses his anthropological training to help figure out who is a good credit risk. Robert Falkner is a corporate lawyer for Motorola, and Katherine Burr is the CEO of the Hanseatic Group (www.hanseaticgroup.com), an organization that manages financial programs for institutions and wealthy individuals. Michael J. Koss, who graduated with an anthropology degree from Beloit College, is the president and CEO of the Koss Corporation (www.koss.com), a leading manufacturer of stereo headphones. You can read more about careers in anthropology at www.ameranthassn.org/careers.htm.

---

ers. The wealth they produce accrues to elites within poor nations as well as people in wealthy nations (E. Wolf 1982). The case of the Turkish women described in the accompanying ethnography illustrates some of the ways in which this process takes place and traditional economies adapt to capitalism. Not all traditional societies are able to make such accommodations, however, and the expansion of capitalism and political power has been accompanied by the wide-scale destruction of traditional societies. This story is told more fully in Chapter 17.

Capitalism is an extremely powerful economic system. It undoubtedly provides a greater

WOMEN AND LABOR IN URBAN TURKEY

Turkey is a modern capitalist nation. A member of the European Economic Community, it produces many goods and services used in the West. Most of the inhabitants of Istanbul, a city of more than 8 million people, are part of a capitalist economy; they sell their labor in enterprises aimed at generating a profit. However, as Jenny B. White (1994) reports, they often attempt to convert relationships between buyers and sellers or bosses and workers into relations of kin. They say that money makes them relatives. This is particularly true for women.

Women in Turkey live in a complex social network that is determined by obligations and relations of reciprocity. They identify themselves by the work they do and the labor demands placed on them by their parents, in-laws, husbands, and children. That is to say, being a good woman means laboring for relatives. This is true even when they knit clothing for the world market.

Turkey is a patrilineal and patriarchal society. Working outside of the home is not considered proper among poor and middle-class Turkish women. However, other work demands on women are very high. When a woman is married, she leaves her parents' home and moves in with her husband. There she is expected to manage all the household chores and to keep her hands busy with knitting, crocheting, or other skilled tasks. At the same time, she has a moral obligation to labor for her family of origin. She may be expected to help clean her mother's home, prepare it for religious ceremonies, and help out when her mother is ill. However, the greatest demands come from mothers-in-law.

A mother-in-law has the right to demand labor and obedience from her son's

Istanbul

TURKEY

wife, and her demands cannot be easily refused. Mothers-in-law insist that their sons' wives help in their household chores. They may live with a son's family or come for frequent extended visits. For example, one mother-in-law in White's study often visited for periods of up to a month. Each time she came to her son's home, she became "ill" and demanded that her daughter-in-law wait on her. At the end of each visit, she invariably became "well" and visited friends all over the city. She once told her daughter-in-law, "I will eat up my son's money. Why else did I bear a son?" (White 1994:48).

Mothers-in-law can exert such pressure on their sons' wives because of the relationship mothers build with their children. Mothers build good relationships with daughters, but these are tempered by the knowledge that daughters will marry and leave. As a result, women put most of their effort into forging very close relationships with their sons. Sons are kings in their houses. They are spoiled by their mothers and are allowed to command their sisters. They are encouraged to demand attention from female family members and may shout and hit in order to get it. It is not unusual for women to tie the shoelaces of their high-school-aged sons or slice and peel fruit for college-

aged sons (White 1994:72). This special relationship between mother and son is the basis of the "milk debt." A mother's love, in theory freely given, incurs a debt that her son can never repay. A son and his family are perpetually paying back this debt, and this responsibility is the cornerstone of Turkish social relations. Other nonfamily relations, including business relations, are patterned on it.

Business in Turkey is often disguised as relations of kinship. Even though buyers and sellers are involved in commerce for profit, they prefer to see their exchanges as social rather than financial. Rather than the emphasis on price and impersonal service we expect in business dealings in the West, Turkish buyers and sellers wrap themselves in social relations. Business may appear as secondary to conversation, and money may be rarely discussed. People who do not know each other at all may buy and sell freely, but the closer the relationship between two individuals is, the less willing they are to discuss money openly. A further difference from Western practice is that, like the milk debt, business relations are open-ended. That is, instead of trying to conclude business deals and settle accounts in full, buyers and sellers remain in constant debt to each other. This indebtedness obligates them to each other and keeps them bound in a social web.

The principles at work here can be seen very clearly in women's piecework. Women in Turkey knit and sew sweaters, blouses, and other garments that are exported and sold in the United States and other Western nations. This is called piecework because the women are paid by the completed piece. The yarns, leathers, and other materials they use are generally supplied to them by an organizer, who also finds a buyer for the finished product. The organizers are very often relatives, neighbors, and friends of the women who do the work. Piecework is very widespread among the poor in Istanbul.

A recent survey showed that about two-thirds of women in a poor neighborhood did piecework (White 1994:13).

It is particularly interesting that women who knit and sew sweaters do not consider their efforts work. In fact, overwhelmingly women think it is improper for them to work, and only 5.5 percent of women in this same neighborhood do paid work outside their homes. Instead, they think of piecework as a way for them to keep their hands busy, and they see knitting as part of their duty as wives. They do it out of obligation to their husband's family. These ideas function as a way of reconciling two opposing cultural values. On one hand, women are not supposed to work in this society; on the other hand, these poor women must earn money. One of the ways to reconcile these opposing claims is to define their work as a gift.

Because women do not think of what they do as work, they do not calculate their wage per hour. Instead, they consider their work as a gift of their labor in return for a gift of money or other support. The price women receive for their efforts is very low but varies with their relationship with the organizer. A woman might work for free for a relative. A neighbor will pay, and people who are more distant will pay more.

Labor organizers also think of female workers as relatives to whom they have social as well as economic responsibilities. Labor organizers rarely pay women in full. When a women returns finished products, the organizer pays her in part and advances her more raw materials. Thus, the organizer stays in debt to the women, and the women, who now have the raw materials, are in debt to the organizer. This exchange of debt tightens the social web between workers and labor organizers and provides increased security for both.

Much anthropological research has shown that for people in noncapitalist

societies and the poor in capitalist societies, the web of social relationships ensures a degree of security. In the emerging capitalist economy of Turkey, the social web continues to have great significance because of the security it affords. Turkish women are understandably reluctant to exchange the safety of the social network for the impersonal interactions of the market, even if it means they are not financially remunerated for all the work they do.

The fact that Turkish hand-sewn garments are produced in a form of economic organization based on reciprocity but are consumed in the market economies of wealthy nations has important implications. As we have shown, Turkish women pieceworkers operate within traditional norms of reciprocity. Labor organizers also attempt to maintain relations of reciprocity with their buyers, the large export firms. However, these firms are governed by market considerations that owe little or nothing to social relations of reciprocity. Relations within this system are fundamentally unequal. Labor organizers generally do not get rich, but they profit more than their workers, and the large export firms benefit the most. Because hand-made garments are produced by people who do not directly calculate their wages, they are available at extremely low prices. Export firms can sell these products in market economies where hand-made clothes command much higher prices. Thus, they are able to profit from the structural differences between the two economic systems.

Critical Thinking Questions

1. White argues that the masking of economic relationships is central to the production of piecework in Istanbul. Piecework performed by women is understood as a household chore rather than a job demanding payment set by its market

WOMEN IN TURKEY KNIT TO FULFILL SOCIAL OBLIGATIONS, BUT THEIR PRODUCTS ARE SOLD FOR HIGH PRICES IN WEALTHY NATIONS.

© Randa Bishop/Pictor.

value. One result is that women's contributions to the economy are undervalued. Does anything similar to this happen in American society? What might be the result of calculating such contributions in purely market terms?

2. White's ethnography raises important questions about international trade and redistribution of wealth among nations. How does this production system redistribute wealth from the poor of Turkey to the wealthy consumers of Europe and North America? Should anything be done about this situation? What sorts of actions might be taken, who could take them, and what might be their results?

Source: Adapted from Jenny B. White, *Money Makes Us Relatives.* Austin: University of Texas Press, 1994.

Alan Oddie/PhotoEdit

PRODUCTIVE RESOURCES BECOME CAPITAL WHEN THEY ARE INVESTED IN WAYS INTENDED TO INCREASE THEIR OWNER'S FINANCIAL WEALTH.

number of goods and services to larger populations than other ways of organizing an economy, but at a cost. Because the private ownership of basic resources results in denying some people access to them, permanently differentiated economic and social classes are an important feature of a capitalist society. Capitalism dictates that although the relative level of wealth may vary among societies, there will always be rich and poor. Often, part of the population lives in extreme poverty, denied virtually all access to basic resources—in American society, this includes the homeless, the landless rural poor, and the permanently unemployed.

Societies organized primarily by capitalism are a late development in the history of humankind. Capitalism in its purest form is best illustrated by the industrial nations of nineteenth-century Europe, the United States, and Japan.

ACCOMMODATION AND RESISTANCE TO CAPITALISM

The fate of those who oppose capitalist expansion is not always submission or annihilation. Even in largely capitalist nations, populations remain that preserve noncapitalist lifestyles. One good example is the Gypsies of Spain (Kaprow 1982). Spanish Gypsies have resisted assimilation and wage labor for hundreds of years. They are self-employed, typically working as scrap dealers, peddlers, contract whitewashers, discount-clothing merchants, and part-time agricultural laborers. These occupations are difficult to regulate and provide the state with few or no taxes. The Gypsy avoidance of wage labor was part of their larger strategy for resisting state controls, but it has also turned out to be economically successful.

Gypsy life may appear exotic to us, but there are many examples of resistance to capitalism closer to home. Consider the inhabitants of Putnam County, New York (Hansen 1995). Located about 50 miles from New York City, Putnam County has been poor since the time of the American Revolution. Even in the preindustrial era, its farms were unable to compete. Today, no commercial farming is done in the county. Its people follow two fundamentally different strategies for survival and belong to two different but related economic systems.

Many of Putnam's inhabitants are new residents who commute to jobs in New York City. They work for union-scale wages as police officers, firefighters, and schoolteachers, using their wages to buy houses, food, and so on. They are deeply in debt to mortgage and credit card companies but believe that higher future earnings will permit them to accommodate this financial burden. They are committed to economic and social advancement, and many hope eventually to leave Putnam County for more prosperous and convenient suburbs closer to the city. Despite the fact that most of them work in public-sector jobs rather than for corporations, this group is deeply committed to capitalism. They own few productive resources, sell their labor for wages, and conduct the economic aspect of their lives almost entirely through the capitalist market.

Putnam County's other residents have lived there for generations. Members of this group very rarely have full-time wage employment. They almost never visit New York City, which to them has become "a metaphor for all the world's evils" (Hansen 1995:146). Instead they follow what Halperin (1990) has called a multiple livelihood strategy. Members of this group acquire their land through inheritance and generally own it outright. Most of these land holdings of 5–50 acres are forest, but all include gardens that provide almost all of the vegetables for those who own them. While women work the gardens, men hunt year-round, taking deer, rabbits, guinea fowl, and pheasants. They fish in ponds and streams and chop wood for fuel. In addition to these subsistence activities, members of this group do carpentry, electrical repair, masonry, plumbing, and other jobs. They barter these skills among themselves and sell them for cash to the commuters. They may also work temporarily for wages at construction jobs. Although Putnam's traditional residents do depend on markets for goods they cannot produce themselves or get through barter, only a small part of their total subsistence comes from the market.

The multiple livelihood strategies of Putnam's traditional residents are aimed at avoiding participation in the capitalist economy. Their financial goals are not to make money or to move to a higher level of consumption. They are concerned with stability rather than mobility and wish to live as independently as possible. Although they own productive resources such as land and equipment, these do not become capital because they are not used with the goal of making high levels of profit. Their productive resources are used to increase the security of their self-sufficiency rather than to accumulate wealth.

Resistance to wage labor and economic marginalization are not always self-chosen, as with the Gypsies of Spain or the traditional residents of Putnam County. Most often, the economic marginalization of certain peoples, whether because of race, ethnicity, or gender, is not voluntary but imposed, a subject that is explored in Chapter 13.

SUMMARY

1. Economics is the study of choice. People around the world make rational choices to allocate scarce resources among competing ends. Such choices do not occur in isolation but are embedded in other aspects of culture. Economic anthropologists study the institutional and cultural arrangements within which these choices occur. They attempt to delineate the factors that motivate economic choices in different cultures.

2. Although technological development has resulted in a dramatic increase in material productivity and consumption in Western societies, it also results in changes in the quality of life.

3. Access to and control over land is basic to every productive system. Among hunters and gatherers, there are few exclusive rights to land; among horticulturalists, land is controlled by the kin group. It is mainly with the rise of intensive agriculture that land becomes subject to private ownership. Generally speaking, the greater the investment of labor and technology and the less land available, the more likely private ownership will be.

4. In tribal and peasant economies, the basic unit of production is a kin group. Resources are produced and used mainly by this group, and production often has social and religious rather than monetary ends. This provides an important contrast with Western societies, where the basic unit of production is the business firm, whose interests are almost solely economic.

5. There is little specialization of labor in tribal and peasant societies, compared with the high degree of occupational specialization in industrial societies. Two universal bases of occupational specialization are sex and age.

6. The sexual division of labor has some almost universal aspects: Hunting, fighting, and clearing land are generally done by men. Women are predominantly responsible for taking care of the children; they also gather crops and do the daily processing of food for domestic use. Beyond this, the sexual division of labor is highly variable; a man's job in one society may easily be a woman's job in another.

7. Productive resources are goods used to produce other goods and are limited in small-scale economies. Productive resources become capital when they are invested primarily for profit. In many traditional societies, most people have access to productive resources and no one group is deprived of the ability to produce.

8. In all societies, goods and services are exchanged in some way. Three systems of exchange are reciprocity, redistribution, and the market. Reciprocity exists in all societies but is the characteristic system of exchange in band and tribal societies. The Kula ring is an example of a system of reciprocity.

9. Redistribution is the characteristic mechanism of integration and exchange in chiefdoms. An example of redistribution is the potlatch of the Kwakiutl of the northwest coast of North America.

10. Leveling mechanisms are norms and activities that result in an evening out of wealth among a population. The many different kinds of leveling mechanisms (obligatory generosity, witchcraft accusations, gossip, religious obligations) force accumulated resources to be used in ways that do not result in significant or permanent economic differences among individuals and groups.

11. Market exchange and capitalism dominate the economies of most societies today. In markets, goods and services are sold at prices that are determined primarily by supply and demand.

12. Most modern economies are capitalist; the owners of productive resources use them to increase their own financial wealth. However, as the ethnography of Turkish women shows, capitalist market relations are sometimes masked as relations of reciprocity.

13. The expansion of the European capitalist system has resulted in far-reaching transformations in many non-European societies. Some groups resist full-scale participation in national economic systems. The Gypsies of Spain and the traditional residents of Putnam County, New York, through their choice of marginal occupations, retain a large measure of control over their own labor.

KEY TERMS

balanced reciprocity	household
capital resources	Kula ring
capitalism	leveling mechanism
cargo system	market exchange
economic system	negative reciprocity
economics	potlatch
economizing behavior	prestige
firm	productive resources
generalized reciprocity	reciprocity
	redistribution

SUGGESTED READINGS

Halperin, Rhoda. 1990. *The Livelihood of Kin: Making Ends Meet "The Kentucky Way."* Austin: University of Texas Press. An ethnography of communities in Appalachia, this is an outstanding analysis of some of the alternative economic forms in the United States.

Mauss, Marcel. 1990. *The Gift.* New York: W. W. Norton. Originally published in 1925, this classic work on reciprocity in tribal societies includes much information on the ceremonial behavior of the potlatch, showing its many social and economic functions.

Miller, Daniel (Ed.). 1998. *Material Cultures: Why Some Things Matter.* Chicago: University of Chicago

Press. This book is a collection of essays by a variety of authors on the ethnography of consumption. Topics range from the role of paper in the workplace to Calypso music to Coca Cola in Trinidad to catalog shopping in Britain. The essays emphasize the ways in which material objects encapsulate and express broader social values, as well as the contradictions in the lives of the people who own them.

Plattner, Stuart. 1989. *Economic Anthropology.* Stanford, CA: Stanford University Press. A more advanced reader in economic anthropology, this work provides theoretical formulations and extensive examples of many of the critical concepts in economic anthropology.

Sahlins, Marshal. 1972. *Stone Age Economics.* Chicago: Aldine de Gruyter. This classic work explores patterns of exchange in traditional societies, focusing on the domestic mode of production. This book is fairly difficult reading, but it is basic to understanding current economic anthropology.

Schneider, Jane, and Rayna Rapp. 1995. *Articulating Hidden Histories: Exploring the Influence of Eric R. Wolf.* Berkeley: University of California Press. This collection of essays, honoring one of the most influential economic anthropologists, explores the ways in which economic and political forces condition the lives of people around the globe. Twenty-one essays cover topics such as peasants, the market, nationalism, and cultural identity.

Wilk, Richard R. 1996. *Economies and Cultures: Foundations of Economic Anthropology.* Boulder, CO: Westview. In this advanced analysis of the history and current place of economics within anthropology, Wilk focuses on the central issue of what motivates people and what that might say about human nature. He sees economic anthropology as a meeting place between materialist and symbolic approaches to anthropology.

INTERNET RESOURCES

The following Internet resources appear in this chapter. Please log on to the Wadsworth anthropology website: **http://anthropology.wadsworth. com**. Click on the Nanda/Warms *Cultural Anthropology* page. Then select the Student Resources section, where you will find a complete presentation of these links and more.

- A link to a website on Potlatch, page 183
- A video link: economic survival in the aftermath of Communism, page 186
- A photo essay on resistance to capitalism, page 190
- Access the Study Guide to InfoTrac College Edition for Anthropology Students

Courtesy of Chander Dembla

AS IN MANY SOCIETIES, MARRIAGE IN INDIA IS CONSIDERED TOO IMPORTANT FOR THE CHOICE OF A SPOUSE TO BE LEFT UP TO
YOUNG PEOPLE. IDEALLY, THE BRIDE LIVES WITH HER HUSBAND'S FAMILY, SO HER ABILITY TO GET ALONG WITH HER IN-LAWS IS AN
IMPORTANT CRITERION OF HER SUITABILITY AS A WIFE. AMONG MODERN INDIAN COUPLES, SUCH AS THE ONE PICTURED HERE,
MARRIAGES CONTINUE TO BE ARRANGED, BUT YOUNG MEN AND WOMEN ARE INCREASINGLY BEING GIVEN AN IMPORTANT VOICE
IN THE SELECTION OF THEIR SPOUSE.

CHAPTER NINE

MARRIAGE, FAMILY, AND DOMESTIC GROUPS

What are some of the universal functions of marriage and the family?

What are some of the rules that regulate marriage in different societies? How can these rules be explained?

How do arranged marriage and romantic love relate to the values of marriage and family in different societies?

What kinds of changes are taking place in the family in the United States?

How does a society's subsistence strategy influence the shape of the family and the household?

All human societies face certain problems for which kinship systems, marriage, and the creation of families offer solutions. Every society must regulate sexual access between males and females, find satisfactory ways to organize labor between males and females, assign responsibility for child care, provide a clear framework for organizing an individual's rights and responsibilities, and provide for the transfer of property and social position between generations. This chapter and the next describe some of the many human solutions to these challenges. Although anthropologists have traditionally described these solutions in terms of the rules that govern them, we must keep in mind that cultural rules always bend to reality. When reality no longer meshes with the rules, the rules themselves change.

FUNCTIONS OF MARRIAGE AND THE FAMILY

The need to regulate sexual access stems from the potentially continuous receptivity of the human female to sexual activity. The human male also has the potential to be sexually aroused continually, rather than just at certain times of the year. Sexual competition could therefore be a source of serious conflict if it were not regulated and channeled into stable relationships that are given social approval. These relationships need not be permanent, and theoretically some system other than marriage could have developed. But in the absence of safe and dependable contraception (as has been the case for most of human history) and with the near certainty that children would be born, a stable union between a male and female that involves responsibility for children as well as economic exchange became the basis for most human adaptations.

Differences in strength and mobility between males and females, as well as women's biological role in infant nurturing, lead to a general sexual division of labor in nonindustrial societies. Marriage is the way most societies arrange for the products and services of men and women to be exchanged and for the care of children. An ongoing relationship between an adult male and an adult female provides a structure (the family) in which the male can provide food and protection and the female can nurse and provide the nurturing needed for the healthy development of children. Another function of marriage that contributes to its near universality in human societies is the way it extends alliances by linking different families and kin groups together. Thus, marriage leads to cooperation among groups of people larger than the primary husband–wife pair. This expansion of the social group within which people can work together and share resources appears to be of great advantage for the survival of the species.

Marriage refers to the customs, rules, and obligations that establish a special relationship between a sexually cohabiting adult male and female, between them and any children they produce, and between the kin groups of husband and wife. Although marriage and the formation of families rest on the biological complementarity of male and female and on the biological process of reproduction, both marriage and family are cultural patterns. As such, they differ in form and functions among human societies.

In the United States, the marriage tie is generally the most important in the formation of the family, but this is not true everywhere. In many societies, the most important family bond is between lineal blood relations (father and children or mother and children), or brothers and sisters, rather than between husband and wife. We must be careful, therefore, not to think of marriage and the family only in terms of the nuclear family. Even in the United States, where "the" family has generally meant the nuclear family, definitions are changing to accommodate new realities: the high divorce rate, same-sex domestic partnerships, the increasing numbers of working mothers and single-parent households, the growing number of couples who live together in long-term relationships with children but who do not formalize these relations in legal marriage, and ethnic variation.

From a cross-cultural perspective, it appears that the most basic tie in society is between mother and child. The provisioning and protective role is generally played by the mother's husband (who is usually a male), but it may be played by the mother's brother, the mother's female husband (see Chapter 11), or even the whole community (Spiro 1958). While all societies construct rules about sex, infant care, labor, and rights and obligations between generations, they do so in very different ways.

MARRIAGE RULES
INCEST TABOOS

Every society has rules prohibiting mating (sexual relations) between people in certain relationships or from certain social groups. The most universal prohibition is that on mating among certain kinds of kin: mother and son, father and daughter, and sister and brother. The taboos on mating between kin always extend beyond this immediate family group, however. In European-based societies, this taboo extends to the children of our parents' siblings (called first cousins in our kinship terminology), although this was not always the case. In other societies, people are not permitted to mate with others who may be related up to the fifth generation. These prohibitions on mating between people classified as relatives are called **incest taboos.**

Because sexual access is one of the most important rights conferred by marriage, incest taboos effectively prohibit marriage among certain kin. The outstanding exception to the taboo on mating and marriage among members of the nuclear family were the preferred brother–sister marriages among royalty in ancient Egypt, in traditional Hawaiian society, and among the Inca in Peru.

Anthropologists have advanced several major theories to explain the universality and persistence of the incest taboo, particularly as it applies to primary (or nuclear) family relationships. In considering these theories, we should

---

marriage The customs, rules, and obligations that establish a special relationship between a sexually cohabiting adult male and female, between them and any children they produce, and between the kin of the bride and groom.

incest taboos Prohibitions on sexual relations between relatives.

keep in mind that the possible origins of the taboo, its functions in contemporary societies, and the motives of individuals in respecting or violating the taboo are all separate issues.

AVOIDING INBREEDING

The inbreeding avoidance theory holds that mating between close kin produces deficient, weak children and is genetically harmful to the species. According to this theory, proposed in the late nineteenth century, the incest taboo is adaptive because it limits inbreeding. Work in population genetics appears to support the view that inbreeding is usually harmful to a human population. Moreover, these disadvantages are far more likely to appear as a result of the mating of primary relatives (mother–son, father–daughter, sister–brother) than of other relatives, even first cousins. However, this theory of the origin of the incest taboo has little credence today. Evidence from animal populations indicates, for example, that debilitating recessive genes are "pruned" out of a population through the process of natural selection. Individuals with these traits are unlikely to reproduce, and lethal recessives frequently result in miscarriages. Furthermore, this theory does not deal with the question of how prescientific peoples could understand the connection between close inbreeding and the biological disadvantages that result.

PREVENTING FAMILY DISRUPTION

Bronislaw Malinowski and Sigmund Freud believed that the desire for sexual relations within the family is very strong. They suggested that the most important function of the incest taboo is preventing disruption within the nuclear family. Malinowski argued that as children grow into adolescence, it would be natural for them to attempt to satisfy their developing sexual urges within the group of people emotionally close to them—that is, within the family. Were this to happen, conflict would occur and the role relationships within the family would be disrupted as fathers and sons, and mothers and daughters, would be competing for sexual part-

ners. This would hinder the family in carrying out the transmission of cultural values in a harmonious and effective way. According to this theory, the incest taboo arose to repress the attempt to satisfy sexual desires within the family and to direct such desires outward.

This theory seems persuasive. Unregulated sexual competition within the family would undoubtedly be disruptive. However, an alternative to the incest taboo could be the regulation of sexual competition among family members. Furthermore, although Malinowski's theory suggests why the incest taboo exists between parents and children, it does not explain the prohibition of sexual relations between brothers and sisters. Regulating sexual activity within the family might solve the problem of disruption through sexual rivalry, but it would not solve the genetic problem. Only the familial incest taboo has both advantages: It prevents disruptions of the family over sexual competition and promotes outbreeding and genetic variability.

FORMING WIDER ALLIANCES

Another theory (Lévi-Strauss 1949/1969) stresses the adaptive value for humans of cooperation among groups larger than the nuclear family. The incest taboo forces people to marry outside the family, thus joining families together into a larger social community. This has undoubtedly contributed to the success of the human species. The alliance theory does not account for the origin of the incest taboo, but alliance between nuclear families certainly seems to be adaptive. The theory can account for the persistence of the familial incest taboo and its extension to groups other than the nuclear family.

Thus, the familial incest taboo appears to have a number of advantages for the human species. In other animal species, incest is often prevented by expelling junior members from family groups as they reach sexual maturity. Because humans take so long to mature, the familial incest taboo seems to be the most efficient and effective means of promoting genetic variability, familial harmony, and community cooperation. These advantages can explain the spread and persistence of the taboo, if not its origins (Aberle et al. 1963).

Exogamy

Two types of marriage rules, exogamy and endogamy, together work to define the acceptable range of marriage partners. **Exogamy** specifies that a person must marry outside particular groups, while **endogamy** requires people to marry within certain groups. Because of the association of sex and marriage, prohibitions on incest produce an almost universal rule of exogamy within the primary family group of parents and children and between brothers and sisters. In every society, exogamous rules also apply to some group larger than the nuclear family. Most often, descent groups based on a blood relationship (such as lineages and clans) are exogamous.

The advantages of exogamy are similar to those proposed for the incest taboo. In addition to reducing conflict over sex within the cooperating group, such as the hunting band, exogamy leads to alliances between different families and groups. Alliance between groups larger than the primary family is of great adaptive significance for humans. Such alliances may have economic, political, or religious components; indeed, these intergroup rights and obligations are among the most important kinds of relationships established by marriage.

Early humans, living in hunting-and-gathering bands, undoubtedly exchanged women in order to live in peace with one another and to extend the social ties of cooperation. One outstanding feature of marriage arrangements among contemporary foragers is a system of exchange and alliance between groups that exchange wives. These alliances are important among peoples who must move around to find food. Different groups take turns visiting and playing host to one another, and this intergroup

sociability is made easier by exogamy. One consequence of exchanging women is that each foraging camp becomes dependent on others for a supply of wives and is allied with others through the bonds that result from marriage. This system contributes to the maintenance of peaceful relations among groups that move around, camp with one another, and exploit overlapping territories. It does not entirely eliminate intergroup aggression, but it probably helps keep it down to a manageable level.

The benefits of exogamy were very clear to the mountain-dwelling Arapesh of New Guinea, who expressed their attitude about exogamous marriage in the following saying:

> *Your own mother*
> *Your own sister*
> *Your own pigs*
> *Your own yams that you have piled up,*
> *You may not eat.*
> *Other people's mothers,*
> *Other people's sisters,*
> *Other people's pigs,*
> *Other people's yams that they have piled up,*
> *You may eat.* (Mead 1935/1963:92)

Just as hoarding one's own food and not sharing or exchanging with the community is unthinkable for the Arapesh, so is keeping the women of one's group to oneself. In many societies, the very mention of incest is often accompanied by protestations of horror. For the Arapesh, incest simply does not make sense. In answer to Margaret Mead's question about incest, an Arapesh informant answered: "No, we don't sleep with our sisters. We give our sisters to other men and other men give us their sisters" (p. 92). When asked about a man marrying his sisters, the Arapesh responded, "What, you would like to marry your sister? What is the matter with you? Don't you want a brother-in-law? Don't you realize that if you marry another man's sister and another man marries your sister, you will have at least two brothers-in-law, while if you marry your own sister you will have none? With whom will you hunt, with whom will you garden, with whom will you visit?" (p. 97).

In peasant societies, rules of exogamy may apply to the village as well. In north India, a

exogamy A rule specifying that a person must marry outside a particular group.

endogamy A rule prescribing that marriage must be within a particular group.

man must take a wife from outside his village. Through exogamy, the Indian village becomes a center in a kinship network that spreads over hundreds of villages. Because the wives will come from many different villages, the typical Indian village has a cosmopolitan character. Village exogamy also affects the quality of family life. In a household where brothers' wives are strangers to one another, peace at any price is an important value. The potential for conflict among sisters-in-law shapes child rearing and personality and helps explain many rules of conduct in the north Indian family, such as the repression of aggression.

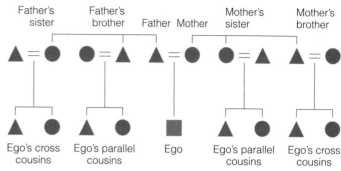

FIGURE 9.1

THIS DIAGRAM INDICATES THE RELATIONSHIPS OF CROSS COUSINS AND PARALLEL COUSINS. IN MANY CULTURES, THESE RELATIONSHIPS ARE IMPORTANT FOR DETERMINING WHO CAN AND CANNOT MARRY, AND FOR DESIGNATING PREFERRED MARRIAGE PARTNERS.

ENDOGAMY

The opposite of exogamy, endogamy requires marriage within one's own group, however that group may be defined. In order to keep the privileges and wealth of the group intact, blood relations may be encouraged or required to marry. This helps explain endogamy among royalty. In India, the caste is an endogamous group. A person must marry someone within the caste or within the specific section of the caste to which he or she belongs. In the United States, although there are currently no named groups within which one must marry, so-called racial groups and social classes tend to be endogamous. In the past, racial endogamy was enforced by law in many states. In the case of social classes, opportunity, cultural norms, and similarity of lifestyle all contribute to maintaining endogamy. It may be as easy to love a rich person as a poor one, but it is a lot harder to meet one unless you are rich yourself. Endogamy is also an important rule for some religious groups in the United States, such as the Amish.

PREFERENTIAL MARRIAGE RULES

In all societies, relatives are classified according to the rules of kinship that are part of culture (see Chapter 10). These classifications of kin are an important basis for choosing marriage partners. In addition to rules about whom one may not marry and the group within which one must marry, some societies have rules about the preferred categories of relatives from which marriage partners are drawn. One of the most common of these preferential marriage rules is that an individual should marry a cross cousin.

Cross cousins are the children of one's parents' siblings of the opposite sex (mother's brother or father's sister). In the United States, cross cousins are not distinguished from **parallel cousins,** children of the parents' same-sex siblings (mother's sister or father's brother). In the United States, both relations are generally excluded as potential mates.

Preferential cross-cousin marriage is related to the organization of kinship units larger than the nuclear family. Where descent groups are **unilineal**—that is, formed by either the mother's or the father's side exclusively—parallel cousins are members of one's own kinship group but cross cousins are not. Because unilineal kinship groups are usually exogamous, a person is prohibited from marrying parallel cousins (who are often considered brothers

cross cousins The children of a parent's siblings of the opposite sex (mother's brothers, father's sisters).

parallel cousins The children of a parent's same-sex siblings (mother's sisters, father's brothers).

unilineal descent A rule specifying that membership in a descent group is based on links through either the maternal or the paternal line, but not both.

and sisters) but is allowed, or even required, to marry cross cousins, who are culturally defined as outside the kinship group. Preferred cross-cousin marriage reinforces ties between kin groups established in the preceding generation. In this sense, the adaptive value of preferential cross-cousin marriage is the same as exogamy: establishing alliances between groups. But where exogamy establishes alliances among several different groups, preferred cross-cousin marriage intensifies the relationship among a limited number of groups generation after generation.

A few societies practice preferred parallel-cousin marriage. Among the Muslim Arabs of North Africa, the preference is for a person to marry the son or daughter of the father's brother. Muslim Arab culture has a rule of patrilineal descent; that is, descent and inheritance are in the male line. Parallel-cousin marriage within this system helps prevent the fragmentation of family property because economic resources can be kept within the family. Another result of parallel-cousin marriage is to reinforce the solidarity of brothers, which has advantages. But by socially isolating groups of brothers, parallel-cousin marriage adds to factional disputes and disunity within the larger social system. Thus, each system of marriage and family has elements that contribute to solidarity and stability at one level but may be disruptive at another level.

THE LEVIRATE AND THE SORORATE

The **levirate** is a custom whereby a man marries the widow of his dead brother. In some cases, the children born to this union are considered children of the deceased man. Among the Nuer, a pastoral people of Africa, a form called ghost marriage exists: A man can marry a woman "to the name of" a brother who has died childless. The offspring of this union are designated as children of the deceased. Thus, the levirate enables the children to remain within the dead husband's descent group and also keeps them from being separated from their mother. The **sororate** is a custom whereby, when a woman dies, her kin group supplies a sister as a wife for the widower. Also, where the sororate exists, the husband of a barren woman marries her sister, and at least some of these children are considered those of the first wife.

The levirate and sororate attest to the importance of marriage as an alliance between two groups rather than between individuals. Through such customs, group alliances are maintained and the marriage contract can be fulfilled even in the event of death. Because marriage involves an exchange of rights and obligations, the family of the wife can be assured that she will be cared for even if her husband dies. This is only fair if she has fulfilled her part of the marriage contract by providing domestic services and bearing children.

But what if there is no one of the right relationship for an individual to marry? Or what if the preferred marriage partner is already married? In this case, other kin may be classified as equals for the purpose of marriage and can thus be chosen as marriage partners. For example, if a man is supposed to marry his father's sister's daughter, the daughters of all women classified as his father's sisters (whether or not they are biologically in this relationship) are eligible as marriage partners. A point to note here is that the levirate and the sororate are ideals; they refer to what people say should happen in their society, not what necessarily does happen. Sometimes, if no brother, sister, or other qualifying relative is available, or if the brother or sister is undesirable, the levirate or sororate will not take place.

NUMBER OF SPOUSES

All societies have rules about how many spouses a person may have at one time. **Monogamy** permits only one man to be married to one woman at any given time. Monogamy is the

---

levirate The custom whereby a man marries the widow of a deceased brother.

sororate The custom whereby, when a man's wife dies, her sister is given to him as a wife.

monogamy A rule that permits a person to be married to only one spouse at a time.

rule in Europe and North America, but not in most of the world's cultures. Given the high divorce rate and subsequent remarriage in the United States, perhaps the term *serial monogamy* is more accurate. In this pattern, a man or woman has one marriage partner at a time but, because of the ease of divorce, does not necessarily remain with that partner for life.

Polygamy is plural marriage. It includes **polygyny,** which is the marriage of one man to several women, and **polyandry,** which is the marriage of one woman to several men. Most societies permit (and prefer) plural marriage. In a world sample of 554 societies, polygyny was favored in 415, monogamy in 135, and polyandry in only 4 (Murdock 1949:28). Thus, about 75 percent of the world's societies prefer plural marriage. However, this does not mean that most people in these societies actually have more than one spouse.

POLYGYNY

The practice of polygyny is related to different factors in different societies. Where women are economically important, polygyny can increase a man's wealth and therefore his social position. Also, because one of the most important functions of marriage is to ally different groups with one another, having several wives from different groups within the society extends a man's alliances. Thus, chiefs, headmen, or leaders of states may have wives from many different clans or villages. This provides leaders with increased economic resources that may then be redistributed among the people, and it also binds the different groups to the leader through marriage. Polygyny thus has important economic and political functions in some societies.

Polygyny is found most characteristically in horticultural societies that have a high level of productivity. Although the most obvious advantages in polygynous societies seem to go to men—additional women in the household increase both the labor supply and the productive yield, as well as the number of children—the status of females in such societies is not uniformly low. In some societies, women welcome the addition of a co-wife because it eases their own workload and provides daily com-

ALTHOUGH THE MORMON CHURCH HAS OFFICIALLY OUTLAWED POLYGYNY, THERE ARE STILL MANY POLYGYNOUS MORMON FAMILIES IN UTAH AND ARIZONA.

panionship. Although polygyny combined with patrilineality may mean that women are restricted by patriarchal authority, polygyny can also be combined with a high degree of sexual and economic freedom for women.

Even in cultures in which polygyny is preferred, the ratio of males to females may be such that few men can have more than one wife. Furthermore, where men must exchange wealth for wives, many men cannot afford more than one wife.

People from cultures where sexual fidelity in marriage is considered essential (particularly

polygamy A rule allowing more than one spouse.

polygyny A rule permitting a man to have more than one wife at a time.

polyandry A rule permitting a woman to have more than one husband at a time.

ETHNOGRAPHY

POLYGYNY: THE TIWI OF NORTH AUSTRALIA

Polygyny appears to be most adaptive in horticultural societies, but it is also adaptive in some foraging societies, such as the Tiwi of Australia (Martin and Voorhies 1975). The Tiwi environment has an ample supply of game, fish, and vegetable foods. Although men hunt kangaroos, lizards, fish, turtles, and geese, the vegetable foods gathered by women provide the staples of everyday meals. Women also make their own tools and, with their dogs, hunt small game. The major problem in the Tiwi environment is not a shortage of food, but collecting the food that is abundantly available.

Among the Tiwi, as in most human groups, the male-female ratio is about equal, except that women predominate in the older age groups because they tend to live longer than men. Because the Tiwi

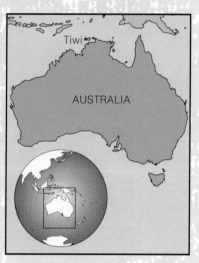

require that every woman be married but do not require this of men, many Tiwi men are polygynous.

Tiwi polygyny is associated with gerontocracy, in which power is held by the elders. Within the constraints of the marriage rules, a Tiwi father betroths his infant daughter to whoever he thinks will bring him the most economic and social

advantage (Hart and Pilling 1960:15). This might be a friend or an ally or someone he wants as a friend or ally. Or he might bestow his daughter on a man who has already bestowed a daughter on him. If he is looking for "old-age insurance," a father might choose a man much younger than himself who shows signs of being a good hunter and fighter and who seems likely to rise in influence. When the older man can no longer hunt, his son-in-law will still be young enough to provide him with food.

In all these cases, the future husband is a great deal older than his future wife. As happens in many societies, where "money follows money," a young man who looks good to one girl's father is also attractive to other fathers. A man who is considered a good catch might have no wives living with him until his late 20s or 30s. Then, as his betrothed wives come of age (around 14), he quickly acquires two or three. As these wives begin to have children, he in turn may become an "in-

in the context of romantic love) may expect to find sexual jealousy in polygynous societies. This is not necessarily the case. Jealousy may occur in polygynous households, but relations between co-wives may also be friendly and helpful. Some polygynous societies have mechanisms to minimize conflict between co-wives. One mechanism is **sororal polygyny,** in which a man marries sisters, who may be more willing to cooperate and can get along better than women who are strangers to each other. Also, co-wives usually live in separate dwellings. A husband who wants to avoid conflict will attempt to distribute his economic resources and sexual attentions evenly among his wives so

there will be no accusations of favoritism. Where women's work is hard and monotonous, co-wives may also provide welcome company for one another.

POLYANDRY

Polyandry (the marriage of one woman to more than one man) is found in parts of Tibet and Nepal and among the Toda and Pahari Hindus of India. Polyandry may be an adaptation to a shortage of females, but such a shortage is created among the Toda and Tibetans by female infanticide. In a society where men must be away from home for long periods of time, polyandry provides a woman with more than one husband to take care of her. In Tibet, polyandry appears to be related to the shortage of land. If several men marry one woman, this

sororal polygyny A form of polygyny in which a man marries sisters.

vestor." By betrothing his own daughters to other men, he may acquire still more wives for himself. In this system, many young men, especially those who are not promising hunters, end up with few or even no wives. Older men who outlive their contemporaries can marry widows, as can younger men who are not sufficiently attractive to acquire wives by bestowal from other men. Being an important, influential man requires having several wives.

The large, multiple-wife Tiwi household can be regarded as an adaptation to the conditions of their existence. The more wives a man has, the more food can be collected. Because of the importance of food collecting, old wives are needed as well as young ones. Older women know the environment and are experienced in finding food. Younger wives serve as apprentices and reinforcements for older wives. For this reason, every man tries to marry an older woman first. Households in which a man has only one or two wives have a much lower standard of living, especially if both wives are young.

Although from a Western perspective Tiwi women appear to be pawns in a marriage game over which they have little control, the Tiwi perspective emphasizes women not simply as wives but as women who have a fluctuating inventory of husbands (Goodale 1971). Early in her married life, the Tiwi girl is introduced to the man who will become the husband of any daughters she may bear. This relationship between a mother-in-law and her prospective son-in-law is very important in Tiwi social structure. The son-in-law must immediately begin to provide food and favors to his mother-in-law, and he often joins her camp at this time. Until her first pregnancy, she enjoys both sexual and social freedom. Young Tiwi women traditionally engage in several extramarital sexual unions with lovers of their own age, a practice that is tolerated although officially not approved of. When a woman gives birth to a girl, who is later given to the prospective son-in-law as a wife, the son-in-law is bound to remain in his mother-in-law's residential group and serve her for life.

As a Tiwi woman gets older, her respect and power increase. As a senior wife, she has power in the domestic group and considerable influence over her sons. Co-wives and their daughters form a cohesive economic and social unit. Thus, rather than viewing women as being socially repressed by male authority, one can view the Tiwi woman as having prestige, power, and independence based on both solidarity with other women and economic complementarity with men.

Critical Thinking Questions

1. From a woman's point of view, what might be some advantages of polygyny in modern industrial society?
2. Present a persuasive argument for monogamy, as it exists in the contemporary United States, to a woman and a man in a polygamous society.

keeps down the number of children a man has to support. If brothers marry the same woman, land can be kept within the family rather than fragmented over the generations.

The Toda of south India are a classic case of **fraternal polyandry.** The Toda female marries one male and at the same time becomes the wife of his brothers. If other brothers are born after the original marriage, they will also share in the marital rights. Sexual access to the wife appears to rotate rather equally, and there is little reported friction or jealousy. When all the brothers live with their wife in one hut, a brother who is with the wife will place his cloak and staff outside as a warning to others. When a wife becomes pregnant, determining the biological father is not considered necessary. Rather, a ceremony called "giving the bow," held in the seventh month of pregnancy, assigns the child a legal or social father. This man makes a ceremonial bow and arrow from twigs and grass and presents these to the wife in front of his relatives. Usually the eldest brother performs this ceremony, and subsequent children are considered his. After two or three children are born, another brother usually gives the bow. Occasionally a woman marries several men who are not biological brothers. When these men live in different villages, the wife lives in the village of each husband for a month. The men arrange among themselves who will give the bow when she becomes pregnant. Because the practice of female infanticide has largely ceased among the Toda, the male-female

fraternal polyandry A custom whereby a woman marries a man and his brothers.

ratio has evened out. For this reason, as well as the influence of Christian missionaries, the Toda today are largely monogamous (Queen and Habenstein 1974).

CHOOSING A MATE

In most societies, marriage is important because it links the kin groups of the married couple. This group interest in marriage often overriding that of the individual partners, accounts for the practice of **arranged marriages.**

In the United States, marriage is primarily an affair of individuals, and the married couple tends to make a new home apart from the parents. Families have less invested in whom their children marry, and certainly less control over marriage, than in other societies. Although choice is not as free in practice as American ideals would lead one to believe, theoretically people are free to choose their own mates. Because sexual compatibility and emotional needs are considered important, mates are chosen on the basis of personal qualities such as physical attractiveness and the complex of feelings Americans call romantic love. Economic considerations are supposed to be subordinated to the ideal of marrying for love.

In societies where the personal satisfactions of the married couple are subordinate to the interests of the family or community, choosing a mate is much less of an individual, haphazard affair. Because of the substantial economic investment of kin groups in marriage, parents and other kin have much more control over the choice of a spouse. Depending on the socioeconomic environment and family structure, different qualities are emphasized for the bride and groom. The economic potential of the groom is of great importance almost everywhere; for brides, reproductive potential and health are important. In addition, each culture has its own special emphases. In India, where a woman is expected to live in a joint family, or at least spend much of her time with her husband's family, a demeanor of submissiveness and modesty is essential. Also, no one wants to arrange a marriage with a family that has the reputation of being quarrelsome or gossipy (Nanda 1999).

Where marriages are arranged, go-betweens are often used. A go-between, or marriage broker, has more information about a wider network of families than any one family can have. Furthermore, neither the family of the bride nor that of the groom loses face if its offer is rejected by the other party. Although the arranged marriage system tends to become less rigid as societies urbanize and industrialize, in most societies families and larger kin groups have a great deal of control over marriage and the choice of a spouse. Important cultural rules guide the arranging of marriages with, to a variable degree, some leeway for individual variation. Different patterns of choosing a mate are closely related to other social and cultural patterns, such as kinship rules, ideals of family structure, transfer of property at marriage, and core cultural values, all of which are rooted in how people make a living.

EXCHANGE OF RIGHTS AND GOODS AT MARRIAGE

The essence of marriage is that it is a publicly accepted relationship involving the transfer of certain rights and obligations. These rights primarily involve sexual access of husband and wife to each other, rights over any children born to the wife, obligations by one or both parents to care for children born to the union, and rights of husband and wife to the economic services of the other.

In many cultures, marriage is also an important means of making alliances between families. Thus, marriage may also give the families or kin groups of the bride and groom certain rights to goods or services from each other. Sometimes this exchange is simply of gifts—items customarily given as a way of winning the goodwill of those with the power to transfer marital rights, though not necessary to complete the transfer. In other cases, the exchange of goods and services is an essential part of the transfer of marital rights (although

arranged marriage The process by which senior family members exercise a great degree of control over the choice of their children's spouses.

the exchanges may still be called gifts). If these exchanges are not completed, the rights in marriage can be forfeited.

BRIDE SERVICE AND BRIDEWEALTH

Three kinds of exchanges made in connection with marriage are bride service, bridewealth, and dowry. In **bride service,** the husband must work for a specified period of time for his wife's family in exchange for his marital rights. Bride service occurs mainly in foraging societies, where accumulating material goods for an exchange at marriage is difficult. Among the Ju/'hoansi, for example, a man may work for his wife's family for as long as 15 years or until the birth of the third child.

The most common form of marriage exchange is **bridewealth,** in which cash or goods are given by the groom's kin to the bride's kin to seal a marriage (Ogbu 1978a). A major function of bridewealth is legitimating the new reproductive and socioeconomic unit created by the marriage. In societies where bridewealth is customary, a person can claim compensation for a violation of conjugal rights only if the bridewealth has been paid. Furthermore, bridewealth paid at marriage is returned (subject to specified conditions) if a marriage is terminated.

Although most studies of bridewealth emphasize its role in entitling the husband to domestic, economic, sexual, and reproductive rights in his wife, bridewealth also confers rights on the wife. By establishing marriage as legal—that is, recognized and supported by public sanctions—bridewealth allows wives to hold their husbands accountable for violations of conjugal rights. In sanctioning the proper exchanges of rights and obligations of both husbands and wives, bridewealth serves to stabilize marriage by giving both families a vested interest in keeping the couple together. However, that does not mean that divorce does not occur in societies with bridewealth.

Bridewealth transactions, although globally widespread, are particularly characteristic of Africa. They are especially common among East African pastoralists such as the Gusii, Turkana, and Kipsigis. Cattle, which dominate these societies culturally and economically, tra-

IN MANY MIDDLE EASTERN SOCIETIES, A WOMAN'S VIRGINITY IS ESSENTIAL TO A VALID MARRIAGE. AMONG THE BEDOUIN OF EGYPT, AS IN MANY OTHER ISLAMIC COMMUNITIES, A VIRGINITY TEST IS PART OF THE MARRIAGE NIGHT. THE PUBLIC DISPLAY OF A SHEET WITH THE BLOOD RESULTING FROM INTERCOURSE CONFIRMS THE HONOR OF THE FAMILY THAT HAS PROVIDED A VIRGIN BRIDE.

ditionally make up the greater part of bridewealth. Bridewealth payments are embedded in the economic strategies of households; they are related to the ways in which men and women engage in labor, distribute property, and maintain or enhance status. Thus, the amount of bridewealth paid varies as people adapt to changing economic, demographic, and social conditions.

This adaptation is illustrated by bridewealth practices among the Kipsigis, a pastoralist/horticultural society in East Africa. A single bridewealth payment, traditionally consisting of livestock but now including some cash, is made at the time of marriage. This contrasts with some societies in which bridewealth payments are made over many years, sometimes only with the birth of each child. The Kipsigis distribute the bridewealth within the immediate families of the bride and the groom. First

bride service Work that the groom performs for his bride's family for a variable length of time either before or after the marriage.

bridewealth Goods presented by the groom's kin to the bride's kin to legitimize a marriage.

BRIDEWEALTH IS THE MOST COMMON FORM OF GIFT EXCHANGE AT MARRIAGE. AMONG THE MEDLPA OF NEW GUINEA, A MARRIAGE IS FORMALIZED BY THE FAMILY OF THE GROOM GIVING GIFTS TO THE FAMILY OF THE BRIDE. THE BRIDE'S FAMILY COMES TO THE GROOM'S VILLAGE TO RECEIVE THE GIFTS. THE BIGMAN OF THE GROOM'S FAMILY (LEFT) PRAISES THE QUALITY OF THE GIFTS, WHILE THE BIGMAN OF THE BRIDE'S FAMILY DENIGRATES THEIR VALUE. TRADITIONALLY, PIGS AND VARIOUS KINDS OF SHELLS WERE PART OF THE BRIDEWEALTH. PIGS ARE STILL GIVEN, BUT THESE DAYS CASH AND PIG GREASE (RENDERED FAT FROM THE PIG), WHICH IS IN THE CAN IN THE CENTER, HAVE REPLACED SHELL MONEY.

marriages are paid for by the groom's father and subsequent marriages by the groom himself, although grooms working for wages may also help with the first payment. The bride's parents are primarily responsible for the negotiation and final acceptance of the bridewealth offer (Borgerhoff Mulder 1995:576). Although young people occasionally pick their own spouses, both young people and their parents are expected to be satisfied by the marriage arrangement, and sometimes the young are brought into line by threats of disinheritance. Personality differences and individual circumstances play a role in bridewealth payments, but certain patterns are also observable.

Kipsigis bridewealth amounts have fluctuated over time. In the past, when agricultural land was available and prices for crops were high, bridewealth was high because of the importance of women's labor in cultivation. Recently, however, bridewealth payments have declined. Land is now scarce and crop prices low. As a result women's agricultural labor has lost its value. Additionally, there are numerous other opportunities for men to invest their wealth, and less is available for bridewealth payments.

The bride's family must balance its desire for higher bridewealth payments with their concern for their daughters' happiness, the need to attract a good son-in-law, and the desire to avoid impoverishing the daughter in her new household. However, Kipsigis parents of girls educated beyond elementary school often demand high bridewealth, both as compensation for the high school fees they have spent on their daughters and because her increased earning potential will benefit her marital home.

Many early Westerners who encountered bridewealth practices assumed that it was both a cause and a symbol of a very low status for women. This is not the case. John Ogbu (1978a) argues that such payments enhance rather than diminish the status of women by enabling both husband and wife to acquire reciprocal rights in each other. Indeed, as the Kipsigis illustrate, it is the higher-status, more educated women who demand higher bridewealth. The low status of women in some parts of Africa has nothing to do with the role of bridewealth in the legitimation of marriage. Despite the general persistence of bridewealth, there has been a decline in women's status with increasing modernization, urbanization, and participation in wage labor economies (Borgerhoff Mulder 1995).

DOWRY

Dowry—a presentation of goods by the bride's kin to the groom's family—is less common than other forms of exchange at marriage. Dowry has somewhat different meanings and functions in different societies. In some cases, this transfer of wealth represents a woman's share of her family inheritance. It may be used by her and her husband to set up a new household, kept by her as insurance in case her husband dies, or spent on her children's future. In other cases, dowry is a payment transferred from the bride's family to the husband's family.

India is one culture where dowry is very common, although it is against the law. The functions of dowry in India are debated. One view is that dowry is a voluntary gift, symbolizing affection for a beloved daughter leaving home and compensating her for the fact that traditionally she could not inherit land or property. Dowry may also be viewed as a source of security for a woman because the jewelry given as part of her dowry is hers to keep. Theories that view dowry as a source of economic security for a woman are challenged in the Indian context on several grounds. First, in reality, most women have no control over their dowries, which remain in the custody of their mothers-in-law or their husbands. Second, if the purpose of dowries were really economic security, they would be of a more productive nature, such as land or a shop, rather than the personal and household goods that constitute the main portion of Indian dowries today.

Another theory holds that dowry in India is a transfer of resources to the groom's family as a recognition of their generosity in taking on an economic burden because upper-class and upper-caste women in India are not supposed to work. Dowry from this standpoint is a compensatory payment from the bride's family, which is losing an economic liability, to the groom's family, which is taking one on. Even as the demanding or giving of dowry has been outlawed in India, a new emphasis on consumerism has increased its importance, especially among members of the middle classes striving for upward social mobility.

Whatever the exact nature of exchanges of goods or services in marriage, they are part of the process of the public transfer of rights that legitimizes the new alliances formed. The public nature of marriage is also demonstrated by the ritual and ceremony that surround it in almost every society. The presence of members of the community at these ceremonies is a way of bearing witness to the lawfulness of the transaction. It is these publicly witnessed and acknowledged ceremonies that distinguish marriage from other kinds of unions that resemble it.

FAMILIES, DOMESTIC GROUPS, AND RULES OF RESIDENCE

Two basic types of families identified by anthropologists are the elementary, or nuclear, family and the extended family. **Nuclear families** are organized around the **conjugal tie,** or the relationship between husband and wife. The **extended family** is based on **consanguineal,** or blood, relations extending over three or more generations.

---

dowry Presentation of goods by the bride's kin to the family of the groom or to the couple.

nuclear family The family organized around the conjugal tie (the relationship between husband and wife). A nuclear family consists of a husband, a wife, and their children.

conjugal tie The relationship between a husband and wife formed by marriage.

extended family Family based on blood relations extending over three or more generations.

consanguineal family People who are related by birth and descent.

A **domestic group,** or household, is not the same as a family. Although domestic groups most often contain related people, nonkin may also be part of a domestic group. In addition, members of a family may be spread out over several households. The composition of a household is affected by the cultural rules about where a newly married couple will live.

THE NUCLEAR FAMILY AND NEOLOCAL RESIDENCE

The nuclear family consists of a married couple and their children. It is most often associated with **neolocal residence,** where the married couple establishes an independent household. This type of family may exist as an isolated and independent unit, as it does in the United States, or it may be embedded within larger kinship units. Only 5 percent of the world's societies are neolocal.

In the United States, in contrast to most other cultures, the neolocal, independent nuclear family is the ideal for most people. It is related to the high degree of mobility required in an industrial system and to a culture that places emphasis on romantic love, the emotional bond between husband and wife, privacy, and personal independence. In nuclear family societies, a newly married couple is expected to occupy its own residence and to function as an independent domestic and economic unit. Larger kin groups are not involved in any substantial way in mate selection or the transfer of goods, and the nuclear family's dissolution (whether from death or divorce) primarily affects only the nuclear family members.

The American nuclear family is ideally regarded as egalitarian, although for most families this is not the case. Although roles in the American nuclear family are less rigidly defined than in other societies, research indicates that even where mothers work full-time, they are also responsible for most of the housework and child care (Lamphere 1997).

domestic group A household unit that usually, but not always, consists of members of a family.

neolocal residence System under which a couple establishes an independent household after marriage.

The idealistic picture of the American independent nuclear family, as touted in political contests over "family values," must be adjusted to some new realities. One of these is the high rates of divorce and remarriage that enmesh nuclear families in ever larger and more complicated kinship networks. With the large numbers of divorces and remarriages in the United States, anthropologist Lionel Tiger (1978) has suggested it is moving toward a new system of marriage and kinship that he calls omnigamy: the marriage of each to all.

As Tiger points out, when parents divorce and remarry, a situation like the following may occur: A and B divorce. Their children, A_1 and B_1, live with A and her new husband, C, but visit B and his new wife, D, on weekends. C's children, C_1, C_2, and C_3, visit him on weekends, and A and C and their five children sometimes spend the weekend together. D also has children, D_1 and D_2, who become friendly with A_1 and B_1 when they visit their father on the weekends when D_1 and D_2 are not visiting theirs. Add to this the sets of grandparents and aunts and uncles that now join these new families, and we can see how complicated it becomes to specify what we mean by the independent nuclear family.

Marriage statistics point to another very important trend in the United States: the increasing number of single-parent (primarily single-mother) households. According to a recent study (Luker 1996), about half the children in the United States will spend at least some of their childhood in a single-parent family. Half of these will do so as the result of divorce or separation; the other half are children of mothers who have never married, many of whom are in their teens. Although there have always been many teenage pregnancies in the United States, increasing numbers of children are being raised by mothers who do not marry. In 1970, 30 percent of teenage mothers were unmarried at the time they gave birth; by 1995, this figure was 70 percent. To some extent, this reflects the overall rise in the number of single mothers of every age. Just after World War II, almost every single mother was either a widow or a divorcee; less than 1 in 100 was an unmarried mother. Today unmarried mothers make up more than a third of the households headed

A PRIMARY FUNCTION OF THE FAMILY—HUSBAND AND WIFE SHARING RESPONSIBILITY FOR TAKING CARE OF THE CHILDREN—IS ILLUSTRATED IN THIS YARN PAINTING OF THE HUICHOL INDIANS OF MEXICO. AS THE WIFE STRUGGLES TO GIVE BIRTH, SHE PULLS ON A CORD ATTACHED TO THE GENITALS OF HER HUSBAND SO THAT HE, TOO, MAY SHARE IN THE BIRTH PAINS.

by single women. This rate is rising, as is the rate of single-parent families. More than half of all U.S. families are headed by a single parent. Although woman-headed households are three times more common among African Americans than among European Americans (Andrews 1992:241), the rates of woman-headed single-parent families and unmarried teenage mothers are increasing among both groups, and the differences between the two groups are shrinking.

The increase in single parenting has a number of possible causes. One was the development of new forms of contraception in the 1960s, making it easier for couples to have an active sex life outside of marriage. With this possibility came a new cultural climate in which marriage and forming a family were disconnected from having and rearing children. As moral disapproval of out-of-wedlock births loses cultural force, the number of unmarried mothers can be expected to grow. Although

much of the concern over single-parent woman-headed households is expressed as political rhetoric about "family values," the real problem is that woman-headed households and teenage pregnancy are correlated with poverty. Although single mothering is often cited as a cause of poverty, it has also been suggested as a symptom, as many unmarried teenage mothers are already disadvantaged by the poverty of their parents (Luker 1996).

The nuclear family is adapted in many ways to the requirements of industrial society. Where jobs do not depend on family connections, and where mobility may be required for obtaining employment and career success, a small, flexible unit such as the independent nuclear family has its advantages. This type of family also seems to be adaptive to the requirements of a hunting and gathering life; more than three-fourths of foraging societies have this type of family unit. In such societies, however, the nuclear family is not nearly as independent or

FAMILY VIOLENCE AND THE CULTURAL DEFENSE

Culture is a powerful concept. When used in a cultural defense, particularly in domestic violence cases, culture can make a difference between life and death. Much, perhaps most, violence in the United States occurs within families, particularly violence by men against women and by parents against their children. When cases of domestic violence involve immigrants to the United States, culture finds its way into court. A cultural defense involves the idea of "state of mind." In United States law, "ignorance of the law is no excuse," but an individual's rational expectations about normal and appropriate behavior (their state of mind) as a member of another culture, may be part of their defense.

Anthropologists are often used as expert witnesses in criminal cases that use a cultural defense. Cultural defenses are controversial because they are frequently used to defend men who have killed their wives, daughters, or others whom they view as having sullied their male "honor" or family's reputation through sexual "transgressions." In a famous case in New York City in 1988, a cultural defense succeeded in freeing a Chinese man who beat his wife to death because he thought she was being unfaithful. The defendant's lawyers, backed by anthropological testimony, argued that the intense shame and dishonor a Chinese man experiences when his wife is unfaithful meant that the husband could not be held fully accountable for his actions (Cardillo 1997). Women's groups, Asian Americans, and legal scholars strongly protested that "there should be only one standard of justice," which should not depend on a defendant's cultural background, and that the court's decision sent out the dangerous message that Asian women cannot be protected by American law (Norgren and Nanda 1996).

In another case, *People* v. *Metallides* (Winkelman 1996), Metallides, a Greek immigrant, killed his best friend after this friend had raped his daughter. Metallides's lawyers, backed by anthropological experts, argued successfully that in Greek culture, maintaining the family honor demanded that Metallides attempt to kill his friend. Similar cases have involved Hmong (Vietnamese) and Laotian refugees, in which anthropological testimony about a Hmong husband's culturally legitimated control over his wife has been used to mitigate homicide charges (Norgren and Nanda 1996:272). The cultural defense was also used in a Hmong case involving rape and kidnapping charges, in connection with the traditional Hmong practice of elopement, or "marriage by capture" (Okin 1999). Hmong elopement begins with a ritualized flirtation, which a woman must strenuously protest by weeping and moaning to demonstrate her virtue, and a man must strenuously overcome to prove he is not weak. Once sexual consummation has occurred, the woman will not be considered marriageable by anyone else. In this case, the defendant claimed that he was following Hmong custom in abducting a girl against her protestations, that the girl in question did want to marry him, and that it was her parents' interference by calling the police that resulted in the rape and kidnapping charges. After hearing anthropological testimony on Hmong marriage customs, the judge decided that although the defendant was sincere in his *belief* that the woman was following the Hmong custom of ritualized protest, his behavior was nonetheless unacceptable. With the agreement of elders in the local Hmong community, the judge dismissed the rape and kidnapping charges, but found the defendant guilty of false imprisonment, sentenced him to three months in jail, and levied a $1200 fine, of which $900 went to the girl's parents.

Domestic violence is a major social problem in the United States, and women from immigrant communities are particularly vulnerable. In many immigrant cultures, patriarchy is strongly entrenched, women have few resources of their own, and spousal abuse is considered a male right. Where a wife's immmigrant visa to the United States is dependent on her marriage, a husband has considerable leverage in ensuring that the wife does not report her abuse to the authorities. Organizations working to protect immigrant women from domestic violence put a high priority on culturally and linguistically sensitive programs and services for battered women and children and acknowledge the need to fight culturally embedded attitudes that deny domestic violence is a problem. To learn more about groups working to protect immigrant women from domestic violence, go to the website of Sakhi for South Asian Women: http://www.sakhi.com.

isolated as it is in U.S. society. The family unit almost always camps together with the kin of the husband or the wife.

COMPOSITE FAMILIES

Composite (compound) families are aggregates of nuclear families linked by a common spouse, most often the husband. Composite families are thus mainly **patrilocal,** structured by rules that require a woman to live in her husband's home after marriage. A polygynous household, consisting of one man with several wives and their respective children, constitutes a composite family. In this case, each wife and her children normally occupy a separate residence.

The dynamics of composite families are different from those of a family that consists of one husband, one wife, and their children, all of whom occupy a common residence. In the composite family, for example, the tie between a mother and her children is particularly strong. The relations between the children of different mothers by the same father is different in a number of ways from the relationship between full siblings in the typical European American nuclear family. In analyzing the dynamics of the composite family, the interaction between co-wives must be taken into account, as well as the different behavior patterns that emerge when a man is husband to several women rather than just one.

Spencer Grant/Photo Researchers, Inc.

ONE OF THE IMPORTANT CHANGES IN THE FAMILY IN THE UNITED STATES OVER THE PAST 50 YEARS IS THE INCREASING NUMBER OF WOMEN WHO WORK OUTSIDE THE HOME. IN MOST FAMILIES, WOMEN'S DOMESTIC RESPONSIBILITIES HAVE NOT DECREASED, BUT IN SOME TWO CAREER FAMILIES, THERE IS A MOVEMENT TOWARD MORE EQUAL SHARING OF DOMESTIC WORK AND CHILD CARE BETWEEN HUSBAND AND WIFE.

EXTENDED FAMILIES

The extended (consanguineal) family consists of two or more lineally related kinfolk of the same sex and their spouses and offspring, occupying a single household or homestead and under the authority of a household head. An extended family is not just a collection of nuclear families. In the extended family system, the ties of lineality—that is, the blood ties between the generations—are more important than the ties of marriage. In more than half of the world's societies, the extended family is the ideal. Even where it is the ideal, however, it is found most often among the landlord and prosperous merchant classes; the nuclear or stem family (a nuclear family with a depen-

dent adult added on) is more characteristic of the less prosperous peasants.

Extended families may be organized around males or females. A **patrilineal** extended family is organized around a man, his sons, and the sons' wives and children. Societies with patrilineal extended families also tend to have patrilocal residence rules; that is, a woman lives with her husband's family after marriage.

composite (compound) family An aggregate of nuclear families linked by a common spouse.

patrilocal residence System under which a bride lives with her husband's family after marriage.

patrilineage A lineage formed by descent in the male line.

INTERNATIONAL RIGHTS OF CHILDREN

Cruelty and violence against children is a global phenomenon. As the case of Elián Gonzalez demonstrates, children are often caught up in politics. In the 1980s, a recurring image in the media that emerged from the world's disaster zones was "a skeletal child with despairing eyes." This image was soon replaced by that of a child soldier, "a gun-toting subteen with a threatening demeanor . . . the kid with a Kalashnikov" (Ryle 1999). According to a report from Amnesty International, *In the Firing Line: War and Children's Rights* (1999), at least 300,000 children under 18 are actively engaged in armed conflicts around the world.

The attempts of international conventions to protect the rights of children run into the issue of cultural differences in the definitions of childhood and the proper treatment of children. For example, the attempts of some European states

to universalize the right of children to choose their own religion is rejected by Islamic states, for whom being raised in Islam is in "the best interests of the child." Sometimes national law protecting children's interests conflicts with international law protecting women's rights. For example, the Jordanian Personal Status Act stipulates that an infant must be breast-fed, either by the mother or by a wet nurse. Finnish law requires men to participate more "actively and creatively" in family life and child rearing so that women can be more active in the community. However, the religiously based Islamic ideal is for women and men to participate in different but complementary ways in raising children. Recognizing children's responsibilities as well as rights also raises possible cultural conflicts. For example, the African Children's Charter requires that children "respect parents and elders at all times." This

may conflict with a Western emphasis on empowering children to resist abuse by their parents and elders and to participate in decisions affecting their lives. The very definition of the age of childhood is also culturally variable. With regard to children as soldiers, however, it may be less relevant whether the age of conscription is 16 or 18 than whether children have been *forcibly* recruited for military service. Rather than focusing solely on age, human rights efforts might be more effectively directed toward control of the arms trade and the issue of forced conscription.

The international human rights efforts on behalf of families and children are an important dimension of globalization in which cultural differences play a key role. The challenge is to produce universally applicable definitions of children's rights that are flexible enough to accommodate these differences (Van Bueren 1995).

A **matrilineal** family is organized around a woman and her daughters and the daughters' husbands and children. Matrilineal families may be associated with **matrilocal residence** rules (a man lives in the household of his wife's family) or with **avunculocal residence** rules (a married couple is expected to live with the husband's mother's brother). If a couple has the choice of living with either the wife's or

the husband's family, the pattern is called **bilocal residence.**

THE PATRILINEAL, PATRILOCAL EXTENDED FAMILY

In premodern China, the patrilineal, patrilocal extended family was the ideal. Lineal descendants—father, son, and grandson—were the backbone of family organization. The family continued through time as a permanent social entity. As older members were lost through death, new ones were added through birth. As in India, marriage in China was viewed more as acquiring a daughter-in-law than taking a wife. It was arranged by the parents, and the new couple lived with the husband's family. The obedient relationship of

---

matrilineage A lineage formed by descent in the female line.

matrilocal residence System under which a husband lives with his wife's family after marriage.

avunculocal residence System under which a married couple lives with the husband's mother's brother.

bilocal residence System under which a married couple has the choice of living with the husband's or wife's family.

the son to his father and the loyalty and solidarity of brothers were given more importance than the ties between husband and wife. In both India and China, the public demonstration of affection between a married couple was severely criticized. In both systems, it was feared that a man's feeling for his wife would interfere with his carrying out responsibilities to his own blood kin.

In these cultures, a good wife is one who is a good daughter-in-law. She must work hard, under the eye of her mother-in-law and her husband's elder brothers' wives. With the birth of a son, a woman gains more acceptance in the household. As the years go by, if she has been patient and played her role well, the relationship between husband and wife develops into one of companionship and a more equal division of power. As her sons grow up, the wife achieves even more power as she begins to arrange for their marriages. When several sons are married, a woman may be the dominant person in the household, even ordering her husband about, as his economic power, and consequently his authority, wanes.

THE MATRILINEAL, MATRILOCAL EXTENDED FAMILY

In the matrilineal extended family, which is also generally matrilocal, the most important ties are between a woman and her mother and her siblings. In a patrilineal society, a child's father is responsible for providing for and protecting the mother-child unit. He has control over women and their children, and owns property with other males in his family. In a matrilineal society, these rights and responsibilities fall to a woman's brother rather than her husband. In matrilineal societies, a man gains sexual and economic rights over a woman when he marries her, but he does not gain rights over her children. The children belong to the mother's descent group, not the father's.

In matrilineal systems, a man usually goes to live with or near his wife's kin after marriage. This means that the man is the stranger in the household, whereas his wife is surrounded by her kin. Because a husband's role in the matrilineal household is less important than in the

patrilineal one, marriages in matrilineal societies tend to be less stable.

A classic ethnographic description of the extended matrilineal family is that of the landowning Nayar caste of Kerala in southern India. The Nayar family was not formed through marriage, but instead consisted of male and female kin descended from a female ancestor. The household group, called the *taravad,* typically contained brothers and sisters, a woman's daughter and granddaughters, and their children. Taravad property was held jointly in the name of the oldest surviving male.

The Nayar family was related to the system of Nayar marriage. Traditionally there were two kinds of marriage among the Nayar: the tali-tying ceremony and the *sambandham* relationship. Every Nayar girl had to undergo the tali-tying ceremony before she reached puberty; this rite marked a girl's transition to womanhood. The man with whom a girl tied the tali had no further rights in her, nor did she have any obligations to him, except for performing certain ceremonies at his death.

After this ceremony, however, a girl could enter into sambandham unions with a number of different men of the proper caste, with whom she would have children. The taravad retained rights over a woman's procreative powers and authority over her children. Even so, for a child to have full birth rights in the taravad, a father had to be acknowledged. Any one of the men with whom the woman had had a sambandham union could acknowledge paternity by bearing certain expenses associated with the birth of a child. Where paternity was doubtful, an assembly of neighbors would attempt to coerce the woman's current sambandham partner to make the payments. If no man of the appropriate caste would take on the role of father, the woman and child were expelled from the taravad and from the caste because it was assumed that the woman was having sexual relations with a lower-caste man. This was considered polluting not only for the woman, but for the entire taravad.

In the Nayar system, then, a woman had several "husbands" (sambandham unions), but the responsibility and care of children were in the hands of a group of brothers and sisters (the taravad). From the perspective of the woman and the taravad, a woman's multiple sambandham unions enhanced both individual and group prestige. Polyandry also gave the Nayar woman access to men in many different occupations, whose services would then be available to the taravad.

The Nayar marriage and family system was well suited to the traditional Nayar occupation of soldiering. Without permanent responsibilities and permanent attachments to wife and children, a young Nayar man was free to pursue a military career. The land owned by the Nayar taravad was worked by lower-caste, landless serfs and managed by an older male of the taravad. This economic system freed younger Nayar men from the necessity of living in the taravad (Mencher 1965).

ADVANTAGES OF EXTENDED FAMILIES

As illustrated by the Nayar, extended families are clearly adaptive under certain economic and social conditions. The extended family system prevails in all types of cultivating societies. Its main advantages are economic. Although the Nayar are somewhat exceptional in that they do not work their own land, one advantage of the extended family is that it provides more workers than the nuclear family. This is useful both for food production and for producing and marketing handicrafts, which are generally more important among cultivators than among foragers. Furthermore, in stable agricultural societies, ownership of land becomes important as a source of pride, prestige, and power. The family becomes attached to the land, knows how to work it, and becomes reluctant to divide it. A system in which land is divided into small parcels through inheritance becomes unproductive. The extended family is a way of keeping land intact, providing additional security for individuals in times of crisis. This relationship between land and family type is supported by evidence from India. The higher castes, who own more land and other property, are more likely to have extended families than are the lower castes. The advantages of matrilineal extended families appear to be important in societies in which warfare takes males

away from home for long distances and periods of time.

Another advantage of the extended family is companionship. Daily activities are carried out jointly by a number of kin working together. The extended family also provides a sense of participation and dignity for the older person, who lives out his or her last years surrounded by respectful and affectionate kin. In the nuclear family, the presumed advantages of privacy and personal autonomy are paid for as people grow old; they are regarded as a burden and a nuisance if they join the household of one of their children.

Although it may be generally true that old people fare better in societies with extended family systems, their life is not always enviable, even in these societies. When sons begin to raise families of their own, extended families often split into parts. As the father loses his productive abilities, he is slowly divested of his status and power. In a Fijian society studied by Marshall Sahlins (1957), the people say "His time is up," and an old man literally waits to die. Although the Fijian ideal is that an old father should be properly cared for by his brothers and sons, "actually he sinks into a pitiable position. In the old days, he might even be killed. Today he is barely kept alive, his counsel is never sought and he is more often considered silly than wise" (p. 451).

Although the nuclear family appears to be adapted to a modern industrialized society, the extended family is not necessarily a liability in some urban settings. The principles of mutual obligation of extended kin, joint ownership of property, and an authority structure in which the male household head makes decisions after consulting with junior members have proved useful among the upper classes of urban India in their successful management of modern corporations (Milton Singer 1968).

Like family types, residence rules are likely to be adaptive to food-producing strategies and other economic factors. Patrilocality, for example, is functional in societies practicing hunting and in agricultural societies, where men must work cooperatively. Matrilocality appears to be adaptive in horticultural societies, where women have an important role in the economy. Nevertheless, many horticultural societies are patrilocal.

Patrilocal residence rules may also be adaptive in societies where males must cooperate in warfare (Ember and Ember 1971). Where fighting between lineages or villages is common, it is useful for men who will fight together to live together. Otherwise, they might wind up having to choose between defending their wife's local group, the one with whom they live, against the families with whom they grew up. Where warfare takes place between societies, rather than within them, and where men must leave their homes to fight, cooperation among women is very important. Because common residence promotes cooperation, matrilocal residence is a functional norm when males engage in warfare that extends beyond local groups, as we saw for the Nayar.

Residence rules and ideals of family structure are related to cultural values. However, they also grow out of the imperatives of real life, in which individuals make choices that do not always accord with the rules. In studying marriage, the family, and domestic groups, anthropologists pay attention to both rules and realities, a dual focus that should be remembered as we study kinship systems in Chapter 10.

IN MUCH OF ASIA, THE PATRILINEAL, PATRILOCAL EXTENDED FAMILY WAS THE IDEAL, EMPHASIZING RESPECT FOR THE ANCESTORS.

SUMMARY

1. Three major functions of marriage and the family are regulating sexual access between males and females, arranging for the exchange of services between males and females, and assigning responsibility for child care.

2. Although marriage and family are rooted in the biological complementarity of male and female and the biological process of reproduction, they are cultural patterns and differ among human societies.

3. Incest taboos are prohibitions on mating between people classified as relatives. Some theories that attempt to account for the universality of such taboos are that they limit inbreeding, they prevent disruption within the family, and they force people to marry out of their immediate families, thus joining people into a larger social community.

4. Exogamy is a rule that requires people to marry outside a particular group. This rule is adaptive in forging alliances between families within a society.

5. Endogamy is a rule requiring marriage within a specified group. Its function may be to keep wealth within the group or to maintain the so-called purity of the blood line.

6. All societies have rules about the number of spouses one may have. Whereas the United States has a rule of monogamy (one spouse only), most of the world's societies allow some form of plural marriage (polygyny or polyandry).

7. Polygyny is found mainly in horticultural societies but also in foraging societies, such as the Tiwi of Australia. Because Tiwi women make important contributions to the food supply, having several wives is advantageous from the man's standpoint. But it is also a source of power for women, especially as they get older and become the center of a cohesive economic and social unit of co-wives and daughters.

8. In many societies, because of the substantial economic investment of kin groups in marriage, family elders have substantial or even total control over choosing their children's spouses.

9. Marriage, a publicly sanctioned relationship, most often is legitimated by an exchange of goods between the bride's kin and the groom's kin. The most common form of exchange is bridewealth, in which the groom's kin gives various goods to the bride's kin.

10. There are two basic types of families. The nuclear family is organized around the tie between husband and wife (the conjugal tie). The extended family is organized around blood ties extending over several generations.

11. The nuclear family is found predominantly in contemporary industrial societies and foraging societies. It appears to be adaptive where geographical mobility is important. The extended family predominates among cultivators. It provides a larger number of workers than does the nuclear family, and it allows land holdings to be kept intact over generations.

12. A domestic group is a household; it usually contains members of a family. The composition of domestic groups is shaped by the postmarital residence rules of a society.

13. The most widespread rule of residence is patrilocality, which requires a wife to live with her husband's family. Matrilocality, which requires the husband to live with his wife's family, is found primarily in horticultural societies. Neolocality, in which the married couple lives independently, is found in a small number of societies, including the United States.

KEY TERMS

arranged marriage
avunculocal
   residence
bilocal residence
bride service
bridewealth
composite
   (compound)
   family
conjugal tie
consanguineal
   family
cross cousins
domestic group
dowry
endogamy
exogamy
extended family
fraternal polyandry

incest taboos
levirate
marriage
matrilineage
matrilocal residence
monogamy
neolocal residence
nuclear family
parallel cousins
patrilineage
patrilocal residence
polyandry
polygamy
polygyny
sororal polygyny
sororate
unilineal descent

SUGGESTED READINGS

Abu-Lugod, Lila. 1993. *Writing Women's Worlds: Bedouin Stories.* Berkeley: University of California Press.

The author uses women's stories to "write against culture," breathing life and complexity into anthropological categories of polygyny, cross-cousin marriage, patrilineality, and other concepts used in studies of the Middle East.

Kilbride, Philip L. 1994. *Plural Marriage for Our Times: A Reinvented Option?* Westport, CT: Greenwood. An exploration of new forms of plural marriage in the United States from the comparative perspective of more traditional forms of polygyny in Africa. The author suggests that plural marriage may be a viable alternative to the contemporary dissolution of families around the world.

Mencher, Joan, and Anne Akongwu (Eds.). 1993. *Where Did All the Men Go? Female-Headed/Female-Supported Households in Cross-Cultural Perspective.* Boulder, CO: Westview. An excellent collection by anthropologists and others who deal with policy issues related to female-headed households that challenge a number of myths, such as their negative effect on children.

Sharff, Jagna Wojcicka. 1997. *King Kong on 4th Street: Families and the Violence of Poverty on the Lower East Side.* Boulder, CO: Westview Press. This deeply moving book grows out of Sharff's innovative and long-term ethnography in this largely Latino but culturally mixed poor neighborhood in New York City.

Werbner, Richard. 1991. *Tears of the Dead: The Social Biography of an African Family.* Washington, DC: Smithsonian Institution Press. The story of an extended family, largely in their own words, from the Bango Chiefdom in Zimbabwe, which emphasizes the many strands of relationships that form the web of life in a small village community.

Internet Resources

The following Internet resources appear in this chapter. Please log on to the Wadsworth anthropology website: **http://anthropology.wadsworth. com**. Click on the Nanda/Warms *Cultural Anthropology* page. Then select the Student Resources section, where you will find a complete presentation of these links and more.

- A video link: on bride service, page 207
- A photo essay on the symbolic elements of an Indian wedding, page 212
- Access the Study Guide to InfoTrac College Edition for Anthropology Students

TIES OF KINSHIP, THROUGH DESCENT AND MARRIAGE, ARE IMPORTANT IN ALL SOCIETIES, THOUGH IN COMPLEX SOCIETIES THEY COMPETE WITH OTHER TIES SUCH AS CITIZENSHIP. AMONG THE MANY KINSHIP OBLIGATIONS IN ALL SOCIETIES IS PARTICIPATION IN IMPORTANT LIFE CYCLE CEREMONIES, SUCH AS THIS MARRIAGE TAKING PLACE IN KOREA.

CHAPTER TEN

KINSHIP

Why is kinship so important in nonstate societies?

Can you explain why hunters and gatherers have kinship classification systems similar to those of industrialized societies?

What are some of the functions of different kinds of kinship systems?

How can people manipulate kinship rules to serve their own interests?

In what ways do kinship terminologies reflect other aspects of a culture?

In societies traditionally studied by anthropologists, kinship is the most important social bond. Although kinship systems are themselves embedded in economic systems, once kinship systems are established in a society, they have an important independent influence on behavior. Kinship is the basis of group formation, and relationships between individuals are governed mainly by kinship norms. The extension of kinship ties is the main way of allying groups to one another and incorporating strangers into a group. In most of the world's cultures, kinship is central in determining people's rights and responsibilities.

In Western societies, other principles of social organization—such as work, citizenship, and common economic and political interests—are also important as bases for group formation and frameworks within which individual rights and obligations are articulated. This does not mean, however, that kinship is insignificant in modern industrialized societies. The nuclear family is a kin group and a core social institution in such societies, and inheritance of property is mainly along kinship lines. Larger groups of relatives also become important on various ritual occasions. For example, in the United States, Thanksgiving is generally thought of as a family holiday among those who celebrate it. A person claiming a kin relation is regarded differently from someone who is not a relative, and there is a strong sentiment that "blood is thicker than water." Although kinship in the United States is not ideally regarded as the basis of occupational choice, it does play a significant role in some important aspects of American life.

Anthropologist Jack Weatherford (1981) makes a persuasive case for the importance of kinship ties in American politics. Among the most important names in United States political history are the Adams, Cabot, Lodge, and Kennedy families of Massachusetts, the Roosevelts of New York, the Gores of Tennessee, and the Bush family from Texas. Some might claim that these family ties in politics are an exception rather than a dominant cultural pattern, but the many examples Weatherford notes, as well as the more familiar examples of the sons and daughters of movie stars who themselves become movie stars, do make a plausible claim for the importance of kinship in American society.

KINSHIP: RELATIONSHIPS THROUGH BLOOD AND MARRIAGE

Kinship includes relationships through blood (**consanguineal**) and relationships through

kinship A culturally defined relationship established on the basis of blood ties or through marriage.

consanguineal Related by blood ties.

Kinship diagrams are more convenient than verbal explanations because they allow us to see immediately how different kinship statuses are linked. In order to make a kinship diagram precise and unambiguous, all relationships in the diagram are viewed from the perspective of one status, labeled **Ego.** Terms of reference rather than terms of address are used—that is, terms we would use in talking about a relative rather than talking to one. In English, for example, we would refer to our mother but might address her as Mom. The symbols used in kinship diagrams are these:

▲ Male   = Marital (affinal) tie

● Female   — Blood (consanguineal) tie

Using these symbols, and English terminology, a kinship diagram of the nuclear family looks like this:

Father | Mother

Brother   Ego   Sister

marriage (**affinal**). In every society, the formation of groups and the regulation of behavior depend to some extent on socially recognized ties of kinship. A **kinship system** includes all relationships based on blood and marriage that link people in a web of rights and obligations, the kinds of groups that may be formed in a society on the basis of kinship, and the system of terms used to classify different kin (**kinship terminology**). Because the formation of kinship groups, the development of kinship ideology, the behavior of different kin toward one another, and the kinship terminology of a society are all interrelated, anthropologists refer to kinship as a system.

Although a kinship system always rests on some kind of biological relationship, kinship systems are cultural phenomena. The ways in which a society classifies kin are cultural; they may or may not be based on a scientifically accurate assessment of biological ties. The term for father, for example, may refer to the child's biological father (**genitor**), or it may refer to a man who takes on responsibility for the child's upbringing or is socially recognized as the father (**pater**). When fatherhood is established by marriage, the "father" is the mother's husband. In some polyandrous societies, such as the Toda of India, biological paternity is irrelevant; fatherhood is established by the performance of a ritual. In this case, social fatherhood is what counts. Because kinship systems are cultural creations, both consanguineal and affinal relatives are classified in different societies in a wide variety of ways. The kinds of social groups formed by kinship and the ways in which kin are expected to behave toward one another also vary widely.

Culturally defined ties of kinship have two basic functions that are necessary for the continuation of society. First, kinship provides continuity between generations. In all societies, children must be cared for and educated so that they can become functioning members of their society. The kinship unit is fundamentally responsible for this task. A society must also provide for the orderly transmission of property and social position between generations. In most human societies, **inheritance** (the transfer of property) and **succession** (the transfer of social position) take place within kin groups.

affinal Related by marriage; in-laws.

kinship system The totality of kin relations, kin groups, and terms for classifying kin in a society.

kinship terminology The system of kinship terms in a particular culture.

genitor A biological father.

pater The socially designated father of a child, who may or may not be the biological father.

Ego The kinship status from which a kinship diagram is constructed.

inheritance The transfer of property between generations.

succession The transfer of office or social position between generations.

Second, kinship defines a universe of others on whom a person can depend for aid. This universe varies widely. In Western societies, the universe of kin on whom one can depend may be smaller than in other societies, where kin groups include a wide range of relations that have significant mutual rights and obligations. The adaptiveness of social groups larger than the nuclear family accounts for the fact that expanded kin groups are found in so many human societies.

RULES OF DESCENT AND THE FORMATION OF DESCENT GROUPS

In anthropological terminology, **descent** is culturally established affiliation with one or both parents. In many societies, descent is an important basis of social group formation. In one sense, of course, the nuclear family is a descent group, but here we use **descent group** to mean a group of consanguineal kin who are lineal descendants of a common ancestor extending beyond two generations. Where descent groups are found, they have important functions in the organization of domestic life, the enculturation of children, the use and transfer of property and political and ritual offices, the carrying out of religious ritual, the settlement of disputes, and political organization and warfare.

Two basic types of descent rules, or kinship ideology, operate in society. In a cultural system with a rule of **unilineal descent,** descent group membership is based on links through either the paternal or the maternal line, but not both. Two types of unilineal descent rules are **patrilineal descent** and **matrilineal descent.** In societies with patrilineal descent rules, a person belongs to the descent group of his or her father. In societies with matrilineal descent rules, a person belongs to the descent group of the mother.

In societies with a system of **bilateral descent,** both maternal and paternal lines are used as the basis for reckoning descent and for establishing the rights and obligations of kinship. A major distinction between systems of unilineal and bilateral descent is that in kinship systems with bilateral descent, nonoverlapping kinship groups are not formed. Bilateral kinship systems are found in few societies throughout the world, although they are basic to Western culture.

The frequency of unilineal descent in the world's cultures reflects two major advantages. First, unilineal rules result in the formation of nonoverlapping descent groups that can perpetuate themselves over time even though their membership changes (as modern corporations can). Corporate descent groups are permanent units that have an existence beyond the individuals who are members at any given time. Old members die and new ones are admitted through birth, but the integrity of the corporate group persists. Such groups may own property and manage resources (just as a modern corporation does). Second, unilineal rules provide unambiguous group membership for everyone in the society. Where descent is traced through only one line, group membership is easily and clearly defined. By knowing the descent group to which they belong and the descent group of others, people can be sure of their rights of ownership, social duties, and social roles. They can also easily relate to a large number of known and unknown people in the society.

Although systems of unilineal descent share certain basic similarities throughout the world, they do not operate exactly the same way in every society. In addition, actual behavior in any society does not correspond exactly to the rules as they are defined in the kinship ideology. Systems of descent and kinship are basically a means by which a society relates to its environment and circumstances. As conditions

descent The culturally established affiliation between a child and one or both parents.

descent group A group of kin who are lineal descendants of a common ancestor, extending beyond two generations.

unilineal descent A rule specifying that membership in a descent group is based on links through either the maternal or the paternal line, but not both.

patrilineal descent A rule that affiliates children with kinsmen of both sexes related through males only.

matrilineal descent A rule that affiliates a person to kin of both sexes related through females only.

bilateral descent System under which both maternal and paternal lines are used in reckoning descent.

KINSHIP AND TRANSMIGRATION

Migration of people across national borders is a significant dimension of globalization. The importance of kinship in this process is apparent in the criteria by which immigration rights and citizenship are granted in most nations of the world. In the United States, for example, the priority of kinship and the cultural importance of bilateral kin relations are basic to contemporary immigration policy. In 1965, 1978, and 1990, new immigration laws abolished the discriminatory national origins quota system of the 1920s and emphasized family reunification. The current preference system, which gives highest priority to members of the nuclear family, indicates American cultural priorities: First preference is given to spouses and married and unmarried sons and daughters and their children, with a lower preference to brothers and sisters, their spouses, and their children. Kinship is also important in the ways in which kin continue ties with their countries of origin through remittances, phone calls, and frequent travel back and forth. A new term, *transmigrant,* has even been coined to indicate these regular connections (Glick-Schiller 1992). The significance of transnational kin relations today means that immigration is often not a traumatic uprooting. Culture is being redefined less in terms of territory than in terms of a portable personal possession that one can carry back and forth across national boundaries.

change, the rules of kinship, like other cultural ideals, are bent and manipulated so that a group may be successful in its environment. The accepted departures from the norm that exist in every society give unilineal systems a flexibility they would otherwise lack—a flexibility necessary for human adaptation.

Anthropologists have offered a number of explanations for the evolution of unilineal descent groups. The common interests that cause people to join together and define themselves as a collective entity justified by kin relations are very diverse. These interests may be economic, such as land or cattle or gardens; they may be political or religious; or they may involve warfare within the society or with other societies. Kinship ideologies, which grow out of these varied common interests, take on a life of their own. With changing economic and historical circumstances, however, kinship ideologies can be manipulated and negotiated to fit new realities.

UNILINEAL DESCENT GROUPS

A **lineage** is a group of kin whose members trace descent from a common ancestor and who can demonstrate those genealogical links among themselves. Lineages formed by descent through the male line are called **patrilineages.** Lineages formed by descent through the female line are called **matrilineages.** Lineages may vary in size, from three generations upward. Where lineages own land collectively and where the members are held responsible for one another's behavior, the lineage is considered a corporate group.

Related lineages may form **clans.** Their presumed common ancestor may be a mythological figure; sometimes, no specific ancestor is known or named. A **phratry** is a unilineal de-

lineage A group of kin whose members trace descent from a known common ancestor.

patrilineage A lineage formed by descent in the male line.

matrilineage A lineage formed by descent in the female line.

clan A unilineal kinship group whose members believe themselves to be descended from a common ancestor but who cannot trace this link genealogically.

phratry A unilineal descent group composed of a number of clans whose members feel themselves to be closely related.

scent group composed of a number of clans who feel themselves to be closely related. Clans are often named and may have a **totem**—a feature of the natural environment with which they are closely identified and toward which the clan members behave in a special way.

Clans and lineages have different functions in different societies. The lineage is often a local residential or domestic group whose members cooperate on a daily basis. Clans are generally not residential units but tend to spread out over many villages. Therefore, clans often have political and religious functions rather than primarily domestic and economic ones.

One of the most important functions of a clan is to regulate marriage. In most societies, clans are exogamous. The prohibition against marriage within the clan strengthens its unilineal character. If a person married within the clan, his or her children would find it difficult to make sharp distinctions between maternal and paternal relatives. Robert H. Lowie (1948:237) wrote of the Crow Indians of North America, among whom clans are very important, that in case of marriage within the clan, "a Crow . . . loses his bearings and perplexes his tribesmen. For he owes specific obligations to his father's relatives and others to his mother's, who are now hopelessly confounded. The sons of his father's clan ought to be censors; but now the very same persons are his joking relatives and his clan." Not only would this person not know how to act toward others, but others would not know how to act toward him. Clan exogamy also extends the network of peaceful social relations within a society as different clans are allied through marriage.

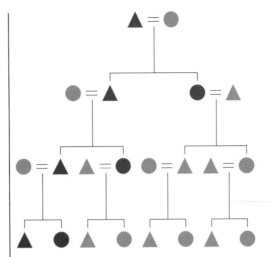

FIGURE 10.1

MEMBERSHIP IN A PATRILINEAL DESCENT GROUP. IN SOCIETIES WITH PATRILINEAL DESCENT GROUPS, MEMBERSHIP IS BASED ON LINKS THROUGH THE FATHER ONLY. SONS AND DAUGHTERS ARE MEMBERS OF THEIR FATHER'S DESCENT GROUP (SHOWN IN DARK GREEN), AS ARE THE CHILDREN OF SONS, BUT NOT OF DAUGHTERS.

PATRILINEAL DESCENT GROUPS

In societies with patrilineal descent groups, a person (whether male or female) belongs to the descent group of the father, the father's father, and so on (see Figure 10.1). Thus, a man, his sisters and brothers, his brother's children (but not his sister's children), his own children, and his son's children (but not his daughter's children) all belong to the same group. Inheritance moves from father to son, as does succession to office.

The Nuer, a pastoral people who live in the Sudan in East Africa, are a patrilineal society. Among the Nuer, all rights, privileges, obligations, and interpersonal relationships are regulated by kinship; one is either a kinsman or an enemy. Membership in a patrilineal descent group is the most significant fact of life, and the father, his brothers, and their children are considered the closest kin. Membership in the patrilineage confers rights in land, requires participation in certain religious ceremonies, and determines political and judicial obligations, such as making alliances in feuds and warfare.

The patrilineage has important political functions among the Nuer. Lineage membership may spread over several villages and thus help create alliances between otherwise independent villages that contain members of several different lineages. Related lineages form still larger groups, or clans. Clans are viewed as composed

totem A plant or animal considered to have an intimate relationship with a human group, sometimes as an ancestor.

of lineages, not of individuals. Each Nuer clan has its members spread out over many villages. Because a person cannot marry someone from within his or her own lineage or clan, or from the lineage of the mother, kinship relations extend widely throughout the tribe. In the absence of a centralized system of political control, kinship-based alliances are an important mechanism for keeping the peace, because the Nuer believe that kin should not fight with one another (Evans-Pritchard 1940/1968).

The degree to which a woman is incorporated into the patrilineage of her husband and the degree of autonomy she has vary in different societies. In some cases a woman may retain rights of inheritance in her father's lineage. In general, however, in a patrilineal system great care is taken to guarantee the husband's rights and control over his wife (or wives) and children because the continuity of the descent group depends on this. Patrilineal systems most often have patrilocal rules of residence, so a wife may find herself living among strangers which tends to undermine female solidarity and support.

Anthropologists have recently begun to focus on the complexity and conflict present within patrilineal families, and in particular on understanding women's roles in kin groups dominated by men. Lila Abu-Lughod's (1993) analysis of families in the Arab world is a good example. Such women have often been portrayed in terms of the kinship patterns of patrilineality, polygyny, and patrilateral parallel-cousin marriage. Analyses have focused on issues of honor and shame, with honor revolving around the male's ability to protect the sexuality of women in his family. According to Abu-Lughod, these generalizations erase many of the conflicts, doubts, and arguments of life as it is really lived. They portray life as timeless, ignoring changing motivations and historical circumstances. Abu-Lughod challenges these static pictures by analyzing the stories Bedouin women tell about themselves: women who refuse their family's choice of a spouse, women who get along (or don't) with their co-wives, women who are sometimes disappointed in their sons, women who assert themselves against their husband's wishes, women who rebel against the norms of their society in

small and sometimes effective ways. The importance of family stories as a way of challenging a static picture of societies dominated by rigid kinship rules is illustrated in the accompanying Cultural Focus box about a conflict over inheritance in a family in a Korean village.

MATRILINEAL DESCENT GROUPS

Two fundamental ties recognized by every society are that between a woman and her children and that between siblings (brothers and sisters). In patrilineal societies, the most important source of male authority and control is the man's position as father and husband; in matrilineal societies, the most important male position is that of the mother's brother. In a matrilineal system, a man gains sexual and economic rights over a woman when he marries her, but he does not gain rights over her children. Children belong to the mother's descent group, not the father's, and many rights and responsibilities belong not to him but to the woman's brother. The membership of a matrilineal descent group (see Figure 10.2) consists of a woman, her brothers and sisters, her sisters' (but not her broth-

FIGURE 10.2

MEMBERSHIP IN A MATRILINEAL DESCENT GROUP. IN A SOCIETY WITH MATRILINEAL DESCENT GROUPS, MEMBERSHIP IN THE GROUP IS DEFINED BY LINKS THROUGH THE MOTHER. SONS AND DAUGHTERS ARE MEMBERS OF THEIR MOTHER'S DESCENT GROUP, AS ARE THE CHILDREN OF DAUGHTERS, BUT NOT THE CHILDREN OF SONS.

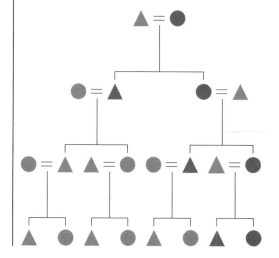

ers') children, her own children, and the children of her daughters (but not of her sons).

Matrilineal systems tend to be correlated with a matrilocal rule of residence: A man goes to live with or near his wife's kin after marriage. This means that in the domestic group, the man is among strangers, whereas his wife is surrounded by her kin. The inclusion of a husband in the household is less important in a matrilineal system than in a patrilineal one, and marriages in matrilineal societies tend to be less stable than those in other systems. As we saw among the Nayar of India, it is possible for a matrilineally organized group to do away with the presence of husbands and fathers altogether, as long as there are brothers who assume responsibilities. It is important to remember that although women usually have higher status in societies where there is a matrilineal reckoning of descent, matrilineality is not the same as matriarchy, in which the formal positions of power are held by women. With a few possible exceptions (A. Wallace 1970), the most important resources and highest political positions in matrilineal societies are in the control of males, although the male with the most power and control in these societies is not the husband (father) but the brother (uncle). The role of the mother's brother is an important or special one even in patrilineal societies, but in matrilineal societies it is particularly important. The mother's brother is a figure of authority and respect, and the children of a man's sister, rather than his own, are his heirs and successors.

In a matrilineal society, the relationship between a man and his son is likely to be affectionate and loving because it is free of the problems of authority and control that exist between fathers and sons in a patrilineal society. A man may feel emotionally close to his sons, but he is committed to pass on his knowledge, property, and offices to the sons of his sister. With his nephews he may have less friendly relations or even conflicts because they are subject to his control. Thus, in a matrilineal system a man's loyalties are split between his own sons and the sons of his sister; in a patrilineal system, this tension does not occur as part of the kinship structure.

Terry Eiler/Stock, Boston

THE HOPI FAMILY IS MATRILINEAL AND REVOLVES AROUND A CORE OF WOMEN. A HUSBAND MOVES TO HIS WIFE'S HOUSEHOLD, IN WHICH HE HAS IMPORTANT ECONOMIC RESPONSIBILITIES BUT FEW RITUAL OBLIGATIONS. THE MOST IMPORTANT MALE ROLE IN HOPI SOCIETY, AS IN OTHER MATRILINEAL SOCIETIES, IS THE RELATION OF A WOMAN'S BROTHER TO HER SON, AND A MAN RETAINS AUTHORITY AND LEADERSHIP IN HIS NATAL HOUSEHOLD EVEN AFTER HE MARRIES.

The Hopi, a Pueblo group in the American Southwest, are a matrilineal society. The matrilineage is conceived of as timeless, stretching backward to the beginnings of the Hopi people and continuing into the future. Both male and female members of the lineage consider their mother's house their home, but men move out to live with their wives after marriage. They return to this home for many ritual and ceremonial occasions, however, and also in the case of separation or divorce. The relationship of a man with his father's lineage and household is affectionate, involving some economic and ritual obligations but little direct cooperation or authority.

RULES AND REALITIES: CONFLICT OVER INHERITANCE IN A KOREAN VILLAGE

The classic anthropological picture of kinship in East Asian villages has been dominated by a focus on the rules of patrilineality, primogeniture (the eldest son inherits all his father's property), seniority, Confucian ethics, and patriarchal authority. This emphasis on rules leaves little room for understanding the realities of family dynamics as they adapt to changing circumstances.

Kinship rules in Korea, as elsewhere, are manipulated by individual family members for their own advantage. Rules of succession to family headship and inheritance are contested as family members try to ensure that their contributions to the family are acknowledged and rewarded in a material way. Occasions on which family property is divided are particularly important as contests in which the balance of credits and debts among family members is reckoned.

According to the local rules of inheritance in Pine Tree, a Korean village studied by anthropologist Soo Ho Choi, the eldest son gets the lion's share of his family's property, including his parents' house and more than half their land. In return, the heir is perpetually obligated to care for his elderly parents and worship them

as ancestors after their deaths. The ancestor worship includes a man's parents and the three preceding generations of lineal ancestors.

However, the realities of contemporary life make it necessary to circumvent these rules in many cases. Most Pine Tree families are so poor that there is not enough property to divide so that any one child will significantly benefit. Sometimes the family property has been acquired through the financial contributions of several family members. When the family property is divided, these people will claim a larger share of the property than the rule of primogeniture would normally allot them. Also, the important Korean value of *chong,* or compassionate generosity, requires elder sons to provide for their younger siblings by contributing to their marriages, education, and living expenses. Any elder son who does not so provide for his younger siblings is highly disapproved of by the community. Finally, in contemporary Korea, an important complicating factor is the practice of spending some of the family's resources on educating one of its sons in the city. This is an enormous expense for a poor or even a well-to-do peasant family.

The poverty of many Korean villages and the pull of industrialization in Korean cities have caused many villagers to migrate. Receiving an education in the city has become a respected alternative to remaining on the farm. Education is highly valued in Korea, for both its traditional importance in Confucian ethics and its pragmatic value; it is a source of great pride to a Korean family to have a highly educated son. However, the high cost of education can be a source of conflict because the money spent on one child's education may be resented by his siblings, who experience his success as having taken place at their expense. This may be exacerbated by a feeling that favoritism plays a role in which son is chosen to be educated. Siblings also resent being left with the economically unrewarding burden of farming, as well as the burdens of ancestor worship and other lineage and village responsibilities. On their father's death, therefore, siblings may try to exclude the educated son from inheriting any family property.

Inheritance rules are also complicated by the status of women, who are legally entitled to an equal share of a family's property. In Pine Tree, however, a daughter's right to family property is consid-

The Hopi household revolves around a central and continuing core of women. The mother-daughter relationship is an exceedingly close one, based on blood ties, common activities, and lifelong residence together. A mother is responsible for the economic and ritual training of her daughters. The daughter behaves with respect, obedience, and affection to her mother and normally lives with her mother and mother's sisters after marriage. A

mother also has a close relationship with her sons, although a son moves to his wife's home after marriage. A son belongs to his mother's lineage and keeps much of his personal and ritual property in her home. A son shows respect for his mother as head of the household and consults her on all important decisions.

The strongest and most permanent tie in Hopi society is between sisters. The foundation of the household group is the relation of sisters to one

ered terminated if her family has given her extensive gifts of cash, furniture, cloth, and jewelry on her marriage. Although a woman who has received such gifts is discouraged from claiming her legal share of family property, many women do make such claims. Contrary to stereotypes, Korean village women are not unassertive. They often participate in the rituals of ancestor worship (formally a male prerogative), which gives them a strong basis for claiming family property. These claims may also lead to conflict between brothers and sisters.

A case study of one family in Pine Tree illustrates many of these conflicting claims. In this family, Sungjo, a frail child who had one brother and two sisters, was his mother's favorite. Because of Sungjo's frailty, he would not be much use as a farmer anyway, and his mother was determined to have him educated in the city. Through her persistence, she finally persuaded her husband to sell one-third of their land to finance Sungjo's education. The sale was opposed by his siblings, who now had to work much harder to compensate for the lost income. To earn additional cash, the women family members wove cotton and silk cloth, and Sungjo's elder brother collected and sold natural lacquer extracted from the woods in the nearby mountains.

After Sungjo's graduation from the university, he was employed by a big corporation and lived in Seoul in comfort. From his family's perspective, he neglected those left behind in the village. When his elder brother and one sister died young, their children attributed it to the sacrifices they had made for Sungjo's education. The elder brother, Sungman, had no sons. According to the cultural rules, his wife should have adopted Sungjo's oldest son as her heir, entitling this boy to perform the ancestral rites and ultimately inherit Sungman's property. But Sungman's wife refused to do this and performed the ancestor rites herself. When she became senile, her eldest daughter took over the performance of these rites and claimed the heir's right to Sungman's property. Sungjo opposed this claim and, after eight years of wrangling, finally prevailed in having his eldest son adopted by Sungman's family. Two years later, Sungman's wife died, and his daughter continued to perform the ancestor rites, although her claim to her parents' property was considerably weakened. As a married daughter, she was no longer considered part of her father's lineage, but that of her husband, and she had neither legal nor cultural support for her claims. Sungjo's eldest sister, who stood to gain more from Sungjo's management of the property than that of her niece, allied with Sungjo to wrest the property from Sungman's daughter.

As stated earlier, one of the most important functions of kinship rules is to smooth the transfer of office and property between generations. The rules are important, but they are not everything. As Sungjo's family history illustrates, cultural rules may be broken to satisfy the demands of changing social circumstances. Conflicting claims based on specific circumstances and individual experiences compete with shared cultural rules and values, and may play decisive roles in family succession and inheritance. However, even though kinship behavior departs from kinship rules, the rules themselves and the kinship categories on which they are based change much more slowly.

Source: Adapted by permission of the author and publisher from Soo Ho Choi, "The Struggle for Family Succession and Inheritance in a Rural Korean Village," *Journal of Anthropological Research* 1995, 51:329–346.

another and to their mother. The children of sisters are raised together; if one sister dies, another looks after her children. Sisters cooperate in all domestic tasks. There are usually few quarrels, and when they occur, they are settled by the mother's brother or their own brothers.

As in all matrilineal societies, a man's relationship to his sister's sons is very important. As head of his sister's lineage and household, a Hopi man is in a position of authority and control. He is the chief disciplinarian and has the primary responsibility for transmitting the ritual heritage of the lineage and clan, which occupies the highest place in Hopi values. A man usually selects his most capable nephew as his successor and trains him in the duties of whatever ceremonial position he may hold; this authority may lead boys to fear their maternal uncles. A woman's brother plays an important role in his nieces' and nephews' lives and is consulted in the choice of a spouse. He instructs his nephews in the proper behavior toward his new relatives and formally welcomes his niece's husband into the household.

Hopi husbands have important economic functions but do not participate in the matrilineage ritual. They may be peripheral in their wives' households, having not only divided residences but divided loyalties. A Hopi father's obligations to his sons are primarily economic. He prepares them to make a living by teaching them to farm and herd sheep. At a son's marriage, a father often presents him with a portion of the flock and a small piece of land. The economic support a son receives from his father is returned in the father's old age, when he is supported by his sons.

Whereas a boy's relationship with his maternal uncle is characterized by reserve, respect, and even fear, his relationship with his father is more affectionate and involves little discipline. A Hopi man's relationship with his daughter is also generally affectionate but not close, and he has few specific duties in regard to her upbringing.

In addition to matrilineages, the Hopi also have matrilineal clans that extend over many different villages. A Hopi man must not marry within his own clan or the clan of his father or his mother's father. Through marriage a Hopi man acquires a wide range of relatives in addition to those resulting from his membership in his mother's clan. Kinship terms are extended to all these people, leading to a vast number of potential sibling relationships and the lateral integration of a great number of separate lineages and clans. This extension of kinship relates a Hopi in some way to almost everyone in the village, in other villages, and even to people in other Pueblo groups who have similar clans. In the clans, men play important political and religious roles, in contrast to the marginal positions they have in domestic life (Eggan 1950).

double descent The tracing of descent through both matrilineal and patrilineal links, each of which is used for different purposes.

DOUBLE DESCENT

When descent is traced through a combination of matrilineal and patrilineal principles, the system is referred to as **double descent.** Double descent systems occur in only 5 percent of the world's cultures. In these societies, a person belongs both to the patrilineal group of the father and to the matrilineal group of the mother. Both matrilineal and patrilineal descent operate as principles of affiliation, but the descent groups formed operate in different areas of life.

The Yako of Nigeria have a system of double descent (Forde 1950). Cooperation in daily domestic life is strongest among patrilineally related kinsmen, who live with or near one another and jointly control and farm plots of land. Membership in the patriclan is the source of rights over farmland and forest products. One obligation of the patriclan is to provide food at funerals. Membership in the men's associations and the right to fruit trees are inherited through the male line. The arbitration of disputes is in the hands of senior patriclan members. Cooperation in ritual and succession to some religious offices are also derived from clan membership.

Matrilineal bonds and clan membership are also important in Yako society, even though matriclan members do not live near one another and do not cooperate as a group in everyday activities. The rights and duties of matrilineal kinship are different from those of patrilineal kinship. Practical assistance to matrilineal kin, the rights and obligations of the mother's brother and sons, and the authority of the priest of a matrilineal clan are based on mystical ideas regarding the perpetuation and tranquility of the Yako world. The Yako believe that the fertility of crops, beasts, and humans, and peace between individuals and within the community are associated with and passed on through women. Life comes from the mother. The children of one mother are bound to mutual support and peaceful relations. The matrilineage is thus held together by mystical bonds of common fertility, and anger and violence between its members are considered sinful.

These sentiments are reinforced in the cult of the matriclan spirits, whose priests are ritually given the qualities of women.

Despite their isolation from one another by the rule of patrilocal residence, matriclan relatives have specific mutual obligations. Rights in the transfer of accumulated wealth, but not land, belong to the matrilineal kinship group. The members of a matriclan supervise a funeral and arrange for the disposal of the dead person's personal property. All currency and livestock customarily pass to matrilineal relatives, who also receive the greater share of tools, weapons, and household goods. The movable property of women passes to their daughters. Matriclans are responsible for the debts of their kin, for making loans to one another at reasonable rates, and for providing part of the bridewealth transferred at the marriage of a sister's son.

Thus, for the Yako, paternity and maternity are both important in descent. Each contains different qualities from which flow the rights, obligations, and benefits, both practical and spiritual, by which people are bound to one another and through which the continuity of the society is ensured.

NONUNILINEAL KINSHIP SYSTEMS

About 40 percent of the world's societies are **nonunilineal,** or bilateral. In systems of bilateral descent (also called **cognatic** or **ambilineal descent**), an individual is considered to be related equally to other kin through both the mother's and the father's side. In a unilineal kinship system, an individual is formally affiliated with a large number of relations extended lineally through time, but only on one side of the family; in a system of bilateral descent, both maternal and paternal lines are used in reckoning descent, in establishing the rights and obligations of kinship, and in forming social groups. Bilateral kinship systems are basic to Western culture, including the United States. They are also the basis of social group formation in some Pacific Island societies, the Northwest Coast of North America, and in Southeast Asia.

ALTHOUGH CORPORATE KIN GROUPS ARE NOT FORMED IN BILATERAL SYSTEMS, IN THE UNITED STATES EXTENDED FAMILY REUNIONS AND "COUSINS CLUBS" BRING BILATERAL KIN TOGETHER. HERE THE NUCLEAR FAMILIES OF THE CURTINS OF ILLINOIS ARE DISTINGUISHED BY DIFFERENT COLOR T-SHIRTS.

Courtesy of Tom Curtin

The people linked by bilateral kin networks are called a **kindred.** A kindred is not a group, but rather a network of relations with Ego at the center. With the exception of brothers and sisters, every individual's kindred is different from every other individual's. Kindreds are actually overlapping categories of kin, rather than social groups, and kindreds are more difficult to organize as cooperative, kin-based collectivities. For example, because it is not a group but rather an Ego-centered network, it cannot own land or have continuity over time.

Ambilineal kinship systems provide a flexible basis for kinship relationships. Each individual has the option of joining either the mother's group or the father's group. Sometimes societies with ambilineal descent rules allow an individual to join only one descent group; in other cases, descent groups may have

nonunilineal descent See **bilateral descent.**

cognatic descent See **bilateral descent.**

ambilineal descent See **bilateral descent.**

kindred Not a group, but a unique kin network made up of all the people related to a specific individual.

overlapping membership. An individual can mobilize a number of relatives from either the father's or the mother's side (or both), depending on the particular enterprise being undertaken. Bilateral kinship systems appear to be particularly adaptive in societies where mobility and independence are important. They predominate among hunters and gatherers and in modern industrial societies.

THE CLASSIFICATION OF KIN

In all societies, kin are referred to by special terms. The total system of kinship terms and the rules for using these terms make up a kinship classification system. In every system of kinship terminology, some relatives are classed together (referred to by the same kinship term), whereas other relatives are differentiated from each other (called by different terms). Kinship systems vary in the degree to which they have different kinship terms for different relatives. Some kinship systems have only a small number of kinship terms, whereas others have a different term for almost every relative.

The ways in which kin are classified are associated with the roles they play in society. For example, if Ego refers to his father and his father's brothers by the same term, the roles he plays in relation to all of these relatives tend to be similar. By the same token, if Ego's father and father's brothers are referred to by different terms, it is expected that Ego will act differently toward each of them and that they will act differently toward him. Furthermore, kinship systems have both an ideal and a real component. Kinship ties include expectations of certain kinds of behavior, but actual behavior is modified by individual personality differences and special circumstances.

Understanding kinship classification systems is not just an interesting anthropological game.

lineal kin Blood relations linked through descent, such as Ego, Ego's mother, Ego's grandmother, and Ego's daughter.

collateral kin Kin descended from a common ancestor but not in a direct ascendant or descendant line, such as siblings and cousins.

Kinship classification is one of the important regulators of behavior in most societies, outlining each person's rights and obligations and specifying the ways in which a person must act toward others and they toward him or her. Kinship classification systems are also related to other aspects of culture: the types of social groups that are formed, the systems of marriage and inheritance, and even deeper and broader cultural values. The Ethnography box on pages 232–234 shows how the differences in kinship classification systems between North America and North India reflect many other cultural patterns in those two societies.

PRINCIPLES FOR CLASSIFYING KIN

Societies differ in the categories of relatives they distinguish and the principles by which kin are classified. Different categories of kin are grouped and distinguished according to seven important principles.

GENERATION

This principle distinguishes ascending and descending generations from Ego. For example, in English we call relatives in the parental generation by such terms as *aunt* or *uncle,* and kin in the descending generation *nephew* or *niece.*

RELATIVE AGE

A kinship system that uses this principle has different kinship terms for one's older brother and one's younger brother, for example. English kinship terminology does not recognize this principle.

LINEALITY VERSUS COLLATERALITY

Lineal kin are related in a single line, such as grandfather–father–son. **Collateral kin** are descended from a common ancestor with Ego but are not Ego's direct ascendants or descendants. For example, brothers and sisters (siblings) and cousins are collateral kin. They are descended from the same ancestors, but are not in a direct ascendant or descendant line. In many societies, collaterality is not distinguished in the kinship terminology. Ego may refer to both his father and father's brother as father. Both the mother and her sisters may similarly be called mother. In these systems, parallel cousins (but not cross cousins) may also be called by the same terms as those for brothers and sisters.

GENDER

In English, some kinship terms differentiate by gender, such as *aunt, uncle,* and *brother;* the word *cousin,* however, does not differentiate by gender. In some other cultures, all kinship terms distinguish gender.

CONSANGUINEAL VERSUS AFFINAL KIN

People related to Ego by blood (**consanguinity**) are distinguished from similar relationships by marriage. For example, English kinship terminology distinguishes *sister* from *sister-in-law, father* from *father-in-law,* and so on. The English word *uncle,* however, does not distinguish between consanguineal and affinal relationships; it is applied equally to the brother of our father or mother, and to the husband of our father's or mother's sister.

SEX OF LINKING RELATIVE

In societies where distinguishing collateral relatives is an important principle of kinship classification, the sex of the linking relative may be important in the kinship terminology. For example, parallel cousins may be distinguished from cross cousins, and may further be distinguished by the gender of the linking relative (for example, matrilateral as opposed to patrilateral cross or parallel cousins). This is particularly important where Ego is prohibited from marrying a parallel cousin but may, or even must, marry a cross cousin.

SIDE OF THE FAMILY

Under this principle, called **bifurcation,** kin terms distinguish between relatives from the mother's side of the family and those from the father's side. An example would be societies

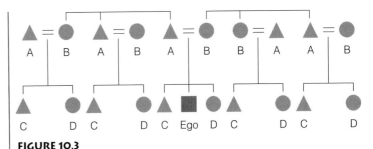

FIGURE 10.3

HAWAIIAN KINSHIP TERMINOLOGY. SYMBOLS WITH THE SAME LETTERS UNDERNEATH ARE REFERRED TO IN THE SAME WAY BY EGO.

where the mother's brother is referred to differently from the father's brother. This principle is not used in English kinship terminology.

TYPES OF KINSHIP TERMINOLOGIES

Systems of kinship terminology reflect the kinds of kin groups that are most important in a society. Anthropologists have identified six systems of kinship terminology: Hawaiian, Eskimo, Iroquois, Omaha, Crow, and Sudanese.

HAWAIIAN

As its name suggests, this system is found in Polynesia. It is rather simple in that it uses the least number of kinship terms. The Hawaiian system emphasizes the distinctions between generations and reflects the equality between the mother's and the father's sides of the family in relation to Ego. All relatives of the same generation and sex—for example, father, father's brother, and mother's brother—are referred to by the same kinship term. Male and female kin in Ego's generation are distinguished in the terminology, but the terms for sister and brother are the same as those for the children of one's parents' siblings (Figure 10.3). This system correlates with ambilineality and ambilocality,

consanguinity Blood ties between people.

bifurcation A principle of classifying kin under which different kinship terms are used for the mother's side of the family and the father's side of the family.

ETHNOGRAPHY

KINSHIP CLASSI-FICATION SYSTEMS IN ACTION: A COMPARISON BETWEEN NORTH AMERICA AND NORTH INDIA

As an anthropologist, I (Nanda) have had the traditional professional interest in kinship classification systems. As an American woman married to a man from North India, however, I have had a more personal interest in understanding how the principles of classification in my culture differ from those of my husband's culture. In order for me to behave properly with the members of my husband's family, I had to learn each of the North Indian kinship terms and the expected behaviors associated with them. At first, I made a lot of mistakes, but as I continued to meet new family members I learned to ask the relevant questions about their relationship so that I could act appropriately. My anthropological experience in making and interpreting kinship diagrams was very helpful in this respect.

As the kinship diagrams of India and the United States indicate, one immediately apparent difference between the North American and North Indian kinship classification systems is the number of terms. North India has 45 different terms, compared with only 22 in the United States. This is because the North Indian system distinguishes several kinds of kin that North Americans group together. Although my husband also had to learn a new kinship classification system, it was easier for him because of the smaller number of categories of relatives and the correspondingly greater flexibility in behavior that is acceptable in North America. For me, learning the many different North Indian kinship terms and the many

corresponding rules of kinship behavior seemed quite a burden. But when I understood the cultural patterns on which these terms and rules of behavior were based, they made more sense to me. I could more easily fit new relatives into the system, and act accordingly.

Many of the North Indian cultural patterns that underlie kinship terminology are based on the importance of the patrilineal, patrilocal extended family: the importance of the male principle in inheritance and seniority; the lower status of the family of the bride compared to that of the groom; the obligations a male child has toward his parents, including the specific ritual obligations of the eldest son; and the ritual roles played by various kin in life cycle ceremonies such as marriage and funerals. These patterns are based on two major principles of Indian culture and social organization: hierarchy and the importance of the group. The contrasting Western values of equality, individualism, and the nuclear family are expressed in North American kinship terminology.

The principle of relative age, which is an aspect of hierarchy, is critical in the Indian kinship system but absent in North

America. Thus, my husband uses different terms to refer to his father's elder brother (*tau*) and his father's younger brother (*chacha*), and this carries over to their wives; his father's elder brother's wife is *tai* and his father's younger brother's wife is *chachi*. This terminological difference reflects the respect attached to seniority. My relationship with my husband's brothers and their wives is also regulated by this principle of seniority. I was instructed that my husband's elder brother is my *jait* and his wife is my *jaitani*. I must treat both of them with deference, similar to that shown to my father-in-law, by adding the suffix *-ji* to their kinship terms, touching their feet when I meet them, and refraining from using their first names. But my husband's younger brother, who is my *deva,* and his wife, who is my *devrani,* may be treated with the friendly informality more characteristic of sister- and brother-in-law relations in the United States. On our trips back to India, I can greet my husband's younger brother with an embrace and talk with him in a joking, familiar manner, but I must never embrace my husband's elder brother, even though I feel equally friendly toward him and like him equally well. Because Indians understand that Americans are generally friendly people who do not recognize these status differences in their own culture, my husband's relatives were very tolerant of my sometimes forgetful lack of deference. For an Indian woman, however, such lapses would be much more serious, and her relations with her husband's elder and younger brothers would be much more strictly differentiated. Indeed, were I an Indian woman, out of respect for the principle of hierarchy, I would probably have to cover my hair, if not my face, in the presence of both my father-in-law and my husband's elder brother.

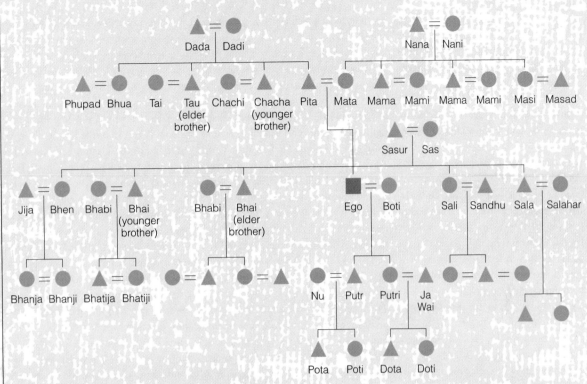

KINSHIP CLASSIFICATION IN NORTH INDIA: TERMS OF REFERENCE

Note: There is no term for a man's nieces and nephews on his wife's side. They are referred to descriptively as wife's sister's daughters or sons. Not shown on this diagram are the terms a wife uses for her husband's sister, her husband's sister's husband, her husband's elder brother, his wife, her husband's younger brother, and his wife. which adds six terms to the 39 used by male Ego.

A second principle that complicates the Indian kinship system from the point of view of a Westerner is the Indian differentiation of kin according to whether they are from the mother's side or the father's side of the family. This principle of bifurcation is absent in English kinship terminology. In North India, the father's brothers and the mother's brothers are called by different terms, as are the father's and mother's parents: *Dadi* and *dada* are the grandparents on the father's side, and *nani* and *nana* are the grandparents on the mother's side. These distinctions reflect the Indian principle of respect and formality associated with the male side of the family and the more open show of affection permitted with the maternal side of the family.

In India, social interaction with one's mother's parents is very different from that with one's father's parents. Ideally the Indian household is based on the patrilineal joint family, composed of a man, his brothers, his father, and his sons. Thus, a son interacts with his father's parents on an everyday basis, whereas his mother's parents live some distance away. Visiting his mother's parents is more like an exciting pleasure trip, and increased fondness and absence of conflict seem to come with distance. Because the parents are expected to give gifts to their daughter and her husband when she visits their home, they also extend this gift-giving to her children, who thus have an additional reason to look forward to such visits.

The patrilineal joint family structure also accounts for another terminological difference between India and the United States: the Indian grouping together of kin that Americans distinguish. In order to highlight the importance of the nuclear family in the United States, the American kinship system distinguishes between siblings (brothers and sisters) and cousins, both of which are collateral relations. But in India this distinction is not made. There is no word for cousin, and what Americans call cousins Indians refer to by the terms for brother and sister.

Kinship Classification Systems in Action: A Comparison Between North America and North India (continued)

The Indian principles of hierarchy and patriarchy turn up again in the higher status accorded the family of the husband's relatives. This status inequality is reflected in a number of ways in Indian kinship terminology and behavior, such as the distinction between Ego's wife's brother (*sala*) and his sister's husband (*jija*). Both relations are called *brother-in-law* in the English system, reflecting the general equality in North America of the husband's and wife's sides of the family. In India, a man's sister's husband is in a higher position relative to him than is his wife's brother. Correspondingly, a sister's husband is treated with great respect, whereas a wife's brother may be treated more ambivalently and may be the target of jokes. The behavioral expectations of this unequal relationship between the bride's and groom's families extend even further. When my husband's sister's husband's sister's husband first visited our home, we treated him with the extra respect due to a man who had taken a "daughter" from our family (the "daughter" referring to both my husband's sister and her husband's sister).

A last example of the importance of kinship terminology in regulating behavior involves the ritual role that different relatives take in life cycle ceremonies, a form of behavior familiar in the United States. For example, in the United States, a woman's father often accompanies her

down the aisle when she marries. In India, the marriage ceremony is much more complex. Each part of the ceremony involves a person in a specific kinship relation to the groom or bride, reflecting all of the important principles by which kin are classified there: relative age, lineality, collaterality, bifurcation, gender, generation, consanguinity, and affinity. Thus, when my husband's sister's son got married, my husband, as the brother of the groom's mother, tied the turban on the groom. However, when my husband's sister's daughter marries, he, as the mother's brother, will give her the ivory and red bangle bracelets that she will wear for a year and the special piece of red cloth that is used in the marriage ceremony. These rituals are concrete symbolic expressions of the continuing warmth and support a girl can expect to find among her mother's male kin, a very important expectation in a culture where a woman is otherwise separated from her own family and incorporated into her husband's family household. This ritual role of the mother's brother in an Indian marriage ceremony also symbolizes the very important kinship tie in India between brother and sister, which is ritually affirmed every year. These rituals, like other aspects of culture involving kinship, reflect the underlying values of a society.

The kinship and other cultural rules that structure relationships between kin

in North India, like those in the Korean village, are important. But their functions in guiding behavior, just like their functions in succession and inheritance described for Korea, are resisted and manipulated in response to pragmatic interest, social circumstances, and emotion. Many members of my husband's family have migrated to the United States, and this has brought a closeness between our families that has lessened the social distance required by the kinship rules. Contesting claims over family property has also led to some alliances within the family that contrast with cultural rules about seniority and patriarchal power. Illness of some family members has also directed the flow of resources in directions not covered, and even in opposition to, kinship rules governing reciprocity.

In short, as close examination of kinship in any society reveals, our understanding of culture and society must be based not just on the "rules of the game" but also the realities of the strategies all people use to negotiate their adaptation to life's contingencies.

Critical Thinking Questions

1. What are the major differences between the kinship systems of North India and the United States?
2. What kinds of behavior in the United States are based on kinship relations and kinship ideology?

which means that a person may choose which descent group he or she wishes to belong to and will live with after marriage. Using the same terms for parents and their siblings establishes closeness with a large number of relatives in the ascending generation, giving Ego a wide choice in deciding which group to affiliate and live with.

ESKIMO

The Eskimo terminology, found among hunting-and-gathering peoples in North America, is correlated with bilateral descent. The Eskimo system emphasizes the nuclear family by using terms for its members (mother, father, sister, brother, daughter, son) that are not used for any other kin. Outside the nuclear family, many kinds of relatives that are distinguished in other systems are lumped together. We have already given the examples of aunt and uncle. Similarly, all children of the kin in the parental generation are called cousins, no matter what their sex or who the linking relative is. The Eskimo system singles out the biologically closest group of relations (the nuclear family) and treats more distant kin more or less equally (Figure 10.4).

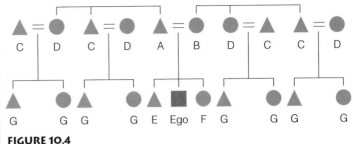

FIGURE 10.4

ESKIMO KINSHIP TERMINOLOGY

IROQUOIS

The Iroquois system is associated with matrilineal or double descent and emphasizes the importance of unilineal descent groups. In this system, the same term is used for mother and mother's sister, and a common term also applies to father and father's brother. Parallel cousins are referred to by the same terms as those for brother and sister. Father's sister and mother's brother are distinguished from other kin, as are the children of father's sister and mother's brother (Ego's cross cousins) (Figure 10.5).

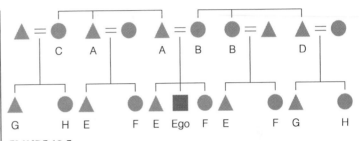

FIGURE 10.5

IROQUOIS KINSHIP TERMINOLOGY

OMAHA

The Omaha system is found among patrilineal peoples, including the Native American group of that name. In this system, the same term is used for father and father's brother and for mother and mother's sister. Parallel cousins are equated with siblings, but cross cousins are referred to by a separate term. A man refers to his brother's children by the same terms he applies to his own children, but he refers to his sister's children by different terms. These terms are extended to all relations who are classified as Ego's brothers and sisters (Figure 10.6). In this system, there is a merging of generations on the mother's side. All men who are members of Ego's mother's patrilineage will be called "mother's brother" regardless of their age or generational relationship to Ego. Thus, the term applied to mother's brother is also applied to the son of mother's brother.

This generational merging is not applied to relations on the father's side. Although father and his brothers are referred to by the same

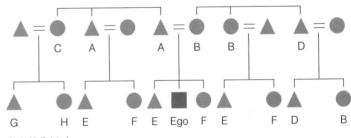

FIGURE 10.6

OMAHA KINSHIP TERMINOLOGY

term, this does not extend to the descending generation. The different terminology applied to the father's patrilineal and the mother's patrilineal groups reflect the different position of Ego in relation to these kin. Generational differences are important on the father's side because members of the ascending generation are likely to have some authority over Ego (as his father does) and be treated differently from patrilineage members of Ego's own generation. The mother's patrilineage is unimportant to Ego in this system, and this is reflected by lumping them all together in the terminology.

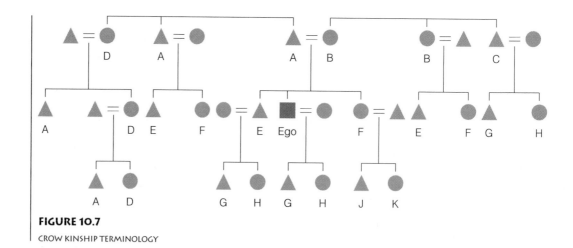

FIGURE 10.7

CROW KINSHIP TERMINOLOGY

CROW

The Crow system, named for the Crow Indians of North America, is the matrilineal equivalent of the Omaha system. This means that the relations on the male side (Ego's father's matrilineage) are lumped together, whereas generational differences are recognized in the mother's matrilineal group (Figure 10.7). In both the Omaha and Crow systems, the overriding importance of unilineality leads to the subordination of other principles of classifying kin, such as relative age or generation.

SUDANESE

The most descriptive terminology systems are sometimes called Sudanese systems, after the groups in Africa, primarily in Ethiopia, that use

them. The types included here use different terms for practically every relative: siblings, paternal parallel cousins, maternal parallel cousins, paternal cross cousins, and maternal cross cousins. Ego refers to his or her parents by terms distinct from those for father's brother, father's sister, mother's sister, and mother's brother (Figure 10.8). Although groups using this system tend to be patrilineal, some elements of matrilineality distinguish them from other patrilineal systems and may account for this distinctive type of terminology.

The great variety in kinship terminologies underscores the fact that kinship systems reflect social relationships and are not based simply on biological relations between people. Kinship classification systems are part of the totality of a kinship system. Each type of classification emphasizes the most important kinship groupings and relationships in the societies in which it is found. Thus, the Eskimo system emphasizes the importance of the nuclear family, setting it apart from more distant relations on the maternal and paternal sides. The Iroquois, Omaha, and Crow systems, found in unilineal societies, emphasize the importance of lineage and clan. In the Hawaiian system, the simplicity of terms leaves the way open for flexibility in choosing one's descent group. At the other extreme, the Sudanese system, with its highly descriptive terminology, may

FIGURE 10.8

SUDANESE KINSHIP TERMINOLOGY

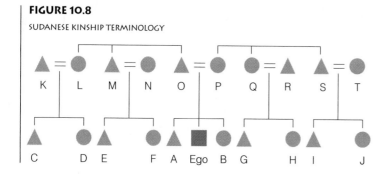

have the same function. In making sense out of kinship systems, anthropologists attempt to understand the relationship of terminologies, rules of descent, and kinship groups to the ecological, economic, and political conditions under which different kinship systems emerge.

SUMMARY

1. Kinship systems are cultural creations that define and organize relatives by blood and marriage. A kinship system includes the kinds of groups based on kinship and the system of terms used to classify different kin.

2. The functions of kinship systems are to provide continuity between generations and to define a group of people who can depend on one another for mutual aid.

3. In traditional societies, kinship is the most important basis of social organization. This contrasts with industrial societies, in which citizenship, social class, and common interests become more important than kinship.

4. In many societies, descent is important in the formation of corporate social groups. In societies with a unilineal rule of descent, descent group membership is based on either the male or female line. Unilineal systems are found among pastoral and cultivating societies.

5. A lineage is a group of kin whose members can trace their descent from a common ancestor. A clan is a group whose members believe they have a common ancestor but cannot trace the relationship genealogically. Lineages tend to have domestic functions, clans to have political and religious functions. Both lineages and clans are important in regulating marriage.

6. In patrilineal systems, a man's children belong to his lineage, as do the children of his sons but not of his daughters. Husbands have control over wives and children, and marriage is surrounded by strong sanctions.

7. In matrilineal systems, a woman's children belong to her lineage, not that of their father. The mother's brother has authority over his sister's children, and relations between husband and wife are more fragile than in patrilineal societies.

8. Patrilineality grows out of patrilocality, which is based on the common economic interests of brothers. Matrilineality grows out of matrilocality, which arises under special circumstances; when these conditions disappear, the kinship system tends to change.

9. In systems of double descent, the individual belongs to both the patrilineage of the father and the matrilineage of the mother. Each group functions in different social contexts. The Yako of Nigeria have a system of double descent.

10. In bilateral systems, the individual is equally related to mother's and father's kin. A bilateral rule of descent results in the formation of kindreds, which are overlapping kinship networks, rather than a permanent group of kin. Bilateral kinship is found predominantly among foragers and in modern industrialized states.

11. Kinship terminology groups together and distinguishes relatives according to various principles such as generation, relative age, lineality or collaterality, sex, consanguinity or affinity, bifurcation, and sex of the linking relative. Different societies may use all or some of these principles in classifying kin. A comparison of kinship terminology in North India and the United States illustrates these differences.

12. The six types of kinship classification systems are the Hawaiian, Eskimo, Iroquois, Omaha, Crow, and Sudanese. Each reflects the particular kinship group that is most important in the society.

KEY TERMS

affinal	**genitor**
ambilineal descent	**inheritance**
bifurcation	**kindred**
bilateral descent	**kinship**
clan	**kinship system**
cognatic descent	**kinship terminology**
collateral kin	**lineage**
consanguineal	**lineal kin**
consanguinity	**matrilineage**
descent	**matrilineal descent**
descent group	**nonunilineal descent**
double descent	**pater**
Ego	**patrilineage**

patrilineal descent **totem**
phratry **unilineal descent**
succession

Suggested Readings

Bohannan, P., and J. Middleton (Eds.). 1968. *Kinship and Social Organization.* Garden City, NY: Natural History Press. Classic articles on kinship and kinship terminology.

di Leonardo, Micaela. 1984. *The Varieties of Ethnic Experience: Kinship, Class, and Gender Among California Italian-Americans.* Ithaca, NY: Cornell University Press. A lively account of ethnicity that emphasizes variability in ethnic experience among different social classes and between women and men. Kinship and family are discussed through individual life histories and in the context of regional, national, and global change.

Pasternak, Burton. 1976. *Introduction to Kinship and Social Organization.* Englewood Cliffs, NJ: Prentice Hall. A good introduction for the beginning student.

Schneider, David M. 1968. *American Kinship: A Cultural Account.* Englewood Cliffs, NJ: Prentice Hall. A look at kinship in the United States and what it suggests about American culture.

Schneider, David M., and Kathleen Gough (Eds.). 1961. *Matrilineal Kinship.* Berkeley: University of California Press. An examination of a variety of matrilineal systems and how matrilineality may be related to subsistence, productivity, and political organization.

Trawick, Margaret. 1990. *Notes on Love in a Tamil Family.* Berkeley: University of California Press. A sensitive, insightful, and skillful interweaving of the author's own life with an ethnography of Tamil (Indian) family relationships. This book gives both a picture of culturally patterned relationships and a vivid experience of the individuals in the family.

Wilson, Monica. 1963. *Good Company: A Study of Nyakyusa Age-Villages.* Boston: Beacon Press (originally published 1951). An interesting study of an African society with an unusual form of social organization.

INTERNET RESOURCES

The following Internet resources appear in this chapter. Please log on to the Wadsworth anthropology website: **http://anthropology.wadsworth. com**. Click on the Nanda/Warms *Cultural Anthropology* page. Then select the Student Resources section, where you will find a complete presentation of these links and more.

- A video link: kinship rules and marriage, page 221
- A link to a kinship tutorial, page 237
- Access the Study Guide to InfoTrac College Edition for Anthropology Students

CULTURAL THEMES ABOUT GENDER RELATIONS OFTEN EMERGE AT A WEDDING AND IN MANY CULTURES INVOLVE PLAYFUL
TRANSFORMATIONS OF GENDER ROLES, AS IN THIS BEDOUIN MARRIAGE.

CHAPTER ELEVEN

GENDER

What are some of the ways in which culture influences gender roles?

What do alternative gender roles tell us about the relationship between sex and gender?

How is masculinity constructed in different cultures?

How are gender hierarchies formed and maintained?

In what ways do men and women contribute to subsistence in different kinds of societies?

How have economic development and participation in world markets affected gender roles?

f you are a male reading this, think about how your life would be different if you woke up tomorrow morning as a female. If you are a female reading this, think about how your life would be different if you woke up tomorrow morning as a male. Which of these differences would be biological and which matters of cultural preference or assignment? Would you experience the changes as positive or negative? Can you imagine making any of these changes without changing from male to female or female to male?

These questions would be answered differently in different cultures. Among some subarctic Indian peoples, for example, where a son was depended on to feed the family through big game hunting, a family that had daughters and no sons would simply select a daughter to "be like a man." When the youngest daughter was about 5 years old, the parents performed a transformation ceremony in which they tied the dried ovaries of a bear to a belt the child always wore. This was believed to prevent menstruation, protect her from pregnancy, and give her luck on the hunt. From then on, she dressed like a male, trained like a male, and often developed great strength and became an outstanding hunter (W. Williams 1996:202). For these Indians, being male or female included both biological elements, such as menstruation and the ability to become preg-

nant, and cultural features, such as the ability to hunt.

In contemporary social science, the distinctions between biological and cultural aspects of being male or female are very important. **Sex** is the biological differences between male and female, particularly the visible differences in external genitalia and the related difference in the role each sex plays in the reproductive process. **Gender** is the cultural and social classification of masculine and feminine. Thus, gender is the social, cultural, and psychological constructs that different societies superimpose on the biological differences of sex (Worthman 1995:598). Every culture recognizes distinctions between male and female, but cultures differ in the meanings attached to these categories, the supposed sources of the differences between them, and the relationship of these categories to other cultural and social facts. Furthermore, all cultures recognize at least two sexes (male and female) and two genders (masculine and feminine), but some cultures recognize additional sexes and genders.

The current anthropological interest in gender emphasizes the central role of gender rela-

sex The biological differences between male and female.

gender The social classification of masculine and feminine.

tions as a basic building block of culture and society (Yanagisako and Collier 1994:190–203). Gender is central to social relations of power, individual and group identities, the formation of kinship and other groups, and meaning and value. As noted in Chapter 3, until the 1970s the central role of gender in society and culture was largely overlooked, and both ethnography and anthropological theory were skewed as a result.

THE CULTURAL CONSTRUCTION OF GENDER

A central assumption of this earlier **androcentric** anthropology was that gender, like sex, was "natural" or biologically determined. The different roles, behaviors, personality characteristics, emotions, and development of men and women were viewed as a function of sex differences, and thus universal. An assumed biological determinism meant that many important questions about the role of gender in culture and society were never asked.

The emergence of feminist anthropology in the 1970s focused attention on cross-cultural variability in the meaning of gender. Biological determinism began to give way to the view that gender is culturally constructed (Ortner and Whitehead 1981). The **cultural construction of gender** emphasizes the different ways cultures think about, distinguish, and symbolize gender.

This new understanding of the cultural construction of gender raised new questions about the culturally patterned nature of women's and men's lives in all cultures. It focused attention on evolutionary and historical changes in gender relations (Zihlman 1989; Spector and Whelan 1989; Lancaster 1989), the role of gender in human development (Chodorow 1974, 1978), and the connections between gender systems

and other sociocultural patterns (Ortner and Whitehead 1981). It also raised questions about the effect of European expansion on gender relations in non-European societies (Nash and Safa 1986) and the changes in gender relations within Europe and North America as a result of industrialism, capitalism, and expansion of the global economy (Warren and Bourque 1989; Andersen and Collins 1995).

THE PIONEERING WORK OF MARGARET MEAD

In the 1930s, Margaret Mead began to question the biologically determined nature of gender (Mead 1935/1963). Mead organized her ethnographic research around the question of whether the characteristics defined as masculine and feminine in Western culture, specifically the United States, were universal. In her studies of three groups in New Guinea—the Arapesh, the Mundugamor, and the Tchambuli—she found that masculine and feminine roles and temperament were patterned differently in each culture.

Among the Arapesh, men and women both were expected to act in ways that Americans considered "naturally" feminine. Both sexes were concerned with taking care of children and nurturing. Neither sex was expected to be aggressive. In Mundugamor society, both sexes were what American culture would call "masculine": aggressive, violent, and with little interest in children. Among the Tchambuli, the personalities of men and women were different from each other but opposite to American conceptions of masculine and feminine. Women had the major economic role and showed common sense and business shrewdness. Men were more interested in esthetics. They spent much time decorating themselves and gossiping. Their feelings were easily hurt, and they sulked a lot. Mead's study showed that the whole repertoire of behaviors, emotions, and interests that go into being masculine and feminine are patterned by culture.

In addition to its importance in gender studies, Mead's work is significant because it reinforces a central anthropological thesis that in order to grasp the potential and limits of di-

---

androcentric Male-centered.

cultural construction of gender The idea that gender characteristics are not inborn but rather constructed within each culture.

ANTHROPOLOGIST MARGARET MEAD WAS A KEY FIGURE IN
EMPHASIZING THE CULTURAL ELEMENT IN GENDER ROLES.
SHE WAS ALSO IMPORTANT IN INTRODUCING THESE
ANTHROPOLOGICAL IDEAS TO THE GENERAL PUBLIC.

versity in human life, we must look at the full
range of human societies—particularly those
outside Western historical, cultural, and economic traditions. Particularly in nonindustrial,
small-scale, kinship-based, more egalitarian societies, gender relationships clearly differ from
those of the West.

ALTERNATIVE SEXES, ALTERNATIVE GENDERS

In the late 1970s, 1980s, and 1990s, new anthropological research and reinterpretation of
older ethnography added weight to the view
of gender as culturally constructed. Particularly important here were cultures that recognized more than two sexes and more than
two genders (Nanda 1999; Williams 1986;
W. Roscoe 1991; Herdt 1994) or where heterosexuality and homosexuality were defined
differently than they were in the United States
(Herdt 1981).

The division of humans into two sexes and
two genders, characteristic of most cultures,
appears to be natural and inevitable. Sex assignment, which takes place at birth, is assumed to
be permanent over a person's lifetime. The
view of sex and gender as a system of two opposing and unchangeable categories is taken

for granted by most social science. It is difficult for most of us even to think about any alternative to this view.

However, a cross-cultural perspective indicates that sex and gender are not necessarily
or universally viewed as identical and limited
to a system of male/female opposites. Among
the Igbo of Nigeria, for example, Amadiume
(1987) notes that members of either sex can
fill male gender roles. Daughters can fill sons'
roles and women can be husbands, without
being considered "masculine" or losing their
femininity. Before the influence of Christianity
among the Igbo, both women and men could
use wealth to take titles (achieve rank) and acquire wives. Although Christian missionaries
attempted to eliminate woman-woman marriage in Africa, the practice continues today. In
some African societies that practice woman-
woman marriages, such as the Nandi of Kenya,
the female husband is considered to be a man
and adopts many aspects of the male gender
role, such as participating in male initiation and
public political discussions (Oboler 1980). The
presence of female husbands has been reported
for more than 30 African groups (D. O'Brien
1977). Although there are important variations
among them, the literature specifically notes
that the relationship between female husband
and wife is not sexual.

Alternative gender roles—neither man nor
woman—have been described for many societies. The xanith of Oman on the Saudi Ara-
bian peninsula (Wikan 1977), the **two-spirit
role** in many Native American tribes (Whitehead 1981; W. Williams 1986; W. Roscoe 1991,
1995), the mahu of Tahiti (Levy 1973; Besnier
1996), and the **hijra** of India (Nanda 1999) are
among the gender roles in which men take on
some of the attributes of women and are classified as an in-between gender.

The Native American two-spirit role has
long been a subject of anthropological inter-

two-spirit role An alternative gender role in native North America
(formerly called *berdache*).
hijra An alternative gender role in India conceptualized as neither
man nor woman.

ETHNOGRAPHY

THE HIJRAS: AN ALTERNATIVE GENDER ROLE IN INDIA

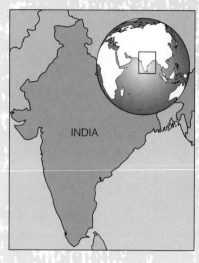

INDIA

The hijra of India is a gender role that is neither masculine nor feminine. Hijras are born as men, but they dress and live as women. The hijras undergo an operation in which their genitals are surgically removed, but unlike transsexuals in the West, this operation turns men into hijras, not into women. Hijras are followers of a Hindu goddess, Bahuchara Mata, and the hijra subculture is partly a religious cult centered on the worship of this goddess. By dressing as women, and especially through emasculation as a ritual expression of their religious devotion, the hijras attempt to completely identify with the goddess. Through this operation, the hijras believe that the procreative powers of the goddess are transferred to them.

Traditionally, the hijras earn their living by performing at life cycle ceremonies, such as the birth of a child (formerly only for male children, who are much desired in India, but sometimes for female children today) and at marriages. Because the hijras are vehicles of the goddess's powers of procreation, their presence is necessary on these occasions. They ask the goddess to bless the newborn or the married couple with prosperity and fertility. Hijras also serve the goddess in her temple.

The word *hijra* may be translated as either *eunuch* or *hermaphrodite;* in both cases, male sexual impotence is emphasized. In fact, few hijras are born hermaphrodites, and as there are many causes for male impotence, there are many reasons that men may choose to join the hijras. In some parts of India, it is believed that an impotent man who does not become a hijra, in deference to the wishes of the hijra goddess, will be reborn impotent for seven future lives.

The concept of the hijra as neither man nor woman emphasizes that they are not men because they cannot function sexually as men, though they were assigned to the male sex at birth. Hijras also claim that they do not have sexual feelings for women, and a real hijra is not supposed to have ever had sexual relations with women. But if hijras, as a third gender, are "man minus man," they are also "man plus woman." The most obvious aspect of hijras as women is in their dress. Wearing female attire is a defining characteristic of hijras. They are required to dress as women when they perform their traditional roles of singing and dancing at births and weddings, and whenever they are in the temple of their goddess. Hijras enjoy dressing as women, and their feminine dress is accompanied by traditionally feminine jewelry and body decoration. Hijras must also wear their hair long like women.

Hijras also adopt female behavior. They imitate a woman's walk, they sit and stand like women, and they carry pots on their hips as women do. Hijras have female names, which they adopt when they join the community, and they use female kinship terms for each other such as *aunt* or *sister.* They also have a special linguistic dialect, which includes feminine expressions and intonations. In public accommodations, such as the movies, or in buses and trains, hijras often request "ladies only" seating. They also request that they be counted as females in the census.

Although hijras are like women in many ways, they are clearly not women. Their

---

est. Two-spirit roles took different forms in different Native American cultures, but most often the two-spirit person was a man who dressed in women's clothing, engaged in women's work, and was often considered to have special supernatural powers and privileges in society (Whitehead 1981). There were also female two-spirit people (Blackwood 1984). Although alternative-gendered people were not equally valued in all Native American cultures, they were very highly valued in some, such as the Zuni (W. Roscoe 1991).

CULTURAL VARIATION IN SEXUAL BEHAVIOR

In addition to varying in the number of sexes and genders they recognize, cultures also vary in their definitions of appropriate sexual be-female dress and mannerisms are often exaggerations almost to the point of caricature, especially when they act in a sexually suggestive manner. Their sexual aggressiveness is considered outrageous and very much in opposition to the expected demure behavior of ordinary Indian women in their roles of wives, mothers, and daughters. Hijra performances are essentially burlesques of women; the entertainment value comes from the difference between themselves, acting as women, and the real women they imitate. Hijras often use obscene and abusive language, which again is considered contrary to acceptable feminine behavior. In some parts of India, hijras smoke the hookah (water pipe) and cigarettes, which is normally done only by men.

The major reason hijras are not considered women, however, is that they cannot give birth. Many hijras wish to be women so that they can give birth, and there are many stories within the community that express this wish. But all hijras acknowledge that this can never be.

As neither man nor woman, the hijras identify themselves with many third-gender figures in Hindu mythology and Indian culture: male deities who change into or disguise themselves as females temporarily; deities who have both male and female characteristics; male religious devotees who dress and act as women in religious ceremonies; and the eunuchs who served in the Muslim courts. Indian culture thus not only accommodates such androgynous figures but views them as meaningful and even powerful.

The emphasis in this ethnography is on the cultural conception of the hijra role. The realities of hijra life do not always match the ideal, and as in other societies, there are some tensions between them. A significant source of conflict among hijras is their widespread practice of prostitution, serving as sexual partners for men, which contradicts their identity as ascetics. Hijras see prostitution as deviant within their community, and many deny that it occurs. Others justify it by reference to their declining incomes from traditional performances.

Unlike many alternative gender roles throughout the world that were suppressed by colonial authorities and Christian missionaries, hijras continue to function as an integral part of Indian culture. Their existence offers strong support for the view of the cultural construction of gender.

Critical Thinking Questions

1. How does a study of the hijras contribute to an understanding of gender as culturally constructed?
2. Can you compare the hijras to similar gender roles in your own society?

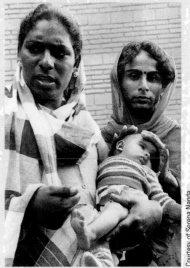

Courtesy of Serena Nanda

HIJRAS ARE CONSIDERED AN ALTERNATIVE SEX AND GENDER IN INDIA. THEY TRADITIONALLY PERFORM AFTER WEDDINGS AND WHEN A CHILD HAS BEEN BORN. HIJRAS PRESENT A PARADOX: THEY ARE THOUGHT OF AS NEITHER MAN NOR WOMAN BECAUSE THEY CANNOT PROCREATE, BUT THROUGH THEIR IDENTIFICATION WITH THE INDIAN MOTHER GODDESS, THEY HAVE THE POWER TO CONFER BLESSINGS OF FERTILITY ON OTHERS. THESE HIJRAS, PERFORMING A BLESSING, ADOPT IN AN EXAGGERATED FORM THE CLOTHING, HAIRSTYLE, AND MANNERISMS OF WOMEN.

Source: Adapted from Serena Nanda, *Neither Man nor Woman: The Hijras of India* (2nd ed.). Belmont, CA: Wadsworth, 1999.

haviors. The cultural component in sexual behavior is not easily understood. Of all the kinds of human behavior, sexual activity is most likely to be viewed as "doing what comes naturally." But a cross-cultural perspective on sexual behavior demonstrates that every aspect of human sexual activity is patterned by culture and influenced by learning.

Culture patterns the habitual responses of different peoples to different parts of the body.

What is considered erotic in some cultures evokes indifference or disgust in others. For example, kissing is not practiced in many societies. The Tahitians learned to kiss from the Europeans, but before this cultural contact, they began sexual intimacy by sniffing. The patterns of social and sexual preliminaries also differ among cultures. The Trobriand Islanders, as described by Malinowski, "inspect each other's hair for lice and eat them . . . to the natives a natural and pleasant occupation between two who are fond of each other" (1929b:335). This may seem disgusting to people from the West, but to the Trobrianders, the European habit of boys and girls going out on a picnic with a knapsack of food is equally disgusting, although it is a perfectly acceptable custom for a Trobriand boy and girl to gather wild foods together as a prelude to sexual activity.

Societies also differ in the extent to which gender and sexuality are culturally elaborated. Whereas some societies have highly complex and explicit views on the relation of gender to sexuality, in societies such as Tahiti (Levy 1973), the Semai of Malaysia (Dentan 1979), and the Tlingit of the northwest coast of North America, gender and sexuality are not central organizing principles.

Who is considered an appropriate sexual partner also differs in different cultures. In some societies, for example, homosexual activity is considered somewhat shameful or abnormal, but in other societies it is a matter of indifference or approval. Among the Sambia of New Guinea, a period of obligatory homosexual relationships is part of the initiation for every adolescent male, who as an adult is expected to enter a heterosexual marriage (Herdt 1981). In this culture, and others in the New Guinea Highlands, it is believed that only men can create men. This process involves a long period during which boys live away from their parents in a men's cult house and engage in homosexual activity as part of their training to be vigorous, strong warriors. The assumptions of Sambia culture contrast strongly with the dominant cultural ideology in the United States, where consistent heterosexuality is considered essential to masculine identity.

Among other variations are the ages at which sexual response is believed to begin and end, the ways in which people make themselves attractive, the importance of sexual activity in human life, and its variation according to gender—all these are patterned and regulated by culture and affect sexual response and behavior. A comparison of two cultures, the Irish of Inis Beag and the Polynesians of Mangaia, makes clear the role of culture in sexuality.

John Messenger describes Inis Beag as "one of the most sexually naive of the world's societies" (1971:15). Sex is never discussed at home when children are near, and parents provide practically no sexual instruction to children. Adults express the belief that "after marriage nature takes its course." (As we shall see, "nature" takes a very different course in Inis Beag than it does in Polynesia!) Women are expected to endure but not enjoy sexual relations; to refuse to have intercourse is considered a mortal sin among this Roman Catholic people. There appears to be widespread ignorance in Inis Beag of the female capacity for orgasm, which in any case is considered deviant behavior. Nudity is abhorred, and there is no tradition of "dirty jokes." The main style of dancing allows little bodily contact among the participants; even so, some girls refuse to dance because it means touching a boy. The separation of the sexes begins very early in Inis Beag and lasts into adulthood. Other cultural patterns related to sexual repression here are the virtual absence of sexual foreplay, the belief that sexual activity weakens a man, the absence of premarital sex, the high percentage of celibate males, and the extraordinarily late age of marriage. According to a female informant, "Men can wait a long time before wanting 'it' but we [women] can wait a lot longer" (p. 16).

Although the idea of total sexual freedom in the South Sea islands is a Western myth, Mangaia, as described by Donald Marshall (1971), presents a strong contrast to Inis Beag. In this Polynesian culture, sexual intercourse is one of the major interests of life. Although sex is not discussed at home, sexual information is taught to boys and girls at puberty by the elders of the group. For adolescent boys, a two-week period of formal instruction about the techniques of intercourse is followed by a culturally approved experience with a mature woman in the village. After this, the boy is considered a man. This contrasts with Inis Beag, where a man is considered a "lad" until he is about 40.

Sexual relations in Mangaia take place in private, but there is continual public reference to sexual activity. Sexual jokes, expressions, and references are expected as part of the preliminaries to public meetings. This pattern of public verbal references to sex contrasts with the public separation of the sexes. Boys and girls should not be seen together in public, but practically every girl and boy has had intercourse before marriage. The act of sexual intercourse itself is the focus of sexual activity. What Westerners call sexual foreplay generally follows intercourse in Mangaia. Both men and women are expected to take pleasure in the sexual act and to have an orgasm. Female frigidity, male celibacy, and homosexuality are practically unknown. The contrast between Inis Beag and Mangaia indicates clearly that societies' different attitudes pattern the sexual responsiveness of males and females in each society.

SEXUALITY AND THE CULTURAL CONSTRUCTION OF GENDER

A culture's construction of gender always includes reference to sexuality and the differences between men and women. Cultural views of gender-related sexuality have often been used to support various sexual ideologies, which also intersect with the construction of race, class, and colonialist relationships. European constructions of masculine and feminine sexuality have been an important part of European images of their own society and of others.

Not all societies so strongly differentiate male and female sexuality. When gender ideologies do make these distinctions, however, they are also likely to use this distinction as the basis of gender hierarchy, in which social control of women's sexuality is central. These controls may take such forms as the seclusion of women (S. Hale 1989); a cultural emphasis on honor and shame as related to female sexuality (Brandes 1981); and control by men, or by the state and organized religion, over marriage, divorce, adultery, and abortion. Controls are also imposed on women through medical/scientific definitions of what constitutes the normal or the pathological in female bodily processes (Martin 1987) and sexuality (Groneman 2000). Society's control of female sexuality is often inscribed on female bodies: female circumcision in some African societies (Barnes-Dean 1989), Chinese footbinding (Anagnost 1989),

gang rape in the United States (Sanday 1992), sati (the Hindu practice of a woman burning herself on her husband's funeral pyre) (Narasimhan 1990), and eating disorders in the United States (Brumberg 1989).

THE CONSTRUCTION OF MASCULINITY IN SPAIN

Like many cultures in the circum-Mediterranean area, Andalusia, in southern Spain, includes a construction of masculinity in which control of female sexuality is central (Gilmore 1996). "Women are the Devil," a butcher in San Blas, Andalusia, explained to anthropologist Stanley Brandes, "because when Eve fell to the temptation of the serpent in the Garden of Eden, she then went on to tempt Adam to eat the apple of the tree of knowledge.... [Woman] was that way from the beginning, and she has been trying to tempt and dominate man ever since."

For San Blas men, this biblical story justifies their view that men are more virtuous than women, more pure (because man sinned only after he was tempted by woman), and closer to God. Consistent with this religiously based view, men in San Blas assert that all women are "seductresses and whores," possessed of insatiable, lustful appetites, who can break down a man's control over his passions and lead him into temptation. Women possess goodness only in their role as mothers, an idealized, pure version of womanhood. Otherwise they are devils who threaten family unity and honor. The ability of women to bring down the reputation of their whole family and kin group through their lustful sexuality underlies the male ambivalence toward women that permeates San Blas social life.

A significant source of this view is early and medieval Christianity, in which Eve's temptation was explicitly interpreted as sexual, and sexual passion was viewed as the mainspring of female nature. The particular suspicion with which medieval Christianity viewed single or widowed women is echoed in the mistrust with which widows are viewed in San Blas. Although wives devote themselves to their husbands, husbands fear that women drive them to a premature death by sapping their strength

H. Armstrong Roberts, Inc./Camerique Stock Photography

IN EARLY AND MEDIEVAL CHRISTIANITY, EVE'S TEMPTATION OF ADAM WAS INTERPRETED AS SEXUAL, AND SEXUAL PASSION WAS VIEWED AS THE MAINSPRING OF FEMININE PERSONALITY. IN THE POPULAR CULTURE OF THE TIME, AS WELL AS IN MANY CULTURES TODAY, THIS VIEW OF WOMEN AS LUSTFUL AND DANGEROUS TO MEN IS A CENTRAL, IF OFTEN UNCONSCIOUS, THEME.

through demands for frequent sexual activity and heavy physical labor. The women do this, men explain, in order to live off their husbands' social security payments without having to share them and to satisfy their voracious sexual appetites without the constraints of marriage (Brandes 1981:225).

The cultural construction of manhood in San Blas explicitly opposes the cultural construction of women. Space is constructed in gender terms: Women belong to the home, men to the streets, bars, and other public spaces. Men most fear that their wives, driven by insatiable sexuality, will be unfaithful, emasculate them, and ruin the honor of their families. They counter this fear by adhering to an image of manliness that centers on aggressive sexuality, a willingness to confront and compete with other men in public, and the demonstrated drive and ability to be successful, whatever the risks, in their marital and economic lives. Even language reflects the sexual inequality of Andalusian culture: Terms from the sexual arena, in which men are supposed to be "on top," are reflected in the language of social stratification in which the rich and powerful not only occupy the higher spaces in Andalusian towns but are considered to be "on top" of the poorer classes, dominating them the way men dominate women (Gilmore 1996).

PROVING MANHOOD: A CULTURAL UNIVERSAL?

The concept of a "real man" as one who proves himself to be virile, controls women, is successful in competition with other men, and is daring, heroic, and aggressive (whether on the streets, in bars, or in warfare) is an almost universal cultural pattern (Gilmore 1990). On the island of Truk, a U.S. trust territory in Micronesia, young Trukese men, who in the past were fierce warriors, are now known as hard drinkers and violent brawlers (M. Marshall 1979). Most young men in Truk go through a turbulent adolescent period of heavy drinking, which generally results in violent fights and serious injuries, particularly on weekends. Through the ethnography of anthropologist Mac Marshall, they have become known as the Weekend Warriors. Masculinity in Truk is defined in terms of competitiveness, assertiveness, risk-taking in the face of danger, physical strength, and, during adolescence, hard drinking, smoking, and physical violence. There is no initiation ritual that turns a boy into a man, and Trukese males must continually demonstrate their manhood in the public arena by cultural competence and effectiveness in everyday affairs (Gilmore 1990:66). This includes being occupationally successful, acquiring consumer goods, and defending one's relatives, particularly women, against danger and dishonor.

We saw in Chapter 6 how becoming a man in many societies is tested by initiation ceremonies in which boys, like the Maasai Tepilit Saitoti, are expected to bear much physical pain without showing any emotion. Among the Sambia of New Guinea, boys were required to undergo a very long and painful process of initiation, which included whipping and beatings, before they were regarded as men (Herdt 1981). In the United States, similar patterns exist in the oppositional cultures of urban streets and schools (see Chapter 13) and in the great attraction of occupations such as firefighting, where the heroic ideal of sacrifice in the face of physical danger is played out on a regular basis (Kaprow 1991).

The near universality of the need to test and prove one's manhood has been called the **manhood puzzle.** Why, in so many different cultures, is the state of manhood regarded as uncertain or precarious, a prize to be won or wrested through struggle? Why does the transformation of a male into a "real man" require trials of skill or endurance, or special rituals? Various attempts to solve this puzzle, particularly in terms of the need for the young boy to separate himself from his mother, are suggested in our discussion of male initiation in Chapter 6.

Some psychological anthropologists offer orthodox Freudian explanations. Thomas Gregor, for example, has described patterns of manhood among the Mehinaku Indians of Brazil (1985). Gregor ascribes the Mehinaku male's preoccupation with a public display of manhood to a culturally conditioned defense against castration anxiety. In order to compensate for their fears about castration, he suggests, Mehinaku men feel compelled to demonstrate their masculinity at every opportunity.

Anthropologist David Gilmore acknowledges the importance of **machismo** in resolving male ambivalence, but suggests that it has important social as well as psychological functions. According to Gilmore (1990), such cultural patterns help ensure that men will fulfill their

ALL MALE GROUPS, WHETHER IN THE STREETS, BARS, OR COFFEE HOUSES, ARE AN IMPORTANT PART OF CIRCUM-MEDITERRANEAN CULTURES AND THEIR LATIN AMERICAN COUNTERPARTS.

roles as procreators, providers, and protectors of their families. This essential contribution to society, he argues, is at the heart of the "macho" role and accounts for its intensity, near universality, and persistence.

GENDER ROLES AND THE STATUS OF WOMEN

Fueled by European and American concerns about male dominance and women's subordination, much of the gendered anthropology in the last three decades has focused on the status of women and gender hierarchy. Studies have examined the significance of women's roles as mothers, sisters, wives, and daughters; women's economic contributions; women's perceptions of their cultures; women's roles in creating symbolic and collective worlds within the context of ideologies of male superiority; the sources of women's power and influence; and the development of women's identities.

> **manhood puzzle** The question of why in almost all cultures masculinity is viewed not as a natural state but as a problematic status to be won through overcoming obstacles.
>
> **machismo** A cultural construction of hypermasculinity as essential to the male gender role.

FEMALE CIRCUMCISION: AN INTERNATIONAL HUMAN RIGHTS ISSUE

Approximately 100 million females in the world today, mainly in Africa and the Middle East, undergo some form of female circumcision, the ritual cutting of a girl's genitals. In the societies traditionally practicing female circumcision, which in Africa include Muslims, Christians, Falasha Jews, and followers of indigenous African religions, it is viewed as an essential gender rite. It is intended to preserve a girl's virginity before marriage, to symbolize her role as a marriageable member of society, and to emphasize her moral and economic value to her patrilineage (Walley 1997). Nubians, for example, view female circumcision and infibulation as symbolic acts that emphasize and embody the essence of femininity: uncontaminated, morally appropriate fertility.

Today, many women from societies where female circumcision is practiced are migrating to Europe and the United States. As a result, this traditional local cultural pattern has taken on global dimensions, as Western cultures consider the rites abusive to women and dangerous to their health (Seddon 1993). France is one of several European countries that have passed laws against female circumcision (Winter 1994), and the World Health Organization has condemned it as a violation of human rights. Some women from these societies have claimed rights of political asylum in Western countries based on the repercussions of their refusal to undergo the rites or to have their daughters undergo them. One such case, that of Lydia Omowunmi Ohuloro, occurred in the United States (Corbin 1994).

The many scholarly and popular publications on female circumcision—or, as it is sometimes called, genital mutilation—are testimony that this is a highly charged cultural issue (Walley 1997). Some women from societies with female genital operations (there are several different kinds with different levels of severity) defend it as affirming a woman's value and enhancing traditional cultural cohesion; others speak out against the practice (El Saadawi 1980). But even for many African women who oppose it, attacks on the practice by outsiders are resented as yet another ethnocentric assault on African cultural integrity by former colonial powers. The international controversy over female genital operations, in which anthropologists have participated in various ways, is yet another demonstration that as the world becomes smaller, local cultural practices can become global issues.

Gender roles are the cultural expectations of men and women in a particular society. Gender roles include expectations about the "natural" abilities of men and women, the occupations considered suitable for each sex, differences in temperament and personality, the kinds of behavior that are most appropriate for men and women, and their attitudes toward themselves and others—in short, almost the entire range of the inner and outer life that characterizes human "nature" and society. **Gender hierar-** chy is the ways in which these attributes are differentially valued and related to the distribution of resources, prestige, and power. Gender roles and gender hierarchy are clearly related to each other because access to material resources, prestige, power, and autonomy depends significantly on what one does, or is allowed to do, in society.

The question of whether (and if so, why) male dominance is universal emerged as an early debate in the anthropology of gender. One theoretical position held that women's subordination to men is universal, based on women's universal role as mothers and homemakers (Rosaldo and Lamphere 1974). In this view, all societies are divided into a less prestigious domestic (private) world, inhabited by women, and a more prestigious public world,

gender role The cultural expectations of men and women in a particular society, including the division of labor.

gender hierarchy The ways in which gendered activities and attributes are differentially valued and related to the distribution of resources, prestige, and power in a society.

dominated by men. This private/public opposition emerged most sharply in highly stratified nineteenth-century capitalist societies, such as those of Victorian Europe and the United States, as productive relationships moved out of the household and middle-class women (but not working-class women) retreated into the home. There they were supposed to concern themselves solely with domestic affairs, repress their sexuality, bear children, and accept a subordinate and dependent role (E. Martin 1987). It became apparent, however, that the **private/ public dichotomy** was not applicable in many non-Western societies, where home and family and economics and politics were not easily separated. Indeed, the dichotomy also obscured the relationship among power, workplace, and family structures critical to understanding much of gender stratification in contemporary Western societies, particularly the United States.

An early critic of the private/public dichotomy as the key to women's status was anthropologist Ernestine Friedl. She attributed widespread male dominance to economic factors. In her comparative examination of foraging and horticultural societies, Friedl (1975) noted that one key factor in women's status was the degree to which they controlled the distribution and exchange of goods and services outside the domestic unit. She argued that in foraging societies the fact that men exercised control over the distribution of meat within the larger community gave them more power and status in society than women. In horticultural societies men cleared the forest for new gardens, and thus were in a position to exercise control over the allocation of land, which put them in a position of power. On the other hand, in societies where women had control over resources beyond distribution within the domestic unit (such as some West African societies, where women sold produce in the market), their status increased. Friedl also suggested that since the care of small children can be shared by older children, neighbors, relatives, and others, women's low status cannot be explained by their obligations in child rearing. Thus cultural norms regarding family size and systems of child care are arranged to conform with women's productive work, rather than the norms of work being an adaptation to pregnancy and childcare.

Marxist-oriented feminist anthropologists added another dimension to the importance of economic factors, emphasizing the cultural and historical variation in women's status, particularly the effects of the expansion of capitalism and European colonialism (Leacock 1981). Eleanor Leacock's work on the Montaignais of eastern North America, for example, was persuasive in documenting that they were egalitarian before European contact, demonstrating in detail how European expansion led to gender inequalities in some non-Western societies. Leacock's work led to a greater focus on changes in gender relations wrought by the European encounter.

In yet another approach to understanding the cultural variability in male dominance, Peggy Sanday (1981) used a controlled cross-cultural comparison to ascertain whether male dominance was universal and, if not, under what conditions it emerged. Sanday concluded that male dominance was *not* universal, but was correlated with ecological stress and warfare. She showed that where the survival of the group rests more on male actions, such as warfare, women accept male dominance for the sake of social and cultural survival.

GENDER RELATIONS: COMPLEX AND VARIABLE

Whatever their position on the universality or variability of gender hierarchy, all sides in this debate agree that gender hierarchies are culturally, not biologically, determined. Both the division of labor by sex and the meanings attached to gendered patterns of activity show great cultural variability and historical specificity. In fact, the debate over the universality of male dominance has been not so much resolved as transcended. As one anthropologist

private/public dichotomy A gender system in which women's status is lowered by their almost exclusive cultural identification with the home and children, while men are identified with public, prestigious economic and political roles.

Betty Press/Woodfin Camp & Associates

IN MANY PARTS OF WEST AFRICA, WOMEN BOTH PRODUCE AND SELL THEIR PRODUCTS IN THE MARKET-PLACE. THIS CONTROL OVER IMPORTANT ECONOMIC RESOURCES IMPROVES THE STATUS OF WOMEN IN SOCIETY, PARTICULARLY IF WOMEN ALSO CONTROL THE CASH THEY RECEIVE FROM THEIR PRODUCTS.

put it, a gendered anthropology has moved from an interest in "woman" to an interest in "women" (Mukhopadhyay and Higgins 1988: 486). This move poses new challenges to old assumptions.

CHALLENGING "MAN THE HUNTER"

New questions and the resulting new data about women's economic roles have affected the most basic ideas about humans in the present and the past. The field of human evolution, for example, had long focused on "man the hunter," omitting the important economic roles of women as gatherers in the origin and development of our species (Slocum 1975). The widespread assumption that a biologically determined division of labor characterized the earliest human groups has also been challenged, providing new starting points for the study of human origins (Spector and Whelan 1989; Cucciari 1981). It is no longer assumed that the earliest human groups elaborated sex differences into differentially valued, gender-exclusive task

groups or gender-structured "families." Instead, the sexual division of labor is being treated as a cultural development that emerged for particular reasons under specific historic conditions.

The interest in the cross-cultural variability of women's roles has led to a reexamination of the sexual division of labor in foraging societies, in which men were previously seen as the sole hunters and male hunting was seen as the basis of male dominance. Contemporary ethnography now documents that, in many foraging societies, women contribute significantly to the food supply by gathering vegetable foods and also by hunting.

As noted in Chapter 9, among the Tiwi of Australia, women make important contributions to the food supply by gathering vegetable foods and hunting small animals (Goodale 1971). These economic contributions give large, multiple-wife households an adaptive advantage over households with fewer wives, which have a much lower standard of living.

Among the foraging Agta of the Sierra Madre in the Philippines, women make an important

Jean Pierre Dutilleux

AMONG THE FORAGING AGTA OF THE PHILIPPINES, MEN FREQUENTLY HUNT LARGE ANIMALS ALONE. A MALE'S POWERFUL HANDS AND ARMS ENABLE HIM TO SHOOT A WILD BOAR WITH A SINGLE ARROW. BUT AGTA WOMEN ALSO HUNT. THE WOMEN, WHO HUNT IN GROUPS, ARE OFTEN MORE SUCCESSFUL THAN MEN IN BRINGING HOME GAME.

economic contribution to their households through hunting. Agta men tend to hunt alone, stalking pigs, deer, and monkeys with their bows and arrows. Women hunt in groups, with men or with other women, using dogs to drive the animals and killing them with long knives or bows and arrows (Estioko-Griffin 1986).

The Agta illustrate Ernestine Friedl's contention that in foraging societies, which rely heavily on women's economic contributions, child rearing is adapted to economic needs. Agta women carry nursing infants on their backs on their forest trips for hunting and gathering. Older children are left with older sisters or grandmothers. Fathers also spend significant amounts of time caring for their children.

WOMEN AND THE DISTRIBUTION OF POWER IN FORAGING SOCIETIES

Anthropologists have also found sources of women's power and influence beyond those of their economic contribution. In many non-Western societies, where the private/public

dichotomy cannot be applied, the power of women cannot be judged solely on the basis of formal political status. In addition to their important roles within households, women in many societies make alliances and participate in networks outside the household. These collectivities provide arenas for entertainment, prestige, influence, and self-esteem.

Because each cultural situation is complex and unique, it is difficult to generalize about the ways in which gender affects the distribution of prestige and power in society. Generally speaking, women had more autonomy and power in egalitarian foraging societies, such as those in native North America (Klein and Ackerman 1995), some tribal populations in Southeast Asia (Ong 1989), some hunters and gatherers in Africa (Shostak 1983), and the Mbuti of the Ituri forest in Africa (Turnbull 1961), than in horticultural or agricultural societies, although there is great variety among these also. Even generalizing about women's status by region becomes risky, as it has been demonstrated that within such regions as aboriginal Australia (Burbank 1989) and sub-Saharan Africa (Potash 1989) there are great variations in women's roles and status.

Although women's economic contributions appear to be an important factor in their social power, other factors are also important. For example, even in foraging societies where women make important economic contributions, men may have greater prestige and power through their (exclusive) participation in hunting large animals (as among the Inuit) or through male-dominated ritual activities, as in native Australia (Kaberry 1939; Bell 1981; Merlan 1988).

Among the most egalitarian societies were native groups in North America (Albers 1989). Egalitarian gender relations in these societies appear to be related to the absence of social hierarchy in most foraging societies and the high degree of individual autonomy accorded both men and women. Even when these groups are not egalitarian, however, gender may be unimportant to social hierarchy.

The Tlingit of the Northwest Coast of North America are a society where social hierarchy is important, but gender relations are egalitarian (Klein 1995). Both women and men could achieve prestige through their own efforts and their kin relationships. Kinship relations and wealth obtained through extensive trade with other coastal societies were the keys to social status for both men and women.

The Tlingit sexual division of labor was clear but not rigid, and economic roles had little bearing on the power and influence of women. The abundant food supply of the Tlingit depended primarily on salmon, which were generally caught by men and smoked and dried by women. The plentiful products of sea and land provided the basis for long-distance trade in "luxury" items such as furs and copper, wood carvings, and woven blankets, which were distributed at festive giveaways (potlatches) as indicators of wealth.

Although long-distance trade was centered on men, women often accompanied men, acting as negotiators and handling the money—a fact commented on by early European traders, missionaries, and anthropologists. Tlingit women regarded men as "being foolish with money," and both girls and boys were expected to "work, save, get wealth and goods" (Klein 1995:35). Becoming a shaman was one route to wealth outside the kinship system, and this role was equally open to men and women.

The private/public dichotomy was not relevant to gender status among the Tlingit. Power and influence were embedded in kinship and rank, which applied equally to men and women. Although Europeans generally recognized only men as chiefs, some women were heads of clans or tribes and Tlingit aristocrats were both male and female. In any case, wealth, kinship connections, and personality were more important sources of status than formal political roles. Titles of high rank were used for both men and women, and the ideal marriage was between a man and woman of equal rank.

The assertive competitiveness that appears to have characterized both women and men in traditional Tlingit society—noticed, not always favorably, by European observers—remains part of Tlingit life (Klein 1976). Tlingit women are found in the highest offices of the native corporations administering Tlingit land and in government, social action groups, and business and cultural organizations. Traditional female roles in accumulating wealth and han-

dling money have served Tlingit women well in their contemporary communities, where they hold political positions and sit on the boards of the influential voluntary associations. With no traditional inhibitions about women appearing in public roles, Tlingit women have taken advantage of opportunities for education and easily enter modern professions. Unlike many societies in which the impact of Europeans resulted in a diminishing of women's economic roles and influence, modernization has led to a broadening of women's roles among the Tlingit.

Anthropologist Laura Klein, who has studied the Tlingit, warns against a Eurocentric reading of women's status as one that diminishes men. Tlingit men and women both take pride in the accomplishments of prominent Tlingit women. Husbands proudly describe the achievements of their wives and daughters, encouraging them to go into public life. Klein concludes that the Tlingit are best described not as a matriarchy, or even as a society where exceptional women can occupy important masculine roles, but rather as a society in which roles are structured more on the basis of individual ability, training, and personality than on the basis of gender (1976:179).

GENDER RELATIONS IN HORTICULTURAL SOCIETIES

Horticultural societies encompass a very wide range of gender relationships, from the highly egalitarian Iroquois of eastern North America (J. Brown 1975) to the highly sex-segregated and male-dominated Yanomamo of South America (Chagnon 1997) and New Guinea (Strathern 1995). There is a correspondingly wide variety in the sexual division of labor in horticultural societies, although some general similarities can be noted (see Chapter 8).

A high degree of segregation between the sexes, paralleled by the importance of males in ritual, is associated with male dominance in some horticultural societies. For example, among the Mundurucu of South America, adolescent boys are initiated into the men's cult and thereafter spend most of their lives in the men's house, only visiting their wives, who live with the children in their own huts in the village. These men's cults are closed to women and surrounded by great secrecy. The men's house itself is usually the most imposing structure in the village, and in or near it are kept the sacred musical instruments and paraphernalia of the cult. The musical instruments, which are often flutelike (shaped like the male genitals), are the symbolic expressions of male dominance and solidarity (Murphy and Murphy 1974). Often, especially in Australia, such cults are associated with circumcision rites for newly initiated boys, after which the initiates are considered men and introduced to the secrets of the cult. Sometimes associated with these cults is a mythology of the cult's origin, which contains an "explanation" of why women are not allowed in them. These myths may also "explain" why women are considered socially inferior to men and why men and women have different roles in these societies.

The solidarity of women in horticultural societies is usually not formalized in cults or associations, but is based on the cooperation of domestic life and strong interpersonal bonds among female kin. In sub-Saharan Africa, for example, the most important economic and emotional ties for both men and women are not between a married couple (conjugal ties) but between generations (consanguineal ties). Women's most important ties are with their children, particularly their sons, on whom women depend for emotional support and security in old age (Potash 1989:199). The importance of kinship ties for African men has long been noted. Ethnographies focusing on the lives of women show how they, too, use kinship ties with their natal groups to gain access to land, gain support in marital disputes, or participate in ritual activities (Sacks 1982).

The impact of European expansion on women in horticultural societies varied. Generally, their role declined as indigenous economies shifted from subsistence horticulture to cash crops to be sold in a world market. This process of change is illustrated by the Polynesian atoll of Nukumanu, a fishing and horticultural society studied by anthropologist Richard Feinberg (1986). Before European contact, Nukumanu depended for its food on the abundant marine life and a few indigenous plants, such as the coconut, pandanus, and taro (a starchy root). Women's primary responsibilities were domestic, whereas men contributed food acquired some distance from the home through fishing, collecting shellfish, and collecting and husking coconuts. Men also made canoes and constructed new buildings, while women cooked food and collected and prepared leaves for thatch.

Both women's and men's roles were highly valued in Nukumanu society. Women exclusively controlled and cultivated swamp taro lands, which were inherited matrilineally. Matrilocality added to women's status, whereas men's power came from their economic contribution and their exclusive occupation of formal positions of power in the chiefly hierarchy.

In the 1880s, under German colonialism, most of Nukumanu was turned over to production of copra (dried coconut meat). Wage laborers were brought in from nearby islands. This resulted in irreversible cultural and economic changes, most of which lowered women's status. Commercial foods such as wheat flour and rice supplanted taro, and men's wages were needed to buy coffee, tea, and sugar (once luxury items). As a result, women's traditional sphere of influence declined, while men's sphere expanded.

In addition, the traditional segregation of men's and women's activities has intensified. With the introduction of kareve (sap of the coconut tree fermented to make a potent alcoholic beverage) in the 1950s, men's economic activities, such as canoe building, took on a social aspect involving drinking. Because the production and consumption of kareve takes up a great deal of men's leisure time and excludes women, sexual segregation has increased.

With the declining importance of taro, women's collective activities have become more individualized, leaving women more isolated and dependent on their husbands and brothers than they were in the past. Male-female tensions have also increased, partly as a result of kareve drinking, which many women vehemently oppose. The traditional tendency for men to travel off the island more than women has also lowered women's status be-

ADVOCATING FOR WOMEN WORKERS IN THE GLOBAL ECONOMY

In the past 25 years, industrial production by multinational corporations in Latin America, Asia, and Africa has exploded. In the search for cheap labor, clothing manufacturing, food processing, pharmaceuticals, and electronics assembly factories have recruited women, particularly young women. These jobs give women a chance to earn on their own, and they offer women an important opportunity to act collectively in their own interests (Lim 1983). But there are also drawbacks.

One of the more heated debates over globalization at the millennium involved the issue of whether the United States should continue normal trade relations with China and permit China to join the World Trade Organization. One concern in this debate, as in other situations where global capitalism is expanding, is the sweatshop working conditions in factories producing for a global market, a situation that particularly affects women.

Pun Ngai, a Hong Kong anthropologist, spent six months tightening screws in computer hardware at an electronics factory in Shenzhen, People's Republic of China, as part of her ethnographic

AN IMPORTANT PART OF THE MULTINATIONAL FACTORY WORKFORCE, AND PARTICULARLY OF THE ASIAN ECONOMIC "MIRACLE," CONSISTS OF YOUNG WOMAN WORKERS.

© Mike Yamashita/Woodfin Camp & Associates

study of how *dagongmei* or "working girls" are responding to the pressure of China's increasing participation in the global economy (Tsui 2000).

The factory directors were interested in Pun Ngai's work because they hoped

to learn more about what the workers want so they know better how to deal with them. At first, the factory directors assumed that Pun Ngai would focus on the factory's operations and inundated her with personnel and administrative

cause it is now mainly men who go overseas for wage labor and higher education. But more recently, the introduction of a Western egalitarian influence is also having an effect, as some women have left the atoll to attend school and pursue careers. With the influence of a new kind of egalitarianism, women may be able to return Nukumanu culture to its tradition of sexual egalitarianism.

ECONOMIC DEVELOPMENT AND THE STATUS OF WOMEN

Women's status in modern, stratified societies varies greatly, affected by economic development and ideologies. With the transition to agriculture, the direct female contribution in food production generally drops drastically. Agricultural societies are a good example of the principle that women lose status in society

documents. They were astounded when she told them she wanted to work on the line and live with the workers, in the participant-observation mode of anthropology. Although the dagongmei were initially suspicious of Pun Ngai, when they saw she was really interested in their lives, they were so eager to talk with her, she didn't have enough time to listen to them all. As an outsider, Pun Ngai quickly became a confidante, dealing with workers' complaints, offering academic guidance, and giving advice on love and other personal relationships.

Pun Ngai found the factory work interesting for the first week, but it soon became a monotonous routine. Dagongmei, most of whom are in their late teens or early 20s, spend 15 hours a day in the factory. They sleep in dormitory-type accommodations, called cagehouses. In addition to boredom on the job, dagongmei also suffer from many physical ailments. Long working hours cause menstrual pain and anemia. Those who weld microchips suffer eyesight problems, while those who wash plates with acids are constantly at risk of chemical poisoning. Accommodation and other expenses are deducted from their already low wages. The dagongmei also work and live under very strict rules. They have to wait their turn to go to the restroom. They are thoroughly searched before they are allowed to leave the factory premises. Security guards wielding electric batons guard the locked quarters at night.

Dr. Pun has followed up her field study with a continuing commitment to improving conditions for dagongmei in China. She represents the interests of dagongmei at labor conferences, fighting for their rights. In China, a residence permit is required to live in a particular city; dagongmei are denied residential rights even if they have been working in the same city for more than 10 years. They are also overcharged for medical and other services and consumer goods. Urban factories recruit dagongmei as cheap labor but then do not want to take proper care of them. When unemployment hits, the first thing people want to do is send the dagongmei back to their rural villages. After years of urban living and participation in a consumer-oriented global lifestyle, dagongmei find it difficult to readapt to village life.

Dagongmei receive little sympathy in China, especially from men who say they are taking away their jobs. In fact, times are getting harder for dagongmei. With China's admission to the World Trade Organization and the opening up of its agricultural market, more people are rushing to the cities. Urban unemployment is high, and thousands of workers have been downsized as a result of the privatization of factories.

Dagongmei see advantages in their factory work, however. It exposes them to a wider view of the world and permits some escape from the rigid patriarchal structure of the village. Some dagongmei, by pooling their earnings, have managed to open small factories. Others have ambitions for a business career, or to improve their education. But out of 70 million dagongmei, few succeed.

Multinational corporations' desire for cheap labor will lead to more women working in the global factory. Anthropologists such as Pun Ngai are trying to make sure their rights are protected when they do.

as the importance of their economic contribution declines. This is usually accompanied by an increase in their work in the home and an increase in the number of children. As women become identified with the domestic sphere, as happens with the rise of plow agriculture and the introduction of a market economy and wage labor, their social status declines. This public/domestic opposition tends to be intensified by the impact of capitalism, Christianity, and colonialism—either directly, as European administrators recognize only male political leaders, or indirectly with the devaluing of women's economic contributions.

The data on women in the global industrial economy vary considerably. Although development projects (often fueled by private or government aid) are expected to improve people's lives and to be readily accepted once their benefits are understood, neither of these assumptions is universally correct. One of the more dismaying results of many economic development projects is that they fail to take women's economic contributions into account. A great deal is being written on the need for development projects to be sensitive to women's status, lest they increase gender inequality (Moser 1993). Some development projects, such as those stimulating the global marketing of women's textiles and pottery in Mexico and Guatemala, result in more prestige, income, and autonomy for women (J. Nash 1993). Unfortunately, this has sometimes led to increasing conflict between women and men, resulting in higher levels of wife abuse as men sense their loss of control over the proceeds from the sale of women's products (J. Nash 1994:15).

TECHNOLOGY AND GENDER ROLES

Changes in technology are undoubtedly one of the most important kinds of transformations a society can experience. The introduction of sophisticated technological innovations, accompanied by androcentric biases in economic development, often worsen women's position in their societies (Warren and Borque 1989). In many rural development programs, women are perceived as peripheral to the agricultural economy, and their work roles are generally ignored in planning and policy making. The transformation of agricultural production through machine technology reduces the overall labor force, and this particularly affects women, whose traditional jobs in cultivation do not include working with this kind of technology. Thus, women are disproportionately excluded from the productive process as their jobs are replaced by technology. The inequality between the sexes is also apparent in the lower wages paid to women as agricultural laborers and in the concentration of women in the labor-intensive aspects of agriculture such as weeding, transplanting, and harvesting.

An example of this process occurred in North India's green revolution, based on the introduction of heavy technology and chemical fertilizers. This widely heralded development program did result in increased agricultural productivity among peasant farmers who were able to afford the new technology. But it also resulted in a lower status for women (Frankel 1971; Dasgupta 1980) and an increase in the disparity of income between men and women (Kelkar 1985).

Despite the important domestic and productive roles of women in rural India, their work is ignored by government planners as unpaid household work and their contribution to agricultural production is regarded as secondary, or supplementary, to men's contributions. In contrast to the stated ideal, women in better-off Indian peasant families do engage in agricultural production, especially in transplanting paddy, weeding, threshing, harvesting, and processing food grains. Indeed, as men increasingly engage in wage labor, women do even more agricultural work, but this work is perceived as merely an extension of women's domestic responsibilities.

With modernization, some valued and remunerative women's work, such as craft production, is being eliminated in the face of competition from urban industry. Women in rural India have always been prohibited from using the plow, and with the introduction of heavier machinery such as tractors and irrigation pumps, women's value in agricultural labor has declined further. Economic development has thus increased gender inequality.

The ideology of many development programs explicitly views the "backwardness" of peasant women as an obstacle to development. Such programs marginalize women's contributions and stigmatize their resistance to change as irrational. Development projects must explicitly take into account their impact on women as well as men, and this calls for a more thorough understanding of cultural and social factors than has previously been the case. By providing this kind of information and illuminating the intersection of class, gender, and culture, anthropologists can make an essential contribution to economic development.

SUMMARY

1. *Sex* refers to biological differences between male and female; *gender* refers to the social classification of masculine and feminine.

2. Beginning with the work of Margaret Mead and emphasized in the work of feminist anthropologists, the prevailing view in anthropology today is that gender is not biologically determined but rather culturally constructed.

3. Although all cultures distinguish between masculine and feminine, some cultures also include alternative, in-between, or third-gender roles. These include woman-woman marriage in parts of Africa, the two-spirit role among Native Americans, and the hijras of India.

4. Hijras are men who dress and act like women, are regarded as ritually powerful devotees of the Mother Goddess, and perform ritually at weddings and childbirths.

5. Views about the nature of male and female sexuality are part of gender ideologies. Attempts to control female sexuality are embedded in gender hierarchies.

6. A male-dominated gender hierarchy is a sociocultural system in which men are dominant, reap most of the social and material rewards of society, and control the autonomy of women.

7. One explanation for gender hierarchy in some societies (mainly more complex ones) is the private/public dichotomy, in which men are associated with public political and economic activities and women are identified with the home and children.

8. The private/public dichotomy is not universal and does not appear to apply to many foraging societies.

9. The contemporary anthropological view is that gender relations are variable and complex and must be understood within particular cultural and historical contexts.

10. A traditional view of hunting as an exclusive male occupation in foraging societies is contradicted by more recent research, which indicates that in some foraging societies, women also hunt (although not as much as men).

11. The Tlingit, a matrilineal society of the northwest coast of North America, are an example of gender egalitarianism. Although there is a gendered division of labor, Tlingit women have high status and a great degree of autonomy and influence.

12. Gender relations in horticultural societies vary considerably. Often, the impact of Western economies has led to a decline in the economic status and prestige of women, as illustrated in Nukumanu atoll in the Pacific.

13. In agricultural societies, women's role tends to decrease and the private/public dichotomy to become more relevant. Development projects, particularly those involving the heavy use of technology, also tend to marginalize women and reduce their autonomy and status.

14. Women are being increasingly incorporated into the world economy, especially working in multinational corporations in developing countries.

KEY TERMS

androcentric

cultural construction of gender

gender

gender hierarchy

gender role

hijra

machismo

manhood puzzle

private/public dichotomy

sex

two-spirit role

SUGGESTED READINGS

Behar, Ruth. 1993. *Translated Woman: Crossing the Border with Esperanza's Story.* Boston: Beacon Press. An engaging literary approach to the life story of a Mexican woman reputed to be a witch. A final chapter contains the anthropologist's reflections on her own life from a feminist perspective.

Freed, Ruth S., and Stanley A. Freed. 1985. *The Psychomedical Case History of a Low-Caste Woman of North India.* New York: Anthropological Papers of the American Museum of Natural History, Vol. 60, part 2. An excellent ethnographically based study using psychology and culture in the analysis of the life history of a young woman who becomes possessed.

Gutmann, Matthew C. 1996. *The Meanings of Macho: Being a Man in Mexico City.* Berkeley: University of California Press. A new and original look at the construction of masculinity in Mexico City, with implications for the rest of Mexico, this ethnography undermines stereotyped views of machismo as the sole basis of Mexican manhood as it reveals the complexities and contradictions of Mexican gender.

Hendrickson, Carol. 1995. *Weaving Identities: Construction of Dress and Self in a Highland Guatemala Town.* Austin: University of Texas Press. This study of women's and men's traje (cloth) examines its role in Indian identity, its relationship to life cycle events, and its role in innovation and change.

Herzfeld, Michael. 1985. *The Poetics of Manhood: Contest and Identity in a Cretan Mountain Village.* Princeton, NJ: Princeton University Press. An important and frequently cited study from Crete on the construction of masculinity. The "poetics" are the praises of their own virility sung by men in coffeehouses.

Lepowsky, Maria. 1994. *Fruit of the Motherland: Gender in an Egalitarian Society.* New York: Columbia University Press. An ethnographic study of the Vanatinai of Papua New Guinea. The author concludes (somewhat in contradiction to her own evidence) that although it is not a perfectly egalitarian society, it comes close.

Nanda, Serena. 2000. *Gender Diversity: Cross-cultural Variations.* Prospect Heights, IL: Waveland. Aimed at introductory students, this short book presents a cross-cultural look at alternative gender roles for both males and females among Native American societies and in India, Brazil, Thailand, the Philippines, Polynesia, Europe, and North America.

Safa, Helen. 1995. *The Myth of the Male Breadwinner: Women and Industrialization in the Caribbean.* Boulder, CO: Westview Press. This study uses comparative data from Puerto Rico, the Dominican Republic, and Cuba to address the changes in women's autonomy and status as a result of their increasing involvement in wage labor outside the home.

INTERNET RESOURCES

The following Internet resources appear in this chapter. Please log on to the Wadsworth anthropology website: **http://anthropology.wadsworth. com**. Click on the Nanda/Warms *Cultural Anthropology* page. Then select the Student Resources section, where you will find a complete presentation of these links and more.

- A link to websites on gender, page 242
- A video link: the Hijras of India, page 244
- A photo essay on gender roles, page 249
- Access the Study Guide to InfoTrac College Edition for Anthropology Students

AS SOCIETIES BECOME MORE COMPLEX, SPECIALIZED POSITIONS OF AUTHORITY DEVELOP AS CENTERS OF POWER AND CONTROL. AMONG THE YORUBA OF NIGERIA, IN WEST AFRICA, THE KING IS SURROUNDED BY MANY SYMBOLS OF HIS OFFICE AS HE PRESIDES OVER A FESTIVAL. ONE SOURCE OF THE KING'S POWER IS HIS MANY WIVES, SOME OF WHOM BEAT IRON GONGS NEAR HIS THRONE.

CHAPTER TWELVE

POLITICAL ORGANIZATION

What roles do politics, law, and religion play in regulating human behavior?

What are the major forms of political organization and how are they related to other features of culture and society?

How do anthropologists explain warfare in tribal societies?

How have anthropologists contributed to alternative forms of conflict management in the United States?

What does the prehistoric Asante state tell us about the connections between political power and social stratification?

In Chapters 7 and 8, we focused on how different societies make a living and how they produce and distribute valued goods. As a result of these economic factors, societies also vary in their systems of **social differentiation**—that is, in the relative access individuals and groups have to basic material resources, wealth, power, and prestige. This chapter describes the ideal types of societies that anthropologists have developed in examining systems of social differentiation and political organization. Although these typologies are useful analytically, they hide a much more complex reality. Social differentiation and political organization are always interrelated, and each ideal type includes many variations.

SOCIAL DIFFERENTIATION

In all societies, individuals differ in talents, physical attractiveness, mental abilities, and skills; equalities and inequalities exist everywhere. But although individuals may be unequally endowed, not all societies formally recognize these inequalities, nor do these differences affect access to important resources. Anthropologists commonly distinguish three types of systems

of social differentiation: egalitarian societies, rank societies, and stratified societies.

EGALITARIAN SOCIETIES

In **egalitarian societies,** no individual or group is barred from access to material resources or has power over others. This does not mean that all individuals are equally regarded. Besides age and sex differences, individual differences in skills and personal qualities are recognized, but no individual is denied the right to make a living or is subject to the control of others. Furthermore, inheritance does not lead to an accumulation of prestige or material goods over generations.

Egalitarian societies have no fixed number of social positions for which individuals must compete. For example, the position of "good hunter" or "wise elder" can be filled by as many people as meet the cultural criteria. Egalitarian

---

social differentiation The relative access individuals and groups have to basic material resources, wealth, power, and prestige.

egalitarian society A society in which no individual or group has more privileged access to resources, power, or prestige than any other.

societies usually operate on the principle of generalized or balanced reciprocity in the exchange of goods and services. Egalitarian societies are associated with the forms of political organization called bands or tribes.

RANK SOCIETIES

Rank societies are characterized by formal differences among individuals and groups in prestige and symbolic resources, which may also be inherited. However, there are no important restrictions on access to basic resources, and all individuals can obtain the material necessities for survival through their membership in kinship groups. Some rank societies had slaves, but slaves had some rights, and their status was not hereditary. Slaves were individuals attached to wealthier families and not, as in some historic stratified societies, an exploited class central to the economic system.

Rank societies are normally based on highly productive horticulture or pastoralism, which permit sufficient accumulation of food so that a surplus can be appropriated and redistributed throughout the society. Redistribution is the characteristic mode of exchange in rank societies, though balanced reciprocity is also important. Social ranking is associated with the form of political organization called a chiefdom.

STRATIFIED SOCIETIES

Stratified societies have formal and permanent social and economic inequalities. Not only are wealth, prestige, and office frequently inherited, but some individuals and groups are denied access to the basic material resources needed to survive. Stratified societies are characterized by permanent and wide differences among groups and individuals in their standard of living, security, prestige, political power, and the opportunity to fulfill one's potential. These differences may be **ascribed** (based on birth) or **achieved** (based on individual accomplishment). Stratified societies are economically organized by market systems, and are normally based on intensive cultivation (agriculture) and industrialism. Stratified societies are the most socially complex, associated with a form of political organization called the state.

POWER AND SOCIAL CONTROL

Power is the ability to control resources in one's own interest. **Authority** is the power that derives from formal political office, but power may also be based on honor, wealth, or knowledge.

LEGITIMATE AND ILLEGITIMATE POWER

In many of the small-scale societies studied by anthropologists (bands, tribes, and chiefdoms), the use of power, decision making, and the coordination and regulation of human behavior are not separate parts of the social system. Rather, they are embedded in other social institutions such as kinship, economics, and religion. Power and leadership may be based on an individual's position as the head of a family, lineage, or clan. Where supernatural intervention is an important aspect of decision making (where to hunt, when to move camp, how to find a thief), individuals with access to supernatural power have important political roles in society. Where authority involves control over the distribution of goods and services, as it often does, power is embedded in economic roles and modes of exchange, as with the chiefs on the Northwest Coast of North America and "bigmen" in New Guinea.

Legitimate power is power exercised with the approval of the community. People conform to legitimate power because they expect that they will benefit from the exercise of

---

rank society A society characterized by institutionalized differences in prestige but no important restrictions on access to basic resources.

stratified society A society characterized by formal, permanent social and economic inequality, in which some people are denied access to basic resources.

ascribed status A social position that a person is born into.

achieved status A social position that a person chooses or achieves on his or her own.

power The ability to control resources in one's own interest.

authority Power exercised through political office or institutions.

legitimate power Power exercised with the consent of the members of a society.

that power (even if only in the long run). The shared values and beliefs that legitimize the distribution and uses of power in a particular society make up its **political ideology. Illegitimate power** is based not on community approval, but on coercion. People obey those in power because they are afraid of some immediate, direct, and specific punishment if they do not. Although some political systems rest more on coercion than others, both coercion and political ideology contribute to maintaining order in a society.

Contemporary anthropologists are primarily interested in **political processes**—that is, how groups and individuals use power to achieve various public goals. These goals may include changing the relationships between groups in society, changing the relationship of a group to its environment (for example, building a road or clearing public land), waging war, making peace, or changing a group's position in the social hierarchy. Political goals have many motivations. Although, by definition, all political behavior affects the public interest, it is not always in the public interest. Groups and individuals may be motivated by personal profit or prestige or by altruism and idealism, though these are not necessarily mutually exclusive. In politically complex societies, those in power use various means to effect a close identification between their own goals and those of the larger society.

FORMAL AND INFORMAL SOURCES OF POWER

Formal political institutions are a source of power, but power also has more informal bases. One source of informal power is **factions**—informal systems of alliance within well-defined political units such as lineages, villages, or political parties. **Leadership,** or the ability to direct an enterprise or action, may be a function of political office, but it can also be wielded through more informal means such as the manipulation of kinship networks or the distribution of wealth. Much of the power of women, for example, derives from these positions, especially among Native Americans (see Chapter 11, pages 253–254). In West Africa, women derive power from their control over

marketing agricultural and other products (Potash 1989). Particularly in matrilineal societies, such as the Minangkabau of Indonesia, women's power is interwoven with their roles in the kinship, ceremonial, and economic systems (Blackwood 2000).

In most of the tribes, chiefdoms, and states studied by anthropologists, women did not hold formal political office. However, there are some important exceptions, particularly in Africa (Potash 1989:205; Matory 1994). Among the Yoruba of Nigeria, certain offices were reserved to represent women's interests. Also in Nigeria, some Igbo groups had a female ruler and council that paralleled that of the king and his council but were concerned with women's affairs. The Mende in Sierra Leone had women paramount chiefs, who were seen as "mothers writ large"; that is, they derived their value and power from the reproductive and supportive roles of women as mothers. The Mende women's secret society, called Sande, was very powerful, reflecting the important economic roles of wives, who were authority figures and who might even succeed a chief in office. One of the most famous Mende women of power was Madam Yoko. Taking advantage of the opportunities offered by the changing political status of Sierra Leone in the nineteenth century, she succeeded her husband in office and was recognized as a paramount chief in 1884 (Hoffer 1974).

The study of political processes emphasizes how power changes hands and how new kinds of political organization and ideologies develop. Political processes are never static. The use of power may stabilize a social order, avoid or resolve conflicts, and promote the general welfare, but power may also be used to contest prevailing political ideologies and to change or

political ideology The shared beliefs and values that legitimize the distribution and use of power in a particular society.

illegitimate power Power exercised by coercion, against the will of the people of a society.

political process The ways in which individuals and groups use power to achieve public goals.

factions Informal systems of alliance within well-defined political units such as lineages or villages.

leadership The ability to direct an enterprise or action.

POLITICAL PROCESSES ARE THE WAYS IN WHICH DIFFERENT, OFTEN CONFLICTING, INTEREST GROUPS MOBILIZE RESOURCES TO ACHIEVE THEIR GOALS. THIS PRO-CHOICE RALLY IS AIMED AT MAINTAINING THE RIGHT OF WOMEN IN THE UNITED STATES TO MAKE THE MOST IMPORTANT DECISIONS ABOUT THEIR BODIES.

even destroy existing political systems. Groups or factions within a society, as well as governments themselves, use legitimate and sometimes illegitimate means (terrorism or torture, for example) to gain their ends, but illegitimate means are no less political than legitimate ones.

Conflict and violence do not necessarily destroy social order. In some societies, violence is a legitimate means of dealing with conflict and solving disputes—for example, blood feuds or legally sanctioned death penalties. Conflict may support the social order, as competition for legitimate goals makes those goals seem worth fighting over. Even violent conflict between competitors for political office does not necessarily destroy the power of the office being sought, as the struggle itself emphasizes that the conflicting groups view the office as politically important. Thus, there is a difference between **rebellion**—the attempt of one group to reallocate resources within an existing political structure—and **revolution,** which is an attempt to overthrow the existing political structure and put another type of political structure in its place.

LAW: SOCIAL CONTROL AND CONFLICT MANAGEMENT

No human society is characterized by eternal peace and harmony. Individuals do not always do what they are supposed to do or expected to do, and often act in ways that disrupt the social order. For a society to function satisfactorily, however, there must be some conformity among its members.

A major basis for conformity in most societies, particularly those organized through kinship and face-to-face social relations, is the internalization of norms and values. This process begins in childhood, but it is also a lifelong process. In stratified state societies and in chiefdoms, in addition to the internalization of norms, the state's or chief's ability to use force and its control over many social institutions and regulatory processes are also important in regulating behavior. Some might argue that these types of control are even more important than the internalization of norms and values.

Every society has some social mechanisms to deal with nonnormative behavior and conflict. Informal mechanisms such as gossip and ridicule are effective because most people value the esteem of (at least some) others. The shame of being gossiped about or ridiculed is a powerful way of ensuring conformity in face-to-face communities and in informal groups within complex societies (Merry 1981). Fear of witchcraft accusations is another informal control mechanism (Evans-Pritchard 1958; Lemert 1997; Seitlyn 1993). In societies with witchcraft beliefs, when something goes wrong, witchcraft accusations are directed at people who stand above the group, are malicious, have a nasty temper, or refuse to share according to group norms. The fear of being accused of witchcraft thus exerts pressure on people to conform.

Avoidance is another informal way of dealing with social deviants. In small-scale societies, where most activities are cooperative, a person shunned by others is at a great disadvantage, both psychologically and economically. Avoidance is also effective in smaller groups

---

rebellion The attempt of a group within society to force a redistribution of resources and power.

revolution An attempt to overthrow an existing form of political organization.

within larger institutions in complex societies, such as the workplace in an industrial society.

Supernatural sanctions are also important in regulating human behavior. A sin is a violation of an important social norm that calls forth punishment by supernatural forces. In the Trobriand Islands, incest is a sin. A person who commits incest is punished by a divinely imposed skin affliction that is caused by an insect spontaneously generated by the sexual act that breaches the incest taboo (Malinowski 1929b: 504). Supernatural forces that punish social deviants are found in every culture, whether ghosts, spirits, ogres, or a Santa Claus who gives presents only to "good" little boys and girls.

Law enters the picture when a social norm is so important that its violation authorizes the community, or some part of it, to punish an offender, resolve a conflict, or redress a wrong. In every society, some offenses are considered so disruptive that force or the threat of force is applied. In more complex societies, these functions belong to separate legal institutions, such as courts. In other societies, law, like power, is often embedded in other social institutions. Nevertheless, law is distinguished from the more general reciprocal rights and obligations that underlie conformity in all societies. A useful definition of **law,** then, is that it is a means of social control through the systematic application of force by a politically organized society. Sanctions are legal when they are imposed by a constituted authority (S. Moore 1978:220).

Law addresses conflicts that would otherwise disrupt community life. In politically complex societies such as contemporary nation-states, crimes against the state are differentiated from grievances people have against one another, although both are addressed by law. In structurally simpler societies, even disputes between individuals may be handled as a potential threat to the social order because they are likely to have ripple effects throughout the community. Conflict management in egalitarian societies is more often directed at maintaining existing social relationships than defining winners and losers. Conflicts may involve the whole community as judge, as in Inuit song duels (see below, p. 268), or a go-between may be authorized to bring the disputants to a settlement. Such go-betweens may have no authority other than

their powers of persuasion in effecting the resolution of a dispute. This is in contrast to courts in state societies, which are authorized to decide disputes.

TYPES OF POLITICAL ORGANIZATION

Political organization is the patterned ways in which power is legitimately used in a society to regulate behavior. All cultures have political organization. A major way in which political organization varies cross-culturally is the degree to which political roles, institutions, and processes are centralized and differentiated from other aspects of social organization. Variations in political organization are related to **social complexity**—the number of different kinds of groups in a society and the ways in which they are connected to one another. Political organization is inextricably related to the forms of social differentiation (egalitarianism, ranking, and stratification) described above. Indeed, though they can be separated for analytical purposes, in reality they are like two sides of a coin.

Anthropologists have identified four ideal types of political organization: bands, tribes, chiefdoms, and states. Typically, bands and tribes are egalitarian societies, chiefdoms are rank societies, and states are stratified societies.

BAND SOCIETIES

Band organization is characteristic of foragers. A **band** is a small group of people (20 to 50) belonging to nuclear families who live together and are loosely associated to a territory

---

law A means of social control and dispute management through the systematic application of force by those in society with the authority to do so.

political organization The patterned ways in which power is legitimately used in a society to regulate behavior.

social complexity The number of different groups and their interrelationships in a society.

band A small group of people, related by blood or marriage, who live together and are loosely associated with a territory in which they forage.

in which they forage. Generalized or balanced reciprocity dominates economic exchanges in band societies, which tend to be egalitarian. Band societies have minimal role specialization and few differences of wealth, prestige, or power. Bands are fairly independent of one another, with few higher levels of social integration or centralized mechanisms of leadership. Bands tend to be exogamous, with ties between them established mainly by marriage. Bilateral kinship systems link individuals to many different bands through ties of blood and marriage. Trading relations also link individuals to other band members. Membership in bands is flexible, and people may change their residence from one band to another fairly easily. The flexibility of band organization is particularly adaptive for a foraging way of life and low population density.

LEADERSHIP

Band societies have no formal leadership; decision making is by consensus. Leaders in foraging bands are usually older men and women whose experience, knowledge of group traditions, and special skills or success in foraging are a source of prestige. Leaders cannot enforce their decisions; they can only persuade, and attract others to their leadership, on the basis of past performance. Thus, among some Inuit, the local leader is called "The One to Whom All Listen," "He Who Thinks," or "He Who Knows Everything Best."

In foraging bands, sharing and generosity are important sources of respect. Among some whaling Inuit, for example, successful whaling captains who do not generously distribute their accumulated wealth are merely called "rich men." They are distinguished from those whose superior ability *and* generosity make them respected leaders in the village.

SOCIAL CONTROL AND CONFLICT RESOLUTION

In band societies, social order is maintained informally by gossip, ridicule, and avoidance. In extreme cases, a person may be killed or driven out of the community. Among the Inuit, super-natural sanctions are an important means of social control (Balikci 1970). Violations of norms are considered sins, and offenders may be controlled through ritual means such as public confessions, which are directed by a shaman. The offender is defined as a patient rather than a criminal and is led to confess all the taboos he or she has violated. The local villagers form the audience and participate as a background chorus. These confessions are mainly voluntary, although a forceful shaman may denounce a member of the community he feels has engaged in acts repulsive to the spirits and therefore dangerous to the whole group.

The romanticized view of band societies as nonviolent is based on a confusion between collective violence and personal violence (Knauft 1987). The Ju/'hoansi, for example, do not engage in collective violence, but men frequently fight, mostly over women, and these fights often result in death (R. Lee 1984). Thus, although the need for cooperation and norms of reciprocity in band societies minimize conflict, it does occur. Because quarrels and conflicts between individuals may disrupt the group, band societies have developed social mechanisms to inhibit conflict from spreading. The flexibility of band membership is one such mechanism. Among the Mbuti of the Ituri Forest, for example, a process called flux operates, as bands regularly break up into smaller units and reform into larger ones throughout the year. Breaking the band down into smaller units separates people who have been in conflict with one another, thus preventing prolonged hostilities (Turnbull 1968).

In Inuit bands, disputes are sometimes resolved through public contests that involve physical action, such as head butting or boxing, or verbal contests, like the famous song duels. Here the weapons are words—"little, sharp words like the wooden splinters which I hack off with my ax" (Hoebel 1974:93). Although murder is normally resolved by killing the murderer, a man may choose to revenge his kin in a song duel if he feels too weak to kill his opponent or if he is confident he will win the song contest. Each contestant in a song duel tries to deliver the traditional compositions with the greatest skill. The one for whom the audience claps the loudest is the winner. Although winning a song duel is not based on the facts of the conflict, it does resolve the quarrel and restore normal relations between the hostile parties. The judgment of the community is accepted by the contestants, and the original complaint is laid to rest.

Because of the low level of technology, lack of formal leadership, and other ecological factors, warfare is largely absent in band societies. They have no formal organization for war, no position of warrior, little or no production for war, and no cultural or social support for sustained armed conflict. When there is violence, its primary objectives are personal and fighting takes place in short skirmishes.

When band societies encounter technologically and culturally dominant groups, bands tend to retreat and isolate themselves in marginal areas rather than fight. Alternatively, they may form peaceful relations with their neighbors. Part of the debate over whether band societies have warfare is the way in which war is defined. If one defines **warfare** as formally organized and culturally recognized patterns of collective violence against another society, or between segments within a larger society, band societies do not have warfare. One of the important contributions of anthropology is to document societies where warfare is absent, as a counterexample to a prevalent belief in the contemporary United States, and elsewhere, that "warfare is in our genes" (Wallman 2000).

IN NATIVE AMERICAN SOCIETIES, THERE WAS NO ROLE OF CHIEF BUT RATHER DIFFERENT LEADERS FOR DIFFERENT ACTIVITIES, SUCH AS WAR LEADERS, PEACE LEADERS, AND DANCE LEADERS.

© Austin MacRae

TRIBAL SOCIETIES

A **tribe** is a culturally distinct population whose members think of themselves as descended from the same ancestor or as part of the same "people." Tribes are found primarily among pastoralists and horticulturalists. Their characteristic economic institutions are reciprocity and redistribution, although as part of larger states, they may participate in market systems as well. Like bands, tribes are basically egalitarian, with no important differences among members in wealth, status, and power. Also like bands, most tribes do not have distinct or centralized political institutions or roles. Power and social control are embedded in other institutions, such as kinship or religion.

Tribes are usually organized into unilineal kin groups, which are the units of political activity and the "owners" of basic economic resources. The emergence of local kin groups larger than the nuclear family is consistent with the larger populations of horticultural and pastoral societies. The effective political unit in tribal societies is a shifting one. Most of the time, the local units of a tribe operate independently; in some societies, such as the Yanomamo (described below, pp. 275–276), the local units may be in a state of ongoing violent conflict among themselves. A higher-level unity among tribal segments most often occurs in response

war (warfare) A formally organized and culturally recognized pattern of collective violence directed toward other societies, or between segments of the larger society.

tribe A culturally distinct population whose members consider themselves descended from the same ancestor.

to the threat of attack from another society or the opportunity to attack another society.

POLITICAL INTEGRATION IN TRIBES

The local segments of a tribal society may be integrated in various ways. One widespread integrating mechanism is groups based on age. An **age set** is a group of people of similar age and sex who move through some or all of life's stages together. Age sets cross kinship lines and are the basis for important social bonds. Most age sets are made up of males and have military and political functions. Cross-cultural comparison of societies in which age sets are important—in Africa, Melanesia, South America, and the Great Plains of North America—suggests that they are associated with frequent warfare and unstable local groups. Where men cannot rely on their kin as allies in warfare because their kin may not be nearby, age sets provide a more dependable source of allies (Ritter 1980).

Age-based groups called **age grades** are also important in some societies. Among the Maasai, a herding people living in Kenya and Tanzania, males follow a well-ordered progression through a series of age grades. Entry into each grade requires a formalized rite of passage, which is at the heart of Maasai culture. A new age grade is opened for recruitment for groups of boys every 14 years. After childhood, boys are initiated into the warrior stage, which lasts about 15 years. Warriorhood is a period of training in social, political, and military skills, and is traditionally geared to warfare and cattle raiding. The warriors then ceremonially graduate to a less active status, during which they can marry. Finally, about 20 years after the formation of the age grade, when another age grade

has become established, the original age grade retires to elderhood in another great ceremony.

Maasai age mates are a cohesive group. They provide reciprocal hospitality when they visit each other's villages, expressing a warm and intimate relationship. Age grade ceremonies periodically bring together Maasai from different sections of the tribe. These gatherings renew their shared identity, sense of unity, and cooperation and confirm a system of leadership under age grade spokesmen. This lends political coherence to a people who live dispersed from one another and have no centralized government (Galaty 1986).

Other kinds of associations may cut across and thus integrate the local segments of a tribe. One example is the military societies that existed among some Plains Indian tribes in North America. Another is the secret societies, such as Poro society for males and Sande society for females, that are found in West Africa.

Local segments of tribes may also be integrated by clan organization. Among the Nuer of East Africa, a **segmentary lineage system** is a significant principle of social organization (Evans-Pritchard 1940/1968). The Nuer are divided into about 20 clans, each of which is further divided into lineages. Below the level of the clan are segments called maximal lineages, which are broken down into major lineages, spread over many villages. Major lineages are subdivided into minor lineages, which in turn are made up of minimal lineages. The minimal lineage contains three to five generations and is the basic descent group that functions in day-to-day activities. Members of a minimal lineage live in the same village and regard one another as close relatives. Minimal lineages are politically independent, and there is no formal or centralized leadership above this level. The higher-order lineages are called upon to function mainly in the context of conflict. They are not groups, and they do not live together. Rather, they are the basis of an alliance network that emerges when lower-order segments come into conflict. In a serious dispute between members of different lower-order lineages, the higher-order lineage members take the side of their nearest kin. This kind of political structure, called **complementary opposition,** is illustrated in Figure 12.1.

age set A group of people of similar age and sex who move through some or all of life's stages together.

age grades Specialized hierarchical associations based on age, which stratify a society by seniority.

segmentary lineage system A form of sociopolitical organization in which multiple descent groups (usually patrilineages) form at different levels and function in different contexts.

complementary opposition A political structure in which higher-order units form alliances that emerge only when lower-order units come into conflict.

FIGURE 12.1

A SEGMENTARY LINEAGE SYSTEM WITH COMPLEMENTARY OPPOSITION. COMPLEMENTARY OPPOSITION FUNCTIONS IN THE FOLLOWING WAY: WHEN Z^1 FIGHTS Z^2, NO OTHER SECTION GETS INVOLVED. WHEN Z^1 FIGHTS Y^1, Z^1 AND Z^2 UNITE AS Y^2. WHEN Y^1 FIGHTS X^1, Y^1 AND Y^2 UNITE, AND SO DO X^1 AND X^2. WHEN X^1 FIGHTS A, X^1, X^2, Y^1, AND Y^2 ALL UNITE AS B. WHEN A RAIDS THE DINKA (ANOTHER TRIBE), A AND B MAY UNITE.

Source: Based on Evans-Pritchard in Marshall Sahlins, "The Segmentary Lineage: An Organization of Predatory Expansion." *American Anthropologist* 1963:332–345. Reprinted by permission of Oxford University Press.

A segmentary lineage system is particularly functional when stronger tribes want to expand into nearby territories held by weaker tribes. Complementary opposition directs the energies of the society upward, away from competition between kin, to an outside enemy. Lineage segments on the borders of other tribes know that if they attack an enemy, they will be helped by other lineages related to them at these higher levels of organization (Sahlins 1961).

LEADERSHIP

Tribal societies have leaders, but no centralized government and few positions of authority. Many Native American societies had different kinds of leaders for different kinds of activities. The Cheyenne had war leaders and peace leaders. The Ojibwa of Canada had different leaders for war, hunting, ceremonies, and clans. Europeans who first came in contact with the Ojibwa often misinterpreted their political system and imposed on the Ojibwa the concept of a supreme leader or chief. When the Canadian government insisted that the Ojibwa must have a chief, the Ojibwa coined a native word, *okimakkan,* which is best translated as "fake chief."

THE BIGMAN IS AN INFORMAL LEADER IN MANY MELANESIAN CULTURES. MUCH OF HIS INFLUENCE IS BASED ON HIS ABILITY TO DISTRIBUTE RESOURCES, AMONG WHICH PIGS ARE MOST IMPORTANT.

Another kind of tribal leader, found throughout Melanesia and New Guinea, is the **bigman**—a self-made leader who gains power through personal achievements rather than through holding office. A bigman begins his career as the leader of a small, localized kin group. Through a series of public actions, such as generous loans, the bigman attracts followers within the community. He skillfully builds up his capital and increases his number of wives. Because women take care of pigs, a polygynous bigman can increase the size of his pig herds. He distributes his wealth in ways that build his reputation as a rich and generous man: sponsoring feasts, paying subsidies to military allies, purchasing high ranks in secret societies, and paying the bridewealth of young men seeking wives. By giving generously, the bigman places many other people under ob-

bigman A self-made leader who gains power through personal achievements rather than through political office.

ANTHROPOLOGY MAKES A DIFFERENCE

ALTERNATIVE FORMS OF CONFLICT RESOLUTION

In many tribal societies, conflicts between parties with ongoing relationships are resolved by mediation, rather than by formal legal adversarial procedures. The aim of mediation is to resolve disputes in such a way that the social relationship between the disputants is maintained and harmony is restored to the social order. The community is involved in resolving conflict, rather than just the two disputants. Mediation takes different forms in different cultures.

An important form of conflict management among the Kpelle of Liberia is the moot. When two Kpelle have a dispute, a moot is called. It takes place before an assembled group that includes kinsmen and neighbors of the disputants (Gibbs 1988). A short ritual begins the proceedings, aimed at reminding the audience of its common interests and unity. The complainant speaks first, but the mediator, or others in the audience, may interrupt with questions. The two parties may also question each other directly. The meeting is spirited and lively, but order is maintained by the mediator. After everyone has been heard, the mediator proposes a solution to the conflict that expresses the consensus of the disputing parties and the audience participating in the moot. The party at fault apologizes to the other party, and a ritual distribution of food and drink again unites the group, as the mediator stresses the importance of the restoration of community harmony. In mediation, a "deviant" is pulled back into a relationship with the wider community, and reconciliation is achieved with a minimum of resentment, so that conflicts do not continue and disrupt the social order (Gibbs 1988).

Another example of a community-oriented mechanism for dispute resolution is the kava drinking circle in Tonga (Olson 1997). Kava is an indigenous drink often consumed in ritual contexts throughout Oceania. In the Kingdom of Tonga, it is a semi-ritualized male activity that serves as a nonviolent alternative to alcohol drinking events. The kava circle is an informal social context in which the status distinctions, otherwise so important in Tonga, are dissolved, and men air their grievances in an atmosphere of social camaraderie.

Anthropological data on the West African moot, the kava circle in Tonga, and other nonadversarial conflict management systems have been used as a key source for reexamining the United States legal system, which depends on adversarial confrontations between disputants. The adversarial system, which operates through formal courts, is costly and time-consuming, and frequently leaves the disputants feeling dissatisfied with outcomes. Anthropologists have introduced alternative forms of conflict management based on what they have learned from small-scale societies like the Kpelle and Tonga. William Ury, an anthropologist and linguist, coauthored a now classic and best-selling account, *Getting to Yes: Negotiating Agreement Without Giving In* (Fisher and Ury 1981), that is widely used in many different kinds of negotiations and conflicts in the United States. Ury's principles for conflict resolution represent a win/win situation, in contrast to the win/lose model of litigation.

---

ligation to him. Bigmen command obedience from their followers through this personal relationship of gratitude and obligation.

A bigman's activities provide leadership above the local level, but it is a fragile mechanism of tribal integration. It does not involve the creation of permanent office, but depends on the personality and constant striving of an individual. Bigmen rise and fall, and with their deaths, their factions may dissolve. Most important, however, the bigman must spur his local group on to ever greater production if he is to hold his own against other bigmen in the tribe. To maintain prestige, he must give his competitors more than they can give him. Excessive giving to competitors means the bigman must begin to withhold gifts to his followers. The resulting discontent may lead to defection among his followers, or even murder of the bigman. A bigman cannot pass on his status to others; each person must begin anew to amass the wealth and forge the internal and external social relationships on which bigman status depends (Sahlins 1971).

Under certain ecological and social conditions, more substantial and permanent political leadership may emerge in tribal societies, which then develop into chiefdoms.

Because mediation and other alternative forms of conflict resolution are less hostile, less costly, and less time-consuming than court procedures, their use has grown enormously in the United States over the past 30 years. As courts become ever more overburdened and litigation ever more expensive, mediation has increasingly been used to resolve many kinds of disputes, especially when the disputants are in long-term relationships. Mediation is now frequently used in divorce proceedings, minor civil disputes, schools, housing projects, neighborhoods, the workplace, and many other situations in the United States.

By introducing the idea of culture as central to conflict, and thus conflict management, anthropologists have also made an important contribution to the development of models of alternative dispute resolution in the international arena (Avruch 1998). International disputes and group conflict within states are both about competition over resources and power, but there are often other, culturally generated contextual subtleties that

Courtesy of Serena Nanda

THE URBAN DOVE: RISE ABOVE THE VIOLENCE. WITH YOUTH VIOLENCE A MAJOR PROBLEM IN THE UNITED STATES, MEDIATION AND OTHER PROGRAMS AIMED AT PREVENTING YOUTH VIOLENCE TAKE ON A PARTICULAR URGENCY. THE NEW YORK–BASED URBAN DOVE IS ONE OF MANY PROGRAMS AIMED AT TEACHING TEENS NONVIOLENT WAYS OF RESOLVING CONFLICTS BY COMBINING MEDIATION WORKSHOPS WITH BASKETBALL.

need to be considered in resolving these conflicts without violence. Anthropological case studies provide an important foundation for discovering the cultural logic of different societies on which nonviolent conflict resolution can be built, and also for identifying and applying cross-culturally applicable principles for the avoidance of violence (Fry and Bjorkqvist 1997).

SOCIAL CONTROL AND CONFLICT RESOLUTION

Tribes, like bands, depend mainly on informal mechanisms for controlling deviant behavior and settling conflicts, but they also have more formal mechanisms of control. The Cheyenne were particularly successful in peacefully resolving intratribal conflict and controlling individual behavior when necessary for the common good. Their formal social control mechanisms came into play during the summer season, when Cheyenne bands came together for great communal buffalo hunts and tribal ceremonies. Order was necessary to prevent disputes at these tribal gatherings. Strict discipline was required on the buffalo hunt; an individual hunter could ruin the hunt for others by alarming and scattering the buffalo. The tribal gatherings and communal hunts were policed by members of military associations. These associations not only punished offenders but also tried to rehabilitate them, bringing them back within the tribal structure. The function of the police was to get the deviant to conform to tribal law in the interest of the welfare of the tribe. People were punished by a variety of methods. Sometimes their tepees were ripped to shreds, or the ears of their horses were cut off, a mark of shame. Offenders might also be whipped. If they resisted, they might be killed on the spot. However, if they accepted the punishment and appeared to have learned a lesson, they were accepted back into the group, and their belongings were often replaced. The Cheyenne military societies operated only during the hunt period. At other times, more informal sanctions and leadership operated at the band level (Hoebel 1960).

Regulating behavior in tribal societies may also involve go-betweens. Among the Nuer, this role is played by the Leopard Skin chief. If someone is killed, retaliation from the victim's kin may begin an ongoing feud. However, a killer may seek sanctuary in the home of the Leopard Skin chief. The chief goes to the killer's family and gets them to promise to pay a certain number of cattle to the victim's family. He then goes to the victim's family and tries to get them to accept this settlement. The Leopard Skin chief can only **mediate;** he cannot compel either family to accept the settlement. In other kinds of disputes, such as those over ownership of cattle, the Leopard Skin chief and perhaps other respected elders in the community may try to get the two sides to reach a settlement through public discussion. They have no means of enforcing their suggestions, however (Evans-Pritchard 1940/1968). Although go-betweens in tribal societies have little or no authority to enforce their decisions, they express the general interest of society in ending tension, punishing wrongs, and restoring social stability. Go-betweens, with the power of public opinion behind them, are usually effective. But if a settlement cannot be agreed upon, a feud will begin.

Another means of conflict resolution, which occurs prominently in New Guinea, is **compensation**—a payment demanded by an aggrieved party to compensate for damage. Compensation is based on the severity of the act that precipitated the dispute. It also tends to

reflect the extent to which other kinsmen are involved as allies, as they must get part of the payment. Payment of compensation generally implies acceptance of responsibility by the donors and willingness to terminate the dispute by the recipients (Scaglion 1981). Currently, in some parts of New Guinea, highly inflated compensation payments are demanded in homicide cases. Rather than facilitating conflict resolution, the size and distribution of these payments have become the basis for further disputes (Ottley and Zorn 1983).

WARFARE IN TRIBAL SOCIETIES

Tribes frequently engage in warfare, a fact for which anthropologists have suggested various explanations. In the absence of strong mechanisms for tribal integration through peaceful means, and the absence of strong motivations to produce food beyond immediate needs, warfare may regulate the balance between population and resources in tribal societies. With slash and burn horticulture, for example, it is much harder to clear forest for cultivation than to work land that has already been used. Thus, a local group may prefer to take land from other groups, by force if necessary, rather than expand into virgin forest. Warfare thus becomes one way for societies that are experiencing a population increase or have reached the limits of expansion into unoccupied land to expand (Vayda 1976). Where there are effective ways other than war for distributing population within the total territory of the tribe, tribes may not engage in war.

Tribal warfare can also be linked to social structure. Patrilineality and patrilocality promote male solidarity, and this makes the use of force in resolving local conflicts more feasible than in matrilineal, matrilocal societies. Matrilocal societies promote solidarity among women and may favor domestic harmony when warfare is carried out over long distances, as among the Iroquois (Ember and Ember 1971). Although anthropologists may not agree about the specific causes of warfare, one area of wide agreement is that war is grounded in historical, material, and ecological conditions, and not in any biologically based human instinct for aggression.

mediation A form of managing disputes that uses the offices of a third party to achieve voluntary consensus to an agreement between disputing parties.

compensation A payment demanded by an aggrieved party to compensate for damage.

Napoleon Chagnon/Anthro-Photo File

A YANOMAMO WARRIOR

One tribal society that experiences both a high level of personal violence and warfare is the Yanomamo of the Amazon areas of Venezuela and Brazil. Violence by men against women, violence among men in the same village, and warfare between villages have all been described as central to Yanomamo culture (Chagnon 1997). Although the high degree of Yanomamo violence described by ethnographer Napoleon Chagnon has been challenged by other anthropologists (Good and Chanoff 1996), persistent warfare among these so-called "fierce people" at certain points in their history has been a subject of much anthropological debate.

Napoleon Chagnon explains ongoing Yanomamo warfare and their military ideology as a way of preserving village autonomy. The high degree of violent conflict between men within villages leads to the division of villages into hostile camps. In order to survive as an independent unit in an environment of constant warfare, a village adopts a hostile and aggressive stance toward other villages, perpetuating inter-village warfare in an endless cycle.

Another explanation for Yanomamo violence and warfare is that of controlling population. William Divale and Marvin Harris (1976) argue that tribal warfare in horticultural societies like the Yanomamo regulates population—not by causing deaths in battles, but indirectly through female infanticide. In societies with constant warfare, there is a cultural preference for fierce and aggressive males who can become warriors. Because male children are preferred over females, female infants are often killed. The shortage of women that results from female infanticide among the Yanomamo provides a strong conscious motivation for warfare—when asked, the Yanomamo say they fight for women, not for land—and a continuing "reason" to keep fighting among themselves. In a Yanomamo raid on another village, as many women as possible are captured.

Another important explanation of Yanomamo warfare involves the effects of European contact. According to Brian Ferguson (1992), the buildup of the extreme Yanomamo violence documented by Napoleon Chagnon in the

1960s was precipitated in the 1940s, as a result of severe depopulation due to European disease epidemics, fatal malnutrition, and intensified competition over European goods. The high death rate led to disruption of Yanomamo family life, and negotiating marriages became particularly difficult due to the deaths of adult males. In addition, the Yanomamo desire for European manufactured goods—particularly metal machetes, axes, and knives, which are very useful for horticulturalists—increased competition among Yanomamo males, and firearms substantially increased the number of fatalities in warfare. Whereas previously such goods were traded into even remote Yanomamo villages, by the 1960s the desire to acquire these goods led to the increasing settlement of Yanomamo around European outposts such as missionary stations. This led to the depletion of game, a highly desired food for Yanomamo cultivators who were also hunters. With the depletion of game, cultural norms of reciprocity broke down, meat was less likely to be shared, and conflict within villages increased. This, in turn, led to enmity between villages. The increasing inter-village warfare reinforced the low status of Yanomamo women and helped further male violence against them, perpetuating the cycle of female infanticide, shortage of women, and raids for women, described by Divale and Harris and Chagnon. Thus, historical factors complement other explanations of Yanomamo "fierceness."

CHIEFDOMS

Two main characteristics distinguish **chiefdoms** from tribes. Unlike a tribe, in which all segments are structurally and functionally similar, a chiefdom is made up of parts that are structurally and functionally different from one another. Chiefdoms have been called the first step in integrating villages as units within a multicommunity political organization (Car-

neiro 1981). Robert Carneiro (1981:45) defines the chiefdom as "an autonomous political unit comprising a number of villages or communities under the permanent control of a paramount chief." Carneiro holds that the reason chiefdoms are such an important human cultural "invention" is that it is in chiefdoms that villagers first surrendered their political autonomy to chiefs from other villages, thereby creating a second level of political authority. Chiefdoms vary greatly in their social complexity (Peoples 1990). Some chiefdoms had monumental architecture, distinct ceremonial centers, elaborate grave goods reflecting high social status, and larger settlements, or administrative centers, surrounded by smaller villages. These geographical units within a chiefdom may each also have has its own chief or council.

Chiefdoms are found mainly among cultivators and pastoralists, although chiefdoms also exist among some foraging groups. Chiefdoms are found in cultivating societies (and in those few foraging societies) where food resources are plentifully available. The abundance of food means that chiefs do not need to put excessive burdens on commoners to extract surpluses (Peoples 1990). The importance of a plentiful food supply helps explain the existence of chiefdoms among the foragers of the Northwest Coast of North America.

LEADERSHIP

Although chiefdoms, like tribes, are organized through kinship, there is an important difference between them. Unlike **acephalous** tribes (tribes without centralized government), chiefdoms have centralized leadership that consists of the political office of the chief. Chiefs are born to that office, and are often sustained in it by religious authority. Chiefdoms keep lengthy genealogical records of the names and acts of specific chiefs, which are used to verify claims to rank and chiefly title.

The rise of a centralized governing center (that is, a chief with political authority) is closely related to redistributive exchange patterns. Goods move into the center (the chief) and are redistributed through the chief's generosity in giving feasts and sponsoring rituals. The economic surplus appropriated by a chief

chiefdom A society with social ranking in which political integration is achieved through an office of centralized leadership called the chief.

acephalous Lacking a government head or chief.

is dispersed throughout the whole society, and is a primary support of the chief's power and prestige. The chief also deploys labor as well as redistributing food, making for a higher level of economic productivity. In addition, the centralized authority of the chief helps prevent violent conflict between segments of the society, and gives a chiefdom more military power than acephalous tribes.

Chiefdoms are ranked societies. Some lineages and the people in them, have higher social status than others, and these statuses are inherited. Among the Nootka, for example, rights to manage all economic resources, such as fishing, hunting, and gathering grounds, were held by individuals, although relatives could not be prevented from using them. Inheritance of these rights passed only through the line of the eldest son. The same was true for the office of chief. The line that went through lesser sons was ranked lower than that of eldest sons, and these differences in rank were typically expressed in terms of wealth. While such wealth consisted partly of important economic resources, it was also symbolic, as in the right to use special names, perform certain ceremonial functions, sponsor potlatches, and wear certain items of clothing and decoration. For example, only chiefs were allowed to wear abalone shell jewelry and sea otter fur on their robes. The right to direct the use of economic resources supported the symbolic ranking system. As manager, a chief of a kin group received resources that formally acknowledged his rank: the first of the salmon catch, the best parts of sea mammals that had been killed, blankets, and furs. It was from this source that a chief could sponsor a potlatch, at which most of these goods were given away.

Some of the most complex chiefdoms were found in Polynesia. In Tahiti, society was divided into the Ari'i, who were the immediate families of the chiefs of the most important lineages in the larger districts; the Ra'atira, who were the heads of less important lineages and their families; and the Manahune, which included the remainder of the population. Social rank in Tahiti had economic, political, and religious aspects. Mana, a spiritual power, was possessed by all people, but in different degrees depending on rank. The Ari'i had the most

mana because they were closest to the ancestral gods from which mana comes. An elaborate body of taboos separated those with more mana from those with less and also regulated social relations between the three ranks. Higher-ranked people could not eat with those of lower rank, and because men had higher rank than women and children, they could not eat with them. The highest-ranking Ari'i was so sacred that anything he touched became poison for those below him. In some Polynesian islands, the highest chief was kept completely away from other people and even used a special vocabulary that no one else was allowed to use.

Chiefdoms are also frequently found among pastoral nomads, such as the Basseri of Iran. To avoid exhaustive grazing of an area, famine of the flocks, and intertribal fighting, nomads such as the Basseri must stick to their migration schedules and fixed routes. Thus, an important role of the chief is to coordinate movements of the tribe and conduct relations with outsiders through whose territories nomadic pastoralists must move (Barth 1964).

SOCIAL CONTROL AND CONFLICT RESOLUTION

Internal violence within chiefdoms is lower than in tribes because the chief has authority to make judgments, punish deviant individuals, and resolve disputes. In the Trobriand Islands, for example, the power of a chief to punish people is achieved partly by hiring sorcerers to kill the offender by magic. The greatest power of the Trobriand chief lies in his authority to control garden magic. As garden magician, he not only organizes the efforts of the villagers under his control but also performs the rituals considered necessary for success at every step: preparing the fields, planting, and harvesting. The ultimate power of the Trobriand chief is his magical control of rain: He is believed to be able to produce a prolonged drought, which will cause many people to starve. This power is used when the chief is angry as a means of collective punishment and enforcement of his will (Malinowski 1935).

Social order in chiefdoms is maintained through both fear and genuine respect for and loyalty to the chief. The chief's authority is backed by his control of symbolic, supernatural, administrative, economic, and military power. As a result, chiefdoms tend to be more stable than acephalous tribes, although sometimes violent competition for the office of chief occurs. Chiefdoms may also be rendered unstable if the burdens the chief imposes on the people greatly exceed the services they receive from him. Chiefs generally suppress any attempt at rebellion or threats from competitors and deal harshly with those who try to take their power. To emphasize the importance of this office for the society, offenses against a chief are often punished by death.

STATE SOCIETIES

The most complex form of political organization is the state. A **state** is a hierarchical, centralized form of political organization in which a central government has a legal monopoly over the use of force. Unlike chiefdoms, where ranking is based on kinship, in state societies kinship does not regulate relations between the different social classes. Each class tends to marry within itself, and kin ties no longer extend throughout the whole society. The legitimacy of the state rests on ties of **citizenship,** which supplant those of blood and marriage. Through the concept of citizenship, the state has an ability to expand without splitting through the incorporation of a variety of political units, classes, and ethnic groups. Thus, states can become much more populous, heterogeneous, and powerful than any other kind of political organization.

THE RISE OF STATE SOCIETIES

The formation of a state is the result of various interrelated events feeding back on one another in complex ways. State societies are associated with the ability to organize large

> **state** A hierarchical, centralized form of political organization in which a central government has a legal monopoly over the use of force.
>
> **citizenship** Membership in a state.

populations for collective and coordinated action, to suppress internal disorder through monopoly over the legitimate use of force, and to defend against external threats. More than any other form of political organization, the state can carry out military action for both defensive and offensive purposes.

The origin of the state, one of humankind's most significant cultural achievements, cannot be explained by any one theory of cause and effect. Rather, it involves different factors interacting in different ways in different circumstances. Some states emerged as cultural solutions to various kinds of problems that demanded more centralized coordination and regulation of human populations (Cohen and Service 1978). Other states may have emerged as a result of particular historical or ecological conditions. Some states, such as the Asante (see Ethnography box), emerged out of military triumph. Prestate societies in various situations respond to different selective pressures by changing some of their internal structures, by subduing a competing group, or by establishing themselves as dominant in a region. This initial shift sets off a chain reaction of other changes that may lead to state formation.

Anthropologist Robert Carneiro (1970) emphasizes the importance of ecology in his theory that a limit on agricultural land available to expanding populations may result in the emergence of a state. This seems to have occurred in pre-Columbian Peru, where independent, dispersed farming villages were confined to narrow valleys bounded by the sea, the desert, or mountains. As the population grew, villages split and populations dispersed until all the available land was used up. At this point, more intensive methods of agriculture were applied to land already being farmed, and previously unusable land was brought under cultivation by terracing and irrigation. As population continued to increase, pressure for land intensified, resulting in war. Because of the constraints of the environment, villages that lost wars had nowhere to go. In order to remain on their land, they had to accept a politically subordinate role. As more villages were defeated, the political organization of the area became more complex and developed into

I N   T H E   F I E L D

WEALTH AND POWER IN THE PRECOLONIAL ASANTE STATE

The Asante are a Twi-speaking Akan people who have long occupied the tropical forest area of what is now south-central Ghana in West Africa. The Asante state emerged in 1701, when the Asante decisively defeated a rival Akan power, and state expansion and elaboration occurred throughout the eighteenth century.

THE MATERIAL BASIS OF THE ASANTE STATE

The major material bases of the Asante state were intensive agriculture; substantial, accessible deposits of alluvial and shallow-reef gold, which by the fifteenth century involved the Akan in trade with Europeans; and participation, in the seventeenth and eighteenth centuries, in the European slave trade (Wilks 1993).

In spite of the difficulties of cultivating the tropical forest, the Asante developed an agricultural economy that not only supported its rural population but produced a sufficient surplus to support a nonproducing urban elite, centered in the state capital of Kumase. This economy initially required outside labor, which the Asante acquired from European slave traders in exchange for gold. Later, the Asante themselves exported slaves, most of whom they acquired in tribute or in warfare.

Asante agricultural productivity rested on a simple, labor intensive technology. Staple crops of yam, plantain, cocoyam, and cassava were supplemented by Indian corn, sweet potato, millet, rice, sugar cane, ginger, tomato, onion, groundnut, orange, lime, banana, custard apple, and pineapple. Gathering of oil palm fruits, palm wine, fungi, and wild yams pro-

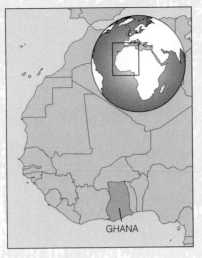

GHANA

vided additional dietary support, as did wild game, freshwater fish (generally smoked), crabs, and snails (also an important trade item). Domestic sheep, fowl, goats, and pigs, though available, were not common; their relatively high cost dictated their use as food mainly on ritual occasions. When the Europeans unilaterally abolished the transatlantic slave trade in the early nineteenth century, the Asante successfully reoriented its export economy to cocoa production.

SOCIAL STRATIFICATION AND THE STATE

The highly productive Asante economy was the basis of a complex social hierarchy, ruled by the Asantehene or king. The state capital, Kumase, which had been a small village in the seventeenth century, had a permanent resident population of about 25,000 by the early nineteenth century. Most of Kumase's population was fully involved in the transaction of government business, in the time-consuming performance of elaborate state ceremonies, or in servicing the state sector through ancillary functions such as producing luxury artifacts. The office-holders and administrators, with their

urban followers, were entirely provisioned and maintained by the intensive agricultural enterprise of the rural peasants, which included non-Asante slaves and less successful members of elite Asante families. This productive agricultural economy was achieved by a systematic rationalization and concentration of labor, organized, overseen, and given direction by the state in order to support the urban elites.

The prodigious food requirements of Kumase reflected the association of high social status with material well-being characteristic of state societies. The Asantehene's household alone—his royal wives and children—daily consumed large quantities of locally grown food, along with imported delicacies such as mutton, turkey, duck, wild game, rice, European biscuits, tea, sugar, and wine. Some of these were gifts from foreign visitors, which were reciprocated by local food supplies.

MANAGING SOCIAL STRATIFICATION

Asante society was composed of several social classes: unfree, alien slaves; peasant commoners living in outlying villages; urban specialists offering their services to the elite; government officials of various classes and positions; and the Asantehene himself, with his royal family, at the top of the hierarchy. It was a dynamic social system, based on achievement, competition, and accumulation of wealth, with widely different levels of material well-being and many opportunities for upward mobility and social competition and conflict. In spite of these potential challenges, the Asante state demonstrated a remarkable stability for well over 150 years, through a balance of coercion, consensus, and regulation of the social hierarchy.

The precolonial Asante state lacked the social infrastructure and technology to

Wealth and Power in the Precolonial Asante State (continued)

command society by coercive force alone. Although it did use such tactics as espionage, detention, fines, confiscation of property, exile, and execution, a most important source of the state's power was its promotion of a central Asante value: that wealth and power went hand in hand, and that the accumulation of wealth by an individual was of benefit to the whole society (reminiscent of the claim by the president of General Motors that what was good for General Motors was good for the United States). Thus, wise investment and the accumulation of wealth resulted in high office, and holding onto high office had to be justified by the accumulation and display of wealth. This Asante value was central to the legitimacy of the state, which maintained its power by redistribution of wealth, regulation of the wealth any individual could accumulate through discretionary use of law and custom, and the control and management of ritual in which wealth was displayed.

Social status in Asante society was based on achievement in the form of accumulated wealth, particularly gold in all its forms: negotiable gold dust, crude rock gold, and gold worked into regalia and ornaments for display. Land and control over human labor, as well as holding high office, were also forms of wealth, but none could compete with gold. Gold was mobile, fluid, desirable, and convertible, giving it immense social value. Gold conferred the highest prestige and was the ultimate purchasing power; it was the currency of the state's taxes and fines, and was internationally negotiable.

STATE CONTROL OVER THE ACCUMULATION OF WEALTH

By the later eighteenth century, and well into the nineteenth, political office became the key to the accumulation of wealth. The Asante state was thus able to control access to wealth and to regulate its distribution, particularly in the form of gold. With the ending of the transatlantic slave trade, desired European goods such as guns, gunpowder, cloth, and luxury articles could only be paid for in gold. Gold ornaments were also necessary for display of social status. Thus, gold became a scarce commodity, exacerbating the Asante tendency to accumulate, hoard, and secrete it, and leading to high interest rates for loans of gold.

The state exploited this scarcity in several ways. For example, the state accepted only gold for payment of fines, tributes, taxes, and levies. Those who didn't have sufficient gold to pay the required amount, or who were unwilling to part with the gold they had, might mortgage land or laborers to acquire the requisite amount in gold, or give these assets directly to the state in lieu of the required amount of gold. As most mortgages wound up in default, the state expanded its assets in either case. These assets might be kept for state expenses or allocated to powerful officeholders as rewards. Through its legal system, then, the state could enrich itself directly and also "redistribute" wealth among the elite according to its own interests.

The state also controlled the allocation of wealth by using discretion in applying legal sanctions. For example, an individual could buy himself out of a mandatory death sentence with a payment of gold that went to the state. The decision was made by the Asantehene, frequently when he wished to ruin a rich officeholder and confiscate his assets. In addition, the state denied individuals the sole right to dispose of their wealth after death. The state levied death duties on self-acquired movable property, and might also impose inheritance taxes on land, before the residue of the deceased person's wealth was restored to the heirs or successors. The state determined death assessments on a case-by-case basis. Thus, it could fine-tune its control over the elite and prevent the emergence of a class of hereditary property owners that might be a threat to its own power.

The state controlled social stratification in other ways. The opportunity to accumulate wealth on the largest scale—by commanding the state's armies, conducting the state's trade, holding state office, or being a favored beneficiary of the state's law—was itself a gift of the state. Sometimes, the state might take the initiative and give an opportunity to some "up-and-comers" to see how they would fare in the competition for wealth and status. The Asantehene, for example, might lend gold to some rising army captains for a couple of years to see if they could not only repay the loan but parlay it into an accumulation of wealth. Thus, lending, repayment, reciprocity, and reward in the circulation and accumulation of wealth were key factors in the Asante state's ability to maintain itself in power.

THE STATE'S CONTROL OF SYMBOLIC CAPITAL

In addition to controlling access to material wealth, the state also controlled "symbolic capital." Only the state could bestow titles or other symbols of high status on individuals in recognition of their success in accumulating wealth. The highest mark of political status granted by the state was the right to use the insignia of the elephant tail. This right and title was surrounded with complex rituals and ceremonies, which combined public display with public acclamation. The ceremonies were punctuated by symbolic and historical references aimed at glorifying the state and recalling the role of public officials as providers and protectors of the people, of which the successful elephant hunt was a symbol.

The aspirant to the title submitted his credentials to public scrutiny by displaying his accumulated wealth in gold, scattering pounded yam mixed with gold dust as he was carried through the streets. He challenged others to display equal wealth, and in other symbolic ways claimed his right to belong to the hallowed tradition of Asante chiefs. Because aspiring to the elephant tail insignia involved the risk of loss of wealth and status, individuals generally attempted it only once in a lifetime, and only when they had indications that they were in favor with the Asantehene.

The equation of accumulated wealth with the social good was an important constraint on officeholders, including the Asantehene, against squandering their wealth. The prestige derived from the possession of the elephant tail was predicated on the identification of individual with social prosperity. A person so honored was recognized as having added significantly to the wealth of Asante society, and nothing was considered more shaming to the posthumous reputation of a titleholder than that he died bankrupt—"boiled and ate the elephant tail." Individual bankruptcy was considered antisocial, a theft from the future wellbeing of Asante society.

These constraints applied to the Asantehene as well. The Asantahene possessed the "Golden Elephant Tail," which took precedence over all the others. It symbolized the commitment of each successive Asantehene to uphold and transmit the inheritance of Asante culture embodied in the concept of the elephant's tail. The Golden Tail, symbolizing wealth, was intimately connected to the Golden Stool, symbolizing political authority and legitimate power. The elephant tail was seen as the "helper" of the stool—wealth helps power. This symbolic conjunction, reinforced in ritual, promoted the political ideology that Asante culture and society were "helped" into being by the processes of accumulation. This ideology gave legitimacy to the state's political authority, which was rooted in effective controls over the right to amass and dispose of wealth. In Asante thought, the objective value of wealth was always firmly situated in relation to purpose: the embedding of culture, the increase of society, and the articulation of political authority.

In addition to managing social stratification and accumulating wealth, the state was also the sole guarantor of membership in the corporate groups (matrilineages) that were the basis of Asante society. The state also controlled the entry of foreign practices, and even foreign ideas, into the society, because alternative cultural values, particularly regarding wealth, were a threat to the state's hegemony.

As European contact increased in the mid-nineteenth century, the Asante state suffered from both internal and external pressures; By the late nineteenth century, it became part of the British Gold Coast colony. Today, however, the Asante continue as a vital ethnic group within the Republic of Ghana, which won its independence from Britain in 1957. The Asantehene retains his power as a ritual, spiritual, and cultural leader of the Asante people.

Critical Thinking Questions

1. What were the economic and political ideologies underlying Asante culture?

2. How did the Asante state establish its control over wealth?

3. What were some important political symbols of the Asante state, and how did these support the Asantehene's power?

Source: Adapted from T. M. McCaskie, *State and Society in Pre-Colonial Asante.* Cambridge: Cambridge University Press, 1995.

---

chiefdoms. The warring units were now larger, and as conquest of larger areas continued, centralization of authority increased. Finally, the entire area was brought under the control of one chief. The next step was the conquest of weaker valley chiefdoms by stronger ones until powerful empires emerged, most notably that of the Inca.

Anthropological theories tend to emphasize either conflict (Fried 1967) or integration (Service 1971) as the dominant factor in the emergence of the state. Integration theories emphasize the benefits of the state to its members: its ability to provide the stability needed for growth and technological development, protection of the rights of its citizens, effective mechanisms for the peaceful settlement of disputes, protection of trade and financial arrangements, defense against external enemies, and ability to expand. Conflict theories tend to emphasize the emergence of the state as directly connected with protecting the power and privileges of an elite class through coercive power and management of political ideology.

ATAHUALLPA, THE LAST INCA KING. THE INCA EMPIRE IN PERU EMERGED AS A RESULT OF ECOLOGICAL CONDITIONS AND WAS DESTROYED BY THE SPANISH CONQUISTADORS.

North Wind Picture Archives

CENTRALIZED GOVERNMENT

States are characterized by **government:** an interrelated set of status roles that become separate from other aspects of social organization, such as kinship. In state societies, groups based on territory become central and an individual belongs to a state through citizenship. The administrative divisions of a state are territorial units, cities, districts, and so on. Each unit has its own government, although these governments are not independent of the central government.

In state societies, the government emerges as a social institution specifically concerned with making and enforcing public policy and engages in other functions that keep the society going. The state, for example, intervenes in every aspect of the economic process. Through taxation, it stimulates the agricultural production of households. It also controls labor. It can order people to work on roads and buildings and to serve in armies, thus affecting the work-

force available for agriculture. The state also intervenes in the exchange and distribution of goods and services through complex market networks. It protects the distribution of goods by making travel safe for traders as they move their goods from one place to another and by keeping peace in the marketplace. The state may also intervene in the consumption process. It can pass laws regarding which people are allowed to use which goods—for example, by reserving for the elite such items as gold, silk, or other costly symbols of high status.

The state also has important military functions. Engaging in warfare strengthens the power of the state. At the same time, it leads to increased political centralization because of a greater need (from the state's perspective) to regulate daily life and to suppress internal conflicts. Because waging war is costly, it often leads to more centralized control over production. Unlike warfare in tribal societies, which is conducted mainly through the voluntary (though sometimes under pressure) contribution of adult males, in a state society coercion replaces voluntary recruitment. Furthermore, going to war in state societies involves divergent interests; some economic and political groups benefit much more than others. As one American yeoman farmer commented about the Civil War, "it is a rich man's war and a poor man's fight" (Foner 1988)—a view that could be applied to many other wars among state societies. As part of the effort to mask this unequal benefit, states also take increasing control over information and channels of communication. This strengthens not only the war effort but also the power of the state.

The many economic, coordinating, and controlling functions of states, in peace and war, require extensive record keeping, giving rise to writing and systems of weights and measures. In some states, cities arose as administrative, religious, and economic centers. These centers then stimulated important cultural achievements in science, art, architecture, and philosophy, which are characteristic of states.

The major defining characteristic of state societies is the government's monopoly over the use of force. A state uses a code of law to make clear how and when it will use force and

---

government An interrelated set of status roles that have the authority to coordinate and regulate behavior within a society.

GLOBALIZATION AND STATE SOVEREIGNTY

States are driven to maintain their sovereignty, or independence from other states, in order to maintain control over their own interests. In the face of an increasingly global economy and globalization of communication through the Internet, the sovereignty of modern states seems increasingly fragile. There is a growing sense in Europe and the United States that national politics and governments are becoming powerless in the face of globalization. In France, for example, the government feels hamstrung in implementing policies to address its all-time-high unemployment rate because of strict spending curbs mandated by France's participation in the European Union. Concerns over globalization are also intensified by the emergence of a European currency, the euro. That the euro was designed to combat perceived American domination of the global economy does not lessen the concern in Europe. Negative French reaction to the proposed sale of a state-owned electronics company to Daewoo, a South Korean multinational, indicates that globalization is not merely a form of Americanization. Indeed, as the United States itself becomes increasingly dependent on an international economy, for both production and markets, concern about the impact of foreign multinational corporations on American politics also intensifies. In addition to globalization of the economy, expansion and globalization of information—through Internet- and satellite-based telecommunications, for example—also undermine the sovereignty of nation-states (Barber 1992). Dissidents involved in the breakup of Yugoslavia, the Zapatista rebellion in Chiapas, Mexico, and the struggle for human rights in China have all used the Internet to rally a global audience for their struggles against the state.

forbids individuals or groups to use force except under the state's authorization. Laws (usually written) are passed by authorized legislative bodies and enforced by formal and specialized institutions of law enforcement. Courts and police forces, for example, have the authority to impose all kinds of punishments: fines, confiscation of property, imprisonment, and even death.

THE STATE AND SOCIAL STRATIFICATION

Most state societies rest on agriculture. The productivity of intensive cultivation enables the central ruling authority or government to appropriate an economic surplus. This, in turn, permits the development of cities, economic and occupational specialization, and extensive trade. With the emergence of specialized, non-food-producing elites, social stratification becomes a key element of the state. Chiefdoms, too, rest on an economic surplus, but in state societies, unlike in chiefdoms, only a part of the surplus goes back to the people directly.

The rest is used to support the activities of the state itself, such as maintaining administrative bureaucracies, standing armies, artists and craftworkers, and a priesthood. States use their power to collect food surpluses through taxation, and part of this wealth is used to support the ruling class in a luxurious lifestyle that differs substantially from that of ordinary people.

The elite classes in state societies are jealous of their control and strive at every turn to keep what they have. They maintain their power in two ways. First, they maintain control over the apparatus of the state—that is, the centralized government and its institutions, particularly its institutions of coercion. Second, they establish hegemony. **Hegemony,** as it is used here, refers to the elite development of ideologies, or patterns of belief, that attempt to justify the stratification system, making it part of the dominant cultural pattern and encoding it in law.

hegemony The development by ruling classes of ideologies that attempt to justify systems of social stratification and embed them in dominant cultural norms.

Even with their great coercive and hegemonic power, however, states are not necessarily peaceful and stable. They persistently experience rebellion, directed at overthrowing those who control the government, and sometimes revolutionary attempts to overthrow the entire structure of government. The state is constantly on the alert to ward off threats to depose the government, outbreaks of violence that might result in civil war, or the disruption of the privileges of vested interests. To the extent that a state wins the loyalty of its people, through its ability to shape political ideology and to implement effective protection of their economic and political rights, the constant use of force is not necessary. It is always there in the background, however, as a potential instrument of social control (Nagengast 1994:116).

In the Ethnography box on pages 279 to 281, we saw the many dimensions of the interaction between social stratification and the state among the Asante of precolonial Ghana.

SUMMARY

1. Social differentiation is an important feature of political organization. Anthropologists have identified three major types of social systems: egalitarian, rank, and stratified. Egalitarian systems, mainly found among foragers and in some horticultural societies, give every individual and group in society equal access to basic resources, power, and prestige.

2. Rank societies, or chiefdoms, recognize differences in prestige among individuals and groups, but no one is denied access to the resources necessary for survival. Rank societies are organized through kinship. The ruling chief and his family maintain their position largely through the distribution of food and other goods throughout the entire society.

3. Stratified societies are associated with the state. Social, political, and economic inequality are institutionalized and maintained through a combination of internalized controls, political power, and force. Kinship ties between the upper and lower classes no longer serve to integrate the society, and there is a wide gap in standards of living.

4. Power in the form of political systems, including law, addresses problems of coordinating and regulating human behavior. The major political processes in any society are making and enforcing decisions affecting the common good and resolving conflicts. Power can be legitimate or illegitimate.

5. Social control is effected through formal and informal means. Informal social control is achieved through gossip, ridicule, and ostracism. Formal sanctions include exile, death, and punishments meted out by courts, judges, police, and other institutionalized forms of regulation.

6. Political organization varies according to the degree of specialization of political functions and the extent to which authority is centralized. These vary with the degree of social complexity. Four major forms of political organization are bands, tribes, chiefdoms, and states.

7. Band societies have little integration of groups beyond the level of the band. Leadership and social control are not centralized, but are diffused throughout the society. Band societies are mainly foragers.

8. Tribal organization is found mainly among horticulturalists and pastoralists. Most often, localized kin groups, the typical political unit in tribes, act independently, but under certain conditions they may act collectively. Tribal societies contain some institutions, such as age groups, clans, and other associations, that integrate the local segments of the tribe.

9. Warfare is common in tribal societies. It may be adaptive in limiting population or redistributing goods, or it may grow out of competition for European goods. Tribal societies also use a wide variety of nonviolent means of conflict resolution to settle differences between people and to control deviance.

10. In chiefdoms, kinship is the most important principle of social organization. Unlike tribes, chiefdoms concentrate power in the office of the chief. The chief's power is bolstered by his role in the redistribution of food and other goods.

11. A state is a hierarchical, centralized form of political organization in which a central government has a legal monopoly over the use of force. The state emerged in different parts of the world in response to different historical and ecological

conditions, all of which demanded more centralized coordination and regulation of human
populations.

12. States are characterized by social stratification
and, unlike chiefdoms, are not organized through
kinship. The elites in state societies maintain their
position through coercive institutions and through
hegemony. An example is provided by the pre-
colonial Asante state.

KEY TERMS

acephalous	leadership
achieved status	legitimate power
age grades	mediation
age set	political ideology
ascribed status	political organization
authority	
band	political process
bigman	power
chiefdom	rank society
citizenship	rebellion
compensation	revolution
complementary opposition	segmentary lineage system
egalitarian society	social complexity
factions	social differentiation
government	state
hegemony	stratified society
illegitimate power	tribe
law	war (warfare)

SUGGESTED READINGS

Barlow, David E., and Melissa Hickman Barlow. 2000.
Police in a Multicultural Society: An American Story.
Prospect Heights, IL: Waveland. An historical and
ethnographic work on a key institution of power
in a state society: the police. With a major focus
on policing and African Americans, this comprehensive but readable study also includes other
groups such as Native Americans.

Blackwood, Evelyn. 2000. *Webs of Power: Women, Kin,
and Community in a Sumatran Village.* New York:
Rowman and Littlefield. This study of an unusual
Islamic matrilineal society in Indonesia analyzes
the different levels and sources of power, their relation to gender, and the ways in which they have
accommodated and resisted colonial, national,
and global processes.

Greenhouse, Carol J., Barbara Yngvesson, and David
Engel. 1994. *Law and Community in Three American Towns.* Ithaca, NY: Cornell University Press.
Three ethnographic studies in different regions
of the United States—the South, the Midwest,
and New England—come to similar conclusions
about the importance of insider/outsider relations
in the use of law and the maintenance of social
order.

Kaplan, Flora E. S. (Ed.). 1997. *Queens, Queen Mothers,
Priestesses, and Power: Case Studies in African Gender.* New York: New York Academy of Sciences.
Eighteen case studies of elite women from a variety of ethnic groups in southern Africa and
West Africa focus on their political and ritual
roles in both the public and the private domain.

Nader, Laura. 1990. *Harmony Ideology: Justice and Control in a Zapotec Mountain Village.* Stanford, CA:
Stanford University Press. This expansion of
Nader's earlier ethnography of a Zapotec village
in Mexico reexamines some theoretical questions
in legal anthropology, as well as issues of methodology and cross-cultural comparison.

Wolf, Eric R. 1998. *Envisioning Power: Ideologies of
Dominance and Crisis.* Berkeley: University of
California Press. In his typically insightful and
original style, Wolf examines three uses of power
in extreme cultural situations: Nazi Germany, the
ancient Aztec, and the Kwakiutl.

INTERNET RESOURCES

WWW

The following Internet resources appear in this
chapter. Please log on to the Wadsworth anthropology website: **http://anthropology.wadsworth.
com**. Click on the Nanda/Warms *Cultural Anthropology* page. Then select the Student Resources section, where you will find a complete presentation of
these links and more.

- A link to a website on political systems, page 263
- A video link: Legal system and the settlement of
  minor disputes, page 273
- A photo essay on the political role played by monuments and ceremony, page 278
- Access the Study Guide to InfoTrac College Edition
  for Anthropology Students

DRESS AND ADORNMENT ARE FREQUENTLY USED AS SIGNS OF WEALTH AND SOCIAL STATUS. AMONG THE KUNA OF THE SAN BLAS ISLANDS OFF THE COAST OF PANAMA, THE TRADITIONAL "MOLA" OR APPLIQUED BLOUSE IS SOLD TO TOURISTS AS AN IMPORTANT SOURCE OF INCOME. WEALTH IS DISPLAYED IN THE JEWELRY, WHICH FREQUENTLY INCLUDES GOLD AND SILVER COINS, WORN BY THE WOMEN.

CHAPTER THIRTEEN

SOCIAL STRATIFICATION IN CONTEMPORARY SOCIETIES: CLASS, CASTE, AND RACE

How do anthropologists explain social stratification?

What are some differences among class, caste, and racially stratified societies?

What are some characteristics of the social stratification system in the United States, and how does it affect the lives and lifestyles of individuals and groups?

How has anthropology contributed to antiracism in the United States?

What are some similarities and differences between the racial stratification systems of Brazil and the United States?

I n this chapter, we continue our examination of social differentiation and the distribution of power by looking at three types of stratification: class, caste, and race. These, along with ethnicity and gender, interact in complex ways, and are the most important bases of stratification in contemporary societies.

Social stratification results from the unequal distribution of goods and services. The ways in which this distribution takes place depend on cultural values, the organization of production, and the access that different individuals and groups have to the means for achieving societal goals.

EXPLAINING SOCIAL STRATIFICATION

Social stratification seems an inevitable part of state societies; indeed, it is one of the criteria by which states are defined. No culture has ever devised a successful means of organizing a large population without stratification and inequality. One reason is that stratification has some clear social functions. From a **functionalist** perspective, inequality and the promise of economic and social rewards for effort motivate people to increase their efforts and engage in difficult, risky jobs, as well as jobs requiring long and arduous training. Society as a whole clearly benefits from having some people undertake such jobs. For example, in the United States, medical doctors are very highly paid. However, becoming a doctor requires 11 or more years of university, medical school, and internship. People must be highly motivated to undertake such an arduous course of study, and prestige and wealth are critical motivators impelling them to do so. If the members of a culture want highly trained medical

functionalism The anthropological theory that specifies that specific cultural institutions function to support the structure of society or serve the needs of individuals in society.

Kevin Horan/Stock, Boston

ONE PRESUMED FUNCTION OF SOCIAL STRATIFICATION IS THAT DIFFERENTIAL FINANCIAL REWARDS ARE NEEDED TO ATTRACT PEOPLE TO DIRTY OR DANGEROUS JOBS.

personnel, they must provide them with rewards commensurate with the length and difficulty of the requisite training.

Although at some level inequality is functional, it is also clear that inequality does not always serve the general good. Every state society has difficult and arduous jobs that are not well rewarded. For example, in the United States, schoolteachers, nurses, and many other professionals do difficult jobs that require substantial training, yet they are not well compensated financially.

Emphasizing the positive, functional aspects of social stratification suggests that inequality benefits society as a whole by drawing the most able people to the most demanding positions. This, too, is not always the case. The effectiveness of social and economic inequality in benefiting society as a whole depends on the degree to which all people start with the same opportunities. However, in no state society do all people have an equal start. Family background, gender, ethnicity, race, social connections, and other factors play important roles in determining the sorts of opportunities available to individuals. As anyone who has ever worked for an inefficient, negligent, or incompetent boss knows, the best-paid and most prestigious positions do not always go to the most able people. And "connections," as noted in the relationship between kinship and political power in the United States, do count!

Furthermore, the motivating power of economic rewards seems to have limits. A person making $25,000 a year would probably agree to work harder and undertake more training for a salary of $50,000 a year. However, would a person making $400,000 a year undertake additional work and training in order to make $450,000 a year? Yet $50,000 is still a great deal of money.

Beyond all these considerations is an issue of the human spirit. Although inequality seems inevitable in large-scale social systems, resentment, however repressed, always seems to accompany substantial inequalities (Scott 1992). Anthropologist Gerald Berreman calls social stratification "painful, damaging, and unjust" and attributes much of the conflict in modern societies—crime, terrorism, ethnic conflict, civil war, and international war—to organized inequality (1981:4-5). Wherever there is inequality, individuals will struggle over rewards. Thus, while social stratification may be inevitable in state societies, and even of some benefit to their populations, it must also be viewed as a source of conflict and instability.

This perspective, rooted in the work of Karl Marx and Max Weber, is known as **conflict theory.** In this view, social stratification results from the constant struggle for scarce goods and services. Inequalities exist because those individuals and groups who have acquired power, wealth, and prestige use their assets and their power to maintain control over the apparatus of the state, particularly its institutions of coercion and ideology. When attempts to establish hegemony falter, elites may fall back on the threat of force or its actual use to maintain the status quo. The description of the Asante state in Chapter 12 illustrates efforts by socially powerful groups to maintain political control, which is at the heart of the inextricable connection between social stratification and the state.

The insights of Karl Marx, Max Weber, and others who focus on the conflicts that under-

conflict theory A perspective on social stratification that focuses on inequality as a source of conflict and change.

lie complex societies are fundamental to a comprehensive analysis of culture and society. The emphasis on conflict and change introduces an historical perspective in understanding social systems. Focusing on conflict also enables us to understand some of the hidden motivations of social actors and to assess institutions by their outcomes, as well as their stated intentions. However, just as the functional view of inequality may lead theorists to ignore the possibility of structural conflict, so too conflict theorists may sometimes ignore the very real mechanisms that promote solidarity across caste, ethnic, and class lines.

CRITERIA OF STRATIFICATION: POWER, WEALTH, AND PRESTIGE

The social stratification system of any society depends on a complex interaction of the three main dimensions of stratification: power, wealth, and prestige. In Chapter 12, we defined **power** as the ability to control resources in one's own interest. Anthropologists analyze power by examining its sources, the channels through which it is exercised, and the goals it is deployed to achieve. For example, in the United States, we might compare the sources, uses, and goals of power among corporate presidents, elected public officials, movie stars, or the heads of organized crime families. From a cross-cultural perspective, we might compare the sources and uses of power of an American president, an Asante king, and the chairman of the Communist party in the People's Republic of China.

Wealth is the accumulation of material resources or access to the means of producing these resources. Many social scientists believe that wealth is the most important dimension of social stratification and the foundation of both power and prestige. For Karl Marx and those who follow his thinking, understanding how material goods are produced and distributed is the critical factor in analyzing social systems. In his analysis of capitalism, Marx differentiated two main strata in society: the capitalists, who own the means of production, and the workers, who must sell their labor in order to survive. According to Marx, the relationship

Kolvoord/The Image Works

IN THE UNITED STATES, AS IN OTHER CLASS SOCIETIES, AN INDIVIDUAL'S CLASS POSITION IS BASED ON SEVERAL INTERRELATED FACTORS, INCLUDING WEALTH, EDUCATION, AND OCCUPATION. WHILE AMERICANS CONSISTENTLY RESIST ACKNOWLEDGING THE CLASS BASIS OF THEIR SOCIETY, THE PRESTIGE OF DIFFERENT OCCUPATIONS IS QUICKLY RECOGNIZED. THIS IS BASED PARTLY ON THE INCOME ASSOCIATED WITH AN OCCUPATION AND PARTLY ON OTHER FACTORS, SUCH AS WHETHER THE OCCUPATION REQUIRES BRAINS OR BRAWN.

of individuals to the means of production is critical in determining how much power and prestige they have. One need not be a Marxist, however, to see the obvious ways in which wealth translates into power. In the United States, for example, rich people are more likely to run for political office and win than others, and wealthy individuals and organizations can influence government in ways that ordinary people cannot.

Prestige, or social honor, is a third dimension of social stratification. Complex societies, which are occupationally specialized, contain many different positions that are ranked high

power The ability to control resources in one's own interest.

wealth The accumulation of material resources or access to the means of producing these resources.

prestige Social honor or respect.

or low in relation to one another. Occupations are ranked differently in different societies. In the Hindu caste system, for example, a central criterion for ranking occupations is the level of spiritual purity or pollution, a concept that is largely absent from occupational rankings in the United States.

As socioeconomic conditions change, the value system that supports a particular system of prestige also changes. Occupations may gain or lose prestige. In eighteenth-century Europe, surgery was performed by barbers and was a lower-class occupation; in contemporary North America, surgeons rank very high in prestige, not least because they make enormous amounts of money.

The prestige awarded to different occupations is related to the power inherent in such occupations, the income derived from them, and their importance to society. Although income is a basis for prestige in American society, the way in which that income is earned is also taken into account. Generally speaking, people who earn their incomes illegally have less prestige than do those whose incomes are legally earned. Who do you think has more prestige in the United States: a basketball player who signs a $5 million annual contract, a heart surgeon who earns $600,000 a year, or the head of an illegal gambling syndicate or drug distribution network who makes hundreds of millions of dollars?

Although wealth is not the sole criteria of social status, money can eventually translate into high social position and legitimate power. Sending one's children to the most prestigious schools, buying a home in the best neighborhood, and joining the right social clubs give people the chance to interact with others in high social positions. All of these opportunities cost money. The social status of a family can thus improve dramatically over just a few generations. The ancestors of some currently promi-

nent political families in the United States made their fortunes illegally, or in ways that today would be considered deviant.

The question of whether prestige or class is more important in social stratification has long been debated by social scientists. Opposing the views of Karl Marx, who argued for the priority of economic or class interests, are those of Max Weber, a German sociologist of the late nineteenth century. Whereas Marx saw people as conscious of their membership in a group of people with similar economic interests (class), Weber believed that people may value prestige and the symbolic aspects of status even more than their economic position. Weber further argued that political action can be motivated by a group's desire to defend its social position as well as, or even in opposition to, its economic self-interest. For example, poor whites in the American South did not join poor blacks in working for improvement of their common economic position because they were more committed to maintaining status differences based on color and race.

ASCRIPTION AND ACHIEVEMENT

In comparing stratification systems in different cultures or over time, an important distinction is made between systems based on **ascription** and those based on **achievement.** In a stratification system based on ascription, an individual's status, or position in the system, is determined mainly by birth. Sex and race, for example, are (with some exceptions) ascribed statuses in the United States. Kinship group and caste membership are other examples of ascribed statuses. In a stratification system based on achievement, a person's social position ideally is determined by his or her efforts. Wife, college professor, criminal, and artist are examples of achieved statuses in the United States. Although different systems of social stratification can be described as based primarily on ascription (**closed systems**) or achievement (**open systems**), most societies contain both. In socially less specialized societies, most important statuses, such as kinship, may be ascribed, but prestige may also be based on individual achievement.

ascribed status A social position that a person is born into.

achieved status A social position that a person chooses or achieves on his or her own.

closed system A system of stratification based primarily on ascription.

open system A system of stratification based primarily on achievement.

The two basic forms of social stratification, class systems and caste systems, are primarily associated with achievement and ascription respectively. In a **class system,** one's class status is held to be achieved, rather than ascribed. The different strata (classes) are not sharply separated from one another but form a continuum, and **social mobility** (movement from one class to another) is possible. A person born into one social class can move, through various means—education, marriage, good luck, hard work, taking risks—into another. In the discussion of class systems, the term *social mobility* generally implies upward mobility, as if downward mobility is deviant or does not occur. As we will see in the Ethnography box later in this chapter, that is not the case. Social mobility can also be downward, and indeed, downward mobility is becoming more widespread in the United States.

IN THE UNITED STATES TODAY, THE ABUNDANCE OF MATERIAL GOODS IS CLOSELY TIED TO THE INDIVIDUAL AND CLASS IDENTITY OF THE MIDDLE CLASS, WHICH IN FACT VARIES CONSIDERABLY AS TO SALARIES AND THE ACCUMULATION OF WEALTH.

SOCIAL CLASS IN THE UNITED STATES

The United States is said to have an open class system: One's position depends largely on achieved statuses such as occupation, education, and lifestyle, and there are many opportunities for upward mobility. The promise of upward mobility, called "The American Dream," is an important part of American national culture and is based on the democratic principle of equality and opportunity for all. Many people in the United States resist accepting that this equality has not yet been fully realized and that social class—as it intersects with gender, race, and ethnicity—is central to the American stratification system.

Many studies show that social class membership in the United States correlates with various attitudinal, behavioral, and lifestyle differences. Anthropological research supports the view that social class is more than an economic phenomenon. A social class is also a subculture; its members share similar life experiences, occupational roles, values, educational backgrounds, affiliations, leisure activities, buying habits, and political views.

In a fascinating and innovative study, anthropologist Richard Wilk (1999) has been examining the consumption patterns that are central to middle-class identity in the United States. As Wilk points out, the North American middle-class lifestyle centers on the home and the "comfort" associated with it. One of the major symbols of this comfort is the recliner chair. Although the recliner was first built in 1927, it was not popular until after World War II, when it became a symbol of working-class domesticity and respectability. For a long while, it was despised by the elite as a symbol of the passive, anti-intellectual, working-class "couch potato." Today the recliner has worked its way into more than one-fourth of all American homes and is associated with the new cultural themes of "relaxation" and deserved compensation for the stresses of work. For the American middle class, it is the overflowing quantity of material goods that is most closely tied to their expression of individual and class identity. Exploring the meanings that Americans of all classes attach to the artifacts and patterns of their lifestyle is a growing field in anthropology.

class system A form of social stratification in which the different strata form a continuum and social mobility is possible.

social mobility Movement from one social class to another.

GLOBALIZATION

A TOUCH OF CLASS, GLOBAL STYLE

A consumer-driven global lifestyle featuring international brands such as Coke, Sony, Porsche, McDonald's, Honda, Benetton, and IKEA is emerging in all the major cities of the world. Trade, travel, and television are the basis of this revolution in global culture, with teenagers as major participants. Propelled by the global diffusion of MTV and worldwide advertising campaigns, more than 250 million teenagers in the United States, Europe, Latin America, and the Pacific Rim share a taste for Levi jeans, Nike shoes, the Red Hot Chili Peppers, hip-hop, reggae, and salsa. Much of the cultural diffusion of fashion, food, and fun originates in the United States, particularly in the African American urban culture. Americans are also importing international cultural fashions at an accelerating pace. In Los Angeles, the specialty of Gurume, a Japanese-run restaurant, is Gurume chicken, made up of chopped chicken and green beans in an Italian marinara sauce, with Japanese cabbage salad, Texas toast, and Louisiana tabasco sauce. Ethnic food is one of the hottest segments in the United States restaurant business, and cappuccino and Perrier are de rigueur in upper-middle-class urban America. The London department store Harrods, owned by an

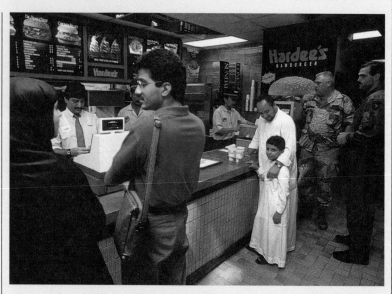

ALL OVER THE WORLD THERE IS A CONVERGENCE AMONG THE ELITES IN CONSUMPTION PRACTICES. EVEN AS CULTURAL NATIONALISM AND RELIGIOUS FUNDAMENTALISM ARE GAINING STRENGTH IN MANY NATIONS, AN INTERNATIONAL LIFESTYLE, INCLUDING A TASTE FOR AMERICAN FAST FOOD, OCCURS IN EVEN THE MOST TRADITIONAL NATIONS, SUCH AS SAUDI ARABIA.

Egyptian, features French peaches, Dutch radishes, Russian button mushrooms, and East African lemon grass, and advertises its famous annual sale in the *New York Times*. Through television, the images of this global lifestyle are available to almost all social classes, but its cost puts it out of reach for most of the world's population. One effect of this class-based global lifestyle is a resurgence of cultural nationalism bent on keeping traditional cultures alive, a movement that often finds its most dedicated adherents among the poorer and more provincial members of society.

Beyond participating in shared cultural patterns, members of a social class also tend to associate more with one another than with people in other classes. Thus, the lifestyle and interactional dimensions of social class reinforce one another. Through interaction based on common residence and schooling, religious participation, voluntary associations, and other social institutions, people learn the lifestyle of their social class. Because lifestyle is an important part of sociability, informal and intimate social relationships, such as friendship and marriage, also tend to bring together people from the same social class.

Some social scientists argue that approaches to social stratification emphasizing lifestyle, cultural patterns, and prestige obscure important economic and power differences in American society. Another way to look at social class that brings economic factors and power into sharper focus is to examine the differences in life chances among social classes. **Life chances** are the opportunities that people have to fulfill their potential in society. Life chances include the chance of survival and longevity, opportunities to obtain an education that will help maximize intellectual and creative potential, opportunities to participate in associations and cultural life, and opportunities to live in comfort and security.

People's life chances are linked to their position in the stratification system. Although the American ideal of equality includes the belief that "anyone can become a millionaire," the demonstrated relationship between life chances and social class contradicts this belief for many people. Social mobility itself, for example, is a life chance that depends on where one already is in the class system. People born into positions of wealth, high status, and power strive to maintain those positions and often have the means to keep others from achieving mobility. People born into the middle class have a better chance of improving their life chances than do people born into a poor class. The high and rising cost of pharmaceuticals and medical care is merely one aspect of the different life chances available to the poor, the middle class, and the wealthy.

Low social position tends to negate not only one's own life chances but also those of one's children. Poverty often perpetuates itself through generations, calling into question the openness of the American class system. The interactional and lifestyle dimensions of social class are reinforced by kinship links, particularly among elites, who use these links both as a basis for exclusive interactional networks and as a way of improving their life chances. As part of the denial of the relevance of class in the United States, many Americans associate the importance of kinship in the elite class with other cultures and nations, not their own. Yet the expression "It's who you know, not what you know that counts" suggests that many Americans are aware of the contradiction between the ideal of a merit-based class system and the reality, in which personal relationships play an important role in improving one's life chances.

CASTE

In contrast to class systems, which are largely based on achieved status, a **caste system** is based on birth. A person belongs to the caste of his or her parents and cannot move from one caste to another. In a class system, people from different classes may marry; in fact, marriage is one route to upward social mobility. In a caste system, a person can marry only within his or her caste. In other words, caste is hereditary, and castes are endogamous. Castes are ranked in relation to one another and are usually associated, though more in the past than today, with a traditional occupation. A caste system, then, consists of ranked, culturally distinct, interdependent, endogamous groups. Unlike class systems, in which no clear boundaries exist between the different classes, a caste system has definite boundaries between castes.

THE CASTE SYSTEM IN INDIA

The unique elements of the Indian caste system are its complexity, its relation to Hindu religious beliefs and rituals, and the degree to which the castes (or, more properly, subcastes) are cohesive and self-regulating groups. Hindu belief includes four caste categories, called *varna*. The varna are ranked according to their ritual purity, which is based on their traditional occupations. The Brahmins, ranked highest, are priests and scholars; second are Kshatriyas, the ruling and warrior caste; third are the Vaisyas, or merchants; and fourth are the Shudras, or menial workers and artisans. Below these four varna is a fifth group, previously called untouchables, now called Harijans (children of God, so named by Gandhi), scheduled castes, or Dalits. Dalits perform spiritually polluting work such as cleaning latrines or tanning leather, and are considered so ritually impure that their mere touch contaminates the purity of the higher castes. A person's birth into any one of these

life chances The opportunities that people have to fulfill their potential in society.

caste system A system of stratification based on birth in which movement from one stratum (caste) to another is not possible.

IN THE FIELD

DOWNWARD MOBILITY AMONG THE MIDDLE CLASS IN THE UNITED STATES

In most discussions of social class in the United States, the openness of the class system and the opportunities for upward social mobility, either within one's lifetime or across generations, occupy a central place. This upward mobility is the core of the American Dream for both the native-born and the millions of immigrants who come to the United States. The belief in opportunities for upward mobility is built into the national mythology and closely tied to core American values: individualism, meritocracy, the work ethic, optimism, a national faith in progress and achievement, and a belief in the ability of individuals to control the circumstances of their lives. The American Dream is based on the belief that if a person works hard and makes personal sacrifices to acquire skills, knowledge, and competence, his or her material standard of living will improve.

This widespread belief in the American Dream leads many people in the United States to deny that a class system exists, despite the reality of millions of people in poverty and the great, persistent inequalities among different segments (racial, gender, ethnic, and regional) of the population. One way in which Americans characteristically deny the existence of class is by applying the label "middle class" to a very wide range of occupations, incomes, and lifestyles, ignoring the diversity of cultures in this group. Another way in which the denial of class operates is the almost exclusive focus on upward, as opposed to downward, mobility.

Anthropologist Katherine Newman defines the downwardly mobile middle class as people who had secure jobs, comfortable homes, and reason to believe that the

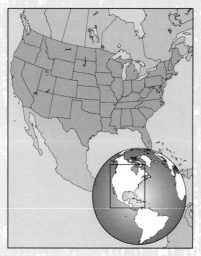

future would be one of continued prosperity for themselves and their children. Through job loss, they experience not only economic decline but also a decline in prestige: They have lost their place in society, and with it their sense of honor and self-esteem. Despite the very high numbers of Americans who have become downwardly mobile, and despite its high toll on both individuals and the economy, downward mobility is almost institutionally invisible. The media more often focus attention on upward mobility and the lives of the rich and famous. These images reflect implicit but dominant assumptions that life gets better from year to year. Although American culture provides many rituals and symbols of upward mobility and success, in the form of displays of wealth and status, there are no such occasions to mark status deterioration. As Newman observes, "Downward mobility is a hidden dimension of our society's experience because it . . . does not fit into our cultural universe."

Because of the glorification of economic success in the United States and the consequent lack of discussion of failure, the economic burdens of downward mobility in the middle class are intensified by the psychological burdens. First, because Americans put so much emphasis

on people's ability to control their lives, failure to do so quickly turns into self-blame. The culture tends to blame the victim rather than investigate possible causes in systemic economic conditions, such as the flight of manufacturing jobs and capital investment to foreign countries, the transition from a manufacturing to a service economy, the recurring downturns that have been part of the capitalist economy for more than 200 years, and changing demographics. This mentality, which is an outgrowth of American culture, means that the government is less responsive to victims of downward social mobility than is true in Japan and many nations of Europe. These governments spend more money on retraining workers who have lost their jobs, require substantial warning periods before plant closings, and have better and longer unemployment benefits.

Economists and sociologists can provide statistical data on downward mobility, but anthropologists have a unique contribution to make in understanding its meaning for the people who experience it. Using the anthropological perspective that culture shapes our interpretations of experience, Newman shows that downward mobility is experienced differently by different segments of the middle class. She compared the experiences of middle managers fired from large corporations, air traffic controllers who lost their jobs as a result of a strike, a town of blue-collar workers who became unemployed when their factory closed, and middle-class women who suffered downward mobility primarily as the aftermath of divorce. An interesting contrast is evident between the middle managers, who experienced downward mobility as a personal failure and an emotionally debilitating experience, and the air traffic controllers. Although both groups were influenced by American cultural values in interpreting their experience, the collective nature of the air traffic controllers' strike led to a very different psychological response than that of the middle managers and executives.

The middle-class managers and executives, mainly white men in their late 40s and early 50s, married suburban dwellers with teenage children, typically lost their jobs as a result of corporate downsizing in response to declining sales or prices. They experienced their unemployment as a personal failure, resulting in demoralization, self-blame, shame, and an excruciating sense of social isolation. Their social networks disappeared rapidly as they were increasingly unable to afford the reciprocity on which social interaction depends. They were isolated in their large suburban homes, where there was rarely a sense of neighborly community. Their economic contacts shrank as their peers were similarly vulnerable and, in fact, became their competition in the job market. Prolonged inability to find a managerial job similar to the one they had lost, or any job at all, brought home the stigma of unemployment as a part of American middle-class culture. Keeping up appearances was critical to these men; some managers did not even tell their wives and families about their firing until long after the fact. Their unemployment and subsequent downward mobility negatively affected all of their family life and routine. Many leisure activities had to be abandoned. The father's status in the family declined as wives and children saw him as the one who had gotten them into financial trouble. Family members were forced into the unfamiliar situation of having to talk to each other more than before. The major interpretation of their downwardly mobile experience for these managers was a feeling of worthlessness, because their self-esteem was so closely tied to their prestigious and high-paying occupations, on which they had built an extremely comfortable lifestyle. When

they lost their jobs and their incomes, their self-esteem was drastically affected.

The air controllers' interpretation of job loss was different. Because they saw themselves as paying a hard price for standing up for what they believed in, their self-esteem was less severely affected. Air traffic controlling requires teamwork in the workplace and among airports. Air traffic controllers had forged many friendships through their occupation, and this collective sense of pride carried over to the initiation of the strike and its aftermath. The air traffic controllers were employed mainly by the federal government. Many of them had achieved upward social mobility from working-class backgrounds through military service, rigorous training, and selection for this high-paying, highly selective, prestigious, and challenging occupation. They were confident that their strike, which took place in August 1981, would be successful, partly because it involved demands for safety measures as well as higher wages. When the strike failed, these workers did not experience paralyzing self-blame, self-doubt, and a sense of loss of control over their lives. Indeed, in their collective struggle against the government, they found dignity and comradeship that survived long after most of them found other jobs and after the public had largely forgotten the strike.

Unlike the managers and executives, who experienced their job loss as individual failure, the air traffic controllers drew on themes in American culture that gave dignity to their actions and made sense of their suffering. They saw their struggle against what they perceived as injustices by a vengeful government as a new kind of patriotism, and their strike as a moral protest. The search for meaning in suffering led them to tie their strike to other honorable rebellions in American history, giving their actions a moral character. The strike became less an effort to gain per-

sonal benefits than a struggle for human rights and professional altruism. The downward mobility that resulted from the strike was interpreted as a tragedy of conflict between the government and the people, not as a personal rejection. In the collective act of the strike, they found self-respect rather than personal failure.

Katherine Newman's anthropological analysis of one aspect of the American class system indicates that social class is defined by more than economic statistics. People interpret their place in society in different ways, even if they label all these different experiences as "middle class." Cultural themes can be used to interpret the same experience in very different ways. In her conclusion, Newman notes that downward social mobility has a cost not just for individuals but also for society. The lack of an ethos of loyalty and commitment to workers on the part of American companies and government contrasts with attitudes in some other nations. For Newman, downward social mobility is a monumental waste of intelligence and motivation that undermines confidence in business and government, leads to a decline in the quality of manufacture and service, and will ultimately leave the United States far behind as a competitor in a global economy.

Critical Thinking Questions

1. What cultural values in the United States support an almost exclusive focus on upward social mobility?

2. Examine the cultural assumptions in your occupational or career goals as these relate to upward and downward mobility.

Source: Adapted from Katherine S. Newman, *Falling from Grace: The Experience of Downward Mobility in the American Middle Class* (2nd ed.). New York: Random House, 1999.

AP/Wide World Photos

IN INDIA, THE UPPER-CASTE VIEW THAT THE LOWEST CASTES ARE CONTENT IN THEIR SOCIOECONOMIC POSITION IS CONTRADICTED BY THE MANY PROTESTS OF DALITS AGAINST THE UNFAIRNESS OF THE CASTE SYSTEM.

caste categories is believed to be a reward or punishment for the quality of his or her actions in a previous life.

Caste interaction is governed by rules of behavior that help maintain caste boundaries. Under traditional norms, members of different castes do not eat with one another, and a higher-caste person will not accept most kinds of food or drink from a lower-caste person. In Indian villages, Dalits are spatially and socially segregated, and are prohibited from drawing water from the same wells as higher castes. Many traditional forms of maintaining caste boundaries, particularly between the upper castes and the Dalits, have been declared null by the constitution of independent India. The constitution incorporates protection of human rights and legal equality for all persons, and outlaws all forms of untouchability and other egregious, public forms of caste inequality.

Caste in India, particularly in villages, has an important economic dimension, involving traditional exchanges of goods and services. Families of various artisan and serving castes—such as carpenters, potters, blacksmiths, water carriers, leather workers (who remove dead cattle from the fields), barbers, and washermen—perform their services for high-caste landown-

ing families and in return receive food from them. In addition, landowning families may pay serving-caste families with grain, clothing, fodder for animals, butter, milk, small amounts of cash, and many other things. Such client–patron or *jajmani* relationships may carry over for several generations. *Jajmani* relationships give landowners a steady supply of workers. The serving castes, in turn, gain stability.

The focus on the integrative functions of the Indian caste system is highly idealized, however, and rests on ethnography carried out mainly among Brahmins and other high castes. Anthropologists with a more conflict-oriented theoretical approach argue that the benefits of the caste system are much greater for the high castes than for the low castes. In this view, social integration in the Indian village is due as much to physical coercion and the absence of alternatives for the lower castes as it is to the integrating force of economic reciprocity (see Mencher 1980).

Although Indian castes are ranked on the basis of prestige rather than wealth, the gains of high-caste position are not just symbolic. The higher castes also benefit materially from their higher status and are in a better position to exercise political power in their own self-interest. The lower castes appear to accept their low position without question, but their conformity also hinges on their awareness that economic sanctions and physical force will be used against them if they try to break out of their caste position. Members of the Indian elites have long used the rationalization that the lower castes are happy where they are. That this is not the case is clear from the many protest movements by poor and oppressed lower and Dalit castes and the attempts of various castes to change their caste rankings.

THE DYNAMICS OF CASTE

Earlier studies of the caste system in India tended to portray it in theoretical and static terms. In fact, lower- and middle-ranked castes often do not accept their caste position and use a number of strategies to rearrange their rank. Such efforts by Dalit castes often bring violent reactions from the higher castes, who see any attempt by Dalits to move up as a threat to their own prestige, wealth, and power.

Unlike in a class system, social mobility in the caste system is primarily a group rather than an individual effort. A caste that has been economically successful in some new occupation may try to raise its prestige by adopting the customs of a higher caste, claiming a new rank for itself. An upwardly mobile caste attempts to change the behavior of its members in the direction of conforming to higher-caste behavior patterns. These new behavior patterns are formulated by caste councils, and nonconforming members will be publicly censured or even outcasted. As part of its striving for social mobility, a lower caste may also invent an origin myth, claiming it originally belonged to a higher-ranked varna.

One aspect of the dynamics of the caste system is illustrated by the Camars, a Dalit caste of leather workers in Agra (site of the Taj Mahal) (Lynch 1969). Traditionally, Camars were shoemakers, and with an increased demand for shoes both in India and abroad, some of them became fairly wealthy. Improved economic circumstances, as well as their potential political power in independent India, stimulated the Camars to try to raise their caste ranking. They claimed to be Kshatriyas (the warrior caste). In an effort to get this claim accepted by the higher castes, they outlawed the eating of beef and buffalo among their members and adopted some high-caste rituals, such as tying the sacred thread. These aspirations for higher status were not acknowledged by others, however.

Subsequently, under the leadership of a Dalit, Dr. B. R. Ambedkar, a lawyer educated in England and the United States, the Camars tried a different strategy: conversion to Buddhism. Instead of trying to raise their status within the Hindu caste system, they sought to improve their position by putting themselves outside the caste system altogether. At the same time, however, they wanted to retain their status as a special caste in order to be eligible for the benefits of affirmative action offered by the Indian government.

Caste studies from the viewpoint of upper castes do not reveal the "cracks" in what is frequently portrayed as a monolithic social system. Ethnographies based on data from lower and particularly Dalit castes, however, reveal that Dalits are caught in a circular bind of stigmatized identity (the view that they are polluting) and economic exploitation. Even with the constitutional prohibition on untouchability, India has not experienced the radical economic reform necessary to eliminate the economic barriers to Dalit social mobility. Without substantially increased economic power, there is little likelihood of change in the stigmatized aspect of their identity. At the same time, old attitudes regarding their stigmatized identity inhibit the possibilities of radical economic change. Whereas high-caste Indians often justify the caste system by reference to Hindu religious beliefs, scheduled caste members almost universally explain their low status by reference to economic factors, such as the unfair concentration of land or capital in the hands of the elite (Mencher 1980).

CHANGES IN THE CASTE SYSTEM

There have been important changes in the caste system in the past 50 years (Fuller 1995). In rural as well as urban India, caste ranking appears to be less sharply defined than formerly, at least within the higher caste categories. This is partly the result of the increasing differentiation of wealth, prestige, and power *within* each caste.

Perhaps the biggest change has occurred in the traditional connection between caste and occupations. New occupations, such as factory work, government service, and the professions, that are not caste related have opened opportunities. At the same time, many low-caste occupations, such as potter and drummer, have declined. These two trends have made caste less relevant for occupation, although the higher castes have the capital and know-how to best exploit new opportunities. Today, members of the middle-class "intelligentsia" feel almost no obligation to follow their caste's traditional occupation (Beteille 1995).

At an ideological level, there has been a significant change in the public discourse about caste (Fuller 1995). Differences in caste are now referred to in public as cultural differences,

Courtesy of The Hispanic Society of America

AS THE SPANISH COLONIZED THE NEW WORLD, THEY ATTEMPTED TO CONTROL THE POPULATION BY CREATING A HIERARCHICAL SOCIETY IN WHICH EACH GROUP HAD ITS OWN SOCIOECONOMIC NICHE. THESE NICHES WERE DEFINED BY "RACE." AT THE TOP WERE THE "PURE BLOOD" SPANISH. MORE THAN 15 OTHER RACES WERE IDENTIFIED IN DESCENDING ORDER, INCLUDING INDIAN, BARBAROUS INDIAN, MULATTO (A MIXTURE OF SPANISH AND AFRICAN), MESTIZA (A COMBINATION OF INDIAN AND SPANISH), AND MANY OTHERS. PAINTINGS OF THESE RACES OR CASTES WERE SENT BACK TO SPAIN TO ASSURE THE GOVERNMENT THAT THE SPANISH WERE MAINTAINING THE SOCIAL HIERARCHY FOUND IN SPAIN.

rather than as a hierarchy based on spiritual purity and pollution. Corresponding to the new trends of public discourse, the more neutral, nonevaluative terms "community" and "association" are replacing the term *jati* (which literally means *species* but refers to subcaste). At the same time, caste boundaries—for example, in eating, drinking, and smoking the hookah—have weakened. It is unclear to what extent these changes reflect a real change in attitude.

The urban upper classes, whose occupations make caste largely irrelevant, may dismiss notions of caste hierarchy, but for the lower castes these ideas are still very relevant. In private, people still speak of caste in a spiritual framework and people still marry within their caste. This ensures that caste as a building block of society will not disappear in the near future.

STRATIFICATION AND RACE

The complexity and ambiguity of caste in India invites comparison with ideas of race. As we noted in Chapters 1 and 2, race is a culturally constructed category, based on perceived physical differences, that is used to imply hereditary differences between peoples and to justify various systems of social stratification. Racial stratification systems are similar to caste systems, in that race is an ascribed characteristic. Caste or class differences (as well as ethnic differences, see Chapter 14) may be conceptualized in racial terms.

In Japan, for example, the Burakumin are a historically stigmatized and oppressed group that are still so treated today, despite their official emancipation in 1871 (De Vos and Wagatsuma 1966). They are called a race in Japan because the Japanese believe that the Burakumin are innately physically and morally distinct from other Japanese, although this is not validated by any objective measures. Burakumin ancestry is manifested only in the family name, occupation, place of residence, and lifestyle. The Burakumin are thus an example of a sociological race that has no physical characteristics distinguishing it from the larger population. Social scientists sometimes refer to them as an "invisible race."

The stigmatization of the Burakumin demonstrates a seemingly universal fact: All systems of inherited stratification include the belief that social distinctions reflect biological, or "racial," differences. These so-called racial differences are associated with traits of character, morality, intelligence, personality, and purity that are seen as natural, inherited, and unalterable. Although it is socially easier to distinguish a race when individuals in the so-called racial groups exhibit obvious physical differences, the Japanese-Burakumin relationship demonstrates that a lack of observable physical differences does not prohibit the invention of racial categories.

A conversation Nanda had in Malaysia highlights the ways in which races may be constructed in socially stratified systems and how race and class intersect. Malaysia has three primary cultural groups—Chinese, Indian, and Malay—as well as a small population of Portuguese descended from sixteenth-century traders who politically dominated Malay society for 100 years. A Malay acquaintance, trying to describe the diversity of Malaysia, began by saying "The Indians are the black people," referring to the dark skin color of the Indians in Malaysia, who are mainly from South India. Joking with him a little, Nanda asked, "If the Indians are the black people, who are the white people?" "Oh," the man answered, without missing a beat, "the Portuguese used to be the white people, but now the Chinese are the white people."

To understand this conversation, it is necessary to know Malaysian history. The Portuguese were the first Europeans to dominate the area. They were later defeated by the British, who colonized Malaysia (then called Malaya), taking over the most important political and economic positions. When the British left, after Malaysia's independence, the Chinese moved into many of the commercial and professional positions and now dominate the Malaysian economy. Having taken over the economic position formerly occupied by the Portuguese and then the British, the Chinese are now defined as having taken over their "racial" category as well.

RACIAL STRATIFICATION IN THE UNITED STATES

Gerald Berreman (1988), an anthropologist who writes about social inequality in the United States and India, holds that inequalities based on gender, race, and caste distinctions are invidious: they give offense and arouse ill will. These distinctions arouse ill will because they are perceived as unfairly related to the treatment a person receives; they are unfair because they are attributes an individual is born with

and cannot change. Invidious distinctions assign people to particular groups and stereotype them on the basis of group characteristics, which are understood as overriding their individual qualities or achievements. In a birth-ascribed system of social stratification, "Everyone is sentenced for life to a social cell shared by others of like birth, separated from and ranked relative to all other social cells" (Berreman 1988:486).

The "life sentence" of individuals in a racially based stratification system has social as well as economic dimensions. For example, the following incident was reported by anthropologist Mitchell Duneier. Duneier, who is white, wrote a book, *Slim's Table* (1992), based on his study of working-class African American men in Chicago in the 1990s. Duneier wanted to use a photograph of other books on African Americans that he had referred to in his work. He planned to take his own copies of these books, place them on a shelf at a local used-book store, and have the photographer, Ovie Carter, take pictures of them. Carter, who is African American, thought they should get permission from the bookstore manager first, but the store employees were busy ringing up sales. Duneier simply put his books on the shelf, Carter photographed them, and Duneier then put them back into his bag. At this point the store manager appeared, and Duneier explained what he was doing. The manager was very understanding, although he said he would have preferred that Duneier and Carter had asked his permission. On leaving the store, Carter pointed out to Duneier how differently he and Duneier were disposed to handle the situation, noting that "as a white man [Duneier] could go through life believing [he] could take liberties that black men would never think of taking." Duneier agreed with Carter's perception: "One can only imagine what would have happened if a black man had been seen putting books in a bag."

The difference between Duneier's and Carter's perspective on this experience highlights the construction of "whiteness" as well as other racial identities. Because being white is taken as the norm in the United States, until recently it has not figured prominently in social science analysis of race. The privileges and advantages that go with being white have been hidden and taken for granted (see Allen 1997; Frankenburg 1993; Hartigan 1997; J. Hill 1998). Peggy McIntosh (1999) notes that white people generally assume that ordinary experiences such as shopping, buying or renting a place to live, finding a hairdresser, or using a credit card will not be problematical; African Americans, as in the incident described by Duneier, have to think twice about what might happen.

"RACIAL" MINORITIES AND SCHOOL ACHIEVEMENT

The interaction between race and social stratification in the United States goes beyond such seemingly trivial but revealing incidents. These everyday situations are only the tip of the racial stratification iceberg. Racial stratification impacts on life chances in the very chance of life itself, as statistics document the higher mortality rate for both infants and mothers among African Americans in the United States (Stolberg 1999). Racial stratification also affects social mobility, through the more limited opportunities open to racial minorities and their vulnerability in exploiting these opportunities based on their historic experiences of discrimination (Harrison 1998). One of these opportunities is education, a key factor in mobility in the American class system.

Research indicates that different racial minorities have different rates of academic success and failure. John Ogbu, a Nigerian anthropologist who has studied the differential success and failure rates of racial groups in American schools, explains his findings through the concept of voluntary and involuntary minorities. Voluntary racial minorities, such as the Japanese, are those who came to the United States voluntarily in order to better their lives. Involuntary minorities, mainly African Americans, were unwillingly incorporated into the United States through slavery. Ogbu's studies indicate that students from involuntary minorities view the social hierarchy of the United States as unfair, permanent, and systematically discriminatory. In response, many of these minority students reject school values and the importance of academic success. Voluntary minorities, on

the other hand—even those who, like the Chinese, have been subjected to severe racial discrimination—tend to emphasize the improvement in their current position over that in their homeland. They have higher expectations about getting ahead in American society and see education as directly linked to their future success (Gibson and Ogbu 1991:211–218).

According to Ogbu, many students from involuntary minorities cope with their subordinated social status by creating a secondary cultural system. In this culture, peer group status is more important than academic achievement, and the peer culture stands in opposition to the school. This oppositional identity—which is furthered by public opinion, peer pressure, and the media—includes behavior patterns, such as cutting classes, clowning, or aggressive disruption, that make academic failure likely (see Smedley 1998a:697).

While Ogbu's distinction between immigrants and involuntary minorities is very powerful, it does not tell the whole story (see Gibson 1997). In addition to the oppositional culture of the peer group, hidden agendas of school policy, restricted budgeting, and classroom practice are also significant in consciously and unconsciously replicating the socially stratified systems of which they are a part. Moreover, an "oppositional culture" may be tied to class as well as race. Such a culture is important in the school failure of working-class boys in Great Britain (Willis 1981), where social classes are relatively rigid and a working-class identity has significant parallels to involuntary racial minority status in the United States.

The role of inner-city schools in perpetuating the racial/class/ethnic stratification system of the United States is described in chilling detail by Phillippe Bourgois (1996), whose ethnography is based on four years of living in East Harlem, a Puerto Rican enclave in New York City. Bourgois notes that many of his informants, who engaged in violent behavior as adults, were school dropouts. Nevertheless, the school played an essential part in their socialization. Many of the "crucial survival skills" of these men—fistfighting, verbal jousting, gang rape, and strategic cruelty—were begun in school at the expense of weaker classmates.

Although these skills have high survival value on the streets, they are counterproductive in achieving upward social mobility in the larger society. Bourgois insists that school ethnographies need to take into account the nexus among the classroom, the halls, the institution, and the streets to gain a fuller understanding of the ways in which class, race, and ethnicity intersect in social reproduction of the stratification system (Bourgois 1996:251).

Whatever the origin, ideology, or rules of racially stratified social systems, they have important economic, political, and psychological consequences for individuals of all races. Gerald Berreman and others before him have suggested that those in the higher social positions put intense energy into rationalizations of racial and other invidious distinctions because, at a deep level, they realize they are unfair. This unfairness as experienced by its victims may also explain why such systems tend to be unstable, maintained only at great cost to society.

Invidious social distinctions are kept in place by outward conformity, not by consensus; by sanctions of coercion and force, often naked violence, not by agreement. The oppressed in such situations may resign themselves to their social position and secure whatever secondary gains they can. Even when resentful of their position, they may not openly resist but rather subvert the system in many ways, even as they display outward compliance (Scott 1992). Thus, conflict and disorder are inherent in birth-ascription systems, whether of race, caste, or entrenched class distinctions. Occasionally, when the oppression is experienced as unbearably severe, the risk of outright revolt may seem worth taking. Where the dominant group has overwhelming power and insists on uncompromising enforcement, they may fail to notice the subtlety of subversion, and social order gives the false impression of being based on legitimacy.

RACIAL STRATIFICATION SYSTEMS: A COMPARISON OF THE UNITED STATES AND BRAZIL

In the United States, race is constructed largely on the basis of skin color and presumed ancestry, rather than any objectively measured phys-

ical characteristics. Apart from a few regional variations on "race"—for example, the Anglo-Hispanic distinction in the American Southwest—the North American system of racial stratification primarily divides people into "blacks" and "whites." This constricted dichotomy simply ignores the reality of the skin color spectrum, which includes many shades, as well as the historical and contemporary reality of racial mixing. The constructed nature of the racial dichotomy is clearly seen, for example, in antebellum Southern court decisions, which considered Chinese as "white"—that is, not black—for purposes of school segregation (Lopez 1997), and changes in the racial designation of some American ethnic groups (Sacks 1994).

This construct of a dual racial system based on ancestry was legally encoded in many American states. In some Southern states, people were defined as black if they had one-thirty-second "Negro blood," even if they had light skin. One of these states was Louisiana. In 1982, a woman named Suzie Phipps, who had been classified as black because her great-great-great-great-grandmother was African, went to court to have herself declared white, a categorization that more accurately reflected her skin color. As a result of anthropological testimony that the Louisiana law was nonsense, it was dropped from the books (Dominguez 1986:3). In an ironic comment on the United States system of racial classification, Haitian dictator Papa Doc Duvalier once told an American reporter that 96 percent of Haitians were white. Surprised at his comment, the reporter asked him on what basis he arrived at this percentage. Duvalier explained that Haiti used the same procedure for counting whites—a "drop" of white blood—that Americans used for counting blacks (Hirschfeld 1996).

The particular American binary form of racism that demands that people be classified as either black or white grew out of specific historical conditions. When attempts to enslave the native inhabitants of the Americas failed, Africans were imported to work the sugar and cotton plantations and slavery soon became identified with Africans. After the abolition of slavery as a result of the Civil War, the freedmen's goals of autonomy clashed with the plantation owners' desires for cheap, subservient labor and this led to laws inhibiting the freedmen's mobility (Foner 1985). Ever more intense rationalizations about the inferiority of blacks emerged to justify these laws. For example, the former plantation owners characterized the freedmen's desire to farm independently as "laziness."

The racial stereotypes that had reinforced slavery and segregation were supported by emerging biological and social sciences that legitimized races as hierarchically arranged natural categories, characterized by physical, cultural, and moral differences (Smedly 1993). By the twentieth century, the system of race in the American South was very much like the caste system in India (Berreman 1959). The castelike aspects of this social system included membership based on birth (one was born white or black and remained in that category for life), marriage within the caste (states had laws against black/white intermarriage), cultural distinctiveness of the two groups, traditional occupations each group could enter or was prohibited from entering, and a rank order in which white was superior. Many of the norms of behavior in the Old South revolved around keeping blacks "in their place" and preventing blacks and whites from mixing except under certain conditions. Ultimately, this system was maintained by physical force, which came into the open whenever the status quo was threatened; each attempt by blacks to better their position, even if only by migrating, was met with violence by whites (Dollard 1937; Powdermaker 1967).

Brazil's race relations are often contrasted with those of the United States (Goldstein 1999). These two countries are the largest multiracial societies in the Americas. Both had plantation slave economies, and slavery in both societies lasted until the second half of the nineteenth century. In both societies, the legacy of slavery continues in the form of racial inequality (Andrews 1992). In contrast to the United States, however, Brazil never encoded its racial system into law. Partly for this reason, Brazil has often been heralded as a multiracial society in which race plays little part in social stratifica-

tion (Sheriff 2000:116). Instead, it has been considered a class-stratified society in which "race" is only one of many criteria, including education, wealth, and land ownership, that govern social status and social mobility (Skidmore 1985:20).

Brazilian and American anthropologists in the 1950s, drawn to focus on the important differences between the two societies, substantially contributed to this characterization of Brazil as a racial democracy (Goldstein 1999). One of these differences is the seemingly unrestricted interracial sexual relations and marriages among the different racial communities of Brazil—European, African, and Indian. Unlike the United States, with its many miscegenation laws, Brazil never legally prohibited sexual relations or marriage among different races. Donna Goldstein (1999) points out, however, that this difference may be more apparent than real. In Brazil, as in the United States, "race" is to a large extent color-coded. Although racially "mixed" individuals are considered more sexually attractive than they are in the United States, notes Goldstein, the most "African" looking individuals are considered the least beautiful. Furthermore, interracial sexual relations are entwined with the power relations of gender and class, which are rarely discussed in public. For the lower-class black women Goldstein studied, interracial sex is mainly the subject of a fantasy in which a young black or mixed woman becomes the mistress of an older, rich, white man, as a way of ensuring economic security. That these relationships benefit both parties is hardly testimony to racial egalitarianism.

Another factor contributing to the image of Brazil as a racial democracy is that American anthropologists generally studied smaller Brazilian communities, which are more economically and racially egalitarian than larger cities. In the village in the northeastern Brazilian state of Bahia studied by Conrad Kottack (1992: 67), for example, the general egalitarianism does include race. Although all the villagers in Kottack's study had slave ancestry, there was marked physical variation among them. Most would have been considered "black" in the United States, but in their own perceptions almost half the villagers were considered mulatto, an intermediate category between black and white. Unlike in the United States, where ancestry determines a person's race, in this village brothers and sisters were often classified as belonging to different races. These Brazilian villagers also used many more criteria than North Americans to assign race. Their racial descriptions included not only skin color, but the length and form of the nose, eye color and shape, hair type and color, and shape of the lips. The villagers actually used 10 to 15 different racial terms to describe people, such as mulatto, *mulatto claro* (light mulatto), or *sarara,* meaning a person with reddish skin and light curly hair. People were inconsistent in applying these terms to themselves and to others, and there was wide disagreement among the villagers in placing themselves and others in racially defined categories.

The kinship, friendship, and ritual kinship relationships in the village spanned all the racial categories. There was no connection between race and social stratification, except for a correlation between landownership and lighter skin color. In this fishing village, landownership was not economically or socially significant as it is in other areas of Brazil, but the correlation is suggestive. As Kottack himself notes, in stratified Brazilian communities, light skin does indeed correlate with higher economic status.

Statistical comparisons of the intersection of race and social stratification indicate both similarities and differences between Brazil and the United States. Important measures of socioeconomic inequality are level of education, distribution of occupations, median income, and level of poverty.

In Brazil the educational disparities between whites and nonwhites are much greater than in the United States (Andrews 1992:243). This difference is based partly on the historical traditions of public education in the two countries. In the United States, providing education is a major obligation of the state and local government, but in Brazil, governments have only assumed this responsibility since World War II. Thus the general level of education in Brazil for both whites and nonwhites is much lower than in the United States. Brazil has a high rate of illiteracy and higher education is almost entirely the province of white elites (Berman, in Danaher and Shellenberger 1995:91). In contrast, most Americans, white and black, are literate and most are high school graduates. Although the percentage of the black population enrolling in college lags far behind that of whites, black college enrollment has doubled since 1950.

Statistics on occupation show important changes over the past half century. In 1950 in the United States there were great job disparities between black and white women, with black women concentrated in the service sectors and white women in white-collar employment. By the 1980s racial inequality between black and white women declined by more than a third. Although the gains for black men were less impressive, the disparity in the distribution of jobs among men also decreased, with more black men working in white-collar jobs and the professions and fewer in manual labor. In Brazil, between 1950 and 1980 the expansion of jobs in the white-collar sector was almost entirely occupied by whites. In sum, whereas racial equality in jobs increased in the United States, it decreased in Brazil.

As might be expected from the job distribution data, salary inequalities by race are much higher in Brazil than in the United States (although in both countries gender inequality in earnings is greater than racial inequality, and accounts significantly for the racial inequalities) (Andrews 1992:250). However, although black-white salary disparities in the United States decreased between 1950 and 1980, since the 1980s those disparities have increased. Salary inequities in Brazil have remained stable.

In Brazil, approximately 45 percent of nonwhite families and 25 percent of white families live below the poverty line; in the United States, 30 percent of nonwhite families and 8 percent of white families live in poverty. Thus, the level of poverty is much higher in Brazil, but the difference between whites and nonwhites is about 21 percent in each nation. In the United States, unlike Brazil, the rate of poverty among nonwhites is related to the increasing number of female-headed households.

ANTHROPOLOGISTS TAKE A STAND AGAINST RACISM

Racism continues to be a major American social problem. In today's more tightly integrated global society, "racial" identities continue to be reproduced and are a source of intergroup violence. At the same time, biological anthropologists are increasingly dismissing the concept of "race" as irrelevant for understanding human variation (Marks 1995).

Beginning with the work of Franz Boas (see Chapter 1), American anthropologists have taken strong stands on educating the American public about race and have played leading roles in critiquing both scientific and popular racism. In 1940, cultural anthropologist Ruth Benedict, a student of Boas, published *Race: Science and Politics,* which was aimed at the general public. In 1942, biological anthropologist Ashley Montagu published another pathbreaking and influential book, *Man's Most Dangerous Myth: The Fallacy of Race.* The horrors of the Nazi Holocaust, with its justification by an appeal to "the science of race," put race in the center of the postwar international agenda (di Leonardo 1998:201), and UNESCO commissioned a committee to produce a definitive scientific repudiation of racism. Most of the members of this committee of experts were anthropologists, including Ashley Montagu, Claude Lévi-Strauss, E. Franklin Frazier, and Juan Comas. On the basis of their work, UNESCO published four statements on race.

In 1998, the first issue of the *American Anthropologist,* in commemoration of 100 years of the American Anthropological Association, was a special issue on race (F. Harrison 1998), and the entire year of the *Anthropology Newsletter* for 1999 was on the theme of race. The American Anthropological Association itself has adopted numerous statements and resolutions on race, including the *American Anthropological Association Statement on the Misuse of "Scientific Findings" to Promote Bigotry and Racial and Ethnic Hatred and Discrimination,* adopted in October 1995:

The American Anthropological Association (AAA) is deeply disturbed and saddened by the spread of bigotry and racial and ethnic hatred around the world, including but not limited to claims of racial supremacy or inferiority, calls for ethnic cleansing and purity, fanning xenophobic fears for political purposes and religious-based discrimination. The AAA also is greatly concerned that promoters of such attitudes and practices often cite alleged scientific findings to support their views. *No such findings exist* [emphasis added].

As stated in the AAA resolution on "race" and intelligence approved in 1994, "differentiating species into biologically defined 'races' has proven meaningless and unscientific as a way of explaining variation (whether in intelligence or other traits)."

The AAA Executive Board therefore finds that the worldwide scientific community has a responsibility to speak out against the use of purported scientific findings used to "justify" racial or ethnic superiority, inferiority or stereotyping and used to "justify" racial, ethnic and religious discrimination. To that end, the AAA Board resolves:

WHEREAS all human beings are members of one species, *Homo sapiens,* and

WHEREAS exclusionary practices and racial, ethnic and religious hatred based on differences among groups are spreading around the world, and

WHEREAS promoters of such attitudes and practices often claim their views are supported by scientific findings, and

WHEREAS no such scientific findings exist, and

WHEREAS the worldwide scientific community has a responsibility to promote responsible uses of scientific findings,

THEREFORE, the American Anthropological Association urges the worldwide scientific community to actively counter such claims whenever and wherever the claims are made, and requests [scientific organizations] to adopt and act on similar resolutions. . . .

FURTHER, the Board directs that copies of this statement and resolution be sent to the scientific organizations [listed] and to the media [and] be published in the *Anthropology Newsletter.*

Several factors help explain the differences in the intersection between race and class in the United States and Brazil. One is demography. In Brazil, for example, a larger percentage of nonwhites live in impoverished rural areas in the northeast, and migrants from these areas to the more economically developed south have mainly been white. In the United

States, on the other hand, many nonwhites migrated to the more economically developed cities of the industrial Northeast and benefited educationally and economically by this move. A second factor is government intervention. In the United States, courts and the efforts of the federal government have not only dismantled legal discrimination but implemented affirmative action programs. In Brazil, although racial discrimination is not supported in law, the federal and state governments cling to their view of Brazil as a multiracial society without discrimination and reject any special treatment of nonwhites as "reverse discrimination." Finally, in both societies, an increase in black consciousness has resulted in greater cultural identification with Africa, particularly on the part of university students (J. M. Turner 1985).

Although statistical methods can be used to measure the role of racial discrimination as a cause of racial inequality, these methods are inexact at best. In both Brazil and the United States, nonwhite populations attribute racial inequalities at least partly to racial discrimination (see Goldstein 1999). It is also clear that growth rates for the economy as a whole play an important but somewhat different role in each society. What comparisons of the United States and Brazil conclusively demonstrate is that racial inequalities are possible within different cultural constructions of race. Racial stratification can occur not only in societies such as the United States, where race is dichotomous, but also in Brazil, where race is viewed as a continuum.

The representation of Brazil as a racial democracy, noted by anthropologists and promoted by the Brazilian government, has been contested in the past 15 years by Brazilian and North American scholars (Fontaine 1985; Sheriff 2000). As the statistics outlined above indicate, these more recent analyses suggest that racial discrimination and significant socioeconomic inequalities between whites and nonwhites exist in both countries despite important differences in the perception of race in Brazil and the United States, a generally more accepting attitude toward interracial sexual and marriage relationships in Brazil, and the role

of law in combating racial stratification in the United States.

SUMMARY

1. Social stratification can be viewed as functional for the social order because it motivates people to undertake all the jobs necessary for the society to survive. Social stratification can also cause conflict, however; different social strata, with opposing interests, can clash with one another over goals and resources.

2. The three major dimensions of social stratification are power, wealth, and prestige. Power is the ability to control people and situations. Wealth is the accumulation of economic resources. Prestige is how one is socially evaluated by others. The particular value system of a culture determines how power, wealth, and prestige interact to determine where a person is placed in the stratification system.

3. Two major types of stratification systems are class and caste. In a class system, social position is largely achieved, although it is also partly determined by the class into which a person is born (ascribed). People may move between social classes, which form a continuum from bottom to top. Social classes are characterized by different lifestyles and life chances.

4. In the United States, the emphasis is on upward social mobility—the improvement of one's material standards and life chances, called the American Dream. But downward mobility among the middle class is also part of the American class system. Downward mobility is experienced differently depending on one's occupation and values.

5. In a caste system, social position is largely ascribed (based on birth). Boundaries between castes are sharply defined, and marriage is within the caste. The caste system in India is the most complex; it is based on Hindu ideas of ritual purity and pollution. The boundaries of caste in India are maintained by prohibitions on many kinds of social interactions, such as sharing food, as well as by cultural differences.

6. The positions of subcastes within the larger caste hierarchy, as well as the importance of the caste system itself, have changed in India with independence. The Indian constitution incorporates protection of individual rights and affirmative

action for lower castes, particularly former untouchables. Other factors for change include the widening of economic and occupational opportunities, particularly in urban India.

7. Racial categories are culturally constructed, designating groups of people who are perceived as sharing similar physical and moral traits transmitted by heredity. Such categories, though scientifically invalid, play an important role in many societies, where they are used by elites to justify unequal distribution of economic and social resources.

8. The biracial system of the United States (which earlier had many aspects of a caste system) and the multiracial system of Brazil are alternative systems of constructing race. In both systems, however, nonwhite status is related to a lower position in the socioeconomic hierarchy.

KEY TERMS

achieved status
ascribed status
caste system
class system
closed system
conflict theory
functionalism

life chances
open system
power
prestige
social mobility
wealth

SUGGESTED READINGS

Danaher, Kevin, and Michael Shellenberger (Eds.). 1995. *Fighting for the Soul of Brazil*. New York: Monthly Review Press. This scholarly yet readable anthology is meant for the nonspecialist. It contains articles by anthropologists and others describing how participation in the global economy has intensified the inequalities of the Brazilian stratification system.

Desjarlais, Robert. 1997. *Shelter Blues: Sanity and Selfhood among the Homeless*. Philadelphia: University of Pennsylvania Press. This innovative, ethnographically based portrait of the personal worlds of 40 homeless men and women living in Boston's Station Street shelter examines the links among culture, illness, personhood, and politics on the margins of contemporary American society.

Lemann, Nicholas. 1999. *The Big Test: The Secret History of the American Meritocracy*. Gordonsville, VA: Farrar, Straus and Giroux. This engrossing history of the Scholastic Aptitude Test (SAT) and its influence in American educational achievement and social policy illuminates the growth of the educational testing culture and its relationship to the perceptions and successes of different racial and ethnic groups in the United States.

Newman, Katherine. 1999. *No Shame in My Game: The Working Poor in the Inner City.* Boston: Harvard University Press. This book focuses on the working poor in urban ghettos, using life stories. It is particularly insightful in analyzing the fast-food service sector of the inner-city job market. Although this sector offers dead-end, low-skilled jobs, it attracts upwardly mobile young people with a strong work ethic that translates into school achievement.

Reed, Adolph, Jr. 2000. *Class Notes: Posing as Politics and Other Thoughts on the American Scene.* New York: New Press. This provocative and insightful analysis of the intersection of race, class, and ethnicity in the United States includes a critical perspective on the effects of the anthropological treatment of the underclass.

Sanjek, Roger. 2000. *The Future of Us All: Race and Neighborhood Politics in New York City.* Ithaca, NY: Cornell University Press. This important, ethnographically based social history of New York City politics and local community relations focuses on one of the most multiethnic and multilingual neighborhoods in the United States, and perhaps the world. Among the topics analyzed are race, class, gender, ritual and politics, and particularly, political alliances that cross ethnic and racial borders.

Stewart, Kathleen. 1996. *A Space on the Side of the Road: Cultural Poetics in an "Other" America.* Princeton, NJ: Princeton University Press. Using narrative language and photographs, this experimental ethnography concerns the "other" America: the one that survives in communities among the ruins of the West Virginia coal camps, largely left behind by "progress."

INTERNET RESOURCES

The following Internet resources appear in this chapter. Please log on to the Wadsworth anthropology website: **http://anthropology.wadsworth. com**. Click on the Nanda/Warms *Cultural Anthropology* page. Then select the Student Resources section, where you will find a complete presentation of these links and more.

- Link to an online Virtual Tour of key sites on social stratification, page 287
- A photo essay on the symbols and activities associated with social stratification across cultures, page 289
- A video link: Homelessness in a large American city, page 291
- Access the Study Guide to InfoTrac College Edition for Anthropology Students

THE CREATION OF NATIONAL AND ETHNIC IDENTITIES REQUIRES CREATING DISTINCTIONS BETWEEN GROUPS. MANY OF THESE DISTINCTIONS ARE PRESENTED AS ROOTED IN ANCIENT TRADITIONS, BUT MAY ACTUALLY BE OF MUCH MORE RECENT VINTAGE.

© Katsuyoshi Tanaka/Woodfin Camp & Associates

CHAPTER FOURTEEN

ETHNICITY

What are some of the meanings of ethnicity, and how are these used in the world today?

What is the nation-state, and how is it related to ethnicity?

What are some sources of contemporary ethnic conflicts?

Who are indigenous peoples, and what are their relationships with nation-states?

How have anthropologists applied their knowledge on behalf of indigenous peoples?

What is the relationship between ethnicity and immigration in the United States?

Ethnicity is a familiar term to most of us. It often appears in the media as a source of conflict and violence—between the Irish and the English in Northern Ireland, between the Hutu and the Tutsi in Central Africa, between Hindus and Muslims in India, between Tamils and Sinhalese in Sri Lanka, between French- and English-speakers in Canada, between Bosnians and Serbs, and Croatians and Albanians, in the former nation of Yugoslavia. In the United States, ethnicity also makes the news, though more often as ethnic politics and ethnic identity than as outbreaks of ethnic violence.

Ethnicity refers to *perceived* differences in culture, national origin, and historical experience by which groups of people are distinguished from others in the same social environment. **Ethnic identity** is the sense of self an individual acquires through identification with an ethnic group or social category characterized by ethnicity. In the contemporary world, ethnic identity is a highly significant basis for self-identity, although it also intersects with other sources of identity such as age, gender, nation, "race," and social class. **Ethnic groups** are categories of people who see themselves as sharing an ethnic identity that differentiates them from other groups or from the larger society as a whole. **Ethnic boundaries** are the perceived

cultural attributes by which ethnic groups distinguish themselves from others.

The perception that one belongs to a particular ethnic group, and the emergence of particular ethnic groups and identities, may originate within the group or be imposed from outside by the larger society. Whatever its origin, however, in the course of time, ethnicity takes on a reality that has cultural meaning and important social consequences.

PERSPECTIVES ON ETHNICITY
AN ESSENTIALIST PERSPECTIVE

Social scientists generally view ethnicity as an ascribed category. Members of ethnic groups, and some social scientists as well, tend to view

ethnicity Perceived differences in culture, national origin, and historical experience by which groups of people are distinguished from others in the same social environment.

ethnic identity The sense of self one experiences as a member of an ethnic group.

ethnic groups Categories of people who see themselves as sharing an ethnic identity that differentiates them from other groups or from the larger society as a whole.

ethnic boundaries The perceived cultural attributes by which ethnic groups distinguish themselves from others.

ethnicity as resting on a "bedrock" of cultural difference from others (Meier and Ribera 1993). Anthropologist Clifford Geertz, for example, defines ethnicity as the "primordial" ties that stem from "common blood, religion, language, attachment to a place, or customs" (1973b:277). For Geertz and others, these ethnic ties, which are passed down from generation to generation, are permanent, natural, and even spiritual. Ethnicity is viewed as inherent in human social life, based on the desire of individuals to belong to a group.

From this perspective, ethnicity appears as an independent force that explains why people act collectively in certain ways—whether voting as a political bloc, protecting economic interests, going to war with other ethnic groups, or rebelling against national governments. Ethnicity is viewed as "a clinging to old loyalties," or to the past, and as underlying a group's resistance to various aspects of modern life. But though it is undeniably true that cultural differences have been—and are—an important basis for group identity in all complex societies (De Vos 1995), it is equally true that ethnicity and ethnic groups are not an inescapable part of human social life. Rather, they are constructed and intensify under specific historical, demographic, and economic conditions.

A CONSTRUCTIONIST PERSPECTIVE

Contemporary anthropology, rather than viewing ethnicity as an explanation of behavior, seeks to explain ethnicity itself: how it emerges, persists, and changes within different social, cultural, and historical contexts. This constructionist view emphasizes that although ethnicity is rooted in preexisting communal solidarities, cultural differences, and historical memories, its specific forms emerge out of specific responses to changing realities, both within the group and in the larger society of which it is a part (di Leonardo 1998). Ethnic traditions and boundaries are viewed not as fossilized "age-old" patterns, but as having been repeatedly reinterpreted and renegotiated over time. Rather than a survival of the past, ethnic identity brings the past into the present, and the present makes the past meaningful in specific ways. From a

constructionist perspective, ethnicity rests less on a bedrock of cultural identity than it does on the shifting sands of history.

Anthropologist Frederik Barth, in his classic study *Ethnic Groups and Boundaries: The Social Organization of Culture Difference* (1969/1998), opened the way for a constructionist view of ethnicity. While Barth agreed that ethnicity has an important cultural content, he demonstrated that there is no simple one-to-one relationship between ethnic units and objectively defined cultural differences. He emphasized that ethnic group development is based not on geographical and social isolation of groups, but on the very process of social interaction, in which different ethnic groups come to occupy different "niches." Barth's ethnography of Pakistan demonstrated that ethnic boundaries persist *despite* frequent and significant interaction among ethnic groups and vitally important social relations across these ethnic boundaries. According to Barth, ethnicity is a socially constructed category that groups perpetuate to differentiate themselves from other, similar groups, in an ongoing process of identity formation. It is "the ethnic boundary that defines the group, not the cultural stuff that it encloses" (1969/1998:15). Ethnicity thus becomes an aspect of relationships with other groups in a society. It is these relationships—which may be competitive, cooperative, conflictual, or a combination of these—that are the essential components of the process of ethnic group formation and definition.

Barth's approach led anthropologists to ask new questions about the circumstances that elicit or mobilize ethnicity as a vehicle for association, collective action, and personal identity. The emphasis now is on how ethnic groups emerge, change, and disappear in response to changing conditions in the economic and social environment, especially in the context of political or economic inequality or competition between groups for resources. As one ethnic constructionist puts it, "Ethnicity is a mask for confrontation" (Vincent 1974:377).

One confrontational situation in which ethnicity emerges or intensifies as a result of external pressures is colonialism. In Africa and native North America, for example, under the impact of European contact, some indigenous groups disappeared. Others regrouped to form new "tribes" (ethnic groups) that competed for the economic rewards created by new economic and political situations (Wolf 1982; Roosens 1995). In India under British rule, to take another example, ethnic conflict intensified as the British disparaged some cultural traditions and rewarded others, largely those that benefited British rule (Luhrmann 1996). Finding favor with the British became an important asset in the competition for important resources now under foreign control. Groups with military traditions, who joined the Indian (British) army, and Anglo-Indians (those of mixed British-Indian parentage) emerged as ethnic groups with special privileges under the British raj.

In modern Africa, ethnicity in the form of "tribalism" frequently persists because of both colonial and contemporary government policies. Colonial governments gave tribal (ethnic) identity institutional and political support. In urban Africa, these identities persisted because of the insecurity of urban employment and the competition for urban jobs. The uneven distribution of government patronage became dependent on ethnic affiliation (Uchendu 1995).

CONSTRUCTED ETHNICITY IN THE SUDAN

The construction of ethnicity in contemporary societies, particularly as a response to changing material conditions of life, is illustrated by West Africans in the Sudan (J. O'Brien 1986). In 1925, the British, who then occupied the Sudan, wanted to expand cotton production there. To ensure sufficient labor for the peak agricultural season, they encouraged local peasants and pastoralists to become part of a seasonally migrant wage labor force. When this local labor force proved insufficient, the British encouraged immigration of poor peasants from West Africa into the Sudan. These peasants, mainly Muslim Hausa-speakers, were given incentives to settle in the Sudan and served as a stable, year-round, cheap labor force. Other groups of West Africans were encouraged to settle in other areas of the Sudan, where they were

given their own land to farm but could also be drawn upon as seasonal wage laborers for the cotton scheme. There was considerable cultural diversity among these West Africans. Even the Muslim Hausa-speaking group included many distinct, named ethnic identities based on different second languages and different customs.

Initially, the local Sudanese people resented the West Africans, who were used by the British to discipline the local labor force. Many of the native Sudanese, who had only recently become cultivators, held agricultural work in low esteem, avoided it when possible, and worked at it only indifferently when necessary. The West African immigrants, on the other hand, had a long history of disciplined agricultural work under exploitive conditions and were more productive.

Within a short time, the West African immigrants came to be known in Sudan as Fulani (many had come from the West African Fulani sultanates), or "Fellata." This term, applied indiscriminately to all of the immigrants from West Africa, took on negative connotations, stereotyping the West Africans as slavish. This became, for the local people, the dominant element of Fulani "ethnicity." The West African immigrants responded to this hostile treatment and confinement to the lowest rungs of the social ladder by a process of cultural realignment. On the one hand, they adopted some of the customs—dress and house type, for example— of the local people. On the other hand, they elaborated some key cultural symbols to which they attached a positive meaning to differentiate themselves from the Arabs. In particular, the immigrants emphasized their more fundamentalist Islamic practices, such as abstaining from alcohol and secluding their women—for example, forbidding them to work in the fields as local Sudanese women did. They also articulated an ethic of hard work and moderate consumption, which gave dignity to their labor.

Gradually, the term *Takari* replaced the term *Fellata*. Since Takari was a positive ethnic label, providing social benefits, it was widely accepted by West Africans. As a result, subgroup differences among them—for example, between Hausa and non-Hausa—tended to be submerged. Today these people of diverse origins consider themselves all to be Takari. As this case illustrates, the emergence of new ethnic identities—and more specifically, the emergence of ethnic hierarchies—must be seen in the context of a particular system of social stratification.

ETHNICITY AND THE NATION-STATE

A constructionist view of ethnicity emphasizes active participation by social groups (whether immigrants, indigenous peoples, or cultural minorities) in defining their group identities and acting collectively. In constructing its ethnicity, a group seeks to determine the terms, modes of adaptation, and outcomes of its accommodation to others. Ethnicity viewed in this way emphasizes a process of negotiation between an ethnic group and the dominant culture, and also among the different ethnic groups in a society.

The most important contemporary context for the emergence, change, and disappearance of ethnicity is the **nation-state.** Nation-states are governments and territories that are identified with culturally homogenous populations and national histories. A nation is popularly felt by its members to be a natural entity, based on bonds of common descent, language, culture, history, and territory. However, all modern nation-states are composed of many ethnic (and other) groups. Benedict Anderson (1991) notes that such states are "imagined communities," because it takes an act of imagination to weld the many disparate groups that actually make up the state into a coherent community. Anthropologists are interested in the historical circumstances under which nation-states evolve, the processes by which they are constructed and maintained, and the circumstances under which they are challenged and destabilized (Stolcke 1995).

The state is a territorial unit whose sovereignty is attached to specific spaces. One way

nation-state A sovereign, geographically based state that identifies itself as having a distinctive national culture and historical experience.

NATION-STATES INTENSIFY NATIONAL IDENTITIES BY PRESENTING HISTORY IN EMOTIONALLY INTENSE WAYS, SUCH AS THIS SCULPTURE OF THE CAPTURE OF IWO JIMA IN WORLD WAR II BY UNITED STATES MARINES.

states construct national identities is to attach new meanings to space, drawing boundaries between spatially defined insiders and outsiders (Handler 1988). Regardless of their differences, the people who live within these boundaries are viewed as having an essential natural identity, based on a common language and shared customs and culture. People outside the national boundary are seen as essentially different, having their own national identities. The importance of the spatial dimension of the nation-state is continuously impressed on us by colorful world maps, which visually represent the world of nations as a discrete spatial partitioning of territory (Alonso 1994:382).

Nation-states are constructed by attaching people to time as well as to space. A common interpretation of the past is essential in creating national identities. Because interpretations of the past are so important in defining the present, the creation of national histories is marked by struggles over which version of history will prevail (J. Friedman 1992). "Tradition," "the past," "history," or "social memory" are all actively invented and reinvented to accord with contemporary national interests and reproduced through rituals, symbols, and ceremonies (Hobsbawm and Ranger 1983). Coronations, inaugurations, a daily pledging of allegiance to the flag, or the singing of national anthems—ceremonies linking the nation's dead to its living, and thus the past to the present—are all essential in maintaining the nation-state.

The importance of the nation-state in conferring identity, at least in the West, is often overlooked because national identities have been so important in the recent historical past. But many European national identities—and more so, contemporary postcolonial identities—have struggled painfully to evolve and even today are problematic for many nations. National identity for Canadians, for example, has always been, and continues to be, insecure and fragmented (Handler 1988). Because of the dual influence of the English and the French on Canada, the current British connection with Canada, the powerful English-speaking United States on its southern border, and the weight of regionalism in a huge territory with a small and geographically scattered population, the search for Canadian national identity is ongoing. In contemporary societies, however, it is subnational identities, such as ethnicity, that is taking center stage.

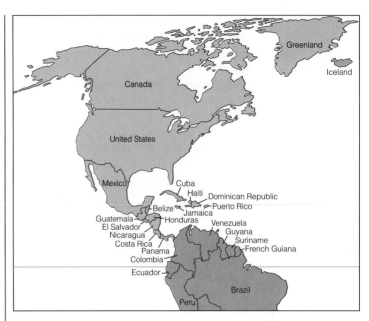

WORLD MAPS REINFORCE THE IMPORTANCE OF THE NATION-STATE AS A TERRITORIAL UNIT.

HOW THE NATION-STATE SHAPES ETHNICITY

In a century in which conflicts are increasingly understood in ethnic terms, it is particularly important to ask questions about the relationship between ethnicity and the state: how and why the state fosters some ethnic groups and identities while disparaging and marginalizing others, exploits cultural diversity for various purposes, and officially ignores the relevance of any cultural unit other than the nation (Foster 1991).

The invention and implementation of a national identity, with its associated rites and symbols, are carried out by nationalist elites, intellectuals, politicians, and institutions. To be successful, a national identity must appear to be a real, unquestionable, timeless, and intrinsic element of personal identity (Foster 1991: 238); the "imagined" or "invented" quality of national unity must be repressed.

The state's power in defining and perpetuating a national identity, and the tolerable limits of ethnicity within it, is substantial. For example, the state generally controls education and textbooks, important means of communicating national histories, which elevate some groups and ignore others. In the United States, as in other nations, textbook selection for public schools is highly political. Different groups battle over which version of American history should be presented to schoolchildren, which historic figures emphasized and which left out. The state, through its records and laws, access to the media, control of education, and other resources, attempts to create a national culture and identity that become the only authorized representation of society.

In the contest between ethnic groups and the state as to which version of culture will dominate, an important source of state power is its control of law (Norgren and Nanda 1996). Conversely, law and courts can also be sites of ethnic resistance (Lazarus-Black and Hirsch 1994). The law may allow ethnic groups to express their cultural differences or repress them, forbidding such expression. It may legitimate ethnicity but, at the same time, marginalize ethnic groups by attempting to construct borders between them and the cultural mainstream. The term *mainstream* conveys an acceptability at the national level denied to subcultures—even though the mainstream, like the subcultures, is a cultural artifact, and its borders are constantly changing.

The political debate in the United States over "family values" provides an illustration of the ways in which the state shapes ethnic cultures through law. The attempt to specify a single cultural form of the family—namely, a unit that is heterosexual, monogamous, and nuclear—is strongly supported by law. State legislation, for example, prohibits homosexuals from marrying and criminalizes Mormon polygyny; zoning laws permit only parents and children to occupy "single-family" residences (Norgren and Nanda 1988:209).

The state can also influence the development of ethnicities by incorporating, for its own purposes, elements of subcultures into the national culture. The Jamaican government, for example, has incorporated some elements of Rastafarian culture, such as Reggae music, while ignoring other aspects such as the Rastafarian rejection of cooperation with the capitalist state (W. Lewis 1993). In Central and South America, Indian ethnicity, if not totally repressed, is defined in ways that serve state purposes. Indians may be identified with a fossilized past as a folkloric irrelevance, a tourist commodity, or a backward culture standing in the way of national development (Alonso 1994:398). Only a few nations incorporate elements of Indian culture in their constructions of national identity. The Mexican government, for example, commonly uses symbols of the Aztec and Maya past. However, identifying "Indianness" with the past actually marginalizes contemporary Indian communities. It masks the important class conflicts that underlie the contemporary resistance of Indian cultures to dominance by the state, conflicts most recently expressed in

the Zapatista rebellion (Maybury-Lewis 1997: 15–21). And even revolutionary Central American governments, such as the Sandanistas in Nicaragua, initially viewed the Miskitu Indians in their country as culturally backward and politically conservative. For the Sandanistas, Miskitu demands for cultural autonomy were an impermissible obstacle to the construction of a new, homogenous, Nicaraguan national identity (C. Hale 1994).

THE NATION-STATE AND ETHNIC CONFLICT

Ethnic conflict today is clearly tied to the rise, maintenance, and collapse of the nation-state (Stolcke 1995). The explanation of ethnic conflicts as "natural" eruptions of "age-old ethnic hatreds" has the virtue of simplicity, but is frequently inaccurate. Many contemporary ethnic conflicts are rooted, at least in part, in relatively recent circumstances, involving peoples whose cultures are only marginally different from each other and who lived together amicably in the past.

History shows that it is only when ethnicity in its local or national form becomes a paramount identity that ethnic violence is likely to occur. Ambitious politicians often promote ethnic identity, building constituencies from groups that hope to gain increased access to economic and political power. Such individuals mobilize a rhetoric of historical abuses and inequities, arousing fears of victimization among group members.

ETHNIC VIOLENCE IN YUGOSLAVIA

Factors such as those described above operated in the ethnic violence resulting from the breakup of Yugoslavia. Yugoslavia became a nation-state following World War II. Earlier, its territory was part of the Ottoman Empire ruled by Muslim Turks. The conflict between the Turks and Christian Europeans became a central force generating Serb nationalism in the nineteenth and twentieth centuries. But current ethnic conflict was not "caused" by the cultural distinctions and hostilities of the past.

Rather a selectively remembered past of cultural differences has been mobilized in contemporary struggles over economic and political power (Maybury-Lewis 1997; Ramet 1996). Economic pressures beginning in the 1980s were more a cause of war among Serbs, Croatians, and Bosnians than long-standing ethnic conflict (Gilliland 1995).

In 1981, after the death of Yugoslav leader Tito, the new political leadership introduced an economic austerity program. In an attempt to increase the amount of hard currency, they tried to halt imports and increase exports. Shortages of consumer goods resulted, undermining faith in the government. Social relationships became more restricted as people depended even more than usual on networks of family and friends. Anxiety and friction increased in everyday life. Much of the resulting frustration was directed at the national government, which was perceived as corrupt and wasteful.

In this atmosphere of political and economic instability, long-standing clashes over points of cultural difference among the three ethnic groups soon became the metaphor for other conflicts. The differences were seized upon by numerous politicians, among them the Croat nationalist leader Franjo Tudjman. Tudjman gained supporters by urging Croats to claim their national rights against Serbs, Muslims, and others. As part of this process, Tudjman tried to rehabilitate the Ustashe government, which during World War II had helped massacre Jews, Communists, Serbs, and Gypsies. During the war, bitter civil wars had been fought between Serb partisans and Croatian fascists. These civil wars are an important source of the current ethnic conflicts. Although Tudjman was imprisoned several times in the 1980s for his radical nationalist views, in 1990, after the breakup of the Yugoslav Communist Party, he led his own nationalist party to victory in Croatian elections. Tudjman's declaration of an independent state in Croatia resulted in a bloody war with Serbia that ended with Croatian independence.

As the ethnic conflicts in the former Yugoslavia heated up, old attributes of similarity were transformed into markers of difference.

RECENT ETHNIC VIOLENCE IN THE FORMER YUGOSLAVIA BEGAN AS A RESULT OF THE POLITICAL EXPLOITATION OF RELATIVELY SMALL CULTURAL DIFFERENCES BETWEEN CROATS AND SERBS.

Croats and Serbs, for example, are both Christian but belong to different sects: the Croats are Catholic and the Serbs Eastern Orthodox. They speak the same language but use different writing systems. Anthropologist Mary Gilliland notes that the original rhetoric of the war was not ethnic, but it became so as a tactic of political manipulation. Croatians, for example, now call their language Croatian rather than Serbo-Croatian, as it was formerly called (Gilliland 1995:202). The representation of the Serb-Croat hostilities as an ethnic conflict was promoted by the Yugoslavian media. The media began to identify the different parties by ethnic labels that dated back to World War II, when the Croats aided the Germans while the Serbs formed the backbone of anti-Nazi resistance.

Gilliland's work demonstrates that contemporary economic and political pressures, as well as long-standing ethnic conflicts, must be considered in analyzing ethnic identity and violence in the contemporary world. In many cases, economic and political considerations growing out of World War II created new states, both in Europe and in former colonies, that included many different ethnic groups, thus setting the stage for contemporary ethnic conflict.

REFUGEES AND POLITICAL ASYLUM: A GLOBAL PROBLEM

One of the by-products of the many wars and racial, religious, ethnic, and political conflicts of the twentieth century has been millions of refugees worldwide. Refugees are people who have been uprooted from their native lands and forced to cross national boundaries into countries that do not necessarily want them or who cannot provide for them. World War I and World War II created millions of refugees; ultimately many of them were resettled, either in their own or in other countries, with the help of the United Nations Relief and Rehabilitation Administration. Since that time, revolutions, wars of national liberation, boundary changes, the end of colonialism, and other situations have kept the refugee problem alive. At the turn of the twenty-first century, there were approximately 16 million refugees worldwide.

The wealthier industrialized nations have been traditional havens for refugees. The United States continues to be a beacon for millions. A recent film, *Well-*

Founded Fear, made by anthropological filmmakers Michael Camerini and Shari Robertson, highlights the process by which refugees are granted political asylum in the United States. In order to be granted political asylum, a refugee must prove a "well-founded fear of persecution based on race, religion, nationality, membership in a particular social group, or political opinion." Any foreigner who finds a way into the United States may apply for refugee protection in the form of political asylum.

This widely acclaimed film, whose aim is to "get Americans to think about the world," is unique in penetrating, with the consent of officers and applicants, the normally closed and confidential hearings of the Immigration and Naturalization Service (INS), whose officers make the decisions to approve or deny applications for political asylum. In 1998, these officers heard 41,000 asylum cases and approved 13,000 applications. Among those documented in the film were applicants claiming asylum from the one-child pol-

icy in China, the rule that women must be veiled in Algeria, the suppression of political dissent in Rumania and Nigeria, and the persecution of Jews in the former Soviet Union.

The willingness of countries to accept refugees appears to be declining, exacerbated by economic downturns. In 1987, for example, Switzerland outlawed asylum, and since the mid-1980s, anti-immigrant political parties in European countries such as Norway, France, and Germany have made significant electoral gains. In 1999, the United States also tightened its acceptance of refugees, reducing the number of people who can apply for asylum, jailing people who arrive at United States borders applying for asylum, and limiting their rights of appeal. Hearing the stories of well-founded fear in Camerini and Robertson's film is a moving reminder of the ways in which the United States is part of a global community.

NATION-STATES AND INDIGENOUS PEOPLES

www Another important source of conflict within nation-states involves their relations with indigenous peoples. **Indigenous peoples,** sometimes referred to as members of the Fourth World, are those small-scale societies designated as bands, tribes, and

indigenous peoples Small-scale, relatively self-sufficient societies distinguished by their cultures and languages and particularly by their historic continuity on their land.

chiefdoms. These societies are typically characterized by close identification with their land, relative social egalitarianism, community-level resource management, and (previously) high levels of self-sufficiency. According to the 1993 UN Declaration of the Rights of Indigenous Peoples, indigenous communities have an historical continuity with the societies that developed on their territories prior to European contact, invasion, and colonialism; they consider themselves distinct from other sectors of society now living in those territories; they are nondominant sectors of the larger societies of which they are a part (nation-states); and they

UNIQUE HANDWOVEN CLOTHING IS AN IMPORTANT ETHNIC BOUNDARY MARKER AMONG INDIANS IN GUATEMALA. IT DISTINGUISHES ONE ETHNIC COMMUNITY FROM ANOTHER, AND INDIANS OF MAYAN HERITAGE FROM THE DOMINANT SPANISH CULTURE OF THE NATION-STATE. WHILE NATIONS SUCH AS GUATEMALA ARE INTERESTED IN CAPITALIZING ON INDIAN ETHNICITY FOR TOURIST DOLLARS, THEY ALSO ATTEMPT TO COERCE INDIAN ASSIMILATION THROUGH FORCE.

are determined to preserve and transmit their lands and culture to future generations in order to continue their existence as a people (R. Lee 2000).

Indigenous peoples today are in a struggle for autonomy and survival in a world dominated by nation-states and a global capitalist economy (Bodley 1999). The process of incorporation of indigenous peoples within larger states began as early as 1450, in the preindustrial stage of capitalist expansion, when European powers began their imperial and colonial projects. With European invasion and conquest, many indigenous societies completely disappeared as a result of epidemics, frontier violence, and military conquest; others survived as remnants in marginal geographic areas (see Chapter 17). Despite the intended and unintended destruction of indigenous peoples, as late as 1800, approximately 50 percent of the

world's territory and 20 percent of the global population were still controlled by relatively autonomous and self-sufficient small-scale indigenous societies (Bodley 2000:398). The destruction of indigenous peoples intensified rapidly by the mid-nineteenth century as new frontiers were opened up in nations such as the United States, Australia, and Brazil. After World War II, when many indigenous peoples were incorporated into new postcolonial states such as Indonesia, Malaysia, and India, few independent, self-sufficient indigenous societies remained (Maybury-Lewis 1997).

The incorporation of indigenous peoples into modern nation-states involved at least partial destruction of their political and economic autonomy. Although these societies were by no means a pushover for expanding state powers, ultimately the military and economic power of nation-states dominated. Because indigenous peoples must maintain control over their land base and subsistence resources in order to remain self-sufficient and politically autonomous, their political defeat was usually accompanied by their economic marginalization. The larger societies in which they were now embedded appropriated—and continue to appropriate—their land, whether through legislation or by enabling others to utilize it in more "productive" ways. These "others" may be the state, or they may be other, nonindigenous, and often politically disempowered groups, such as the marginal peasants who have expanded into the borderlands of the Amazon in Brazil (Dombrowski 2000; Moran 1988:160). Without their land base, indigenous peoples were pushed into participation in the global market economy, which indeed was the express motivation of many European colonial projects.

Participation by indigenous peoples in larger economies was—and is—furthered by the "pull" of their desire for Western goods. However, whenever indigenous people were reluctant to acquiesce to colonial agendas, including participation in capitalist consumer-oriented economies, colonialism always fell back on threatened or actual coercion through military conquest.

THE IMPOSITION OF WESTERN LAW

The colonial agenda was also imposed on indigenous peoples through Western law. European colonial powers defined acceptable behavior in terms of their own ideologies and enforced that behavior through the establishment of written penal codes, constitutions, and Western-style courts, with severe sanctions for nonconformity (Merry 1991, 2000). A wide array of indigenous cultural practices—polygamy, sati (widow immolation in India), witchcraft accusations, use of peyote and marijuana in religious contexts, potlatching, drumming, dancing, warfare, collective land tenure, headhunting, slash and burn horticulture, transvestism, and many others—were outlawed in the name of social reform and the European civilizing mission (Merry 1991). Many colonial laws involved restraints on sexuality. Sexual relations between Europeans and native women,

which dissolved the line between the colonial power and the subordinate "natives," were often explicitly prohibited. Sexual practices of indigenous peoples were often criminalized as uncivilized and un-Christian (W. Roscoe 1995).

Western law was also a key factor in effecting the transfer of land from indigenous peoples to Europeans and Americans. Most land in non-Western, small-scale societies was held collectively and could not be sold even when individuals or kinship groups had exclusive use rights to the land. Under European and American colonialism, indigenous collective rights to the land and norms of land tenure were undermined, and individual ownership of land was legally established. This permitted land to be sold and resulted in the transfer of much land to Europeans (Parker 1989).

European courts in colonized areas became alternative forums for resolving disputes, traditionally handled in other ways. Some colonized areas became characterized by legal pluralism, or the operation of several different levels of law (Sheleff 2000). One level of law, like the moots of West Africa (described in Chapter 12), operated at the village level and handled specific kinds of domestic conflicts; state-run courts were established to handle other kinds of conflicts and deviance. In New Guinea, for example, killings in response to witchcraft accusations were viewed as murder by British and Australian colonial authorities and were handled in colonial courts (Ottley and Zorn 1983). Local New Guinean mechanisms of conflict resolution, such as compensation, were not considered acceptable punishment. Instead, European courts imposed jail sentences, disrupting the social order in ways that local conflict resolution mechanisms did not.

After World War II, the establishment of the United Nations provided an international framework within which the concept of human rights was steadily expanded to include indigenous peoples as cultural groups and to legitimize their struggle for self-determination. Since the United Nations policy worked within the framework of the nation-state, however, it did little to support indigenous rights in any substantial way. National policies were frequently based on the expectation that indigenous peo-

SAAMI REINDEER HERDERS HAVE BECOME CAUGHT UP IN THE GLOBAL ECONOMY BY THE NEED TO EARN CASH TO BUY FOOD, CLOTHING, HOUSEHOLD APPLIANCES, AND PARTICULARLY SNOWMOBILES AND THE GAS TO RUN THEM. WITHOUT SNOWMOBILES, SAAMI HERDERS CANNOT COMPETE IN HERDING LARGE NUMBERS OF ANIMALS.

ples would eventually disappear, as they assimilated into national cultures and participated in national and global economic "development" programs. This was also the presumption of international financial organizations, such as the World Bank and the International Monetary Fund, whose lending practices supported economic "development" programs that adversely affected the subsistence economies of indigenous peoples (Bodley 2000:378).

Saami Reindeer Herders and the Nation-State

The struggle of indigenous peoples to retain traditional livelihoods and cultures in the face of opposition by modern nation-states is illustrated by the reindeer-herding Saami of Scandinavia. More than 100,000 Saami live in Norway, Sweden, Finland, and parts of Russia. The Saami are an indigenous people who have oc-

cupied this area for more than 2000 years, for most of that time as hunters of wild reindeer. In the past 400 years, the Saami have become reindeer herders, primarily using reindeer dairy products rather than the meat; reindeer are slaughtered only reluctantly, even for ritual occasions. Saami livelihood depends on access to the lichen-rich subarctic tundra areas of northern Norway and Sweden, which provide winter pasture for their reindeer (Stephens 1987).

Many Saami today do not herd reindeer, but make their living by fishing, small-scale agriculture, crafts, logging, roadbuilding, and some government welfare payments. Even for the Saami who do not herd reindeer, reindeer herding has important historical and symbolic meanings.

About 60,000 Saami live in Norway. The Norwegian government considers the Saami a culturally distinct ethnic group and is officially committed to furthering the Saami reindeer-herding way of life. At the same time, however, Norway is committed to national economic development and environmental conservation, both of which, the government says, are impeded by unregulated Saami reindeer herding (Paine 1994).

In attempting to achieve its goals as a progressive, modern, egalitarian, multicultural nation, Norway considers it essential to regulate Saami reindeer herding and to change Saami cultural values and practices. This has been the source of conflict between the Saami and the government.

The essence of the Saami reindeer-herding culture is the close connection between herding families and their reindeer herds. Reindeer are individually owned and inherited, by men, women, and children, but are herded collectively by a few families who make up a work unit. Reindeer herding is physically exacting and demands extensive knowledge of the animals' terrain. Herders need to adjust their herd management to changing seasonal weather patterns and other ecological factors, all of which involve risk. While the Saami value reindeer as a market commodity, reindeer also have intrinsic cultural value, both as a form of wealth and as a source of Saami cultural distinctiveness.

The Norwegian government regards many traditional Saami herd management practices as "unproductive," "irrational," and detrimental to the environment. The government's objectives, encoded since 1978 in the Reindeer Management Act, are to reduce the overall number of Saami reindeer, to equalize the number of reindeer in each family's herd, and to rationalize reindeer marketing practices. The government has taken a number of steps to achieve these objectives. One is the official restricting of reindeer pastureland. Norway now requires Saami herders to register themselves in one of several officially designated "reindeer districts" and limits the number of herders in each one. This regulation directly conflicts with—and overrides—Saami cultural knowledge about the importance of pasture flexibility.

In its insistence on the economic rationalization of the reindeer industry, the Norwegian government calls for more efficient, pro-

ductive, and profitable herding, slaughtering, and marketing. Since World War II, a market has developed for reindeer meat as a luxury item in Scandinavia and other parts of northern Europe. Reindeer hides are a popular tourist souvenir item, and even reindeer antlers have a market in the Far East, where antler powder is believed to have aphrodisiac powers (Stephens 1987:37). As part of its marketing efforts, the Norwegian government has agreed to pay a minimum price for slaughtered reindeer and has set up regional slaughtering and marketing centers, where the reindeer are slaughtered in sanitary conditions and the meat certified as to grade. This requires, however, that Saami bring their reindeer to these centers to be slaughtered, which many Saami are reluctant to do.

The government has also formalized reindeer herd management, and provides the Saami with government "experts" to counsel them. Most Saami feel that these experts do not really know or care about the Saami way of life. They resent the government's intervention, even when some of the suggested changes have already been adopted by the Saami themselves (Paine 1994). Nor do many Saami think that formal training can match their own knowledge of the environment and herd management gained from years of experience.

Like many indigenous peoples, through their own desire to selectively "modernize," the Saami have become fully engaged in the cash-based global economy. At one time, reindeer herding supplied herding families with most of their needs—food, clothing, transportation, and hides for tents—but now Saami need money to buy many things: houses, furniture, radios, televisions, video recorders, clothes, food, cars, and snowmobiles (and the gasoline to run them), the latter essential to compete in herding large numbers of animals. Today more Saami lead a settled way of life, and many Saami children go further in school, leading them away from their traditionally based livelihood.

In spite of many cultural changes, however, the distinctive Saami culture still rests upon values that treat reindeer and reindeer herding as something more than an "economic bottom line." But now Saami culture must compete with other national needs as well. Their area is desired for tourism, mining, and hydroelectric development, and large tracts have been set aside for military developments, such as the NATO bases in northern Norway.

The decade from 1979 to 1989 was a time of unprecedented state intervention in Saami reindeer pastoralism. Essentially, it resulted in Norway's placing an ethnically distinct livelihood under state license. Although this provides a strong guarantee that at least some Saami, at the state's discretion, will be able to continue reindeer herding, it will not be reindeer herding as the Saami have traditionally practiced it. The Reindeer Management Act is caught up in the contradiction between the government's official support of Saami culture and the national priorities of social egalitarianism and economic development. The government objective of reducing herd size while increasing income (rationalizing herd management) gives the state the power to decide how many and which Saami may register as pastoralists and what the size and composition of their herds will be.

The premises of the modern, progressive Norwegian state embrace cultural difference represented by Saami reindeer herders only with difficulty. The state views pastoralism as productively inferior to agriculture. It sees the pastoral way of life as a gift from the state that will continue only so long as it does not interfere with other state objectives, including economic progress in the form of agricultural and industrial development. Government intervention, if it is successful, will transform Saami pastoralism, whose aim is to *keep* all animals except those slaughtered for domestic needs, into Norwegian reindeer ranching, whose aim is to *sell* all animals except those needed to feed the family.

The conflict between the Saami and the Norwegian state illustrates that even a benevolent state, based on universalism, bureaucracy, and economic rationalism, can negatively impact indigenous peoples. Even though, after 10 years, the Reindeer Management Act has failed in almost all its objectives to rationalize Saami

reindeer herding, this does not ensure a future of cultural autonomy for the Saami. Nor does the Saami example offer reassurance of a secure future for other indigenous peoples, even those within democratic and progressive nation-states.

CULTURAL DIVERSITY AND ETHNICITY IN THE UNITED STATES

The United States, even before it was a nation, has always been a culturally diverse society. This diversity consisted first of Native Americans, themselves a culturally diverse population; then European immigrants, initially mainly Dutch, Spanish, French, and English; and soon after, Africans, brought to the new colony as slaves. Historically, however, it has been the concept of ethnicity, and the ways in which it interacts with the larger national identity, that has dominated the American discourse on cultural diversity.

The significance of ethnic identity fluctuates with the situation in which people find themselves. African Americans in Africa, for example, may feel that they share a common identity with those around them, but Africans regard them primarily as Americans (Bruner 1996). Margaret Mead (1995) contended that an American national identity was more likely to be experienced in contrast to others who were perceived as not American, or not 100 percent American, than as a set of distinctive American cultural characteristics. Thus, the experiencing of one's American ethnicity, like the experiencing of most ethnicities, comes into play mainly when interacting with others.

No one criterion of ethnic identity holds for all groups. Language, for example, may or may not be an important ethnic boundary marker, and it may be more important for outsiders than for insiders. Spanish is a major criterion of Latino/Hispanic ethnic identity for the United States government. However, many people whose mother tongue is Spanish reject the ethnic category of Hispanic; they prefer to be identified by their place of origin, such as Cuban Americans, Puerto Ricans, Colombians, and Mexican Americans. But because the United

ANTHROPOLOGISTS AS ADVOCATES FOR INDIGENOUS PEOPLES

Anthropology has always been very closely linked to indigenous peoples. Indeed, in the popular imagination, indigenous peoples have been *the* subject matter of anthropology, both for ethnography and for cross-cultural comparison. Anthropological documentation of the cultural particularity of indigenous peoples—their arts, folklore, and cultural traditions; of their communally based, communal, noncapitalist values; and particularly, their sense of place—has been the staple of cultural anthropology (R. Lee 2000). Anthropologists today have taken a major role in supporting human rights for indigenous peoples and advocating on their behalf to popular, governmental, and other audiences. This role is consistent with efforts indigenous peoples today are making on their own behalf.

Indigenous peoples have learned by experience that they cannot rely on state benevolence. Thus, in the past 30 years, many indigenous peoples have organized politically to gain their rights through national and international courts and in the court of world public opinion. By the 1960s, indigenous peoples began to press their demands for full control over their traditional lands and communities. Indigenous peoples want strong international guarantees of their rights to self-determination. They have urged removal of older international conventions which, from their point of view, ethnocentrically privilege national integration and national economic development at the expense of indigenous cultures.

Many anthropologists have participated actively with indigenous peoples in their struggles for justice. In the United States, for example, anthropologists have used their knowledge of historical movements of the indigenous peoples of North America to testify in land claims cases on the behalf of Native Americans against the United States government's efforts to remove them from their land. John H. Bodley's *Victims of Progress* (1990), originally published in the early 1970s, was one of the first critiques of ethnocidal national and international policies toward indigenous peoples worldwide. Bodley has made a significant contribution in alerting the general public as well as anthropology students to the fragile position of indigenous peoples today.

Cultural Survival, an anthropological group begun at Harvard University in 1972 under the leadership of David Maybury-Lewis, has also been very active in promoting the rights of indigenous peoples. Cultural Survival works toward increasing the ability of indigenous peoples to improve their position within multiethnic or culturally pluralist nation-states. It helps indigenous peoples retain their cultural identities while they adapt gradually to the changes accompanying national economic development.

Cultural Survival's advocacy for indigenous peoples is based on the conviction that such societies have been wronged over the past centuries and that anthropologists have an obligation to right those wrongs (Maybury-Lewis 1993). One important activity of Cultural Survival is to educate the public about indigenous peoples and to debunk the argument that they stand in the way of national economic development. Cultural Survival also helps indigenous peoples understand the implications of individual ownership of land and helps them become more effective in negotiating to protect their land base. Cultural Survival does not aim to preserve indigenous peoples in some mythical original state of cultural "purity," but rather to help indigenous peoples create conditions under which they can maximize their power to make decisions about their own future.

An important part of Cultural Survival's agenda is to help indigenous peoples develop and sustain satisfactory alternatives to traditional subsistence economics. For example, in the 1980s, when policies of the South African government had almost destroyed the foraging way of life of the Ju/'hoansi, Richard Lee, an anthropologist who has worked with them for many years, led an international campaign through Cultural Survival to help the Ju/'hoansi reorient their economy around cattle husbandry and subsistence farming supplemented by foraging. Cultural Survival provided direct assistance in the form of livestock, medicine and medical services for livestock, and tools for improving the water holes around which the Ju/'hoansi traditionally settled (R. Lee 1992).

Courtesy of Cultural Survival

CULTURAL SURVIVAL IS AN ORGANIZATION OF ANTHROPOLOGISTS THAT TRIES TO HELP INDIGENOUS PEOPLES ADAPT TO THE MODERN WORLD. CULTURAL SURVIVAL RAISES MONEY TO SUPPORT ITS EFFORTS THROUGH THE SALE OF POSTERS SUCH AS THIS ONE, REPRESENTING INDIGENOUS PEOPLES AROUND THE WORLD.

Terance Turner, along with other an-thropologists, also advocates for the rights of indigenous peoples. Turner has testified before Congressional committees exam-ining the abuses of indigenous peoples' rights in the Amazon and also writes about indigenous peoples in the popular media. Turner has worked for more than 30 years among the Kayapo of the Brazilian Amazon. He is helping them implement a project of video self-documentation, through which they hope to compile a comprehensive archive of Kayapo culture as the basis of a course for their young people. The Kayapo also see video as an effective means of reaching out to a non-Kayapo, global audience, gaining support and respect for their efforts to preserve their autonomy within the context of Brazilian society.

States government uses "Hispanic" ethnicity as a significant bureaucatic criterion for access to resources, such as bilingual education or legal redress for discrimination based on national origin, its importance as an ethnic marker has increased.

For many older ethnic groups of European origin, language as an ethnic boundary marker has lost its relevance today. Nonetheless, ethnic group differences do exist in the United States, often persisting over several generations. In addition to the more obvious ethnic markers, such as food, these ethnic group differences show up in subtle ways: verbal and nonverbal means of communication (Cerroni-Long 1993); the experience of health, illness, and pain; occupational choices; and voting patterns (Shensul 1997).

At the same time, it is important to remember that ethnicity in the United States, as well as in other places, is an "invented tradition." The relevance of ethnic groups, their relation to American identity, and their relations to each other have changed over time (di Leonardo 1998:80ff). Specific constructions of ethnicity and ethnic communities serve diverse interests—those of political elites as well as of ethnic communities themselves. In some historical periods, ethnicity and ethnic groups have been viewed as repositories of "good" characteristics, such as placing a high value on the traditional family; at other times, ethnics have been designated as having the "bad" characteristics of being old-fashioned and culturally behind the times, obstacles to the furtherance of modernity and social unity (di Leonardo 1998: 82). In the 1960s, when those in power saw widespread protest movements as threatening to the status quo, the United States experienced the "invention" of the "white ethnics"—ethnic groups of European origin who formed the "silent majority" that was presumed to support the social and political status quo. Just 40 years earlier, these same white ethnics had been characterized as undesirable "races," their immigration curtailed by discriminatory immigration laws! Indeed, some social scientists see the contemporary focus on ethnicity as a means of obscuring the more important role of class and race in the unequal distribution of wealth and power in the United States (Steinberg 1989; di Leonardo 1998; Reed 2000).

ETHNICITY AND IMMIGRATION

Ethnicity in the United States, more than in many societies, is based on immigration. Thus, U.S. immigration history is an essential context for understanding contemporary constructions of American ethnicity and the relations between ethnic groups (J. Ryan 1999). Though the United States is for the most part a nation of immigrants, there is no single immigrant experience (Lamphere 1992; di Leonardo 1984). Different groups have faced historically different circumstances. Depending on these circumstances, their national origin, and the degree to which their culture was perceived as alien, they have met with greater or lesser hostility from those already established.

The continuous process of adaptation of immigrants in the United States also intersected with the continuous, self-conscious project of creating a national identity—a key element in American culture that began with the American Revolution and continues up until the present (A. Wallace 1999). American efforts at creating a national identity led to ethnicity's becoming equated with "national origin," which thus became the primary framework within which American cultural diversity was understood. This translation of diversity into ethnicity based on national origin meant that each group of newcomers had to negotiate its particular place within this constructed framework.

The concept of ethnicity has not been equally applied to all immigrants and nationalities, however, and this has led to different patterns of individual and group adaptation. English national origin, for example, was not seen as ethnic, but as the American norm, even though the English were immigrants in a land already inhabited by Native Americans and, in different sections of the country, by other European nationalities as well. It was these other nationalities, such as the Dutch in New York and the Spanish in Florida, rather than the English, that became "ethnicized."

© L. P. Winfrey/Woodfin Camp & Associates

THE LARGE NUMBERS OF IMMIGRANTS FROM SOUTHERN AND EASTERN EUROPE AROUND THE TURN OF THE TWENTIETH CENTURY SOUGHT ECONOMIC IMPROVEMENT AND HOPE OF A BETTER FUTURE.

Although outsiders often lump together immigrants with a common national origin, immigrant groups are not homogeneous, but are divided by varying combinations of regional origin, dialect, class, politics, and religion (Lamphere 1992). Thus, within an immigrant group there are competing interpretations of authentic identity. A group's understanding of its ethnic identity emphasizes different interpretations as social and economic circumstances change. Ethnic identity is dynamic and must be flexible enough to provide a basis for ethnic group solidarity despite differences within the group. Such solidarity is essential if the group is going to compete successfully for access to political and economic resources. Ethnic groups also attempt to defuse actual or potential hostility from the larger society—for example, by depicting ethnic values as compatible with mainstream culture, or seeking economic niches that do not compete with other Americans (Gjerde 1998; also see the Ethnography box later in this chapter).

THE AMERICAN DISCOURSE ON IMMIGRATION

Immigration has always been an intensely debated topic in the United States. Early idealistic visions of America as a land of economic opportunity and political freedom for immigrants from Europe were actually narrowly defined to encompass mainly those from northern and western Europe. In considering questions of citizenship in the creation of the United States Constitution, the framers effectively limited it to those who were "free and white."

By the 1830s, increasing immigration of Irish Catholics and Germans to the United States heightened earlier concerns that the new immigrants would undermine American republicanism—either because their previous poverty in Europe had denied them the experience of political freedom, or because their authoritarian religion would make them hostile to it and draw their loyalties elsewhere (Gjerde 1998). In addition, some Americans feared that an influx of immigrants would result in lower urban wages, or that immigrants would flood and then dominate the western part of the country. These concerns coalesced in strongly anti-Catholic and anti-immigrant nativist movements, some of which, like the Know Nothing Party, experienced short-term political success before flickering out.

Meanwhile, immigration continued to increase. Between 1850 and 1910, many immigrants gravitated to cities, where they lived in ethnic (actually multiethnic)—and poor—neighborhoods, generating the fear that they would be corrupted by urban political machines. On the basis of common culture and national origin, immigrants formed social and ethnic institutions. These organizations, which helped them retain some of their ethnic culture and separateness from the larger society, at the same time mediated their connections with it.

The largest and most varied immigration to the United States occurred between 1880 and the 1920s. In these years, the discourse on immigration moved from ethnicity to race. African Americans had always been viewed as a racial group, but by 1880 "racial" typologies were fashionable (a situation in which anthropologists unfortunately played a role) and began to be applied to Europeans as well. Southern and Eastern Europeans were racially distinguished from the Nordic "races" from Northern and Western Europe and by the 1920s restrictive immigration laws effectively limited immigration to these "Nordic" groups.

Throughout this period the Supreme Court grappled with the definition of "whiteness" in a series of cases involving nationals from such countries as India and Lebanon, who appealed the denial of their immigration status based on their "nonwhite" racial status (Gjerde 1998). Proponents of restrictive immigration claimed that people who were members of different "races" could never become good American citizens and that the United States would "degenerate" if it incorporated them.

MODELS OF CULTURAL DIVERSITY

The huge increase in immigration around the turn of the twentieth century was accompanied by popular and scholarly concern as to how immigrants should be incorporated into American society. Three main models of ethnic relations emerged: the assimilationist model, prevalent at the turn of the twentieth century; the "melting pot" model, popular through the 1970s; and the "mosaic" model, which is current today.

THE ASSIMILATIONIST MODEL

The **assimilationist model** holds that immigrants should, to the greatest extent possible, abandon their cultural distinctiveness and be-

assimilationist model A model of immigration that holds that immigrants should abandon their cultural traditions and become wholly absorbed in mainstream American culture.

come "mainstream" Americans. At its height, assimilationism resulted in the building of urban Settlement Houses, designed to teach immigrants "American" ways, and the institution of citizenship programs in the public schools. Assimilationists supported only minimal further immigration to the United States, and triumphed in the 1920s with the passage of the restrictive immigration acts mentioned previously. Nations such as England, seen as similar to the United States, were allowed almost unrestricted immigration. Nations such as Greece and Poland, seen as different, were allowed only minimal immigration. Immigration of Asians was all but completely halted.

The assimilationist model was also applied to Native Americans. As Anthony Wallace (1999) points out, the commitment of Thomas Jefferson and the Founding Fathers to a national rather than an imperial model of government put culturally different and politically autonomous groups like the Native Americans in a very precarious position. With few dissenting voices, assimilationism soon became the dominant American policy toward the Indians—though even those groups, like the Cherokee, who had adopted many "American" cultural patterns, were still subject to removal and appropriation of their land by whites (Norgren 1996).

By the mid-nineteenth century, forced onto reservations, Indians became a captive audience for the teaching of American values of individualism, Christianity, agricultural production, and the English language by missionaries and Indian agents of the United States government. Native Americans were also forced to send their children to American boarding schools, often hundreds of miles from their local communities, so that they would be permanently alienated from their native cultures and languages.

By the early 1870s, it became clear that the reservation policy had failed to transform Indians into mainstream Americans. Thus, in 1887, the United States Congress passed the General Allotment (Dawes) Act, which provided that Native American families would be given an allotment of land to be owned privately, not communally. The Dawes Act was based on the belief that only by becoming invested in the system of private ownership and individual enterprise could Indians "progress" and become "civilized." Indians who participated, or who otherwise left their tribal cultures, would be given American citizenship. By the 1920s, it became clear that the Dawes Act, too, had failed in assimilating Native Americans. Only in the 1930s, under the directorship of John Collier, an anthropologist who headed the Bureau of Indian Affairs, were government policies reversed to support the strengthening of Indian cultures and societies (Norgren and Nanda 1996:18–22).

THE MELTING POT MODEL

The **melting pot model** was both a theory and an ideal. It envisioned that each new immigrant group would lose some of its cultural traditions in the United States, but retain others. The result would be the disappearance of ethnic groups and ethnic identity and the emergence of a new American identity comprised of elements of the different immigrant cultures. By the late 1950s, however, it was clear that the melting pot theory had only limited application. While much of the cultural distinctiveness of ethnic groups had in fact disappeared, ethnic groups themselves persisted, mainly as interest groups organized around political goals and mobilized for gaining access to economic resources (Glazer and Moynihan 1970). By the mid-twentieth century, it also became clear that as an ideal vision of American society, the melting pot was highly selective. It incorporated the cultures of European immigrants, but excluded Asians, Native Americans, Mexican Americans, and African Americans.

THE MOSAIC MODEL

The **mosaic model** holds that ethnic groups do not and should not assimilate completely. This model uses the metaphor of a salad bowl rather than a melting pot: Just as a salad has many different sorts of greens and vegetables, which are individually recognizable yet contribute to the value of the whole, so too will American society benefit by the cultural distinctiveness of its many groups. The mosaic model, sometimes incorporated under the umbrella of "multiculturalism," arose partly in response to the swell of immigration in the past 25 years. It reflects the "politics of identity" movements that began in the 1960s and continue today, incorporating groups identified not only by the cultural differences expressed in ethnicity, but also by "race," gender, and indigenous status.

In 1965, a new Immigration and Nationality Act replaced the discriminatory immigration laws of the 1920s. The new law was explicitly aimed at reversing the discriminatory basis of earlier immigration laws. It greatly expanded the number of people permitted to immigrate from previously discriminated against nations, abolished immigration quotas, gave high priority to the social goal of family unification, and put refugee immigration on a less ad hoc basis (Lamphere 1992:Introduction; Fix and Passel 1994).

While the new law has resulted in an historic high of immigration, the percentage of the United States population that is foreign-born (about 8.5 percent) is actually about half what it was at its historic peak (Fix and Passel 1994). The major change has been in the composition of the immigrant flow. The "new" immigrants have come in great numbers from nations that had hitherto been restricted because of "race": from the Middle East, the Indian subcontinent, China, Korea, the Caribbean, and parts of Central and South America. The new immigrants bring languages and cultures from all over the world, and the mosaic of American culture is palpable in any major American city today: One hears many languages, sees many forms of dress, can eat many different kinds of food, and can participate in cultural activities drawn from many sources. This has created dynamic synergies not seen in American society since the early 1900s.

melting pot model A model of immigration that holds that as immigrants lose some of their cultural differences, they will melt together into a new American culture.

mosaic model A model of immigration that holds that cultural diversity is a positive aspect of American national identity.

I N   T H E   F I E L D

THE NEW CHINESE IMMIGRANTS IN SAN FRANCISCO

San Francisco's Chinatown, the oldest and largest in the United States, was established when the California Gold Rush of 1849 brought thousands of mostly unskilled, uneducated, male Chinese laborers from southern China into northern California to work in the mines and on the transcontinental railroad. Racism, fear of economic competition, and hostility greeted these immigrants, prompting them to live and work in the relative safety of Chinese settlements amidst those who spoke their language and shared their culture. By 1850, San Francisco's Chinatown included scores of Chinese-owned and -run general stores, restaurants, laundries, food markets, and boardinghouses—economic niches that required little capital investment and avoided competition with white workers.

As Chinese women and families were not permitted to immigrate to the United States, Chinese men in the "bachelor societies" of the San Francisco Bay Area worked mainly to save enough money to eventually return home. These "sojourners" lived in cramped quarters, worked long hours for low pay, and were continually subjected to legislative and physical attacks by whites. Legally barred from many occupations, lacking English skills and political power, and prohibited from educating their children in American schools, the first generations of Chinese immigrants organized their own ethnic economy and protective associations. After the 1882 Chinese Exclusion Act, Chinese immigration and reentry by the sojourners were forbidden. Not until the 1940s were Chinese immigrants able to

interact socially and economically with the European American mainstream.

The passage of the 1965 U.S. immigration law, emphasizing family reunification, dramatically changed the ethnic and economic composition of the new Chinese immigration. Most new immigrants now became permanent residents or naturalized citizens. Many of these new arrivals initially lived in rented quarters in the older Chinatowns, and worked the same long hours for low pay in the same ethnic economic niches as their forebears. Eventually, however, by pooling family resources, many were able to establish businesses and buy commercial or residential property outside historically Chinese neighborhoods, often in rundown areas that had been abandoned by more prosperous whites. While the new immigrants continued to shop and attend cultural events in Chinatown, they educated their children in the culturally diverse American public schools, and the isolated "sojourner" ethnic mentality of the pre-1965 generations largely disappeared.

The differences between the earlier and the "new" Chinese immigrants stem from both the backgrounds of the new immi-

grants and the changed conditions of the American economic and social environment. Although sporadic arrivals of poor, uneducated, and terribly exploited illegal Chinese immigrants occur, most of today's new legal immigrants are educated, technically skilled, urban people. Those from Taiwan or Hong Kong are motivated primarily by economic and educational opportunities; they frequently arrive with access to capital, professional training and experience, or expertise in manufacturing, finance, or engineering. Many are relatively westernized and proficient in English, a crucial factor in their successful adaptation. The new immigrants from mainland China are more likely to be intellectuals escaping repression in their homeland, and are somewhat less westernized. As a group, however, despite continued discrimination and other hardships, the new Chinese immigrants have been able to use a much wider range of adaptive strategies, both socially and economically, than those of the nineteenth century and their American-born descendants.

The new Chinese immigrants to the San Francisco Bay Area mainly engage in family-type entrepreneurship—the establishment and management of commercial enterprises using family resources and kinship networks. Some of these businesses expand upon traditional ethnic enterprises such as gift stores, restaurants, and hotels. Others are financial institutions geared to the growing ethnic communities in the area. Still others, like garment manufacturing or construction, unknown in earlier Chinese enclaves, serve both Chinese and non-Chinese customers. Many new immigrants are also employed in the computer industry, initially as professionals or academics working for American corporations or universities, but later branching out as owners of or employees in Chinese family-type firms. Still other immigrants engage in transnational commerce. Central to successful Chinese entrepreneurship is the convergence of the new immigrants' cultural values with the requirements of modern business practices. The Chinese cultural core of Confucian ethics and tightly woven kinship networks are highly adaptive to the American, and indeed the global, marketplace.

The Confucian emphasis on the family is a valuable resource for Chinese entrepreneurs, who marshal family connections to borrow capital to start and develop their businesses. They also employ siblings, spouses, and children as loyal, trustworthy, industrious, and often nonsalaried or low-paid help. Confucian hierarchical values, which privilege fathers over sons, husbands over wives, and older siblings over young ones, mesh well with the clear-cut chain of command in both small and large, more complex businesses. "Filial piety," which encompasses respect to living parents and ancestors alike, ensures that family members will subordinate their own desires to the demands of the family enterprise, and save and share the family's wealth for the present and future success of the business. The Confucian ideal of glorifying one's lineage and the Confucian emphasis on education mean that even when the younger generations leave the family business for university study or the professions, they still feel obligated to succeed and to be available resources for their parents and the family firm. The achievements of each generation, whether in business or scholarship, give "face" (honor) to the family and assurance that its immigration was not in vain.

Ninety percent of new immigrant businesses in San Francisco Bay Area are "family" firms, although as they grow, "family" may include fictive kin from the same village, town, school, or "last name" association. Nuclear family members (husband/wife or adult siblings) retain authority and financial control, but owners and their children often work alongside their employees at whatever jobs need doing, whether operating a sewing machine or clearing restaurant tables. All the workers, "bosses" included, work longer hours for less pay than would be the case in an American business.

These business practices allow owners to operate their businesses at a profit, which although small, permits the accumulation of capital to expand or modernize the business. Employees benefit from profitable business management by increases in salary, responsibilities, or expertise that eventually result in their own accumulation of wealth. This economic niche provides an important transitional period for non-English-speaking employees, in a personalized, family-style atmosphere. Employees eat together as a family, consult the firm's owner about personal problems, receive time off for Chinese holidays, and sometimes can secure jobs for their children or their own recently arrived relatives. Since employees are hired because of kinship or friendship ties, the immigrant worker feels an obligation to repay this debt through loyal and industrious service.

The difficulties of capitalization and the small profit margin of many immigrant businesses, the long hours and grinding work required for success, increasing competition, the instability of the American economy, and the Chinese value on higher education have directed some new immigrants with the necessary qualifications into professional and technical areas. But although American society is now more economically and socially hospitable to Chinese immigrants than in the past, hostility still exists. Chinese labor practices are seen by some, including younger Chinese, as exploitative. Other Americans sometimes resent the influx of Chinese students into California colleges and universities, and glass ceilings in corporate work stall promotion of immigrant Chinese to higher managerial levels. Immigrants encounter hostility toward Chinese specialty business and residential expansion into formerly "American" suburbs (Horton 1992). All these factors have led many new immigrants to expand their economic strategies. This may take the form of entrepreneurship in the global marketplace, using kin and friendship networks to gain employment in international firms or to expand their own businesses beyond American borders. Some Chinese have also returned to their homelands as academics, businesspeople, or government consultants. While this transnationalism is economically adaptive, it can put extreme stress on family relationships if the breadwinning husband must be away from the home for long periods, leaving a wife and children to cope in an unfamiliar and sometimes uncomfortable environment.

Anthropologist Bernard Wong holds that transnational entrepreneurship is only a temporary adaptive strategy for new Chinese immigrants, most of whom are committed to their American communities and their identity as Americans. Although understandably reluctant to surrender their ethnicity totally, the majority seek to combine their Chinese cultural traits with American values, synthesizing the more intimate scale of interaction in Chinese culture with American pragmatism, technological progress, democracy, and equality. Like many other ethnic

---

groups, the Chinese have developed ethnic institutions, including an ethnic press and business and professional groups, to help them adapt to American society. Also like other immigrant groups, they have become more proactive in using affirmative action and the political process to fight discrimination and assist them in achieving their goals. The children of new Chinese immigrants, like many American-born Chinese, look forward to complete acceptance into American society based on a greater American understanding of their continued contributions to their local and national communities.

Critical Thinking Questions

1. How are the "new" Chinese immigrants different from earlier Chinese immigrants to the United States?

2. What are some of the values of the new Chinese immigrants that have helped them adapt to the United States?

Source: Adapted from Bernard Wong, *Ethnicity and Entrepreneurship: The New Chinese Immigrants in the San Francisco Bay Area*. Needham Heights, MA: Allyn and Bacon, 1988.

The immigrants of the late twentieth century differ in significant ways from those of early 1900s. Many of them entered the United States at the time of economic contraction. Corporate downsizing was curtailing the number of jobs for legal immigrants, while providing jobs at the lowest wages and under the most difficult conditions for illegal immigrants (Stull, Broadway, and Erickson 1992; Benson 1999). Also, immigrants in the 1990s were entering the United States when the pursuit of group interests, backed by policies such as affirmative action, had greater legitimacy than it did a century earlier. These new immigrants live in a world where communication—by telephone, e-mail, and the internet—is abundant, relatively simple, and inexpensive, and air travel is within the reach of the middle class. Thus, many immigrants, especially those from nearby areas such as the Caribbean (Hamid 1990), are able to retain much closer social and economic ties with their families and cultures in their homelands. Anthropologists refer to this pattern of close ties and frequent visits as **transnationalism** (Glick-Schiller, Basch, and Szanton-Blanc 1992). Though there are important class and educational differences among immigrant groups, in general, they are more familiar with American culture through its global diffusion than were immigrants of the past. The Ethnography box highlights the many ways in which the new immigration both builds upon and differs from immigration and models of ethnicity in the past.

The extent to which ethnic differences will persist among immigrants in the United States is unclear. On the one hand, it appears that ethnic cultural differences do not disappear entirely (Cerroni-Long 1993). On the other hand, it also seems unlikely that cultural distinctions on a scale seen in the United States today will persist indefinitely (Ryan 1999). While some immigrants and their families travel frequently to their homelands, most people cannot afford to take their families for extended stays in distant lands. Will the grandchildren of today's immigrants speak their grandparents' native language? Will they retain more than basic elements of their ancestors' culture? The jury is still out, but if past experience is a guide, it seems unlikely. While attempts to legislate "Americanness" have mostly faded, today's immigrants and their children face enormous pressures from the marketplace, the media, and the schools to conform to a mainstream vision of American culture. Mainstream culture in the United States itself continues to be enormously flexible, absorbing distinctive cultural characteristics from all over the world.

Although our focus has been on immigration in the United States, immigration is in fact

Transnationalism A pattern of immigration in which immigrants maintain close social and economic ties with their families and cultures in their homelands.

a global issue. The enormous movements of populations in the twentieth century have a global aspect that makes immigration, multiculturalism, and ethnicity central to contemporary anthropological concerns.

Summary

1. Ethnicity, or the perceived cultural distinctions between groups, is an increasingly important force in today's world. The essentialist view of ethnicity is that it is an unreflecting, basically emotional, sense of collective selfhood based on shared cultural traits. The constructionist view sees ethnicity, ethnic groups, and ethnic boundaries as contingent and dynamic cultural creations. The Takari of the Sudan illustrate the construction of ethnicity.

2. The nation-state is a significant development within which modern ethnicity takes shape. The nation-state emerges when governments and elites succeed in identifying the state with a group of people defined as culturally homogenous.

3. Within states, many contesting voices try to shape the creation of national identities. Among these, the government has the advantage of greater resources and control over its population, partly through the passage of laws. One goal of contemporary anthropology is to identify the processes by which states define and bring into existence both the nation and the ethnic groups that compose it.

4. Extreme ethnic conflict is a product of contemporary constructions of ethnicity. The example of ethnic violence in the former Yugoslavia suggests that political manipulation of cultural differences, not ethnicity per se, is at the root of interethnic violence.

5. Indigenous peoples are small-scale, relatively separate societies with historical ties to a given territory that antedate European contact, invasion, or colonization. Nation-states are often in conflict with indigenous peoples whom they have conquered and deprived of their land, leading to the destruction of indigenous cultures. Law has been an important tool in the arsenal of modern nation-states in their coercion of indigenous peoples.

6. The conflict between the government of Norway and the indigenous Saami pastoralists, arising from Norway's attempts to rationalize reindeer herding, illustrates the kinds of conflicts experienced by indigenous peoples worldwide. Nation-states frequently view indigenous peoples as standing in the way of "progress" and economic development.

7. The cultural diversity of the United States has largely been framed in terms of ethnicity based on the national origin of immigrants. Three major models of ethnic relations have been the assimilationist model, the melting pot model, and the mosaic model.

8. The assimilationist model holds that immigrants should abandon their cultural traditions and be absorbed into mainstream American culture. The melting pot model holds that as immigrants lose some of their cultural differences, they will melt together into a new American culture. The mosaic model sees cultural diversity as a positive aspect of American national identity.

9. A consistent theme in United States history has been a concern with the numbers and national origins of its immigrants. From the 1880s through the 1920s, restrictive and racist immigration laws were passed, giving preference to immigration from certain European countries. In 1965, changes in American immigration laws led to increasing immigration from a wide diversity of nations and "races." The adaptive strategies of these new immigrants is illustrated by the Chinese in the San Francisco Bay Area.

Key Terms

assimilationist model	indigenous peoples
ethnic boundaries	melting pot model
ethnic groups	mosaic model
ethnic identity	nation-state
ethnicity	transnationalism

Suggested Readings

Carnes, Jim. 1995. *Us and Them: A History of Intolerance in America.* Montgomery, AL: Southern Poverty Law Center. This award-winning short anthology of historical events describes experiences of discrimination by many different groups in the United States.

Falla, Ricardo. 1994. *Massacres in the Jungle.* Boulder, CO: Westview Press. Written by a Catholic priest turned anthropologist, this outstanding example of action anthropology documents the massacres and counterinsurgency terror by the Guatemalan military in the 1980s against indigenous Maya of the recently colonized northern border regions.

Glick-Schiller, Nina, Linda Basch, and Cristina Szanton-Blanc (Eds.). 1992. *Towards a Transnational Perspective on Migration: Race, Class, Ethnicity, and Nationalism Reconsidered.* New York: New York Academy of Sciences. This collection of articles develops the concept of migration called transnationalism, using research on migrants from many countries to the United States. A major thesis of the book is that migrants' experiences in their new home have important connections with their status in their countries of origin.

Lamphere, Louise (Ed.). 1992. *Structuring Diversity: Ethnographic Perspectives on the New Immigration.* Chicago: University of Chicago Press. In a welcome emphasis on the daily lives of immigrants in various cities in the United States, this interdisciplinary project focuses on social relations between newcomers and established residents within the context of the major "mediating" institutions of school, workplace, and neighborhood.

Maybury-Lewis, David. 1997. *Indigenous Peoples, Ethnic Groups, and the State.* Boston: Allyn and Bacon. An anthropologist prominent in advocating for the rights of indigenous peoples explains many of the ethnic conflicts in the world today, involving both indigenous peoples and ethnic groups in European and African states. This volume is part of a series, Cultural Survival Studies in Ethnicity and Change.

Trask, Haunani-Kay. 1993. *From a Native Daughter: Colonialism and Sovereignty in Hawai'i* (rev. ed.). Monroe, ME: Common Courage Press. An eye-opening account from a feminist indigenous perspective of the impact of United States colonialism on the native peoples of Hawai'i.

INTERNET RESOURCES

The following Internet resources appear in this chapter. Please log on to the Wadsworth anthropology website: **http://anthropology.wadsworth. com**. Click on the Nanda/Warms *Cultural Anthropology* page. Then select the Student Resources section, where you will find a complete presentation of these links and more.

- A photo essay on marketing Native American identity in the United States, page 316
- A video link: A story of the demise of an indigenous people, page 322
- A link to the Borders and Identity website, page 326
- Access the Study Guide to InfoTrac College Edition for Anthropology Students

WORSHIPING THE GODS IN DAILY RITUALS IS AN ESSENTIAL PART OF HINDU RELIGIOUS PRACTICE. THESE DEVOTIONAL ACTIVITIES ARE CARRIED OUT IN THE HOME BY WOMEN, WHILE MALE PRIESTS OFFICIATE IN HINDU TEMPLES.

CHAPTER FIFTEEN

RELIGION

What is religion?

What does religion do in society?

How are religious beliefs and rituals different in various cultures?

What roles do sacred stories and symbols play in religion?

What are some common key elements in religious rituals?

What are the differences between prayer, sacrifice, and magic?

How do priests differ from shamans?

Under what conditions do religions change, and when do new religions form?

In Trinidad, before harvesting, farmers make sacrifices to the di, the spirits of the first owners of their fields. They believe that failure to do so will result in a poor harvest. Because many fields are owned by absentee landlords, they also set aside a portion of the harvest to pay rent. Most people from industrialized societies would say that sacrifices to the di are supernatural and rent payments are part of the natural world. But is it really so simple? After all, as anthropologist Morton Klass (1995) points out, the farmer may have never seen a di or the landlord. He knows of people who have been evicted because they failed to pay the rent, but he also knows people whose crops have failed when they did not sacrifice to the di. Some people say that the di do not really exist, but others say that landlords really don't exist and everyone has a right to the land they live on and work. If we assume that the payments the farmer makes to the di constitute religion but those he makes to the landlord are something completely different, we seem to miss something essential.

All societies have something anthropologists identify as religion; yet as Klass's example of the di and the landlord suggests, defining religion is surprisingly difficult. Most definitions focus on the supernatural. Because American culture makes a clear distinction between natural and supernatural, that seems logical enough. The problem is that some religions explicitly deny that supernatural beings exist, and others do not distinguish them from what Americans call the natural. Even in the United States, the difference may be problematic. Is God's presence in the world supernatural to the devout, or is it simply part of the natural order of the world?

Because different societies perceive reality in different ways, there is no agreed upon way to distinguish the natural from the supernatural. But our problems are even greater than this. Religions around the world show enormous variation. Religion scholars Carmody and Carmody have noted that "religion ranges almost endlessly—into every geographical area, into every temporal period, into so many uses of the human body, mind, imagination, social instinct, artistic genius, and all the rest that no library could contain all the studies that the full range of religion, actual and potential, would require" (1992:4).

It is probably true that no single belief is shared by all the world's people. Differences vary from issues as grand as the nature of life itself (do we live once, as the Judeo-Christian-Islamic tradition teaches, or repeatedly, as the Hindu and Buddhist traditions teach) to issues as specific as sexual relations between men (discouraged by the Judeo-Christian-Islamic tradition but compulsory among the Sambia of New Guinea [Herdt 1987]). Despite this confusion, every culture has some process among its members, and between them and the world, that helps to order their society and provides them with meaning, unity, peace of mind, and the degree of control over events they believe is possible (Klass 1995:38). This process is **religion.**

Religion is a human universal, and most anthropologists believe that it goes back to the beginnings of the human species. In the nineteenth and early twentieth centuries, many anthropologists were concerned with trying to find the origin, and trace the development, of religion. For the most part, they wanted to demonstrate that religion had evolved from primitive superstition to enlightened Christianity. This view has long been discredited; no religion is any more evolved than another. Anthropologists today are interested in the functions that religion serves in society and the ways in which it lends meaning to human life.

WHAT RELIGION DOES IN SOCIETY

Religion has many functions in a society. It may provide meaning and order in people's lives. It may reduce social anxiety and give people a sense of control over their destinies. Religion can promote and reinforce the status quo or, in some situations, can be the means

religion A social process that helps to order society and provide its members with meaning, unity, peace of mind, and the degree of control over events they believe is possible.

cosmology A system of beliefs that deals with fundamental questions in the religious and social order.

of changing existing conditions. Religion may critically affect the way a culture relates to its environment.

SEARCHING FOR ORDER AND MEANING

One of the most important functions of religion is to explain aspects of the physical and social environment that are important in the lives of individuals and societies and give them meaning. Although there is no single question answered by every religion, belief systems all provide responses to the central concerns of their followers. Religions usually support the fundamental assumptions their believers make about the nature of reality. They provide a **cosmology**—a set of principles or beliefs about the nature of life and death, the creation of the universe, the origin of society, the relationship of individuals and groups to one another, and the relation of humankind to nature. Human societies create symbolic images of reality that serve as a framework for interpreting events and experiences. Through religion, humans impose order and meaning on their world and often gain the feeling that they have some measure of control over it.

By defining the place of the individual in society and through the establishment of moral codes, religions provide people with a sense of personal identity, belonging, and meaning. When people suffer a profound personal loss or when life loses meaning because of radically changed circumstances, religion can supply a new identity and become the basis for personal and cultural survival. Giving meaning to our lives and the world is fundamental to human existence. Psychologist Victor Frankl, a survivor of the Nazi death camps, found that those whose lives retain meaning, even in hopeless situations, are more likely to survive than those whose lives lose meaning (1946). Although there are many possible ways to give one's life meaning, historically and cross-culturally, religion is the principal means that people have used.

Science and religion are often opposed in Western thought, but both are means through

RELIGION AND ECOLOGY

Religious belief and ritual may not only contribute indirectly to the survival of a society but may also directly affect the relationship between a social group and its physical environment. A classic study by Roy Rappaport (1967) of the Tsembaga of New Guinea shows how religious belief and ritual may produce "a practical result on the external world."

The Tsembaga, who live in the valleys of a mountain range in New Guinea, are swidden cultivators who also raise pigs. Small numbers of pigs are easy to keep, as they eat anything and help keep residential areas free from garbage. Although pigs can ruin gardens, they are also useful for cultivation. Before planting, they are allowed into garden areas to root after old seeds, tubers, and other plants. This not only disposes of weeds but also helps churn and soften the soil, preparing it for planting. If pig herds grow too large, however, feeding them becomes a problem; people must grow additional food just for the pigs. Furthermore, when there are too many pigs, they are more likely to invade gardens and eat crops meant for people. When this happens, it creates disputes among neighbors and friends. Thus, it becomes necessary to reduce the size of the pig herd. However, the Tsembaga kill pigs only on ritual occasions or in times of misfortune such as illness, death, or warfare.

The Tsembaga have a ritual cycle that they perform in order to rearrange their relationships with the supernatural world. This cycle can be viewed as beginning with the rituals performed during warfare. In Tsembaga warfare, opponents generally occupy territories next to each other. After hostilities have broken out, each side performs certain rituals that formally designate the other group as the enemy. Fighting may continue on and off for weeks, sometimes ending with one group's being routed. In this case, the survivors go to live with their kinsmen, and the victors destroy the losers' gardens, slaughter their pigs, and burn their houses. The victors do not occupy their land, however, as it is believed to be guarded by the ancestors of the defeated group.

Most Tsembaga warfare ends in truce, however, with both groups remaining on their territory. When a truce is declared, each group performs a ritual called "planting the rumbin." The rumbin is a type of plant. At the ritual, the rumbin is dedicated to the ancestors, who are thanked for helping in the fight. Then there is a wholesale slaughter of adult pigs. Some of the meat is eaten by the local group itself, and the rest is distributed to other groups that have helped it fight. After the feast, there is a period in which the fighting groups are still considered to be in debt to their allies and their ancestors. This period will not end until the rumbin plant is uprooted. Uprooting the rumbin also requires a pig feast and occurs when there are enough pigs. But how many pigs are enough?

When pig herds exceed four per woman caretaker, they become too troublesome to manage and begin to compete with humans for food. At this point, the wives of the owners of large numbers of pigs begin agitating for the ritual to uproot the rumbin. This ritual is followed by a pig festival lasting about a year, which involves much entertaining among villages. Food is exchanged, and hosts and guests spend the nights dancing. During this time, future alliances may be established between hosts and guests. Much trade also takes place, involving such items as axes, bird plumes, and shell ornaments. For one festival, Rappaport observed that 4500–6000 pounds of pig meat were distributed over 163 occasions to 2000–3000 people in 17 local groups. The pig festival ends with another pig slaughter and the public presentation of a salted pig belly to one's allies. This concludes the ritual cycle. A local group would now consider itself free to attack its neighbors, knowing that assistance from both human allies and ancestors would be forthcoming because their obligation to feed them pork had been fulfilled.

Although the Tsembaga see their rituals in religious terms, it is clear that they have many ecological functions as well. The rituals form a complex system of cultural switches that control the production of pigs, warfare, trade, and the consumption of pig meat, turning each of these off and on. In addition to mediating the relationship between the Tsembaga and their ancestors and gods, religious rituals keep the Tsembaga in balance with their environment. They regulate the relationship between people and pigs, ensuring that neither exceeds the carrying capacity of the environment or the ability of the Tsembaga culture to handle stress.

Courtesy of Yuko Miyazaki

RELIGIONS PROVIDE A SENSE OF ORDER AND MEANING IN A WORLD THAT OFTEN SEEMS CHAOTIC.

and dead ancestors, power and leadership are often believed to have divine origins, rules of behavior are given divine sanction, and breaches of these rules are punished by the gods. The success of even ordinary undertakings in the physical world is ensured by enlisting the help of supernatural powers. Natural disasters, illness, and misfortune are believed to be caused by extrahuman or supernatural spirits. Natural and supernatural, human and natural, past, present, and future may be perceived as a unity in a way that violates the logic of Western thought. This makes it difficult for us to understand many non-Western religions and accounts for our ethnocentric labeling of them as irrational, contradictory, or the products of faulty thinking.

REDUCING ANXIETY AND INCREASING CONTROL

Many religious practices are aimed at ensuring success in human activities. Prayers, sacrifice, and magic are done in the hope that they will aid a particular person or community. Rituals are performed to call on supernatural beings and to control forces that appear to be unpredictable. Although such practices are widespread, they seem more common in situations in which there is less predictability of outcome and thus less feeling of being in control. For example, if you have studied for a test and know the material well, you are unlikely to spend much time praying for success. You are more likely to pray for success if you have not studied, and you may even bring your lucky pencil or another charm to the test.

Prayer and magic are prevalent in sports and games of chance. Anthropologist and former professional baseball player George Gmelch (2000) has noted that professional baseball players are likely to use magic for the least predictable aspects of the game: hitting and pitching. Fielding has little uncertainty, and few magical practices are connected with it.

Even if prayer and magic do not "work" from the standpoint of Western science, they may be effective in achieving results indirectly, mainly by reducing the anxiety of those who practice them. Sometimes, technology and science are

which people seek to understand the world, and both provide organizing principles to guide that search. In fact, many early European scientists, such as Copernicus and Newton, were deeply religious. They felt that their study of the world brought them close to the mind of its creator. In the modern world, however, there are some key differences between scientific and religious understanding. Scientific explanations depend on empirical data based on observation and measurement, whereas religious systems tend not to be open to empirical testing and are based on faith. Conversely, science can deal only with certain types of questions and problems. When people cannot agree on the kinds of research questions, data, or means of measurement that are central to an issue, science must remain mute. Thus, questions of beauty, love, and the existence of what we call the supernatural lie beyond the reach of scientific answers.

The separation between religion and science in the United States corresponds to the sharp separation of the supernatural and the natural typical of American culture. Other societies make less of a distinction between the two, or sometimes none at all. Thus, in many societies, kin groups may include both living relatives

able to increase predictability and control over events. Then ritual practices tend to become less important. However, like getting an "A" in this course or hitting a baseball, many aspects of life remain intrinsically unpredictable.

REINFORCING OR MODIFYING THE SOCIAL ORDER

Religion is closely connected with the survival of society and generally works to preserve the social order. Through religion, beliefs about good and evil are reinforced by supernatural means of social control. Sacred stories and rituals provide a rationale for the present social order and give social values sacred authority. Religious ritual also intensifies social solidarity by creating an atmosphere in which people experience their common identity in emotionally moving ways. Finally, religion is an important educational institution. Initiation rites, for example, almost always include transmission of information about cultural practices and tradition.

Religion can also be a catalyst for social change. When the image of the social order that a religion presents fails to match the daily experience of its followers, prophets may emerge who create new religious ideas or call for a purification of existing practices. Sometimes prophecies encourage people to invest themselves in purely magical practices that have little real effect on the social order. At other times, however, prophets call on their followers to pursue their goals through political or military means, which may result in rapid social change. The American civil rights movement, the Iranian revolution, the rise of the Taliban government in Afghanistan, and the conflict between Pakistan and India over the state of Kashmir are all examples of social movements in which religion has played a critical role.

At times, religion provides an escape from reality. In the religious beliefs of a glorious future or the coming of a savior, powerless people who live in harsh and deprived circumstances can create an illusion of power through the manipulation of religious symbols. Religion in these circumstances has both individ-

ual and social functions. It provides an outlet for frustration, resentment, and anger and serves to drain off energy that might otherwise be turned against the social system. In this way, religion contributes indirectly to maintaining the social order.

CHARACTERISTICS OF RELIGIONS

Although there are no points of faith or doctrine adhered to by all the world's religions, most religions do have common characteristics. All religions include a body of sacred narratives and symbols. Most religions fill their worlds with beings such as gods, spirits, ghosts, and tricksters. All have rituals in which groups come together to celebrate the critical stories and symbols of their tradition, communicate with gods or spirits, and try to affect their physical and social worlds. In addition, they have individual and communal ways of addressing the supernatural world through prayer, sacrifice, and magic. Finally, all religions have clerics, people who take leading roles in performing religious rituals for society.

SACRED NARRATIVES AND SYMBOLS

Anthropologists may attempt to analyze the functions of religion within a society. However, members of the society do not experience religion in these terms. They experience it through their beliefs and understandings. These are generally expressed through the use of symbols and the telling of stories. Therefore, anthropologists study the meanings and structure of the sacred narratives and symbols.

Sacred stories or narratives have often been called myths, but this is problematic. We generally use the word *myth* to denote a false belief, or a religious belief we do not share. Thus, we are likely to claim that our own religion is composed of history and sacred story, but other people have myths. For example, we may say that Christians, Jews, and Muslims have Bible stories, but Native Americans have myths. Clearly, we should apply the same terminol-

A MOSAIC OF RELIGIONS

Although many people think of the United States as having an extremely secular culture, it is actually one of the world's most religious industrialized nations. When De Tocqueville arrived in America in 1831, the religious aspect of the country was the first thing that struck his attention (1835–1840/1956:319). Today, 96 percent of Americans say they believe in God, and church attendance has risen steadily in recent years (Warner 1995). In 1940, only about 37 percent of Americans attended church regularly; today, according to the world value survey (Morin 1998), 44 percent do. This compares with 27 percent in Great Britain, 21 percent in France, and 4 percent in Sweden. Not only are more Americans participating in religion, but they are joining an extremely broad range of religious organizations. Immigration, ease of transportation, and electronic communication have all made common religions that were once considered exotic in the United States.

A recent survey of the membership of religious organizations in the United States (Britannica 1996:298) shows that in 1995 the great majority of Americans were Christians. However, other religions showed surprisingly large memberships. For example, there were 300,000 Baha'i, 780,000 Buddhists, 910,000 Hindus, more than 5 million Muslims, and 5.5 million Jews. Furthermore, many of these religions were increasing their membership at a faster rate than Christian churches. Whereas the annual rate of increase of Christians is about 0.83 percent, non-Christians are increasing at a rate of about 1.77 percent. Religions that are traditionally considered Asian are increasing particularly rapidly (Buddhism 4.33 percent and Hinduism 9.15 percent). Christians have no need to fear for their majority status for many years to come, but as a percentage of the population they are steadily declining. Almost 91 percent of Americans were Christians in 1970, but by 2000 that number had declined to less than 85 percent. Temples and mosques are increasingly joining churches and synagogues as part of the American scene.

ogy to others' religious beliefs that we apply to our own.

Sacred narratives are stories that tell of historical events, heroes, gods, spirits, and the origin of all things. Such stories are powerful symbolic means of communicating religious ideas. These narratives are not merely explanatory stories of the cosmos, but have a sacred power in themselves that is evoked by telling them or acting them out ritually. Sacred narratives may recall historic events, although these are often clothed in poetic and sometimes esoteric language.

By explaining that things came to be the way they are through the activities of sacred beings, sacred narratives validate or legitimize beliefs, values, and customs, particularly those having to do with ethical relations. As Bronislaw Malinowski pointed out more than half a century ago, there is an intimate connection between the sacred tales of a society and its ritual acts, moral deeds, and social organization. These stories are not merely idle tales, wrote Malinowski, "but a hard-worked active force; the function of myth, briefly, is to strengthen tradition and endow it with a greater value and prestige by tracing it back to a higher, better, more supernatural reality of initial events" (1954:146).

A clear example of what Malinowski meant is provided by a portion of the origin narrative of the Hopi, an agricultural people who live in New Mexico. Traditionally, they have been vegetarians, subsisting mostly on blue corn. Blue corn is more difficult to grow than most other varieties, but it is a strong, resistant strain. Hopi life is difficult; the Hopi say "it is hard to be a Hopi but good to be a Hopi" (Loftin 1991:5). Through the growing of blue corn, the Hopi reexperience the creation of their world.

According to Hopi belief, in earlier, imperfect creations they lived underground. Just be-

sacred narratives Stories held to be holy and true by members of a religious tradition. Sacred narratives tell of historical events, heroes, gods, spirits, and the origin of all things.

fore the Hopi appeared on the Earth's surface, they were given their choice of subsistence activities. They chose blue corn and were given the *sooya,* or digging stick, to plant it. The techniques for the farming of blue corn were established by the god Maasaw, who taught the Hopi to treat the earth respectfully, as a relative. The Hopi believe that doing so recreates the feelings of humility and harmony that the ancestors chose when they selected the blue corn. Before the twentieth century, the Hopi farmed their fields in work groups made up of clan members. Because their tradition holds that clans were given land to farm together as they became members of the tribe, Hopi reexperience the settlement of their land by various clans as they farm (Loftin 1991:5–9). It is easy to see how the Hopi creation story serves as a charter for society. The Hopi live their religious understanding of their world as they grow blue corn. The telling of such stories and the actions that accompany them or are implied in them reinforce social tradition and enhance solidarity.

Religious symbolism may be expressed in material objects such as the cross, the Star of David, and the crescent moon and star of Islam. Masks, statues, paintings, costumes, body decorations, or objects in the physical environment may also be used as symbols. In addition, religions frequently use verbal symbols. The names for gods and spirits, certain words, phrases, or songs are often believed to be powerful in themselves.

In religious ritual, ideas are often acted out in dance, drama, and physical movements. Because such ideas are often complex and abstract, they require symbolic representation in order to be grasped by most people. The Christian ritual of the communion service, for example, symbolizes the New Testament story of the Last Supper, which communicates the abstract idea of communion with god. This idea is present in other religions but is represented by different symbolism. In Hinduism, for example, one of the most popular representations of communion with god is the love between the divine Krishna, in the form of a cowherd, and the gopis, or milkmaids, who are devoted to him. In the dramatic enactment of the stories of Krishna and in the singing of songs to him, the Hindu religion offers a path to communion with god that ordinary people can understand.

THE WORLD OF SPIRITS AND SACRED POWERS

A great many important religious narratives and symbols concern the world of spirits and sacred powers. Although many religions do not separate the natural from the supernatural, most propose that the world is full of beings and powers that have life and consciousness separate from that of human beings but whose existence cannot be proven through scientific measurement. Spirits may be **anthropomorphic,** or human in form; **zoomorphic,** with the form of an animal; or **naturalistic,** associated with features of the natural environment. They are generally **anthropopsychic;** that is, they have features of personality similar to those of human beings.

Spirits have volition. They can be happy or unhappy, stingy or generous, or can experience any other human emotion. The understanding of the spirits and souls of animals in hunting societies provides a good illustration. Among the Netsilik Inuit, the souls of bear, caribou, and seal were particularly important. The Netsilik believed that if the soul of an animal they killed received the proper religious attention, it would be pleased. Such an animal would reincarnate in another animal body and let itself be killed again by the same hunter. In this sense, a hunter who treated the spirits of the animals he killed properly would always hunt and kill the same animals. An animal soul that did not receive proper attention, however, would be angered and would not let itself be killed a second time. As a result, the hunt would fail. Particularly offended animal souls might become

---

anthropomorphic Having human shape.

zoomorphic Having an animal shape.

naturalistic Endowing features of the natural world, such as rivers and mountains, with spirit, soul, or other supernatural characteristics.

anthropopsychic Having thought processes and emotions similar to humans.

Bob Burch/Bruce Coleman Inc.

IN RELIGIOUS CEREMONIES, HUMANS MAY BE TRANSFORMED INTO SUPERNATURAL BEINGS. THIS MASKED DANCER FROM CÔTE D'IVOIRE IS NOT SIMPLY A PERSON WEARING A MASK, BUT A PERSON WHO HAS BECOME A SUPERNATURAL BEING.

bloodthirsty monsters and terrorize people (Balikci 1970:200–201).

The term **god** is generally used for a named spirit who is believed to have created or to control some aspect of the world. In some religions, gods are of central importance, but this is not always the case. High gods—that is, gods understood as the creator of the world and ultimate power in it—are present in only about half of all societies (Levinson 1996:229). In about one-third of these societies, such gods are distant and withdrawn, having little inter-

god A named spirit who is believed to have created or to control some aspects of the world.

polytheism Belief in many gods.

monotheism Belief in a single god.

trickster A supernatural entity that does not act in the best interests of humans.

mana Religious power or energy that is concentrated in individuals or objects.

est in people, and prayer to them is unnecessary. An example is the creator god of the Igbo of Nigeria. Like other remote gods, he is accessible only through prayer to lesser spirits (Uchendu 1965:94).

A religion may be **polytheistic** (having many gods) or **monotheistic** (having only one god). However, the difference between them is not clear-cut. In polytheistic religions, the many gods may really be different aspects of one god. In India, for example, it is said that there are literally millions of gods; yet all Indians understand that in some way they are all aspects of one divine essence. Conversely, in monotheistic religions, the one god may have several aspects. In Roman Catholicism, for example, there is God the Father, God the Son, and God the Holy Spirit; yet these are all part of a single, unitary God.

One class of spirit that may be singled out for special treatment is the **trickster.** Trickster spirits come in many guises, but their key characteristic is that they are interested in their own benefit, not that of human beings. Some tricksters, such as the Christian Devil, are personifications of evil. Others are much more sympathetic. They often combine attributes such as greed, lust, and envy with humor and wisdom. Tricksters are powerful, but they themselves are often fooled. In African religions, monkey and hyena spirits are often tricksters. In many Native American cultures, the key trickster spirit is Coyote.

In addition to spirits, religions often hypothesize that a special sort of religious power or energy, called **mana,** infuses the universe. Mana may be concentrated in individuals or in objects. For example, as noted in Chapter 12, chiefs in Tahiti had a much higher degree of mana than ordinary people. Mana gives one spiritual power, but it can also be dangerous. That is why belief in mana is often associated with an elaborate system of taboos, or prohibitions. Mana is like electricity; it is a powerful force, but it can be dangerous when not approached with the proper caution.

Mana is most often found in areas (spatial, temporal, verbal, or physical) that are the boundaries between clear-cut categories. Hair, for

C U L T U R A L   F O C U S

AZTEC HUMAN SACRIFICE

Human sacrifice was an important aspect of Aztec religion. Aztec gods such as the jaguar and the serpent were bloodthirsty and fierce and required human victims to appease their appetites. The Aztec ritual calendar had many festivals that required human sacrifice; on these occasions, such sacrifices were made in towns throughout central Mexico. Special occasions, such as the coronation of a new king, also called for human sacrifice. On one particularly famous occasion, as many as 80,400 captives were sacrificed at the dedication of a temple (Hassig 1988:221). Most victims of sacrifice were partially consumed in cannibal feasts.

Michael Harner (1977) and Marvin Harris (1989) have suggested that Aztec human sacrifice was ecologically determined by a shortage of dietary protein. Because the Aztec had no large domesticated animals and little access to wild game, human meat was an important supplement to their diet. Although this is an interesting explanation, it is incompatible with archaeological and nutritional evidence, and most anthropologists consider it discredited (Ortiz de Montellano 1990; Conrad and Demarest 1984). Many anthropologists now view Aztec sacrifice from a political perspective. They argue that it was part of the strategy of intimidation the Aztecs used to demonstrate their power and to rule subjugated peoples (Hassig 1988).

A symbolic approach to understanding Aztec cannibalism suggests that for the Aztecs the consumption of human flesh was less important than the sacred character of the sacrificial rite. The aim of this rite was to bring humans into communion with the gods. Without the proper nourishment of human hearts and human blood, the gods could not work on behalf of humans. The gods depended on human sacrifice for energy; without it, the sun would not come up, the sky would fall down, and the universe would return to its original state of chaos. The sustenance given to the gods in the sacrificial offering, and to humans in their houses, ensured the regeneration of every individual and of Aztec society (Sahlins 1978; Sanday 1986).

Whatever we think of the Aztec rationale for human sacrifice, we might argue that from their perspective they were correct. The cessation of human sacrifice brought about by Spanish conquest was simultaneous with the collapse of the Aztec way of life. When the gods stopped receiving sustenance, Aztec society disintegrated.

---

example, is believed to contain supernatural power in many different cultures (as in the Old Testament story of Samson and Delilah). Hair is a symbol of the boundary between the self and the not-self, both part of a person and separable from the person. Doorways and gates—which separate the inside from the outside and can thus serve as symbols of moral categories such as good and evil, pure and impure—are also widespread symbols of power. Because these boundary symbols contain supernatural power, they are often used in religious ritual and surrounded by taboos.

RELIGIOUS RITUALS

Sacred narratives, symbols, spirits, and sacred power all find their place in religious ritual. A **ritual** is a ceremonial act or a repeated stylized gesture used for specific occasions (Cunningham et al. 1995). A religious ritual is one that involves the use of religious symbols. Through ritual, people enact their religion. Rituals may involve the telling or acting out of sacred stories as well the use of music, dance, drugs, or pain to move worshipers to an ecstatic state of trance.

The specific content of religious rituals—the stories and symbols they use, and the spirits and powers they address—varies enormously from culture to culture. However, certain patterns of religious behavior are extremely widespread, if not universal. Rites of passage and rites of intensification are found in almost all cultures. In addition, almost all people address

---

ritual A patterned act that involves the manipulation of religious symbols.

the supernatural through prayers, sacrifices, magic, and divination.

RITES OF PASSAGE

Rites of passage are public events that mark the transition of a person from one social status to another (see Chapter 6). Rites of passage almost always mark birth, puberty, marriage, and death and may include many other transitions as well. Rites of passage involve three phases (van Gennep 1961). The first phase is **separation,** in which the person or group is detached from a former status. The second, or **liminal,** phase is one of limbo, in which the person has been detached from the old status but not yet attached to a new one. The third stage is **reincorporation,** in which the passage from one status to another is symbolically completed. After reincorporation, the person takes on the rights and obligations of his or her new social status.

Anthropologists have been particularly interested in analyzing the liminal stage of ritual. The liminal stage mediates between two statuses; a person in the liminal stage is "neither here nor there." To emphasize this, the symbols of the liminal stage often focus on nothingness and ambiguity. The liminal stage often involves a dissolution of many of the structured and hierarchical classifications that normally separate people in society (such as caste, class, or kinship categories) and puts people in a temporary state of equality and oneness called **communitas.**

Communitas has many different expressions, but it is often characterized by what anthropologists call **antistructure,** and it frequently includes role reversals. Behavior that would be virtually unthinkable under usual circumstances becomes normal. For example, ritual transvestism was once a prominent feature of community festivals in Japan. All members of the community would dance wearing the clothing of the opposite sex (Norbeck 1974:51). At the Wubwang'u ritual among the Ndembu of Zambia, men and women publicly insult each other's sexual abilities and extol their own, but no one is allowed to take offense (Turner 1969: 78–79).

As society becomes more complex and differentiated, some institutionalized liminal statuses emerge. Organizations such as monasteries, where people live permanently as members of a religious community, embody communitas or are the medium for bringing it about. Institutionally liminal individuals or groups are often of low status and ambiguous nature. They are frequently associated with danger or supernatural power and sacredness. Their very marginality, paradoxically, is the source of their power. For example, the hijras of India (see Chapter 11) are in between the classifications of male and female. Because of their sexual ambiguity, they are believed to have the power to confer blessings for fertility.

Rituals that include a state of communitas are extremely widespread and are often depicted in religious art, symbols, and sacred narratives. This suggests that humans need the bonds of communitas. Societies must be structured to provide order and meaning. But antistructure— the temporary ritual dissolution of the established order—is also important, helping people to more fully realize the oneness of the self and the other (Turner 1969:131).

RITES OF INTENSIFICATION

In addition to rites of passage, most societies have **rites of intensification.** These are rituals directed toward the welfare of the group or community rather than the individual. They

---

rite of passage A ritual that marks a person's transition from one status to another.

separation The first stage of a rite of passage in which individuals are removed from their community or status.

liminal The stage of a ritual, particularly a rite of passage, in which one has passed out of an old status but not yet entered a new one.

reincorporation The third stage of a rite of passage during which participants are returned to their community with a new status.

communitas A state of perceived solidarity, equality, and unity among people sharing a religious ritual, often characterized by intense emotion.

antistructure The socially sanctioned use of behavior that radically violates social norms. Antistructure is frequently found in religious ritual.

rite of intensification A ritual structured to reinforce the values and norms of a community and to strengthen group identity.

are structured to reinforce the values and norms of the community and to strengthen group identity. Through these rituals, the community maintains continuity with the past, enhances the feeling of social unity in the present, and renews the sentiments on which cohesion depends (Elkin 1967).

In some groups, rites of intensification are connected with totems. A **totem** is an object, an animal species, or a feature of the natural world that is associated with a particular descent group. **Totemism** is a prominent feature of the religions of the Australian aborigines. People are grouped into societies or lodges, each of which is linked with some species in the natural environment that is its totem. Under most circumstances, members of a group are prohibited from eating their totem. In religious rituals, members of the same society or lodge assemble to celebrate their totems. The ceremonies, which often take place at night, explain the origin of the totem (and hence, of the group) and reenact the time of the ancestors. Through singing and dancing, both performers and onlookers are transported to an ecstatic state. In a classic description, French sociologist Émile Durkheim wrote:

> When they are once come together, a sort of electricity is formed by their collecting which quickly transports them to an extraordinary degree of exaltation. . . . [O]n every side one sees nothing but violent gestures, cries, veritable howls, and deafening noises of every sort. . . . One can readily conceive how, when arrived at this state . . . a man does not recognize himself any longer . . . [and feels] himself dominated and carried away by some sort of external power. . . . [E]verything is just as though he really were transported into a special world. (1915/1961:247–251)

Durkheim believed that when people worship their totem, which is a symbol of their common social identity, they are actually worshiping the moral and social order that is the foundation of social life. In doing so, they bind themselves to each other, creating and worshiping their shared identity. Although not all

RITES OF INTENSIFICATION CREATE AND REINFORCE GROUP IDENTITY. THEY CAN BE USED FOR RELIGIOUS, POLITICAL, OR ECONOMIC PURPOSES. THE NAZI NUREMBERG RALLY, HELD ANNUALLY FROM 1933 TO 1938, WAS DESIGNED TO REINFORCE ENTHUSIASM FOR THE NAZI PARTY AND SHOWCASE ITS POWER.

aspects of his theory are considered correct today, his analysis of the role of religious rites in heightening social solidarity is an important contribution to understanding human behavior.

The religious rituals of the Australian aborigines may seem exotic, but Americans participate in similar observances all the time—and to the same effect. Some American rites of intensification are religious, but many are secular. One with which most students are familiar is the college football game and the rallies associated with it. If the game is "good" or the school has "spirit," these gatherings produce enormous excitement among their fans and transport them to "a special world." They also increase collective identity. If you are a fan, you will probably feel intense identification with your school and your team at such an event. Identification with your team and the excite-

---

totem An animal, plant, or other aspect of the natural world held to be ancestral or to have other intimate relationships with members of a group.

totemism Religious practices centered around animals, plants, or other aspects of the natural world held to be ancestral or to have other intimate relationships with members of a group.

ment of sporting events will help to keep you "loyal" to your school (and hopefully encourage you to donate to it as an alumnus/a). Schools have totems (animal mascots) as well.

MEANS OF ADDRESSING THE SUPERNATURAL

Most religious rituals involve a combination of prayer, sacrifices, and magic to contact and control supernatural spirits and powers. The difference between these common ways of worship lies in the degree of control that humans believe they exert over the spirit world. In addition, people may also use divination to attempt to discover hidden truths.

PRAYER

Prayer is any conversation held with spirits and gods. In prayer, people petition, invoke, praise, give thanks, dedicate, supplicate, intercede, confess, repent, and bless (Levinson 1996). The critical feature of prayer is that people believe that its results depend on the will of the spirit world rather than on actions humans perform. Thus, the failure of a spirit to respond to a request is understood as resulting from its disinclination rather than from improper human action. Prayer may involve a request, a pleading, or merely praise for the deity. Other forms of prayer are less familiar to Westerners. In some cultures, gods may be lied to or ridiculed. Among the many Northwest Coast tribes of North America, the insulting tone used to one's political rivals was also used to the gods. In these ranked societies, the greatest insult was to call a man a slave; when calamities fell or their prayers were not answered, people vented their anger against the gods by saying, "You are a great slave" (Benedict 1934/1961:221).

prayer Any communication between people and spirits or gods in which people praise, plead, or request without assurance of results.

sacrifice An offering made to increase the efficacy of a prayer or the religious purity of an individual.

magic A religious ritual believed to produce a mechanical effect by supernatural means. When magic is done correctly, believers think it must have the desired effect.

SACRIFICE

Sacrifice occurs when people make offerings to spirits to increase the efficacy of their prayers. People may sacrifice animal lives or human lives in order to propitiate a deity. In Western culture, it is more common to offer changes in behavior. People may offer to give up smoking or drinking if god will grant a request.

Bargaining with spirits or making offerings and sacrifices to them are also widespread religious practices. In many religions, including Christianity, it is common to make a vow to carry out a certain kind of behavior, such as going on a pilgrimage or building a place of worship, if the spirits will grant a particular wish. Offerings to spirits may consist of the first fruits of a harvest. In some societies, animals or humans may be sacrificed as an offering to the gods.

Cattle sacrifices are central to religion among cattle pastoralists of East Africa, such as the Nuer and the Pokot. The essence of the East African cattle complex is that cattle are killed and eaten only in a ritual and religious context. This may seem an inefficient use of resources, but it may be quite adaptive. Cattle sacrifices are offered in community feasts that occur about once a week in any particular neighborhood. The feasts are thus an important source of meat in the diet. Furthermore, the religious taboo that a person who eats ritually slaughtered meat may not take milk on the same day has the effect of making milk more available to those who have no meat or of conserving milk, which can be consumed as sour milk on the following day. In the absence of refrigeration, sacrifices and feasts offer access to fresh meat. One family could not consume a whole steer by itself, but this problem is solved by offering it to the community in a ceremonial setting. Because the portions are distributed according to age and sex by a rigid formula, meat can be shared without quarreling over the supply (Schneider 1973).

MAGIC

When people do **magic,** they believe that their words and actions compel the spirit world to behave in certain ways. Failure of a magical request is understood as resulting from incorrect performance of the ritual rather than the refusal of spirits to act. Magic is an attempt to mechanistically control supernatural forces. In performing magic, people are expressing their belief that ritual procedures, if done correctly, will compel a specific and predictable result.

Two of the most common magical practices are imitation and contagion. In **imitative magic,** the procedure performed resembles the result desired. A Vodou doll is a form of imitative magic with which many people are familiar. The principle is that mistreatment of a doll-like image of a person will cause injury to that person. The Christian practice of baptism can also be seen as a form of imitative magic. Most Christians believe that in baptism original sin, often ritually compared with dirt or a stain, is washed away with holy water. Christians generally do not see themselves as compelling god in the baptism ritual, but they do believe that if the ceremony is done properly by duly constituted authority, god will not fail to remove original sin from the child.

Contagious magic is based on the idea that an object that has been in contact with a person retains a magical connection with that person. For example, a person might attempt to increase the effectiveness of a Vodou doll by attaching a piece of clothing, hair, or other object belonging to the person they wish to injure. People in the United States often attribute special power and meaning to objects that have come in contact with famous or notorious people. Signed baseballs, bits of costumes worn by movie stars, and pens used to sign famous documents all become collectors' items and are imbued with special power and importance.

In many cultures, magical practices accompany most human activities. Among the Asaro of New Guinea, when a child is born, its umbilical cord is buried so that it cannot later be used by a sorcerer to cause harm. In order to prevent the infant's crying at night, a bundle of sweet-smelling grass is placed on the mother's head, and her wish for uninterrupted sleep is blown into the grass. The grass is then crushed over the head of the child who, in breathing its aroma, also breathes in the mother's command not to cry. When a young boy kills his

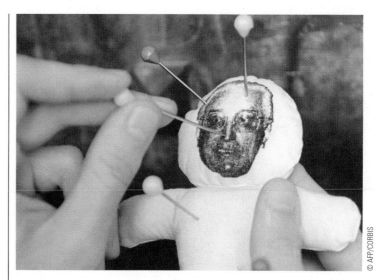

A VODOU DOLL IS AN EXAMPLE OF BOTH IMITATIVE AND CONTAGIOUS MAGIC.

first animal, his hand is magically "locked" into the position of the successful kill. When he later tries to court a girl, he will use love magic, which in a particularly powerful form will make him appear in front of her with the face of another man to whom she is known to be attracted. Both magical and technical skills are used to make gardens and pigs grow. One technique is to blow smoke into the ear of a wild pig to tame it. This is based on the belief that the smoke cools and dries the pig's "hot" disposition. Magical techniques are used to treat serious illness: blowing smoke over the patient to cool a fever (which is hot) or administering sweet-smelling leaves with a command for the illness to depart.

DIVINATION

Divination, a ritual practice directed toward obtaining useful information from a supernatural authority, is found in many societies. Div-

imitative magic The belief that imitating an action in a religious ritual will cause the action to happen in the material world.

contagious magic The belief that things once in contact with a person or object retain an invisible connection with that person or object.

divination A religious ritual done to find hidden objects or information.

ination discovers the unknown or the hidden. It may be used to predict the future, diagnose disease, find hidden objects, or discover something about the past. In many cultures, divination is used to discover who committed a crime.

The Naskapi, who hunt caribou on the Labrador peninsula, use a form of divination called **scapulomancy.** In this divination ritual, a shoulder blade (scapula) of a caribou or other animal is scorched by fire. The scorched bone is used as a map of the hunting area, and the cracks in the bone are read as giving information about the best place to hunt (O. Moore 1969). This technique was also used in ancient China and Japan (de Waal Malefijt 1968:220). Scapulomancy may be adaptive because it randomizes the choices of hunting sites, a strategy that modern game theorists know results in the least chance of repeated failures.

Most Americans are familiar with a wide variety of divination techniques. Tarot cards, palmistry, flipping coins, and reading auras are all forms of divination. Some farmers use a divination technique called water witching or dowsing to find sources of well water. In one technique, the dowser holds a forked willow branch (a willow is a tree found by river banks and is "sympathetic" to water) in his hands as he walks over a property. When he stands above water, the wand is supposed to bend downward. The effect of this ritual is to help a homesteader make a decision and be able to move forward confidently in developing his farm. In fact, because of the great variability of the water table, the method of the dowser appears to be no more or less reliable than scientific techniques in determining which spots will have water.

The practice of divination makes people more confident in their choices when they do not have all the information they need or when several alternative courses of action appear equal.

Divination may also be practiced when a group decision has to be made and there is disagreement. If the choice is made by divination, no member of the group feels rejected.

Prayer, sacrifice, and magic can be found in most religious traditions, and the distinctions between them are more a matter of degree than of exclusive classification. For example, a great many prayers contain elements of sacrifice, and most magical practitioners agree that, in theory, it is possible that the spirit world will not honor their request, although in practice it may never happen.

RELIGIOUS PRACTITIONERS

Every society has people who are considered to have a special relationship with the religious world. These religious practitioners, or **clerics,** are charged with organizing and leading major ritual events. There are many different kinds of clerics, but anthropologists generally organize them into two broad categories: shamans and priests.

SHAMANS

Shamans are part-time clerics. In many respects, they are average members of the community; they must hunt, gather, garden, or get up and go to work like anyone else. Their shamanic activities are reserved for specific ceremonies, times of illness, or crisis.

Although learning to be a shaman may involve arduous training, a critical aspect of shamanism is that shamans have direct, personal experiences of the supernatural. Study alone cannot make a person a shaman; he or she must be chosen by the spirit world and be able to enter into it. Shamans use prayer, meditation, song, dance, pain, drugs, or any combination of techniques to achieve a trance state in which they understand themselves (and are understood by their followers) as able to enter into the real world of the supernatural. They may use such contact to bring guidance to themselves or their group, heal sick people, or divine the future. Almost all societies have some

---

scapulomancy Divination using the shoulder blade of an animal.

cleric A religious practitioner or authority.

shaman An individual who is socially recognized as having the ability to mediate between the world of humanity and the world of gods or spirits but who is not a recognized official of any religious organization.

PRESERVING SHAMANISM

In the past hundred years, anthropologists have played a critical role in the preservation and maintenance of traditional religious practices. In the early years of the twentieth century, Franz Boas and his students interviewed elders in many Native American tribes. They collected religious lore and described the ceremonial practices of these societies. Half a century later, when the descendants of these elders sought to revive their traditional practices, the work of Boas and his students proved an invaluable source of information for them.

The work of documenting and preserving religious traditions continues today, and Michael Harner is one of the anthropologists at its forefront. Harner's fieldwork among the Jivero of Ecuador convinced him that, although Western medicine has much to offer traditional peoples, their religious and medical practices not only are of great value in their own right but offer important insights for people living in modern society. Harner went on to do fieldwork on shamanism in the western United States, Lapland, and the Canadian Arctic. He has published several books on the subject, including *The Way of the Shaman, Hallucinogens and Shamanism,* and *The Jivaro: People of the Sacred Waterfalls.*

Harner's conviction that traditional religious practices were of great value led him, in 1986, to organize the Foundation for Shamanic Studies (FSS), a nonprofit educational and research organization dedicated to the preservation, study, and teaching of shamanic knowledge. Through a worldwide network of anthropologists in the field, the FSS works to prevent shamanic knowledge from being lost. Places where the Foundation works include Nepal, Siberia, Finland, China, Central Asia, the Ecuadorian Amazon, Mexico, and West Africa. The Foundation also promotes research on altered states of consciousness and ecstatic religious trance.

One of the main goals of the FSS is education. The Foundation studies the effectiveness of shamanic healing techniques and promotes their use as a complement to mainstream medical practice. The FSS offers more than 200 courses and trains more than 5000 students, including both medical personnel and lay people, each year. Harner and his wife, a clinical psychologist, have also developed a method for using the insights gained from traditional shamans in modern psychotherapy.

The FSS maintains a website at www.shamanism.org. Many other websites are also devoted to shamanism. The Center for Shamanism and Consciousness Studies, led by anthropologist Michael Ripinsky-Naxon, also sponsors research into shamanism and offers courses. Their website can be found at www.csacs.org. A third site of interest is www.shamanism.com, the home page of the Dance of the Deer Foundation. This organization is devoted to preserving the culture and shamanic practices of the Huichol, a Native American group from the Pacific coast of Mexico.

shamans, but they are likely to be the only clerics in band and tribal societies.

VISION QUEST

In come cultures, almost every adult may be expected to achieve direct contact with the real world of the supernatural. The **vision quest,** common among many Native American groups, was an example of this. In these cultures, a person was expected to develop a special relationship with a particular spirit that would give the person power and knowledge of specific kinds. The spirit acted as a personal protector or guardian. The vision seeker was under a strong emotional impulse and by various means, such as fasting, isolation in a lonely spot, or self-mutilation, intensified his or her emotional state.

The Thompson Indians of western Canada had a vision quest that included most of the traits typical of this pattern. Boys began their search for guardian spirits between the ages of

vision quest An individual, emotionally intense search for a special relationship with a particular spirit that will provide protection, knowledge, and power.

IN MANY SOCIETIES, SHAMAN ACT AS CURERS, OFTEN TRAVELING INTO THE SUPERNATURAL TO DISCOVER THE SOURCE AND TREATMENT OF A DISEASE. IN THIS PICTURE A SHAMAN TREATS A CHILD IN LADAKH, INDIA.

© Chris Lisle/CORBIS

12 and 16. Before beginning the quest, boys prepared themselves with ordeals such as running until they were exhausted and diving into ice-cold water. They also prepared by painting their faces and wearing special clothing. The nights before the quest were spent in dancing, singing, and praying around a fire on a nearby mountain peak.

The boy then went on lonely pilgrimages into the mountains, eating nothing for several days on end. He intensified his physical suffering by sweating himself with heated rocks over which he threw water and by whipping his body with nettles. This strenuous regimen continued until the boy had a dream of some animal or bird and received the inspiration for a spirit song that he would then always use to call his protector. He also prepared a medicine bag of the skin of the spirit animal and filled it with a variety of objects that had taken on symbolic significance for him during his quest. These became the symbols of his power (Pettitt 1972).

Although the vision quest was an intensely individual experience, it was shaped by culture. Among the Crow Indians, for example, several informants related the same vision and interpretation to the anthropologist Robert Lowie (1963). They told Lowie that they saw a spirit or several spirits riding along and how the rocks and trees around the riders turned into enemies who attacked them but were unable to do any harm. They interpreted this to mean that the spirits were making them invulnerable. This motif is common in Crow religious narratives and the vision seekers worked it unconsciously into their experience. Another cultural influence is that most Crow Indians obtained their spiritual blessing on the fourth night of their seclusion, and four is considered a mystical number among the Crow.

SHAMANIC CURING

Among the Inuit as well as other groups, shamans are often called on to cure illness. Illness is cured by discovering which supernatural being has been offended by a broken taboo. Often, the shaman extracts a confession from the victim and then exorcises the possessing spirit through a ritual procedure.

In shamanic curing, the shaman, usually in a trance, travels into the supernatural world to discover the source of illness and what might be done to cure it. This may consist of combat, pitting the shaman, in his or her supernatural state, against the spirits that are responsible for the illness. Following is a description of a Netsilik Inuit curing performance:

> The shaman, adorned with his paraphernalia, crouched in a corner of the igloo . . . and covered himself with a caribou skin. The lamps were extinguished. A protective spirit called by the shaman entered his body and, through his mouth, started to speak very rapidly, using the shaman's secret vocabulary. While the shaman was in trance, the tupiliq [an evil spirit believed to be round in shape and filled with blood] left the patient's body and hid outside the igloo. The shaman then dispatched his protective spirits after the tupiliqs; they, assisted usually by the benevolent ghost of some deceased shaman, drove the tupiliqs back into the igloo through the entrance; the audience encouraged the evil spirits, shouting: "Come in, come in, somebody is here waiting for you."

No sooner had the tupiliqs entered the igloo than the shaman, with his snow knife, attacked them and killed as many as he could; his successful fight was evidenced by the evil spirits' blood on his hands. (Balikci 1970: 226–227)

If the patient died, it was said that the tupiliqs were too numerous for the shaman to kill or that after the seance evil spirits again attacked the patient.

In the modern world, shamanic curing often exists alongside modern technological medicine. People go to shamans for healing when they have diseases that are not recognized by technological medicine, they lack money to pay for modern medical treatment, or they have tried such treatment and it has failed.

Shamanistic curing has important therapeutic effects. First, shamans generally do treat their patients with drugs. All traditional cultures have a **pharmacopoeia,** or collection of preparations used as medication. Scientific testing has shown that many (though not all) traditional medicines are effective (Fábrega 1997:144). Second, shamanic curing ritual uses story, symbolism, and dramatic action to bring together cultural beliefs and religious practices in a way that enables patients to understand the source of their illness and the actions they must take to be cured. These ceremonies express and reinforce the values of a culture and the solidarity of a society. They often involve participation by the audience, whose members may experience various degrees of ecstasy themselves. Shamanic curing ceremonies work by cultivating an awareness that "one's body is located at a central intersection within a system of relations. Illness ruptures this pattern, and healing restores the perception of harmony" (Glucklich 1997:95). Such ceremonies are cathartic in the sense that they release the anxiety caused by various disturbing events. The natural and supernatural forces that have the power to do evil in a society are brought under control, and seemingly inexplicable misfortunes are given meaning within the traditional cultural pattern. As a result, both the individual and community are better able to carry out their normal activities.

PRIESTS

In most state societies, religion is bureaucratized; that is, it is an established institution consisting of a series of ranked offices that exist independently of the people who fill them. Anthropologists use the term **priest** to refer to a person who is formally elected, appointed, or hired to a full-time religious office. Priests are responsible for performing certain rituals on behalf of individuals, groups, or the entire community. Members of the community are supposed to have access to supernatural power only through these intermediaries.

Priests are most often associated with gods who are believed to have great power. They may be members of a religion that worships several high gods, as in the religions of the ancient Greeks, Egyptians, and Romans, or only one high god, as in the Judeo-Christian-Islamic tradition. Where priests exist, there is a division between the lay and priestly roles. Lay people participate in ritual largely as passive respondents or audience rather than as managers or performers.

People become priests through training and apprenticeship. For example, to become a cleric in any mainstream American religion, you would enter the training program (usually a seminary) of the appropriate religion. If you were successful, at graduation you would be certified by the religious body (or church) as a cleric and generally given an assignment. Your authority in that assignment would derive from your certification by the religion you represent.

In most mainstream religions in the United States, it is generally not considered necessary for priests to have ecstatic religious experiences. However, this is not the case in all priestly religions. Although ultimately the priest's authority derives from position, such status may give a person the right to seek direct contact with gods and spirits.

For example, in ancient Maya states, priests were members of a ranked bureaucracy. In many

pharmacopoeia A collection of preparations used as medication.

priest One who is formally elected or appointed to a full-time religious office.

MAYAN TEMPLES WERE ELABORATE STAGES FOR RITUALS DURING WHICH PRIESTS AND RULERS USED DRAMATIC TECHNIQUES TO TRAVEL INTO THE SUPERNATURAL WORLD.

George Holton/Photo Researchers, Inc.

cases, they were also political leaders; kings and members of the nobility exercised not only secular political authority but priestly authority as well. Their religious position gave them the right to use ecstatic techniques to travel in the spiritual world. At the dedication of buildings consecrated to the royal lineage, priests, including the king and other nobles, would let blood by perforating their penises and other body parts with special lancets and take hallucinogenic drugs. These methods created ecstatic states in which the priest/kings would travel to the supernatural underworld to inform their ancestors of the new building and invite the souls of these former rulers to inhabit it. A Mayan ritual might have looked like this:

> Against a backdrop of terraced architecture, elaborately costumed dancers, musicians, warriors, and nobles entered the courts in long processions. Dancers whirled across the plaza floors and terrace platforms to music made on rattles, whistles, wooden trumpets and drums of all sizes. A crowd of participants wearing bloodletting paper or cloth

witchcraft The ability to harm others by harboring malevolent thoughts about them; the practice of sorcery.

tied in triple knots sat on platforms and terraces around the plaza. According to Bishop Landa [an early Spanish writer], these people would have prepared themselves with days of fasting, abstinence and ritual steam baths. Well into the ceremony, the ruler and his wife would emerge from within a building high above the court, and in full public view, he would lacerate his penis, she her tongue. Ropes drawn through their wounds carried the flowing blood to paper strips. The saturated paper—perhaps along with other offerings, such as rubber (the chicle resin from which chewing gum is made)—were placed in large plates, then carried to braziers and burned, creating columns of black smoke. The participants, already dazed through deprivation, public hysteria and massive blood loss, were culturally conditioned to expect a hallucinatory experience. (Schele and Miller 1986:178)

As among the Maya, priests in state societies may pursue ecstatic religious experience, but states generally attempt to suppress independent shamans as a source of power competing with that of the state.

WITCHCRAFT AND SORCERY

Witchcraft and sorcery are common elements of belief in many cultures. Although the words *witchcraft* and *sorcery* are often used interchangeably, many anthropologists differentiate between the two.

WHAT ARE WITCHCRAFT AND SORCERY?

In some societies, **witchcraft** is understood as a physical aspect of a person. People are witches because their bodies contain a magical witchcraft substance. They generally acquire this substance through inheritance and may not even be conscious that they possess it. If a person's body contains the witchcraft substance, his or her malevolent thoughts will cause ill to befall those around them. The Azande, an East African group, are a classic example. They believe that witches' bodies contain a substance called mangu, which allows them to cause misfortune and death to others (Evans-Pritchard 1937/1958). This sort of witchcraft is always understood as causing evil to others. Since people are witches because of what they are rather than what they do, they are generally thought of as unable to prevent themselves from causing evil.

Sorcery is the conscious manipulation of words and ritual objects with the intent of magically causing either harm or good. Bone pointing, a magical technique of sorcerers in Melanesia described by Malinowski, is a good example of using sorcery to cause illness. The sorcerer ritually imitates throwing a magical stick, either an arrow or the spine of some animal, in the direction of the person the magic is intended to kill. For the magic to work, the sorcerer must perform the procedure with an expression of hatred. He thrusts the bone in the air, twists it in the ground, and then pulls it out with a sudden jerk. Both the physical act and the emotional state of passion have to be imitated to achieve results.

Cases of magical death, or death from sorcery, have been observed by anthropologists in many parts of the world. In a survey of numerous reports of death from sorcery, Walter Cannon (1942) concluded that death was usually caused by the victim's extreme terror. Individuals who are psychologically vulnerable to begin with, are aware that they are the victims of sorcery, and believe in its effectiveness generally exhibit stress reactions that disorder various physiological functions. The intended victim may despair, lose his or her appetite, and slowly starve to death, unable to overcome the inertia caused by the belief that he or she is a victim. Persistent terror and the weakening effects of hunger may make the victim vulnerable to infectious agents as well as stroke and heart attack.

ACCUSATIONS OF WITCHCRAFT OR SORCERY

Although people do actually practice witchcraft and sorcery, their main effects on society are probably through accusations. Accusing relatives, friends, and neighbors of witchcraft

IN EUROPEAN AND NORTH AMERICAN CULTURE, WITCHES WERE OFTEN IMAGINED TO BE OLD WOMEN DRESSED IN BLACK. THE WICKED WITCH OF THE WEST FROM THE 1939 FILM "THE WIZARD OF OZ" IS A CLASSIC EXAMPLE.

Bettmann/CORBIS

or sorcery is common in many cultures and serves various purposes.

The most common form of witchcraft accusation serves to stigmatize differences. People who do not fit into conventional social categories are often suspected of witchcraft. The European and American image of the witch as an evil old hag dressed in black is a good example. In traditional Western European society, social norms dictated that women should have husbands and children (or alternatively, they might become nuns). Impoverished women who remained in the community yet were un-

sorcery The conscious and intentional use of magic.

married or widowed without children violated this social convention and might be subject to witchcraft accusations. It is they who would have appeared as old hags dressed in black (Brain 1989; Horsley 1979). Those accused of witchcraft because they fail to conform may be ostracized and harassed but are unlikely to be killed or driven out of the community. They are valuable as negative role models, examples of what not to be. The lesson that a young girl might derive from the witch is: Get married and have children or you might end up a witch.

Witchcraft and sorcery accusations may also be used to scapegoat. In times of great social change, when war, disease, calamity, or technological change undermines the social order, people's lives lose meaning. Under such circumstances, they may well turn to accusations of witchcraft and blame their misfortunes on the presence of evildoers. If people's lives have changed for the worse, they may conclude that witches and sorcerers are to blame. Those responsible must be found and destroyed in order for their own lives to be improved.

We often think of the era of European witch-hunting as belonging to the Middle Ages, but this was not the case. During the Middle Ages, the social order remained stable and accusations of witchcraft were fairly rare. The witch craze belongs to the Renaissance, a time of great artistic and technological achievement but social disaster. Plague swept repeatedly through Europe, and the medieval social and religious order collapsed in war and chaos. Under these circumstances, people were willing to believe that witches were the cause of their misery and pursue reprisals against people they suspected of witchcraft. The accused witch who is a social deviant may be scorned and ostracized, but witches who are believed responsible for wide-scale social disaster are often dealt with more harshly. Their lot is more likely to be death or banishment. Although the number of people who were murdered in the witch craze has of-

ten been overestimated (Hester 1988), it is certain that thousands of suspected witches were put to death.

MODERN WITCHES, WICCANS, AND NEOPAGANS

Recent times in Europe and the United States have seen the emergence of religious worshipers who call themselves witches, **Wiccans,** or **neopagans.** Many Wiccan beliefs are derived from the work of English author Gerald Gardner. Gardner claimed to have rediscovered the ancient beliefs of an aboriginal fairy race, and many Wiccans today say that they practice an ancient pre-Christian religion of nature worship. However, most scholars believe that Gardner composed his religion from a variety of modern sources (A. Kelly 1991; Orion 1995).

A basic principle of most Wiccan belief is the threefold law, which proclaims that whatever good or ill people do in the world returns to them three times. Wiccans are no more likely to commit evil acts than are members of more mainstream religions. Many Wiccans are very well educated; a recent survey showed that more than 65 percent had at least one college degree and at least 25 percent had master's degrees or higher (Orion 1995:66).

RELIGION AND CHANGE

As we have seen, religion is generally a force that preserves the social order. This may be particularly evident in socially stratified societies, where the elite may invoke religious authority to control lower social orders. In such situations, the priesthood and religion act not only as a means of regulating behavior, which is a function of religion in all societies, but also as a way of maintaining social, economic, and political inequalities.

RELIGION AND RESISTANCE

Under certain circumstances, religions become vehicles of resistance to domination and catalysts for social change. Prophecy and the found-

Wiccan A member of a new religion that claims descent from pre-Christian nature worship; a modern-day witch.

neopagan See **Wiccan.**

ing of new religions are common among oppressed groups and peoples caught in eras of rapid social change. For such people, the socially equilibrating functions of established religion no longer work.

Most religions contain implicit or explicit visions of the ideal society—an image of the way a correct, just social order should look. No society actually achieves its vision; people never live exactly the way they are supposed to. However, most of the time religion validates society. The image of society as it should be is not so different from life in society as it is. As a result, most people feel that the society they live in is essentially good (or the best available). If it hasn't achieved the perfection their beliefs tell them to strive for, it is at least on the right path.

However, if societies change very rapidly (as a result of colonization, disease, or technological change) or if groups are systematically enslaved and oppressed, the vision of the ideal world painted by people's religious beliefs may move far from their daily experience. People may feel that they are lost, that their vision of the ideal cannot be attained, or that, in light of new developments, it is simply wrong. Under these conditions, prophets may emerge, and new religions may be created.

RELIGIOUS NATIVISM AND VITALISM

Some religious movements are **nativistic;** that is, they aim to restore a golden age believed to have existed in the past. Others are **vitalistic** and look toward a utopian future; an example is the Rastafarians, described in the accompanying Ethnography box. In some cases, these movements reject most elements of the old cultural systems under which they suffer; in others, they attempt to combine new customs with the old and to dissolve the social boundaries between the dominant and powerless groups in society. Many religious **revitalization movements,** such as the cargo cults found on certain Pacific Islands (see Chapter 17) arose in response to colonization. Religious movements vary in the effectiveness with which they bring social and political change. Even those

that fail in this respect may create powerful new identities among their members.

Often, the poor and powerless in a society create religions that challenge those of the mainstream. Such religions may rationalize their lower social position and emphasize an afterlife in which their suffering will be rewarded. In some cases, these religions have a **messianic** outlook; they focus on the coming of a messiah who will usher in a utopian world. In others, they are **millenarian;** they look to a future cataclysm or disaster that will destroy the current world and establish in its wake a world characterized by their version of justice. In many messianic and millenaristic religions, members participate in rituals that give individuals direct access to supernatural power. They experience states of ecstasy heightened by singing, dancing, handling dangerous objects such as snakes, or using drugs.

The holiness churches common in Appalachia among coal miners and other rural poor who lead difficult and dangerous lives are a good example of a religion of resistance. Church members cite biblical passages as the basis for their practices of faith healing, glossolalia (speaking in tongues), drinking poison, and handling poisonous snakes. Holiness church congregations view these activities as demonstrations of the power of god, working through people whose beliefs allow them to become god's instruments (Covington 1995; T. Burton 1993). In church services, the loud music, singing, and dancing cause some members to experience "being filled with the holy spirit." In this state, they handle poisonous snakes, which proves to them that "Jesus has the power to deliver them

---

nativism A religious movement that aims to restore a golden age believed to have existed in the past.

vitalism A religious movement that looks toward the creation of a utopian future that does not resemble a past golden age.

revitalization movement A movement that proposes that society can be improved through the adoption of a set of new religious beliefs.

messianic Focusing on the coming of a messiah who will usher in a utopian world.

millenarian The belief that a coming catastrophe will signal the beginning of a new age and the eventual establishment of paradise.

I N   T H E   F I E L D

THE RASTAFARI: RELIGION AND RESISTANCE TO DOMINATION

The Rastafari religion began on the Caribbean island of Jamaica in the 1930s, a time when much of the Jamaican peasantry was being incorporated into the emerging capitalist economy as wage labor. Since that time, the Rastafari have spread throughout the Caribbean, into parts of the African states of Kenya and Ethiopia, and to the urban centers of the United States, England, and Canada. The Rastafari are an example of the successful emergence of a new religion that resists the culture that surrounds it.

In the nineteenth century, after slavery had ended in Jamaica, a peasant economy developed, organized around a system of localized, small-scale exchanges involving interpersonal networks of extended kin. But by the 1920s, capitalism, primarily in the form of the American United Fruit Company, had considerably undermined the peasant economy. Some Jamaicans benefited, but there was substantial racial stratification. Whites and mulattos accumulated wealth at the expense of black peasants. Lacking either land or wages, these peasants soon found themselves penniless. As Jamaica became increasingly tied to the capital provided by the international economy, the pool of landless unemployed grew. By the mid-1930s, they numbered in the hundreds of thousands.

It was out of this milieu that the Rastafarians emerged. In 1930, Ras (Duke) Tafari was crowned emperor Haile Selassie I of Ethiopia. In Jamaica, the splendid coronation ceremonies, which included a retinue of European dignitaries paying homage to the emperor, drew enormous publicity. During them, Ras Tafari was proclaimed "King of Kings" and "Lion of Judah."

Shortly after this event, Leonard Howell, a former soldier in the United States Army, had a prophetic revelation. Born in 1898, Howell lived in the United States from 1918 to 1932. Probably influenced by Trinidadian black nationalist George Padmore (Chevannes 1994), on his return to Jamaica in 1932 Howell declared that the coronation of Haile Selassie fulfilled biblical prophecies: Haile Selassie was the messiah and the hope of freedom for all black people. Howell proclaimed:

> People, you are poor but you are rich, because God planted mines of diamonds and gold for you in Africa, your homeland. Our King has come to redeem you home to your motherland, Africa. (W. Lewis 1993)

Although Howell is generally credited with being the first preacher of Rastafari, others had similar visions—among them, Robert Hinds, Joseph (Teacher) Hibbert, and Archibald Dunkley.

The Rasta leaders founded communities in and around Kingston that emphasized what they understood as traditional African values. Haile Selassie became their central symbol, embodying the value of cooperative work efforts, respect for life, and the unity of all peoples of African descent. Through their belief that he is the messiah (a faith that his overthrow and assassination in 1974 did nothing to diminish), the Rastas affirm blackness and their African roots. Through him, they proclaim their rejection of the values of capitalist society and the competitive marketplace.

A central theme in Rasta philosophy is repatriation to Africa. The concept of repatriation (like all symbols) has several meanings. It may mean a literal passage to Africa, and some Rastas did actually move to Africa (though with little economic or social success). Alternatively, repatriation may be interpreted as a call to live what Rastafarians believe are African lifestyles in whichever country they find themselves.

Two other important symbols of Rastafarian culture are the use of marijuana and a special vocabulary. The use of ganja (marijuana) has been common on Jamaican agricultural estates since the turn of the century and is considered a legitimate part of Jamaican working-class life. Although it was illegal, the upper classes approved of ganja use because it acted as a stimulant and an incentive to work. Rastafari, however, have reversed these meanings. To them, ganja is a tool of illumination. They use it to stimulate discussion at "reasoning sessions," where they gather

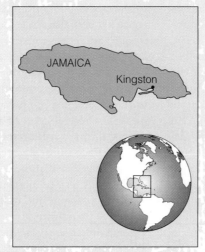

to interpret biblical passages and share beliefs about freedom, slavery, colonialism, and racism. Ganja, they believe, allows them to see through the evils of the bourgeois world, understand the roots of their oppression, and verify the authenticity of the Rasta lifestyle. Thus, whereas traditional use of ganja in Jamaica supported the dominant society, Rasta use subverts it.

In addition, the illegal sale of marijuana is part of the underground economy of many Rasta groups. The networks for growing it, preparing it for sale, and distributing it are all based on friendship, alliances, and reciprocity. Although the Rastas have encountered difficulties with law enforcement in connection with their use and sale of marijuana, ganja has provided the Rastas with a livelihood that allows them independence and freedom from the capitalist system, a position they value highly. Ultimately, many Rastafarians hope that their world will become more and more based on reciprocity and redistribution and that money as a medium of exchange will disappear from their community.

Rastafarian linguistic usages include the invention of *i*-centered words, phrases, and suffixes, such as *ital* for *vital,* and the replacement of such diminutive prefixes as *under-* and *sub-* by their opposites. For example, *understand* is rendered *overstand*. In rejecting diminutives and emphasizing *i*-centered words, the Rastafari appear to be disavowing the hierarchical nature of relations in the marketplace. Rasta language contradicts the submissiveness that an employer expects of an employee. Their language is an assertion of their black self-worth, and this keeps them separate from the world of the boss and the worker.

Rejecting aspirations of social mobility and participation in wage labor, the Rastas fashion a livelihood by forming networks of cooperation. In Jamaica, they engage in fishing, handicrafts, and hustling in the cities and, in the rural areas, in a family-based subsistence agriculture with minimal involvement in the market economy. The small group of Rastas living in Shashemane, Ethiopia, rely on their agricultural produce and financial donations from abroad. In urban England, Canada, and the United States, Rasta economic activities tend to be small-scale cooperative businesses such as eateries, craft shops, small clothing stores, and the illegal sale of marijuana. All of these enterprises are based on the productivity and input of extended family networks, and Rastafari circulate their wealth through the community in the form of gifts, loans, parties, and many other personalized relationships.

The Rastas draw boundaries around themselves to exclude the outside world from participation in their economic and social relationships. There is strong solidarity against outsiders, particularly those in positions of authority. Rastas have rejected much of the social and psychological orientation of modern society, which they call Babylon. Although much of Rastafarian culture reflects the milieu out of which it emerged, including sources in the Hebrew and Christian testaments, Rastas have created a new religion and culture that allow them to survive in a manner consistent with their own worldview.

Critical Thinking Questions

1. The Rasta movement arose in Jamaica but has gained enormous popularity worldwide. What sorts of people are likely to be attracted to the Rasta message, and what elements of that message are likely to be particularly appealing to them?

2. Rastafarians are probably better known worldwide for their association with reggae music than with specific religious beliefs. Consider a reggae song by a major artist such as Bob Marley, Burning Spear, or Peter Tosh (do some research if you are not familiar with any of these artists). How do the lyrics reflect Rasta religious belief?

3. There are many new religions in the United States. Are any of them similar to the Rasta movement? In what ways are they similar?

RASTAFARIANS ARE MEMBERS OF A RELIGION OF RESISTANCE THAT STARTED IN THE 1930S.

Jacques Charlas/Stock, Boston

Source: Adapted with permission from William F. Lewis, *Soul Rebels: The Rastafari*. Prospect Heights, IL: Waveland, 1993.

Courtesy of Serena Nanda

SANTERIA, AN AFRICAN-BASED RELIGION THAT ORIGINATED IN CUBA, IS AN EXAMPLE OF SYNCRETISM, OR THE MERGING OF TWO RELIGIOUS TRADITIONS.

from death here and now," even though they are often bitten and sometimes die. But their beliefs prove to them that however oppressed and poor they are, they have access to holiness that other, more affluent, members of society lack (Daugherty 1976/1993:344). These beliefs, though satisfying in some ways, do not accomplish changes in the social structure that creates the poverty in which they live.

Religious **syncretism**—the merging of two or more religious traditions to form a new religion—is often found in religions of resistance. One example is Santeria, an African-based religion originating in Cuba (J. Murphy 1989). Santeria emerged from slave

---

syncretism The merging of elements of two or more religious traditions to produce a new religion.

oricha A Yoruba deity identified with a Catholic saint in Vodou and Santeria.

Ghost Dance A Native American religious movement of the late nineteenth century.

---

society. Europeans attempted to suppress African religions, but the slaves resisted by combining African religion, Catholicism, and French spiritualism to create a new religion (Lefever, 1996). They identified African deities, called **orichas,** with Catholic saints and used them for traditional purposes: curing, casting spells, and influencing other aspects of the worshiper's life. Each oricha-saint has distinct attributes and is believed to control a specific aspect of human life. For example, Orunmila, identified with Saint Francis of Assisi, is believed to know each person's destiny and can therefore give guidance about how to improve one's fate. Santeria has spread through the Spanish Caribbean, Brazil, and North America, taking different forms in different locations.

RELIGIOUS CHANGE IN NATIVE NORTH AMERICA

The history of native North America provides a particularly good example of religious innovation. The European and (involuntary) African invasion brought disaster to Native American societies. Disease, warfare, and technological change undermined traditional native lifeways and belief systems. In this situation, a series of prophets and religious movements emerged. These included the prophetic movements of Handsome Lake, the Delaware Prophet, the Shawnee Prophet, and the Ghost Dance movement. As with the Rastafarian movement described in the Ethnography box, the timing and particular beliefs of these movements were closely tied to the social and political positions of their followers.

The visions of the Ghost Dance prophets of the second half of the nineteenth century were directly related to the expansion of European American power. In the late 1860s, Wodziwab, a Northern Paiute Indian living in the Sierra Nevada, became the first **Ghost Dance** prophet. Wodziwab foresaw the return of the ancestors on an immense train. Following this, a cataclysm would swallow up all the whites but leave their goods behind for the Native Americans who became his followers. Heaven on earth would follow, and the Great Spirit

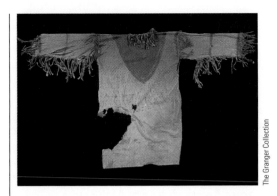

SOME FOLLOWERS OF THE GHOST DANCE PROPHET WOVOKA BELIEVED THAT SPECIAL GHOST SHIRTS WOULD PROTECT THEM FROM GUNFIRE, BUT 350 INDIAN MEN, WOMEN, AND CHILDREN DIED AT THE MASSACRE AT WOUNDED KNEE ON DECEMBER 29, 1890, INCLUDING THE INDIVIDUAL WHO WORE THIS GHOST SHIRT.

would return to live with the people. Wodziwab taught that only his followers' ancestors would return to earth (de Waal Malefijt 1968: 344). Wovoka, the second Ghost Dance prophet, was the son of an early follower of Wodziwab and had probably seen the Ghost Dance and heard its prophecies as a boy. In 1889, during a total eclipse of the sun, Wovoka had a vision in which "he saw God, with all the people who had died long ago engaged in their old-time sports and occupations, all happy and forever young" (Mooney 1896/1973:771). Wodziwab and Wovoka taught that the arrival of paradise could be hastened by specific rituals, including a series of dances, songs, and, in the case of Wovoka, the wearing of ghost shirts (special clothing painted with designs he saw in his visions). Some of Wovoka's followers believed that these shirts had the power to protect them from bullets. Although Wovoka called for peace with the whites, he also taught that the whites would either be carried away by high winds or become Indians (Lesser 1933), and he urged Indians to return to their traditional practices.

The Ghost Dance prophecy was welcomed by many Native Americans. Numerous tribes sent representatives, generally by train, to speak with Wovoka and learn the rituals of the Ghost Dance. The tribes heard the Ghost Dance vision in diverse ways, but it received its most radical interpretation among the Sioux, for whom the conditions of conquest and reservation life were particularly oppressive. Although the Sioux had defeated Custer at the Little Big Horn in 1876, they were eventually forced into submission. Starved and expected to survive by agriculture on nonproductive lands, they found a vision that promised the disappearance of their oppressors and the return of traditional ways extremely appealing.

During the fall of 1890, Ghost Dancing spread among the Sioux. Government agents were frightened by the popularity of the dance, the threat that the Sioux would return to their traditional life, and the Sioux belief that the whites would shortly disappear. They ordered the Sioux to stop the dance; some but not all Sioux groups obeyed. The government tried to suppress the remaining dancers, but they fled into the badlands to perform the Ghost Dance ceremonies and await the cataclysm that would sweep the oppressors from the plains. A complex series of moves followed as the government tried to force an end to the Ghost Dance. The final act of the drama occurred on December 28 and 29, 1890, when the Seventh Cavalry, the same unit that had been destroyed by the Sioux at the Little Bighorn, captured the last remaining band of Ghost Dancers. In the battle that ensued at Wounded Knee, about 350 Sioux Ghost Dancers, including many women and children, were killed, and the notion that doing Ghost Dance rituals would hasten the disappearance of the whites or protect Native Americans from them lost credibility.

The Ghost Dance religion did not end with the battle at Wounded Knee. Especially in Oklahoma, people continued to do the Ghost Dance into the 1930s, and one group of adherents continued to practice until the 1960s. Wovoka himself lived until 1932 and continued to promote his vision (Kehoe 1989). However, the battle at Wounded Knee marked a critical junction in the history of the prophecy. After Wounded Knee, the Ghost Dance declined, and by the first years of the twentieth century, few people practiced it.

Another religion that appeared at about the same time as the Ghost Dance, however, prospered and has become a major force in Native American communities. The **Native American Church,** sometimes known as the Peyote religion, now has between 250,000 and 500,000 members in the United States and Canada ("For Indian Church" 1995, "Field Full of Buttons" 1999).

Peyote is a small, hallucinogenic cactus that grows only in south Texas and northern Mexico. While peyote has always been part of religious rituals for some indigenous peoples, including the Huichol and Tarahumara, before the late nineteenth century its use was confined to groups in southern Texas and the Mexican desert. The modern peyote ceremony probably originated with the Carrizo Apache in south Texas; however, the spread of the ritual was due largely to the efforts of Comanche, Kiowa, and Caddo leaders, including Quannah Parker, Apiaton (Wooden Lance), and John Wilson. Some of them had visited Wovoka, the Ghost Dance prophet, but all had rejected his teachings (Stewart 1987:80). Peyote leaders (called Roadmen) taught that the use of peyote was a sacrament and that god was accessible through it. In all-night meetings, members of the Native American Church chew peyote, pray and sing, and experience the presence of god. Quannah Parker said, "When a Indian Peyotist goes to [a peyote ceremonial meeting] he talks to God, and not about what man has written in the scriptures about what God said" (quoted in Brito 1989:14).

Although the use of a hallucinogen to achieve communion with the supernatural may seem like an affront to mainstream American society, other aspects of the peyote religion were definitely not. Church leaders preached a vi-

sion they called the **Peyote Road.** The elements of the Peyote Road include abstinence from alcohol, attentiveness to family obligations, marital fidelity, self-support, helpfulness among members of the group, and attempting to live at peace with all peoples (Brito 1989; Stewart 1987). These are all values that are likely to be supported by Americans of any ethnic origin. The teachings of the Native American Church provide a pathway through which Native Americans can operate successfully in mainstream American society. At the same time, the notion that communion with the Great Spirit is possible through the use of peyote and the rituals surrounding it separates them from other Americans and allows them to affirm their identity as Native Americans. Thus, the church has been successful because it simultaneously allows its members to reinforce their identity and adapt to the demands of the larger society.

More recently, in the United States, rapid cultural and economic change, economic oppression, powerlessness, and anomie experienced by different social groups have led to new religious movements, often with dire results. The prophecies of People's Temple leader Jim Jones or the Branch Davidian David Koresh provided new lives for their followers. But in both cases, these leaders' actions led to the violent deaths of their followers. Jones and Koresh presented their congregations with consistent and meaningful (if, in others' view, misguided) ways of understanding the world. Participants in these groups constructed a collective identity through the use of stories, symbols, and organization. For members of the People's Temple, personal annihilation may have been preferable to a public admission of the failure of the prophet's vision and the recriminations that would have followed such an act (J. Hall 1993:107). The same may well be true for other, similar groups.

Examples such as the Native American Church and the People's Temple show something of the range and effectiveness of religious movements. In most circumstances, religion is likely to support the status quo, but it can also become a powerful force for change. Religion offers a series of principles, encapsu-

Native American Church A religious revitalization movement among Native Americans, also known as the Peyote religion.

peyote A small hallucinogenic cactus found in southern Texas and northern Mexico.

Peyote Road The moral principles followed by members of the Native American Church.

lated in story, symbol, and interpretation. Believers organize their lives around these, with varying results. Religion can be a powerful force for social change, providing people with the rationale and motivation for political involvement and personal renewal. From the Iranian Revolution to the Christian Coalition, religious leaders can have a powerful political impact. However, prophets may also give their followers convincing models that cannot exist in our material, social, and political world. When that happens, the results may be explosive.

Summary

1. Religion is a process among the members of a society and between them and their world that helps to order their society and provides them with meaning, unity, peace of mind, and the degree of control over events they believe is possible. Religion is a universal cultural pattern and goes back to the beginnings of the human species.

2. Through religion, people create meaning and order in their world. Religion has many functions. Some of the most significant are explaining aspects of the physical and social environment, reducing anxiety in risky situations, increasing social solidarity, educating, ensuring conformity, maintaining social inequalities, and regulating the relationship of a group of people to their natural environment.

3. Religious ideas are expressed through sacred narratives and symbols. Sacred narratives explain and validate or legitimize beliefs, values, and customs. Religious symbols are a means by which abstract ideas can be expressed in terms that most people can grasp.

4. Most religions assume the world to be populated with nonempirical beings we call gods and spirits. Religions teach that such beings have life, personality, and power. Some common forms are gods, spirits, spirits of human origin, and tricksters. Additionally, religions usually postulate that people, objects, or places may be imbued with spiritual power, or mana.

5. Many kinds of rituals are used to communicate with, manipulate, and influence religious powers. Two common types of religious ritual are rites of passage and rites of intensification. Rites of passage mark the transition from one social status to another. Rites of intensification reinforce the values of the group and increase feelings of solidarity and purpose among group members.

6. People use prayer, sacrifice, and magic to interact with the world of the supernatural. Most religions include examples of all three. The key difference between the three is the degree to which people believe their own actions determine outcomes. Also common is the use of divination, a religious technique to discover the hidden.

7. All religions have clerics, people who are charged with taking leading roles in performing religious ritual for other members of their society. Anthropologists divide these clerics into two classes: shamans and priests.

8. Shamans are religious clerics whose legitimacy depends on their ability to achieve direct contact with the supernatural world. They are not members of bureaucracies and often mediate between their communities and the supernatural world. Shamans are found in most societies.

9. Priests are professional religious specialists who hold offices in bureaucracies. Although priests' authority depends on their official positions, they may also use ecstatic techniques to contact the supernatural. Priests are typical of socially stratified societies.

10. Witchcraft and sorcery are common elements of belief in many societies. Some anthropologists differentiate between witches and sorcerers. Witches are people who unconsciously use their evil thoughts to harm people. Sorcerers use magic for both good and evil purposes.

11. Although people do perform magic, accusations that others are sorcerers or witches probably have a greater effect on society. Such accusations may function to promote conformity and explain catastrophic events.

12. Religion is often used to resist cultural domination. Such resistance movements are often syncretic; that is, they combine features of two or more religions so that a new religion emerges. Santeria, a syncretism of Yoruba religion, Catholicism, and spiritualism, is an example of a syncretic religion originating in resistance.

13. Religious revitalization movements are consciously organized efforts to construct a new culture and

personal identity. These movements arise in situations in which a group of people has been oppressed and has suffered cultural loss and loss of personal identity. Native American religious movements such as the Ghost Dance and the Native American Church are good examples.

14. Religious movements may catalyze changes in political and social structure as well as individual personality. However, when religious movements cannot cause the changes they desire in the material world, their members may turn to self-destruction.

priest
reincorporation
religion
revitalization movement
rite of intensification
rite of passage
ritual
sacred narratives
sacrifice
scapulomancy

separation
shaman
sorcery
syncretism
totem
totemism
trickster
vision quest
vitalism
Wiccan
witchcraft
zoomorphic

Key Terms

anthropomorphic
anthropopsychic
antistructure
cleric
communitas
contagious magic
cosmology
divination
Ghost Dance
god
imitative magic
liminal
magic
mana

messianic
millenarian
monotheism
Native American Church
nativism
naturalistic
neopagan
oricha
peyote
Peyote Road
pharmacopoeia
polytheism
prayer

Suggested Readings

Brown, Karen McCarthy. 1991. *Mama Lola: A Vodou Priestess in Brooklyn*. Berkeley: University of California Press. This outstanding person-centered account illustrates that ethnography is a human relationship and introduces a fascinating religion to the reader.

Covington, Dennis. 1995. *Salvation on Sand Mountain: Snake Handling and Redemption in Southern Appalachia*. Reading, MA: Addison-Wesley. This powerful account of a snake-handling church in Alabama gives readers a sense of the meaning of holiness worship and raises important questions about the nature of faith and community in the modern world.

Faris, James C. 1990. *The Nightway, a History: And a History of Documentation of a Navajo Ceremonial.* Albuquerque: University of New Mexico Press. This text is among the best ethnographies on Navajo religion, representing Navajo knowledge using biographical, linguistic, and behavioral data to convey the Navajo worldview.

Kehoe, Alice B. 1989. *The Ghost Dance: Ethnohistory and Revitalization.* New York: Holt, Rinehart, & Winston. An interesting and easy-to-read book describing the history and practice of the Ghost Dance.

Myerhoff, Barbara. 1976. *Peyote Hunt: The Sacred Journey of the Huichol Indians.* Ithaca, NY: Cornell University Press. A fascinating account of the search for peyote, which figures prominently in the annual rituals of the Huichol Indians of northern Mexico.

Numbers, Ronald L. 1992. *The Creationists: The Evolution of Scientific Creationism.* Berkeley: University of California Press. This social history of the creationist movement in the United States highlights one prominent area of conflict between science and some religious traditions. The book is well balanced and tries to present an objective view of creationists and their claims.

Turner, Victor. 1977. *The Ritual Process: Structure and Anti-Structure.* Ithaca, NY: Cornell University Press. A discussion of the roles and rituals that represent communitas in different societies, with a case study from the Ndembu of south central Africa, by a leading figure in symbolic anthropology.

Wafer, Jim. 1991. *The Taste of Blood: Spirit Possession in Brazilian Candomble.* Philadelphia: University of Pennsylvania Press. A winner of the Victor Turner Prize in ethnographic writing, this ethnography conveys the personal experiences of candomble, an Afro-Brazilian religion, and calls into question some traditional anthropological divisions of experience into oppositions such as rational and irrational.

INTERNET RESOURCES

www The following Internet resources appear in this chapter. Please log on to the Wadsworth anthropology website: **http://anthropology.wadsworth. com**. Click on the Nanda/Warms *Cultural Anthropology* page. Then select the Student Resources section, where you will find a complete presentation of these links and more.

- Link to websites on world religions and faith practices, page 348
- A photo essay on religious syncretism in the New World, page 358
- Access the Study Guide to InfoTrac College Edition for Anthropology Students

THE PRE-COLUMBIAN ART OF THE INDIGENOUS PEOPLES OF MEXICO IS AN IMPORTANT ELEMENT OF MEXICAN NATIONAL IDENTITY. MUCH OF THIS ART WAS DESTROYED IN THE SPANISH CONQUEST. THE PRESERVATION OF THIS ART IN NATIONAL MUSEUMS, AS A WAY OF INCORPORATING THE PAST INTO THE NATIONAL PRESENT, IS A HIGH PRIORITY OF THE MEXICAN GOVERNMENT.

CHAPTER SIXTEEN

THE ARTS: EXPRESSING CULTURAL IDENTITIES

Why is art universal, but the role of the artist found only in modern society?

How do societies differ in their artistic emphases and styles?

What are some universal functions of the arts?

What are some of the different ways in which the arts express cultural identities?

How have the global economy and the global culture affected the arts of indigenous peoples?

In every society, people express themselves in ways that go beyond the need for physical survival. Every culture has characteristic forms of creative expression that are guided by aesthetic principles involving imagination, beauty, skill, and style. These expressive activities are sometimes called the arts. In this chapter we use the broadest definition of that term to include the graphic and plastic arts, such as painting, architecture, sculpture, carving, pottery, and weaving; crafts, or the application of aesthetic principles to the production of utilitarian objects and activities; the structured use of sound in music, song, poetry, folklore, and myth; the movements of the human body in dance, sports, games, and play; and combined forms of these in dramatic and ritual performance. From the very broad anthropological perspective used in this chapter, tea drinking is an art form in Japan, cockfighting is an art form in Bali, and calligraphy is an art form in China and the Islamic Middle East, even though these are not art forms for most people in the United States.

ANTHROPOLOGICAL PERSPECTIVES ON ART

Art is a universal aspect of human experience; there is no known culture in which art is not present. The arts are a universal means of expressing the basic themes, values, perceptions of reality, and the very identity of a culture. Evidence of art appears very early in the human fossil record, indicating that artistic expression is a fundamental dimension of our species. Tools manufactured according to aesthetic principles, the embellishment of burial sites beyond the merely practical, and the sophisticated and complex cave paintings of prehistoric peoples all indicate the inherent connection between the arts and being human.

art Forms of creative expression that are guided by aesthetic principles and involve imagination, skill, and style.

THE ARTIST IN SOCIETY

The importance of the arts in communicating cultural themes means that the arts must be understood in relation to their cultural context. For most anthropologists, claims to universal criteria of art independent of cultural context are based on Western ethnocentrism. Although art is universal, the high value placed on art for art's sake in the West is by no means universal. In fact, the opposite is true. In most societies, art is not produced or performed solely for the purpose of giving pleasure but is inseparable from other activities. The separation of art from social behavior, and the separation of a class of objects or acts labeled art, is characteristic only of the more fragmented nature of modern society. In nonindustrial societies, art is embedded in all aspects of culture; no separate class of material products, movements, or sounds is created solely to express aesthetic values.

The Inuit, who have a highly developed artistic skill, do not have a separate word for art. Rather, all artificial objects are lumped together as "that which has been made," regardless of the purpose of the object. This does not mean that Inuit do not have aesthetic values, but that their plastic art was traditionally applied to the manufacture of objects that have primarily instrumental value, such as tools, amulets, and weapons. The Inuit, like most other nonindustrial societies, do not make a distinction between artist and craftworker, a distinction that does exist in Western societies. Similarly, many creative acts (such as dancing, weaving, singing, and playing a musical instrument) that in the West are performed as a special category of behavior called the arts are used in other societies in connection with other cultural activities such as religion, exchange, or storytelling. In all societies, some people are recognized as more competent in these skills than others, but this competence does not necessarily translate into the specialized role of artist.

The contemporary Western identification of creativity with originality, when imposed on other cultures, is also ethnocentric. Although anthropologists, and particularly art historians,

THE "COLON" TRADITION IN AFRICAN ART, REPRESENTING AFRICANS IN EUROPEAN DRESS OR SERVING EUROPEAN COLONIAL POWERS, HAVE BECOME IMPORTANT COLLECTOR'S ITEMS. CONSISTENT WITH THE DEMANDS OF THE WESTERN ART MARKET THAT "PRIMITIVE" ART BE ANONYMOUS, AFRICAN ARTISTS GENERALLY DO NOT SIGN THEIR CREATIONS.

Courtesy of Serena Nanda

have not generally investigated aesthetics in non-Western, nonindustrial societies, evidence indicates that the making of art in all cultures is recognized as a creative process, though not necessarily an innovative one (Price 1989). Many cultures do not prize originality—the creation of something entirely new—in their arts. In many societies in Africa, for example, improvisation is more highly valued than artistic originality. In much of African art, whether verbal, musical, or visual, creativity is expressed in creating interesting and endless variations on a theme (Vogel 1991:20). Indifference or even inhibition of originality in art occurs particularly when the arts are connected with religion. Among the Navajo, for example, there is believed to be only one right way to sing a song. Improvisation is not valued in Navajo singing, which has ritual connections, and the Navajo believe that "foreign music is dangerous and not for Navajo" (McAllester 1954). In other Navajo arts, such as weaving, styles remain stable but innovation is permitted; indeed, where marketing is the motive, traders may encourage innovation to increase sales.

Cultural attitudes toward the arts also shape artistic form. Art in Africa is much more public than Western art; its interaction with its audience is of central importance. As part of this interaction, African artists emphasize the content of art (the message it contains) and its function in community life. This contrasts with the Western emphasis on the individual aspect of artistic expression and the more private nature of much of Western art collection and display.

In studying the artist in society, anthropologists have been limited by a lack of ethnographic data. In many small-scale societies, the artist as a specialist does not exist. Even if certain people are recognized as exceptionally skilled, they are unlikely to identify themselves as artists; rather, they express their artistic creativity as part of other, often religious, activities. Thus, artistic expression in these societies may be carried out by religious specialists rather than artists. The Western emphasis on originality has also led to underestimating the role of the artist in societies where art conforms more to cultural tradition. The Western emphasis on innovation and difference has led to conceptualizing the artist as a special person, often a deviant, working alone, and more likely to be in opposition than in harmony with society. This perception is usually absent in art production in non-Western cultures (and historically not true in the West itself).

Because "primitive art" (the term used by the Western art world for the art of non-Western "tribal" societies) is now part of an international art market, Western conceptions of such art have become important to its producers as

CONTRARY TO THE WESTERN VALUATION OF ANONYMITY IN MUCH TRIBAL ART, THE VALUE OF NATIVE AMERICAN ART IN THE AMERICAN SOUTHWEST DEPENDS ON THE INDIVIDUAL ARTIST. HERE, MARIA MARTINEZ, THE MAJOR FIGURE IN THE DEVELOPMENT OF AN ART MARKET FOR NATIVE AMERICAN POTTERY, MAKES ONE OF HER SIGNATURE BLACK-ON-BLACKWARE PIECES.

George Haling/Photo Researchers, Inc.

well as those who market it. Often an important (and commercially valuable) dimension of the Western notion of primitive art is that of the anonymous artist. Thus, even when an individual artist can be tracked down, dealers and collectors are generally not interested in doing so (Price 1989). Art middlemen in West Africa know that an object is worth more to Westerners "if it is perceived by the buyer to have been created by a long departed and unknown artist and to have come directly out of a remote village community" (Steiner 1995: 157). Art middlemen are quite willing to manipulate both the objects and the information about their production to meet these demands of Western buyers.

MANAGING NATIVE AMERICAN CULTURAL RESOURCES

This chapter underscores the importance of the arts and cultural resources in maintaining a group's cultural identity. Anthropologists have been useful to indigenous peoples and ethnic groups in helping them to preserve their material culture and their associated cultural histories. Although some of these relationships were problematical in the past, today relationships between anthropologists and indigenous peoples are collaborative. One important area in which anthropologists have been helpful is in the repatriation of religious and cultural objects to tribal ownership.

Anthropologist T. J. Ferguson owns and operates Heritage Resources Management Consultants in Tucson, Arizona, which collects information needed to manage Native Americans' cultural resources (Ferguson 2000). Most of this work is done as a consultant under contract to Indian tribes who "set the research agenda, participate in the collection and analysis of data, and control the work product." Ferguson finds that his work, which incorporates archaeology, cultural anthropology, and ethnohistory, offers "exciting research opportunities and challenging ethical questions." He describes his work in this way:

At the beginning of my career . . . I was hired by the Pueblo of Zuni to help develop one of the first tribally based cultural resource management programs in the United States. As Tribal Archaeologist, I advised the Zuni Tribal Council on the management of cultural resources . . . . After several years, Pueblo leaders asked me to assist them with efforts to repatriate Zuni War Gods (sacred artifacts that had been stolen from shrines on Zuni land) and to interview tribal elders to collect information needed to litigate land claims against the U.S. government. Both of these assignments required the application of ethnographic and ethnohistoric approaches [beyond archaeology].

Through this work, Ferguson became interested in how archaeological sites and historic places functioned as cultural properties used to retain and transmit traditional Native American cultures. This led him into research on the significance of places and landscapes in the living history of contemporary peoples.

Ferguson emphasizes that in addition to the technical skills needed in his work, "to be done well, this work must be undertaken in close collaboration with the Native Americans who use the traditional

cultural properties." He points out that "many Native Americans are antagonistic toward scholarly research because they feel that their cultures have been violated by publications that divulge esoteric information."

Ferguson addresses this issue in the following way:

I structure my work so that the tribes I work for make the decisions about what information to reveal and to whom it will be revealed. The fact that I have consciously not learned the languages of the people I work for creates a situation in which I must collaborate with native speakers in the research and reports I produce. This means that my Native American clients remain the cultural experts, and my role is essentially that of a facilitator . . . rather than an advocate. I simply try to help people explain their cultural concerns in a manner that effectively communicates with the state and federal agencies that regulate historic preservation.

In this work, there is an ethical obligation to conduct research that both meets project objectives and is congruent with tribal cultural values. The ethics of this research are challenging because they are constantly evolving

---

Although omitting identification of the artist may increase the value of African art, this is not true for all tribal arts, each of which has its own history of relations with the West. The value of Native American art, for example, increases with identification of the artist.

In native North America, Anglo interest in indigenous arts has been responsible for creating the status of artist in societies where it did not previously exist. One of the best-known examples is in the life and work of the renowned Pueblo Indian potter Maria Martinez of San Ildefonso (Babcock 1995). In the early 1920s, as part of an Anglo interest in reviving Native American arts, a number of wealthy Easterners and museum directors who had moved to

as the tribes gain a better understanding of scholarly research and historical preservation.

As Ferguson notes, there are many complicated issues involved:

My professional ethic to share what I learn with my colleagues is often at odds with tribal ethics to keep esoteric information from being divulged to outsiders. This and other potential conflicts in research are minimized by carefully constructed contracts that require reports and publications to undergo tribal review. . . . [T]he tribes I work for . . . own my products. These tribes graciously allow me to publish some aspects of my work, and the review that precedes this is always helpful in making sure my perspectives accurately reflect tribal knowledge and concerns.

AMONG NATIVE AMERICANS, TRADITIONALLY MADE ADOBE HOMES AND RELIGIOUS BUILDINGS (KIVAS), AS WELL AS SPECIFIC GEOGRAPHICAL SITES, ARE AN ESSENTIAL PART OF THEIR CULTURES. ANTHROPOLOGISTS ARE HELPING PUEBLO GROUPS TO PRESERVE THIS CULTURAL HERITAGE.

Phil Borden/Photo-Edit

Ferguson finds his work in applied anthropology very satisfying:

I enjoy helping tribal leaders and elders effectively interact with land managing agencies and historic preservation regulators. . . . I am personally enriched by the history Native Americans choose to share with me. . . . [I]t feels good to conduct research that the people I am studying find useful for their own ends and, at the same time, contributes to a greater anthropological understanding of past and present peoples.

T. J. Ferguson, in applying his anthropological knowledge to ensure that Native Americans gain control over their cultural heritage, is another anthropologist who makes a difference.

Source: Based on T. J. Ferguson, "Applied Anthropology in the Management of Native American Cultural Resources: Archaeology, Ethnography, and History of Traditional Cultural Places." In P. L. W. Sabloff (Ed.), *Careers in Anthropology: Profiles of Practitioner Anthropologists* (pp. 15–17). Washington, DC: National Association of Practicing Anthropologists, 2000.

the Southwest "reinvented" Native American pottery as a fine art. The pottery was sold to wealthy Americans, in the newly established Santa Fe Indian market, and exhibited in museums (Mullin 1995). Maria Martinez and her husband, Julian, produced a matte-and-polish black-on-blackware that was an almost instant success in the Anglo market. To award Maria Martinez status as an artist within the Western meaning of that term, she was encouraged to sign her pots as a way of increasing their value for collectors. When other San Ildefonso potters asked her to sign their pots too, she willingly did so, expressing the egalitarian quality of Indian pueblo life—but causing havoc among her sponsors (Babcock 1995:137).

Maria and Julian Martinez shared their techniques with other members of their pueblo, and several members of her family actually participated in the various stages of making her pots. As a result, San Ildefonso as a community became identified with fine pottery. It was Maria Martinez, however, who became the star in the Pueblo pottery revival. Maria Martinez's image was reproduced in photographs, videotapes, books, and other media, and she became identified with a romanticized image of the Native American woman potter.

ARTISTIC STYLES

Although all cultures experience some stylistic changes in art, aesthetic principles are often very stable. Archaeological evidence indicates that the artistic styles of many cultures changed very slowly over very long periods. The widespread integration of art with religion often limits the range of variation that individual artists display; this was true in earlier periods of Western history and is true for many contemporary non-Western cultures. Where religion and art have become separated, as in much of the contemporary world, experimentation, innovation, and real change in artistic style are much more likely to occur.

Cultures also differ in the attention they give to various types of art. In some cultures, masks and painting are the most important media for the expression of aesthetic values and technical skill. In other cultures, verbal skills are more important, reflected in a wealth of myths, folktales, and word games. Calligraphy (writing) is an important art form in both China and the Islamic Middle East, but is associated with quite different meanings.

In China, written language is considered one of the defining attributes of Chinese civilization and is a key source of Chinese cultural identity and unity. Writing was the ruler's instrument of legitimation, and it appeared on state monuments and documents. Gradually, it became revered as an art form.

In Islam, calligraphy is the most respected of the graphic arts because it is the visual representation of the Word (the Koran). Islam forbids the worship, or even the creation, of graven human images, a prohibition often extended to the depiction of animals. In the Islamic cultures influenced by Persia (Iran), such as Mughal India and Ottoman Turkey, animals and even humans are portrayed in paintings and carpets, but the religious prohibition has led to an emphasis on abstract geometric designs and calligraphy in much Islamic Arabic art (Schuyler 1995).

Whatever its artistic emphasis, no culture, no matter how simple its technology or how difficult its environment, lacks art. In fact, cultures in which making a living is not easy and in which social structure is simple, such as Inuit and aboriginal Australian groups, often exhibit artistic skills of a very high level.

For convenience, discussions of the arts ordinarily divide them into five types: graphic and plastic arts, music, dance, folklore, and sports and games. Certain general approaches in cultural anthropology can be applied to the study of all these arts, but because of their different natures, they are usually studied by specialists. Some of the generalized approaches to the study of the various arts consider content, themes, or subjects, style, changes over time, social and psychological functions, the relationship of art to other aspects of culture and society, the creative process, and the interaction of artists and their audience.

SOME FUNCTIONS OF ART

Among the many functions of art are ritual control of the environment, display of cultural themes, social integration, and historical continuity.

ART IN RITUAL: CONTROLLING THE ENVIRONMENT

In many cultures, artistic expression in the form of ritual acts and ritual objects is a powerful form of communication with and means of control over the natural and supernatural world. In hunting and gathering cultures, dance movements that imitate the movements of animals are believed to exert control over those animals.

THE WORLD BEAT OF MUSIC

One of the fastest growing global phenomena is the diffusion of music around the world. One dimension of this globalization is the emergence of world music. World music is local musical traditions—produced for local occasions, in local languages, shared by genuine cultural communities—that fuse together in new musical compositions and performances as genuine cross-cultural interactions. Underlying the premise of world music is a philosophy that all the folk and ethnic musics of the world are connected at some fundamental level. Another dimension of the glob-

alization of music is the incorporation of bits of traditional music—Indonesian gamelan, Andean panpipes, Tibetan chants—into Western performance and recording.

Many cultures are contributing to musical fusion, but the influence of Africa and African-derived music stands out. For centuries, African and New World music have traded ideas, creating endless variations from shared foundations in call-and-response and polyrhythm. The music of African religious ceremonies was preserved by slaves and adapted into the sacred and secular music of the New World (Pareles 1996). From the poly-

rhythmic basis of North American ragtime and early New Orleans jazz, through the African-Cuban percussionist influence of Mongo Santamaria, to the performance combination of Youssou N'Dour of Senegal and American Paul Simon, to the contemporary albums of griots from West Africa (such as Mory Kante from Guinea, who merges African melodies with dance music technology), to the wild enthusiasm of Europeans for hip-hop music of urban African American culture, music has transcended narrow cultural identities to become a significant part of global culture.

In these foraging societies, dependence on nature leads to a perception of it as an active and personal force that people must appeal to in order to survive.

Prehistoric cave paintings and other artistic expressions in contemporary hunting societies represent the ritual restoration to nature of the animals that are killed. Whenever an animal was killed, its essence was restored to nature by a ritual drawing of the animal's image at a sacred spot. Where restitution to nature is believed not only possible but necessary, drawing images is one way of accomplishing it (Levine 1957). Taking a life is dangerous. Ritual art, dedicated to the powerful spirits who protect life, is one way of lessening the danger.

Similarly, in some cultures artistic products such as paintings, masks, or sculptures are believed not merely to represent but to be—to partake of the spirit of—the thing visualized. Under certain ritual conditions, the spirit travels into the mask, painting, or dancer; taking these forms, it can be more easily manipulated and controlled by humans. Because the objects, dances, songs, or other artistic forms are be-

lieved to be powerful in themselves, they are often created in ways that are strictly guided by traditional processes.

HUNTING PEOPLES OFTEN MAKE ARTISTIC PRODUCTS AS A WAY OF SATISFYING AND APPEALING TO NATURE. THIS 15,000-YEAR-OLD PAINTING OF A HORSE, FOUND IN A CAVE IN FRANCE, HAD THE SPOTS AND HANDPRINTS ABOVE IT ADDED AFTER THE ORIGINAL OUTLINE WAS MADE, SUPPORTING THE ARGUMENT THAT SUCH PREHISTORIC PAINTINGS HAD RITUAL SIGNIFICANCE FOR THEIR CREATORS.

Alexander Marshack

ART AND THE DISPLAY OF CULTURAL THEMES

Even in cultures where forms are not themselves viewed as containing spiritual power, the arts are always powerful means of symbolic communication, conveying knowledge and provoking interpretations and emotions that have both individual and cultural dimensions. Each culture, for example, has specific traditional artistic symbols that stand for references in nature and human society or are associated with particular emotions. Because these symbolic elements are culturally specific, one needs to know the particular cultural meanings assigned to a particular artistic element to understand it.

THE ALL-POWERFUL HAND IS A HIGHLY SYMBOLIC IMAGE. DATING FROM THE COLONIAL PERIOD, IT IS STILL POPULAR IN MEXICO TODAY. SEVERAL LAYERS OF MEANING ARE REFERENCED IN THE IMAGE. THE EUCHARIST IS SYMBOLIZED IN THE BLEEDING HAND; THE NAIL WOUND AT THE CENTER IS MEANT TO RECALL THE WOUNDS CHRIST RECEIVED ON THE CROSS. THE SEVEN LAMBS DRINKING THE BLOOD RECALL REVELATIONS. THE EXTENDED FAMILY OF CHRIST IS REPRESENTED BY THE INDIVIDUAL FIGURES ON EACH OF THE FIVE FINGERS.

Unknown Artist Mano Poderosa/The Brooklyn Museum

In Western music, for example, the use of the minor scale conveys the emotion of sadness; various other musical forms are traditionally associated with other emotions. The traditional element is important in evoking the emotion because people in that culture have been taught the association. In Western culture, the phrase "Once upon a time" is a signal that this is not going to be a story about real events and people, and sets the stage for people to respond emotionally in certain ways.

The arts are also used to communicate elements of social structure. The totem poles of the Native American groups on the Northwest Coast of North America reflect and are a powerful message about the importance of social hierarchy in their societies, as are the many artistic products and performances associated with the potlatch (Jonaitis 1991). After the Spanish conquest of Peru, indigenous artists were commissioned by Inca royalty to paint portraits of the Inca kings in order to keep alive the memory of Inca rulers for those claiming royal descent and noble status. Upper-class natives of Peru thus asserted their claims to high status and power in the colonial hierarchy by depicting their own illustrious forbears in the visual language of European culture.

Messages about social structure are also an important dimension in folktales and other oral traditions. These may reverse, ridicule, or question the social order and, in doing so, may provide satisfactory solutions to the conflicts that arise out of domination and control. African American oral traditions, for example, commonly contain the figure of the trickster, or clever hero, who is smaller and weaker than his opponent but triumphs through his wits rather than through force. The trickster tales, popular in one form as the Br'er Rabbit stories, have an obvious relation to slavery in the pre–Civil War South. At the same time that they conveyed a representation of the social structure based on race, these stories conveyed a message about how to overcome the system and provided an outlet for justifiable anger (Friedheim and Jackson 1996:24). As the American social structure changed and possibilities of open protest against the racial caste system increased, African American oral traditions also changed. The "badman," who openly displays his arrogance and virility, came to supplant the trickster as hero (Abrahams 1970).

Much of the power of the arts comes from their symbolic nature, which leaves their production and performance open to a variety of interpretations. An artistic product or performance may convey a basic cultural theme, or it may combine several themes, some of which may even be in opposition to one another. An important anthropological perspective on the arts is to understand both the surface and the deep structures through which the arts communicate and elicit responses from their participants and audiences.

In examining an audience's response to art, anthropologists take into account the culturally mediated perspective through which art is not only produced but viewed. Art historians, as the gatekeepers of the Western response to art, generally claim that great art is measured and responded to in terms of universal intrinsic artistic qualities. Anthropologists, in contrast, emphasize the cultural factors—such as education, social status, and knowledge about the reputation of the artist or the commercial value of the art—that shape the response of audiences to the arts. The anthropological view has been expressed by Marshall Sahlins, who quipped, "There is no such thing as an immaculate perception," and by Franz Boas, who called "the seeing eye . . . an organ of tradition" (Price 1989:19, 22).

THE INTEGRATIVE FUNCTION OF THE ARTS

The power of the arts to convey cultural themes is related to one of its most important functions: cultural and social integration. The art forms of a society do not merely reflect the society and its culture. Participation in the arts, whether as performers or audiences, can foster the unity and harmony of a community or society in a way that is intensely felt by its members. The powerful artistic symbols of a society express universal emotions—death, masculinity, pride, gender relations, aggression, solidar-

ity, and identity—in culturally compelling ways, even when (some might say particularly when) their content is not consciously articulated. The arts make dominant cultural themes visible, tangible, and thus more real. Likewise, the arts can also give voice to disunity and conflict within a society.

CULTURAL IDENTITY: ART, POWER, AND THE MAKING OF HISTORY

An important function of the arts is to express people's sense of their cultural identity and history. The use of art to link the present with the sacred past is very widespread. In many cultures, the most important artistic efforts and performances are those representing ancestors and the continuity of group identity. This is true for both literate and nonliterate societies, although oral performances and visual arts are particularly important in a society without writing. Because they display cultural identity and history in ways that are visible, tangible, and emotionally compelling, the arts are an important way of interpreting and remembering the past.

In all cultures people have a sense of their own identity. The "we" group may be constructed in terms of kinship, space, ethnicity, race, gender, nationality, political alliance, or several of these criteria intersecting in particular ways. As we noted in Chapter 14, these identities are products of specific cultural histories and emerge and change, sometimes radically, over time. Very often, in hierarchical societies, the power embodied in the ruler is represented in the graphic, oral, architectural, or performing arts. These artistic displays reiterate and legitimate the divine source of the ruler's power, and are thus central to the making of a society's history.

Among the Luba of Zaire, works of art play a central role in reconstructing memory and making history (Roberts and Roberts 1996). The Luba were an important central African kingdom from the seventeenth to the nineteenth centuries. They value highly the recounting of history, particularly as it relates to the most important statuses in their society. Kings, chiefs, titleholders, and members of associations all use the vocabulary of art—in memory boards, beaded emblems, sculpted wooden stools, staffs, figures, divination objects, and works in metal—to recall the significant events, royal lineages, and political relationships that make up Luba collective memory.

The most prestigious Luba histories are traced to their founding ancestral kings. The members of an association called Mbudye, or "men of memory," were rigorously trained to narrate family lineages and episodes in the founding of kingship with the assistance of memory boards. Although the Luba kingdom declined in the wake of European colonialism and its aftermath, the Mbudye Society still performs public dances to reenact these historical narratives.

Luba memory boards are small, flat, wooden objects, studded with beads and pins or covered with carved ideograms, that can be read to recite sacred lore about culture heroes, the beginning of the kingdom, and clan migrations. They contain the official history of the Luba. In addition to these memory boards, other artistic memory devices recall other histories. Carved staffs are used to remember family and clan history and migration. High-level officeholders carry staffs to public meetings to perform historical recitations to honor the ancestors and teach their descendants about family ties to Luba kingship. Carved thrones and stools, as the seat of the past, depict female figures that represent important women, who in turn represent previous male rulers. Divination objects, such as sculptures, baskets, and gourds, are used to reconstruct personal histories and use the knowledge of the past to solve current problems.

The specific elements in Luba art all convey meaning. Kings, for example, are represented on memory devices by anvil-shaped metal pins. These pins symbolize their association with iron smelting and blacksmithing, which was introduced by the Luba cultural hero. Every object associated with a Luba king contains these metal pins. The personal history of a Luba woman is represented on her body, which is considered a canvas on which her beauty will be perfected through intricate scarification, elaborate hairstyles, beaded apparel, and gleaming skin.

Jerry L. Thompson/Courtesy of the Museum for African Art, New York

LUBA WOODEN FEMALE SCULPTURES EMBODY ALL THE MARKS OF THE SPIRITUAL AND MORAL PERFECTION WHICH THE LUBA SEE AS A HALLMARK OF THEIR CULTURAL IDENTITY: SCARIFICATION, GLEAMING SKIN, AN ELEGANT COIFFURE, BEADED ACCESSORIES AND APPAREL, FILED TEETH, EYES MADE OF COWRIE SHELLS, A SERENE, COMPOSED ATTITUDE, AND METAL TACKS IN THE HEAD AND COIFFURE TO KEEP OUT ENEMIES AND KEEP IN THE SPIRIT. THE STATUES MUST BE BEAUTIFULLY CARVED AND ADORNED TO BE SPIRITUALLY EFFECTIVE.

In imperial China, the arts were central in the legitimation of the emperor (Hearn 1996). The Chinese believed that only those with a knowledge of the past could have a vision of the future, and it was essential for the imperial courts to possess historical writings and paintings to display that knowledge. Throughout Chinese imperial history, figure painting was directed toward commemorating the emperor. Life-size portraits of the emperor had to incorporate the two main Chinese ideals of imperial rule: moral authority and the power of the emperor's central role in a controlled bureaucratic administration. Thus, paintings of the emperor had to show him with individualized features representing the humanistic Confucian values of compassion and virtue while conveying the imposing demeanor of the absolute ruler, the Son of Heaven.

Another artistic representation that conveyed imperial power was a series of almost life-size portraits of Chinese cultural heroes, commissioned by some emperors in the twelfth century. By displaying these paintings in the court, the emperor demonstrated his rightful place in the lineage of Confucian rulers, much as the Luba king identified himself with the Luba cultural hero who was the founder of the ruling dynasty.

DEEP PLAY AS A FORM OF ART

Deep play (Geertz 1973a) refers to cultural performances in which participants and spectators are joined together in experiences that have functions similar to those of art. Examples of deep play include cockfighting in Bali and football in the United States. Both are expressive forms of culture that heighten emotions, display compelling aspects of social structure, and reinforce cultural identities.

THE BALINESE COCKFIGHT

Cockfights are a consuming passion of the Balinese that reveal much of Balinese culture. According to anthropologist Clifford Geertz (1973a), it is "only apparently cocks that are fighting there. Actually it is men."

Balinese men have an intense identification with their fighting cocks and spend much time caring for them, discussing them, and looking at them. The cocks embody two opposing Balinese themes. They are both a magnification of the owner's masculine self and an expression of animality, the direct inversion of human status in Bali. Thus, in identifying with his animal, the Balinese man is identifying with his ideal masculine self but also with what he most fears, hates, and is fascinated by: "the powers of darkness." The cockfight embodies the oppo-

COCKFIGHTING AMONG THE BALINESE IS A FORM OF DEEP PLAY THAT EMBODIES IMPORTANT CULTURAL THEMES, SUCH AS MASCULINITY AND SOCIAL STATUS.

Wendy Bass/Viesti Associates, Inc.

sition of man and beast, good and evil, the creative power of aroused masculinity and the destructive power of loosened animality, fused in a bloody drama of violence as cocks with razor-sharp, 5-inch-long steel spurs on their feet fight to the death.

Geertz interprets the cockfight as a sociological event closely tied to Balinese society. The pivot of cockfighting around which all other aspects turn is gambling. There are two kinds of bets. One is the large bet, for even money, between the owners of the cocks and several of their kinsmen or village mates. The other is the many side bets around the ring between members of the audience. In a large-bet, well-made match, there is a mob scene atmosphere—a sense of sheer chaos about to break loose—as all the waving, shouting men try desperately to find a last-minute partner.

deep play Cultural performances, such as sports and games, in which participants and spectators are joined together in emotionally compelling experiences.

This frenzy is heightened by the intense stillness that falls as the cocks are put down in the ring and the battle begins. When the fight ends, all bets are immediately paid.

Large, center bets, in which the cocks are evenly matched and the outcome is less predictable, are the focal points of the competition for prestige that forms the deep play aspect of Balinese cockfighting. In deep play, the stakes are so high that, from a utilitarian standpoint, it is irrational for men to engage in it at all. Yet men often engage in such play and with great passion. For the Balinese, esteem, honor, and dignity are more at stake than material gain. This does not mean that the money at stake is not important; on the contrary, it is very important. Because so much money is involved, risking it publicly is also risking one's status, especially one's masculinity. This belief increases the meaning of the cockfight for the Balinese.

The Balinese cockfight is a symbolic contest between male egos; more important, it is also a symbolic expression of the Balinese social hierarchy. Prestige is the driving force in Balinese society and the central driving force of the cockfight, transforming the fight into a status bloodbath. The more nearly a match involves men of equal status, especially personal enemies or high-status men, the deeper and more emotional the match is felt to be.

The Balinese are aware of the deep status concerns involved in cockfighting, which they refer to as "playing with fire without getting burned." Cockfighting activates village and kin group rivalries and hostilities in "play" form. It comes dangerously and entrancingly close to the expression of open and direct interpersonal and intergroup aggression, something that almost never happens in the course of ordinary Balinese life. But then, the Balinese say, it is not quite the same as "real" aggression because, after all, "it is only a cockfight."

REPRESENTING THE OTHER IN ART

In representing cultural identity, art depicts not only the self (that is, the culture in which it is created) but also the "other"—the alien, the foreigner, the outsider. Indeed, artistic forms are important aspects of cultural ideologies of difference, communicating in subtle but significant ways the nature of we/they distinctions.

This artistic rendering of the "other" appears in many aspects of European (or Western) art. One result of the encounters between Europeans and other peoples was a profound rethinking of European cultural identity (S. Schwartz 1994). Although these encounters were experienced differently in different times and places, Europeans most often responded by creating opposite categories of "them" and "us" (Bitterli 1986). These dichotomies take many forms: East and West, primitive and civilized, traditional and modern, developed and undeveloped. Anthropology itself was closely connected to this process, and anthropological representations and their extensions into museums were an important element in these constructions of the "other" (di Leonardo 1998). Today, mass media continue these ascriptions of cultural difference, most often in ways that implicitly and explicitly reinforce the superiority of the West and the subordination of the "others" (Shohat and Stam 1994).

ORIENTALISM IN EUROPEAN ART: PICTURING THE MIDDLE EAST

Artistic products can be a source of insight into the fantasies one group of people entertains about another (Bassani and Fagg 1988). Artistic images of outsiders may be useful as historical documents, portraying details of behavior and costume. But the unknown aspects of foreigners also act as invitations to engage in fantasies having less to do with the reality of the observed than the needs and fantasies of the observers. Thus, repeated images of an "other" in a culture's art forms may reveal more about the creating culture's own basic concerns and fantasies than it does about the "other" (Tsurua 1989).

In the nineteenth century, Europeans explored, wrote about, painted, and excavated North Africa, Arabia, the Levant, and the Ottoman Empire. This region, today called the Middle East, was then called the Orient. European artists of the nineteenth and twentieth centuries offered armchair travelers a vividly

Otto E. Nelson/The Metropolitan Museum of Art, Gift of Lincoln Kirstein, 1959

THE IMPORTANCE OF EUROPEAN AND AMERICAN CONTACT WITH JAPAN IS REPRESENTED IN MANY WOODCUTS AND OTHER PORTRAYALS OF WESTERNERS. MANY OF THESE IMAGES REFLECT THE AMBIVALENCE WITH WHICH THE JAPANESE VIEWED THESE INVADERS, WHO WERE POWERFUL YET REGARDED AS CULTURAL BARBARIANS.

graphic image of the Islamic, largely Arabic cultures inhabiting this world. One important impetus for these representations, particularly in France, was the Napoleonic campaigns in Egypt (1798–99). By the mid-nineteenth century, the Egyptian experience had become part of the French cultural spirit (Hauptman 1985:48).

Europeans saw the Oriental "other" as threatening because they perceived it as the opposite of European civilization. The Orient was despotic, static, and irrational, whereas Europe was democratic, dynamic, and rational. But the Orient was also enchanting: a land of mystery, fairy tales, and exotic beauty. This perception of the Orient was reflected in and reinforced by its depiction in European paintings. Although many Europeans traveled to the Orient, painters generally worked from second-hand sources or, in some cases, purely from

imagination. However, their works were rendered in exquisite detail, which gave the viewer a sense of historical accuracy.

Many of the early nineteenth-century images of the Middle East to reach Europe were archaeological. Artists were inspired by the romantic spirit to seek out the picturesque and the awesome (fabled ruins, biblical sites, deserts, and mountains). The Orient was viewed as an area of enchantment, and Orientalist paintings emphasized the exoticism and glamour of Oriental markets, camel caravans, and snake charmers. Islam was captured not in its religious experience (to which Europeans were generally hostile) but in the architecture of its mosques and its practice of prayer, all portrayed in lavish, opulent detail.

Gender roles and relationships were a central theme in Orientalist painting. Men were perceived as clearly dominant and pictured in public places, where women were mostly absent. The Arab warrior was the most common symbol of Oriental masculinity, but men were also painted in more relaxed poses, drinking coffee or smoking the hookah. But it was Oriental women who were central to European fantasies of the period (Thornton 1994). The difficulty of finding women to pose in no way inhibited their depiction; indeed, this difficulty gave free rein to artists' imaginations. Women were portrayed as the Orient's greatest temptation, whether hidden behind the veil or revealed in the harem.

Harems and slave markets, painted for male patrons by male artists, offered a convenient way of feeding European lust by displaying the dominant men and vulnerable women of another culture, far removed from home. Pornographic scenes disguised as either documentation or art were integral to the European market for Orientalist painting. These images were not confined to "fine" art but found frequent expression in other elements of culture such as the picture postcard, a genre that Alloula (1986) calls the "comic strip of colonial morality." In early twentieth-century Algeria, the French sent home postcards that reveal the preoccupation of Europeans with the veiled female body. The native models for these cards were photographed in studios reenacting exotic rituals in costumes provided by photographers. The models represent the French fantasy of the inaccessible Oriental female, more tempting because she is behind the veil in the forbidden harem.

In deconstructing the symbolism of Orientalist representations, Alloula notes that many of the photographs have women behind the bars of their own home, representing the European perception that if women are inaccessible, it is because they are imprisoned. The harem is portrayed as a lascivious world of idle women who lie adorned as if ready for unending festivities (Alloula 1986:35). Women are often represented pouring coffee, a metaphor of sweetness; another stereotypical prop is the hookah, which in fact was little used in Algeria. But the association of the hookah with hashish brought to life "a world of dreamy feminine presences in various states of self abandonment and lasciviousness" (Alloula 1986:74).

Alloula connects these represented fantasies to colonial reality, noting that the raiding of women has always been the dream and the obsession of the total victor: "These raided bodies are the spoils of victory, the warrior's reward." The postcards are an "enterprise in seduction directed to the troops, the leering wink in the encampment" (1986:122).

Orientalist representations of women reflected the long-standing conflict between Christian Europeans and Middle Eastern Muslims. Since the Middle Ages, Europeans had faulted Muslims for sanctioning the practice of polygyny and associated it with promiscuity. Popular images of slave girls, harems, and concubines provided a continual source of horror and titillation for Western critics of the Muslim world. Even today, Western thinking about the contemporary Middle East is preoccupied with the veiling, segregation, and oppression of women (Hale 1989).

REPRESENTING EUROPEANS: PERFORMING THE CONQUEST IN LATIN AMERICA

The Spanish conquest of the Americas was one of the world's great cultural encounters, both in its impact on Europe and its disastrous impact on indigenous populations (see Chapter 17). For Europeans, the narrative of the conquistadors evoked adventure, imagination, glory, triumph, and riches; for the Indians, the conquest meant the end of an era and the ruin of their civilizations (Wachtel 1977:12). Most of the information about these events comes from Spanish records. The dominant European historical narrative, as well as "official" Latin American narratives, picture indigenous peoples as accepting and benefiting from Spanish rule.

But other sources tell a different story (Ronald Wright 1992). One of these sources is contemporary performances associated with village festivals in parts of Mexico, Guatemala, and Peru, which reenact the events of the conquest using dialogue, song, dance, and costume. Although all of these plays have been influenced by Spanish culture—particularly the Spanish play *Moors and Christians,* celebrating the Spanish triumph over Islam in 1492—the Latin American plays present a counternarrative to the European conquest that is part of the collective history of Indian peoples (Wachtel 1977). These plays indicate that indigenous peoples throughout the New World resisted Spanish invasion and domination and keep the memories of that resistance alive in their popular arts.

Portents and prophecies in Maya, Inca, and Aztec cosmology anticipated the coming of foreigners that would result in great upheavals for their societies. They were nevertheless unprepared for the pillage, massacres, violence, and disease that accompanied the conquest. These events began a traumatic experience for indigenous peoples in which they had to deal with a totally different world. This trauma continues in the culture and psychology of the present, as the Indian people continue to experience Spanish domination as a source of humiliation and subjection (Burgos-DeBray 1984).

Every year, in various parts of Central and South America, peasants reenact the Spanish conquest in village festivals. These plays seem to have appeared quite soon after the conquest. In Peru and Bolivia, the performance of "The Tragedy of the Death of Atahuallpa" (the last of the Incas) begins with dreams predicting the arrival of the Spanish: bearded men coming by sea in iron ships. It then enacts preliminary meetings between the servants of the Incas and the Spanish lieutenants, followed by the meet-

THE ENIGMA OF THE MIDDLE EASTERN WOMAN, WHETHER HIDDEN BEHIND HER VEIL OR REVEALED
IN THE HAREM, WAS A CORE IMAGE OF ORIENTALIST PAINTING. IN MANY CASES THE ARTIST WAS NOT
PAINTING FROM LIFE. THIS SCENE BY JUAN GIMENEZ-MARTIN, CALLED "IN THE HAREM," WAS ACTUALLY
PAINTED IN ROME.

ing of the Inca and Spanish chieftains face to face. A central theme in all these meetings is the Inca incomprehension at the Spanish, who bring the news of the true god in a letter, which of course the Inca cannot read. Atahuallpa first offers Pizarro gold and silver, which Pizarro rejects as insufficient. Atahuallpa then surrenders, begging Pizarro to spare his life. Pizarro refuses, and Atahuallpa readies himself for death. He makes his son promise to retreat and refuse the Spanish yoke and to drive out the bearded enemy at a later time. Then Atahuallpa curses Pizarro, saying the conquistador will be sullied with the blood of Atahuallpa whose subjects will never accept Spanish rule.

Pizarro then kills Atahuallpa, and his death is followed by lamentations. Because the Inca was identified with the Sun and worshiped as a god, his death indicated not only the collapse of the polity but the birth of chaos and the swallowing up of the universe. The Incas experienced the Spanish dominion as bereavement, martyrdom, and inconsolable loss. In the last act, a chorus pronounces a curse on Pizarro. The final scene shows the meeting of Pizarro and the king of Spain, in which Pizarro offers Atahuallpa's head to the king. The king is indignant at Pizarro's crime, praises the Inca, and tells Pizarro that he will be punished. Cursing his sword, and the day he was born, Pizarro falls to the ground dead (Wachtel 1977:37). Thus, these plays emphasize the victory of the Indians over the Spanish; indeed, some versions end with the resurrection and triumph of Atahuallpa, heralding the ultimate expulsion of the Spanish.

MARKETING CULTURAL IDENTITIES THROUGH THE ARTS

Current anthropological perspectives on art now include an interest in the role of the arts in a globally interconnected economic and cultural system (Mullin 1995). One result is an examination of the political and cultural meanings implicit in how creative works are classified (Clifford 1988). Another result is that the boundaries between "high" and "low" arts are increasingly contested (Bright

I N   T H E   F I E L D

THE ARTS, TOURISM, AND CULTURAL IDENTITY AMONG THE TORAJA

The connection between the arts, tourism, and the construction of cultural identity is well illustrated by the Toraja of South Sulawesi, Indonesia. The Toraja are mainly subsistence cultivators who also raise water buffalo, pigs, and chickens, all of which are killed and eaten on ritual occasions. Two artistic productions among the Toraja that have particular spiritual importance in their society are *tongkonan,* or ancestral houses (which represent the links among ancestors, living kin, and future kin), and the *tau-tau,* which are wooden effigies of nobles carved in connection with mortuary ritual.

Although the Toraja today are predominantly Christian, they continue to perform and have expanded their traditionally elaborate mortuary rituals. In fact, for outsiders and for the Toraja themselves, these ritual performances, and the artistic works associated with them, have emerged as a major component of contemporary Toraja cultural identity (Volkman 1984). Tourism has been essential in this process.

By the late 1960s, tourism began to expand in the Toraja area, almost all of it oriented toward viewing the Toraja mortuary rituals of animal sacrifice, the spectacularly carved tongkonan, and the eerie

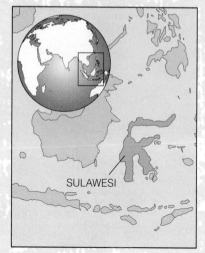

SULAWESI

tau-tau. Organized tourism to Tana Toraja was an important part of Indonesia's tourist development program, aimed at increasing the flow of Western capital (Volkman 1984:162). Tourism increased rapidly, from only 650 foreign visitors in 1972 to more than 179,000 tourists (domestic and foreign) by 1987 (Adams 1990:31). Among the early tourists was a British film crew, so the Toraja became known throughout Europe in connection with their rituals and their art, specifically the tongkonan and the tau-tau.

The importance of these elements in creating a Toraja identity was illustrated in the tourist brochure issued by the American Museum of Natural History to promote a one-day tour to the Toraja country, led by anthropologist Clifford Geertz. The Toraja were described as "a fascinating people who practice unique burial rituals, create beautiful artworks,

and build striking, intricately carved houses" (Volkman 1984:163). Indeed, because of the artistic attraction of ancestral houses, which have upward-curving eaves resembling a boat and spectacularly carved side panels, Toraja were forbidden by Indonesian tourist officials to alter them. These officials even questioned whether Toraja should be permitted to inhabit their houses because human occupancy could damage these "tourist objects" (Adams 1990:33). Reflecting the tourist demand for "portable art," the Toraja began carving miniature ancestral houses for sale in tourist shops.

The other significant artistic element in Toraja cultural identity is the tau-tau. These effigies represent the spirit of the dead person; they are the vessel of the Torajan soul (Adams 1993). Tau-taus are permitted to be carved only for the wealthiest nobility and are therefore an important symbol of aristocratic status among the Toraja. Tau-taus are commissioned by the family of the deceased, and the carving is surrounded at every step by religious ritual. When the funeral begins, the tau-tau is adorned with finely woven clothing, a betel nut bag filled with silver and bamboo utensils, a head dressing, gold jewelry, and a sacred knife—all heirlooms associated with nobility or deities. The tau-tau is supposed to resemble the dead person; it makes his or her soul visible. During the funeral, the tau-tau is placed near the body of the deceased, from where it observes the mortuary ritual. When the mortuary rites are completed,

and Bakewell 1995). Also included in these new anthropological approaches to art is an examination of the Western and international art worlds (Marcus and Myers 1995; Price 1989).

The arts have always been important in marking cultural boundaries. They retain that importance in the contemporary world, particularly with regard to the construction of ethnic identities of indigenous peoples (Graburn 1976). The linking of the arts to cultural identity is promoted by popular television shows about non-Western "exotic" cultures, the worldwide

the tau-tau is placed with its relatives on platforms chiseled into limestone cliffs, where it becomes a visual link between the community of the living and the community of the dead.

Christian missionaries disapprove of tau-taus, but tau-taus continue to be part of Christian Toraja identity and may incorporate such Christian elements as Bibles and crosses. Tau-taus also incorporate other Western cultural elements, such as digital watches, eyeglasses, and Western clothing (Adams 1993). Although tau-taus were always carved as individualized portraits of the deceased, today they are carved and painted as very realistic resemblances. Indeed, in an attempt to reconcile their attachment to the tau-tau with church prohibitions, Christian Toraja explain the tau-tau as three-dimensional pictures of the dead.

Traditionally, tau-taus were closely associated only with noble identity, but for tourists the tau-tau have become emblematic of a generalized Torajan identity. Miniature tau-taus are sold in the tourist markets, along with large carvings of the burial cliffs. Thus, tourism began a process by which ritually significant objects have been transformed into art objects of economic significance.

As the tau-taus became known as art objects in the Western world, hundreds of them were stolen and sold to American, European, and Asian art collectors. Redesignated by Western curators and collectors as archaic Indonesian art, some effigies have also found a home in Western museums. For the Toraja, the theft of a tau-tau is tantamount to the abduction of an ancestor, and the loss must be redressed by ritual propitiation. Additionally, the Toraja realize that without the tau-taus, tourism will decline, depriving them of an important source of income and prestige.

Unlike other artistic forms such as music or dance that, if appropriated or stolen, can be reenacted, the tau-tau is irreplaceable. Legal, political, and economic obstacles stand in the way of repatriation, and tau-taus today are openly sold for thousands of dollars in international galleries. The Indonesian government, more to maintain tourist interest than address Torajan concerns, has replaced stolen tau-taus with newly made ones, but the Torajans reject these as being not only clumsily made but without spiritual significance because they were not made under ritual conditions (Adams 1993).

Paradox and pathos thus attend the tau-tau today. The tau-tau's meaning has changed from ritual to art object, and where once the tau-tau served as a protection for the family of the deceased, today the family of the deceased must protect the tau-tau (Adams 1993).

TAU-TAUS, OR EFFIGIES OF THE SPIRIT OF A RECENTLY DECEASED NOBLE PERSON, HAVE TAKEN ON NEW IDENTITIES, BOTH FOR THE TORAJA AND FOR OUTSIDERS, AS THEY BECOME TRANSFORMED INTO ARTISTIC COMMODITIES FOR TOURISTS AND INTERNATIONAL COLLECTORS.

Wendy Bass/Viesti Associates, Inc.

Critical Thinking Questions

1. One of the effects of tourism is to make people more self-conscious of their culture. This can have both positive and negative effects. What effects has tourism had on Toraja cultural identity?

2. What forms of artistic expression are particularly important in relation to your own cultural identity?

3. What does it mean to say that culture has become a commodity? How does the buying and selling of cultural symbols affect the identities of those who sell them and those who buy them?

Source: Adapted from Kathleen M. Adams, "Theologians, Tourists and Thieves: The Torajan Effigy of the Dead in Modernizing Indonesia." *Kyoto Journal,* 1993: 38–45.

sale of ethnic arts, traveling museum shows in which indigenous peoples are represented through their arts, the circulation of tribal arts among Western art collectors, and tourism. In addition to providing new sources of income, artistic objects and performances that have their origin in the ritual and social life of these societies become artistic products around which modern cultural identities may be constructed, by outsiders if not by the societies themselves.

The growth of tourism has been of particular relevance to indigenous peoples. Since

World War II, there has been an enormous increase in the number of Europeans, Americans, and Japanese visiting what were previously remote areas of the world. With greater accessibility, primarily through the development of airports, islands in the middle of the Indian Ocean, villages in the center of deep jungle in South America, and Inuit communities in the Canadian and American Arctic are feeling the impact of tourism. Although 90 percent of the world's tourists both come from and visit countries in Europe, the United States, and Japan, tourist spending is often a major part of the economy in the developing nations in which indigenous peoples live.

The anthropological view of tourism is generally that it has negative impacts on local cultures, unless it is carefully controlled by indigenous peoples, and that it is bad for art. Tourism often does debase indigenous, culturally authentic, and creative art into mass-produced souvenirs of low quality, lacking any cultural meaning, but its effects on art and cultural identity have actually been mixed.

Tourism can support and reaffirm cultural identities by reviving respect for traditional art forms, as has occurred to some extent in the American Southwest (Mullin 1995). In Bali, the interest of tourists in cultural performances has stimulated an improvement in the artistic quality of some of the dance and dramatic performances. The economic boost from tourist patronage of these performances has allowed local troupes to buy new instruments for their gamelan orchestras and new costumes, and it has encouraged the opening of schools and institutes throughout Indonesia for training in traditional art forms. An expert and professional group of Indonesian artists has maintained tight control over performances and is acting to conserve the quality of the arts. Similarly, interest in the Inuit arts has been an extremely important alternative source of income for them, especially as their traditional hunting declines. This connection between art, tourism, and the strengthening of cultural identity is also seen in the weaving of Indian women in Guatemala and Mexico, although this has increased conflicts within the society (J. Nash 1986).

The changing meanings of ritually and socially significant cultural elements as they become part of staged performances for tourists, or move from their original cultural contexts into the world art market, are part of a larger process in which culture itself has become a marketable commodity, reshaped and packaged in part in response to the demands of a world market. Will this marketing of culture move the world inevitably toward cultural homogenization? Or will the global economy and global village always leave spaces for the emergence of meaningful local artistic expressions of cultural identity?

SUMMARY

1. From an anthropological perspective, the arts include a wide range of activities in which creative expression is guided by standards of beauty in a particular culture.

2. Although art exists in every society, art for art's sake and the specialized role of the artist do not. In most nonindustrial societies, art and the artist are part of other cultural activities, such as ritual.

3. Aesthetic values differ among cultures. In some cultures, such as those in the West, originality is essential to art. In other societies, improvisation is more important. In some cases, artistic products are produced according to strict, often religious, rules.

4. Artistic emphasis also differs among peoples. Writing is an art form in one culture, tea drinking in another, and cockfighting in yet another, depending on cultural values.

5. Art is often regarded as inherently powerful. In prehistoric cultures, cave paintings of animals were believed to exert control over hunting.

6. One of the powerful elements in art is the symbolic meanings it has for its audience. One of the compelling elements of art is its multilayered levels of meaning communicating several cultural themes.

7. The arts have many connections with social structure. Artistic objects may be made for, owned by, or represent powerful elites. Art can also contest power by mocking those in power or questioning society's rules.

8. The arts, in both their production and their display, are significant elements in cultural integra-

tion, bringing people into a common emotional state as they respond to culturally meaningful symbols.

9. Art forms, as among the Chinese and the Luba, are significant in expressing a people's cultural identity and their interpretation of their history.

10. Deep play, such as the Balinese cockfight and American football, help integrate society by revealing its social structure and embodying cultural themes.

11. Art is used to represent one's own cultural identity and to represent the "other"—those felt to be different in basic ways from oneself. Europeans represented the Oriental "other" through painting. Indigenous peoples of Latin America represent the European "other" through performances re-enacting the Spanish conquest of the New World.

12. The arts are important ethnic boundary markers in the contemporary world. Indigenous peoples, particularly, are known to the West through their arts. With the increase in tourism, these objects, performances, and rituals, which originally had spiritual meanings, become transformed into staged displays of cultural identity for tourists or commodities in international art markets.

KEY TERMS

art
deep play

SUGGESTED READINGS

Brownell, Susan. 1995. *Training the Body for China: Sports in the Moral Order of the People's Republic.* Chicago: University of Chicago Press. An exceptionally readable look into the ways in which China has developed a sports culture consistent with some traditional Chinese values, written from the ethnographic site of a university track team in Beijing.

Dalby, Liza. 1993. *Kimono: Fashioning Culture.* New Haven, CT: Yale University Press. An anthropologist who lived and worked in a geisha community for 14 months, the author discusses both historical and contemporary aspects of the kimono and its relationship to Japanese culture.

Dubin, Lois Sherr. 1999 *North American Indian Jewelry and Adornment: From Prehistory to the Present.* New

York: Harry N. Abrams, Inc. An astonishingly beautiful book that interweaves anthropological and Native American perspectives. Dubin undermines stereotypes of Native Americans through her emphasis on the connections between past and contemporary artistic creativity and by highlighting the voices of Native Americans as they explain the meaning of their art.

Rice, Timothy. 1994. *May It Fill Your Soul: Experiencing Bulgarian Music.* Chicago: University of Chicago Press. Compact disc included. An accessible yet scholarly introduction to the field of ethnomusicology, in which the reader gets to know the people as well as the music. Particularly interesting is the discussion of the relationship between the music, the musicians, and the state.

Shohat, Ella, and Robert Stam. 1994. *Unthinking Eurocentrism: Multiculturalism and the Media.* London: Routledge. A spectacular, encyclopedic, and essential resource on the ways in which European films have represented non-Europeans and the contemporary ways non-Europeans are representing themselves.

Waterman, Christopher Alan. 1990. *Juju: A Social History and Ethnography of an African Popular Music.* Chicago: University of Chicago Press. A scholarly treatment of a non-Western African performance tradition, examining the urban and colonial context, social relations, and aesthetic aspects of a popular musical form in contemporary Nigeria.

INTERNET RESOURCES

The following Internet resources appear in this chapter. Please log on to the Wadsworth anthropology website: **http://anthropology.wadsworth. com**. Click on the Nanda/Warms *Cultural Anthropology* page. Then select the Student Resources section, where you will find a complete presentation of these links and more.

- A video link: The place of a musician within his village and community, page 366
- A photo essay on the muralist tradition in Mexico, combining art and politics, page 373
- Link to websites that demonstrate how the Internet is being used to promote and market ethnographic goods, page 379
- Access the Study Guide to InfoTrac College Edition for Anthropology Students

ALTHOUGH PEOPLE STILL USE TRADITIONAL TECHNOLOGIES AND CULTURAL PRACTICES, CHANGE HAS AFFECTED PEOPLE IN ALL THE WORLD'S CULTURES.

Barbara Backer

Chapter Seventeen

CULTURAL CHANGE

What factors enabled the peoples of Europe to expand their power?

What were some effects of European expansion on non-European cultures?

Why did European nations colonize, and what was the effect of colonization on people of other cultures?

What are some of the problems faced by poor nations today?

Culture, as we have seen, is dynamic and changing. Environmental and population pressures, internal conflict, innovation, and discovery are always active processes in human groups: No people have ever been frozen in time. At the same time, there can be no doubt that the pace of change is increasingly rapid, not only for ourselves but for people all over the world.

We can see the increasing speed of change in terms of world population and resource use. Consider the rate of population growth. Scientists believe that about 2 million years ago, our remote ancestors numbered perhaps 100,000. By the time the first agricultural societies were developing 10,000 years ago, world population had reached 5 to 10 million people. Two thousand years ago, at the time of the Roman Empire, there were still only about 250 million people in the world. By 1750, this had tripled to 750 million. Then things really began to speed up. Fifty years later, in 1800, there were 1 billion people in the world; by 1930, there were 2 billion. In the last two-thirds of the twentieth century, world population tripled, surpassing the 6 billion mark in the summer of 1999 (Erickson 1995; Fetto 1999). If this enormous rate of population growth continues, a person born in 1975 who lives to be 75 years old will have seen the world's population increase from 4 to 10 billion (Haub and Richie 1994).

This huge increase in population is related to many other changes. Ten or twelve thousand years ago, almost all the world's people lived by hunting and gathering. By 1500, only 1 percent of them did. Today there are virtually no hunter-gatherers left (Lee and Devore 1968). One thousand years ago, the vast majority of the world's population consumed at similar levels, although substantial differences in wealth existed. Today, about one-fifth of the Earth's population takes home 64 percent of the world's income. Even more shockingly, the net worth of the 358 richest people in the world is equal to the combined income of the world's poorest 2.3 billion people (United Nations Development Programme 1996). The average person in an industrialized nation consumes 3 times as much fresh water, 10 times as much energy, and 19 times as much aluminum as someone in a developing nation (Durning 1994).

We all know that the pace of change has been extremely rapid in the past several centuries; we know less about the patterns of change and their effects on cultures around the world. The story of these patterns is complex and diverse. It is a story of contact between cultures. In general, it is the story of the expansion of the wealth and power of places that are now considered industrialized nations. This expansion occurred in thousands of locations and had many different effects. Sometimes cultural con-

EUROPEAN EXPANSION WAS OFTEN ACCOMPANIED BY VIOLENCE AND SLAUGHTER. HERE, BARTOLOMEO, THE BROTHER OF CHRISTOPHER COLUMBUS AND FOUNDER OF SANTA DOMINGO (PRESENT-DAY CAPITAL OF THE DOMINICAN REPUBLIC), DESTROYS A VILLAGE THAT RESISTED HIS RULE.

Antman Archives/The Image Works

tact was accidentally genocidal, sometimes intentionally so. Many traditional cultures have been destroyed; others have prospered, though in altered forms. Members of different cultures often confronted each other through a veil of suspicion and accusations of savagery, but sometimes common interests, common enemies, mutual curiosity, and occasionally friendship among people overrode their differences.

Our world, the current result of this process, is an enormously contradictory place. All around us, we see increasing cultural homogeneity; you can find a bottle of soda, a radio, or a tape recorder almost anywhere in the world. At the same time, people around the world are insisting, sometimes violently, on their right to preserve their cultural or ethnic identity.

In this chapter, we describe the overall pattern of change during the past several hundred years. Of all the innumerable changes in that time, the expansion of European influence has probably had the greatest impact worldwide. For that reason, we begin with a bird's-eye view of Europe and the rest of the world as it might have appeared in 1400 and a discussion of the growth of European power.

THE WORLD IN 1400

As surprising as it may seem now, a visitor touring the world on the eve of European expansion in 1400 would probably have been amused by the notion that European societies would soon become enormously wealthy and powerful. Other areas of the globe would have seemed much more likely prospects for power. Europeans had devised oceangoing vessels, but Arab and Chinese ships regularly made much longer voyages. The cities of India and China made those of Europe look like mere villages. Almost no European states could effectively administer more than a few hundred square kilometers. Certainly there were none to compare to China's vast wealth and centralized bureaucracy. Europeans were masters of cathedral and castle construction, but other than that, their technology was backward. War, plague, and economic depression were the order of the day (Scammell 1989). Moreover, other areas of the world seemed to be expanding. Despite occasional setbacks, the Islamic powers had expanded steadily in the five centuries leading up to 1400, so that Islamic nations stretched from Spain to Indonesia. Not only had these empires preserved the scholarship of India and the ancient Mediterranean civilizations, but they had greatly expanded technical knowledge in astronomy, mathematics, medicine, chemistry, zoology, mineralogy, and meteorology (Lapidus 1988:96, 241–252).

China also had an extraordinarily ancient and powerful civilization. As late as 1793, Emperor Ch'ien Lung, believing China to be the most powerful state in the world (or perhaps showing bravado in the face of foreign traders), responded to a British delegation's attempt to open trade by writing to King George II: "Our dynasty's majestic virtue has penetrated into every country under heaven and kings of all nations have offered their costly tribute by land and sea. As your Ambassador can see for himself, we possess all things . . . we have never valued ingenious articles, nor do we have the slightest need of your country's manufacturers" (Peyrefitte 1992:288–292). Unfortunately for the Chinese, by the time the emperor wrote this letter, it was no longer accurate. Half a century later, by the end of the First Opium War, Britain virtually controlled China.

EUROPEAN EXPANSION: MOTIVES AND METHODS

From slow beginnings in the fifteenth century, European power grew rapidly from the sixteenth to the twentieth centuries. Many theories have been suggested to account for the causes and motives of European expansion. Although often a cover for more worldly aims, the desire of the pious to Christianize the world was certainly a motivating factor. The archives of the Jesuit order, for example, include more than 15,000 letters, written between 1550 and 1771, from people who wanted to be missionaries abroad (Scammell 1989:60). The desire to find a wide variety of wonders, both real and imagined, was also important. The Portuguese looked for routes to the very real wealth of Eastern empires such as China, but also for the mythical kingdom of Prester John, a powerful but hidden Christian monarch, the fountain of youth, and the seven cities of Cibola.

Beyond this, there was always the desire for wealth. Nations and nobles quickly lost their aversion to exploration as gold and diamonds were discovered. The poor and oppressed of Europe often saw opportunities for wealth and respect in the colonies. There, they often fulfilled their dreams of wealth by recreating the very social order they had fled.

Europeans were aided in their pursuit of expansion by various social and technological developments. These included the rise of a banking and merchant class, a growing population, and the development of the caravel, a new ship design that was better at sailing into the wind. Two further developments, the monoculture plantation and the joint stock company, were to have critical impacts on the world's people.

In many cases, however, the key advantage Europeans had over other people was the diseases they carried. Almost every time Europeans met others who had been isolated from the European, African, and Asian land masses, they brought death and cultural destruction in the form of microbes. In many instances, virtually the entire native population perished of imported diseases within 20 years. Although Europeans too died of diseases, they did so in far smaller numbers.

The European search for wealth depended on tactics that, in their basic form, were ancient. Two of the quickest ways to accumulate wealth are to steal it from others and to get other people to work for you for free. State societies have always practiced these methods. War, slavery, exploitation, and inequality were present in most of the world before European contact, so there was nothing fundamentally new about their use by Europeans. However, no earlier empire had been able to practice these tactics on the scale of the European nations. All previous empires, however large, were regional affairs. European expansion, for the first time in history, linked the entire world into an economic system. This system created much of the wealth of Europe and ultimately that of many of today's industrialized nations. At the same time, it systematically impoverished much of today's developing world.

PILLAGE

One of the most important means of wealth transfer was **pillage.** In the early years of expansion, Europeans were driven by the search for precious metals, particularly gold and silver. When they found such valuables, they moved quickly to send them back to their home countries. Metals belonging to indigenous peoples were quickly dispatched back to Europe, and mines were placed under European control. The profits of this enterprise were enormous.

In 1531, Pizarro captured the Inca emperor Atahuallpa and received $88.5 million in gold and $2.5 million in silver (current value) as his ransom. A gang of Indian smiths worked nine forges day and night to melt down this treasure, which was then shipped back to Spain (Duncan 1995:158). In the early seventeenth century, 58,000 Indian workers were forced

---

pillage To strip an area of money, goods, or raw materials through the use of physical violence or the threat of such violence.

WHY THE NATIVES DIED:
DISEASE IN EUROPEAN EXPANSION

Can you imagine a society in which no one ever gets a cold or the flu? Where measles, mumps, smallpox, tuberculosis, and most other contagious diseases are unknown? Though it may seem hard to imagine, the Americas were like that before Columbus. Europeans brought disease and death to almost every place they visited outside of Europe, Africa, and Asia. The impact of disease in the Americas is particularly well documented, although smallpox and tuberculosis decimated the population of the Pacific islands as well (Owsley, Gill, and Ousley 1994). In the wake of contact with Europeans, up to 95 percent of the total population of the New World died of epidemic diseases. In the 50 years after Cortés arrived in Mexico, its population, estimated at between 25 and 30 million, declined to 3 million (Karlen 1995). Mesoamerica had at least 14 major epidemics between 1520 and 1600 (Wolf 1982). In New Mexico, between 60 and 70 percent of Pueblo Indians died between 1606 and 1638 (Palkovich 1994).

The founding of European colonies in New England led to rapid native population declines. By the mid-1600s, only 30 years after the Pilgrims landed at Plymouth, Naragansett, and Massachuset Indian populations had declined 86 percent, the Pocumtut by 95 percent, and the Mohegan and Pequot by 81 percent (B. Baker 1994). Although occasionally epidemics may have been intentionally caused, neither Europeans nor natives had any knowledge of contagion or germs, and the vast majority of deaths were not premeditated. Although Europeans later came to believe that the deaths of the natives demonstrated their biological inferiority and confirmed the "manifest destiny" of Europeans, initially even the

Europeans were bewildered at the extent and impact of these epidemics.

All of this happened because natives of the New World had no immunity to Old World diseases. This, however, raises an interesting question. Why didn't Europeans return home with New World diseases? If isolation were the only important factor, Europeans should have died of New World diseases as rapidly as New World natives died of European diseases. There are two principal answers to this question.

First, the key diseases that killed indigenous populations were smallpox, influenza, tuberculosis, malaria, plague, measles, and cholera. These diseases all have several characteristics in common. They spread easily and rapidly. They quickly kill those susceptible to them, and they confer immunity on those that survive them. Such diseases do not survive without infected humans to spread them. As a result, they are all diseases of crowds, requiring a large human population. To understand why, consider what would happen if one of these diseases attacked a small, relatively isolated group. All those susceptible to the disease would soon die. Those who survived, as well as their nursing infants, would be immune. A new generation of susceptible individuals would take a while to develop. Thus, epidemics can only sustain themselves if the population is so large that children without resistance are always available to be infected. For some diseases, the numbers required are quite high, perhaps a half million for measles (Diamond 1992). The result is that small groups are generally free of such diseases. They catch imported diseases easily but have few of their own to give back.

This explains the high death rate among small groups like the Naragansett and

Massachuset, Indians of eastern North America. But what of the dense populations of Mexico and South America? While the Aztec and other groups certainly had populations high enough to sustain these diseases, they happened not to have been exposed to them. To understand why, we must consider the sources of crowd diseases. All of the diseases mentioned above had their origins in domesticated animals. Measles, for example, probably came from a virus that affects cows; influenza had its likely origin in swine. Horses were the apparent source of the common cold. Sheep and goats together have contributed more than 46 diseases to humans (Karlen 1995). Europeans and others in the Old World had long been in contact with many domesticated animals. They had been exposed to these diseases and, as a result, both carried their germs and had developed a degree of immunity. But in the Americas, domesticated animals were extremely rare. Most of the wild animals that could have been domesticated became extinct at the end of the last Ice Age, about 11,000 years ago. The only domesticates present at the time of contact with Europe were turkeys, ducks, guinea pigs, and llamas. Of these, turkeys and ducks do not live in large enough flocks to develop crowd diseases and llamas were generally not kept in close contact with people. Guinea pigs may be the source of one human disease, an infection carried by a trypanosome parasite that causes Chagas' disease, but they were limited to Peru. Because Native Americans had so few domesticated animals, they had neither immunity to European diseases nor crowd diseases to give to Europeans. This imbalance had fundamental implications for the course of history.

FORCED LABOR WAS CRITICAL TO EXTRACTING WEALTH FROM NEWLY ACQUIRED LANDS. GROWING SUGAR IN THE WEST INDIES WAS EXTREMELY PROFITABLE BUT DEMANDED HUGE AMOUNTS OF HUMAN LABOR. THIS DEMAND FOR LABOR LED TO THE IMPORTATION OF MILLIONS OF AFRICAN SLAVES. THIS 1855 WOODCUT SHOWS MEN AND WOMEN MAKING HOLES FOR PLANTING SUGARCANE, A PROCESS KNOWN AS "CANE-HOLING."

into silver mining in the town of Potosi in the Peruvian Andes (Wolf 1982:136). Between 1500 and 1660, Spanish colonies in the Americas exported 300 tons of gold and 25,000 tons of silver (Scammell 1989:133).

Such plunder was not limited to the New World. After the British East India Company came to power in India, it plundered the treasury of Bengal, sending wealth back to investors in England (Wolf 1982:244). In addition, art, artifacts, curiosities, and occasionally human bodies were stolen around the world and sent to museums and private collections in Europe.

FORCED LABOR

Forced labor was also a key element of European expansion. The most notorious example was African slavery, but impressing local inhabitants for labor, debt servitude, and other forms of **peonage** were common. Europeans forced both the peoples whose lands they conquered and their own lower classes into **vassalage.** Europeans invented neither slavery in general nor African slavery in particular; non-Europeans probably exported more than 7 million slaves

to the Islamic world between 650 and 1600 (Lovejoy 1983). However, Europeans did practice African slavery on a larger scale than any people before them. Between the end of the fifteenth century and the end of the nineteenth, approximately 11.7 million slaves were exported from Africa to the Americas. More than 6 million left Africa in the eighteenth century alone (Coquery-Vidrovitch 1988). Although we are fairly certain that about 12 million slaves were transported across the Atlantic, no one really knows how many died in the process of capturing and transferring slaves within Africa. Estimates vary from one to five deaths for each slave transferred.

The massive transport of people had two important economic effects. First, the use of slave labor was extremely profitable for both slave shippers and plantation owners. Second, it im-

peonage The practice of holding a person in bondage or partial slavery in order for them to work off a debt or serve a prison sentence.

vassalage A condition of hereditary bondage in which the use of land is granted in return for payment, homage, and military service or its equivalent.

poverished areas from which slaves were drawn. The loss of so many people to the African continent was probably sufficient to stop population growth and radically alter African societies (Coquery-Vidrovitch 1988).

The demand for slaves was created by **monoculture plantations**—farms devoted to the production of a single crop for sale to distant consumers. Sugar and cotton were produced in the Americas and spices in Asia for sale to consumers located primarily in Europe. Through the eighteenth century, sugar was probably the most important monoculture crop. British consumption of sugar increased some 2500 percent between 1650 and 1800. Between 1800 and 1890, sugar production grew another 2500 percent, from 245,000 tons to more than 6 million tons (Mintz 1985:73). Growing and processing sugar was extremely labor intensive, and the massive labor power required was largely provided by slaves. Between 1701 and 1810, for example, Barbados, a small island given over almost entirely to sugar production, imported 252,500 slaves; almost all of them were involved in growing and processing sugar (Mintz 1985:53).

JOINT STOCK COMPANIES

The **joint stock company** was another innovation that allowed extremely rapid expansion and led to enormous abuses of power. Most early European exploration was financed and supported by aristocratic governments or small private firms. By the turn of the seventeenth century, however, the British and Dutch had established joint stock companies. The French, Swedes, Danes, Germans, and Portuguese followed by mid-century. Based on the sale of shares to many private owners, these companies enjoyed enormous financial power and were much more profitable than those that preceded them. The **Dutch East India Company** (**VOC,** after its initials in Dutch), founded in 1602, is a model of this form. Based on money raised from the sale of shares, the VOC was chartered by the Dutch government to hold the monopoly on all Dutch trade with the societies of the Indian and Pacific oceans. Shares in the VOC were available on reasonable terms and were held by a wide cross-section of Dutch society (Scammell 1989:101). In many ways, the company functioned as a government. Led by a board of directors called the **Heeren XVII** (the Lords Seventeen), it was empowered to make treaties with local rulers in the name of the Dutch Republic, occupy lands, levy taxes, raise armies, and declare war. The fundamental difference was that whereas governments are to some degree beholden to those they govern, the VOC was interested solely in returning dividends to its shareholders. Through the seventeenth and early eighteenth centuries, the VOC distributed annual dividends of 15.5 to 50 percent. It returned dividends of 40 percent per year for six consecutive years from 1715 to 1720 (Boxer 1965:46).

Through the seventeenth century, the VOC used its powers to seize direct or indirect control of many of the Indian Ocean islands. Among these were Java, including the port of Jakarta (which became their headquarters, renamed Batavia), Sri Lanka (Ceylon), and Malacca. In addition, the VOC acquired from the sultan of Ternate the right to control the production and trade of the most valuable spices of the area (cloves, nutmeg, and mace). The sultan's permission was not enough to prevent other people from participating in this commerce, however, and the VOC took brutal steps to keep its monopoly. For example, during the 1620s, virtually the entire population of the nutmeg-producing island of Banda was deported, driven away, starved to death, or massacred. They were replaced with Dutch col-

monoculture plantation An agricultural plantation specializing in the large-scale production of a single crop to be sold on the market.

joint stock company A firm that is managed by a centralized board of directors but owned by shareholders. Shares may be transferred from one owner to another, and shareholders are directly responsible for the firm's debt.

Dutch East India Company A joint stock company chartered by the Dutch government to control all Dutch trade in the Indian and Pacific oceans. Also known by its Dutch initials, VOC.

VOC The Dutch East India Company (Verenigde Oostindische Compagnie), after its Dutch initials.

Heeren XVII The "Lords Seventeen," members of the board of directors of the Dutch East India Company.

onists using slave labor (Ricklefs 1993:30). The VOC sent expeditions to destroy all clove plantings that they could not control, and by the 1670s had effectively complete control of all spice production (Wolf 1982).

Natives of this region did not submit passively to VOC control, and the company did not have a clear-cut military advantage. Instead, the VOC rapidly (and ultimately disastrously) became embroiled in the area's wars. For example, in the seventeenth century, the Maratram Dynasty controlled most of central Java. In 1677, when the dynasty was about to be overthrown, the VOC intervened on its behalf. In a bloody campaign, the combined VOC and dynasty forces crushed the rebellion, and Emperor Amangkurat II was established on the throne. Trouble quickly ensued. The VOC had intervened in hopes of cash payment and trading concessions but received neither. In 1686, the VOC sent an armed force to demand payment and concessions. It was defeated by Amangkurat II's forces, and the company was unable to recoup its losses or claim its trading privileges (Ricklefs 1990). This was just the beginning of a series of extremely brutal wars pitting different factions of Javanese kingdoms against each other and against the VOC. Kingdoms alternately allied with and fought against the VOC as their interests dictated. These conflicts lasted until 1757.

The company often acted with extraordinary brutality. The treatment of the Chinese in Batavia is a good example. The Chinese had come to Batavia as traders, skilled artisans, sugar millers, and shopkeepers. Despite harsh measures against them, by 1740 roughly 15,000 lived there. VOC officials believed they were plotting rebellion, and after an incident in which several Europeans were killed, VOC governor general Adriaan Valckenier hinted that a massacre would not be unwelcome. In the melee that followed, Europeans and their slaves massacred 10,000 Chinese. The Chinese quarter of the city burned for several days, and the VOC was able to stop the looting only by paying its soldiers a premium to return to duty (Ricklefs 1993:90).

The burden of continual warfare, as well as corruption and inefficiency, forced the VOC into serious financial difficulties. By the last quarter of the eighteenth century, large areas of coastal Java had been depopulated by years of warfare, but the VOC had not succeeded in controlling the principal kingdoms of the island. The Heeren XVII were dismissed by the Netherlands government in 1796 after an investigation revealed corruption and mismanagement in all quarters. On December 31, 1799, the VOC was formally dissolved, and its possessions were turned over to the Batavian Republic, a Dutch client state of France.

The story of the VOC brings several key points to light. Europeans fundamentally altered the communities with which they came into contact. In some cases, brutal policies and disease destroyed entire cultures. However, at least until the late nineteenth century, many of those affected by European expansion were not simply overrun and demolished. Rather, they sought to use Europeans to their own advantage when possible. Although some groups, particularly tribal peoples, suffered horrifically as the result of European expansion, others benefited by using the foreigners to increase their own wealth and power. Through it all, however, the key beneficiaries remained the Europeans. In the case of the VOC, the enormous profits reaped by shareholders in the Netherlands helped make it one of the wealthiest and most powerful nations of the seventeenth and eighteenth centuries. In the Dutch East Indies (modern-day Indonesia), however, the VOC left poverty in its wake.

THE ERA OF COLONIALISM

Colonialism differs in important ways from earlier forms of European expansion. Whereas much of the initial phase of European expansion was carried out by private companies and often took the form of raid and pillage, colonialism involved the active possession of foreign territory by European governments. Colonies were created when nations established

colonialism The active possession of a foreign territory and the maintenance of political domination over that territory.

and maintained political domination over geographically separate areas and political units (Kohn 1958). European colonies were of fundamentally different types. Some, as in Africa, existed primarily to exploit native people and resources. In other areas, such as North America and Australia, the key goal was the settlement of surplus European population. Still other locales, such as Yemen, which borders on the Red Sea, were seized because they occupied key strategic locations.

At one time or another, much of the world came under direct European colonization, but the timing of colonialism varied from place to place. The Americas were colonized in the 1500s and 1600s, but most other areas of the world did not come under colonial control until the nineteenth century. This is because it was only in the nineteenth century that Europeans (and their North American descendants) were able to acquire clear technological superiority.

COLONIZING THE AMERICAS

In the Americas, the quick success of the conquistadors was largely the result of disease. Cortés's conquest of Mexico is a good example. There is currently much dispute over the European narrative of this event, which tells us that the Aztecs greeted Cortés as a god when he first appeared in 1519 and were intimidated and overwhelmed by Spanish military superiority. It is more likely that Montezuma, following Aztec tradition, intended his gifts to Cortés and his opening of the city of Tenochtitlán to the Spanish to be a show of strength rather than a sign of surrender.

When it became clear that the Spanish were their enemies, the Aztecs expelled them from the city in a fierce battle that cost the Spanish and their allies perhaps two-thirds of their total army. The Aztecs believed that this decisive victory ended their confrontation with the Spanish, but Cortés and his men were back in 1521. By that time, a smallpox epidemic had killed half the Aztecs. Even after such crushing losses

---

industrialization The process of the mechanization of production.

---

to disease, the Spanish conquest of Tenochtitlán took more than four months to accomplish (Clendinnen 1991; Berdan 1982; Karlen 1995). Had the Aztecs not been devastated by disease, they might have again defeated Cortés.

Disease played an even bigger part in the conquest of the Incas in Peru. Disease swept across Central and South America well in advance of the Europeans themselves. By the time Spanish conquistador Francisco Pizarro reached Peru, the Inca empire had already been decimated. Without the disease factor, the situation in the Americas might have been much like that in Java. Europeans would not have been able to rapidly establish control over vast areas of the Americas and would have had to fight protracted battles against powerful local kingdoms.

COLONIZING IN THE NINETEENTH CENTURY

By the beginning of the nineteenth century, **industrialization** was under way in Europe and North America. This had two immediate consequences. First, it enabled Europeans and Americans to produce weapons in greater quantity and quality than any other people. Second, it created an enormous demand for raw materials that could not be satisfied in Europe. In addition, discoveries in medicine, particularly vaccines and antimalarial drugs, improved the odds of survival for Europeans in places previously considered pestilential. Thus, Europeans had the means to colonize as well as uses for the products of colonization.

Acting in their own self-interest, however, Europeans and Americans generally did not move rapidly to place other areas under colonial control. The primary goal of European expansion was always the pursuit of wealth, and plundering was a rapid and cost-effective way to get it. The financial burden of establishing mercantile companies such as the VOC was borne by their shareholders. However, colonizing an area required some level of government expenditure (for example, for government officials and the troops to back them). In most cases, infrastructure such as roads, bridges, and railways also had to be built. These were expensive undertakings, and governments were generally not enthusiastic about funding them. Most often, European governments felt forced to assume control either because of the scandals surrounding the collapse of mercantile companies or out of fear that their national commercial interests were threatened, generally by other European nations. It was this fear that led to the Berlin conference partitioning Africa among European powers in the late nineteenth century.

After European governments had established colonies, they cloaked their actions in the ideology of social betterment. They were, in poet Rudyard Kipling's words, taking up "the white man's burden" of bringing civilization to the "savage." This notion provided an ideology that helped maintain support for colonialism at home and was useful in controlling the native population in the colonies, who were taught that they were being colonized for their own benefit.

MAKING COLONIALISM PAY

Once they had seized control of an area, European administrators had to make it profitable for their national firms; that is, they had to find ways to exploit it economically. In many cases, that meant the systematic disruption of indigenous ways of life, as wage labor and transition to cash crops disrupted traditional economic patterns based on reciprocity and kin structures.

Sometimes colonial powers seized direct control of the political leadership, but more often colonialists ruled indirectly, through native leaders. Leaders not sympathetic to colonial rule were rapidly replaced by those who were. Where colonists could not easily identify ethnic groups or leaders, they often created new chiefly offices. Sometimes colonialists and missionaries forged entire new ethnic groups, lumping together people with different traditions and sometimes different languages (Harries 1987). Dozon (1985) has shown that the Bété, an ethnic group of central Ivory Coast in Africa, did not exist before the era of colonialism but was created by the actions of colonial and postcolonial governments.

One of the most direct ways that European governments tried to make their colonies prof-

itable was by requiring **corvée labor**—unpaid work demanded of native populations. Until World War II, most colonial governments insisted on substantial labor from their subjects. The British often compelled subjects to work for up to a month per year, the Dutch two months. In 1926, the French enacted a law that permitted an annual draft of labor for their West African colonies. Conscripts were compelled to work for three years on bridge and road building, irrigation projects, and other public works. At the turn of the century, conditions were perhaps worst in the Congo (ruled by Belgium), where, at least in theory, each native owed the government 40 hours a month in exchange for a token wage (Bodley 1990: 116). In addition to public works, the British and French both drafted natives into their armed forces. They used these armies to capture and control their colonies, fight colonial wars, and augment their regular armies wherever needed. Natives resisted these demands by concealing workers or by fleeing from authorities when such work was demanded.

Particular projects might be done with forced labor, but to make a colony truly profitable, colonial masters had to encourage the population to work for them voluntarily or produce the goods they desired. Taxation was a key mechanism for accomplishing this. Taxation was needed to support the colonial government, but its main purpose was to force native subjects into the market system. This participation in wage labor was viewed as the essential precondition for "civilizing" the natives. Taxes generally had to be paid in colonial money, which native subjects could obtain only by working for a colonist or producing something that the colonists wanted to buy. Taxation thus had a double effect in enmeshing the colonial subject in the market system. For example, farmers who spent time cultivating cotton to sell to a European company had less time to spend on their own crops. If they could not produce enough to eat, they had to buy it from the market, dominated by companies owned

---

corvée labor Unpaid labor required by a governing authority.

AFRICAN SOLDIERS OF MISFORTUNE

Europeans saw in their colonies not only opportunities for the extraction of mineral and agricultural wealth, but also reservoirs of manpower. This was particularly true in Africa, which had traditionally served Europeans as a source of labor. Both the British and the French were quick to see the military potential of African labor, and both formed armies composed of Africans. The British unit was known as the King's African Rifles, and the French as the Tirailleurs Sénégalais (Senegalese Riflemen). The French began using African military manpower in the eighteenth century, but the Tirailleurs Sénégalais was officially created in 1857. Most of its soldiers were slaves, bought by the French for army service. Armed with French weaponry and led by French officers, their first task was the capture and control of colonies in sub-Saharan Africa.

The French empire in Africa was completed by the turn of the century, but the Tirailleurs Sénégalais was not disbanded. Instead, powerful interests in France argued that Africans had an obligation to serve the French state and could revitalize its army. The first practical trial of this idea was in 1912, when Africans were used to quell a rebellion in Morocco, but the real test came in World War I. The practice of filling army ranks through the purchase of slaves had been abandoned in the late nineteenth century; by the time of World War I, men were drafted into military service. More than 135,000 African troops served for the French in the trenches of Europe in World War I, and almost 30,000 of these died there (Page 1987). The men who made their way back to Africa in 1918–1919, like

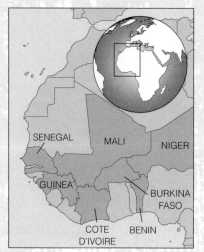

many other veterans of World War I, had witnessed horrors incomprehensible to most of their countrymen. Like European and American soldiers suffering from "shell shock," members of this group were often considered deranged.

Though manpower needs slackened after World War I, France determined to continue to draft African men into the Tirailleurs Sénégalais. Historian Myron Echenberg writes that French conscription in West Africa was "indeed a tax in sweat and blood" (1991:47). Between World War I and World War II, hundreds of thousands of Africans were conscripted into the army, and by 1939, on the eve of World War II, about 9 percent of the French army in France was composed of Africans. By the end of that war, France had recruited (most often drafted) more than 200,000 Africans, and of these as many as 25,000 perished.

The role played by African troops was critical for France in World War II. Most people have heard of de Gaulle's Free French, but few realize that between the fall of France in 1940 and the summer of 1944, the majority of the members of

the Free French Army were Africans. Even in late 1944, sub-Saharan Africans constituted as much as one-fifth of the total French army. For political reasons, both during and after the war, de Gaulle concealed the importance of African contributions to the war effort, but it is clear that events in France might have taken a very different course without African soldiers (Echenberg 1991:104). In addition to providing soldiers, France's African possessions were also taxed heavily to provide food, cotton, latex (raw rubber), and other products for the war effort (Lawler 1992).

After the war, the returned soldiers occupied an important place in African society. Frequently veterans were respected by their peers because they understood modernity, foreigners, and in particular, the French (Lawler 1992:212). In addition, the sacrifices they had made, as well as the sacrifices of their countrymen, gave veterans a degree of moral suasion over the French colonialists. Veterans emerged as leaders, organizers, and agitators in the fight for African independence. The French, meanwhile, continued to enlist Africans in the Tirailleurs Sénégalais and used them against natives fighting wars of independence in Indochina (Vietnam) and Algeria in the 1950s.

Most of the French colonies in Africa received their independence in the early 1960s. The years since then have not been kind to the veterans of the Tirailleurs Sénégalais. The military service that gave them moral power as subjects of France was something of an embarrassment after independence. Members of radical governments and younger people saw them as men who had wasted their time in the service of a discredited authority. They were considered promoters of colonialism rather than, more accurately, its victims. Today, the veterans of the Tirailleurs Sénégalais are all but forgotten. They are rapidly aging, and their struggles and trials seem irrelevant to the young. Most rarely talk about their experiences except with those who shared them. Veterans live throughout the former French possessions in Africa. More than 100 live in and around the town of Bougouni in Mali. In 1992 and 1995, Richard Warms was privileged to speak with many of them.

A soldier who had served the equivalent of 15 years in the Tirailleurs Sénégalais was entitled to a small pension. Some veterans had been able to use this money to marry several wives and raise large families. These men often became prosperous and well-respected members of their community. Such veterans sometimes look back on their military careers with pride and some fondness. One said, "Well, [my military career was] the work of God. It's the way God made it to be.... I had love for the army, and because of my love for the army, I was able to continue serving" (Warms 1995).

Most veterans, however, served only the required three years. They received no pension, and in some cases, were not even permitted to keep their uniforms. When they returned, they often faced hostility or isolation. Fellow villagers couldn't understand their experiences and often thought poorly of them because they had returned with nothing to show for their labors. For them, military service was something best forgotten. One said, "When you come back, you have to follow the ideas of the people in the village. If not, if you try to tell them all about the army and what you have seen, they are never going to understand you. You can explain things and there are those who will just say you are lying. You just let

VETERANS OF THE TIRAILLEURS SÉNÉGALAIS, BOUGOUNI, MALI, 1995.

them alone, at least that's the way I've gotten along" (Warms 1995).

Even those veterans who do receive pensions are given far less than French veterans and receive few services. Though they are proud of their accomplishments, they often feel like forgotten men, and many are profoundly disillusioned. In 1992, a 15-year pensioned veteran of World War II put it like this: "We gave our blood and our bodies so that France could be liberated. But now, since they have their freedom, they have thrown us away, forgotten us. If you eat the meat, you throw away the bone. France has done just that to us" (Warms 1996).

Critical Thinking Questions

1. The Tirailleurs Sénégalais often fought for the French empire to keep rebelling subjects from gaining their political freedom. How, as oppressed people themselves, did

they justify their participation in France's colonial wars? How do you suppose the soldiers thought about their wars?

2. While France is a wealthy country, Mali is extremely poor. Many veterans live in inadequate housing, with no access to safe drinking water or an adequate food supply. What obligations, if any, does France have to these men and their families?

3. Veterans who returned to their villages with no money were often poorly treated. The fact that, in many cases, they had seen much of the world did not necessarily make them respected. Why do you think that this was the case? Why weren't veterans seen as a valuable source of information about the outside world?

by colonialists. In this way, native subjects became increasingly dependent on the market.

Even when subject populations were not forced into labor gangs, economic and social policies of colonial regimes required them to radically alter their lifestyles. For example, Portuguese colonial policy in Mozambique forced almost a million peasants to grow cotton. The colonial government controlled not only what these growers produced, but where they lived, with whom they traded, and how they organized their labor. Although a few growers prospered, the great majority were impoverished and struggled to survive against famine and hardship (Isaacman 1996). By the 1960s, the brutality and terror used by the colonial regime to control their subjects resulted in a civil war that continued into the 1990s.

In addition to policies aimed at forcing subjects to participate in an economy centered in the industrial world, colonial governments took more direct aim at cultures through educational policies. Colonial education was often designed to convince subjects that they were the cultural, moral, and intellectual inferiors of those who ruled them. For example, education in nineteenth-century India encouraged children to aspire to be like the ideal Englishman (Viswanathan 1988). In French colonies in Africa, children were taught directly to obey their colonial masters, as illustrated in this passage from a turn-of-the-century reader designed to teach French to schoolchildren and used in the colonies:

> It is . . . an advantage for a native to work for a white man, because the Whites are better educated, more advanced in civilization than the natives, and because, thanks to them, the natives will make more rapid progress . . . and become one day really useful men. . . . You who are intelligent and industrious, my children, always help the Whites in their task. (cited in Bodley 1990:104)

Education was often aimed at the children of elites. These children were taught that, although they might never reach the level of the colonists, they were considerably more intellectually evolved than their uneducated countrymen. Thus, schooling both reinforced the colonizers'

position and created a subservient educated class convinced of its superiority (G. Kelly 1986).

COLONIALISM AND ANTHROPOLOGY

The origins and practice of modern anthropology are bound up with the colonial era. The evolutionary theories of nineteenth-century anthropologists pictured a world in which all societies were evolving toward the civilization already attained by Europeans. This convenient philosophy could be pressed into service as a rationale for colonization (Godelier 1993; Ghosh 1991). Some argued that because they were "civilized," European nations had the right (or the obligation) to colonize. Through colonization, they claimed, other people could be hurried on the path to civilization.

In the first half of the twentieth century, colonial governments faced with the practical problems of governing their possessions often relied on information provided by anthropologists. Anthropologists, anxious to find funding for their research, argued that it had practical value to colonial administrators (Malinowski 1929a). However, anthropology did not come into being to promote or enable colonialism, which would have gone on with or without it (J. Burton 1992). Anthropologists did not generally question the political reality of colonialism, but they often self-consciously tried to advance the interests of the people they studied. Because of this, they were often looked at with mistrust by colonial officials. Prah (1990), for example, reports that although colonial officials in the Sudan used information provided by anthropologists to govern native groups in that colony, they were also deeply suspicious of them. Colonial officials generally believed that anthropologists were much too sympathetic to colonial subjects. Furthermore, as Goody (1995) points out, most anthropological research was financed not by governments but by private charitable foundations, most of which had reformist agendas. Some anthropologists financed their own research. The great French ethnographer Marcel Griaule, for example, put on a circus and promoted boxing matches to finance his ethnographic expeditions (Goody 1995:17).

INDEPENDENCE AND DEVELOPMENT

The eras of Western expansion and colonization radically and permanently changed the world. By the time of World War II, there were no "pristine" groups anywhere in the world. All peoples had been affected by Western expansion, and their cultures had been altered by this experience. Some, attempting to resist foreign influences and protect their ways of life, had moved as far away from outsiders as possible. However, most lived in societies where the presence and influence of outsiders, their demands for goods and labor, and their attempts to change culture were fundamental facts of life.

Most of the nations of the Americas gained their independence in the eighteenth and nineteenth centuries. In Africa and Asia, independence from European colonialism was not achieved until after World War II. Many nations that were part of the Soviet Union only received their independence in the late 1980s and early 1990s. There were as many reasons for the granting of independence as there were for exploration and colonialism, but two were of particular importance. First, civil disobedience, and in some cases civil war, made the colonies ungovernable. The purpose of a colony was to make money, but suppressing rebellion was expensive. The resistance of colonial subjects ultimately made continued colonization too expensive for the colonial powers. Second, the geopolitical situation was fundamentally altered by World War II. Before the war, Britain and France, the two largest colonial powers, were also extremely important economic and military powers. The war left their economies devastated. Political and economic problems at home became their first priority. Suppressing revolt abroad was, in most cases, unpopular at home.

After the war, the United States and the Soviet Union (and a bit later, China) emerged as the world's dominant powers. These nations were rapidly embroiled in the Cold War. Despite their many differences, neither the United States nor the Soviet Union was a major colonial power in Africa or Asia, and both promoted an end to colonialism.

DEVELOPMENT PROGRAMS OFTEN INCLUDE THE MECHANIZATION OF AGRICULTURE. IN SOME PLACES YIELDS HAVE INCREASED GREATLY, BUT SMALL FARMERS AND LABORERS HAVE BEEN IMPOVERISHED.

Paul S. Howell/The Gamma Liaison Network

The end of colonial rule brought numerous challenges to the newly independent nations. They were beset by issues of poverty, the presence of multinational corporations, urbanization, population growth, war, and instability. A few nations, such as Singapore (formerly a British colony) and Korea (a Japanese colony from 1905 to 1945), have done extremely well, but the vast majority of the world's nations remain extremely poor.

Economists often measure national wealth in **per capita GNP,** a figure that gives a very rough estimation of prosperity. In the United States in 1998 (the most recent year for which figures are available), the per capita GNP was $29,340. Nine nations had GNP per capita greater than that. In that same year, of the 210 nations listed by the World Bank, 72 had per capita GNPs of less than $1,000, and 158 had per capita GNPs of less than $10,000. Worse yet, almost 30 of the world's poorest nations grew even poorer between 1990 and 1997, a time of unprecedented prosperity for most of

per capita GNP The total market value of all goods and services produced in a country in a year divided by the population of that country; often used as a general measure of the wealth of a nation and the quality of life of its citizens.

I N   T H E   F I E L D

CARGO CULTS IN MELANESIA

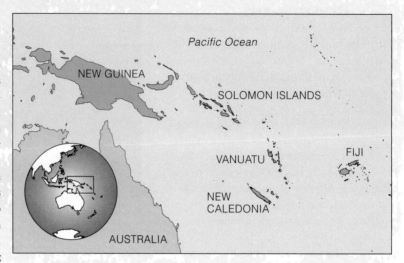

Pacific Ocean

NEW GUINEA

SOLOMON ISLANDS

VANUATU

FIJI

NEW CALEDONIA

AUSTRALIA

For the past 400 years, Western culture has spread through the islands of Melanesia, including the Solomon Islands and New Guinea. Initially, Melanesians were receptive to Western culture, which reached them primarily through trade goods, called "cargo" in Pidgin English, and Christianity, which was introduced by missionaries. Islanders believed that they would receive cargo and the riches of the Europeans through the missions and colonial governments. However, they found that accepting Christianity and colonial rule did not bring the cargo any nearer. Treated unequally by Europeans, Melanesians soon realized that the preaching of Western religion and promises of the benefits of European rule were different from the reality.

With the expansion of a cash crop plantation economy in the Pacific, Europeans removed men from their villages to work on plantations in Fiji and Australia. This trapped them into a global market in rubber and copra in which prices, and thus wages, changed frequently. As these tribal peoples sought to understand the power of the white man, and their own poverty and powerlessness, they concluded that ritual was the key. Ritual action was a major basis of power in their own societies, and this explanation made sense of their observations of the whites. Whites did not

work but made "secret signs" on scraps of paper, for which they were given shiploads of goods; Melanesians, who worked so hard, got nothing. Plainly, the whites knew the secret of cargo and were keeping it from the islanders.

So-called cargo cults appeared all over Melanesia. Though there was some variety, the cults shared certain common features. A local prophet announced that the world was about to end in a terrible catastrophe, after which God (or the ancestors, or a local culture hero) would appear, and a paradise on earth would begin. The riches (cargo) of the Europeans would come to the Melanesians. Americans figured prominently in some cargo cults because of the generosity and friendliness of American soldiers encountered by the Melanesians during World War II and because many of these soldiers were black.

In 1946, when Australian government patrols arrived in one part of the New Guinea highlands, they found themselves viewed as the fulfillment of a prophecy—the sign that the end of the world was at hand. The native butchered all their pigs in the belief that after three days of darkness, "great pigs" would appear from the sky. Food, firewood, and other necessities were stockpiled to see the people through until the great pigs arrived.

In other places, native prophets announced that Europeans would soon leave, abandoning their property to the natives. In Guadalcanal, people prepared airfields, roads, and docks for the magic ships and planes they believed were coming from America. In Dutch New Guinea, where the Dutch had been driven out by the Japanese, it was believed that on the return of Mansren, the native culture hero,

the world's wealthy nations. The situation is particularly grave in the nations of the former Soviet Union. In 1989, about 14 million people in those territories were living on less than four dollars a day. By the mid-1990s, that number had increased more than tenfold, with 147 million people living below the four-dollar

line (World Bank 2000). In other places, things are even worse. About 1.3 billion people in the world still live in absolute poverty, defined as an income of less than one dollar a day (Cernea 1995).

Most of the world's traditional peoples live in the poor nations and have been dramatically

the existing world order would be reversed. White men would turn black like the Papuans (indigenous peoples of New Guinea), Papuans would turn white, root crops would grow in trees, and coconuts would grow on the ground. In some groups, the believers sat around tables dressed in European clothes, making signs on paper, in the belief that this mysterious custom was the clue to the white man's extraordinary power over goods and people.

The first Europeans to write about cargo cults were colonial administrators, who saw them as the irrational beliefs and activities of a primitive, savage, unpredictable, and therefore potentially dangerous people who had succumbed to a kind of "madness." This view explicitly opposed Melanesian irrationality to European rationality (Lindstrom 1993). The attribution of irrationality also justified tighter control over New Guinea by the Australian colonial administration (Buck 1989).

Anthropologists, who began describing cargo cults in the 1950s, attempted to understand their logic from the Melanesian perspective. The Melanesian desire for cargo was interpreted as symbolic of the Melanesian desire for social equality with Europeans. It was also seen as a religious form of resistance against European colonial rule. Anthropologists viewed cargo cults as rational attempts by Melanesians to make sense out of a seemingly chaotic and senseless social

order, whose economy, politics, and society were beyond their comprehension (Worsley 1959). The repressive colonial regime made it necessary to clothe their resistance in the religious form, as political rebellion would have been immediately suppressed. When Melanesians became independent of colonial rule, they would organize their activities politically, and cargo cults would disappear.

These anthropological interpretations viewed the Melanesians not as irrational, but rather as working off the false premise that ritual action could compel the appearance of cargo. Far from seeing cargo cults as "madness," anthropologists saw them as deriving from important themes in Melanesian culture: the importance of wealth, the seeking of economic advantage through ritual activities, and the role of ritual leader as supernaturally inspired prophet.

In attempting to understand the European preoccupation with cargo cults, anthropologists Lamont Lindstrom has investigated writing on the subject by anthropologists and journalists, Westerners and Melanesians. He found that while cargo cults have lost much of their power in contemporary Melanesia, the term is increasingly being applied to events in the West. The wishful thinking of the inner-city poor who hope that jobs will somehow appear to rescue them from poverty, the craving of Eastern Europeans, newly liberated from communism, for wealth and consumer goods, and the ex-

travagant consumerism of the West have all been identified as cargo cult thinking (Lindstrom 1993:53).

One study of American schools commented that the Protestant ethic, promoting steady progressive effort and hard work, has been beaten down by a cargo cult ideology that holds that fortune depends on luck and is animated by ritual strategies. What is advertising, the study asks, but a cargo cult orientation, in that an advertised product is supposed to bring about a desired state of affairs (Conforti 1989, quoted in Lindstrom 1993:53).

Are we, then, also cargo cultists, Lindstrom asks? Does the European preoccupation with cargo cults reveal as much about ourselves as compulsive and eternally unfulfilled consumers as it reveals about Melanesians? If we are all cargo cultists, is the fixation on infinite and unfulfilled desire an expression of a universal human nature? Not necessarily, says Lindstrom. The current Western preoccupation with cargo is more likely a particular cultural development that grows out of the period of late capitalism and admirably serves the market economy. To project a cargo cult mentality as part of a universal human nature is just an ethnocentric imposition of our own, culturally specific passions onto the rest of humankind.

affected by these issues. They have had to adapt culturally to extraordinary circumstances. In the face of economic and political change, and despite technological innovation that increasingly ties all people together, some cultures have simply disappeared. Many others have managed to adapt, preserve many of their ways of

life, and maintain a degree of integrity. New identities have been forged as people and cultures adapt to modernization. However, no culture has been left unchanged. Some of the most important forces behind these changes are economic development projects sponsored by the wealthy nations, the influence of multinational corporations, the movement from rural to urban lifestyles, the explosive growth of population, and high levels of political instability. We will examine each of these in turn.

DEVELOPMENT

The end of colonialism did not mean the end of forced cultural change or foreign intervention. If anything, the pace of cultural contact and change increased when nations became independent. In some cases, even the number of foreign nationals living in newly independent nations increased. For example, after Côte d'Ivoire, in West Africa, gained its independence from France in 1960, ties between the two countries grew stronger. In the 20 years following independence, the total French population there grew from 30,000 to 60,000 (Handloff 1991:170).

There were, however, critical differences between colonies and newly independent nations. Before independence, economic plans generally concentrated on how to make colonies most productive for the nations that controlled them; after independence, the notion of economic **development** became ascendent. The idea championed by economists and development experts from industrialized nations was that former colonies were poor because they had underdeveloped, backward economies, but if they pursued the proper political and economic policies, they could become developed like the Western industrialized world. In order to develop, nations and cultures had to transform their traditional practices.

Development served the interests of both the industrialized nations and elites in the former colonies. Industrialized nations promoted development to spread their economic and political influence. This was particularly important during the Cold War, when both Eastern and Western blocs used development aid to spread their ideology and advance their economic systems in the nonindustrialized world. In the former colonies, elites and government officials benefited from the prestige associated with development projects; because donated money generally passed through their hands, they gained economic advantages as well. Money from development aid supported an elite lifestyle and opened many possibilities for political patronage, not to mention bribery, graft, and other forms of corruption.

In the West, the most popular ideology of development has been **modernization theory.** Modernization models describe a modern/traditional dichotomy in which non-Western societies move from tradition to modernity. Modernity is defined as the technological and sociocultural systems of industrialized nations. The notion of modernization was used, by anthropologists and others, both as a description of reality and as a prescription for what should happen in order for economic development to take place. Early modernization plans were based on the notion that poor nations would become wealthy and developed by repeating the historical experience of the industrialized nations. To this end, foreign advice and financial aid were designed to alter the structural, cultural, and psychological features that stood in the way of modernization. For example, because most traditional societies are agrarian, modernization models envisioned a change from using "simple" traditional technology and intensive human and animal labor to using machine technology. Economically, modernization assumes a shift from subsistence economies to cash economies. Indigenous peoples would move into the world market economy by increasing their cultivation of cash crops and moving from agriculture into industrial wage labor. Both of these shifts were presumed to result in economic development and higher standards of living.

Unfortunately, the record of development projects has not been encouraging. Almost a half a century after the first development efforts began, the world remains divided into haves and have-nots, industrialized and nonindustrialized nations. There are a great many

---

development The notion that some countries are poor because they have small industrial plants and few lines of communication and that they should pursue prosperity by acquiring these things.

modernization theory A model of development that predicts that nonindustrial societies will move in the social and technological direction of industrialized nations.

reasons for this failure, but some are fundamental. Many of the assumptions of modernization theorists ignored history or were simply incorrect. Theorists often assumed that the societies they wished to develop were traditional and timeless—that they had remained static for a great many years. As we have recounted, however, the actions of the wealthy nations had helped to create poverty in other parts of the world. The societies that development planners considered traditional were in many cases creations of colonialism and European expansion. Furthermore, it was impossible for undeveloped nations to repeat the historic experiences of the industrialized world. After all, the very existence and exploitation of these areas had been a fundamental part of the rise of industrialism.

Beyond this, development projects were often poorly designed. Sometimes they were based on technologies that did not work well. Often they had deleterious effects on both environment and culture. For example, Ostergaard (1990) reports that in lowland Sumatra (Indonesia), the introduction of improved rice varieties worked poorly because under existing political, economic, and ecological conditions, yields of the improved rice were often lower than those of traditional varieties.

Determining success or failure, moreover, depends on what the evaluator decides to measure. Economic success may carry a heavy noneconomic price. Stonich , Murray, and Rossart (1994) note that aid projects helped to increase the export of shrimp in Honduras by more than 1500 percent, but the price of this growth was pollution, environmental destruction, and the impoverishment of people who lived near the shrimp farms. These environmental and social justice issues resulted in widespread tension and increasingly violent confrontations.

Despite their difficulties, aid projects are a seemingly permanent part of life in the poor nations. In 1995, the **World Bank,** one of the largest development agencies, was involved in 1800 development projects costing $150 billion. Moreover, some progress has been made. In the poor nations, life expectancy has increased 20 percent and literacy 25 percent in the past generation. Children are only half as likely to die before the age of 5 as they were a generation ago.

Anthropologists play increasingly important roles in the planning of development. The World Bank hired its first full-time anthropologist in 1974; today its staff includes 50 to 60 anthropologists, sociologists, and political scientists, who make important contributions in the design of development projects and their increased success rate. Anthropologists have demonstrated that development can be more successful when it gives a prominent place to issues of culture and social organization. Anthropological input has been especially critical to the success of resettlement programs (particularly on the Senegal River in West Africa) and to the formulation of policy on issues such as urban growth, primary education, forestry, and the use of water resources (Cernea 1995).

MULTINATIONAL CORPORATIONS

The power of **multinational corporations** is another important factor in cultural change. Because such corporations control vast amounts of wealth, they play major roles in politics throughout the world. However, two factors make their presence in poor nations particularly important. First, while large corporations may have vast wealth, no corporation controls more than a small percentage of the economy of any of the rich nations. However, in poor nations, individual multinationals may have yearly budgets that are greater than those of national governments and may control large portions of the national economy. Thus, while large corporations are politically powerful everywhere, they are particularly powerful in poor nations. In addition, multinational corporations try to ensure that their operations around the world contribute wealth to their shareholders, the vast majority of whom live in the

World Bank An agency of the United Nations, officially called the International Bank for Reconstruction and Development, that provides loans to promote international trade and economic development, especially to poor nations.

multinational corporation A corporation that owns business enterprises or plants in more than one nation.

DEVELOPMENT ANTHROPOLOGY

In the second half of the twentieth century, many newly independent nations turned their attention to economic and social development. They wished to preserve the richness of their traditional cultures while, at the same time, achieving economic prosperity. The history of economic development programs has been rich and controversial. From the beginning, anthropologists have played an important role.

A reforestation project in Haiti is one example of the successful application of anthropology to economic development. Anthropologist Gerald R. Murray had an opportunity to help Haitians work on the problem of deforestation. Based on ethnographically gained knowledge about the cash-oriented foundation of Haitian peasant horticulture, Murray suggested that Haitians plant fast-growing trees and market the timber as a cash crop. Since Murray understood the local system of classification, he knew that Haitians did not generally think of wood trees as a cash crop. Thus, he designed a program to get the message across that wood can be a crop just like coffee or corn. His ethnographically gained knowledge of Haitian peasant land tenure led Murray to suggest individual and family ownership of trees rather than the community forest schemes then preferred by development planners. On Murray's return visit to Haiti, he was able to see the fruits of successful development: Several houses

had been built using wood from the trees planted through the project, charcoal made from the trees was being sold in local markets, and poles of wood from the trees were bringing in cash in markets (Murray 1986).

Anthropologist Mari H. Clarke has been working as a consultant in international development for more than 18 years. She has trained local nurse-midwives to design and use instructional materials in Kenya, Egypt, Turkey, and Sierra Leone; developed training materials for Peace Corps health volunteers; examined household economics in Greece; worked in strategic planning for the United States Agency for International Development; and helped design education programs in Egypt. Clarke says that anthropology makes a major contribution to international development. Because anthropologists take a holistic approach, they tend to look for links between different facets of society that others may miss. They think in terms of understanding the entire system rather than single elements. While economists and development planners often assume that all people think alike and respond to the same incentives, anthropologists use their skills in listening and observing to understand local people's perceptions of the world and to access their knowledge (Clarke 2000).

Clarke notes that, with the end of the Cold War and the emphasis on financial restraint in the wealthy nations, the job

market in international development is increasingly tight. However, jobs in development still employ many anthropologists. Clarke advises students to have qualifications in addition to their anthropology degrees. She has a master's degree in instructional media as well as graduate training in anthropology. In addition, she says that experience in development really makes a difference on a résumé. Volunteering for the Peace Corps is a good way to get international experience, as are internships in both government agencies and private charitable organizations.

A great many highly informative websites provide information about economic development. Large governmental development organizations, such as the World Bank (www.worldbank.org), the United States Agency for International Development (www.usaid.gov), and the United Nations (www.un.org), are often controversial. But whether you support their programs or not, their websites contain an enormous wealth of information. Volunteer opportunities abound on the web. The Peace Corps (www.peacecorps.gov) maintains an extensive and highly informative website, including information on volunteering as well as stories from former volunteers. Other volunteer associations with interesting websites are WorldTeach (www.worldteach.org), Global Citizens Network (www.globalcitizens.org), and Operation Crossroads Africa (www.igc.org/oca).

world's wealthiest nations. Thus, the conversion of non-Western societies into economic colonies serving the needs of outsiders that began with the expansion of Europe has continued into the current era.

Multinational corporations use modern technology to move goods and information around the globe at high speed. As a result, they are able to seek out and move to the least expensive places to produce goods and services as well as the most profitable places to sell them. Multinational corporations bring employment opportunities as well as goods and services to people who would not otherwise have them. However, such advantages often carry a very high price. Multinationals have a powerful influence on the natural, economic, and social environments as they attempt to exploit natural resources for profit, cause worldwide shifts in population as economic opportunities open up in some societies and decline in others, and are implicated in the transformation of agricultural populations into wage labor on a huge scale.

Because much of the cheap labor multinational corporations depend on for their profits is provided by women and children, there is a clear link between feminist concerns in anthropology and the extension of the global economy. The operations of multinational corporations affect land rights in many countries as national governments, including the United States, attempt to persuade or coerce indigenous populations to give up their land to make it available for the economic investments that only multinational corporations can afford.

Multinational corporations may also create major flows of labor; the Mexican maquiladora program is a good example. **Maquiladoras** are plants owned by multinational corporations and located in Mexico to take advantage of inexpensive labor there. Most are assembly plants that import almost all of their supplies. In theory, maquiladoras can be located anywhere in Mexico, but almost all are within a few miles of the U.S. border. The promise of jobs in maquiladoras has drawn millions of Mexicans to the border, and the growth rate of Mexican border cities is almost double that of the rest of the nation (E. Williams 1995). On the border, many live in shanty towns without running water or sewage facilities. Pollution, disease, and social strife have become common in these areas (La Botz 1994). Conditions in Juarez/El Paso, for example, are particularly bad. In 1996, Juarez still had no water treatment facility, and the city's 350 factories dumped 55 million gallons of raw sewage into the Rio Grande daily. Air quality was so poor that 75 percent of days in the first 11 months of 1995 had unhealthy

ozone levels. However, multinational corporations have benefited greatly from access to cheap labor. For example, the AFL-CIO (1995) reported that the CEO of Allied Signal made $12.4 million in 1995, whereas the company's 3800 Mexican employees combined made an estimated $7.8 million.

The activities of multinational corporations raise important questions about the rights of different people to a share of the benefits that accompany their economic activities (Bonsignore 1992), as well as questions about how the social, cultural, and health costs of their operations should be borne. These questions become particularly urgent in the face of major disasters such as the *Exxon Valdez* oil spill of March 24, 1989, when an oil tanker ran aground and spilled more than 10 million gallons of crude oil in Prince William Sound in Alaska, and the accidental release of a lethal gas in December 1984 in Bhopal, India, in which at least 1700 people were killed and as many as 50,000 were injured.

URBANIZATION

Although cities had important cultural roles in preindustrial societies, urban migration has increased dramatically in the contemporary world. In 1950, only about 16 percent of the total population of nonindustrialized nations lived in large cities. By 1985, this figure had increased to 30 percent, and it is expected to reach 50 percent early in the twenty-first century (Kasarda and Crenshaw 1991). In 1990, 12 of the world's 20 most populous cities were in poor nations (including China and Korea). More than 40 percent of the population in Korea, Argentina, and Colombia lived in cities of over 1 million, compared with 39 percent for the United Kingdom, 34 percent for Germany, and 22 percent for France (Angotti 1993). While the percentage of people living in cities is rising in most countries, it is rising much more rapidly in poor than in wealthy nations.

maquiladora A manufacturing plant owned by an international company, located in Mexico to take advantage of inexpensive labor there.

MORE THAN HALF OF THE WORLD'S LARGEST CITIES ARE IN POOR NATIONS. THESE PICTURES OF RIO DE JANEIRO, BRAZIL, SHOW THE ENORMOUS CONTRASTS PRESENT IN SUCH CITIES. WHILE RIO DE JANEIRO HAS AN EXTREMELY PROSPEROUS ELITE, MOST OF ITS RESIDENTS LIVE IN ABJECT POVERTY. MODERN OFFICE AND APARTMENT BUILDINGS, AS WELL AS LUXURY RESORTS (LEFT), EXIST ALONGSIDE SHANTY TOWNS WITH ONLY MINIMAL ACCESS TO SAFE DRINKING WATER OR SANITATION.

The World Bank reports that between 1970 and 1997, the percentage of population living in the cities in high-income nations increased by about 5 percent; in low-income nations, it increased by 47 percent (World Bank 2000:30).

Rural people come to cities seeking jobs and the social, material, and cultural advantages they perceive to be related to urban living. They are forced out of rural areas by high population levels, inability to acquire land, environmental degradation, and sometimes violence. Urbanization affects traditional societies in many different ways. Graves and Graves (1974) characterized the adaptations of traditional societies to urbanization as a three-ring circus, referring to the three arenas within which adaptation to urbanization takes place: among members of the home community left behind, among the urban migrants themselves, and within the urban host community to which the migrants go.

Many migrants who leave their local communities do so only temporarily. They return to participate in a variety of economic or social activities and maintain important ties with those left behind. The degree to which urban migration is permanent depends on the personal involvements of the migrating person, on the ability of the local community to reabsorb its returning migrants, and on the barriers to assimilation the migrant group meets in the urban area.

Whether temporary or permanent, urban migration is both a direct and an indirect source of change in traditional societies. Not only are urban migrants changed in the process of adapting to urban life, but the communities of origin are also changed. Most modern influences enter the countryside through urban centers, either by mass communication or through the links between urban migrants

THE NEW 100-PERCENT AMERICAN

In the 1930s, Ralph Linton wrote a famous essay called "100% American." At that time, isolationism and nativism were important political forces in the United States. Nazism was on the rise in Europe, and many Americans were sympathetic to its ideas of racial and cultural purity. In his essay, Linton attacked the national chauvinism of prominent Americans such as Henry Ford and Charles Lindbergh.

While isolationism continues to have its champions, most Americans today are aware that our nation is diverse and a great many of our customs originated elsewhere in the world. Anthropologists today are less concerned with the foreign origins of American cultural practices than with the extent to which facets of our culture affect members of other groups—the extent to which other parts of the world have become "Americanized."

American culture, and industry's ability to promote it, have proven remarkably powerful. Eating at McDonalds, for example, has become a status symbol in Thailand, and *The Cosby Show* was one of the most popular television programs in South Africa in the 1980s. Political scientist Benjamin Barber notes that such cultural elements have become an extraordinary force in globalization: "What is the power of the Pentagon compared with Disneyland? Can the Sixth Fleet keep up with CNN? McDonald's in Moscow and Coke in China will do more to create a global culture than military colonization ever could" (1992). Essayist Pico Iyer sees the same issue in spiritual terms. When he visits the Himalayas, for example, "most of the people that I see are Westerners from Germany, California, or the Netherlands, who are wearing sandals, Indian smocks, and are in search of enlightenment, antiquity, peace, and all the things they can't get in the West. Most of the people they meet are Nepali villagers in Lee jeans, Reeboks, and Madonna T-shirts who are looking for the paradise that they associate with Los Angeles—a paradise of material prosperity and abundance" (quoted in London 1996).

and those who remain at home. New ideas and values as well as consumer goods may be passed on to villagers through urban migrants.

Urban life can be extremely difficult. Many of the urban poor are unemployed and face hunger, unsafe drinking water, inadequate sanitation facilities, and substandard shelter. Disease and early death are rampant in the slums of the world's large cities. Many of those who are employed fare little better, and most migrants to cities live in poverty for many years. In one study, researchers used a storytelling technique to evaluate three groups of Kenyan women: rural women in a traditional village, poor urban women, and middle-class urban women. The researchers showed each woman a picture and asked her to tell a story about it. The stories provided information on the ways that the women perceived their lives. The researchers found that the traditional women almost always told very positive stories that usually had a happy ending. Middle-class urban women told stories that emphasized their own power and competence. Poor urban women's stories were generally tragic and focused on powerlessness and vulnerability. The researchers note that many poor urban women have "lost the security and protection of the old [traditional] system without gaining the power or rewards of the new system" (Friedmann and Todd 1994).

With urbanization, a great variety of social groups based on voluntary membership develop. These **voluntary associations** are adaptive in helping people to achieve their goals in complex and changing societies. They are especially helpful for migrants making the transition from traditional, rural society to an urban lifestyle. Although not all voluntary associations formed in newly urbanized societies have

voluntary association A social group based on voluntary membership, typically found in complex, urban societies.

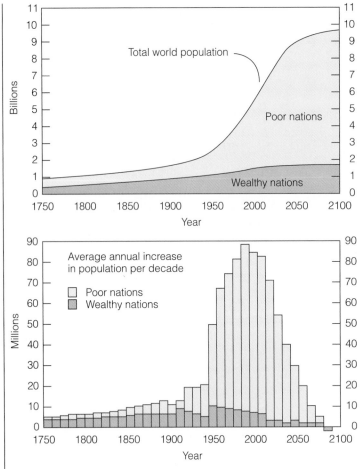

IF CURRENT TRENDS CONTINUE, WORLD POPULATION WILL INCREASE TO ABOUT
10 BILLION BY THE MIDDLE OF THE TWENTY-FIRST CENTURY BEFORE LEVELING OFF.
THE GREAT MAJORITY OF THIS INCREASE WILL COME IN THE POOR NATIONS.

POPULATION PRESSURE

As noted at the beginning of this chapter, the increase in world population is a powerful indicator of the accelerated speed of change in the modern world. It is also a critical problem for poor nations and traditional peoples. In the past several decades, most of the economic gains made by poor countries have been consumed by the increasing size of their populations. In some cases, high population levels mean that traditional subsistence strategies can no longer provide enough food. In other cases, the population explosion and the search for land and wealth have pushed people onto land previously occupied only by indigenous groups. For example, the lands occupied by the Yanomamo in Brazil are increasingly threatened by land-poor peasants and gold miners moving in from densely populated areas of eastern Brazil (Gorman 1991).

Traditional economic strategies may not be able to support extremely high levels of population growth. In parts of East Africa, the amount of arable land per person declined 40 percent between 1965 and 1987 (World Bank 1992), and this has resulted in important cultural changes. Among the Waluguru in the Uluguru Mountains of Tanzania, for example, population increase has made it impossible for people to be self-sufficient in food (van Donge 1992). This is a recent phenomenon; in the 1950s, self-sufficiency was the rule. Solidarity and authority were powerfully structured within the area, and the economy was based on high levels of cooperation. People gained access to land through their lineage; therefore, the lineage head was a powerful figure. Today, not only has the institution of the lineage head completely disappeared, but it is hardly even remembered. Van Donge reports that people have few interactions involving economic cooperation, solidarity, or authority. Instead, as land has become scarce, women in this matrilineal society have tightened their hold over it. This has weakened the position of men in marriages to the point where many prefer to migrate to the cities to marry. More than 37 percent of women over

goals that are directly economic or political, these associations often serve as vehicles through which such goals can be achieved.

Voluntary associations that emerge among newly urbanized populations may serve as mutual aid societies, lending money to members, providing scholarships for students, arranging funerals, and taking care of marriage arrangements for urban migrants. Some develop along kinship or ethnic lines that were relevant in the traditional culture; others, such as labor unions, are based on relationships deriving from new economic contexts and have no parallel in traditional rural society.

20 are now unmarried, compared with 15 percent of men.

Programs to control population growth are often extremely controversial. In many cultural groups, a woman's value is measured to some degree by the number of children she bears. In addition, religious authorities often take active stands against the use of birth control. Furthermore, intellectuals and governments in many poor nations are deeply suspicious of population control programs coming from the wealthy nations. They note that the economies of wealthy nations have often prospered in times of population growth; the period 1945–1965, for example, was a time of great population growth and great prosperity in the United States. They suspect that the wealthy nations are promoting their own interests when they attempt to limit population in other countries. Sometimes, they accuse the promoters of population control programs of racist intentions, noting that such programs usually consist of efforts by wealthy white people to limit the population growth of poor nonwhite people (Lichtenberg 1994).

Behind these accusations lies a central issue. Population growth is only part of a larger problem of distribution of resources. The poor nations of the world have high levels of population growth but still consume small portions of many of the world's resources. For example, the United States has a population growth rate of only 1 percent, but each additional American consumes 860 kilograms of grain a year (most of this is grain fed to animals, which are then eaten). Tanzania has a population growth rate more than three times as high, but each Tanzanian consumes only 145 kilograms of grain a year (World Bank 1995; Postel 1994). If our concern is the ability of the world to support us, we had best look to our own consumption rather than the population growth of the poor. Furthermore, a major factor behind high population growth is the search for security. In conditions of poverty and economic uncertainty, having large numbers of children improves the odds that some will prosper and increase the family wealth. Improving the life chances of people in poor countries may ulti-

mately prove to be one of the keys to controlling population growth.

INSTABILITY

The political instability of many nations has had dire consequences for cultures worldwide. Violent confrontation is nothing new. Traditional societies often fought with one another, and Western expansion was accompanied by great loss of life and culture. However, the twentieth century must be considered the most violent in human history. It is safe to say that in this century, people unleashed more brutality on other human beings than at any other time in human history. Furthermore, the industrialized and wealthy societies are most responsible for this savagery. It was they who created the trenches of World War I, the death camps of World War II, nuclear weapons, the purge, and the Gulag.

The nonindustrial world was deeply affected by Europe's wars. For example, about 50,000 Africans died in the East African campaigns of World War I (Page 1987), and enormous loss of life occurred during the Solomon Island campaigns of World War II. However, the era since World War II has been most devastating in many places. In some, such as French Indochina (later Vietnam), World War II faded into wars of independence that did not end until the 1970s. Other countries, such as Ethiopia, Somalia, Nicaragua, El Salvador, and Mozambique, were caught between the great powers in the Cold War and fought proxy wars. During the Cold War, both the United States and the Soviet Union furnished guerilla movements, impoverished governments, and rebel armies with vast amounts of weaponry. Throughout the world, traditional people became involved in networks of warfare that connected them with competition between the great powers.

The foraging peoples of southern Africa are a good example. Most anthropology students are familiar with the Ju/'hoansi. They are well studied and often used as an example of a foraging society. However, students may be unaware that many Ju/'hoansi, along with other

VIOLENCE AND DISASTER OFTEN OVERWHELM ANY INFLUENCE ANTHROPOLOGISTS MAY HAVE IN THE WORLD. IN 1994 IN RWANDA, IN A MATTER OF WEEKS OVER 800,000 TUTSI AND THEIR HUTU FRIENDS AND SUPPORTERS WERE SLAUGHTERED BY HUTU TROOPS AND CITIZENS, ACTING UNDER THE ENCOURAGEMENT OF THE GOVERNMENT.

© Peter Turnley/CORBIS

southern African foraging people, eventually became soldiers in the South African Army. Through the 1970s and 1980s, South Africa fought a long war against the Southwest African People's Organization (SWAPO), a guerilla organization fighting for the independence of Namibia. South Africa had the support of the United States and other capitalist nations; SWAPO was supported by the Soviet Union. In 1974, the South African Defense Forces (SADF) began to recruit foraging peoples to act as trackers in their war; by 1981, Omega, the SADF base at Caprivi, included 850 soldiers, 900 women, and 1500 children. By this time, virtually the entire foraging population of the Caprivi was supported directly or indirectly by the military. The military plans for these people were based on the assumption that they should become as much like whites as possible. They were trained in the religion of the Dutch Reformed Church, agriculture, hygiene, sewing, and baking. In 1990, a few days before Namibia became independent, almost 4000 of them were resettled in South Africa by the SADF (Gordon 1992:185–192). It is clear that not much remains of the hunting-and-gathering lifestyles documented by anthropologists in the 1950s and 1960s.

The end of the Cold War brought some relief to the nonindustrialized nations. In some cases, wars that were fueled by great power rivalries, such as those in Mozambique, Namibia, El Salvador, and Nicaragua, came to a rapid end. In other cases, however, rival elites that had been held in check by external threats or enormous flows of wealth began to battle each other. Traditional hatreds that had been muted by the Cold War reemerged in new violent forms. Yugoslavia, Somalia, Liberia, Sudan, Sri Lanka, and Sierra Leone are all examples of nations that fell apart as rival ethnic groups fought for control.

One particularly violent recent example is the 1994 destruction and genocide in Rwanda. Most Rwandans are members of one of two ethnic groups, Hutu and Tutsi. Although Hutu and Tutsi speak the same language, the Hutu majority are farmers and the Tutsi are herders. Rivalry between Hutu and Tutsi is quite ancient but was greatly exacerbated by colonial rule. Since 1959, there have been numerous violent clashes between the two groups, but in 1994 a new level of violence was reached when, in a matter of weeks, Hutus murdered 800,000–850,000 Tutsis and their Hutu friends and supporters. Only about 130,000 Tutsis in Rwanda survived the massacre. Every level of society was involved, and in many cases, women led the killings (Prunier 1995; Fenton 1996). Tutsis were massacred by their clergy in churches where they sought sanctuary: 2800 in Kibungo, 6000 in Cyahinda, 4000 in Kibeho, and more in many other places. Although most of the killing was done with machetes, technology played an important part, as the Hutu-controlled Radio Mille Collines—called "the radio that kills" by its opponents—spewed out a daily message of hate and encouragement to slaughter (Destexhe 1995). In the weeks that followed the genocide, a rebel Tutsi army took over the government, and more than 2 million Hutu refugees fled to neighboring countries. By 1995, more than one-third of the Rwandan population was either dead or living in exile. Today most of the living have returned, but their fate, and that of the nation of Rwanda, is very uncertain.

The changes that have rocked many of the world's societies in the last half century overwhelm the ability of social scientists to influence events, or perhaps even fully comprehend them. It is hard to imagine, for example, how anthropologists could have altered the situation in Rwanda. The forces of change at work in the world are simply too great. Students sometimes ask anthropologists whether they are afraid of changing, somehow contaminating, the people they study. Anthropologists reply that this idea is the sin of hubris, or excessive pride; anthropologists are too small, and the forces affecting society are too large. However, even if anthropological contributions cannot change the underlying patterns of history, they can have some impact. As recent essays on the plight of Haitians show (Martinez 1996; Chierici 1996), they can document and publicize the stories of peoples around the world. If anthropologists were powerless to prevent the tragedies of places such as Rwanda and Haiti, they can at least try to ensure that they are not forgotten.

Beyond this, anthropologists can contribute to public policy and development efforts. They can apply ethnographic strategies to the study of local communities as these are affected by the transformations introduced by the forces of the global economy. A holistic, cross-cultural perspective gives anthropologists a unique view of the global economy and the communities that participate in it.

Addressing the processes of change exerted by internal and external forces is doing what anthropologists have been committed to all along: describing and analyzing cultures in their local contexts and illuminating how people adapt to and make sense of the ecological, economic, and political changes in their world.

Summary

1. Cultures are always changing, and no one lives today as they did in the "Stone Age." Cultural change has been increasingly rapid in the last several hundred years.

2. Some characteristics of recent change are rapid increases in population, increasing disparity between rich and poor, and expansion of the power of industrialized nations at the expense of nonindustrialized nations.

3. In the fifteenth century, Europe was neither wealthy nor technologically advanced. The centers of world power lay primarily in the Middle East and Asia. However, Europe was poised on the brink of a great expansion.

4. A combination of religious faith, greed, new social arrangements, and new technologies drove European expansion. Europeans were particularly successful in the Americas, where they were aided by the diseases they carried. They met far more resistance in Asia.

5. Plunder of precious metals, the use of slave labor, and the joint stock company, as well as political and military maneuvering, drew wealth from around the world into Europe. European nations became prosperous, but other areas of the world were impoverished.

6. Colonialism occurred when European governments took direct control of overseas territories. This happened very early in the Americas but was a much later development elsewhere in the world.

7. Although European governments often justified colonialism by calling it a civilizing mission, governments colonized to increase their wealth and protect their trade. They used forced labor, taxation, and education programs designed to discredit local culture to compel natives to produce for European interests.

8. Most colonies gained their independence between the end of World War II and 1965. Civil unrest in the colonies and the emergence of the United States and the Soviet Union as superpowers played critical roles in the timing of independence.

9. After independence, development became a critical issue for former colonies. Economists believed that many nations were poor because they had undeveloped economies. Projects designed to change traditional practices served the interest of both the industrialized world and elites in the nonindustrialized countries.

10. Multinational corporations have also become extremely important in the world's poor nations. They are able to use inexpensive natural resources and labor in the nonindustrialized countries to benefit consumers and shareholders in industrialized nations.

11. Nonindustrialized nations are beset with problems of urbanization. More than half of the world's

most populous cities are in poor nations, and urbanization has been a major force in changing traditional cultures. Providing services to poor people in large cities is beyond the financial capacity of many poor countries.

12. Rapid population increases in the past several decades have led to the collapse of traditional subsistence strategies in many places. They have created a problem for poor nations' governments because even high rates of economic growth have failed to keep pace with population growth.

13. Political instability has had dire consequences for people worldwide. Wars of independence, the Cold War, and ethnic rivalries have led to violence that has destroyed cultures and societies.

Key Terms

colonialism
corvée labor
development
Dutch East India Company
Heeren XVII
industrialization
joint stock company
maquiladora
modernization theory
monoculture plantation
multinational corporation
peonage
per capita GNP
pillage
vassalage
VOC
voluntary associations
World Bank

Suggested Readings

Bodley, John H. 1998. *Victims of Progress* (4th ed.). Mountain View, CA: Mayfield. A comprehensive review of the effects of Western expansion on tribal and indigenous people. Bodley has written several books detailing the relationship of the industrialized powers to native peoples. Other titles include *Tribal Peoples and Development Issues: A Global Overview* (1988) and *Anthropology and Contemporary Human Problems* (3rd ed.) (1995).

Destexhe, Alain. 1995. *Rwanda and Genocide in the Twentieth Century* (Alison Marschner, Trans.). New York: New York University Press. An important work detailing the 1994 massacre of Tutsi by Hutu in Rwanda. Destexhe's work raises important questions about the nature of ethnic conflict and genocide in the context of modern history.

Kottak, Conrad Phillip. 1999. *Assault on Paradise: Social Change in a Brazilian Village* (3rd ed.). New York: McGraw-Hill. Chronicles almost 30 years of Kottak's work in the Brazilian village of Arembepe and the changes wrought by the village's increasing connection with the outside world and the global economy.

Larsen, Clark Spencer, and George R. Miller (Eds.). 1994. *In the Wake of Contact: Biological Responses to Conquest*. New York: Wiley. This is a collection of rather technical essays that explore the effects of disease in the wake of contact between Europeans and others. Most of the focus is on the Americas, but there are also essays on Pacific Islands.

Lawler, Nancy Ellen. 1992. *Soldiers of Misfortune: Ivoirien Tirailleurs of World War II*. Athens: University of Ohio Press. This historical work chronicles the contributions of soldiers from Côte d'Ivoire to the French effort in World War II. It explores the political and economic consequences of World War II for France's colonial subjects in Africa.

Mintz, Sidney W. 1985. *Sweetness and Power: The Place of Sugar in Modern History*. New York: Elisabeth Sifton Books. A fascinating account of the ways in which sugar has changed the world economy. Mintz explores the ways in which sugar production and consumption changed both Europe and the Americas and altered our eating habits and diet. Mintz has recently published *Tasting Food, Tasting Freedom: Excursions into Eating, Culture, and the Past* (1997), a collection of essays that updates and expands his original work.

Scammell, G.V. 1989. *The First Imperial Age: European Overseas Expansion c. 1400–1715*. London: Harper-Collins. This work explores Europe's rise to world power, focusing on the precapitalist period. It is a particularly good source for understanding European involvement in Asia.

Wolf, Eric R. 1982. *Europe and the People Without History*. Berkeley: University of California Press. A classic and highly readable introduction to the history of Western expansion, written by a prominent anthropologist. Wolf explores the effects of European expansion on native peoples throughout the world. His work underscores the relationship between wealth and poverty and highlights the importance of history to understanding current societies. In the recently published *Envisioning Power: Ideologies of Dominance and Crisis* (1999), Wolf uses case studies of the Kwakiutl, the Aztecs, and Nazi Germany to further explore his ideas about the historical relationship between power and culture.

INTERNET RESOURCES

The following Internet resources appear in this chapter. Please log on to the Wadsworth anthropology website: **http://anthropology.wadsworth. com**. Click on the Nanda/Warms *Cultural Anthropology* page. Then select the Student Resources section, where you will find a complete presentation of these links and more.

- A photo essay on social changes and contacts through history, page 386
- Link to a website for social and economic development, page 400
- A video link: A classic example of the interplay between modern development and traditional practices, page 402
- Access the Study Guide to InfoTrac College Edition for Anthropology Students

APPENDIX

A BRIEF GUIDE TO ANTHROPOLOGICAL THEORY

People have probably been curious about their neighbors since the emergence of the species *Homo sapiens.* They have investigated these neighbors systematically in many places and at many times. However, for our purposes, we may date the origins of anthropology as an intellectual and academic discipline to the beginning of the nineteenth century. In fact, the word *anthropologist* was first used in print in 1805 in *The Edinburgh Review* (Kuklick 1991:6). Since that time, numerous different theoretical schools have appeared, each related to its predecessors, but each with its own understanding of the critical issues that surround the analysis of culture. In this appendix, we provide very brief chronological descriptions of the principal schools of anthropological thought and introduce some of the key thinkers in each school.

NINETEENTH-CENTURY EVOLUTIONISM

Various forms of social evolutionary theory held sway throughout most of the nineteenth century. These theories were loosely based on evolutionary models drawn from biology, particularly the work of **Jean Baptiste Lamarck** (1744–1829) and **Charles Darwin** (1809–1882). Lamarck is best known for his notion of inheritance of acquired characteristics. He argued that organs improve with repeated use and grow weak with disuse and that living things are able to pass these strengths and weaknesses on to their offspring. Lamarck reasoned that over time this would give rise to new species. Darwin reasoned that chance endowed certain individuals with traits that allowed them to produce relatively more offspring and that such individuals were able to pass these successful

traits along to their offspring. Darwin's theory of natural selection is described more fully in Chapter 2. As interpreted by social thinkers, the key tenet of evolutionary thought was that the history of humanity could be described as progress toward increasingly complex forms of society. This progress followed discoverable natural laws and could be understood by using scientific methodology.

Herbert Spencer (1820–1903) was a key early thinker in social evolutionism. He compared societies to biological organisms and proposed that both progressed by increasing in complexity. Although much of Spencer's theoretical position was established before Darwin published his theory of natural selection, Spencer rapidly incorporated elements of Darwin's work into his own. The Englishman **Sir Edward Burnett Tylor** (1832–1917) and the American **Lewis Henry Morgan** (1818–1881) both proposed that all human societies progressed from a state of savagery, through barbarism, to civilization. Societies progressed at different speeds, however. Western European and European American societies had achieved the fastest progress. Others, such as the Australian aborigines, had been left far behind in savagery. Although from our perspective, this notion is deeply ethnocentric, it is important to point out that the evolutionary anthropological theorists were deeply critical of their own societies, particularly the entrenched hereditary privilege of the aristocracy and upper classes.

Karl Marx (1818–1883), along with **Friedrich Engels** (1820–1895), and **Sigmund Freud** (1856–1939) also proposed evolutionary theories that had profound impacts on anthropology. Marx viewed evolution in terms of conflict between different social groups (see Chapter 13 for some additional information on Marx). Freud wrote in the twentieth century, but drew largely on nineteenth-century sources. He saw evolution as a psychological process and believed that the psychological development of the individual repeated that of human society. The children of the "civilized" were thus the emotional equals of adult "savages."

THE EARLY SOCIOLOGISTS

The key sociological thinker in turn-of-the-century France was **Émile Durkheim** (1858–1917). Durkheim believed that each group of people shared a "collective conscience." The collective conscience consisted of a shared system of beliefs and values that molded and controlled individual behavior, similar to what many anthropologists today call culture. Durkheim thought that the collective conscience had an existence independent of the people who shared it. It was something that operated by its own laws and could be studied on its own terms. The task of sociologists was to discover the contents of the collective conscience (which Durkheim referred to as social facts and collective representations) and the laws by which they functioned. One of the key laws that Durkheim believed he discovered was that the human mind divided things into opposites. The most basic of these divisions was between the sacred and the profane.

Durkheim and his students are often referred to as *L'Année Sociologique,* after a journal they published that reviewed each year's developments in sociology. His students were some of the brightest minds of Europe, including his nephew **Marcel Mauss** (1872–1950) and **Robert Hertz** (1881–1915). Sadly, most of Durkheim's students died in the trenches in World War I.

While Durkheim and his students focused on questions of social cohesion or solidarity, **Max Weber** (1864–1920) was more concerned with conflict. Weber was profoundly influenced by Marx, but did not believe that social classes necessarily acted in solidarity. Weber is also known for promoting the notion that social scientists must develop empathetic understanding of those they study in order to understand their behavior.

AMERICAN HISTORICAL PARTICULARISM

In the United States, much of anthropology in the late nineteenth and early twentieth centuries had been devoted to the attempt to find scientific justification for institutionalized racism. The German-trained scholar **Franz Boas** (1858–1942) created a new American anthropology that was utterly opposed to this thinking. Boas asserted that all human beings were biological equals and that differences among human societies were the result of culture alone. The form each culture took depended almost entirely on its own specific history (hence *historical particularism*—a term coined long after Boas's death) rather than any pan-human pattern of development as the evolutionists proposed. Boas went on to debunk many nineteenth-century thinkers, showing that the cultural traits they believed showed general patterning actually arose from quite different histories.

The claim of particular historical development for each culture had important implications. First, it meant that cultures could be evaluated only on their own terms rather than any universal yardstick of development. Therefore, cultural relativism became a cornerstone of Boasian anthropology. Second, though Boas wrote that controlled cultural comparison was possible and general laws of growth could be found (1896/1988), his insistence that cultures are unique results of their history and context suggests that this is virtually impossible. No two cultures have histories so similar that no objection could be raised to their comparison and comparing similar elements of different cultures removes them from their context and thus violates Boasian principles. In any event, Boas and his students assiduously avoided making such comparisons or proposing general laws. Instead, Boasians focused on collecting ethnographic data through fieldwork, which became central to American anthropology.

Boas's influence on American anthropology was extraordinary. During his long career at Columbia University, he trained many of the most important American anthropologists of the first half of the twentieth century, including **A. L. Kroeber, Robert Lowie, Edward Sapir, Ruth Benedict, Paul Radin,** and **Ashley Montague.**

FUNCTIONALISM

In Europe, the trauma of World War I led to the abandonment of social evolutionism. However, many of the ideas of Spencer and Durkheim were retained in British functionalism. Like Spencer, functionalists tended to view societies as analogous to biological organisms. Instead of being interested in their evolution, however, functionalists were concerned with the relations among their parts.

The two critical thinkers in functionalism were **A. R. Radcliffe-Brown** (1881–1955) and **Bronislaw Malinowski** (1884–1942). Radcliffe-Brown is considered a structural functionalist. Profoundly influenced by his reading of Durkheim, he wanted to discern and describe the role of social institutions such as kinship in maintaining the smooth working of society and preserving social solidarity. Malinowski's psychological functionalism focused on human physical and psychological needs. He proposed seven universal human needs: nutrition, reproduction, bodily comfort, safety, relaxation, movement, and growth. He examined cultural institutions in terms of the ways they functioned to meet these needs.

Although their theoretical positions were very different, Boas and Malinowski shared some interesting similarities. Like Boas, Malinowski set extremely high standards for fieldwork among his students. Also like Boas, Malinowski trained many important anthropologists, including **E. E. Evans-Pritchard, Meyer Fortes, Audrey Richards,** and **Raymond Firth,** during his long academic career at the London School of Economics.

CULTURE AND PERSONALITY

Boas transmitted to his students his insistence on the historical uniqueness of each culture, but he did not give them any unifying principle around which to organize their work. To remedy this, many of them turned to the notion of personality. **Ruth Benedict** (1887–1948), **Margaret Mead** (1901–1978), and others analyzed culture as "personality writ large." They believed that each culture had a unique configuration that shaped the personality of its members, molding them to fit the culture's dominant type. Benedict, for example, described the Zuni as having an Appolonian configuration; that is, the Zuni were reserved and levelheaded and avoided excess of any kind.

To solve the problem of how cultural configurations were formed and maintained, culture and personality theorists, particularly **Abram Kardiner** (1891–1981) and **Cora DuBois** (1903–1991), turned to Freud. Although they rejected Freud's evolutionary theories, they accepted the notion that early childhood experiences determine later life personality. Thus, they saw child-rearing practices as critical to understanding cultural institutions.

With the coming of World War II, the culture and personality theorists turned to writing national character studies of the United States, its allies, and its opponents. These works, produced by analyzing written data rather than fieldwork, were substantially less successful than their earlier efforts.

Although few anthropologists today would consider themselves culture and personality theorists, some of the best-known books in American anthropology are associated with this school of thought. These include Margaret Mead's **Coming of Age in Samoa** (1928) and **Sex and Temperament in Three Primitive Societies** (1935) and Ruth Benedict's **Patterns of Culture** (1934).

CULTURAL ECOLOGY AND NEO-EVOLUTIONISM

By the mid-1930s, a second school of American anthropological thought emerged to compete with the ideas of Boas and his intellectual descendants. Cultural ecology and neo-evolutionism reevaluated the insights of the nineteenth-century evolutionists and, through new research, attempted to raise their scientific standards. Key thinkers in this enterprise were **Julian Steward** (1902–1972), **Leslie White** (1900–1975), and **George Peter Murdock** (1897–1985). All three searched for general laws of cultural development. Steward, who coined the term *cultural ecology,* was particularly interested in the relationship between culture and environment. He believed that cultures at similar technological levels, in similar environments, would develop broadly similar institutions. His work thus depended on cross-cultural comparisons. Leslie White was deeply influenced by his reading of Morgan and Marx. This led him to a concern with cultural evolution and the nature of production. He proposed that cultures evolve as the amount of energy they capture increases. Changes in the technology of production were critical to increasing the ability to capture energy. George Peter Murdock was an intellectual descendant of Spencer. He believed that general principles of culture could be derived from cross-cultural analysis on a massive scale. Thus, he began a project to index and tabulate information on all the world's known cultures. This project, known as the Human Relations Area Files (HRAF), still continues today (see Chapter 3).

NEO-MATERIALISM: EVOLUTIONARY, FUNCTIONALIST, ECOLOGICAL, AND MARXIST

Steward, White, Murdock, and others set the stage for many of the anthropological theorists of the 1960s and 1970s. These combined earlier anthropological work with insights from the physical and biological sciences and, sometimes, a deep understanding and appropriation of Marxist thought.

Evolutionary theorists such as **Morton Fried** (1923–1986), **Marshal Sahlins** (born 1930), and **Elman Service** (1915–1996) looked for ways to combine the insights of Steward and White into a single theory of cultural evolution. They developed the band–tribe–chiefdom–state model commonly used in much of modern anthropology (see Chapter 12).

Ecological functionalists took the position that cultures were adaptations that permitted their members to exploit their environments successfully. They examined the ways in which cultural practices were related to physical, technological, and economic aspects of the environment. **Marvin Harris** (born 1927) is perhaps the best-known functional ecologist. He uses the term *cultural materialism* to describe his approach. Harris's analysis of Indian cattle worship (see Chapter 4) and Aztec cannibalism (see Chapter 15) are good examples of his approach.

Neo-Marxists were a third group of thinkers within this tradition. Most neo-Marxists were particularly concerned with issues of colonialism and international economic relations, but their approaches to these questions varied. In Europe, French scholars such as **Claude Meillassoux** (born 1925) and **Maurice Godelier** (born 1925) broke with the Soviet scholars who had dominated Marxist anthropology. They proposed new ways of adapting Marx's critical insights to the anthropology of nonindustrial society. In the United States, political economy theorists, led by **Eric Wolf** (1923–1999), focused on the historical development of capitalism and the conflicts it generated. Wolf and others rejected the notion of cultures as bounded wholes that could be studied independently. They urged anthropologists to see issues of conflict, domination of one group by another, and appropriation of wealth as central to understanding culture.

STRUCTURALISM

Structural anthropology is based largely on the work of **Claude Lévi-Strauss** (born 1908). Lévi-Strauss was inspired by Durkheim's work on the nature of human thought as well as advances made in linguistics in the first half of the twentieth century. At that time, linguists were exploring the sound system of languages. They discovered phones and phonemes (see Chapter 5), which they considered the most fundamental units of language. In a similar fashion, Lévi-Strauss sought to uncover the basic units of culture and the rules by which they operated. He suggested that the human mind had certain fundamental features and that the same basic units and rules of culture found expression in all cultures. Lévi-Strauss reasoned that the basics of culture could best be discovered in the folktales and mythologies of "primitive" people, which might present such units and rules in their most pristine form. Much of Lévi-Strauss's life work has been in analyzing myths from different cultures to show what he believes to be the basic units and rules of culture. Like Durkheim, Lévi-Strauss holds that the most fundamental rule of culture is the tendency of human thinking to make binary distinctions. He adds, however, that human thinking is not satisfied with such distinctions and always tends to add a third category that in some way transcends or reconciles the opposition. His insights are fundamental to the analysis of myth and the interpretation of the symbolic aspects of culture.

ETHNOSCIENCE AND COGNITIVE ANTHROPOLOGY

Ethnoscience and cognitive anthropology were largely American developments. Some of the key scholars associated with these approaches are **Ward Goodenough** (born 1919), **Harold Conklin** (born 1926), **Stephen Tyler** (born 1932), and **James Spradley** (1933–1981). Ethnoscience is based on a critique of anthropological method but draws heavily on Boasian anthropology and structuralism. Ethnoscientists and cognitive anthropologists claimed that existing anthropological reporting was unreliable because there was no regular, consistent anthropological methodology. Projects such as Murdock's HRAF were flawed because different ethnographers observed and reported on differing aspects of the societies they studied. Thus, generalizations about cultures could not be made.

Ethnoscientists and cognitive anthropologists proposed a way around this dilemma. They asserted that culture was a shared mental model through which people organized their world. Further, they claimed that language was the key means through which this organization was accomplished. Thus, the distinctions that people made in speaking could be used to construct a model for each culture. Ethnoscientists and cognitive anthropologists developed a

fieldwork method called the structured interview, which was designed to discover the linguistic models that members of different cultures used to classify their worlds. They claimed that if done properly, structured interviews could provide the information needed to behave like a member of the culture. Some ethnoscientists and cognitive anthropologists suggested that a person who fully understood the mental model of another culture could think like a member of that culture as well, though this was hotly disputed.

One key tenet of ethnoscience and cognitive anthropology reflected its Boasian heritage: the belief that each culture had a unique mental model. Like Boas, thinkers in this school believed that, given enough time and data collection, some universal theory of culture might emerge. However, such a theory was only a long-term possibility for the distant future.

In the 1980s and 1990s, cognitive anthropologists turned away from the linguistic model. Realizing that many forms of knowledge and behavior did not involve linguistic processing, they began to look at insights from psychology and physiology. The result was the emergence of schema theory and connectivism. Schema theory describes knowledge in terms of generalized representations of experiences, events, and objects that are stored in memory. Connectivists argue that knowledge is structured in "processing units" and examine the ways in which such units might be distributed, linked, and networked. Current cognitive anthropologists attempt to describe the relationship among culture, schema, and behavior (D'Andrade 1995).

SOCIOBIOLOGY, EVOLUTIONARY PSYCHOLOGY, AND BEHAVIORAL ECOLOGY

Perhaps the most controversial theoretical position in anthropology is sociobiology. It was developed and promoted largely by biologists and anthropologists in the 1960s and 1970s. Some of its key thinkers are biologists **W. D. Hamilton** (1936–2000), **Robert Trivers** (born 1943), and **E. O. Wilson** (born 1929), sociologist **Lionel Tiger** (born 1937), and anthropologists **Robin Fox** (born 1934), **Jerome Barkow** (born 1944), **Napoleon Chagnon** (born 1938), and **Kristen Hawkes** (born 1944).

Sociobiologists applied the Darwinian idea of natural selection directly to human cultural behavior. They believed that culture reflected an underlying genetic patterning. Further, as in biology, those genetically based culture traits that led to increased reproduction would be selected and transmitted, and thus would appear increasingly in the population. Thus, they viewed much of cultural behavior as a mechanism through which individuals tried to increase their chances of reproduction. In the 1970s, sociobiologists were particularly concerned with the problem of altruism, in which an individual sacrifices his or her own reproductive chances to benefit those of another, and tried to show how such a trait could evolve.

In the 1980s and 1990s, sociobiologists split into three groups: evolutionary psychologists, human behavioral ecologists, and the study of human universals. Evolutionary psychologists theorize that the mind is composed of a collection of specialized suborgans designed for particular tasks. They try to describe these and show what they were designed to accomplish. Human behavioral ecologists emphasize human populations rather than cultures and try to test the hypothesis that culturally patterned traits enhance fitness. Some anthropologists focus on discovering and describing human universals, or characteristics found in all societies.

Sociobiologists have insisted that understanding the connections between biology and culture should be the focus of anthropology. The vast majority of cultural anthropologists, however, believe that culture is almost completely independent of biology. As a result, sociobiology has been strongly criticized by cultural anthropologists, and it has remained a relatively small and isolated theoretical position.

ANTHROPOLOGY AND GENDER

The feminist critique of anthropology developed along with the women's movement in the late 1960s and 1970s (see Chapters 3, 4, and 11). Despite the fact that some very prominent anthropologists had been women, anthropology in general had been overwhelmingly concerned with men's activities. Though women constituted half the population, they were often invisible in ethnographic writing. Feminist anthropologists such as **Michelle Zimbalist Rosaldo** (1944–1981), **Louise Lamphere** (born 1940), **Sherry Ortner** (born 1941), and **Micaela di Leonardo** (born 1949) tried to rectify this situation by focusing attention on women's worlds. Feminist anthropologists actually took many different theoretical positions, from structuralism to neo-Marxism to postmodernism. However, they all shared an interest in women's position in society. Much of feminist anthropology in the 1970s was concerned with trying to explain female subordination, which some scholars considered to be universal. More recently, feminist anthropologists have focused on the social construction of gender, the relationship of gender to social, economic, and political power, and the cultural variation among different groups of women.

SYMBOLIC AND INTERPRETIVE ANTHROPOLOGY

Like ethnoscientists and cognitive anthropologists, symbolic and interpretive anthropologists are fundamentally concerned with the ways in which people formulate their reality. However, unlike the former, who thought of culture in terms of formal linguistic models, symbolic and interpretive anthropologists use models from psychology and the study of literary texts to analyze culture. Some major figures in this group are **Clifford Geertz** (born 1926), **Mary Douglas** (born 1921), and **Victor Turner** (1920–1983). Geertz, one of the best-known modern anthropologists, believes that people use symbols to help them understand their own culture. Culture is like a story that people tell themselves about themselves, and in so doing give meaning and poignancy to their lives. Turner, on the other hand, followed the tradition of Durkheim and British functionalist anthropology, viewing symbols in terms of their role in the maintenance of society. He was particularly interested in the study of ritual and outlined the characteristics of symbols. Douglas drew particular inspiration from her reading of Durkheim. She suggested that shared symbols helped hold societies together. Douglas was particularly interested in beliefs about purity and contamination and held that such notions symbolized beliefs about the social order.

Most anthropologists have argued that their theoretical position rests on scientific principles. Symbolic and interpretive anthropologists make no such claim. Rather, they suggest that anthropology is an art of cultural interpretation, more of a humanity than a science. For this reason, those who favor an anthropology modeled on the natural sciences are deeply critical of symbolic and interpretive anthropology. Nonetheless, symbolic and interpretive thinkers have had a powerful impact on current anthropology.

POSTMODERNISM

Postmodernism grew from the insights of the feminist anthropologists, interpretive and symbolic anthropologists, and neo-Marxists, but its development was critically dependent on the thinking of cultural historian **Michel Foucault** (1926–1984) and literary critic **Jacques Derrida** (born 1930). Anthropological postmodernists hold that all accounts of culture are partial and conditioned by the observer's personal history and experiences. One result, according to postmodernists, is that anthropological writing tells us a great deal about anthropologists and their society but rather little about the societies that anthropologists observe.

Issues of power and "voice" are critical to postmodern scholars. They assert that a great many different interpretations of history or culture are valid. The interpretations held by the wealthy and powerful are likely to be considered legitimate, while others are discredited. For postmodernists, culture is often viewed as a constant battle between opposing, contesting interpretations. Some postmodernists, such as **Renato Rosaldo** (born 1941), focus on explanations of culture that highlight conflicting interpretations. Others, such as **Vincent Crapanzano** (born 1939) or **Gananath Obeyesekere** (born 1930), study anthropological writing itself. They analyze ethnographies to show the ways in which they are constructed and explain what they tell us about anthropologists and Western society.

At its most radical, postmodernism asserts that objectivity is impossible, implying that no interpretation or analysis can ever be better or worse than another. If this is the case, fieldwork is irrelevant and anthropology should be understood as a branch of literature, less accurate than fiction because of its pretensions to authority and fact. While anthropology does have a long history of interpretive analysis, postmodernism's radical rejection of objectivity has been highly controversial and few anthropologists would whole-heartedly describe themselves as postmodernists. However, even postmodernism's detractors would agree that it has made anthropologists more sensitive to the ways that knowledge is generated in anthropology and to issues of whose story they are telling as well as their own motivations and agendas in telling it.

INTERNET RESOURCES

The following Internet resource appears in the Appendix. Please log on to the Wadsworth anthropology website: **http://anthropology.wadsworth. com.** Click on the Nanda/Warms *Cultural Anthropology* page. Then select the Student Resources section, where you will find this link and more.

- Link to a website on theory in anthropology, page 412

GLOSSARY

A

acephalous: Lacking a government head or chief.

achieved status: A social position that a person chooses or achieves on his or her own.

adaptation: A change in the biological structure or life ways of an individual or population by which it becomes better fitted to survive and reproduce in its environment.

affinal: Related by marriage; in-laws.

African American Vernacular English (AAVE): See **Ebonics.**

age grades: Specialized hierarchical associations based on age, which stratify a society by seniority.

age set: A group of people of similar age and sex who move through some or all of life's stages together.

agriculture (intensive cultivation): A form of food production in which fields are in permanent cultivation using plows, animals, and techniques of soil and water control.

allophones: Two or more different phones that can be used to make the same phoneme in a specific language.

ambilineal descent: See **bilateral descent.**

androcentric: Male-centered.

androcentric bias: The distortion in anthropological theory and ethnography focusing primarily on male activities or male perceptions of female activities.

anthropology: The comparative study of human societies and cultures.

anthropomorphic: Having human shape.

anthropopsychic: Having thought processes and emotions similar to humans.

antistructure: The socially sanctioned use of behavior that radically violates social norms. Antistructure is frequently found in religious ritual.

applied anthropology: The application of anthropology to the solution of human problems.

arboreal: Tree-dwelling.

archaeology: The subdiscipline of anthropology that focuses on the reconstruction of past cultures based on their material remains.

arranged marriage: The process by which senior family members exercise a great degree of control over the choice of their children's spouses.

art: Forms of creative expression that are guided by aesthetic principles and involve imagination, skill, and style.

artifacts: The material remains of past cultures; any object made or modified by human beings.

ascribed status: A social position that a person is born into.

assimilationist model: A model of U.S. immigration that holds that immigrants should abandon their cultural traditions and become wholly absorbed in mainstream American culture.

atlatl: A spear thrower; a device used to increase and extend the power of the human arm when throwing a spear.

australopithecines: Members of an early hominid genus found in Africa and characterized by bipedal locomotion and small brain size.

authority: Power exercised through political office or institutions.

avunculocal residence: System under which a married couple lives with the husband's mother's brother.

B

balanced reciprocity: An exchange of goods of nearly equal value, with a clear obligation to return them within a specified time limit.

band: A small group of people related by blood or marriage, who live together and are loosely associated with a territory in which they forage.

bifurcation: A principle of classifying kin under which different kinship terms are used for the mother's side of the family and the father's side of the family.

bigman: A self-made leader who gains power through personal achievements rather than through political office.

bilateral descent: System under which both maternal and paternal lines are used in reckoning descent.

bilocal residence: System under which a married couple has the choice of living with the husband's or wife's family.

biological/physical anthropology: The subdiscipline of anthropology that specializes in the study of humankind from a biological perspective. It includes osteology, nutrition, demography, epidemiology, and primatology.

biopsychological equality: The notion that all human groups have the same biological and mental capabilities.

bipedalism: Walking on two feet, a distinctive characteristic of humans and our ancestors.

Black English Vernacular (BEV): See **Ebonics.**

blending: The combination of two calls to produce a new call; a hypothesized early phase in language evolution.

bound morpheme: A unit of meaning that must be associated with another.

bride service: The cultural rule that a man must work for his bride's family for a variable length of time either before or after the marriage.

bridewealth: Goods presented by the groom's kin to the bride's kin to legitimize a marriage.

bureaucracy: Administrative hierarchy characterized by specialization of function and fixed rules.

C

call system: The form of communication among nonhuman primates composed of a limited number of sounds that are tied to specific stimuli in the environment.

capital: Productive resources that are used with the primary goal of increasing their owner's financial wealth.

capitalism: An economic system in which people work for wages, land and capital goods are privately owned, and capital is invested for individual profit.

cargo cult: Revitalization movements in Melanesia which involve ritual attempts to bring the wealth (cargo) of Europeans to the indigenous peoples.

cargo system: A ritual system common in Central and South America in which wealthy people are required to hold a series of costly ceremonial offices.

caste system: A system of stratification based on birth in which movement from one stratum (caste) to another is not possible.

chiefdom: a society with social ranking in which political integration is achieved through an office of centralized leadership called the chief.

citizenship: Membership in a state.

clan: A unilineal kinship group whose members believe themselves to be descended from a common ancestor but who cannot trace this link genealogically.

class system: A form of social stratification in which the different strata form a continuum and social mobility is possible.

cleric: A religious practitioner or authority.

clinical distribution: The frequency change of a particular trait as you move geographically from one point to another.

closed system: A stratification system based primarily on ascription.

cognatic descent: See **bilateral descent**.

cognitive anthropology: A theoretical approach that defines culture in terms of the rules and meanings underlying human behavior, rather than behavior itself.

collateral kin: Kin descended from a common ancestor but not in a direct ascendant or descendant line, such as siblings and cousins.

colonialism: The active possession of a foreign territory and the maintenance of political domination over that territory.

communication: The act of transmitting information that influences the behavior of another organism.

communitas: A state of perceived solidarity, equality, and unity among people sharing a religious ritual, often characterized by intense emotion.

compensation: A payment demanded by an aggrieved party to compensate for damage.

complementary opposition: A political structure in which higher-order units form alliances that emerge only when lower-order units come into conflict.

composite (compound) family: An aggregate of nuclear families linked by a common spouse.

conflict theory: A perspective on social stratification that focuses on inequality as a source of conflict and change.

conjugal tie: The relationship between a husband and wife formed by marriage.

consanguineal: Related by birth.

consanguineal family: People who are related by birth and descent.

consanguinity: Blood ties between people.

contagious magic: The belief that things once in contact with a person or object retain an invisible connection with that person or object.

controlled cross-cultural comparison: An anthropological method that uses comparable ethnographic data from many societies and tests particular hypotheses.

conventionality: The notion that, in human language, words are only arbitrarily or conventionally connected to the things for which they stand.

core vocabulary: A list of 100 or 200 terms that designate things, actions, and activities, likely to be named in all the world's languages.

corvée labor: Unpaid labor required by a governing authority.

cosmology: A system of beliefs that deals with fundamental questions in the religious and social order.

cross-cousins: The children of a parent's siblings of the opposite sex (mother's brothers, father's sisters).

cross-cultural survey (also called **controlled cross-cultural comparison**): A research method that uses statistical correlations of traits from many different cultures to test generalizations about culture and human behavior.

cultural anthropology: The study of human behavior that is learned rather than genetically transmitted, and that is typical of groups of people.

cultural construction of gender: The idea that gender characteristics are not inborn but rather constructed within each culture.

cultural ecology: A theoretical approach that regards cultural patterns as adaptive responses to the basic problems of human survival and reproduction.

cultural materialism: A theoretical perspective that holds that the primary task of anthropology is to account for the similarities and differences among cultures and that this can best be done by studying the material constraints to which human existence is subject.

cultural relativism: The notion that there are no universal standards by which all cultures may be evaluated. Cultures must be analyzed with reference to their own histories and culture traits understood in terms of the cultural whole.

culture: The learned behaviors and symbols that allow people to live in groups. The primary means by which humans adapt to their environments. The way of life characteristic of a particular human society.

culture and personality: A theoretical perspective that focuses on culture as the principal force in shaping the typical personality of a society as well as on the role of personality in the maintenance of cultural institutions.

D

deep play: Cultural performances, such as sports and games, in which participants and spectators are joined together in emotionally compelling experiences.

descent: The culturally established affiliation between a child and one or both parents.

descent group: A group of kin who are lineal descendants of a common ancestor, extending beyond two generations.

descriptive or **structural linguistics:** The study and analysis of the structure and content of particular languages.

development: The notion that some countries are poor because they have small industrial plants and few lines of communication and that they should pursue wealth by acquiring these things.

diffusion: The spread of cultural elements from one culture to another through cultural contact.

displacement: The capacity of all human languages to describe things not happening in the present.

divination: A religious ritual done to find hidden objects or information.

domestic group: A household unit that usually, but not always, consists of members of a family.

double descent: The tracing of descent through both matrilineal and patrilineal links, each of which is used for different purposes.

dowry: Presentation of goods by the bride's kin to the family of the groom or to the couple.

duality of patterning: The ability to produce arrangements of blended sounds; the hypothesized second step in the evolution of language.

Dutch East India Company: A joint stock company chartered by the Dutch government to control all Dutch trade in the Indian and Pacific oceans. Also known by its Dutch initials, VOC.

E

ecological functionalism: A theoretical perspective that holds that the ways in which cultural institutions work can best be understood by examining their effects on the environment.

economic system: The norms governing production, distribution, and consumption of goods and services within a society.

economics: The study of the ways in which the choices people make combine to determine how their society uses its scarce resources to produce and distribute goods and services.

economizing behavior: Choosing a course of action to maximize perceived benefit.

efficiency: Yield per person per hour of labor invested.

egalitarian society: A society in which no individual or group has more privileged access to resources, power, or prestige than any other.

Ego: The kinship status from which a kinship diagram is constructed.

emic (perspective): Examining society using concepts, categories, and distinctions that are meaningful to members of that culture.

empirical science: An approach to understanding phenomena based on attempts to observe and record a presumed objective reality.

enculturation: The ways in which humans learn to become members of their society.

endogamy: A rule prescribing that marriage must be within a particular group.

ethnic boundaries: The perceived cultural attributes by which ethnic groups distinguish themselves from others.

ethnic groups: Categories of people who see themselves as sharing an ethnic identity that differentiates them from other groups or from the larger society as a whole.

ethnic identity: The sense of self one experiences as a member of an ethnic group.

ethnicity: Perceived differences in culture, national origin, and historical experience by which groups of people are distinguished from others in the same social environment.

ethnobotany: An anthropological discipline devoted to describing the ways in which different cultures classify plants.

ethnocentrism: Judging other cultures from the perspective of one's own culture. The notion that one's own culture is more beautiful, rational, and nearer to perfection than any other.

ethnographic method: The intensive study of a particular society and culture as the basis for generating anthropological theory.

ethnography: The major research tool of cultural anthropology; includes both fieldwork among people in society and the written results of fieldwork.

ethnology: Comparative statements about cultural and social processes that are based on cross-cultural ethnographic data.

ethnomedicine: An anthropological discipline devoted to describing the medical systems of different cultures.

ethnoscience: A theoretical approach that focuses on the ways in which members of a culture classify their world and holds

that anthropology should be the study of cultural systems of classification.

etic (perspective): Examining society using concepts, categories, and rules derived from science; an outsider's perspective, which produces analyses that members of the society being studied may not find meaningful.

exogamy: A rule specifying that a person must marry outside a particular group.

extended family: Family based on blood relations extending over three or more generations.

extensive cultivation: See **horticulture.**

F

factions: Informal systems of alliance within well-defined political units such as lineages or villages.

feminist anthropology: A theoretical perspective that focuses on describing and explaining the social roles of women.

fieldwork: The firsthand, systematic exploration of a society. It involves living with a group of people and participating in and observing their behavior.

foraging (hunting and gathering): A food-getting strategy that does not involve food production or domestication of animals.

forensic anthropology: The application of biological anthropology to the identification of skeletalized or badly decomposed human remains.

fourth world: Indigenous peoples living in nation-states.

fraternal polyandry: A custom whereby a woman marries a man and his brothers.

free morpheme: (linguistics) a unit of meaning that may stand alone as a word.

functionalism: The anthropological theory that specific cultural institutions function to support the structure of society or serve the needs of individuals in society.

G

gender: The social classification of masculine and feminine.

gender hierarchy: The ways in which gendered activities and attributes are differentially valued and related to the distribution of resources, prestige, and power in a society.

gender role: The cultural expectations of men and women in a particular society, including the division of labor.

genderlect: The consistent variations in private and public speaking patterns between males and females.

genealogy: A family history; a chart of family relationships.

generalized reciprocity: A distribution of goods with no immediate or specific return expected.

genetic drift: Changes in the frequencies of specific traits caused by random factors.

genitor: A biological father.

genus: In biological classification, a group of similar species.

gerontocracy: A society in which most of the power resides with the elders.

Ghost Dance: A Native American religious movement of the late nineteenth century.

glottochronology: A statistical technique that linguists have developed to estimate the date of separation of related languages.

god: A named spirit who is believed to have created or to control some aspect of the world.

government: An interrelated set of status roles that have the authority to coordinate and regulate behavior within a society.

grasslands: A plain characterized by coarse grass and scattered tree growth.

H

Heeren XVII: The "Lords Seventeen," members of the board of directors of the Dutch East India Company.

hegemony: The development by ruling classes of ideologies that attempt to justify systems of social stratification and embed them in dominant cultural norms.

hijra: An alternative gender role in India conceptualized as neither man nor woman.

historical linguistics: A branch of linguistics concerned with discovering the histories of languages.

holistic/holism: The physical proposition that the whole is greater than the sum of its parts. In anthropology, an approach that focuses on the elements of culture, the relationships among these elements,

and the relationship of culture to biology and environment.

Homo erectus: A species of early human found in Africa, Asia, and Europe. *Homo erectus* were present between 1.8 million and about 200,000 years ago.

Homo habilis: A species of early human found in Africa. *Homo habilis* were present between 2.5 and 1.8 million years ago.

Homo sapiens: A species of human found throughout the world. The earliest *Homo sapiens* appeared about 500,000 years ago.

horticulture (extensive cultivation): Production of plants using a simple, nonmechanized technology; fields are not used continuously.

Human Relations Area File (HRAF): An ethnographic database including cultural descriptions of more than 300 cultures.

human variation: The subdiscipline of anthropology concerned with mapping and explaining physical differences among modern human groups.

hunting and gathering: See **foraging.**

hybridization model: A theory that seeks to explain the transition from archaic to modern *Homo sapiens* by proposing that modern and archaic forms interbred.

I

ideal type: A description of a phenomenon that defines it in contrast to others of its kind but may not exist in a pure form in the real world.

illegitimate power: Power exercised by coercion, against the will of the people of a society.

imitative magic: The belief that imitating an action in a religious ritual will cause the action to happen in the material world.

incest taboos: Prohibitions on sexual relations between relatives.

indigenous peoples: Groups of people who have occupied a region for a long time but who have a minority position and usually little or no influence in the government of the nation-state that ultimately controls their land.

industrialism: An economic strategy involving the mechanization of production and associated characteristics such as bureaucratization, extreme

occupational specialization, and social stratification.

industrialization: The process of the mechanization of production.

informant: A person from whom anthropologists gather cultural data.

inheritance: The transfer of property between generations.

initiation ritual: A ritual that marks the passage from childhood to adult status.

innovation: A new variation on an existing cultural pattern that is subsequently accepted by other members of the society.

intensive cultivation: See **agriculture.**

International Phonetic Alphabet (IPA): A system of writing designed to represent all the sounds used in the different languages of the world.

interpretive or **symbolic anthropology:** A theoretical approach that emphasizes that culture as a system of meaning and proposes that the aim of cultural anthropology is to interpret the meanings that cultural acts have for their participants.

invention: New combinations of existing cultural elements.

J

joint stock company: A firm that is managed by a centralized board of directors but owned by shareholders. Shares may be transferred from one owner to another, and shareholders are directly responsible for the firm's debts.

K

key informant: A person particularly knowledgeable about his or her own culture who is a major source of the anthropologist's information.

kindred: Not a group, but a unique kin network made up of all the people related to a specific individual.

kinship: A culturally defined relationship established on the basis of blood ties or through marriage.

kinship system: The totality of kin relations, kin groups, and terms for classifying kin in a society.

kinship terminology: The system of kinship terms in a particular culture.

Kula ring: A pattern of exchange among trading partners in the Trobriands and other South Pacific islands.

L

law: A means of social control and dispute management through the systematic application of force by those in society with the authority to do so.

leadership: The ability to direct an enterprise or action.

legitimate power: Power exercised with the consent of the members of a society.

leveling mechanism: A practice, value, or form of social organization that evens out wealth within a society.

levirate: The custom whereby a man marries the widow of a deceased brother.

lexicon: The total stock of words in a language.

life chances: The opportunities that people have to fulfill their potential in society.

liminal: The stage of a ritual, particularly a rite of passage, in which one has passed out of an old status but not yet entered a new one.

lineage: A group of kin whose members trace descent from a known common ancestor.

lineal kin: Blood relations linked through descent, such as Ego, Ego's mother, Ego's grandmother, and Ego's daughter.

linguistics: A field of cultural anthropology that specializes in the study of human languages.

M

machismo: A cultural construction of hypermasculinity as essential to the male gender role.

magic: A religious ritual believed to produce a mechanical effect by supernatural means. When magic is done correctly, believers think it must have the desired effect.

mana: Religious power or energy that is concentrated in individuals or objects.

manhood puzzle: The question of why in almost all cultures masculinity is viewed not as a natural state but as a problematic status to be won through overcoming obstacles.

maquiladora: A manufacturing plant, owned by an international company, located in Mexico to take advantage of inexpensive labor there.

market exchange: An economic system in which goods and services are bought and sold at a money price determined primarily by the forces of supply and demand.

marriage: The customs, rules, and obligations that establish a special relationship between a sexually cohabiting adult male and female, between them and any children they produce, and between the kin of the bride and groom.

matrilineage: A lineage formed by descent in the female line.

matrilineal descent: A rule that affiliates a person to kin of both sexes related through females only.

matrilocal residence: System under which a husband lives with his wife's family after marriage.

mediation: A form of managing disputes that uses the offices of a third party to achieve voluntary consensus to an agreement between disputing parties.

melanin: A pigment found in the skin, hair, and eyes of human beings, as well as many other species, and responsible for variations in color.

melting pot model: A model of U.S. immigration that holds that as immigrants lose some of their cultural differences, they will melt together into a new American culture.

menarche: A girl's first menstruation.

messianic: Focusing on the coming of a messiah who will usher in a utopian world.

millenarian: One who believes that a coming catastrophe will signal the beginning of a new age and the eventual establishment of paradise.

modernization theory: A model of development that predicts that nonindustrial societies will move in the social and technological direction of industrialized nations.

monoculture plantation: An agricultural plantation specializing in the large-scale production of a single crop to be sold on the market.

monogamy: A rule that permits a person to be married to only one spouse at a time.

monotheism: Belief in a single god.

morpheme: The smallest unit of a language that has a meaning.

morphology: A system for creating words from sounds.

mosaic model: A model of immigration that holds that cultural diversity is a positive aspect of American national identity.

multinational corporation: A corporation that owns business enterprises or plants in more than one nation.

multiregional model: A theory that seeks to explain the transition from *Homo erectus* to *Homo sapiens* by arguing that different populations of *Homo sapiens* are descendant from different populations of *Homo erectus.*

mutation: A random change in genetic material; the ultimate source of all biological variation.

N

nation–state: A sovereign, geographically based state that identifies itself as having a distinctive national culture and historical experience.

Native American Church: A religious revitalization movement among Native Americans, also known as the Peyote religion.

native anthropologist: An anthropologist who does fieldwork in his or her own culture.

nativism: A religious movement that aims to restore a golden age believed to have existed in the past.

naturalistic: Endowing features of the natural world, such as rivers and mountains, with spirit, soul, or other supernatural characteristics.

natural selection: The mechanism of evolutionary change; changes in traits of living organisms that occur over time as a result of differences in reproductive success among individuals.

Neandertal: Members of a population of archaic *Homo sapiens* that lived between 130,000 and 35,000 years ago.

negative reciprocity: Exchange conducted for the purpose of material advantage and the desire to get something for nothing.

neo-evolutionism: A theoretical perspective concerned with the historical change of culture from small-scale societies to extremely large-scale societies.

neolocal residence: System under which a couple establishes an independent household after marriage.

neo-Marxism: A theoretical perspective concerned with applying the insights of Marxist thought to anthropology; neo-Marxists modify Marxist analysis to make it appropriate to the investigation of small-scale, non-Western societies.

Neopagan: See **Wiccan.**

nomadism: The constant mobility of human groups in pursuit of food (as in foraging) or a form of pastoralism in which the whole social group (men, women, children) and their animals move in search of pasture.

nonunilineal descent: See **bilateral descent.**

norm: An ideal cultural pattern that influences behavior in a society.

nuclear family: A family organized around the conjugal tie (the relationship between husband and wife). A nuclear family consists of a husband, a wife, and their children.

O

oasis: A fertile concentration of soil in a desert environment.

Oedipus complex: Defined by Freud as the sexual attachment of a male child to his mother, accompanied by hatred and jealousy of his father.

Oldowan tools: Stone tools made by *Homo habilis.*

omnivore: An animal that eats both plant and animal foods.

open system: A stratification system based primarily on achievement.

oricha: A Yoruba deity identified with a Catholic saint in Vodou and Santeria.

P

paleoanthropology: The subdiscipline of anthropology concerned with tracing the evolution of humankind in the fossil record.

parallel cousins: The children of a parent's same-sex siblings (mother's sisters, father's brothers).

participant-observation: The fieldwork technique that involves gathering cultural data by observing people's behavior and participating in their lives.

pastoralism: A food-getting strategy that depends on the care of domesticated herd animals.

pater: The socially designated father of a child, who may or may not be the biological father.

patrilineage: A lineage formed by descent in the male line.

patrilineal descent: A rule that affiliates children with kin of both sexes related through males only.

patrilocal residence: System under which a bride lives with her husband's family after marriage.

peasants: Food-producing populations that are incorporated politically, economically, and culturally into nation-states.

peonage: The practice of holding a person in bondage or partial slavery in order for them to work off a debt or serve a prison sentence.

per capita GNP: The total market value of all goods and services produced in a country in a year divided by the population of that country; often used as a general measure of the wealth of a nation and the quality of life of its citizens.

peyote: A small hallucinogenic cactus found in southern Texas and northern Mexico.

Peyote Road: The moral principles followed by members of the Native American Church.

pharmacopoeia: A collection of preparations used as medications.

phone: A sound made by humans and used in any language.

phoneme: The smallest significant unit of sound in a language. A phonemic system is the sound system of a language.

phonology: The sound system of a language.

phratry: A unilineal descent group composed of a number of clans whose members feel themselves to be closely related.

pillage: To strip an area of money, goods, or raw materials through the use of physical violence or the threat of violence.

plasticity: The ability of humans to change their behavior in response to a wide range of environmental demands.

political ideology: The shared beliefs and values that legitimize the distribution and use of power in a particular society.

political organization: The patterned ways in which power is legitimately used in a society to regulate behavior.

political process: The ways in which individuals and groups use power to achieve public goals.

polyandry: A rule permitting a woman to have more than one husband at a time.

polygamy: A rule allowing more than one spouse.

polygyny: A rule permitting a man to have more than one wife at a time.

polytheism: Belief in many gods.

population density: The number of people inhabiting a given area of land.

positivism: A philosophical system concerned with positive facts and phenomena and excluding speculation on origins or ultimate causes.

postmodernism: A theoretical perspective focusing on issues of power and voice. Postmodernists suggest that anthropological accounts are partial truths reflecting the background, training, and social position of their authors.

potlatch: A form of competitive giveaway practiced by the Kwakiutl and other groups of the Northwest Coast of North America.

power: The ability to control resources in one's own interest.

prayer: Any communication between people and spirits or gods in which people praise, plead, or request without assurance of results.

prehistoric: Societies for which we have no usable written records.

prelanguage: A language of human ancestors consisting of blended sounds; a hypothesized phase in the evolution of language.

prestige: Social honor or respect.

priest: One who is formally elected or appointed to a full-time religious office.

primate: A member of a biological order of mammals that includes human beings, apes, and monkeys as well as prosimians (lemurs, tarsirs, and others).

private/public dichotomy: A gender system in which women's status is lowered by their almost exclusive cultural identification with the home and children, while men are identified with public, prestigious economic and political roles.

productive resources: Material goods, natural resources, or information that is used to create other goods or information.

productivity: (1) The idea that humans can combine words and sounds into new meaningful utterances they have never before heard. (2) Yield per person per unit of land.

psychological anthropology: A specialization in cultural anthropology that seeks to understand the relation between psychological processes and cultural practices.

R

racialism: An ideology that claims there are biologically fixed races with different moral, intellectual, and physical characteristics that determine individual aptitudes and that such races can be ranked on a single hierarchy. Racialists propose that political action should be taken to order society so that it reflects this hierarchy.

racism: The belief that some human populations are superior to others because of inherited, genetically transmitted characteristics.

rain forest: Tropical woodland characterized by high rainfall and a dense canopy of broad-leaved evergreen trees.

random sample: A selection of items from a total set, chosen on a random, or unbiased, basis.

rank society: A society characterized by institutionalized differences in prestige but no important restrictions on access to basic resources.

rebellion: The attempt of a group within society to force a redistribution of resources and power.

reciprocity: A mutual give-and-take among people of equal status.

redistribution: A form of exchange in which goods are collected from or contributed by members of the group and then redistributed to the group, often in the form of ceremonial feasts.

reincorporation: The third phase of a rite of passage during which participants are returned to their community with a new status.

religion: A social process that helps to order society and provide its members with meaning, unity, peace of mind, and the degree of control over events they believe is possible.

replacement model: The theory that modern people evolved first in Africa and then spread out to inhabit virtually all the world, outcompeting or destroying other human populations in the process.

revitalization movement: A movement that proposes that society can be improved through the adoption of a set of new religious beliefs.

revolution: An attempt to overthrow an existing form of political organization.

rickets: A childhood disease characterized by softening and bending of leg and pelvis bones. Rickets is related to dietary insufficiency of vitamin D and/or calcium.

rite of intensification: A ritual structured to reinforce the values and norms of a community and to strengthen group identity.

rite of passage: A ritual that marks a person's transition from one status to another.

ritual: A patterned act that involves the manipulation of religious symbols.

S

sacred narratives: Stories held to be holy and true by members of a religious tradition. Sacred narratives tell of historical events, heroes, gods, spirits, and the origin of all things.

sacrifice: An offering made to increase the efficacy of a prayer or the religious purity of an individual.

Sapir–Whorf hypothesis: The hypothesis that perceptions and understandings of time, space, and matter are conditioned by the structure of a language.

scapulomancy: Divination using the shoulder blade of an animal.

sedentary: Settled, living in one place.

segmentary lineage system: A form of sociopolitical organization in which multiple descent groups (usually patrilineages) form at different levels and function in different contexts.

semantics: The subsystem of a language that relates form to meaning.

separation: The first stage of a rite of passage in which individuals are removed from their community or status.

sex: The biological difference between male and female.

shaman: An individual who is socially recognized as having the ability to mediate between the world of humanity and the world of gods or spirits but who is not a recognized official of any religious organization.

slash and burn: See **swidden.**

social birth: Time at which an infant is considered a person.

social complexity: The number of groups and their interrelationships in a society.

social differentiation: The relative access individuals and groups have to basic material resources, wealth, power, and prestige.

social mobility: Movement from one social class to another.

social stratification: A system of institutionalized inequalities of wealth, power, and prestige.

society: The set of social relationships among people in their status and roles within a given geographical area.

sociobiology: A theoretical perspective that explores the relationship between human cultural behavior and genetics.

sociolinguistics: A subdiscipline of anthropology that focuses on speech performance.

sorcery: The conscious and intentional use of magic.

sororal polygyny: A form of polygyny in which a man marries sisters.

sororate: The custom whereby, when a man's wife dies, her sister is given to him as a wife.

species: In biological classification, a group of organisms whose members are similar to one another and are able to reproduce with one another but not with members of other species.

Standard Spoken American English (SSAE): The form of English spoken by most of the American middle class.

state: A hierarchical, centralized form of political organization in which a central government has a legal monopoly over the use of force.

stratified society: A society characterized by formal, permanent social and economic inequality in which some people are denied access to basic resources.

structural anthropology: A theoretical perspective that holds that all cultures reflect similar deep, underlying patterns and that anthropologists should attempt to decipher these patterns.

structural linguistics: See **descriptive linguistics.**

subculture: A system of perceptions, values, beliefs, and customs that are significantly different from those of a larger, dominant culture within the same society.

subsistence strategies: The ways in which societies transform the material resources of the environment into food, clothing, and shelter.

succession: The transfer of office or social position between generations.

swidden (slash and burn): A form of cultivation in which a field is cleared by felling the trees and burning the brush.

symbol: Something that stands for something else; central to culture.

syncretism: The merging of elements of two or more religious traditions to produce a new religion.

syntax: The part of grammar that has to do with the arrangement of words to form phrases and sentences.

T

termite fishing: The learned use of twigs or blades of grass to extract termites from their mounds characteristic of some groups of chimpanzees.

Tirailleurs Sénégalais: Regiments of the French army recruited and drafted from France's African colonial possessions between the mid-nineteenth century and 1960.

totem: An animal or plant, or other aspect of the natural world held to be ancestral or to have other intimate relationships with members of a group.

totemism: Religious practices centered around animals, plants, or other aspects of the natural world held to be ancestral or to have other intimate relationships with members of a group.

transculturation: The transformation of adopted cultural traits, resulting in new cultural forms.

transhumance: A pastoralist pattern in which herd animals are moved regularly throughout the year to different areas as pasture becomes available.

Transnationalism: A pattern of immigration in which immigrants maintain close social and economic ties with their families and cultures in their homelands.

tribe: A culturally distinct population whose members consider themselves descended from the same ancestor.

trickster: A supernatural entity that does not act in the best interests of humans.

two-spirit role: An alternative gender role in native North America (formerly called *berdache*).

U

unilineal descent: A rule specifying that membership in a descent group is based on links through either the maternal or the paternal line, but not both.

universal grammar: A basic set of principles, conditions, and rules that underlie all languages.

V

values: Culturally defined ideas of what is true, right, and beautiful.

vassalage: A condition of hereditary bondage in which the use of land is granted in return for payment, homage, and military service or its equivalent.

"Venus" figurines: Small stylized statues of females made in a variety of materials by early modern humans.

vitalism: A religious movement that looks toward the creation of a utopian future that does not resemble a past golden age.

VOC: The Dutch East India Company (Verenigde Oestendische Compagnie), after its Dutch initials.

voluntary association: A social group based on voluntary membership, typically found in complex, urban societies.

voluntary minorities: Groups of people who have voluntarily migrated to the United States.

W

war (warfare): A formally organized and culturally recognized pattern of collective violence directed toward other societies, or between segments within a larger society.

wealth: The accumulation of material resources or access to the means of producing these resources.

Wiccan: A member of a new religion that claims descent from pre-Christian nature worship; a modern-day witch.

witchcraft: The ability to harm others by harboring malevolent thoughts about them; the practice of sorcery.

word: The smallest part of a sentence that can be said alone and still retain its meaning.

World Bank: An agency of the United Nations, officially called the International Bank for Reconstruction and Development, that provides loans to promote international trade and economic development, especially to poor nations.

Z

zoomorphic: Having an animal shape.

REFERENCES

Aberle, David F., Urie Bronfenbrenner, Eckhard Hess, Daniel Miller, David Schneider, and James Spuhler. 1963. "The Incest Taboo and Mating Patterns of Animals." *American Anthropologist* 65: 253–265.

Abrahams, Roger D. 1970. *Deep Down in the Jungle.* Chicago: Aldine.

Abu-Lughod, Lila. 1987. *Veiled Sentiments: Honor and Poetry in a Bedouin Society.* Berkeley: University of California Press.

Abu-Lughod, Lila D. 1993. *Writing Women's Worlds: Bedouin Stories.* Berkeley: University of California Press.

Acheson, James M. 1989. "Management of Common-Property Resources." In S. Plattner (Ed.), *Economic Anthropology.* (pp. 351–378). Stanford, CA: Stanford University Press.

Adams, Kathleen M. 1990. "Cultural Commoditization in Tana Toraja, Indonesia." *Cultural Survival Quarterly* 40(1): 31–34.

Adams, Kathleen M. 1993. "Theologians, Tourists and Thieves: The Torajan Effigy of the Dead in Modernizing Indonesia." *Kyoto Journal* 22:38–45.

Adams, Kathleen M. 1995. "Making-Up the Toraja? The Appropriation of Tourism, Anthropology, and Museums for Politics in Upland Sulawesi, Indonesia." *Ethnology* 34:143–152.

AFL-CIO. 1995. "NAFTAmath: A Tale of Two Countries." AFL-CIO Discussion Paper, June 12.

Albers, Patricia C. 1989. "From Illusion to Illumination: Anthropological Studies of American Indian Women." In S. Morgen (Ed.), *Gender and Anthropology: Critical Reviews for Research and Teaching* (pp. 132–170). Washington, DC: American Anthropological Association.

Alland, Alexander, Jr. 1972. *The Human Imperative.* New York: Columbia University Press.

Allen, Catherine. 1989. *The Hold Life Has: Coca and Cultural Identity in an Andean Community.* Washington, DC: Smithsonian Institution.

Allen, J. P. B., and Paul van Buren (Eds.). 1971. *Chomsky: Selected Readings.* London: Oxford University Press.

Allen, Theodore W. 1997. *The Invention of the White Race* (Vols. 1 and 2). London: Verso.

Alloula, Malek. 1986. *The Colonial Harem* (Myrna Gozich and Wlad Godzich, Trans.). Minneapolis: University of Minnesota Press.

Alonso, Ana Maria. 1994. "The Politics of Space, Time and Substance: State Formation, Nationalism, and Ethnicity." In B. Siegel (Ed.), *Annual Review of Anthropology* (Vol. 23, pp. 379–405). Stanford, CA: Stanford University Press.

Altorki, Soraya, and Camillia Fawzi El-Solh (Eds.). 1988. *Arab Women in the Field: Studying Your Own Society.* Syracuse, NY: Syracuse University Press.

Amadiume, Ifi. 1987. *Male Daughters, Female Husbands.* Atlantic Highlands, NJ: Zed Books.

American Anthropological Association. 1983. *Professional Ethics: Statements and Procedures.* Washington, DC: Author.

American Anthropological Association. n.d. *Careers in Anthropology: Anthropology Education for the 21st Century.* Washington, DC: Author.

Amit-Talai, Vered, and Helena Wulff (Eds.). 1995. *Youth Cultures: A Cross Cultural Perspective.* London: Routledge.

Amnesty International. 1999. *In the Firing Line: War and Children's Rights.* London: Author.

Anagnost, Ana. 1989. "Transformations of Gender in Modern China." In S. Morgen (Ed.), *Gender in Anthropology: Critical Reviews for Research and Teaching*

(pp. 313–342). Washington DC: American Anthropological Association.

Anderson, Jervis. 1996. "Black and Blue." *The New Yorker,* April 29–May 6, pp. 62–64.

Anderson, Margaret L., and Patricia Hill Collins (Eds.). 1995. *Race, Class, and Gender: An Anthology* (2nd ed.). Belmont, CA: Wadsworth.

Andrews, George Reid. 1992. "Racial Inequality in Brazil and the United States: A Statistical Comparison." *Journal of Social History* 26(2):229–263.

Angotti, Thomas. 1993. *Metropolis 2000: Planning, Poverty, and Politics.* London: Routledge.

Arens, William. 1975. "The Great American Football Ritual." *Natural History* 84:72–80.

Arens, William. 1976. "Professional Football: An American Symbol and Ritual." In W. Arens and S. P. Montague (Eds.), *The American Dimension* (pp. 1–9). Port Washington, NY: Alfred.

Arens, William. 1979. *The Man Eating Myth: Anthropology and Anthropophagy.* New York: Oxford University Press.

Aries, Philippe. 1962. *Centuries of Childhood.* New York: Vintage.

Arnould, Eric J. 1989. Anthropology and West African Development: A Political Economic Critique and Auto-Critique. *Human Organization* 48: 135–148.

Arth, Malcolm. 1972. "Aging: A Cross-cultural Perspective." In R. K. Donald, P. Kent, and Sylvia Sherwood (Eds.), *Research Planning and Action for the Elderly: The Power and Potential of Social Science* (pp. 352–364). New York: Behavioral Publications.

Avruch, Kevin. 1998. *Culture and Conflict Resolution.* Washington, DC: United States Institute of Peace.

Babcock, Barbara. 1995. "Marketing Maria: The Tribal Artist in the Age of Mechanical Reproduction." In Brenda Jo Bright and Liza Bakewell (Eds.), *Looking High and Low: Art and Cultural Identity* (pp. 125–150). Tucson: University of Arizona Press.

Baker, Brenda J. 1994. "Pilgrims' Progress and Praying Indians: The Biocultural Consequences of Contact in Southern New England." In C. S. Larsen and G. R. Miller (Eds.), *In the Wake of Contact: Biological Responses to Conquest* (pp. 35–45). New York: Wiley.

Baker, Lee D. 1998. "Unraveling the Boasian Discourse: The Racial Politics of 'Culture' in School Desegregation 1944–1954." *Transforming Anthropology* 7(1):15–32.

Baker, Paul T. (Ed.). 1978. *The Biology of High Altitude Peoples.* Cambridge: Cambridge University Press.

Baker, Randall. 1981. "'Development' and the Pastoral People of Karamoja, Northeastern Uganda: An Example of Treatment Symptoms." In D. Bates and S. Lees (Eds.), *Contemporary Anthropology: An Anthology* (pp. 66–78). New York: Knopf.

Balick, Michael J., Elaine Elisabetsky, and Sarah A. Laird (Eds.). 1996. *Medicinal Resources of the Tropical Forest: Biodiversity and Its Importance to Human Health.* New York: Columbia University Press.

Balikci, Asen. 1970. *The Netsilik Eskimo.* Prospect Heights, IL: Waveland.

Barber, Benjamin R. 1992, March. "Jihad vs. McWorld." *Atlantic Monthly,* pp. 53–65.

Barfield, Thomas J. 1993. *The Nomadic Alternative.* Englewood Cliffs, NJ: Prentice Hall.

Barker, Joan C. 1999. *Danger, Duty, and Disillusion: The Worldview of a Los Angeles Police Officer.* Prospect Heights, IL: Waveland.

Barlow, Kathleen. 1995. "Achieving Womanhood and the Achievements of Women in Murik Society: Cult Initiation, Gender Complementarity, and the Prestige of Women." In Nancy C. Lutkehaus and Paul B. Roscoe (Eds.), *Gender Rituals: Female Initiation in Melanesia* (pp. 85–112). New York: Routledge.

Barnes-Dean, Virginia Lee. 1989. "Clitoridectomy and Infibulation." *Cultural Survival Quarterly* 9(2): 26–30.

Barrera Caraza, Estanislao. 1995. La Virgen de Guadalupe en la cultura Otomi. *America Indigena* 55(3): 139–159.

Barth, Fredrik. 1964. *Nomads of South Persia.* New York: Humanities Press.

Barth, Fredrik. 1998. *Ethnic Groups and Boundaries: The Social Organization of Culture Difference.* Prospect Heights, IL: Waveland. (Originally published 1969)

Bascom, William. 1970. "Ponapean Prestige Economy." In T. G. Harding and B. J. Wallace (Eds.), *Cultures of the Pacific: Selected Readings* (pp. 85–94). New York: Free Press.

Bassani, Ezio, and William Fagg. 1988. *Africa and the Renaissance: Art in Ivory.* New York: Center for African Art.

Basso, Keith. 1979. *Portraits of "The Whitemen".* New York: Cambridge University Press.

Bates, Daniel G. 1998. *Human Adaptive Strategies: Ecology, Culture, and Politics.* Boston: Allyn and Bacon.

Bates, Daniel G., and Susan H. Lees (Eds.). 1996. *Cast Studies in Human Ecology.* New York: Plenum.

Bates, Marston. 1967. *Gluttons and Libertines: Human Problems of Being Natural.* New York: Random House.

Battaglia, Deborah. 1992. "The Body in the Gift: Memory and Forgetting in Sabarl Mortuary Exchange." *American Ethnologist* 19:3–18.

Baum, A., and V. M. Epstein (Eds.). 1978. *Human Response to Crowding.* New York: Wiley.

Behar, Ruth, and Deborah A. Gordon (Eds.). 1995. *Women Writing Culture.* Berkeley: University of California Press.

Beidelman, Thomas O. 1966. "The Ox and Nuer Sacrifice." *Man* 1:453–467.

Beidelman, Thomas O. 1971. *The Kaguru: A Matrilineal People of East Africa.* New York: Holt, Rinehart and Winston.

Bell, D. 1981. "Women's Business Is Hard Work: Central Australian Aboriginal Women's Love Rituals." *Signs* 7:318–337.

Benedict, Ruth. 1934. "Anthropology and the Abnormal." *Journal of General Psychology* 10:791–808.

Benedict, Ruth. 1940. *Race: Science and Politics.* New York: Viking.

Benedict, Ruth. 1946. *The Chrysanthemum and the Sword.* Boston: Houghton Mifflin.

Benedict, Ruth. 1961. *Patterns of Culture.* Boston: Houghton and Mifflin. (Originally published 1934)

Benet, Sula. 1976. *How to Live to Be 100: The Lifestyle of the People of the Caucasus.* New York: Dial Press.

Benfer, Robert A., Jr. 1996. "Science and Antiscience in Anthropology." *Anthropology Newsletter* 37(4): 74,76.

Bennion, Janet. 1998. *Women of Principle: Female Networking in Contemporary Mormon Polygyny.* New York: Oxford University Press.

Benson, Janet E. 1999. "Undocumented Immigrants and the Meatpacking Industry in the Midwest." In D. W. Haines and K. E. Rosenblum (Eds.), *Illegal Immigration in America: A Reference Handbook* (pp. 172–192). Westport, CT: Greenwood.

427

Berdan, Frances F. 1982. *The Aztecs of Central Mexico: An Imperial Society.* New York: Holt, Rinehart and Winston.

Berdan, Frances F. 1989. "Trade and Markets in Precapitalist States." In S. Plattner (Ed.), *Economic Anthropology* (pp. 78–107). Stanford, CA: Stanford University Press.

Bereiter, Carl, and Siegfried Engelmann. 1966. *Teaching Disadvantaged Children in Preschool.* Englewood Cliffs, NJ: Prentice Hall.

Berreman, Gerald D. 1959. "Caste in India and the United States." *American Journal of Sociology* 66: 120–127.

Berreman, Gerald D. 1962. *Behind Many Masks: Ethnography and Impression Management in a Himalayan Village.* Ithaca, NY: Cornell University Press.

Berreman, Gerald D. 1981. *Social Inequality: Comparative and Developmental Approaches.* New York: Academic Press.

Berreman, Gerald D. 1988. "Race, Caste, and Other Invidious Distinctions in Social Stratification." In J. Cole (Ed.), *Anthropology for the Nineties: Introductory Readings* (pp. 485–518). New York: Free Press.

Berreman, Gerald D. 1990. "The Incredible Tasaday: Deconstructing the Myth of Stone-Age People." *Cultural Survival Quarterly* 15(1):3–25.

Besnier, Niko. 1996. "Polynesian Gender Liminality Through Time and Space." In G. Herdt (Ed.), *Third Sex, Third Gender: Beyond Sexual Dimorphism in Culture and History* (pp. 285–328). New York: Zone.

Bettelheim, Bruno. 1962. *Symbolic Wounds* (rev. ed.). New York: Collier.

Birdwhistell, R. 1955. Background to Kinesics. *ETC* 13:10–18.

Bitterli, Urs. 1986. *Cultures in Conflict: Encounters Between European and Non-European Cultures, 1432–1800.* Stanford, CA: Stanford University Press.

Blackwood, Evelyn. 1984. "Sexuality and Gender in Certain Native American Tribes: The Case of Cross-Gender Females." *Signs: Journal of Women in Culture and Society* 10:27–42.

Blackwood, Evelyn. 2000. *Webs of Power: Women, Kin, and Community in a Sumatran Village.* New York: Rowman and Littlefield.

Boas, Franz. 1988a. "The Limitations of the Comparative Method of Anthropology." In P. Bohannan and M. Glazer (Eds.), *High Points in Anthropology* (2nd ed.) (pp. 85–93). New York: McGraw-Hill. (Originally published 1896)

Boas, Franz. 1988b. *Race, Language, and Culture.* Chicago: University of Chicago Press. (Originally published 1940)

Boas, Noel T., and Alan J. Almquist. 1999. *Essentials of Biological Anthropology.* Upper Saddle River, NJ: Prentice Hall.

Bodley, John H. 1999. *Victims of Progress* (4th ed.). Mountain View, CA: Mayfield.

Bodley, John H. 2000. *Cultural Anthropology: Tribes, States, and the Global System* (3rd ed.). Mountain View, CA: Mayfield.

Bonsignore, John J. 1992. "Multinational Corporations: Getting Started." *Focus on Law Studies* 7(1):10–11.

Bonvillain, Nancy. 1997. *Language, Culture, and Communication* (2nd ed.). Englewood Cliffs, NJ: Prentice Hall.

Bordes, Francois. 1968. *The Old Stone Age.* New York: McGraw-Hill.

Borgerhoff Mulder, Monique. 1995. "Bridewealth and Its Correlates: Quantifying Changes over Time." *Current Anthropology* 36:573–603.

Borofsky, Robert. 1994. "On the Knowledge and Knowing of Cultural Activities." In R. Borofsky (Ed.), *Assessing Cultural Anthropology* (pp. 331–347). New York: McGraw-Hill.

Bossen, Laurel. 1989. "Women and Economic Institutions." In S. Plattner, (Ed.), *Economic Anthropology* (pp. 318–350). Stanford, CA: Stanford University Press.

Bott, Elizabeth. 1957. *Family and Social Network: Roles, Norms, and Extended Relationships in Ordinary Urban Families.* London: Tavistock.

Bourgois, Philippe. 1989. "Crack in Spanish Harlem: Culture and Economy in the Inner-City." *Anthropology Today* 5(4):6–11.

Bourgois, Philippe. 1996. "Confronting Anthropology, Education, and Inner-City Apartheid." *American Anthropologist* 98:249–265.

Bowen, Elenore Smith [Laura Bohannan]. 1964. *Return to Laughter.* New York: Anchor/Doubleday.

Boxer, C. R. 1965. *The Dutch Seaborne Empire 1600–1800.* New York: Knopf.

Bracey, Dorothy. 1985. "The System of Justice and the Concept of Human Nature in the People's Republic of China." *Justice Quarterly* 2:139–144.

Bracken, Christopher. 1997. *The Potlatch Papers: A Colonial Case History.* Chicago: University of Chicago Press.

Bradby, Barbara. 1999. "Will I Return or Not? Migrant Women in Bolivia Negotiate Hospital Birth." *Women's Studies International Forum* 22:287–301.

Bradford, Phillips Verner, and Harvey Blume. 1992. *Ota Benga: The Pygmy in the Zoo.* New York: Delta.

Brady, Ivan. 1982. "The Man Eating Myth." *American Anthropologist* 84:595–610.

Brain, James L. 1989. "An Anthropological Perspective on the Witchcraze." In Jean R. Brink, A. P. Coudert, and M. C. Horowitz (Eds.), *The Politics of Gender in Early Modern Europe* (pp. 15–27). Kirksville, MO: Sixteenth Century Journal Publishers.

Brandes, Stanley. 1981. "Like Wounded Stags: Male Sexual Ideology in an Andalusian Town." In S. B. Ortner and H. Whitehead (Eds.), *Sexual Meanings: The Cultural Construction of Gender and Sexuality* (pp. 216–239). Cambridge: Cambridge University Press.

Brecher, Jeremy. 1972. *Strike.* San Francisco: Straight Arrow Books.

Briggs, Jean L. 1991. "Expecting the Unexpected: Canadian Inuit Training for an Experimental Lifestyle." *Ethos* 19:259–287.

Briggs, Jean L. 1998. *Inuit Morality Play: The Emotional Education of a Three-Year-Old.* New Haven, CT: Yale University Press.

Bright, Brenda Jo, and Liza Bakewell (Eds.). 1995. *Looking High and Low: Art and Cultural Identity.* Tucson: University of Arizona.

Brito, Silvester J. 1989. *The Way of a Peyote Roadman.* New York: Peter Lang.

Broadhead, Robert, Yael Van Hulst, and Douglas Heckathorn. 1999. "Termination of an Established Needle Exchange: A Study of Claims and Their Impact." *Social Problems* 46(1):48–56.

Brookfield, Harold C. 1988. "The New Great Age of Clearance and Beyond." In Julie Sloan Denslow and Christine Padoch (Eds.), *People of the Tropical Forest* (pp. 209–224). Berkeley: University of California Press.

Brooks, Charles R. 1989. *The Hare Krishnas in India.* Princeton, NJ: Princeton University Press.

Brosius, Peter J. 1999. "Green Dots, Pink Hearts: Displacing Politics from the Malaysian Rain Forest." *American Anthropologist* 101:36–57.

Brown, Judith. 1965. "A Cross Cultural Study of Female Initiation Rites." *American Anthropologist* 65: 837–855.

Brown, Judith. 1975. "Iroquois Women: An Ethnohistoric Note." In R. R. Reiter (Ed.), *Toward an Anthropology of Women* (pp. 235–251). New York: Monthly Review Press.

Brown, Karen McCarthy. 1991. *Mama Lola: A Vodou Priestess in Brooklyn.* Berkeley: University of California Press.

Brown, P., and A. Podelefsky. 1976. "Population Density, Agricultural Intensity, Land Tenure, and Group Size in the New Guinea Highlands." *Ethnology* 15:211–238.

Brownell, Susan. 1995. *Training the Body for China: Sports in the Moral Order of the People's Republic.* Chicago: University of Chicago Press.

Brumberg, Joan Jacobs. 1989. *Fasting Girls: The History of Anorexia Nervosa.* New York: Penguin.

Brumfiel, Elizabeth. 1991. "Weaving and Cooking: Women's Production in Aztec Mexico." In J. M. Gero and M. W. Conkey (Eds.), *Engendering Archaeology: Women and Prehistory* (pp. 224–251). Cambridge, MA: Basil Blackwell.

Bruner, Edward. 1996. "Tourism in Ghana: The Representation of Slavery and the Return of the Black Diaspora." *American Anthropologist* 98:290–304.

Buck, Pem Davidson. 1989. "Cargo-Cult Discourse: Myth and the Rationalization of Labor Relations in Papua New Guinea." *Dialectical Anthropology* 13:157–171.

Burbank, Victoria K. 1989. "Gender and Anthropology Curriculum: Aboriginal Australia." In S. Morgen (Ed.), *Gender and Anthropology: Critical Reviews for Research and Teaching* (pp. 116–131). Washington DC: American Anthropological Association.

Burenhult, Goran (Ed.). 1993. *The First Humans: Human Origins and History to 10,000 BC.* San Francisco: Harper.

Burgoon, Judee K., David B. Buller, and W. Gill Woodall. 1996. *Nonverbal Communication: The Unspoken Dialogue* (2nd ed.). New York: McGraw-Hill.

Burgos-DeBray, E. (Ed.). 1984. *I, Rigoberta Menchu: An Indian Woman in Guatemala* (A. Wright, Trans.). New York: Verso.

Burton, John W. 1992. "Representing Africa: Colonial Anthropology Revisited." *Journal of Asian and African Studies* 27:181–201.

Burton, Thomas G. 1993. *Serpent-handling Believers.* Knoxville: University of Tennessee Press.

Cancian, Frank. 1989. "Economic Behavior in Peasant Communities." In Stuart Plattner (Ed.), *Economic Anthropology* (pp. 127–170). Stanford, CA: Stanford University Press.

Cane, Scott. 1996. "Australian Aboriginal Subsistence in the Western Desert." In Daniel G. Bates and Susan H. Lees (Eds.), *Case Studies in Human Ecology* (pp. 17–51). New York: Plenum.

Cannon, Walter B. 1942. "The 'Voodoo' Death." *American Anthropologist* 44:169–180.

Cardillo, Cathy. 1997. "Violence Against Chinese Women: Defining the Culture Role." *Women's Rights Law Reporter* 19(1):85–96.

Carlson, Robert G., Harvey A. Siegal, Jichuan Wang, and Russel S. Flack. 1996. "Attitudes Toward Needle 'Sharing' Among Injection Drug Users: Combining Qualitative and Quantitative Research Methods." *Human Organization* 55:361–369.

Carmody, Denise Lardner, and John Tully Carmody. 1992. "Introduction." In D. L. Carmody and J. T. Carmody (Eds.), *The Range of Religion: An Introductory Reader* (pp. 1–6). New York: Macmillan.

Carneiro, Robert. 1970. "A Theory of the Origin of the State." *Science* 169:733–738.

Carneiro, Robert. 1981. "The Chiefdom: Precursor of the State." In Grant Jones and Robert Kautz (Eds.), *The Transition to Statehood in the New World* (pp. 37–79). Cambridge: Cambridge University Press.

Carneiro, Robert. 1988. "Indians of the Amazonian Forest." In J. S. Denslow and C. Padoch (Eds.), *People of the Tropical Rain Forest* (pp. 73–86). Berkeley: University of California Press.

Casey, Geraldine J. 1991. "Eleanor Leacock, Marvin Harris, and the Struggle over Warfare in Anthropology." In A. E. Hunter (Ed.), *On Peace, War and Gender: A Challenge to Genetic Explanations* (pp. 1–33). New York: Feminist Press.

Cashdan, Elizabeth. 1989. "Hunters and Gatherers: Economic Behavior in Bands." In S. Plattner (Ed.), *Economic Anthropology* (pp. 21–48). Stanford, CA: Stanford University Press.

Cernea, Michael M. 1995. "Social Organization and Development Anthropology." *Human Organization* 54:340–352.

Cerroni-Long, E. L. 1993. "Teaching Ethnicity in the USA: An Anthropological Model." *Journal of Ethno-Development* 2(1):106–112.

Cerroni-Long, E. L. 1995. "Introduction." In E. L. Cerroni-Long (Ed.), *Insider Anthropology* (Napa Bulletin, Vol. 16). Washington, DC: American Anthropological Association.

Chagnon, Napoleon. 1997. *Yanomamo* (5th ed.). Fort Worth: Harcourt Brace Jovanovich.

Chevannes, Barry. 1994. *Rastafari: Roots and Ideology.* Syracuse, NY: Syracuse University Press.

Chierici, Rose-Marie. 1996. "Lifting the Veil of Anonymity: A Haitian Refugee's Tale: Lessons for the Anthropologist." *Identities* 2:407–417.

Childe, V. Gordon. 1951. *Man Makes Himself.* New York: Mentor.

Chodorow, Nancy. 1974. "Family Structure and Feminine Personality." In M. Rosaldo and L. Lamphere (Eds.), *Women, Culture, and Society* (pp. 43–66). Stanford, CA: Stanford University Press.

Chodorow, Nancy. 1978. *The Reproduction of Mothering.* Berkeley: University of California Press.

Choi, Soo Ho. 1995. "The Struggle for Family Succession and Inheritance in a Rural Korean Village." *Journal of Anthropological Research* 51:329–346.

Chomsky, Noam. 1965. *Syntactic Structures.* London: Mouton.

Chomsky, Noam. 1975. *The Logical Structure of Linguistic Theory.* New York: Plenum Press.

Clark, J. D. 1989. "The Origins and Spread of Modern Humans: A Broad Perspective on the African Evidence." In P. Mellars and C. Stringer (Eds.), *The Human Revolution: Behavioural and Biological Perspectives on the Origins of Modern Humans* (pp. 565–588). Edinburgh: Edinburgh University Press.

Clark, Margaret. 1973. "Contributions of Cultural Anthropology to the Study of the Aged." In L. Nader and T. W. Maretski (Eds.), *Cultural Illness and Health* (pp. 78–88). Washington, DC: American Anthropological Association.

Clarke, Mari H. 2000. "On the Road Again: International Development Consulting." In Paula Sabloff (Ed.), *Careers in Anthropology: Profiles of Practitioner Anthropologists* (pp. 71–74). Washington, DC: National Association for the Practice of Anthropology.

Clendinnen, Inga. 1991. *Aztecs: An Interpretation.* Cambridge: Cambridge University Press.

Clifford, James. 1988. *The Predicament of Culture: Twentieth-Century Ethnography, Literature, and Art.* Cambridge, MA: Harvard University Press.

Clifford, James, and George E. Marcus (Eds.). 1986. *Writing Culture: The Poetics and Politics of Ethnography.* Berkeley: University of California Press.

Cohen, Abner. 1969. *Custom and Politics in Urban Africa.* London: Routledge and Kegan Paul.

Cohen, Lawrence. 1998. *No Aging in India: Alzheimer's, the Bad Family, and Other Modern Things.* Berkeley: University of California Press.

Cohen, Ronald, and Elman R. Service. 1978. *Origins of the State: The Anthropology of Political Evolution.* Philadelphia: Institute for the Study of Human Issues.

Cohen, Yehudi. 1971. *Man in Adaptation: The Institutional Framework.* Chicago: Aldine.

Condon, Richard G., with Julia Ogina and the Holman Elders. 1996. *The Northern Copper Inuit: A History.* Toronto: University of Toronto Press.

Connolloy, Bob, and Robin Anderson. 1987. *First Contact: New Guinea's Highlanders Encounter the Outside World.* New York: Penguin.

Conrad, Geoffrey W., and Arthur Demarest. 1984. *Religion and Empire: The Dynamics of Aztec and Inca Expansionism.* Cambridge: Cambridge University Press.

Coquery-Vidrovitch, Catherine. 1988. *Africa: Endurance and Change South of the Sahara.* Berkeley: University of California Press.

Corbin, Beth. 1994. "Deportation vs. Female Genital Mutilation." *National NOW Times Special Edition,* June 5.

Counts, Dorothy Ayers, and David R. Counts. 1985. *Aging and Its Transformations: Moving Toward Death in Pacific Societies.* New York: Lanham/University Press of America.

Covington, Dennis. 1995. *Salvation on Sand Mountain: Snake Handling and Redemption in Southern Appalachia.* Reading, MA: Addison-Wesley.

Crapanzano, Vincent. 1980. *Tuhami: Portrait of a Moroccan.* Chicago: University of Chicago Press.

Cucciari, Salvatore. 1981. "The Gender Revolution and the Transition from Bisexual Horde to Patrilocal Band: The Origins of Gender Hierarchy." In S. B. Ortner and H. Whitehead (Eds.), *Sexual Meanings: The Cultural Construction of Gender and Sexuality* (pp. 31–79). Cambridge: Cambridge University Press.

Culotta, Elizabeth. 1999. "Neanderthals Were Cannibals, Bones Show." *Science* 286:18b–19b.

Cunningham, Lawrence S., John Kelsay, R. Maurice Barineau, and Heather Jo McVoy. 1995. *The Sacred Quest: An Invitation to the Study of Religion* (2nd ed.). Englewood Cliffs, NJ: Prentice Hall.

D'Andrade, Roy G. 1995. "What Do You Think You're Doing?" *Anthropology Newsletter* 36(7):1, 4.

D'Andrade, Roy G., Nancy Scheper Hughes, et al. 1995. "Objectivity and Militancy: A Debate." *Current Anthropology* 36:399–420.

Dalton, George. 1961. "Economic Theory and Primitive Society." *American Anthropologist* 63:1–25.

Dalton, George. 1967. "Primitive Money." In G. Dalton (Ed.), *Tribal and Peasant Economics* (pp. 254–281). Garden City, NY: Natural History Press.

Damon, Frederick H. 1983. "What Moves the Kula: Opening and Closing Gifts on Woodlark Island." In J. W. Leach and E. Leach (Eds.), *The Kula: New Perspectives on Massim Exchange* (pp. 309–342). Cambridge: Cambridge University Press.

Danaher, Kevin, and Michael Shellenberger (Eds.). 1995. *Fighting for the Soul of Brazil.* New York: Monthly Review Press.

Dart, Raymond Arthur. 1996. "The Discovery of *Australopithecus.*" In Brian M. Fagan (Ed.), *Eyewitness to Discovery* (pp. 37–45). New York: Oxford University Press. (Originally published 1959)

Dasgupta, B. 1980. *The New Agrarian Technology and India.* New York: Macmillan.

Daugherty, Mary Lee. 1993. "Serpent-Handling as Sacrament." In A. C. Lehmann and J. E. Myers (Eds.), *Magic, Witchcraft, and Religion: An Anthropological Study of the Supernatural* (pp. 343–348). Mountain View, CA: Mayfield. (Originally published 1976)

De Vos, George, and Lola Romanucci-Ross. 1995. "Ethnic Identity: A Psychocultural Perspective." In Lola Romanucci-Ross and George A. De Vos (Eds.), *Ethnic Identity: Creation, Conflict, and Accommodation* (3rd ed.) (pp. 349–380). London: Sage.

De Vos, George A., and Hiroshi Wagatsuma. 1966. *Japan's Invisible Race: Case Studies in Culture and Personality.* Berkeley: University of California Press.

de Waal Malefijt, Annemarie. 1968. *Religion and Culture: An Introduction to the Anthropology of Religion.* Prospect Heights, IL: Waveland Press.

Defleur, Alban, Tim White, and Patricia Valensi. 1999. "Neanderthal Cannibalism at Moula-Guercy, Ardeche, France." *Science* 286:128–131.

Dei, Kojo. 1996. "Illicit Drugs and Minority Youths in a Low-Income Urban Neighborhood." Unpublished doctoral dissertation, Columbia University, New York.

Dentan, Robert Knox. 1979. *The Semai: A Nonviolent People of Malaya* (Fieldwork Edition). New York: Holt, Rinehart and Winston.

Desjarlais, Robert. 1997. *Shelter Blues: Sanity and Selfhood Among the Homeless.* Philadelphia: University of Pennsylvania Press.

Destexhe, Alain. 1995. *Rwanda and Genocide in the Twentieth Century* (Alison Marschner, Trans.). New York: New York University Press.

Dettwyler, Katherine A. 1994. *Dancing Skeletons: Life and Death in West Africa.* Prospect Heights, IL: Waveland.

DeVita, Phillip R. 2000. *Stumbling Towards Truth: Anthropologists at Work.* Prospect Heights, IL: Waveland.

DeVita, Phillip R., and James D. Armstrong. 1993. *Distant Mirrors: America as a Foreign Culture.* Belmont, CA: Wadsworth.

di Leonardo, Micaela. 1984. *The Varieties of Ethnic Experience: Kinship, Class, and Gender among California Italian-Americans.* Ithaca, NY: Cornell University Press.

di Leonardo, Micaela (Ed.). 1991. *Gender at the Crossroads of Knowledge: Feminist Anthropology in the Postmodern Era.* Berkeley: University of California Press.

di Leonardo, Micaela. 1998. *Exotics at Home: Anthropologies, Others, American Modernity.* Chicago: University of Chicago Press.

Diamond, Jared. 1992. "The Arrow of Disease." *Discover* 13(10):64–73.

Diamond, Jared. 1994. "Race Without Color." *Discover* 15(11):82–89.

Divale, William Tulio, and Marvin Harris. 1976. "Population, Warfare and the Male Supremacist Complex." *American Anthropologist* 78:521–538.

Dollard, John. 1937. *Caste and Class in a Southern Town.* New Haven, CT: Yale University Press.

Dombrowski, Kirk. 2000, March. "Comments on Richard Lee's 'Indigenism and Its Discontents.'" Paper presented at the annual meeting of the American Ethnological Society, Tampa, FL.

Dominguez, Virginia. 1986. *White by Definition.* New Brunswick, NJ: Rutgers University Press.

Douglas, Mary. 1970. *Purity and Danger.* Baltimore: Penguin.

Dow, James W. 1996. "The Cultural Context of Scientific Anthropology." *Anthropology Newsletter* 37(2):48.

Dozon, Jean-Pierre. 1985. "Les Bété: une creation coloniale." In J. L. Amselle and E. M'bokolo (Eds.), *Au Coeur de l'ethnie* (pp. 49–85). Paris: Editions La Decouvere.

Drucker, P., and R. F. Heizer. 1967. *To Make My Name Good.* Berkeley: University of California Press.

DuBois, Cora. 1944. *The People of Alor.* Minneapolis: University of Minnesota Press.

Duncan, David Ewing. 1995. *Hernando de Soto: A Savage Quest in the Americas.* New York: Crown.

Duncan, David James. 2000, March/April. "Salmon's Second Coming." *Sierra,* pp. 30–41.

Dundes, Alan (Ed.). 1980. *Into the Endzone for a Touchdown: A Psychoanalytic Consideration of American Football.* Bloomington: Indiana University Press.

Duneier, Mitchell. 1992. *Slim's Table: Race, Respectability, and Masculinity.* Chicago: University of Chicago Press.

Duranti, Alessandro. 1997. *Linguistic Anthropology.* Cambridge: Cambridge University Press.

Durkheim, Emile. 1961. *The Elementary Forms of the Religious Life.* New York: Collier. (Originally published 1915)

Durning, Alan Thein. 1994. "The Conundrum of Consumption." In L. A. Mazur (Ed.), *Beyond the Numbers: A Reader on Population, Consumption, and the Environment* (pp. 40–47). Washington, DC: Island Press.

Eaton, S. Boyd, and Melvin Konner. 1989. Ancient Genes and Modern Health. In A. Podolefsky and P. J. Brown (Eds.), *Applying Anthropology* (pp. 43–46). Mountain View, CA: Mayfield.

Echenberg, Myron. 1991. *Colonial Conscripts: The Tirailleurs Sénégalais in French West Africa, 1857–1960.* Portsmouth, NH: Heinemann.

Edgerton, Robert. 1992. *Sick Societies.* New York: Free Press.

Eggan, Fred. 1950. *The Social Organization of Western Pueblos.* Chicago: University of Chicago Press.

El Saadawi, Newal. 1980. *The Hidden Face of Eve.* London: Zed Books.

Elkin, A. P. 1967. "The Nature of Australian Totemism." In J. Middleton (Ed.), *Gods and Rituals.* (pp. 159–176). Garden City, NY: Natural History Press.

Ember, Melvin, and Carol R. Ember. 1971. "The Conditions Favoring Matrilocal vs. Patrilocal Residence." *American Anthropologist* 73:571–594.

Ember, Melvin, and Carol R. Ember. 1996. "Comparing Cultures: What Have We Learned from Cross-Cultural Research?" *Bulletin of the Council for General Anthropology* 2(2):1.

Engelmann, Siegfried, and Therese Englemann. 1966. *Give Your Child a Superior Mind: A Program for the Preschool Child.* New York: Simon and Schuster.

Erickson, Jon. 1995. *The Human Volcano: Population Growth as Geologic Force.* New York: Facts on File.

Estioko-Griffin, Agnes. 1986. "Daughters of the Forest." *Natural History* 5:37–42.

Evans-Pritchard, E. E. 1958. *Witchcraft, Oracles, and Magic among the Azande.* Oxford: Clarendon Press. (Originally published 1937)

Evans-Pritchard, E. E. 1967. "The Nuer Concept of Spirit in Its Relation to the Social Order." In J. Middleton (Ed.), *Myth and Cosmos* (pp. 109–126). Garden City, NY: Natural History Press.

Evans-Pritchard, E. E. 1968. *The Nuer.* Oxford: Clarendon Press. (Originally published 1940)

Fábrega, Horacio. 1997. *Evolution of Sickness and Healing.* Berkeley: University of California Press.

Fagan, R. 1993. "Primate Juveniles and Primate Play." In Michael E. Pereira and Lynn A. Fairbanks (Eds.), *Juvenile Primates: Life History, Development and Behavior* (pp. 182–196). New York: Oxford University Press.

Fairbanks, Lynn A. 1988. "Vervet Monkey Grandmothers: Interactions with Infant Offspring." *International Journal of Primatology* 9:425–441.

Falk, Dean. 1984, September. "The petrified brain." *Natural History,* pp. 36–39.

Falla, Ricardo. 1994. *Massacres in the Jungle.* Boulder, CO: Westview Press.

Farb, Peter. 1974. *Word Play: What Happens When People Talk.* New York: Knopf.

Farb, Peter. 1978. *Man's Rise to Civilization.* New York: Dutton.

Feinberg, Richard. 1986. "Market Economy and Changing Sex-Roles on a Polynesian Atoll." *Ethnology* 25:271–282.

Feinberg, Richard. 1994. "Contested Worlds: Politics of Culture and the Politics of Anthropology." *Anthropology and Humanism* 19:20–35.

Feldman, Douglas. 1986. *The Social Dimensions of AIDS: Method and Theory.* New York: Praeger.

Fenton, James. 1996. "A Short History of Anti-Hamitism." *New York Review of Books* 43(3):7–9.

Ferguson, R. Brian. 1984. *The Ecology and Political Economy of War: Anthropological Perspectives.* New York: Academic Press.

Ferguson, R. Brian. 1992. "A Savage Encounter: Western Contact and the Yanomamo War Complex." In R. B. Ferguson and N. L. Whitehead (Eds.), *War in the Tribal Zone: Expanding States and Indigenous Warfare* (pp. 199–227). Santa Fe, NM: School of American Research Press.

Ferguson, R. Brian, and Neil L. Whitehead (Eds.). 1992. *War in the Tribal Zone: Expanding States and Indigenous Warfare.* Santa Fe, NM: School of American Research Press.

Ferguson, T. J. 2000. "Applied Anthropology in the Management of Native American Cultural Resources: Archaeology, Ethnography, and History of Traditional Cultural Places." In P. L. W. Sabloff (Ed.), *Careers in Anthropology: Profiles of Practitioner Anthropologists* (pp. 15–17). Washington, DC: National Association of Practicing Anthropologists.

Fernandez Kelley, Maria Patricia. 1997. "Maquiladoras: The View from the Inside." In C. B. Brettell and C. F. Sargent (Eds.), *Gender in Cross-Cultural*

Perspective (2nd ed.) (pp. 525–537). Upper Saddle River, NJ: Prentice Hall.

Fernea, Elizabeth Warnock. 1995. *Children in the Muslim Middle East.* Austin: University of Texas Press.

Ferraro, Gary P. 1994. *The Cultural Dimension of International Business* (2nd ed.). Englewood Cliffs, NJ: Prentice-Hall.

Fetto, John. 1999, June. "Six Billion Served." *American Demographics,* p. 14. "A Field Full of Buttons." 1999. *The Economist,* April 3.

Fisher, Roger, and William Ury. 1981. *Getting to Yes: Negotiating Agreement Without Giving In.* New York: Penguin.

Fix, Michael, and Jeffrey Passel. 1994. *Immigration and Immigrants: Setting the Record Straight.* Washington, DC: Urban Institute.

Flannery, K. 1973. "The Origins of Agriculture." In B. J. Siegel (Ed.), *Annual Review of Anthropology* (pp. 271–310). Palo Alto, CA: Annual Reviews.

Fleagle, J. G. 1988. *Primate Adaptation and Evolution.* San Diego: Academic Press.

Flood, Merielle K. 1994. "Changing Gender Relations in Zinacantan, Mexico." *Research in Economic Anthropology* 15:145–173.

Foner, Eric. 1985. *Reconstruction: America's Unfinished Revolution 1863–1877.* New York: Harper.

Fontaine, Pierre-Michel. 1985. *Race, Class, and Power in Brazil.* Los Angeles: University of California, Center for Afro-American Studies.

"For Indian Church, A Critical Shortage." 1995. *New York Times,* March 20, p. A8.

Ford, Clellan S. 1938. "The Role of a Fijian Chief." *American Sociological Review* 3:542–550.

Forde, Daryll. 1950. "Double Descent among the Yako." In A. R. Radcliffe-Brown and D. Forde (Eds.), *African Systems of Kinship and Marriage* (pp. 285–332). London: Oxford University Press.

Fordyce, E. James, Roy Shum, Tejinder Pal Singh, and Susan Forlenza. 1998. "Economic and Geographic Diversity in AIDS Incidence among HIV Exposure Groups in New York City: 1983–1995." *AIDS and Public Policy Journal* 13(3):103–114.

Fortune, Reo F. 1932. *Sorcerers of Dobu.* Prospect Heights, IL: Waveland Press.

Foster, Robert J. 1991. "Making National Cultures in the Global Ecumene." *Annual Reviews of Anthropology* 20:235–260.

Fouts, Roger. 1983. "Chimpanzee Language and Elephant Tails: A Theoretical Synthesis." In J. D. Luce and H. T. Wilder (Eds.), *Language in Primates* (pp. 63–75). New York: Springer-Verlag.

Fouts, Roger, and Deborah Fouts. 1989. "Loulis in Conversation with the Cross-Fostered Chimpanzees." In R. Allen Gardner, Beatrix T. Gardner, and Thomas Van Cantfort (Eds.), *Teaching Sign Language to Chimpanzees* (pp. 293–307). Albany: State University of New York Press.

Francher, J. Scott. 1973. "'It's the Pepsi Generation': Accelerated Aging and the Television Commercial." *International Journal of Aging and Human Development* 4: 245–255.

Frankel, Francine R. 1971. *India's Green Revolution: Economic Gains and Political Costs.* Princeton, NJ: Princeton University Press.

Frankenberg, Ruth. 1993. *White Women, Race Matters: The Social Construction of Whiteness.* Minneapolis: University of Minnesota Press.

Frankl, Victor. 1946. *Man's Search for Meaning.* Boston: Beacon Press.

Freed, Ruth S., and Stanley A. Freed. 1985. "The Psychomedical Case History of a Low-Caste Woman of North India." *Anthropological Papers of the American Museum of Natural History* 60(2).

Fried, Morton. 1967. *The Evolution of Political Society.* New York: Random House.

Friedan, Betty. 1993. *The Fountain of Age.* New York: Simon and Schuster.

Friedheim, William, with Ronald Jackson (Eds.). 1996. *Freedom's Unfinished Revolution: An Inquiry into the Civil War and Reconstruction.* New York: New Press.

Friedl, Ernestine. 1975. *Women and Men: An Anthropologist's View.* New York: Holt, Rinehart and Winston.

Friedman, Ariella, and Judith Todd. 1994. "Kenyan Women Tell a Story: Interpersonal Power of Women in Three Subcultures in Kenya." *Sex Roles* 31: 533–546.

Friedman, Jonathan. 1992. "The Past in the Future: History and the Politics of Identity." *American Anthropologist* 94:837–859.

Fry, Douglas P., and Kaj Bjorkqvist (Eds.). 1997. *Cultural Variation and Conflict Resolution: Alternatives to Violence.* Mahwah, NJ: Erlbaum.

Fuller, Christopher J. (Ed.). 1995. *Caste Today.* Delhi: Oxford University Press.

Galanter, Marc. 1992. *Competing Equalities: Law and the Backward Classes in India.* Oxford: Oxford University Press.

Galaty, John G. 1986. "Introduction." In Tepilit Ole Saitoti, *The Worlds of a Maasai Warrior* (pp. xiv–xxi). New York: Random House.

Gallo, Patrick J. 1981. *Old Bread, New Wine: A Portrait of the Italian-Americans.* Chicago: Nelson-Hall.

Gardner, B. T., and R. A. Gardner. 1967. "Teaching Sign Language to a Chimpanzee." *Science* 165:664–672.

Gardner, Peter. 1966. "Symmetric Respect and Memorate Knowledge: The Structure and Ecology of Individualistic Culture." *Southwestern Journal of Anthropology* 22:389–413.

Gates, Hill. 1987. *Chinese Working Class Lives: Getting by in Taiwan.* Ithaca, NY: Cornell University Press.

Geertz, Clifford. 1963. *Agricultural Involution: The Process of Ecological Change in Indonesia.* Berkeley: University of California Press.

Geertz, Clifford. 1973a. "Deep Play: Notes on the Balinese Cockfight." In C. Geertz (Ed.), *The Interpretation of Cultures* (pp. 412–453). New York: Basic Books.

Geertz, Clifford (Ed.). 1973b. *The Interpretation of Cultures.* New York: Basic Books.

Geertz, Clifford. 1988. *Works and Lives: The Anthropologist as Author.* Stanford, CA: Stanford University Press.

Geertz, Clifford. 1995. "Culture War." *New York Review of Books* 15(19):4–6.

Ghosh, Anjan. 1991. "The Structure of Structure, or Appropriation of Anthropological Theory." *Review* 14(1):55–77.

Gibbs, James L., Jr. 1988. "The Kpelle Moot: A Therapeutic Model for the Informal Settlement of Disputes." In J. B. Cole (Ed.), *Anthropology of the Nineties* (pp. 347–359). New York: Free Press.

Gibson, Margaret A. 1997. "Ethnicity and School Performance: Complicating the Immigrant/Involuntary Minority Typology." *Anthropology and Education Quarterly* 28(3):431–454.

Gibson, Margaret A., and John Ogbu. 1991. *Minority Status and Schooling: A Comparative Study of Immigrant and Involuntary Minorities.* New York: Garland.

Gilliland, Mary. 1995. "Nationalism and Ethnogenesis in the Former Yugoslavia." In Lola Romanucci-Ross and George A. De Vos (Eds.), *Ethnic Identity: Creation, Conflict, and Accommodation* (3rd ed.) (pp. 197–221). London: Sage.

Gilmore, David D. 1990. *Manhood in the Making: Cultural Concepts of Masculinity.* New Haven, CT: Yale University Press.

Gilmore, David D. 1996. "Above and Below: Toward a Social Geometry of Gender." *American Anthropologist* 98:54–66.

Gimbutas, M. 1989. *The Language of the Goddess.* London: Thames and Hudson.

Gjerde, Jon. 1998. *Major Problems in American Immigration and Ethnic History.* Boston: Houghton Mifflin.

Glazer, Nathan. 1983. *Ethnic Dilemmas 1964–1982.* Cambridge, MA: Harvard University Press.

Glick-Schiller, Nina. 1992. "Transnationalism: A New Analytic Framework for Understanding Migration." In N. Glick-Schiller, L. Basch, and C. Szanton-Blanc (Eds.), *Towards a Transnational Perspective on Migration: Race, Class. Ethnicity and Nationalism*

Reconsidered (pp. 1–24). New York: New York Academy of Sciences.

Glick-Schiller, Nina, Linda Basch, and Christina Szanton-Blanc (Eds.). 1992. *Towards a Transnational Perspective on Migration: Race, Class, Ethnicity and Nationalism Reconsidered.* New York: New York Academy of Sciences.

Glucklich, Ariel. 1997. *The End of Magic.* New York: Oxford University Press.

Gmelch, George. 2000. "Baseball Magic." In James Spradley and David McCurdy (Eds.), *Conformity and Conflict* (pp. 322–331). Boston: Allyn and Bacon.

Godelier, Maurice. 1993. "L'Occident, miroir brisé: une evaluation partielle de l'anthropologie sociale assortie de quelques perspectives." *Annales* 48: 1183–1207.

Goldman, Lawrence R. 1998. *Child's Play: Myth, Mimesis and Make Believe:* Berg.

Goldstein, Donna. 1999. "'Interracial' Sex and Racial Democracy in Brazil: Twin Concepts?" *American Anthropologist* 101:563–578.

Gonzalez-Wippler, Migene. 1989. *Santeria: The Religion.* New York: Harmony Books.

Good, Kenneth, and David Chanoff. 1996. *Into the Heart: One Man's Pursuit of Love and Knowledge Among the Yanomamo.* Old Tappan, NJ: Addison-Wesley.

Goodale, J. 1971. *Tiwi Wives.* Seattle: University of Washington Press.

Goodall, J. 1968. "A Preliminary Report on Expressive Movements and Communication in the Gombe Stream Chimpanzees." In P. Jay (Ed.), *Primates: Studies in Adaptation and Variability* (pp. 313–382). New York: Holt, Rinehart and Winston.

Goodenough, Ward. 1956. "Componential Analysis and the Study of Meaning." *Language* 32:195–216.

Goody, Jack. 1995. *The Expansive Moment: Anthropology in Britain and Africa 1918–1970.* Cambridge: Cambridge University Press.

Gordon, Robert J. 1992. *The Bushman Myth: The Making of a Namibian Underclass.* Boulder, CO: Westview Press.

Gorman, Peter. 1991. "A People at Risk: The Yanomami of Brazil." *The World and I* 6:670–681.

Graburn, Nelson H. H. (Ed.). 1976. *Ethnic and Tourist Arts: Cultural Expressions from the Fourth World.* Berkeley: University of California Press.

Gragson, Ted L. 1993. "Human Foraging in Lowland South America: Pattern and Process of Resource Procurement." *Research in Economic Anthropology* 14:107–138.

Grant, Madison. 1916. *The Passing of the Great Race, or the Racial Basis of European History.* New York: Charles Scribner's Sons.

Graves, Nancy B., and Theodore D. Graves. 1974. "Adaptive Strategies in Urban Migration." In B. J. Siegel (Ed.), *Annual Review of Anthropology* (pp. 117–151). Palo Alto, CA: Annual Reviews.

Greaves, Thomas. 1995. *Cultural Rights and Ethnography.* Washington, DC: Council for General Anthropology.

Greenhouse, Carol J., Barbara Yngvesson, and David M. Engel. 1994. *Law and Community in Three American Towns.* Ithaca, NY: Cornell University Press.

Gregg, Joan. 1988. *Contrastive Rhetoric: An Exploration of Chinese and American Expository Patterns.* Philadelphia: Temple University Working Papers in Composition.

Gregg, Joan. 1997. *Devils, Women, and Jews: Reflections of the Other in Medieval Sermon Stories.* Albany: State University of New York Press.

Gregor, Thomas. 1985. *Anxious Pleasures: The Sexual Life of an Amazonian People.* Chicago: University of Chicago Press.

Grindal, Bruce, and Frank Salamone (Eds.). 1995. *Bridges to Humanity: Narratives on Anthropology and Friendship.* Prospect Heights, IL: Waveland.

Grine, Frederick. 1993. "Australopithecine Taxonomy and Phylogeny: Historical Background and Recent Interpretation." In R. L. Ciochon and J. G. Gleagle (Eds.), *The Human Evolution Source Book* (pp. 198–210). Englewood Cliffs, NJ: Prentice Hall.

Groneman, Carol. 2000. *Nymphomania: A History.* New York: Norton.

Gruzinski, Serge. 1992. *Painting the Conquest: The Mexican Indians to the European Renaissance* (Deke Dusinberre, Trans.). Paris: Flammarion.

Gulevich, Tanya. 1990. "Economic Integration, Proletarianization, and Gender Transformation along the U.S.-Mexican Border." In J. Hurtig and K. Gillogly (Eds.), *Gender Transformations: Michigan Discussions in Anthropology* (Vol. 9, pp. 75–88). Ann Arbor: University of Michigan, Department of Anthropology.

Guthrie, R. D. 1984. "Ethnological Observations from Paleolithic Art." In *La contribution de la zoologie et de l'ethnologie à l'interpretation de l'art des peuples chasseurs prehistoriques: 3ème Colloque de la Société Suisse de Sciences Humaines* (pp. 35–73). Fribourg: Editions Universitaires.

Gutmann, Matthew C. 1996. *The Meanings of Macho: Being a Man in Mexico City.* Berkeley: University of California Press.

Hacker, Andrew. 1997. *Money: Who Has How Much and Why.* Riverside, NJ: Simon and Schuster.

Hale, Charles R. 1994. *Resistance and Contradiction: Miskitu Indians and the Nicaraguan State 1894–1987.* Stanford, CA: Stanford University Press.

Hale, Sondra. 1989. "The Politics of Gender in the Middle East." In S. Morgen (Ed.), *Gender and Anthropology: Critical Reviews for Research and Teaching* (pp. 246–267). Washington, DC: American Anthropological Association.

Hall, Edward T. 1959. *The Silent Language.* Greenwich, CT: Fawcett.

Hall, Edward T. 1966. *The Hidden Dimension.* New York: Doubleday.

Hall, Edward T. 1968. "Proxemics." *Current Anthropology* 9:83–109.

Hall, Edward T. 1983. *The Dance of Life: The Other Dimension of Time.* New York: Anchor/Doubleday.

Hall, Edward T., and Mildred Reed Hall. 1987. *Hidden Differences: Doing Business with the Japanese.* New York: Doubleday.

Hall, John R. 1993. "Apocalypse at Jonestown." In A. C. Lehmann and J. E. Myers (Eds.), *Magic, Witchcraft, and Religion: An Anthropological Study of the Supernatural* 3rd ed.) (pp. 96–107). Mountain View, CA: Mayfield. (Originally published 1979)

Halperin, Rhoda H. 1990. *The Livelihood of Kin: Making Ends Meet "The Kentucky Way."* Austin: University of Texas Press.

Halperin, Rhoda H. 1994. *Cultural Economies Past and Present.* Austin: University of Texas Press.

Hamid, Ansley. 1990. "The Political Economy of Crack-Related Violence." *Contemporary Drug Problems* 17:31–73.

Hamid, Ansley. 1992. "The Developmental Cycle of a Drug Epidemic: The Cocaine Smoking Epidemic of 1981–1991." *Journal of Psychoactive Drugs* 24:337–348.

Hamid, Ansley. 1998. *Drugs in America.* Gaithersburg, MD: Aspen.

Hamilton, James W. 1987. "This Old House: A Karen Ideal." In D. W. Ingersoll, Jr., and G. Bronitsky (Eds.), *Mirror and Metaphor: Material and Social Constructions of Reality* (pp. 229–245). Lanham, MD: University Press of America.

Hammar, Lawrence. 1989. "Gender and Class on the Fringe: A Feminist Critique of Ethnographic Theory and Data in Papua New Guinea." Working paper 189, Women and International Development Program, Michigan State University, East Lansing.

Handler, Richard. 1988. *Nationalism and the Politics of Culture in Quebec.* Madison: University of Wisconsin Press.

Handloff, Robert E. (Ed.). 1991. *Côte d'Ivoire: A Country Study.* Washington, DC: Library of Congress, Federal Research Division.

Hansen, Edward C. 1995. "The Great Bambi War: Tocquevillians versus Keynesians in an Upstate New York County." In J. Schneider and R. Rapp (Eds.), *Articulating Hidden Histories: Exploring the Influence of Eric R. Wolf* (pp. 142–155). Berkeley: University of California Press.

Harding, Susan, and Fred Myers (Eds.). 1994. "Further Inflections: Toward Ethnographies of the Future." *Cultural Anthropology* 9:3.

Harlow, Harry. 1959. "Love in Infant Monkeys." *Scientific American* 200:163–186.

Harlow, Harry, and Margaret Harlow. 1961. "A Study of Animal Affection." *Natural History* 70:48–55.

Harner, Michael. 1977. "The Ecological Basis for Aztec Sacrifice." *American Ethnologist* 4:117–133.

Harries, Patrick. 1987. "The Roots of Ethnicity: Discourse and the Politics of Language Construction in South-East Africa." *African Affairs* 87:25–52.

Harris, Marvin. 1966. "The Cultural Ecology of India's Sacred Cattle." *Current Anthropology* 7:51–66.

Harris, Marvin. 1974. *Cows, Pigs, Wars, and Witches: The Riddles of Culture.* New York: Random House/Vintage.

Harris, Marvin. 1989. *Our Kind: Who We Are, Where We Came From, Where We Are Going.* New York: Harper Perennial.

Harris, Marvin. 1990. *The Rise of Anthropological Theory: A History of Theories of Culture.* New York: Harper.

Harris, Michael S. 1991. "Diversity in a Bangladeshi Village: Landholding Structure, Economic Differentiation, and Occupational Specialization of Moslems and Hindus." *Research in Economic Anthropology* 13:143–160.

Harrison, Faye V. 1998. "Introduction: Expanding the Discourse on 'Race.'" *American Anthropologist* 100: 609–631.

Harrison, Robert. 1973. *Warfare.* Minneapolis: Burgess.

Hart, C. W. M. 1967. "Contrasts between Pre-pubertal and Post-pubertal Education." In R. Endelman (Ed.), *Personality and Social Life* (pp. 275–290). New York: Random House.

Hart, C. W. M., and Arnold R. Pilling. 1960. *The Tiwi of Northern Australia.* New York: Holt, Rinehart and Winston.

Hartigan, John. 1997. "Establishing the Fact of Whiteness." *American Anthropologist* 99:495–505.

Hasenbalg, Carlos A. 1985. "Race and Socioeconomic Inequalities in Brazil." In P.-M. Fontaine (Ed.), *Race, Class, and Power in Brazil* (pp. 25–41). Los Angeles: University of California, Center for Afro-American Studies.

Hassig, Ross. 1988. *Aztec Warfare: Imperial Expansion and Political Control.* Norman: University of Oklahoma Press.

Haub, Carl, and Martha Farnsworth Richie. 1994. "Population by the Numbers: Trends in Population Growth and Structure." In L. A. Mazur (Ed.), *Beyond the Numbers: A Reader on Population, Consumption, and the Environment* (pp. 95–108). Washington, DC: Island Press.

Hauptman, William. 1985. "Renoir's Master." *EMR* 15:48–66.

Headland, Thomas N. (Ed.). 1992. *The Tasaday Controversy: Assessing the Evidence.* Washington, DC: American Anthropological Association.

Hearn, Maxwell K. 1996. *Splendors of Imperial China: Treasures from the National Palace Museum, Taipei.* New York: Metropolitan Museum of Art.

Heimer, Robert, Ricky Bluthenthal, Merill Singer, and Kaveh Khoshnood. 1996. "Structural Impediments to Operational Syringe-Exchange Programs." *AIDS Public Policy Journal* 11:169–184.

Helman, Cecil G. 1998. "Medicine and Culture: Limits of Biomedical Explanation." In G. Ferraro (Ed.), *Applying Cultural Anthropology: Readings* (pp. 3–6). Belmont, CA: Wadsworth. (Originally published 1991)

Henry, Jules. 1973. *Pathways to Madness.* New York: Random House/Vintage.

Herdt, Gilbert H. 1981. *Guardians of the Flutes: Idioms of Masculinity.* New York: McGraw-Hill.

Herdt, Gilbert H. 1987. *The Sambia.* New York: Holt, Rinehart and Winston.

Herdt, Gilbert H. 1990. "Mistaken Gender: 5-alpha Reductase Hermaphroditism and Biological Reductionism in Sexual Identity Reconsidered." *American Anthropologist* 92:433–446.

Herdt, Gilbert H. (Ed.). 1996. *Third Sex, Third Gender: Beyond Sexual Dimorphism in Culture and History.* New York: Zone.

Herrnstein, Richard J., and Charles A. Murray. 1994. *The Bell Curve: Intelligence and Class Structure in American Life.* New York: Free Press.

Hertzfeld, Michael. 1985. *The Poetics of Manhood: Contest and Identity in a Cretan Mountain Village.* Princeton, NJ: Princeton University Press.

Hertzfeld, Michael. 1987. *Anthropology through the Looking-Glass: Critical Ethnography in the Margins of Europe.* Cambridge: Cambridge University Press.

Hester, Marianne. 1988. "Who Were the Witches?" *Studies in Sexual Politics* 26–27:1–22.

Hewes, Gordon W. 1973. "Primate Communication and the Gestural Origins of Language." *Current Anthropology* 14:5–12.

Hickerson, Nancy Parrott. 1980. *Linguistic Anthropology.* New York: Holt, Rinehart and Winston.

Hill, Jane H. 1998. "Language, Race, and White Public Space." *American Anthropologist* 100:680–689.

Hill, K. H., K. Hawkes, and A. M. Hurtado. 1985. "Men's Time Allocation to Subsistence Work Among the Aché of Eastern Paraguay." *Human Ecology* 13(1):29–48.

Hinshaw, Robert E. 1980. "Anthropology, Administration, and Public Policy." In B. J. Siegel (Ed.), *Annual Review of Anthropology* (pp. 497–522). Palo Alto, CA: Annual Reviews.

Hirschfeld, Lawrence A. 1996. *Race in the Making.* Cambridge, MA: MIT Press/Bradford Books.

Hitchcock, Robert K. 1997, April. "Indigenous Peoples, Multinational Corporations, and Human Rights." Paper presented at the International Symposium on Indigenous Peoples, University of Nebraska, Lincoln.

Hobsbawm, Eric, and Terence Ranger (Eds.). 1983. *The Invention of Tradition.* Cambridge: Cambridge University Press.

Hochschild, Jennifer L. 1995. *Facing Up to the American Dream: Race, Class, and the Soul of the Nation.* Princeton, NJ: Princeton University Press.

Hockett, Charles F. 1973. *Man's Place in Nature.* New York: McGraw-Hill.

Hockett, Charles F., and R. Ascher. 1964. "The Human Revolution." *Current Anthropology* 5:135–168.

Hodge, William. 1981. *The First Americans: Then and Now.* New York: Holt, Rinehart and Winston.

Hoebel, E. Adamson. 1960. *The Cheyennes: Indians of the Great Plains.* New York: Holt.

Hoebel, E. Adamson. 1974. *The Law of Primitive Man.* New York: Henry Holt.

Hofer, Tamas (Ed.). 1994. *Hungarians between "East" and "West": Three Essays on National Myths and Symbols.* Budapest: Museum of Ethnography.

Hoffer, Carol P. 1974. "Madam Yoko: Ruler of the Kpa Mende Confederacy." In M. Z. Rosaldo and L. Lamphere (Eds.), *Women, Culture and Society* (pp. 173–188). Stanford, CA: Stanford University Press.

Hoijer, Harry. 1964. "Cultural Implications of Some Navajo Linguistic Categories." In D. Hymes (Ed.), *Language in Culture and Society* (pp. 142–160). New York: Harper and Row.

Holland, Dorothy C., and Margaret A. Eisenhart. 1990. *Educated in Romance: Women, Achievement, and College Culture.* Chicago: University of Chicago Press.

Holmberg, Allan R., et. al. 1965. "The Vicos Case: Peasant Society in Transition." *American Behavioral Scientist* 8(7):3–33.

Holmquist, R., M. M. Miyamoto, and M. Goodman. 1988. "Higher Primate Phylogeny: Why Can't We Decide?" *Molecular Biology and Evolution* 5:201–216.

Hooks, Bell. 1989. *Talking Back: Thinking Feminist, Thinking Black.* Boston: South End Press.

Hopkins, Nicholas. 1987. "Mechanized Irrigation in Upper Egypt: The Role of Technology and the State in Agriculture." In B. Turner, II and S. B. Brush (Eds.), *Comparative Farming Systems* (pp. 223–247). New York: Guilford.

Horsley, Richard A. 1979. "Who Were the Witches? The Social Roles of the Accused in the European Witch Trials." *Journal of Interdisciplinary History* 9:689–715.

Horton, Donald. 1943. "The Functions of Alcohol in Primitive Societies: A Cross-Cultural Study." *Quarterly Journal of Studies on Alcohol* 4:199–320.

Horton, John. 1992. "The Politics of Diversity in Monterey Park." In L. Lamphere (Ed.), *Structuring Diversity: Ethnographic Perspectives on the New Immigration* (pp. 215–246). Chicago: University of Chicago Press.

Howard, Jane. 1984. *Margaret Mead: A Life.* New York: Simon and Schuster.

Huang, Shu-min. 1993. "A Cross-Cultural Experience: A Chinese Anthropologist in the United States." In P. R. DeVita and J. D. Armstrong (Eds.), *Distant Mirrors: America as a Foreign Culture* (pp. 39–45). Belmont, CA: Wadsworth.

Huang, Wanpo, et al. 1995. "Early *Homo* and Associated Artifacts from Asia." *Nature* 378:275–278.

Huffman, Michael A., and Duane Quiatt. 1986. "Stone Handling by Japanese Macaques (*Macaca fuscata*): Implications for Tool Use of Stone." *Primates* 27:413–423.

Hunt, George T. 1940. *The Wars of the Iroquois.* Madison: University of Wisconsin Press.

Hurtado, A., K. Hawkes, K. Hill, and H. Kaplan. 1985. "Female Subsistence Strategies Among Aché Hunter-Gatherers of Eastern Paraguay." *Human Ecology* 13(1):1–28.

Hymes, Dell. 1972. *Reinventing Anthropology.* New York: Random House/Vintage.

Isaac, Barry L. 1993. "Retrospective on the Formalist-Substantivist Debate." *Research in Economic Anthropology* 14:213–233.

Isaacman, Allen. 1996. *Cotton Is the Mother of Poverty: Peasants, Work, and Rural Struggle in Colonial Mozambique (1938–1961).* Portsmouth, NH: Heinemann.

Itard, Jean-Marc-Gaspard. 1962. *The Wild Boy of Aveyron* (George and Muriel Humphrey, Trans.). Englewood Cliffs, NJ: Prentice-Hall. (Original work published 1806)

Jennie, Keith, et al. (Eds.). 1994. *The Aging Experience: Diversity and Commonality Across Cultures.* Thousand Oaks, CA: Sage.

Jensen, Arthur. 1969. "How Much Can We Boost IQ and Scholastic Achievement?" *Harvard Educational Review* 39(1):1–123.

Jia, Lan-Po, and Haung Weiwen. 1990. *The Story of Peking Man.* New York: Oxford University Press.

Johanson, Donald. 1996. "Lucy." In Brian M. Fagan (Ed.), *Eyewitness to Discovery* (pp. 53–60). New York: Oxford University Press. (Originally published 1981)

Johnson, Allen. 1978. "In Search of the Affluent Society." *Human Nature* 1(9):50–59.

Johnson, Allen. 1989. "Horticulturalists: Economic Behavior in Tribes." In S. Plattner (Ed.), *Economic Anthropology* (pp. 49–77). Stanford, CA: Stanford University Press.

Johnston, David Cay. 1996, November 10. "Voting, America's Not Keen On. Coffee Is Another Matter." *New York Times,* p. D2.

Jolly, Alison. 1985. *The Evolution of Primate Behavior* (2nd ed.). New York: Macmillan.

Jonaitis, Aldona (Ed.). 1991. *Chiefly Feasts: The Enduring Kwakiutl Potlatch.* Seattle: University of Washington Press.

Jones, Delmos J. 1995. "Anthropology and the Oppressed: A Reflection on 'Native' Anthropology." In E. L. Cerroni-Long (Ed.), *Insider Anthropology*

(Napa Bulletin, Vol. 16, pp. 58–70). Washington, DC: American Anthropological Association.

Kaberry, P. 1939. *Aboriginal Woman: Sacred and Profane.* New York: Gordon Press.

Kalish, R. A. (Ed.). 1980. *Death and Dying: Views from Many Cultures.* Amityville, NY: Baywood.

Kaplan, Flora E. S. (Ed.). 1997. *Queens, Queen Mothers, Priestesses, and Power: Case Studies in African Gender.* New York: New York Academy of Sciences.

Kaprow, Miriam Lee. 1982. "Resisting Respectability: Gypsies in Saragossa." *Urban Anthropology* 11: 399–431.

Kaprow, Miriam Lee. 1991. "Magical Work: Firefighters in New York." *Human Organization* 50:97–103.

Kardiner, Abram. 1945. *The Psychological Frontiers of Society.* New York: Columbia University Press.

Karlen, Arno. 1995. *Man and Microbes: Disease and Plagues in History and Modern Times.* New York: G. P. Putnam's Sons.

Kasarda, John D., and Edward M. Crenshaw. 1991. "Third World Urbanization: Dimensions, Theories, and Determinants." *Annual Review of Sociology* 17:467–501.

Kaufman, Sharon R. 2000. "In the Shadow of 'Death with Dignity': Medicine and Cultural Quandaries of the Vegetative State." *American Anthropologist* 102:69–83.

Keesing, Roger M. 1987. "Anthropology as Interpretive Quest." *Current Anthropology* 28:161–176.

Kehoe, Alice Beck. 1989. *The Ghost Dance: Ethnohistory and Revitalization.* Fort Worth, TX: Holt, Rinehart and Winston.

Keith, Jennie, Christine L. Fry, Anthony P. Glascock, Charlotte Ikels, Jeanette Dickerson-Putman, Henry C. Harpending, and Patricia Draper. 1994. *The Aging Experience: Diversity and Commonality Across Cultures.* Thousand Oaks, CA: Sage.

Kelkar, Govind. 1985. "Tractors Against Women." *Development* 3:18–23.

Kelly, Aidan A. 1991. *Crafting the Art of Magic.* St. Paul, MN: Llewellyn.

Kelly, Gail P. 1986. "Learning to Be Marginal: Schooling in Interwar French West Africa." *Journal of Asian and African Studies* 21:171–184.

Kelly, Robert L. 1995. *The Foraging Spectrum: Diversity in Hunter-Gatherer Lifeways.* Washington, DC: Smithsonian Institution.

Kensinger, Kenneth M. 1995. *How Real People Ought to Live: The Cashinahua of Eastern Peru.* Prospect Heights, IL: Waveland.

Kilker, Ernest Evans. 1993. "The Culture and Politics of Racial Classification." *International Journal of Politics, Culture, and Society* 7:229–258.

Kimbel, W. H., et al. 1996. "Late Pliocene Homo and Oldowan Tools from the Hadar Formation (Kada Hadar Member), Ethiopia." *Journal of Human Evolution* 31:549–561.

Kinsey, Alfred C., Wardell B. Pomeroy, and Clyde E. Martin. 1948. *Sexual Behavior in the Human Male.* Philadelphia: Saunders.

Klass, Morton. 1995. *Ordered Universes: Approaches to the Anthropology of Religion.* Boulder, CO: Westview Press.

Klein, Laura F. 1976. "'She's One of Us, You Know': The Public Life of Tlingit Women: Traditional, Historical, and Contemporary Perspectives." *Western Canadian Journal of Anthropology* 6(3):164–183.

Klein, Laura F. 1995. "Mother as Clanswoman: Rank and Gender in Tlingit Society." In L. F. Klein and L. A. Ackerman (Eds.), *Women and Power in Native North America* (pp. 28–45). Norman: University of Oklahoma Press.

Klein, Laura F., and Lillian A. Ackerman (Eds.). 1995. *Woman and Power in Native North America.* Norman: University of Oklahoma Press.

Kleinman, Arthur, and Byron Good. 1985. *Culture and Depression: Studies in the Anthropology and Cross-Cultural Psychiatry of Affect and Disorder.* Berkeley: University of California Press.

Kluckhohn, Clyde. 1959. "The Philosophy of the Navaho Indians." In M. H. Fried (Ed.), *Readings in Anthropology* (Vol. 2). New York: Crowell.

Knauft, Bruce. 1987. "Reconsidering Violence in Simple Human Societies: Homicide among the Gebusi of New Guinea." *Current Anthropology* 28: 457–482.

Koester, Stephen K. 1994. "Coping, Running, and Paraphernalia Laws: Contextual Variables and Needle Risk Behavior among Injection Drug Users in Denver." *Human Organization* 53:287–295.

Kohn, Hans. 1958. "Reflections on Colonialism." In R. Strausz-Hupe and H.W. Hazard (Eds.), *The Idea of Colonialism* (pp. 2–16). New York: Praeger.

Kottak, Conrad P. 1992. *Assault on Paradise: Social Change in a Brazilian Village* (2nd ed.). New York: McGraw-Hill.

Kottak, Conrad P. 1999. "The New Ecological Anthropology." *American Anthropologist* 101:23–35.

Krings, M., A. Stone, R. W. Schmitz, H. Krainitzki, M. Stoneking, and S. Pääbo. 1997. "Neandertal DNA Sequences and the Origin of Modern Humans." *Cell* 90:19–30.

Kuklick, Henrika. 1991. *The Savage Within: The Social History of British Anthropology 1885–1945.* Cambridge: Cambridge University Press.

Kunstadter, Peter. 1988. "Hill People of Northern Thailand." In J. S. Denslow and C. Padoch (Eds.), *People of the Tropical Rain Forest* (pp. 93–110). Berkeley: University of California Press.

Kuper, Hilda. 1986. *The Swazi: A South African Kingdom* (2nd ed.). New York: Holt, Rinehart and Winston.

La Barre, Weston. 1969. *And They Shall Take Up Serpents.* New York: Schocken Books.

La Botz, Daniel. 1994. "Manufacturing Poverty: The Maquiladorization of Mexico." *International Journal of Health Services* 24:403–408.

Labov, William. 1969. "The Logic of Nonstandard English." *Georgetown Monographs on Language and Linguistics* 22:1–22,26–32.

Labov, William. 1972. *Language in the Inner City.* Philadelphia: University of Pennsylvania Press.

Labov, William. 1983. "Recognizing Black English in the Classroom." In J. Chambers (Ed.), *Black English: Educational Equity and Law* (pp. 29–55). Ann Arbor, MI: Karoma.

Ladefoged, Peter. 1982. *A Course in Phonetics.* New York: Harcourt Brace Jovanovich.

Laitman, Jeffrey T. 1984. "The Anatomy of Human Speech." *Natural History* 93:22–27.

Lamphere, Louise (Ed.). 1992. *Structuring Diversity: Ethnographic Perspectives on the New Immigration.* Chicago: University of Chicago Press.

Lamphere, Louise. 1997. "The Domestic Sphere of Women and the Public World of Men: The Strengths and Limitations of an Anthropological Dichotomy." In C. B. Brettell and C. F. Sargent (Eds.), *Gender in Cross Cultural Perspective* (2nd ed.) (pp. 82–91). Upper Saddle River, NJ: Prentice Hall.

Lancaster, Jane B. 1989. "Women in Biosocial Perspective." In S. Morgen (Ed.), *Gender and Anthropology: Critical Reviews for Research and Teaching* (pp. 95–115). Washington, DC: American Anthropological Association.

Lansing, J. Stephen. 1991. *Priests and Programmers: Technologies of Power in the Engineered Landscape of Bali.* Princeton, NJ: Princeton University Press.

Lapidus, Ira M. 1988. *A History of Islamic Societies.* Cambridge: Cambridge University Press.

Larsen, Clark Spencer. 1995. "Biological Changes in Human Populations with Agriculture." *Annual Review of Anthropology* 24:185–213.

Lawler, Nancy Ellen. 1992. *Soldiers of Misfortune: Ivoirien Tirailleurs of World War II.* Athens, OH: Ohio University Press.

Lazarus-Black, Mindie, and Susan F. Hirsch (Eds.). 1994. *Contested States: Law, Hegemony, and Resistance.* New York: Routledge.

Leacock, Eleanor Burke. 1981. *Myths of Male Dominance.* New York: Monthly Review Press.

Leacock, Eleanor Burke, and Helen I. Safa (Eds.). 1986. *Women's Work: Development and the Division of Labor by Gender.* South Hadley, MA: Bergin and Garvey.

Leakey, Mary, and Louis Leakey. 1996. "The Discovery of *Zinjanthropus boisei.*" In Brian M. Fagan (Ed.), *Eyewitness to Discovery* (pp. 46–52). New York: Oxford University Press. (Originally published 1984)

Leathers, Dale G. 1997. *Successful Nonverbal Communication* (3rd ed.). Boston: Allyn and Bacon.

Lee, Dorothy. 1959. *Freedom and Culture.* Englewood Cliffs, NJ: Prentice-Hall.

Lee, Richard B. 1968. "What Hunters Do for a Living, or How to Make Out on Scarce Resources." In R. B. Lee and I. DeVore (Eds.), *Man the Hunter* (pp. 30–48). Chicago: Aldine.

Lee, Richard B. 1974. "Eating Christmas in the Kalahari." In J. Spradley and D. W. McCurdy (Eds.), *Conformity and Conflict.* Boston: Little, Brown.

Lee, Richard B. 1984. *The Dobe !Kung.* New York: Holt, Rinehart and Winston.

Lee, Richard B. 1992. "Art, Science, or Politics? The Crisis in Hunter-Gatherer Studies." *American Anthropologist* 94:31–54.

Lee, Richard B. 2000, March. "Indigenism and Its Discontents: Anthropology and the Small Peoples at the Millennium." Keynote Address at the annual meeting of the American Ethnological Society, Tampa, FL.

Lee, Richard B., and Irven DeVore (Eds.). 1968. *Man the Hunter.* New York: Aldine.

Lefever, Harry G. 1996. "When the Saints Go Riding In: Santeria in Cuba and the United States." *Journal for the Scientific Study of Religion* 35:318–330.

Lemert, Edwin M. 1997. *The Trouble with Evil: Social Control at the Edge of Morality.* Albany: State University of New York Press.

Lesser, Alexander. 1933. *The Pawnee Ghost Dance Hand Game: Ghost Dance Revival and Ethnic Identity.* Lincoln: University of Nebraska.

Lévi-Strauss, Claude. 1969. *The Elementary Structures of Kinship.* Boston: Beacon Press. (Originally published 1949)

Lévi-Strauss, Claude. 1974a. *Structural Anthropology* (Vol. I). New York: Basic Books.

Lévi-Strauss, Claude. 1974b. *Structural Anthropology* (Vol. II). Chicago: University of Chicago Press.

Levine, Morton. 1957. "Prehistoric Art and Ideology." *American Anthropologist* 59:949–962.

Levinson, David. 1996. *Religion: A Cross-cultural Dictionary.* New York: Oxford University Press.

Levy, Robert. 1973. *Tahitians: Mind and Experience in the Society Islands.* Chicago: University of Chicago Press.

Lewis, Arnold. 1980. "The Ritual Process and Community Development." *Community Development Journal* 15(3):190–199.

Lewis, Oscar. 1960. *Tepoztlan, Village in Mexico.* New York: Holt, Rinehart and Winston.

Lewis, Oscar. 1966. *La Vida.* New York: Random House.

Lewis, Richard D. 1996. *When Cultures Collide: Managing Successfully Across Cultures.* London: Nicholas Brealey.

Lewis, Tom. 1991. *Empire of the Air: The Men Who Made Radio.* New York: Harper Perennial.

Lewis, William F. 1993. *Soul Rebels: The Rastafari.* Prospect Heights, IL: Waveland.

Lewis-Williams, J. D., and T. A. Dowson. 1988. "The Signs of All Times." *Current Anthropology* 29:201–217.

Lichtenberg, Judith. 1994. "Population Policy and the Clash of Cultures." In L. A. Mazur (Ed.), *Beyond the Numbers: A Reader on Population, Consumption, and Environment* (pp. 273–280). Washington DC: Island Press.

Lieberman, Leonard, and Rodney C. Kirk. 1996. "The Trial of Darwin Is Over: Religious Voices for Evolution and the 'Fairness' Doctrine." *Creation/Evolution* 16(2):1–9.

Lieberman, Philip. 1984. *The Biology and Evolution of Language.* Cambridge, MA: Harvard University Press.

Lim, Linda Y. C. 1983. "Capitalism, Imperialism, and Patriarchy: The Dilemma of Third-World Women Workers in Multinational Factories." In J. Nash and M. P. Fernandez-Kelly (Eds.), *Women, Men, and the International Division of Labor* (pp. 70–92). Albany: State University of New York Press.

Lindenbaum, Shirley. 1979. *Kuru Sorcery: Disease and Danger in the New Guinea Highlands.* Palo Alto, CA: Mayfield.

Lindholm, Charles. 1982. *Generosity and Jealousy: The Swat Pukhtun of Northern Pakistan.* New York: Columbia University Press.

Lindstrom, Lamont. 1993. *Cargo Cult: Strange Stories of Desire from Melanesia and Beyond.* Honolulu: University of Hawaii Press.

Linton, Ralph. 1936. *The Study of Man: An Introduction.* New York: Appleton-Century.

Linton, Ralph. 1937. "One Hundred Per Cent American." *American Mercury* 40:427–429.

Locke, John L. 1994. "Phases in the Child's Development of Language." *American Scientist* 82:436–445.

Loftin, John D. 1991. *Religion and Hopi Life in the Twentieth Century.* Bloomington, IN: Indiana University Press.

London, Scott. 1996, January. "Postmodern Tourism: An Interview with Pico Iyer." *Sun.*

Long, Norman. 1977. *An Introduction to the Sociology of Rural Development.* London: Tavistock.

Lopez, Ian F. Haney. *White by Law: The Legal Construction of Race.* New York: New York University Press.

Lovejoy, Paul E. 1983. *Transformations in Slavery: A History of Slavery in Africa.* Cambridge: Cambridge University Press.

Lowie, Robert H. 1948. *Social Organization.* New York: Holt, Rinehart and Winston.

Lowie, Robert H. 1963. *Indians of the Plains.* Garden City, NY: Natural History Press. (Originally published 1954)

Luhrmann, Tanya M. 1996. *The Good Parsi: The Fate of a Colonial Elite in Postcolonial Society.* Cambridge, MA: Harvard University Press.

Luhrmann, Tanya M. 2000. *Of Two Minds: The Growing Disorder in American Psychiatry.* New York: Knopf.

Luker, Kristin. 1996. *Dubious Conceptions: The Politics of Teenage Pregnancy.* Cambridge, MA: Harvard University Press.

Lutkehaus, Nancy C., and Paul B. Roscoe (Eds.). 1995. *Gender Rituals: Female Initiation in Melanesia.* New York: Routledge.

Lynch, Owen K. 1969. *The Politics of Untouchability.* New York: Columbia University Press.

Lynd, Robert, and Helen Lynd. 1937. *Middletown in Transition.* New York: Harcourt, Brace and World.

Macintyre, Martha. 1983. "Kune on Tubetube and in the Bwanabwana Region of the Southern Massim." In J. W. Leach and E. Leach (Eds.), *The Kula: New Perspectives on Massim Exchange* (pp. 369–379). Cambridge: Cambridge University Press.

Maher, Lisa. 1997. *Sexed Work: Gender, Race, and Resistance in a Brooklyn Drug Market.* Oxford: Clarendon Press.

Mails, Thomas E. 1973. *Plains Indians: Dog Soldiers, Bear Men and Buffalo Women.* New York: Bonanza.

Malinowski, Bronislaw. 1929a. "Practical Anthropology." *Africa* 2:22–38.

Malinowski, Bronislaw. 1929b. *The Sexual Life of Savages.* New York: Harcourt, Brace and World.

Malinowski, Bronislaw. 1935. *Coral Gardens and Their Magic.* New York: American Book Company.

Malinowski, Bronislaw. 1944. *A Scientific Theory of Culture and Other Essays.* Chapel Hill: University of North Carolina Press.

Malinowski, Bronislaw. 1953. *Sex and Repression in Primitive Society.* London: Routledge and Kegan Paul. (Originally published 1927)

Malinowski, Bronislaw. 1954. *Magic, Science, and Religion.* Garden City, NY: Doubleday.

Malinowski, Bronislaw. 1961. *Argonauts of the Western Pacific.* New York: E. P. Dutton. (Originally published 1922)

Malinowski, Bronislaw. 1967. *A Diary in the Strict Sense of the Term.* New York: Harcourt, Brace and World.

Marcus, George E. (Ed.). 1992. *Rereading Cultural Anthropology.* Durham, NC: Duke University Press.

Marcus, George E., and Michael M. J. Fischer. 1986. *Anthropology as Culture Critique: An Experimental Moment in the Human Sciences.* Chicago: University of Chicago Press.

Marcus, George E., and Fred R. Myers (Eds.). 1995. *The Traffic in Culture: Refiguring Art and Anthropology.* Berkeley: University of California Press.

Marks, Jonathan. 1995. *Human Biodiversity: Genes, Race, and History.* New York: Aldine de Gruyter.

Marks, J., C. W. Schmidt, and V. M. Sarich. 1988. "DNA Hybridization as a Guide to Phylogeny: Relations of the Hominoidea." *Journal of Human Evolution* 17:769–786.

Marshall, Donald. 1971. "Sexual Behavior on Mangaia." In D. S. Marshall and R. C. Suggs (Eds.), *Human Sexual Behavior: Variations in the Ethnographic Spectrum* (pp. 163–172). New York: Basic Books.

Marshall, Mac. 1979. *Weekend Warriors.* Palo Alto, CA: Mayfield.

Martin, Emily. 1987. *The Woman in the Body.* New York: Beacon Press.

Martin, M. K., and Barbara Voorhies. 1975. *Female of the Species.* New York: Columbia University Press.

Martinez, Samuel. 1996. "Indifference within Indignation: Anthropology, Human Rights, and the Haitian Bracero." *American Anthropologist* 98:17–25.

Matory, J. Lorand. 1994. *Sex and the Empire That Is No More: Gender and the Politics of Metaphor in Oyo Yoruba Religion.* Minneapolis: University of Minnesota Press.

Matsuda, Mari J. 1988. "Law and Culture in the District Court of Honolulu, 1844–45: A Case Study in the Rise of Legal Consciousness." *American Journal of Legal History* 32:17–41.

Matsumoto, David, and Tsutomu Kudoh. 1993. "American-Japanese Cultural Differences in Attributions of Personality Based on Smiles." *Journal of Nonverbal Communication* 17(4):231–243.

Matthews, Richard. 1997. "The Ebonic Plague Will Kill America Yet." *Atlanta Journal and Constitution,* January 23, p. A18.

Matute-Bianchi, Maria. 1991. "Situational Ethnicity and Patterns of School Performance among Immigrant and Nonimmigrant Mexican-Descent Students." In M. A. Gibson and J. U. Ogbu (Eds.), *Minority Status and Schooling: A Comparative Study of Immigrant and Involuntary Minorities* (pp. 205–248). New York: Garland.

Mauss, Marcel. 1990. *The Gift: Form and Reason of Exchange in Archaic Societies* (W. D. Halls, Trans.). New York: W. W. Norton. (Originally published 1924)

Maybury-Lewis, David. 1993. "A Special Sort of Pleading: Anthropology at the Service of Ethnic Groups." In W. A. Haviland and R. J. Gordon (Eds.), *Talking About People: Readings in Contemporary Cultural Anthropology* (pp. 16–24). Mountain View, CA: Mayfield.

Maybury-Lewis, David. 1997. *Indigenous Peoples, Ethnic Groups, and the State.* Boston: Allyn and Bacon.

Mayer, Adrien. 1995. "Caste in an Indian Village." In C. J. Fuller (Ed.), *Caste Today* (pp. 37–63). Delhi: Oxford University Press.

McAllester, David P. 1954. *Enemy Way Music.* Cambridge, MA: Harvard University, Peabody Museum.

McCaskie, T. C. 1995. *State and Society in Pre-Colonial Asante.* Cambridge: Cambridge University Press.

McDermott, LeRoy. 1996. "Self-Representation in Upper Paleolithic Female Figurines." *Current Anthropology* 37:227–275.

McGee, R. Jon. 1990. *Life, Ritual, and Religion Among the Lacandon Maya.* Belmont, CA: Wadsworth.

McGee, R. Jon, and Richard L. Warms. 2000. *Anthropological Theory: An Introductory History* (2nd ed.). Mountain View, CA: Mayfield.

McHenry, Henry. 1992. "Body Size and Proportions in Early Hominids." *American Journal of Physical Anthropology* 87:404–431.

McIntosh, Peggy. 1999. "White Privilege: Unpacking the Invisible Knapsack." In A. Podolefsky and P. J. Brown (Eds.), *Applying Cultural Anthropology: An Introductory Reader* (4th ed.) (pp. 134–137). Mountain View, CA: Mayfield.

Mead, Margaret. 1963. *Sex and Temperament in Three Primitive Societies.* New York: Dell. (Originally published 1935)

Mead, Margaret. 1971. *Coming of Age in Samoa.* New York: Morrow. (Originally published 1928)

Mead, Margaret. 1995. "Ethnicity and Anthropology in America." In Lola Romanucci-Ross and George A. De Vos (Eds.), *Ethnic Identity: Creation, Conflict, and Accommodation* (pp. 298–320). London: Sage.

Meek, Charles K. 1972. "Ibo Law." In J. D. Jennings and E. A. Hoebel (Eds.), *Readings in Anthropology* (pp. 247–258). New York: McGraw-Hill.

Meggitt, Mervyn. 1977. *Blood Is Their Argument: Warfare among the Mae Enga Tribesmen of the New Guinea Highlands.* Palo Alto, CA: Mayfield.

Meier, Matt S., and Feliciano Ribera. 1993. *Mexican Americans/American Mexicans: From Conquistadors to Chicanos.* New York: Hill & Wang.

Mencher, Joan P. 1965. "The Nayars of South Malabar." In M. F. Nimkoff (Ed.), *Comparative Family Systems* (pp. 162–191). Boston: Houghton Mifflin.

Mencher, Joan P. 1974. "The Caste System Upside Down: Or the Not-So-Mysterious East." *Current Anthropology* 15:469–494.

Mencher, Joan P. 1980. "On Being an Untouchable in India: A Materialist Perspective." In Eric Ross (Ed.), *Beyond the Myths of Culture: Essays in Cultural Materialism* (pp. 261–294). New York: Academic Press.

Merlan, F. 1988. "Gender in Aboriginal Social Life." In R. Berndt and R. Tonkinson (Eds.), *Social Anthropology and Australian Aboriginal Studies: A Contemporary Overview* (pp. 15–72). Canberra: Aboriginal Studies Press.

Merry, Sally E. 1981. *Urban Danger: Life in a Neighborhood of Strangers.* Philadelphia: Temple University Press.

Merry, Sally E. 1990. *Getting Justice and Getting Even: Legal Consciousness among Working Class Americans.* Chicago: University of Chicago Press.

Merry, Sally E. 1991. "Law and Colonialism." *Law and Society Review* 25:891–922.

Merry, Sally E. 1996. "Legal Vernacularization and Ka Ho'okolokolonui Kanaka Maoli, the People's International Tribunal, Hawaii 1993." *POLAR* 19(1):67–82.

Merry, Sally E. 2000. *Colonizing Hawai'i: The Cultural Power of Law.* Princeton, NJ: Princeton University Press.

Messenger, John C. 1971. "Sex and Repression in an Irish Folk Community." In D. S. Marshall and R. C. Suggs (Eds.), *Human Sexual Behavior: Variations in the Ethnographic Spectrum* (pp. 3–37). New York: Basic Books.

Mestel, R. 1994, October. "Ascent of the Dog." *Discover,* pp. 90–98.

Miles, H. Lyn. 1978. "Language Acquisition in Apes and Children." In F.C.C. Peng (Ed.), *Language Acquisition in Man and Ape* (pp. 103–120). Boulder, CO: Westview Press.

Miles, H. Lyn. 1983. "Apes and Language: The Search for Communicative Competence." In J. D. Luce and H. T. Wilder (Eds.), *Language and Primates* (pp. 43–61). New York: Springer-Verlag.

Mintz, Sidney W. 1985. *Sweetness and Power: The Place of Sugar in Modern History.* New York: Penguin.

Moberg, Mark, and Christopher L. Dyer. 1994. "Conservation and Forced Innovation: Responses to Turtle Excluder Devices among Gulf of Mexico Shrimpers." *Human Organization* 53:160–166.

Moffatt, Michael. 1989. *Coming of Age in New Jersey.* New Brunswick, NJ: Rutgers University Press.

Molnar, Stephen. 1983. *Human Variation: Races, Types, and Ethnic Groups* (2nd ed.). Englewood Cliffs, NJ: Prentice Hall.

Monaghan, Leila. 1997. "Ebonics Discussion Continues." *Anthropology Newsletter* 38(2):44–45.

Montagu, Ashley. 1942. *Man's Most Dangerous Myth: The Fallacy of Race.* New York: Columbia University Press.

Montagu, Ashley. 1978. *Touching: The Human Significance of the Skin* (2nd ed.). New York: Harper and Row.

Montague, Susan, and Robert Morais. 1976. "Football Games and Rock Concerts: The Ritual Enactment." In W. Arens and S. P. Montague (Eds.), *The American Dimension* (pp. 33–52). Port Washington, NY: Alfred.

Mooney, James. 1973. *The Ghost-Dance Religion and the Sioux Outbreak of 1890.* Glorieta, NM: Rio Grande Press. (Originally published 1896)

Moore, Molly. 1997. "To Guatemalan Scientist, Dead Men Do Tell Tales." *Washington Post,* July 19. p. A22.

Moore, Christopher W. 1993. "'Have Process, Will Travel': Reflections on Democratic Decision Making Management Practice Abroad." *Forum,* Winter, pp. 1–12.

Moore, Omar Khayyam. 1969. "Divination: A New Perspective." In Andrew P. Vayda (Ed.), *Environment and Cultural Behavior* (pp. 121–128). Austin: University of Texas Press.

Moore, Sally Falk. 1978. *Law as Process: An Anthropological Approach.* London: Routledge and Kegan Paul.

Moran, Emilio F. 1979. *Human Adaptability: An Introduction to Ecological Anthropology.* Boulder, CO: Westview Press.

Moran, Emilio F. 1988. "Following the Amazonian Highways." In J. S. Denslow and C. Padoch (Eds.), *People of the Tropical Rain Forest* (pp. 155–162). Berkeley: University of California Press.

Morgan, Lynn M. 1996. "When Does Life Begin? A Cross-Cultural Perspective on the Personhood of Fetuses and Young Children." In W. A. Haviland and R. J. Gordon (Eds.), *Talking About People: Readings in Contemporary Cultural Anthropology* (2nd ed.) (pp. 24–34). Mountain View, CA: Mayfield.

Moser, Caroline. 1993. *Gender Planning and Development: Theory, Practice, and Training.* New York: Routledge.

Mourant, A. E., A. C. Kopec, and K. Domaniewska-Sobczak. 1976. *The Distribution of the Human Blood Groups and Other Polymorphisms.* London: Oxford University Press.

Mukhopadhyay, Carol C., and Patricia J. Higgins. 1988. "Anthropological Studies of Women's Status Revisited: 1977–1987." *Annual Review of Anthropology,* 17:461–495.

Mullin, Molly H. 1995. "The Patronage of Difference: Making Indian Art, Not Ethnology." In George E. Marcus and Fred R. Myers (Eds.), *The Traffic in Culture: Refiguring Art and Anthropology* (pp. 166–200). Berkeley: University of California Press.

Munn, Nancy D. 1983. "Gawan Kula: Spatiotemporal Control and the Symbolism of Influence." In J. W. Leach and E. Leach (Eds.), *The Kula: New Perspectives on Massim Exchange* (pp. 277–309). Cambridge: Cambridge University Press.

Munroe, Robert L., and Ruth H. Munroe. 1977. *Cross-Cultural Human Development.* New York: Aronson.

Murdock, George Peter. 1949. *Social Structure.* New York: Free Press.

Murdock, George Peter. 1996. "Family Stability in Non-European Cultures." In R. J. McGee and R. Warms (Eds.), *Anthropological Theory: An Introductory History* (pp. 258–266). Mountain View, CA: Mayfield. (Originally published 1950)

Murphy, Joseph M. 1989 *Santeria: An African Religion in America.* Boston: Beacon Press.

Murphy, Michael Dean, and Agneta Johannsen. 1990. "Ethical Obligations and Federal Regulations in Ethnographic Research and Anthropological Education." *Human Organization* 49:127–134.

Murphy, Robert. 1964. "Social Distance and the Veil." *American Anthropologist* 66:1257–1273.

Murphy, Yolanda, and Murphy Robert. 1974. *Women of the Forest.* New York: Columbia University Press.

Murray, Gerald F. 1986. "Seeing the Forest While Planting the Trees: An Anthropological Approach to Agroforestry in Haiti." In D. W. Brinkerhoff and J. C. Garcia-Zamor (Eds.), *Politics, Projects, and Peasants: Institutional Development in Haiti* (pp. 193–226). New York: Praeger.

Muwahidi, A. A. 1989. "Islamic Perspectives on Death and Dying." In A. Berger, P. Badham, A. Kutscher, J. Berger, M. Perry, and J. Beloff (Eds.), *Perspectives on Death and Dying: Cross-Cultural and Multidisciplinary Views* (pp. 38–54). Philadelphia: Charles Press.

Myerhoff, Barbara. 1978. *Number Our Days.* New York: Simon and Schuster.

Myers, Fred. 1986. *Pintupi Country, Pintupi Self: Sentiment, Place, and Politics among Western Desert Aborigines.* Washington, DC: Smithsonian Institution Press.

Nader, Laura, and Thomas W. Maretzki (Eds.). 1973. *Cultural Illness and Health.* Washington, DC: American Anthropological Association.

Nagashima, Kenji, and James A. Schellenberg. 1997. "Situational Differences in Intentional Smiling: A Cross-cultural Exploration." *Journal of Social Psychology* 137:297–301.

Nagengast, Carole. 1994. "Violence, Terror, and the Crisis of the State." In B. J. Siegel (Ed.), *Annual Review of Anthropology.* (Vol. 23, pp. 109–136). Stanford, CA: Stanford University Press.

Nanda, Serena. 1999. *Neither Man nor Woman: The Hijras of India* (2nd ed.). Belmont, CA: Wadsworth.

Nanda, Serena. 2000a. "Arranging a Marriage in India." In P. R. DeVita (Ed.), *Stumbling Towards Truth: Anthropologists at Work* (pp. 196–204). Prospect Heights, IL: Waveland.

Nanda, Serena. 2000b. *Gender Diversity: Crosscultural Variations.* Prospect Heights, IL: Waveland.

Narasimhan, Sakuntala. 1990. *Sati: Widow Burning in India.* New York: Anchor/Doubleday.

Narayan, Kirin. 1993. "How Native Is a 'Native' Anthropologist?" *American Anthropologist* 95:671–686.

Narotzky, Susana. 1997. *New Directions in Economic Anthropology.* London: Pluto Press.

Nash, June. 1986. *Women and Change in Latin America.* South Hadley, MA: Bergin and Garvey.

Nash, June. 1993. "Introduction: Traditional Arts and Changing Markets in Middle America." In June Nash and Helen Safa (Eds.), *Crafts in the World Market* (pp. 1–24). Albany: State University of New York Press.

Nash, June. 1994. "Global Integration and Subsistence Insecurity." *American Anthropologist* 96:7–30.

Nash, June, and Helen Safa (Eds.). 1986. *Women and Change in Latin America.* South Hadley, MA: Bergin and Garvey.

Nash, Manning. 1967. "The Social Context of Economic Choice in a Small Society." In G. Dalton (Ed.), *Tribal and Peasant Economies* (pp. 524–538). Garden City, NY: Natural History Press.

Nations, James. 1988. "The Lacandon Maya." In J. S. Denslow and C. Padoch (Eds.), *People of the Tropical Rain Forest* (pp. 87–88). Berkeley: University of California Press.

Netting, Robert. 1977. *Cultural Ecology.* Menlo Park, CA: Cummings.

Newman, Katherine S. 1999a. *Falling from Grace: Downward Mobility in an Age of Affluence* (2nd ed.). Berkeley: University of California Press.

Newman, Katherine S. 1999b. *No Shame in My Game: The Working Poor in the Inner City.* New York: Knopf.

Nielsen, Joyce McCarl. 1990. *Sex and Gender in Society: Perspectives on Stratification* (2nd ed.). Prospect Heights, IL: Waveland.

Norbeck, Edward. 1974. *Religion in Human Life: Anthropological Views.* Prospect Heights, IL: Waveland.

Norgren, Jill. 1996. *The Cherokee Cases: The Confrontation of Law and Politics.* New York: McGraw-Hill.

Norgren, Jill, and Serena Nanda. 1988. *American Cultural Pluralism and Law.* New York: Praeger.

Norgren, Jill, and Serena Nanda. 1996. *American Cultural Pluralism and Law* (2nd ed.). New York: Praeger.

O'Brien, Denise. 1977. "Female Husbands in Southern Bantu Societies." In A. Schlegel (Ed.), *Sexual Stratification* (pp. 109–127). New York: Columbia University Press.

O'Brien, Jay. 1986. "Toward a Reconstitution of Ethnicity: Capitalist Expansion and Cultural Dynamics in Sudan." *American Anthropologist* 4:898–907.

O'Kelly, Charlotte G. 1980. "Center, Periphery, and Hierarchy: Gender in Southeast Asia." In S. Morgen (Ed.), *Gender and Anthropology: Critical Reviews for Research and Teaching* (pp. 294–312). Washington, DC: American Anthropological Association.

Oboler, Regina Smith. 1980. "Is the Female Husband a Man? Woman/Woman Marriage among the Nandi of Kenya." *Ethnology* 19:69–88.

Ochs, Elinor, and Bambi B. Schieffelin. 1984. "Language Acquisition and Socialization: Three Developmental Stories and Their Implications." In R. Shweder and R. Levine (Eds.), *Culture Theory: Essays on Mind, Self and Emotion* (pp. 276–320). Cambridge: Cambridge University Press.

Ogbu, John. 1974. *The Next Generation: An Ethnography of Education in an Urban Neighborhood.* New York: Academic Press.

Ogbu, John. 1978a. "African Bridewealth and Women's Status." *American Ethnologist* 5:241–260.

Ogbu, John. 1978b. *Minority Education and Caste: The American System in Cross-Cultural Perspective.* New York: Academic Press.

Okin, Susan Moller. 1999. *Is Multiculturalism Bad for Women?* Princeton, NJ: Princeton University Press.

Ong, Aihwa. 1989. "Center, Periphery, and Hierarchy: Gender in Southeast Asia." In S. Morgen (Ed.), *Gender and Anthropology: Critical Reviews for Research and Teaching* (pp. 294–303). Washington, DC: American Anthropological Association.

Oriard, Michael. 1993. *Reading Football: How the Popular Press Created an American Spectacle.* Chapel Hill: University of North Carolina Press.

Orion, Loretta. 1995. *Never Again the Burning Times.* Prospect Heights, IL: Waveland.

Ortiz, Fernando, 1947. *Cuban Counterpoint: Tobacco and Sugar* (Harriet de Onis, Trans.). New York: Knopf.

Ortiz de Montellano, Bernard R. 1978. "Aztec Cannibalism: An Ecological Necessity?" *Science* 200: 611–617.

Ortiz de Montellano, Bernard R. 1990. *Aztec Medicine, Health, and Nutrition.* New Brunswick, NJ: Rutgers University Press.

Ortner, Sherry B., and Harriet Whitehead. 1981. *Sexual Meanings: The Cultural Construction of Gender and Sexuality.* Cambridge: Cambridge University Press.

Ostergaard, Lene. 1990. "The New Rice and Agricultural Change in Lowland Sumatra: A Case Study from Kuantan, Riau Province." *Research in Economic Anthropology* 12:53–86.

Ottley, Bruce L., and Jean G. Zorn. 1983. "Criminal Law in Papua New Guinea: Code, Custom and the Courts in Conflict." *American Journal of Comparative Law* 31:251–300.

Ovchinnikov, Igor V., et al. 2000. "Molecular Analysis of Neanderthal DNA from the Northern Caucasus." *Nature* 404:490–493.

Owsley, Douglas W., George W. Gill, and Stephen D. Ousley. 1994. "Biological Effects of European Contact on Easter Island." In C. S. Larsen and G. R. Milner (Eds.), *In the Wake of Contact: Biological Responses to Conquest* (pp. 161–177). New York: Wiley.

Pacini, Deborah, and Christine Franquemont. 1986. *Coca and Cocaine: Effects on People and Policy in Latin America.* Cambridge, MA: Cultural Survival Publications.

Page, Melvin E. 1987. "Introduction: Black Men in a White Men's War." In M. E. Page (Ed.), *Africa and the First World War* (pp. 1–27). New York: St. Martin's.

Paine, Robert. 1994. *Herds of the Tundra: A Portrait of Saami Reindeer Pastoralism.* Washington, DC: Smithsonian Institution.

Palkovich, Anna M. 1994. "Historic Epidemics of the American Pueblos." In C. S. Larsen and G. R. Milner (Eds.), *In the Wake of Contact: Biological Responses to Conquest* (pp. 87–95). New York: Wiley.

Pareles, Jon. 1996. "A Small World After All. But Is That Good?" *New York Times,* March 24, p. B34.

Parenti, Michael J. 1967. "Black Nationalism and the Reconstruction of Identity." In R. Endelman (Ed.), *Personality and Social Life* (pp. 514–524). New York: Random House.

Parker, Linda S. 1989. *Native American Estate: The Struggle over Indian and Hawaiian Lands.* Honolulu: University of Hawaii Press.

Patterson, Francine, and Ronald H. Cohn. 1978, Oct. "Conversations with a Gorilla." *National Geographic,* pp. 438–465.

Peacock, Nadine R. 1991. "Rethinking the Sexual Division of Labor: Reproduction and Women's Work among the Efe." In M. di Leonardo (Ed.), *Gender and the Crossroads of Knowledge: Feminist Anthropology in the Postmodern Era* (pp. 339–360). Berkeley: University of California Press.

Peoples, James G. 1990. "The Evolution of Complex Stratification in Eastern Micronesia." *Micronesia Suppl.* 2:291–302.

Pettitt, George A. 1972. "The Vision Quest and the Guardian Spirit." In J. Jennings and E. A. Hoebel (Eds.), *Readings in Anthropology* (pp. 265–272). New York: McGraw-Hill.

Peyrefitte, Alain. 1992. *The Immobile Empire* (Jon Rothschild, Trans.). New York: Knopf.

Pfeiffer, John. 1972. *The Emergence of Man.* New York: Harper and Row.

Phillip, Hornick (Ed.). 1993. *The Immigration Act of 1990 Handbook.* Deerfield, IL: Clark, Boardman, and Callaghan.

Picchi, Debra. 1991. "The Impact of an Industrial Agricultural Project on the Bakairi Indians of Central Brazil." *Human Organization* 50:26–38.

Picturing the Middle East: A Hundred Years of European Orientalism. 1995. New York: Dahesh Museum.

Pilbeam, David. 1972. *The Ascent of Man.* New York: Macmillan.

Pilbeam, David. 1996. "Genetic and Morphological Records of the Hominoidea and Hominid Origins: A Synthesis." *Molecular Phylogenetic Evolution* 5:155–168.

Pinker, Steven. 1994. *The Language Instinct.* New York: William Morrow.

Plattner, Stuart. 1989a. "Economic Behavior in Markets." In S. Plattner (Ed.), *Economic Anthropology* (pp. 209–221). Stanford, CA: Stanford University Press.

Plattner, Stuart. 1989b. "Marxism." In S. Plattner (Ed.), *Economic Anthropology* (pp. 379–396). Stanford, CA: Stanford University Press.

Polyani, Karl. 1944. *The Great Transformation.* New York: Holt, Rinehart and Winston.

Posey, Darrell. 1988. "Kayapo Indian Natural-Resource Management." In J. S. Denslow and C. Padoch (Eds.), *People of the Tropical Rain Forest* (pp. 89–90). Berkeley: University of California Press.

Pospisil, Leopold. 1963. *The Kapauku Papuans of West New Guinea.* New York: Holt, Rinehart and Winston.

Post, Peter, Farrington Daniels, Jr., and Robert T. Binford, Jr. 1975. "Cold Injury and the Evolution of White Skin." *Human Biology* 47:65–80.

Postel, Sandra. 1994. "Carrying Capacity: The Earth's Bottom Line." In L. A. Mazur (Ed.), *Beyond the Numbers: A Reader on Population, Consumption, and the Environment* (pp. 48–70). Washington, DC: Island Press.

Potash, Betty. 1989. "Gender Relations in Sub-Saharan Africa." In S. Morgen (Ed.), *Gender and Anthropology: Critical Reviews for Research and Teaching* (pp. 189–227). Washington, DC: American Anthropological Association.

Potter, Jack M. 1967. "From Peasants to Rural Proletarians: Social and Economic Change in Rural Communist China." In Jack M. Potter, May M. Diaz, and G. M. Forster, (Eds.), *Peasant Society: A Reader* (pp. 407–418). Boston: Little, Brown.

Powdermaker, Hortense. 1967. *Stranger and Friend.* New York: Norton.

Prah, Kwesi K. 1990. "Anthropologists, Colonial Administrators, and the Lotuko of Eastern Equatoria, Sudan: 1952–1953." *African Journal of Sociology* 3(2):70–86.

Price, Sally. 1989. *Primitive Art in Civilized Places.* Chicago: University of Chicago Press.

Pringle, H. 1998. "The Slow Birth of Agriculture." *Science* 282:1446.

Prunier, Gerard. 1995. *The Rwanda Crisis: History of a Genocide.* New York: Columbia University Press.

Queen, Stuart, and Robert W. Habenstein. 1974. *The Family in Various Cultures.* New York: J. B. Lippincott.

Radcliffe-Brown, A. R. 1956. *Structure and Function in Primitive Society.* Glencoe, IL: Free Press.

Radcliffe-Brown, A. R. 1964. *The Andaman Islanders.* New York: Free Press.

Radcliffe-Brown, A. R. 1965. *Structure and Function in Primitive Society.* New York: Free Press. (Originally published 1952).

Ramet, Sabrina P. 1996. *Balkan Babel: Politics, Culture, and Religion in Yugoslavia* (2nd ed.). Boulder, CO: Westview.

Ramet, Sabrina P. 1999. *Balkan Babel: The Disintegration of Yugoslavia from the Death of Tito to the Ethnic War.* Boulder, CO: Westview.

Rapoport, Amos. 1982. *The Meaning of the Built Environment: A Nonverbal Communication Approach.* Beverly Hills, CA: Sage.

Rapp, Rayna. 1991. "Family and Class in Contemporary America: Notes Toward an Understanding of Ideology." In E. Jelin (Ed.), *Family, Household and Gender Relations in Latin America* (pp. 197–215). London: Kegan Paul International and UNESCO.

Rappaport, Roy A. 1967. "Ritual Regulation of Environmental Relation among a New Guinea People." *Ethnology* 6:17–30.

Rappaport, Roy A. 1971. "The Flow of Energy in an Agricultural Society." *Scientific American* 225: 116–132.

Rathje, William, and Cutten Murphy. 1993. *Rubbish! The Archaeology of Garbage.* New York: Harper Perennial.

Ratliff, Eric A. 1999. "Women as 'Sex-Workers,' Men as 'Boyfriends': Shifting Identities in Philippine Go-Go Bars and Their Significance in STD/AIDS Control." *Anthropology and Medicine* 6(1):79–101.

Reed, Aldoph, Jr. 2000. *Class Notes: Posing as Politics and Other Thoughts on the American Scene.* New York: New Press.

Redfield, Robert. 1971. "Art and Icon." In C. M. Otten (Ed.), *Anthropology and Art* (pp. 39–65). Garden City, NY: Natural History Press.

Renfrew, Colin. 1989. "Models of Change in Language and Archaeology." *Transactions of the Philological Society* 87(2):103–155.

Reynolds, Larry T. 1992. "A Retrospective on 'Race': The Career of a Concept." *Sociological-Focus* 25(1): 1–14.

Reynolds, Vernon. 1965. *Budongo: An African Forest and Its Chimpanzees.* Garden City, NY: Doubleday.

Rhoades, Robert E. 1984. *Breaking New Ground: Agricultural Anthropology.* Lima, Peru: International Potato Center.

Richards, Audrey I. 1956. *Chisungu: A Girl's Initiation Ceremony among the Bemba of Northern Rhodesia.* New York: Grove Press.

Rickford, John Russell. 1997. "Suite for Ebony and Phonics." *Discover* 18 (December): 82–87.

Rickford, John Russell, and Russell John Rickford. 2000. *Spoken Soul: The Story of Black English.* New York: Wiley.

Ricklefs, Merle C. 1990. "Balance and Military Innovation in 17th Century Java." *History Today* 40(11): 40–47.

Ricklefs, Merle C. 1993. *A History of Modern Indonesia since c. 1300* (2nd ed.). Stanford, CA: Stanford University Press.

Rifkin, Jeremy. 1993. *Beyond Belief: The Rise and Fall of the Cattle Culture.* New York: NAL/Dutton.

Ritter, M. L. 1980. "The Conditions Favoring Age-Set Organization." *Journal of Anthropological Research* 36:87–104.

Roberton, John. 1827. *Observations on the Mortality and Physical Management of Children.* London: Longman, Rees, Orme, Brown and Green. Available at http://www.neonatology.org/classics/roberton/roberton.html

Roberts, Mary N., and Allen F. Roberts. 1996. *Memory: Luba Art and the Making of History.* New York: Museum for African Art.

Robins, A. H. 1991. *Biological Perspectives on Human Pigmentation.* Cambridge: Cambridge University Press.

Rohner, Ronald, and Evelyn Rohner. 1970. *The Kwakiutl: Indians of British Columbia.* New York: Holt, Rinehart and Winston.

Roland, Alan. 1988. *In Search of Self in India and Japan.* Princeton, NJ: Princeton University Press.

Roosens, Eugene. 1995. "Subtle 'Primitives': Ethnic Formation among the Central Yaka of Zaire." In Lola Romanucci-Ross and George A. De Vos (Eds.), *Ethnic Identity: Creation, Conflict, and Accommodation* (3rd ed.) (pp. 115–124). London: Sage.

Root, Maria P. (Ed.). 1992. *Racially Mixed People in America.* Newbury Park, CA: Sage.

Rosaldo, Michelle Z., and Louise Lamphere. 1974. "Introduction." In M. Z. Rosaldo and L. Lamphere (Eds.), *Women, Culture and Society* (pp. 1–16). Stanford, CA: Stanford University Press.

Rosaldo, Renato. 1993. *Culture and Truth: The Remaking of Social Analysis.* Boston: Beacon Press.

Roscoe, Paul B. 1995. "Initiation in Cross-Cultural Perspective." In Nancy C. Lutkehaus and Paul B. Roscoe (Eds.), *Gender Rituals: Female Initiation in Melanesia* (pp. 219–238). New York: Routledge.

Roscoe, Will. 1991. *The Zuni Man-Woman.* Albuquerque: University of New Mexico Press.

Roscoe, Will. 1995. "Strange Craft, Strange History, Strange Folks: Cultural Amnesia and the Case of Lesbian and Gay Studies." *American Anthropologist* 97:448–452.

Rosman, Abraham, and Paula G. Rubel. 1971. *Feasting with Mine Enemy: Rank and Exchange among Northwest Coast Societies.* Prospect Heights, IL: Waveland.

Royal, Robert. 1992. *1492 and All That: Political Manipulations of History.* Boston: Ethics and Public Policy Center.

Ryan, Alan. 1996. "Too Nice to Win?" (Review of *Time Past: A Memoir* by Bill Bradley). *New York Review of Books* 43(5):8–12.

Ryan, John Paul (Ed.). 1999. "Immigration: A Dialogue on Policy, Law, and Values." *Focus on Law Studies* 14(2).

Ryle, John. 1999. "Children in Arms." *New York Review of Books,* March 4, p. 16.

Sacks, Karen Brodkin. 1982. *Sisters and Wives.* Westport, CT: Greenwood.

Sacks, Karen Brodkin. 1994. "How Did Jews Become White Folks?" In Steven Gregory and Roger Sanjek (Eds.), *Race* (pp. 78–102). New Brunswick, NJ: Rutgers University Press.

Sahlins, Marshall. 1957. "Land Use and the Extended Family in Moala, Fiji." *American Anthropologist* 59:449–462.

Sahlins, Marshall. 1961. "The Segmentary Lineage: An Organization of Predatory Expansion." *American Anthropologist* 63:332–345.

Sahlins, Marshall. 1971. "Poor Man, Rich Man, Big Man, Chief." In J. P. Spradley and D. W. McCurdy (Eds.), *Conformity and Conflict* (pp. 362–376). Boston: Little, Brown.

Sahlins, Marshall. 1972. *Stone Age Economics.* Chicago: Aldine.

Sahlins, Marshall. 1978. "Culture as Protein and Profit." *New York Review of Books* 25(18):45–53.

Said, Edward W. 1978. *Orientalism.* New York: Random House.

Said, Edward W. 1993. *Culture and Imperialism.* New York: Knopf.

Saitoti, Tepilit Ole. 1986. *The Worlds of a Maasai Warrior.* New York: Random House.

Salzman, Philip C. 1972. "Multi-Resource Nomadism in Iranian Baluchistan." In W. Irons and N. Dyson-Hudson (Eds.), *Perspectives on Nomadism* (pp. 61–69). Leiden, The Netherlands: E. J. Brill.

Salzmann, Zdenek. 1993. *Language, Culture and Society.* Boulder, CO: Westview Press.

Sanchez, Rene. 1997. "Ebonics Debate Comes to Capitol Hill; 'Political Correctness Gone Out of Control,' Sen. Faircloth Says." *Washington Post,* January 24, p. A15.

Sanday, Peggy Reeves. 1981. *Female Power and Male Dominance.* New York: Cambridge University Press.

Sanday, Peggy Reeves. 1986. *Divine Hunger: Cannibalism as a Cultural System.* New York: Cambridge University Press.

Sanday, Peggy Reeves. 1992. *Fraternity Gang Rape: Sex, Brotherhood, and Privilege on Campus.* New York: New York University Press.

Sanday, Peggy Reeves. 1996. *A Woman Scorned: Acquaintance Rape on Trial.* New York: Doubleday.

Sanjek, Roger. 1991. "The Ethnographic Present." *Man* 26:609–628.

Sanjek, Roger. 1994. "Intermarriage and the Future of Races." In S. Gregory and R. Sanjek (Eds.), *Race* (pp. 103–130). New Brunswick, NJ: Rutgers University Press.

Sanjek, Roger. 2000. *The Future of Us All: Race and Neighborhood Politics in New York City.* Ithaca, NY: Cornell University Press.

Sapir, Edward. 1949a. *The Selected Writings of Edward Sapir in Language, Culture and Personality* (D. Mandelbaum, Ed.). Berkeley: University of California Press.

Sapir, Edward. 1949b. "The Status of Linguistics as a Science." In D. Mandelbaum (Ed.), *The Selected Writings of Edward Sapir in Language, Culture and Personality* (pp. 160–166). Berkeley: University of California Press.

Savage-Rumbaugh, E. S., D. M. Rumbaugh, and S. Boysen. 1980. "Do Apes Use Language?" *American Scientist* 68:49–61.

Scaglion, Richard. 1981. "Homicide Compensation in Papua New Guinea: Problems and Prospects." In *Law Reform Commission of Papua New Guinea Monograph 1.* New Guinea: Office of Information.

Scammell, G.V. 1989. *The First Imperial Age.* London: HarperCollins Academic.

Scammell, G.V. 1992. *The First Imperial Age: European Overseas Expansion c. 1400–1715.* New York: Routledge.

Schele, Linda, and Mary Ellen Miller. 1986. *The Blood of Kings: Dynasty and Ritual in Maya Art.* New York: Braziller.

Schensul, Stephen L. 1997. "The Anthropologist in Medicine: Critical Perspectives on Cancer and Street Addicts." *Reviews in Anthropology* 26(1): 57–69.

Schepartz, L. A. 1993. "Language and Modern Human Origins." *Yearbook of Physical Anthropology* 36: 91–96.

Scheper-Hughes, Nancy. 1989. "Lifeboat Ethics: Mother Love and Child Death in Northeast Brazil." *Natural History* 98(10):8–16.

Scheper-Hughes, Nancy. 1992. *Death Without Weeping: The Violence of Everyday Life in Brazil*. Berkeley: University of California Press.

Scheper-Hughes, Nancy. 1994. "Embodied Knowledge: Thinking with the Body in Critical Medical Anthropology." In Robert Borofsky (Ed.), *Assessing Cultural Anthropology* (pp. 229–249). New York: McGraw-Hill.

Schlegel, Alice (Ed.). 1977. *Sexual Stratification: A Cross-Cultural View*. New York: Columbia University Press.

Schmink, Marianne. 1988. "Big Business in the Amazon." In J. S. Denslow and C. Padoch (Eds.), *People of the Tropical Rain Forest* (pp. 163–171). Berkeley: University of California Press.

Schneider, Harold K. 1973. "The Subsistence Role of Cattle among the Pokot in East Africa." In E. P. Skinner (Ed.), *Peoples and Cultures of Africa*. Garden City, NY: Natural History Press.

Schuler, Sidney Ruth, and Syed M. Hashemi. 1995. "Family Planning Outreach and Credit Programs in Rural Bangladesh." *Human Organization* 54: 455–461.

Schultes, Richard Evans, and Siri von Reis (Eds.). 1995. *Ethnobotany: Evolution of a Discipline*. Portland, OR: Dioscorides Press.

Schumacher, William. 1975. *Small Is Beautiful*. New York: Harper and Row.

Schuyler, Phillip. 1995. "The Arts of the Arabic-Speaking Middle East." In *What in the World Is Culture?* (pp. 49–53). 651 World Series Festival Booklet. New York: King's Majestic Corporation.

Schwartz, Norman B. 1978. "Community Development and Cultural Change in Latin America." *Annual Review of Anthropology* 7:235–261.

Schwartz, Norman B. 1981. "Anthropological Views of Community and Community Development." *Human Organization* 40:313–322.

Schwartz, Stuart B. 1994. *Implicit Understandings: Observing, Reporting, and Reflecting on the Encounters Between Europeans and Other Peoples of the Early Modern Era*. Cambridge: Cambridge University Press.

Scoditti, Giancarlo M., with Jerry W. Leach. 1983. "Kula on Kitava." In J. W. Leach and E. Leach (Eds.), *The Kula: New Perspectives on Massim Exchange* (pp. 249–273). Cambridge: Cambridge University Press.

Scott, James. 1992. *Domination and the Arts of Resistance: Hidden Transcripts*. New Haven, CT: Yale University Press.

Seddon, Judith S. 1993. "Possible or Impossible? A Tale of Two Worlds in One Country." *Yale Journal of Law and Feminism* 5:265–288.

Seitlyn, David. 1993. "Spiders In and Out of Court, or 'The Long Legs & the Law': Styles of Spider Divination in Their Sociological Contexts." *Africa* 63:219–240.

Service, Elman. 1971. *Profiles in Ethnology*. New York: Harper and Row.

Shanklin, Eugenia. 1994. *Anthropology and Race*. Belmont, CA: Wadsworth.

Sharff, Jagna W. 1997. *King Kong on 4th Street: Families and the Violence of Poverty on the Lower East Side*. Boulder, CO: Westview.

Shawcross, William. 2000. *Deliver Us From Evil: Peacekeepers, Warlords and a World of Endless Conflict*. New York: Simon and Schuster.

Sheleff, Leon. 2000. *The Future of Tradition: Customary Law, Common Law, and Legal Pluralism*. Ilford, England: Frank Cass.

Sheriff, Robin E. 2000. "Exposing Silence as Cultural Censorship." *American Anthropologist* 102: 114–132.

Shohat, Ella, and Robert Stam. 1994. *Unthinking Eurocentrism: Multiculturalism and the Media*. London: Routledge.

Shostak, Marjorie. 1983. *Nisa: The Life and Words of a !Kung Woman*. New York: Random House.

Sibley, C. G., and J. E. Ahlquist. 1987. "DNA Hybridization Evidence of Hominoid Phylogeny: Results from an Expanded Data Set." *Journal of Molecular Evolution* 26:99–121.

Sibley, C. G., J. A. Comstock, and J. E. Ahlquist. 1990. "DNA Hybridization Evidence of Hominoid Phylogeny: A Reanalysis of the Data." *Journal of Molecular Evolution* 30:202–236.

Simeone, William E. 1995. *Rifles, Blankets, and Beads: Identity, History, and the Northern Athapaskan Potlatch*. Norman, OK: University of Oklahoma Press.

Singer, Merrill. 1992. "AIDS and U.S. Ethnic Minorities: The Crisis and Alternative Anthropological Responses." *Human Organization* 51:89–95.

Singer, Merrill. 2000. "Update on Projects Recovery and CONNECT." In P. L. W. Sabloff (Ed.), *Careers in Anthropology: Profiles of Practitioner Anthropologists* (NAPA Bulletin, Vol. 20). Washington, DC: National Association of Practicing Anthropologists.

Singer, Merrill, Ray Irizarry, and Jean J. Schensul. 1991. "Needle Access as an AIDS Prevention Strategy for IV Drug Users: A Research Perspective." *Human Organization* 50:142–153.

Singer, Milton. 1968. "The Indian Joint Family in Modern Industry." In M. Singer and B. Cohn (Eds.), *Indian Society: Structure and Change* (pp. 413–423). Chicago: Aldine.

Skidmore, Thomas. 1985. "Race and Class in Brazil: Historical Perspectives." In Pierre-Michel Fontaine (Ed.), *Race, Class, and Power in Brazil* (pp. 11–24). Los Angeles: University of California Press.

Skin Cancer Foundation Australia. 1998. http://www.scfa.edu.au

Skin Cancer Research Foundation. n.d. "Get Serious About Sun Exposure." http://skincancer.cool.net.au.

Slocum, Sally. 1975. "Woman the Gatherer: Male Bias in Anthropology." In R. R. Reiter (Ed.), *Toward an Anthropology of Women* (pp. 36–50). New York: Monthly Review Press.

Sluka, Jeffrey. 1990. "Participant Observation in Violent Social Contexts." *Human Organization* 49: 114–126.

Small, M. F. 1989, January. "MS monkey." *Natural History*, pp. 10–12.

Smedley, Audrey. 1998a. "'Race' and the Construction of Human Identity." *American Anthropologist* 100:690–702.

Smedley, Audrey. 1998b. *Race in North America: Origin and Evolution of a Worldview* (2nd ed.). Boulder, CO: Westview.

Smith, J. David, and George Lee Johnson, Jr. 1997. "Margaret Mead and Mental Retardation: Words of Understanding, Concepts of Inclusiveness." *Mental Retardation* 35:306–309.

Sokolovsky, Jay. 1997. *The Cultural Context of Aging*. Westport, CT: Bergin and Garvey.

Southworth, F. C., and C. J. Daswani. 1974. *Foundations of Linguistics*. New York: Free Press.

Spector, Janet D., and Mary K. Whelan. 1989. "Incorporating Gender into Archaeology Courses." In S. Morgen (Ed.), *Gender and Anthropology: Critical Reviews for Research and Teaching* (pp. 65–94). Washington, DC: American Anthropological Association.

Spicer, Edward H., and Theodore E. Downing. 1974. "Training for Non-Academic Employment: Major Issues." In E. Leacock, N. Gonzalez, and G. Kushner (Eds.), *Training Programs for New Opportunities in Applied Anthropology* (pp. 1–12). Washington, DC: American Anthropological Association.

Spiro, Melford. 1982. *Oedipus in the Trobriands*. Chicago: University of Chicago Press.

Spiro, Melford. 1995. "On the Strange and the Familiar in Recent Anthropological Thought." In C. R. Ember, M. Ember, and P. N. Peregrine (Eds.), *Research Frontiers in Anthropology*. Englewood Cliffs, NJ: Prentice Hall.

Sponsel, Leslie E. (Ed.). 1995. *Indigenous Peoples and the Future of Amazonia: An Ecological Anthropology of an Endangered World*. Tucson: University of Arizona Press.

Spradley, James. 1970. *You Owe Yourself a Drunk*. Boston: Little, Brown.

Spuhler, J. N. 1989. "Raymond Pearl Memorial Lecture, 1988: Evolution of Mitochondrial DNA in Human and Other Organisms." *American Journal of Human Biology* 1:509–528.

Stack, Carol. 1974. *All Our Kin: Strategies for Survival in a Black Community*. New York: Harper and Row.

Stack, John, Jr. (Ed.). 1981. *Ethnic Identities in a Transitional World*. Westport, CT: Greenwood Press.

Stark, Rodney. 1996. *Sociology* (6th ed.). Belmont, CA: Wadsworth.

Steadman, Lyle B., and Charles F. Merbs. 1982. "Kuru and Cannibalism." *American Anthropologist* 84: 611–627.

Stearns, M. L. 1975. "Life Cycle Rituals of the Modern Haida." In D. B. Carlisle (Ed.), *Contributions to Canadian Ethnology* (pp. 129–169). Ottawa: National Museum of Man.

Steegmann, A. T., Jr. 1975. "Human Adaptation to Cold." In A. Damon (Ed.), *Physiological Anthropology* (pp. 130–160). New York: Oxford University Press.

Steele, James. 1999, May. "Palaeoanthropology: Stone Legacy of Skilled Hands." *Nature*, pp. 24–25.

Stein, Philip L., and Bruce M. Rowe. 2000. *Physical Anthropology* (7th ed.). Boston: McGraw-Hill.

Steinberg, Stephen. 1989. *The Ethnic Myth: Race, Ethnicity, and Class in America* (2nd ed.). Boston: Beacon.

Steiner, Christopher B. 1994. *African Art in Transit*. Cambridge: Cambridge University Press.

Steiner, Christopher B. 1995. "The Art of the Trade: On the Creation of Value and Authenticity in the African Art Market." In G. E. Marcus and F. R. Myers (Eds.), *The Traffic in Culture: Refiguring Art and Anthropology* (pp. 151–165). Berkeley: University of California Press.

Stephens, Sharon. 1997, December. "Lapp Life After Chernobyl." *Natural History*, pp. 33–40.

Stern, Pamela R. 1999. "Learning to Be Smart: An Exploration of the Culture of Intelligence in a Canadian Inuit Community." *American Anthropologist* 101:502–514.

Steward, Julian. 1972. *The Theory of Culture Change: The Methodology of Multilinear Evolution*. Urbana: University of Illinois Press.

Stewart, Omer Call. 1987. *Peyote Religion: A History*. Norman, OK: University of Oklahoma Press.

Stocking, George W., Jr. 1992. *The Ethnographer's Magic, and Other Essays in the History of Anthropology*. Madison: University of Wisconsin Press.

Stolberg, Sheryl Gay. 1999. "Black Mother's Mortality Rate is Under Scrutiny." In *New York Times*, August 8. p. A1.

Stolcke, Verena. 1995. "Talking Culture: New Boundaries, New Rhetorics of Exclusion in Europe." *Current Anthropology* 36:1–7.

Stone, Linda, and Caroline James. 1997. "Dowry, Bride-Burning, and Female Power in India." In C. B. Brettell and C. F. Sargent (Eds.), *Gender in Cross-Cultural Perspective* (pp. 270–279). Upper Saddle River, NJ: Prentice Hall.

Stonich, Susan C., Douglas L. Murray, and Peter R. Rossart. 1994. "Enduring Crises: The Human and Environmental Consequences of Nontraditional Export Growth in Central America." *Research in Economic Anthropology* 15:239–274.

Strathern, Marilyn. 1995. *Women in Between: Female Roles in a Male World: Mount Hagen, New Guinea*. Latham, MD: Rowman and Littlefield.

Strauss, Lawrence G. 1991. "Southwestern Europe at the Last Glacial Maximum." *Current Anthropology* 32:189–199.

Strier, Karen B. 2000. *Primate Behavioral Ecology*. Boston: Allyn and Bacon.

Stull, Donald D., Michael J. Broadway, and Ken C. Erickson. 1992. "The Price of a Good Steak: Beef Packing and Its Consequences for Garden City, Kansas." In L. Lamphere (Ed.), *Structuring Diver-*

437

sity: Ethnographic Perspectives on the New Immigration (pp. 35–64). Chicago: University of Chicago Press.

Stull, Donald D., and Jean J. Schensul (Eds.). 1987. Collaborative Research and Social Change. Boulder, CO: Westview Press.

Sturtevant, Edgar H. 1947. An Introduction to Linguistic Science. New Haven, CT: Yale University Press.

Swisher, Carl, et al. 1994. "Age of the Earliest Known Hominids in Java, Indonesia." Science 263: 1118–1121.

Taheri, Amir. 1986. The Spirit of Allah: Khomeini and the Islamic Revolution. Bethesda, MD: Adler and Adler.

Talmon, Yohina. 1964. "Mate Selection in Collective Settlements." American Sociological Review 29: 491–508.

Tannen, Deborah. 1990. You Just Don't Understand: Women and Men in Conversation. New York: Morrow.

Tedlock, Barbara. 1991. "From Participant Observation to the Observation of Participation: The Emergence of Narrative Ethnography." Journal of Anthropological Research 47:69–94.

Templeton, Alan R. 1985. "The Phylogeny of the Hominoid Primates: A Statistical Analysis of the DNA-DNA Hybridization Data." Molecular Biology and Evolution 2:420–433.

Templeton, Alan R. 1986. "Further Comments on Statistical Analysis of DNA-DNA Hybridization Data." Molecular Biology and Evolution 3:290–295.

Templeton, Alan R. 1996. "Gene Lineages and Human Evolution." Science 272:1363–1364.

Templeton, Alan R. 1998. "Human Races: A Genetic and Evolutionary Perspective." American Anthropologist 100:632–650.

Terrace, H. S. 1979. Nim. New York: Knopf.

Terrace, H. S. 1983. "Apes Who 'Talk': Language or Projection of Language by Their Teachers?" In J. de Luce and H. T. Wilder (Eds.), Language in Primates (pp. 19–42). New York: Springer-Verlag.

Thornton, Lynne. 1994. Women as Portrayed in Orientalist Painting. Paris: PocheCouleur.

Tiger, Lionel. 1978. "Omnigamy: The New Kinship System." Psychology Today.

Tobin, Joseph J., David Y. H. Wu, and Dana Davidson. 1989. Preschool in Three Cultures: Japan, China, and the United States. New Haven, CT: Yale University Press.

Tocqueville, Alexis de. 1956. Democracy in America. New York: Penguin. (Originally published 1835–1840)

Todorov, Tzvetan. 1993. On Human Diversity: Nationalism, Racism, and Exotism in French Thought (Catherine Porter, Trans.). Cambridge, MA: Harvard University Press.

Traphagan, John W. 1998. "Contesting the Transition to Old Age in Japan." Ethnology 37:333–350.

Trask, Haunani-Kay. 1999. From a Native Daughter: Colonialism and Sovereignty in Hawai'i. Honolulu: University of Hawai'i Press.

Trice, Harrison M., and Janice M. Beyer. 1993. The Cultures of Work Organizations. Englewood Cliffs, NJ: Prentice-Hall.

Tsui, Clarence. 2000. "A Hong Kong Anthropologist Spent Months at a Mainland Electronic Plant to Study Lives of Its Female Workers: Hardship, Hope and Dreams in a Factory." South China Morning Post, January 9, p. 1.

Tsuruta, Kinua. 1989. The Walls Within: Images of Westerners in Japan and Images of the Japanese Abroad. Vancouver: Institute of Asian Research.

Turnbull, Colin. 1961. The Forest People. New York: Simon and Schuster.

Turnbull, Colin. 1968. "The Importance of Flux in Two Hunting Societies." In R. B. Lee and I. DeVore (Eds.), Man the Hunter (pp. 132–137). Chicago: Aldine.

Turnbull, Colin. 1983. The Mbuti Pygmies: Change and Adaptation. New York: Holt, Rinehart and Winston.

Turner, J. Michael. 1985. "Brown into Black: Changing Racial Attitudes of Afro-Brazilian University Students." In P.-M. Fontaine (Ed.), Race, Class, and Power in Brazil (pp. 73–84). Los Angeles: University of California Center for Afro-American Studies.

Turner, Victor. 1967. The Forest of Symbols: Aspects of Ndembu Ritual. Ithaca: Cornell University Press.

Turner, Victor. 1969. The Ritual Process: Structure and Antistructure. Chicago: Aldine.

Tylor, Edward. 1920. Primitive Culture (2 vols.). New York: G. P. Putnam's Sons.

Uchendu, Victor Chikezie. 1965. The Igbo of Southeastern Nigeria. New York: Holt, Rinehart and Winston.

Uchendu, Victor Chikezie. 1995. "The Dilemma of Ethnicity and Polity Primacy in Black Africa." In Lola Romanucci-Ross and George A. De Vos (Eds.), Ethnic Identity: Creation, Conflict, and Accommodation (3rd ed.) (pp. 125–135). London: Sage.

Ucko, P., and A. Rosenfeld. 1967. Paleolithic Cave Art. New York: McGraw-Hill.

United Nations. 2000. Human Development Report 2000. New York: Oxford University Press.

United Nations Development Programme. 1996. Human Development Report. New York: Oxford University Press.

United States Commission on Civil Rights. 1992. Civil Rights Issues Facing Asian Americans in the 1990s. Washington, DC: Author.

Urdaneta, Maria Luisa, Delia Huron Saldana, and Anne Winkler. 1995. "Mexican-American Perceptions of Severe Mental Illness." Human Organization 54:70–77.

Van Buren, Geraldine. 1995. "The International Protection of Family Members' Rights as the 21st Century Approaches." Human Rights Quarterly 17: 732–765.

van Donge, Jan Kees. 1992. "Agricultural Decline in Tanzania: The Case of the Uluguru Mountains." African Affairs 91:73–94.

van Gennep, Arnold. 1960. The Rites of Passage. Chicago: University of Chicago Press.

van Willigen, John. 1993. Applied Anthropology: An Introduction (rev. ed.). Westport, CT: Bergin and Garvey.

Vatuk, S. 1990. "'To Be a Burden on Others': Dependency Anxiety Among the Elderly in India." In Owen Lynch (Ed.), Divine Passions: The Social Construction of Emotion in India (pp. 64–88). Berkeley: University of California Press.

Vayda, Andrew P. 1976. War in Ecological Perspective. New York: Plenum.

Victor, David A. 1992. International Business Communication. New York: HarperCollins.

Vincent, Joan. 1974. "The Structuring of Ethnicity." Human Organization 33:375–379.

Vincent, Susan. 1998. "The Family in the Household: Women, Relationships, and Economic History in Peru." Research in Economic Anthropology 19:179–187.

Viswanathan, Gauri. 1988. "Currying Favor: The Politics of British Educational and Cultural Policy in India 1813–1854." Social Text 19–20 (Fall): 85–104.

Vogel, Susan. 1991. Africa Explores: 20th Century African Art. New York: Center for African Art.

Volkman, Toby Alice. 1984. "Great Performances: Toraja Cultural Identity in the 1970s." American Ethnologist 11:152–168.

von Graeve, Bernard. 1989. The Pacaa Nova: Clash of Cultures on the Brazilian Frontier. Peterborough, Ontario: Broadview Press.

Wachtel, Nathan. 1977. The Vision of the Vanquished: The Spanish Conquest of Peru Through Indian Eyes, 1530–1570. New York: Barnes and Noble.

Wafer, Jim. 1991. The Taste of Blood: Spirit Possession in Brazilian Candomble. Philadelphia: University of Pennsylvania Press.

Wagner, Roy. 1975. The Invention of Culture. Englewood Cliffs, NJ: Prentice-Hall.

Waite, Linda. 1991. New Families, No Families? The Transformation of the American Home. Berkeley: University of California Press.

Wallace, Anthony. 1966. Religion: An Anthropological View. New York: Random House.

Wallace, Anthony. 1970. Death and Rebirth of the Seneca. New York: Knopf.

Wallace, Anthony. 1999. Jefferson and the Indians: The Tragic Fate of "The First Americans." Cambridge, MA: Harvard University Press.

Wallace, Ben J. 1995. "How Many Trees Does it Take to Cook a Pot of Rice? Fuelwood and Tree Consumption in Four Philippine Communities." Human Organization 54:182–186.

Wallerstein, Immanuel. 1974. The Modern World System: Capitalist Agriculture and the Origins of the European World Economy in the Sixteenth Century. New York: Academic Press.

Wallerstein, Immanuel. 1995. Historical Capitalism. London: Verso.

Wallman, Joel. 2000. "Common Sense about Violence: Why Research?" In Year 2000 Report of the Harry Frank Guggenheim Foundation: Research for Understanding and Reducing Violence, Aggression, and Dominance (pp. 7–25). New York: Harry Frank Guggenheim Foundation.

Wally, Christine J. 1997. "Searching for 'Voices': Feminism, Anthropology, and the Global Debate over Female Genital Operations." Cultural Anthropology 12:405–438.

Warms, Richard L. 1995, November. "Making War Abroad, Negotiating Social Standing at Home: Relations Between Malian Veterans and Their Families and Communities." Paper presented at the 38th annual meeting of the African Studies Association, Orlando, FL.

Warms, Richard L. 1996. "Throwing Away the Bones: The Story of Mory Samake, an African Veteran of the French Colonial Army." In A. Marcus (Ed.), Anthropology for a Small Planet: Culture and Community in a Global Environment (pp. 1–18). St. James, NY: Brandywine Press.

Warren, D. Michael, L. Jan Slikkerveer, and David Brokensha (Eds.). 1995. The Cultural Dimension of Development: Indigenous Knowledge Systems. London: Intermediate Technology Publications.

Warren, Kay B., and Susan C. Bourque. 1989. "Women, Technology, and Development Ideologies: Frameworks and Findings." In S. Morgen (Ed.), Gender and Anthropology: Critical Reviews for Research and Teaching (pp. 382–410). Washington, DC: American Anthropological Association.

Waterston, Alisse. 1993. Street Addicts in the Political Economy. Philadelphia: Temple University Press.

Weatherford, J. 1981. Tribes on the Hill. New York: Rawson, Wade.

Weiner, Annette B. 1976. Women of Value, Men of Renown: New Perspectives on Trobriand Exchange. Austin: University of Texas Press.

Whilte, T. D., Suwa G., and Asfaw B. 1995. "Australopithecus ramidus, a New Species of Early Hominid from Aramis, Ethiopia." Nature 375:88.

White, Benjamin. 1980. "Rural Household Studies in Anthropological Perspective." In H. Binswanger, R. Evenson, C. Florencio, and B. White (Eds.), Rural Household Studies in Asia (pp. 3–25). Singapore: Singapore University Press.

White, Geoffrey M. 1993. "Three Discourses on Custom." Anthropological Forum 6:475–494.

White, Jenny B. 1994. Money Makes Us Relatives. Austin: University of Texas Press.

White, Leslie A. 1949. "Energy and the Evolution of Culture." In L. A. White (Ed.), The Science of Culture (pp. 363–393). New York: Farrar, Straus and Cudahy.

Whitehead, Harriet. 1981. "The Bow and the Burden Strap: A New Look at Institutionalized Homosexuality in Native North America." In S. B. Ortner and H. Whitehead (Eds.), Sexual Meanings: The Cultural Construction of Gender and Sexuality (pp. 80–115). Cambridge: Cambridge University Press.

Whiting, Beatrice (Ed.). 1963. Six Cultures: Studies of Child Rearing. New York: Wiley.

Whiting, John, and Irvin L. Child. 1984. *Child Training and Personality: A Cross-Cultural Study*. Westport, CT: Greenwood.

Whiting, John, Richard Kluckhohn, and Albert Anthony. 1967. "The Function of Male Initiation Ceremonies at Puberty." In R. Endelman (Ed.), *Personality and Social Life* (pp. 294–308). New York: Random House.

Whiting, John, and Beatrice Whiting. 1973. "Altruistic and Egotistic Behavior in Six Cultures." In L. Nader and T. W. Maretski (Eds.), *Cultural Illness and Health* (pp. 56–66). Washington, DC: American Anthropological Association.

Whorf, B. L. 1956. *Language, Thought and Reality*. Cambridge, MA: MIT Press.

Wikan, Unni. 1977. "Man Becomes Woman: Transsexualism in Oman as a Key to Gender Roles." *Man* (new series) 12:304–319.

Wilk, Richard. 1999. "Consuming America." *Anthropology Newsletter* 40(2):1.

Wilkie, David S. 1988. "Hunters and Farmers of the African Forest." In J. S. Denslow and C. Padoch (Eds.), *People of the Tropical Rain Forest* (pp. 111–126). Berkeley: University of California Press.

Wilkins, Wendy K., and Jennie Wakefield. 1995. "Brain Evolution and Neurolinguistic Preconditions." *Behavioral and Brain Sciences* 18:161–226.

Wilks, Ivor. 1993. *Forests of Gold: Essays on the Akan and the Kingdom of Asante*. Athens, OH: Ohio University Press.

Williams, Edward J. 1995, September. "The Maquiladora Industry and Environmental Degradation in the United States–Mexican Borderlands." Paper presented at the annual meeting of the Latin American Studies Association, Washington, DC.

Williams, Terry Moses. 1989. *The Cocaine Kids: The Inside Story of a Teenage Drug Ring*. Reading, MA: Addison-Wesley.

Williams, Terry Moses, Eloise Dunlap, Bruce D. Johnson, and Ansley Hamid. 1992. "Personal Safety in Dangerous Places." *Journal of Contemporary Ethnography* 21:343–374.

Williams, Vernon J., Jr. 1996. *Rethinking Race: Franz Boas and His Contemporaries*. Lexington: University of Kentucky Press.

Williams, Walter. 1986. *The Spirit and the Flesh* (2nd ed.). Boston: Beacon Press.

Williams, Walter. 1996. "Amazons of America: Female Gender Variance." In Caroline B. Brettell and Carolyn F. Sargent (Eds.), *Gender in Cross-Cultural Perspective* (2nd ed.) (pp. 202–213). Upper Saddle River, NJ: Prentice Hall.

Willis, Paul. 1981. *Learning to Labor*. New York: Columbia University Press.

Wilson, Edward. 1975. *Sociobiology: The New Synthesis*. Cambridge, MA: Harvard University Press.

Winkelman, Michael. 1996. "Cultural Factors in Criminal Defense Proceedings." *Human Organization* 55:154.

Winter, Bronwyn. 1994. "Women, the Law and Cultural Relativism in France: The Case of Excision." *Signs* 19:939–974.

WoldeGabriel, Giday, Tim White, and Suwa Gen. 1994. "Ecological and Temporal Placement of Early Pliocene Hominids at Aramis, Ethiopia." *Nature* 371:330–333.

Wolf, Arthur. 1968. "Adopt a Daughter-in-Law, Marry a Sister: A Chinese Solution to the Incest Taboo." *American Anthropologist* 70:864–874.

Wolf, Eric R. 1966. *Peasants*. Englewood Cliffs, NJ: Prentice-Hall.

Wolf, Eric R. 1981. "The Mills of Inequality: A Marxian Approach." In G. D. Berreman (Ed.), *Social Inequality: Comparative and Developmental Approaches* (pp. 41–57). New York: Academic Press.

Wolf, Eric R. 1982. *Europe and the People Without History*. Berkeley: University of California Press.

Wolf, Eric R. 1994. "Perilous Ideas: Race, Culture, People." *Current Anthropology* 35:1–7.

Wolf, Eric R. 1998. *Envisioning Power: Ideologies of Dominance and Crisis*. Berkeley: University of California Press.

Wong, Bernard. 1988. *Ethnicity and Entrepreneurship: The New Chinese Immigrants in the San Francisco Bay Area*. Needham Heights, MA: Allyn and Bacon.

Woodburn, James. 1968. "An Introduction to Hadza Ecology." In R. B. Lee and I. DeVore (Eds.), *Man the Hunter* (pp. 49–55). Chicago: Aldine.

Woodburn, James. 1998. "Sharing Is Not a Form of Exchange: An Analysis of Property-Sharing in Immediate Return Hunter-Gatherer Societies." In C. M. Hann (Ed.), *Property Relations: Renewing the Anthropological Tradition* (pp. 48–63). Cambridge: Cambridge University Press.

World Bank. 1992. *Development and the Environment: World Development Report 1992*. New York: Oxford University Press.

World Bank. 1995. *Workers in an Integrating World, World Development Report 1995*. New York: Oxford University Press.

World Bank. 2000. *World Development Indicators 2000*. Washington, DC: Author.

Worsley, Peter M. 1959. "Cargo Cults." *Scientific American* 200:117–128.

Worthman, Carol M. 1995. "Hormones, Sex, and Gender." In William Durham, E. Valentine Daniel, and Bambi Schieffelin (Eds.), *Annual Review of Anthropology* (Vol. 24, pp. 593–618). Stanford, CA: Stanford University Press.

Wright, Ronald. 1992. *Stolen Continents: The "New World" Through Indian Eyes*. Boston: Houghton Mifflin.

Yanagisako, Sylvia, and Jane Collier. 1994. "Gender and Kinship Reconsidered: Toward a Unified Analysis." In R. Borofsky (Ed.), *Assessing Cultural Anthropology* (pp. 190–203). New York: McGraw-Hill.

Yanagisako, Sylvia, and Carol Delaney (Ed.). 1994. *Naturalizing Power: Essays in Feminist Cultural Analysis*. New York: Routledge.

Yellen, J. E., A. S. Brooks, E. Cornelissen, M. J. Mehlman, and K. Stewart. 1995. "A Middle Stone Age Worked Bone Industry from Katanda, Upper Semliki Valley, Zaire." *Science* 268:553–556.

Yewell, John. 1992. "The Day, the Pledge, the Myth." In J. Yewell, C. Dodge, and J. DeSirey (Eds.), *Confronting Columbus: An Anthology* (pp. 167–172). Jefferson, NC: McFarland.

Zihlman, Adrienne L. 1989. "Woman the Gatherer: The Role of Woman in Early Hominid Evolution." In S. Morgen (Ed.), *Gender and Anthropology: Critical Reviews for Research and Teaching* (pp. 21–40). Washington, DC: American Anthropological Association.

INDEX

442